Irene C. Fountas & Gay Su Pinnell

The Writing Minilessons Book

Your Every Day Guide for Literacy Teaching

GRADE 4

HEINEMANN
Portsmouth, NH

Heinemann
145 Maplewood Avenue, Suite 300
Portsmouth, NH 03801
www.heinemann.com

Offices and agents throughout the world

The authors and publisher wish to thank those who have generously given permission to reprint borrowed material: Please see the Credits section beginning on page 691.

Library of Congress Cataloging in Publication data is on file at the Library of Congress.

Library of Congress Control Number: 2022949191

ISBN: 978-0-325-11883-3

Editors: Kerry L. Crosby and Sue Paro
Production: Cindy Strowman
Production Assistant: Anthony Riso
Cover and Interior Designs: Ellery Harvey and Kelsey Roy
Illustrators: Sarah Snow and Will Sweeney
Typesetter: Sharon Burkhardt
Manufacturing: Jaime Spaulding

Printed in the United States of America on acid-free paper

1 2 3 4 5 6 7 8 9 10   BB   28 27 26 25 24 23
June 2023 Printing / PO 4500869423

CONTENTS

Introductory Chapters

1   Management

2 — Genres and Forms

Functional Writing

Narrative Writing

Informational

3 Craft

4 Conventions

5 Writing Process

Planning and Rehearsing

Editing and Proofreading

Publishing

Introduction

Welcome to *The Writing Minilessons Book, Grade 4*

For fourth graders, writing and drawing have become powerful ways to communicate their thoughts, ideas, and plans. For you, your students' writing and drawing provide a window into their understandings of written language. Through their writing, you can infer what your students understand about genre, craft, conventions, and the writing process. Through your teaching, your students will grow and deepen their understandings across these areas. And now, the journey begins.

Organization of Lessons

In this book, you will find 225 writing minilessons that help students develop as artists and writers. The minilessons are organized across five sections:

- ❱ Section 1: Management (MGT)
- ❱ Section 2: Genres and Forms (GEN)
- ❱ Section 3: Craft (CFT)
- ❱ Section 4: Conventions (CNV)
- ❱ Section 5: Writing Process (WPS)

The sections contain groups of minilessons, or "umbrellas." Within each umbrella, the minilessons are all related to the same big idea so you can work with each concept for several days. The umbrellas are numbered sequentially within each section, and the minilessons are numbered sequentially within each umbrella. Each writing minilesson is identified by section, umbrella, and minilesson. For example, MGT.U1.WML1 indicates the first minilesson in the first umbrella of the Management section.

Content of Lessons: *The Literacy Continuum*

Almost all lessons in this book are based on the behaviors and understandings presented in *The Fountas & Pinnell Literacy Continuum: A Tool for Assessment, Planning, and Teaching*. This volume presents detailed behaviors and understandings to notice, teach for, and support for prekindergarten through middle school across eight instructional reading, writing, and language contexts. In sum, *The Fountas & Pinnell Literacy Continuum* describes proficiency in reading, writing, and language as it changes over grades and over levels. When you teach the lessons in this book, you are teaching for the behaviors and understandings that fourth graders need to become proficient readers and writers over time.

Organized for Your Students' Needs

We have provided a suggested sequence of lessons (see pp. 4–5) for you to try out and adjust based on your observations of your students. The sequence provides one path through the lessons. If this is your first time teaching minilessons, you may want to stick to it. However, with 225 lessons from which to choose, you will not have time to teach every minilesson in this book. Choose the lessons that make sense for your class and omit any lessons that would be too advanced or too easy. You will be able to locate the lessons easily because they are organized into sections. We organized the lessons into sections for these reasons:

▶ Students in any given fourth-grade class will vary greatly in their literacy experiences and development. Lessons organized by topic allow you to select specific umbrellas or lessons that respond to your students' needs. You can find lessons easily by section and topic through the table of contents.

▶ Writing is a complex process and involves many levels of learning— from figuring out the idea to communicate, to putting the thinking into language, to thinking about what to draw and write, to applying the conventions of the written language. Having the lessons organized by section enables you to focus on the areas that might be most helpful to your students at a specific point in time.

Key Words Used in Minilessons

The following is a list of key terms that we will use as we describe minilessons in the next chapters. Keep them in mind so that together we can develop a common language to talk about the minilessons.

▶ **Umbrella** A group of minilessons, all of which are directed at different aspects of the same larger category of understanding.

▶ **Minilesson** A short, interactive lesson to invite students to think about one idea.

▶ **Principle** A concise statement of the concept students will learn and be invited to apply.

▶ **Writing** All the kinds of writing, including drawings, that fourth-grade students will do to communicate meaning and a message.

▶ **Mentor Text** A fiction or nonfiction text in which the author or illustrator offers a clear example of the minilesson principle. Students will have previously heard the text read aloud and talked about it. Mentor texts can be books you have read to them as well as texts that you have written or ones that you and the students have written together. Occasionally, student writing can also serve as a mentor text.

▶ **Text Set** A group of either fiction or nonfiction books or a combination of both that, taken together, help students explore an idea, a topic, or a type of book (genre). You will have already read the books to them before a lesson. Students will have also made important connections between them.

> ▶ **Anchor Chart** A visual representation of the lesson concept using a combination of words and images. You create it as you talk with the students. It summarizes the learning and can be used by the students as a reference tool.

The chapters at the beginning of this book help you think about the role of talking, drawing, and writing in fourth grade, how the lessons are designed and structured, and the materials and resources you will need to teach the lessons.

Suggested Sequence of Lessons

If you are new to fourth-grade minilessons, you may want to use the Suggested Sequence of Lessons (Figure I-1) for teaching writing minilessons across the year. This sequence weaves in lessons from the different sections so that students receive instruction in all aspects of writing and drawing throughout the school year. Lessons are sequenced in a way we think will support most fourth-grade students, but you need first to observe what most of your students are doing as talkers, artists, and writers. Then choose the specific lessons that will lead them forward.

Every group of fourth graders is different, so it is impossible to prescribe an exact sequence of lessons. However, this sequence will give you a good starting place and a menu of choices to consider as you begin to teach the lessons in *The Writing Minilessons Book, Grade 4*. As you use the suggested sequence, consider the following:

> ▶ You will most likely not be able to teach every minilesson this book has to offer, so pick the lessons that will be most important for your group of learners. Minilessons within an umbrella work together but they also can stand alone, so don't worry if you skip minilessons within an umbrella.

> ▶ Pick and choose genres you want to introduce to your students and also provide time for them to make their own genre choices. There are many craft, conventions, and writing process minilessons that can be applied to any genre. Your students are learning how to be writers who make decisions to clearly communicate to an audience no matter what genre they are writing in.

If you use *Fountas & Pinnell Classroom™ Shared Reading Collection* (2023) or *Interactive Read-Aloud Collection* (2020), or *The Reading Minilessons Book, Grade 4* (2020), note that the Suggested Sequence of Lessons follows the sequences found in these resources to help organize

Months	Texts from *Fountas & Pinnell Classroom™ Shared Reading Collection*	Text Sets from *Fountas & Pinnell Classroom™ Interactive Read-Aloud Collection*	Reading Minilessons (RML) Umbrellas	Writing Minilessons (WML) Umbrellas	Teaching Suggestions for Extending Learning
Months 1 & 2	Stinky, Slimy, Sludgy Poems	Friendship	MGT.U1: Being a Respectful Member of the Classroom Community	**MGT.U1: Being a Respectful Member of the Classroom Community**	If you have taught the first umbrellas in the Management and Literary Analysis sections of *The Reading Minilessons Book, Grade 4*, you may not need to teach similar lessons in WML MGT.U1 because the RML and WML books establish the same basic routines. The lessons in WML MGT.U1 provide a context for applying the umbrella's behaviors and routines by inviting students to interview classmates and create slides to introduce them to the class. They are also invited to make public service announcements about their class values.
		Figuring Out Who You Are	MGT.U2: Getting Started with Independent Reading	**WPS.U1: Introducing and Using a Writer's Notebook, WML1–WML4**	We recommend introducing a writer's notebook as soon as you can in the school year so that students can write in it daily. Teach most of this umbrella at one time or interweave these lessons with MGT.U1 or MGT.U2. Consider teaching more than one minilesson a day for the first couple of weeks of school. For example, teach a lesson from MGT.U1 or MGT.U2 and WPS.U1 on the same day. Leave the last lesson in WPS.U1 until you have introduced most sections of the writer's notebook thoroughly.
			WAR.U1: Introducing a Reader's Notebook		
		Empathy	MGT.U3: Living a Reading Life		

reading and writing instruction across the year. If you do not have the texts suggested in the lessons as mentor texts, simply pick similar books and examples from your own classroom library or school library. Characteristics of the books used in the lessons are described on the opening page of the umbrellas for the writing minilessons. It is our intention that whenever possible students will have already seen and heard the mentor texts by the time they are used in a lesson. To read more about using the Suggested Sequence of Lessons to plan your teaching, see Chapter 6.

Figure I-1: The complete Suggested Sequence of Lessons is on pages 665–682 in this book and in the online resources.

Chapter 1

The Role of Writing in Literacy Learning

Writing can contribute to the building of almost every kind of inner control of literacy learning that is needed by the successful reader.

—Marie Clay

LOOK AROUND A FOURTH-GRADE CLASSROOM, bustling with the energy of independent learners. Some students are busy observing, sketching, and writing notes in their writer's notebooks about the latest observation in the science center. Other students are deep into their research about a topic they love and care about. Still others are off making books. They are writing picture book biographies, making poetry anthologies, and writing about their favorite memories. They are composing multimedia presentations and narrating digital photo essays on computers. Partners read each other their writing and offer suggestions, and the teacher confers with individual writers who are eager to share the latest additions to their writing. The classroom is filled not only with the excitement of exploration but with the tools of literacy.

Students in your fourth-grade classroom are learning to be part of a community of talkers, scientists, mathematicians, artists, readers, and writers. The writing minilessons in this book play an important role in this process.

In the lessons, students will draw and write in many different ways for many different purposes and audiences across the curriculum (Figure 1-1).

The writing minilessons in this book will help students see the stories in their lives and will help you provide time and space for them to share their stories—orally as well as in written form. We recommend that fourth graders use a writer's notebook to collect ideas for writing. Several minilessons in the Writing Process section are dedicated to helping students build a writer's notebook and develop the habit of using quick writes to write in their notebooks for at least ten minutes a day outside of writers' workshop. They learn that a writer's notebook is a place to generate and try out ideas, play with craft moves, and learn about their identities and interests. Students begin to live their lives with a writer's eye—seeing ideas for writing in everyday occurrences. If they have daily opportunities to write and draw, they will learn to see themselves as writers and artists.

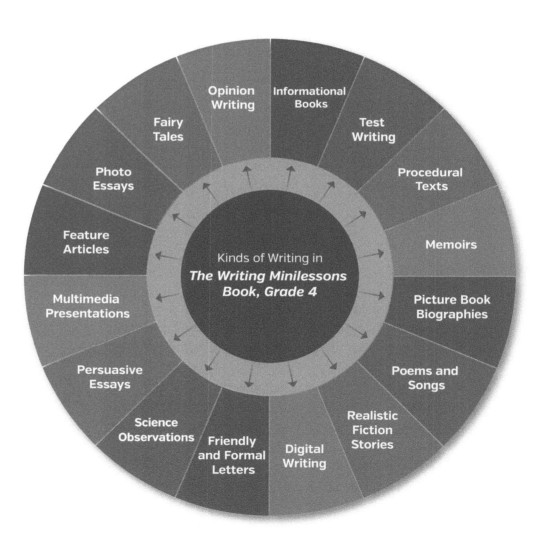

Figure 1-1: Students will have opportunities to write and draw in a variety of ways across the year.

Students' Writing Shows What They Know

Students learn differently from one another, but all make progress toward the kind of writing they see in the world, from books to digital media. Observing fourth graders write and looking at their writing will give you evidence of what they know. Notice whether they

- initiate writing quickly,
- have things to write about,
- choose topics and stories they care about,
- show enthusiasm for their writing,
- draw pictures with details,
- write words with standard spellings,
- talk about their pictures and messages,
- try out different kinds of writing (different genres and forms),
- write several sentences or paragraphs to communicate a continuous message,
- read and reread what they have written,
- try out new learning in their writing,
- use capitalization and punctuation to clarify their writing, or
- revise, or change, their writing to make it more interesting, more detailed, or clearer.

When you notice what your students are doing with writing and drawing, you can build on their strengths and help them take the next steps as writers and illustrators. In Figure 1-2, notice all the things fourth-grader Dan is doing in his writing. Also notice areas in which he can grow based on his budding understandings. It is important to note that students take on new behaviors and understandings over time. Your foremost goal in analyzing students' writing is not to "fix" a particular piece of writing (though you might use one piece to teach one or two important new concepts) but to give students the tools to think and write in new ways. Analyzing your students' writing gives you direction for what you might teach to lead them forward. When you meet students where they are and build on their strengths, they are more engaged and interested in learning how to make their writing and art more like the texts they are reading.

Chapter 6 includes information about the tools provided in the online resources to assess your students' writing. *The Fountas & Pinnell Literacy Continuum* and the assessment sections in the writing minilessons will guide your observation of students' writing behaviors and your analysis of their writing pieces. When you take time to talk to students and read their writing, you learn what they have understood from your teaching, what they have yet to understand, and what you might teach them next.

Fourth Graders Connect Oral Language, Reading, and Writing

A child's journey to becoming literate begins at birth. Dan has developed the understandings he demonstrates in Figure 1-2 over many years. As caregivers engage a child in language interactions, the child learns to communicate, and this oral language foundation paves the way for learning about written language—reading and writing. All aspects of students' oral and written language—listening, speaking, reading, and writing—develop together and support each other as the students' literacy understandings grow. Each literacy experience they have contributes to what they are able to show in their own writing.

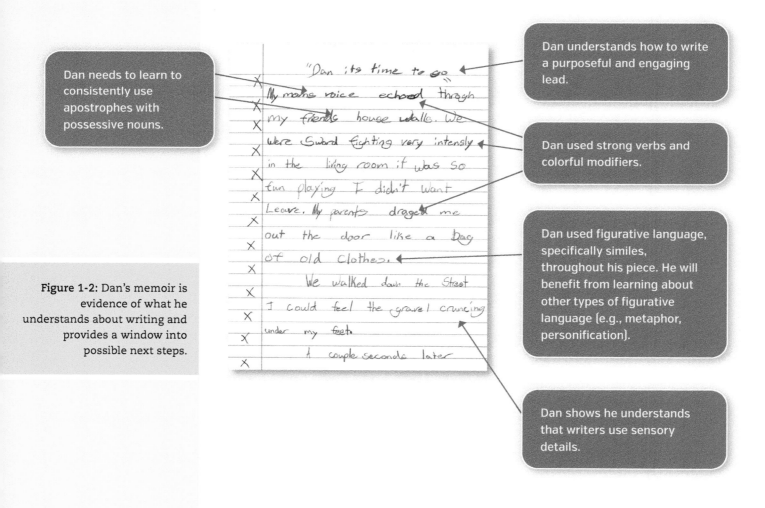

Dan needs to learn to consistently use apostrophes with possessive nouns.

Dan understands how to write a purposeful and engaging lead.

Dan used strong verbs and colorful modifiers.

Dan used figurative language, specifically similes, throughout his piece. He will benefit from learning about other types of figurative language (e.g., metaphor, personification).

Dan shows he understands that writers use sensory details.

Figure 1-2: Dan's memoir is evidence of what he understands about writing and provides a window into possible next steps.

Dan needs to learn how to recognize run-on sentences and use more conventional punctuation and capitalization.

Dan demonstrates an understanding of how to integrate dialogue into a piece of writing, but he needs to learn to punctuate dialogue more consistently.

Dan understands how to use transitions to help his writing flow and shows that he understands he can edit his work. Here, he used a caret to add an omitted word.

Dan understands how to use dialogue to show a character's feelings. He elongated the word "please" to show how much he wants to climb the fence.

Dan understands how to use ellipses to create suspense and tension. He also clearly understands how to tell a story in chronological order and use words to show the passage of time.

Dan shows a beginning understanding of how to use paragraphs to break up his writing and start new ideas.

[Student handwriting, first page:]

we took a left turn down a dirt
so path. Down the dirt path the
tree's were beutiful they were all
diffrent colors red, orange, yellow,
brown they were all draping leafs
by the minute. As we walked
my legs were draging me so
I asked my Dad "Can I go
on your shoulders' after a
few feets droped. He spoke
"Sure get on my back"
As we walked ^we aproached
a fence. It was a pale blue

[Student handwriting, second page:]

fence with a shinning glare.
showing of it. All of a suddent all I wanted to do
was climb it. I looked down
at my dad and asked "Can
I pleaaase climb that
fence" my dad looked at
my mom she noded so
he replied "go ahead".
I ran over to the
fence.
It had started to drissle
When I reached the
fence I looked back

[Student handwriting, third page:]

at my parents they were
going around the fence
because there were two paths
around it. So I started
to climb. I Climbed up the
first bar the Second and
third. then suddenly I sliped
I could feel the cold
hard Ciment under my arm.
I burst out into tears
my mom and dad ran
over to me like a
stamped of buffloa

Dan still needs to work on paragraphing to show a new speaker in dialogue.

Dan would benefit from learning how to introduce new characters in his writing.

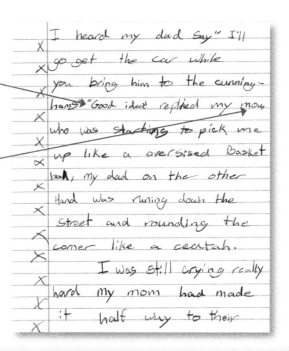

I heard my dad say" I'll go get the car while you bring him to the cunninghams" "Good idea" replied my mom who was starting to pick me up like a oversised Basket ball, my dad on the other Hand was runing down the street and rounding the corner like a ceatah.
I was still crying really hard my mom had made it half way to their

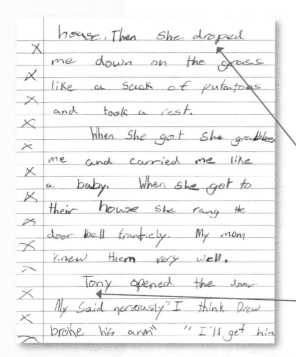

house, Then She droped me down on the grass like a sack of putatoos and took a rest.
When she got she grubbed me and carried me like a baby. When she got to their house She rang the door bell franticly. My mom Knew them very well.
Tony opened the door My Said nervously"I think Drew broke his arm" '' I'll get him

Dan needs to learn to review the rule for doubling consonants when adding the suffixes -ed and -ing and apply it more consistently.

Dan would benefit from minilessons about proofreading and from rereading his work to find missing words and inconsistent punctuation.

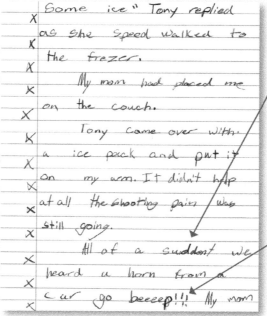

Some ice" Tony replied as she speed walked to the frezer.
My mom had placed me on the couch.
Tony came over with a ice pack and put it on my arm. It didn't help at all the shooting pains was still going.
All of a suddent we heard a horn from a car go beeeep!!! My mom

Though Dan has a beginning understanding of how to vary sentences, he would benefit from minilessons on how to vary sentence length and use transitions.

Dan infused his writing with voice through his word choices, punctuation decisions, and spelling choices.

The Writing Minilessons Book, Grade 4

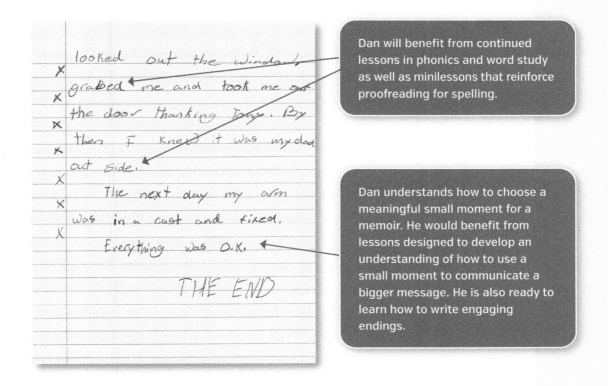

Fourth graders understand that their thoughts and ideas can be put into language, language can be put into writing, and the writing can be read (Figure 1-3).

Students benefit from opportunities to tell their stories orally. Whenever possible, have students share their ideas and stories aloud in small groups or with a partner so they have a chance to rehearse what they want to say before putting it on paper. The minlessons in MGT.U1: Being a Respectful Member of the Classroom Community are designed to build a classroom culture of acceptance and respect in which students feel comfortable sharing their stories and receiving feedback. In addition to sharing stories and ideas, students articulate how they plan to apply a new writing minilesson principle. The Have a Try section of the minilesson often invites students to share how they will apply the new understanding to their current writing. As fourth graders listen to, read, and discuss more complex texts, they also grow in their understanding of plot and text structures. They develop the ability to use increasingly more sophisticated patterns of language and build strong vocabularies. As they write their own texts, they have conversations about their writing that deepen their ability to explain their thinking. They learn to organize their ideas, to elaborate with story details, to use content-specific vocabulary, and to more accurately describe what they want to say.

The Contributions of Writing to Language, Literacy, and Learning

As students take on literacy, they grow in oral language, reading, and writing. As they write, they

- Link spoken language to written language
- Work on communicating meaningful messages
- Break multisyllable words into smaller parts
- Experiment with more complex language structures
- Read and reread their writing
- Use technical vocabulary they have heard or read
- Use punctuation to craft the way they want their audience to read their writing

Figure 1-3: Contributions of writing to literacy learning

Oral storytelling and rehearsal are not only useful for writing stories. Talking about what to write also helps with nonfiction writing. For example, it is helpful for students to say something in their own words before they jot down notes while doing research on a topic. Fourth graders can more easily move from research to writing when they have opportunities to talk about their learning before writing.

Students also benefit from orally sharing what they have written. As they engage in quick writes in their writer's notebooks, build in opportunities for them to turn and talk about their writing. Not only does this oral interaction inspire writing ideas across the classroom, but it also develops students' ability to listen deeply and respond to their peers. Community building is fostered across the year as students share writing and drawing that is important to them within the minilesson structure. Students learn to value and honor each individual's identity when you give them opportunities to write about themselves and space to share their writing with one another.

Students Have Opportunities to Write Across the Day

In the fourth-grade classroom, it is important to carve out a dedicated time for writing as well as to embed writing opportunities into a variety of daily classroom activities across the curriculum. From the time they enter the literacy-rich classroom, students are engaged in writing. They answer survey questions on charts, create writing pieces with their class members, write explanations for their math solutions, and make sketches of their scientific observations. They talk about the decisions authors make for their books, and they make their own books. Providing fourth graders with a predictable

Structure of Writers' Workshop		
Whole Class	Writing Minilesson	5–15 minutes
Individuals and Small Groups	Independent Writing Individual Conferences Guided Writing Groups	35–50 minutes (The time will expand as students build stamina across the year.)
Whole Class	Group Share	5–10 minutes

time to write each day allows them the opportunity to experiment with writing, to work on writing projects over several days, and to apply their new learning from writing minilessons. Consider setting aside the following times in your day for writing, and think about how you might build writing across content areas and into other established routines in your classroom.

Independent Writing Time During Writers' Workshop Independent writing time is typically bookended by a writing minilesson and a chance for students to share their writing (Figure 1-4). They learn about an aspect of writing during a writing minilesson and then have a chance to apply what they learned in that lesson as they write independently. The teacher has the opportunity to confer with individual writers or to work with small groups in guided writing (see pages 24–25 for information about guided writing). Students engage in both print and digital writing across a variety of genres and forms. They choose their own writing topics and often also select the genre and form that best fit their purpose and audience. They spend time exploring and growing ideas in a writer's notebook (Figure 1-5) and engage in both print and online research. The writers' workshop ends with a whole-group meeting in which students share their writing and, if applicable, the ways they used their new understandings from the writing minilesson. Chapter 2 describes how the writing minilessons in this book follow and support this structure. Using the Management minilessons will help you establish a productive and engaging independent writing time with your fourth graders.

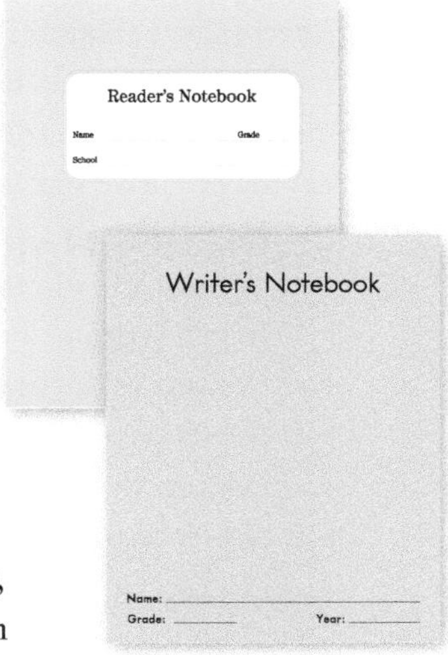

Ten-Minute Daily Quick Writes Students need regular, daily opportunities to write in their writer's notebooks in addition to the time they spend writing in their notebooks during independent writing time. Carving out ten minutes every day for students to engage in notebook writing helps them develop the habit of

Figure 1-4: A writers' workshop structure allows for whole-class learning, individual and small-group instruction from the teacher, independent writing, and whole-class sharing.

Reader's Notebook

Name   Grade

School

Writer's Notebook

Name: _____

Grade: _____   Year: _____

Figure 1-5: Students use reader's notebooks and writer's notebooks as tools to collect their thinking and ideas. A reader's notebook is used primarily for writing about reading. The writer's notebook is used for collecting and experimenting with ideas for writing original pieces.

writing every day, increases stamina, and inspires creativity and engagement in writing. Some teachers invite students to write first thing in the morning when they are often brimming with things they want to talk about. Other teachers use small windows of time they have between specials or after lunch to give students the opportunity to settle back into the classroom. This time should feel relaxing and low-pressure for students. Whether you offer a generative prompt that is open-ended enough to allow for choice or you ask them to reread their notebooks and add to a notebook entry or write about something that piques their interest, you are teaching students that writing is valued in your classroom. Providing this time outside of writers' workshop frees them to experiment with writing in a different way from the way they work on a writing project or in their writers' notebooks during independent writing. They get to exercise their writing muscles in a different manner, which fuels the work they do in writers' workshop. These daily ten-minute quick writes not only generate ideas for future writing projects but also help keep the writer's notebook fresh and relevant for use during writers' workshop.

Writing About Reading During Readers' Workshop After engaging in an inquiry-based reading minilesson, students spend time independently reading and writing about their reading. For example, they might write a weekly letter to their teacher about their reading, record character traits on a web, summarize a story, or write an opinion about a book in a book review. During this time, teachers often confer with individual readers about applying what they learn from the reading minilesson to their independent reading, or they work with small groups in a guided reading lesson. Students also might write about guided reading books as part of a reading lesson.

We recommend that fourth graders collect their thinking and writing about books in a reader's notebook (Figure 1-5). The *Reader's Notebook, Intermediate* (Fountas and Pinnell 2011) provides sections for students to record their reading, take notes about reading minilessons, and write about their reading in a variety of ways. *The Reading Minilessons Book, Grade 4,* has an extensive section of reading minilessons dedicated to writing about reading to support students in using a reader's notebook and in writing about reading in different genres and forms.

Though writing about reading is a wonderful way for students to grow as both readers and writers, be cautious about how much time you have them spend engaged in writing during reading time. Fourth graders need time to gradually increase their reading stamina. Nevertheless, you can certainly use this time to make important reading and writing connections.

Shared/Interactive Writing Time During shared writing, students have an opportunity to collaborate on a piece of writing with you as the scribe. Though shared writing is often a part of writing minilessons, you might also find it helpful to dedicate a time to writing as a whole group a few times a week. The pieces you create as a class can be used as mentor texts during

When you teach multilingual learners, you can adjust your teaching—not more teaching, but different teaching—to assure effective learning throughout each lesson. Look for the symbol below to see ways to support multilingual learners.

ML CONNECTION

writing minilessons or writing conferences. Shared writing can be done with either a whole class or a small group. Some of the students in your class, particularly multilingual learners, might also benefit from interactive writing, which is the same as shared writing except that students "share the pen" with you to write letters, word parts, or words. Interactive writing is used mostly in small groups because fewer fourth graders need this high level of support in connecting letters and sounds.

Fourth Graders Make Literacy Connections Across Content Areas

Besides having dedicated times for writing in a writers' workshop, students need to be immersed in a variety of literacy experiences throughout the day so they can make important connections between reading, writing, and word study. In a literacy-building environment, students are immersed in talking, reading and writing. They hear books read aloud, read independently, write their own books, experience reading and phonics lessons, share poetry, and write and draw about their reading. They learn to observe and write like scientists and research like historians. They learn about language and word origins and grow in vocabulary across the content areas. They learn to try out new craft techniques as they begin to think like the authors and illustrators of the mentor texts they study. All of this supports students' writing development.

Interactive Read-Aloud and Shared Reading Reading aloud to fourth graders is essential. We call it "interactive" because it is so important for students to talk with each other about the books they hear (Figure 1-6). They also love shared reading with enlarged print books and charts, reading together from the same book, song, or poem. Books enjoyed over several readings become "theirs." Interactive read-aloud and shared reading expose students to a variety of stories, informational books, songs, and poems. As fourth graders listen to and discuss these books and poems, they hear the way written language sounds and notice what other writers and illustrators do in their books. When you spend

Figure 1-6: Students develop an understanding of different text structures, an appreciation for writer's craft, and knowledge about the conventions of print through interactive read-aloud (shown here) and shared reading.

Figure 1-7: Students apply what they learn in a reading minilesson when they read independently.

time teaching students to notice how the illustrator designed the cover, the colors used in the illustrations, an interesting choice of words, or the rhythm of a repeating line, they become aware of the author's or illustrator's craft in a simple and authentic way.

Reading Minilessons, Guided Reading, and Independent Reading

Reading minilessons build on the literary understandings developed during interactive read-aloud and shared reading. Students learn more about what illustrators and writers do, how written language sounds, and how stories and information are organized. They learn about the author's message, how illustrations and print work together, and about different genres of writing. They participate in shared writing as they work with you to create anchor charts for reading minilessons and learn how to write and draw about their reading. Fourth graders grow in all of these understandings as they participate in brief, small-group guided reading lessons in which they read books at their instructional level. Students are also given opportunities throughout the day to read independently (Figure 1-7). As they engage with a variety of texts independently, they not only apply what they have learned during reading minilessons and guided reading but also make their own discoveries about print, writer's and illustrator's craft moves, and other literary elements. We have written extensively about reading minilessons and guided reading in The *Reading Minilessons Book, Grade 4* and in *Guided Reading: Responsive Teaching Across the Grades* (Fountas and Pinnell 2017). Good teaching in reading is essential to the teaching of writing and vice versa. Writing minilessons help students transfer what they have learned in reading to their own writing. In turn, what they learn about writing will make them stronger readers. It is a deeply reciprocal process.

Writing Across the Curriculum Writing plays an important role in the content areas as well (Figure 1-8). Students draw and write as they solve math problems and explain their solutions. They record information during science experiments, they write predictions and wonderings about scientific phenomena, and they take notes about what they read and experience in social studies. Writing, along with talking and reading, is one of the vehicles for learning across the curriculum. Encourage your students to make books in science and social studies—

for example, a how-to book for conducting a science experiment, a picture book biography of a current or historical figure, or a lab book of science observations. In the Genres and Forms section, you will find several umbrellas that introduce different kinds of writing that can be used across the curriculum. For example, GEN.U9: Making Informational Multimedia Presentations provides a way for students to display their learning about any topic they study in the content areas. In the Writing Process section,

Figure 1-8: Examples of fourth graders' writing across the curriculum

Cyrus made a comic strip about immigration through Ellis Island in 1908.

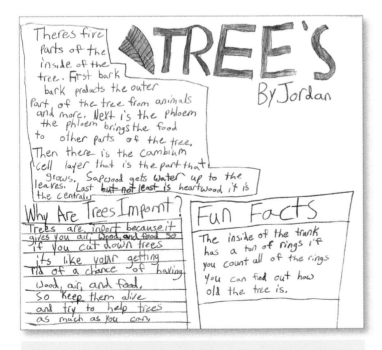

Minh made an informational poster to tell about some of the things she has learned about trees. She incorporated features and graphics she has seen in informational mentor texts (e.g., fun facts).

During independent reading, Minh wrote about the theme of Patricia Polacco's book *The Junkyard Wonders* in her reader's notebook.

as part of the planning process, there is an umbrella that demonstrates how to observe and write like a scientist. GEN.U16: Making Photo Essays offers students yet another creative way to tell about something they have learned.

As described earlier, fourth graders also have several opportunities throughout the day to write about their reading in a reader's notebook. You can teach them a variety of ways to respond to their reading through modeled or shared writing. The writing minilessons in this book focus on having students write their own original pieces, but writing about reading is still an important part of becoming a writer.

Phonics and Word Study Through inquiry-based writing minilessons, students have opportunities to revisit important word-solving actions and be reminded of key principles about the way words work to support their use of conventional spelling. For example, in CNV.U1: Writing Words, students learn to break words into syllables, to use what they know about words to write new words, and to pay close attention to writing plurals and homophones. Writing provides the opportunity to apply what they have learned through phonics and word study lessons. It is important for fourth-grade teachers to provide a specific time for daily word study lessons (see *Fountas & Pinnell Word Study System, Grade 4,* 2020) in addition to writing minilessons. The following list has a few simple ways to help students develop in these areas.

- Demonstrate making words and word parts with magnetic letters.

- Use word webs (e.g., write a word in the middle of the web and brainstorm words with the same root or same word part for the spokes of the web).

- Use word ladders to change parts of words to make new words (e.g., *port, part, past, last, list*).

- Provide games (e.g., lotto, bingo, concentration) that focus on a word study principle, and teach students how to play.

- Use shared reading of songs, poems, and big books to highlight high-frequency words, different spelling patterns, and vocabulary.

Students Engage in the Writing Process

All writers, regardless of age or experience, engage in the same aspects of the writing process every time they write. Although components of the writing process are usually listed in a sequence, writers can and will use any or all of the components at any point while writing (Figure 1-9). Throughout the process, writers and illustrators often use a writer's notebook to generate ideas, make plans, and try out new craft moves. The lessons in the Writing Process section will help you set up this tool if you want to use it with your

The Writing Process

Planning and Rehearsing

Gather ideas in your writer's notebook and plan your writing.

Drafting and Revising

Start a writing project on draft paper. Organize, change, add to, or delete words or sentences from your writing to make it interesting, focused, and clear.

Editing and Proofreading

Read over your writing to make sure it makes sense. Check your spelling, capitalization, and punctuation to make it clear for your readers.

Publishing

Make your writing ready to share with an audience. Choose a title, add book and print features, and choose how you want your final piece to look.

Figure 1-9: The writing process is not linear. Sometimes writers will go forward (the solid arrows) and sometimes they will go back (the dotted arrows) before they move forward again. Individual writers develop their own writing process. Not all writing projects go entirely through to publishing, but all projects provide an opportunity to apply what students are learning in writing minilessons.

students. You can read more about the writing process and the writer's notebook in Chapter 5.

- ▶ **Planning and Rehearsing** In this part of the writing process, students gather ideas and talk about them with others. Fourth graders learn to become more intentional planners. They think about their purpose and audience and choose the genre or form of writing that is most effective for their purpose and best communicates their message. During planning, students are often engaged in collecting ideas in their writer's notebooks or rereading entries to decide what they might want to develop into a more in-depth writing piece.

- ▶ **Drafting and Revising** This part of the process is focused on getting ideas down on paper and learning how to make changes to improve the writing. Through writing minilessons, students learn the craft moves authors and illustrators make. They use their writer's notebooks to experiment with ideas for writing and to try out the new craft moves.

▶ **Editing and Proofreading** For fourth graders, editing and proofreading mean applying what they have learned about the conventions of writing to make their writing clear for readers.

▶ **Publishing** This part of the process means sharing a finished piece with an audience. Fourth grade is a good time to think about broadening these audiences to give students authentic experiences for sharing their writing. There are a variety of ways to publish both formally and informally using different materials and tools.

Of course, drawing and reading are fundamental parts of this process, as well. The minilessons in the Writing Process section are designed to support students as they engage in each step of this process.

Fourth Graders Learn About Writing by Seeing and Doing

Students benefit from seeing examples and demonstrations of drawing and writing before they try drawing and writing on their own. Use modeled, shared, interactive, or guided writing so that students see writing happening.

Modeled Writing

Modeled writing, which includes drawing, has the highest amount of teacher support (Figure 1-10). Students see what it looks like to produce a piece of writing as you demonstrate creating a particular genre, or type of writing. As you draw and write, talk through the decisions you are making as an artist or writer. Sometimes, you will have prepared the writing before class, but you will still talk about your thought process. Modeled writing or drawing is often used within a writing minilesson to demonstrate what a particular kind of writing looks like and how it is produced.

Modeled writing is a powerful way to teach writing because it allows you to teach from experience. When you are a teacher who writes, you can talk about the mentor texts you might have consulted, explain why you chose a certain craft move, and share your struggles with the writing process. You will also discover what is helpful to a writer and what might actually be limiting. Write from your own experiences and interests. You don't have to oversimplify your writing to demonstrate important writing principles from it. You also don't have to share your entire writing piece. Excerpts of modeled writing work just fine during a minilesson. Your students will value the fact that the example comes from a real piece of writing that you care about. Students will connect with the authenticity of your writing and get even more excited about their own.

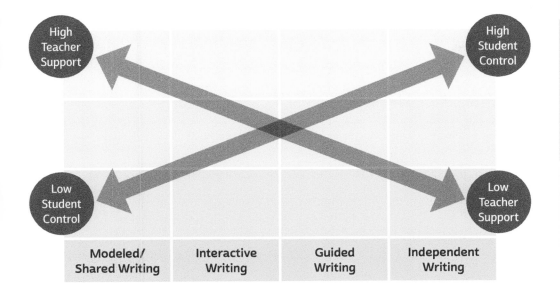

| Modeled/ Shared Writing | Interactive Writing | Guided Writing | Independent Writing |

Figure 1-10: Each instructional context for writing has a different amount of teacher support and student control (from *The Literacy Quick Guide* by Irene C. Fountas and Gay Su Pinnell, 2018).

Shared Writing

In shared writing, use the students' experiences and language to create a collaborative text. Multilingual learners especially benefit from being able to read a text to which they have contributed. Shared writing is used for most of the charts in the writing minilessons, though you might decide to use modeled, or occasionally, interactive writing. Although you are the scribe who writes the text on chart paper displayed on an easel or whiteboard, students participate by contributing ideas. First, students talk about their experiences and ideas. Then, you and your students decide together what to say and how to say it (composing). Fourth graders benefit from participating in the process of putting complex thoughts together and getting them on paper. The process begins with a plan you make together, and then you move to writing the message as the students observe and talk about the content and process.

Shared writing provides the opportunity to occasionally pause and ask students to say multisyllable words slowly, breaking them into syllables to support their writing of more complex words. It is important for the students to say the word for themselves. Other times, you (with the students' input) will write the word, sentence, or phrase on the chart quickly to keep the lesson moving. Reread what you have written as you go along so that students can rehearse the language structure, anticipate the next word, and check what has been written. The chart then becomes a model, example, or reference for future reading, writing, and discussion.

Shared writing is often integrated into writing minilessons (Figure 1-11), but you may want to occasionally carve out a time focused solely on creating a piece of writing with your students. This process can be particularly helpful

ML CONNECTION

when introducing a new genre. For example, you might spend a day or two writing about a class memory before you embark on GEN.U5: Writing Memoirs.

Interactive Writing

 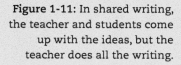

Interactive writing and shared writing are very similar. The only difference is that in interactive writing students share the pen by writing letters, word parts, or words. Occasionally, while making teaching points about various features of letters and words as well as punctuation, invite a student to the easel to contribute a letter, a word, a part of a word, or a type of punctuation. This process is especially helpful to multilingual learners and students who need support with letter/sound relationships and spelling. Consider using interactive writing with small groups of these students during independent writing time.

Guided Writing

Guided writing allows for differentiated learning in order to address the common needs of a small, temporary group of students. By conducting conferences with students and examining their writing, you determine which students would benefit from small-group teaching. For example, you may have introduced a new kind of writing to the whole group but notice that there are a few students who need more support to take on the new learning. Or, you have noticed a few students experimenting with writing poetry and you want to support their new interest. In each case, you can pull a guided writing group together to deepen and expand students' understandings about genre, craft, conventions, and the writing process. When the new learning is accomplished, the group is disbanded. Whether you are reviewing or teaching something new that the whole class is not quite ready for, the small-group setting of guided writing allows you to closely observe your students' writing behaviors and provide specific guidance. Guided writing lessons are brief and focused. Typically a guided writing lesson lasts only ten to fifteen minutes and can take place while the rest of the class is engaged in independent writing (Figure 1-12).

Figure 1-11: In shared writing, the teacher and students come up with the ideas, but the teacher does all the writing.

Choose the point of view that best fits your story.	
First person	Third person
• How important is it for the reader to know inner thoughts?	• Do I want to create suspense?
• Do I want the main character to tell the story?	• Do I want the reader to know more about all the characters?
• How do I want my reader to connect to the main character?	• Which events do I want to zoom into?
• Does writing in first person help the story flow?	• Which events do I want to zoom out of?
	• Does writing in third person make my story flow?

Structure of a Guided Writing Lesson	
Teach a Minilesson	Teach a single principle that is useful for a small group of writers at a particular point in time. Keep the lesson brief, and allow student inquiry to drive the learning.
Students Have a Try	Provide a piece of writing and invite students to apply the new thinking. Support students' learning with additional teaching, as needed. Point out effective applications of the principle by group members.
Students Apply the Principle to Their Own Writing	Invite students to try out the principle using an existing piece of writing or, as appropriate, by beginning a new piece of writing. Students continue to work at the small table as you observe and provide guidance that deepens individual students' understanding of the principle.
Students Share	Invite students to share what they noticed and learned during the lesson. Reinforce the principle, and encourage students to share the next steps they will take in their writing.

Independent Writing

When students write and draw for themselves, all their understandings about writing and drawing—literacy concepts, word solving, purpose, audience—come together in a way that is visible. Sometimes they will write about their reading. Sometimes they will write in the content areas (e.g., science or social studies). Sometimes they will write from their personal experiences, and other times they will write about what they know or have learned about a topic through their observations and research. Through their participation in writing minilessons, students take on new understandings. Through independent writing, they try them out.

Figure 1-12: Structure of a guided writing lesson from *The Literacy Quick Guide* (Fountas and Pinnell 2018)

Levels of Support for Writing	
Type of Writing	**Characteristics**
Modeled	• Whole class or small group • Teacher composes the text (creates and says the sentences) • Teacher writes the print and/or draws images • Used to demonstrate ideas and refer to • Used as a resource to read
Shared	• Whole class or small group • Teacher and students compose the text (create and say the sentences) • Teacher writes what the students decide together • Used to record ideas to read or refer to later • Often included in writing minilessons to show something about writing or drawing

Levels of Support for Writing (cont.)

Type of Writing	Characteristics
Interactive	• Whole class or small group • Teacher and students plan what to write and/or draw • Teacher and students share the pen to write and illustrate the text • Slows down the writing/drawing and allows focus on specific drawing and writing concepts (e.g., saying words slowly to hear sounds, breaking words into syllables, techniques for drawing) • The writing/drawing can be used as a mentor text during writing minilessons and as a reference for independent writing • Often used as a shared reading text later • In fourth grade, mostly used in small groups to support students who need help with particular aspects of spelling, writing words, or craft techniques
Guided	• Small group • Teacher provides a brief lesson on a single writing principle that students apply to their own writing • Allows for close observation and guidance • Used to differentiate instruction • Teaching might involve modeled, shared, or interactive writing • Similar to a writing minilesson but in a small-group setting
Independent	• Individuals • Students decide what to say or draw and then write or illustrate their own texts (in a variety of genres and forms) • Supported by writing conferences with the teacher • Engages students in all aspects of the drawing and writing process

Figure 1-13: Choose the level of support that helps you reach your goals for your students. These supports apply to both writing and drawing.

Figure 1-13 summarizes the features of modeled writing, shared writing, interactive writing, guided writing, and independent writing. In writing minilessons, you might use any one or more levels of support: modeled, shared, and interactive writing. The ultimate goal of writing minilessons is to support students in developing their own independent drawing and writing.

Chapter 2 | What Is a Writing Minilesson?

Every minilesson should end with students envisioning a new possibility for their work, and the key to successful minilessons is helping the group of students sitting in front of us to envision the difference this lesson might make in their work.

—Katie Wood Ray and Lisa Cleaveland

A WRITING MINILESSON IS BRIEF. It focuses on a single writing concept to help students write successfully. A writing minilesson uses inquiry, which leads students to discover an important understanding that they can try out immediately.

Writing minilessons provide ways to make the classroom a community of learners. Writing minilessons engage students in conversations, storytelling, and reflection as they think about what it means to be in a community of writers. They engage students in writing in a variety of genres, learning about writer's and illustrator's craft, exploring the conventions of writing, and navigating through the writing process. Writing minilessons help fourth graders emerge as readers and writers by allowing them to think about one small understanding at a time and apply it for themselves independently.

> In an **inquiry lesson**, students engage in the thinking and develop the thinking for themselves. They learn from the inside, instead of simply being told what to understand. *Telling* is not the same as teaching.

Five Types of Writing Minilessons

This book has 225 lessons in five color-coded sections (Figure 2-1):

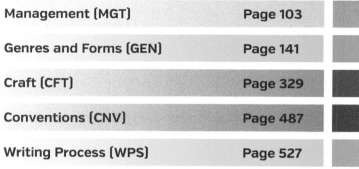

Management [MGT]	**Page 103**
Genres and Forms [GEN]	**Page 141**
Craft [CFT]	**Page 329**
Conventions [CNV]	**Page 487**
Writing Process [WPS]	**Page 527**

Minilessons in the Management section help students become a strong community of diverse learners who work and learn together peacefully and respectfully. Most of your minilessons at the beginning of the school year will focus on organizing the classroom and building a community in which students feel safe to share ideas and learn about one another. Repeat any of the lessons as needed across the year. A guiding principle: teach a minilesson on anything that prevents the classroom from running smoothly. In these lessons, students will learn

- how to get to know one another and value each individual's interests, ideas, and identities,
- routines that will help them work well with their classmates,
- ways they can participate,
- the importance of listening, taking turns, and other listening and speaking conventions when in a group, and
- how to work independently and manage materials, including their writer's notebooks and writing folders.

Minilessons in the Genres and Forms section support students by helping them see that they can write and draw like the authors of the books that they read. Through inquiry, students study the characteristics and qualities of different genres and forms. They learn how to

- teach others something they know how to do in procedural texts,
- use ideas from their own lives to write memoirs and realistic fiction,
- tell what they know about a topic in feature articles and multimedia presentations,

Figure 2-1: The writing minilessons are organized within five sections.

- write friendly and formal letters,

- make picture book biographies,

- write about their opinions,

- write persuasive essays,

- plan and create photo essays, and

- write and craft different types of poems.

Each time students are exposed to a different genre or form, they expand their understanding of ways they can write and learn more about how illustrators and authors craft their writing. The minilessons in this section primarily address behaviors in the Genres and Forms section in the grade 4 Writing continuum in *The Fountas & Pinnell Literacy Continuum*.

Minilessons in the Craft section help fourth graders learn about the decisions writers and illustrators make as they craft their pieces of writing. Through the umbrellas in this section, students explore the way authors use details in their writing to describe characters and settings. They look at the ways authors add dialogue to stories and text features to nonfiction writing. They experiment with different ways to start and end their writing and examine the ways authors choose words and shape sentences to make their writing interesting. The minilessons in this section address the behaviors and understandings in the Craft section of the grade 4 Writing continuum in *The Fountas & Pinnell Literacy Continuum*.

Minilessons in the Conventions section help students develop more sophisticated understandings of "how print works." They learn, for example, that

- you can use what you know about words to write other words,

- words can be broken into syllables to help in spelling them,

- punctuation and capitalization play important roles in communicating a writer's message, and

- writers use paragraphing to organize their writing and signal new ideas.

The lessons in this section address the behaviors primarily in the Conventions section of the grade 4 Writing continuum in *The Fountas & Pinnell Literacy Continuum*.

Minilessons in the Writing Process section guide fourth graders through the phases of the writing process: planning and rehearsing, drafting and revising, editing and proofreading, and publishing. The minilessons in this section support your students in using a writer's notebook regularly, looking for writing ideas in their own lives, and getting inspired by other writers and artists. Other lessons teach fourth graders to think about why they are writing, whom they are writing for, and what kind of writing will serve their purpose. Finally, minilessons in this section help students learn how to add to their writing, how to cut and reorganize it, how to proofread it, and how to publish and assess it.

Writing Minilessons Are Grouped into Umbrella Concepts

Within each of the five major sections, lessons are grouped in what we call "umbrellas." Each umbrella is made up of several minilessons that are related to the larger idea of the umbrella. Lessons are placed together in an umbrella to show you how the lessons build the concept. When you teach several minilessons about the same idea, students deepen their understandings and develop shared vocabulary. These connections are especially helpful to multilingual learners.

In most cases, it makes sense to teach the minilessons in an umbrella one right after another. But for some umbrellas, it makes sense to allow time between the minilessons so that students gain more experience with the first idea before moving on to the next.

ML CONNECTION

Figure 2-2: Constructing anchor charts with and in front of your class provides verbal and visual support for all learners.

Anchor Charts Support Writing Minilessons

Anchor charts are an essential part of each writing minilesson (Figure 2-2). They capture your students' thinking during the lesson and hold it for reflection at the end of the lesson. The chart is a visual reminder of the important ideas and the language used in the minilesson. Each writing minilesson features at least one sample chart, but use it only as a guideline. Your charts will be unique because they are built from ideas offered by the students in your class.

Each minilesson provides guidance for adding information to the chart. Read through lessons carefully to know whether any parts of the chart should be prepared ahead or whether the chart will be constructed during the lesson or left until the end. After the lesson, the charts become a resource for students to refer to throughout the day and on following days. They are a visual resource for students who need to not only hear

Sketch and take notes about your observations.

Tuesday, November 8

Amount of Stretch	Distance Flown
10 cm	1 meter
20 cm	2 meters
30 cm	3 meters

10cm, trial #1

but also see the information. Students can revisit these charts as they apply the minilesson principles to their writing or as they try out new routines in the classroom. You can refer to them during guided writing lessons and when you confer with students about their independent writing. When you create charts with fourth graders, consider the following:

Make your charts simple, clear, and organized. Keep the charts simple without a lot of dense text. If the topic requires more information on the chart, make sure to print neatly in dark, easy-to-read colors.

Make your charts visually appealing and useful. All of the minilesson charts contain visual support in the form of words and sometimes drawings, which will be helpful for all students, especially multilingual learners. Any drawings are intentionally simple to give you a quick model on which to base your own drawings. You might find it helpful to prepare them on separate pieces of paper or sticky notes ahead of the lesson and tape or glue them onto the chart as the students construct their understandings. This time-saving tip can also make the charts look more interesting and colorful because certain parts will stand out for the students.

 **ML CONNECTION**

Some of the art you see on the sample charts is available from the online resources to represent concepts that are likely to come up as you construct the charts with students. The downloadable chart art is provided for your convenience. Use it when it applies to your students' responses, but do not let it determine or limit their responses. Valuing the ideas of the class should be your primary concern.

Make your charts colorful. The sample minilesson charts are colorful for the purposes of engagement and organization. Color can be useful, but be careful about the amount and type you choose. Color can support multilingual learners by providing a visual link to certain words or ideas. However, color can also be distracting if overused. Be thoughtful about when you choose to use color to highlight an idea or a word on a chart so that students are supported in reading continuous text. Text that is broken up by a lot of different colors can be very distracting for readers. You will notice that the minilesson principle is usually written in black or a dark color across the top of the chart so that it stands out and is easily recognized as the focus of the lesson. In most cases, the minilesson principle is added at the end of the lesson after students have constructed their own understanding of the concept.

Use the charts to support language growth. Anchor charts support language growth in all students, especially multilingual learners. Conversation about the minilesson develops oral language and then connects oral language to print when you write words on the chart, possibly with picture support. By constructing an anchor chart with the students, you provide print that is immediately accessible to them because they helped create it and have

Figure 2-3: Characteristics of high-quality anchor charts

ownership of the language. After a chart is finished, revisit it as often as needed to reinforce not only the ideas but also the printed words (Figure 2-3).

Umbrellas and Minilessons Have Predictable Structures

Understanding how the umbrellas are designed and how the minilessons fit together will help you keep your lessons focused and brief. Each umbrella is set up the same way, and each writing minilesson follows the same predictable structure (Figure 2-4). Use mentor texts that you have previously read and enjoyed with your students to streamline the lessons. You will not need to spend a lot of time rereading large sections of the text because the students will already know the texts well.

A Closer Look at the Umbrella Overview

All umbrellas are set up the same way. They begin with an overview and end with questions to guide your evaluation of students' understanding of the umbrella concepts plus several extension ideas. In between are the writing minilessons.

At the beginning of each umbrella (Figure 2-5 on page 35), the minilessons are listed and directions are provided to help you prepare to teach them. There are suggestions for books from *Fountas & Pinnell Classroom™ Interactive Read-Aloud* Collection and *Shared Reading Collection* to use as mentor texts. There are also suggestions for the kinds of books you might select if you do not have these books.

A Closer Look at the Writing Minilessons

The 225 writing minilessons in this book help you teach specific aspects of writing. An annotated writing minilesson is shown in Figure 2-6 on page 36. Each section is described in the text that follows.

Before the Lesson

Each writing minilesson begins with information to help you make the most of the lesson. There are four types of information:

The Writing Minilesson Principle describes the key idea the students will learn and be invited to apply. The minilesson principles are based on the behaviors in the grade 4 sections of *The Fountas & Pinnell Literacy*

Structure of a Writing Minilesson	
Minilesson	• Show examples/provide demonstration. • Invite students to talk about their noticings. • Make an anchor chart with clear examples.
Have a Try	• Have students try out what they are learning (usually with a partner).
Summarize and Apply	• Summarize the learning. • Write the minilesson principle on the chart. • Invite students to apply the principle during independent writing time.
Confer	• Move around the room to confer briefly with students.
Share	• Gather students together and invite them to talk about their writing.

Figure 2-4: Once you learn the structure of a writing minilesson, you can create your own minilessons with different examples.

Continuum, but the language has been carefully crafted to be accessible and memorable for fourth graders.

The minilesson principle gives you a clear idea of the concept you will help students construct. The lessons are designed to be inquiry-based because the students need to do the thinking to understand the concept for themselves instead of hearing it stated at the beginning.

Although we have crafted the language to make it appropriate for the age group, you can shape the language to fit the way your students talk. When you summarize the lesson, be sure to state the principle simply and clearly so that students are certain to understand what it means. State the minilesson principle the same way every time you refer to it.

The Goal of the minilesson is based on behaviors in *The Fountas & Pinnell Literacy Continuum*. Each minilesson is focused on one single goal that leads to a deeper understanding of the larger umbrella concept.

The Rationale is the reason the minilesson is important. It is a brief explanation of how this new learning leads students forward in their writing journey.

Assess Learning is a list of suggestions of specific behaviors and understandings to look for as evidence that students understand and can apply the minilesson concept. Keep this list in mind as you teach.

Minilesson

The **Minilesson** section provides an example of a lesson for teaching the writing minilesson principle. We suggest some precise language and open-ended questions that will keep students engaged and the lesson brief and focused. Effective minilessons, when possible, involve inquiry. That means students actively think about the idea and notice examples in a familiar piece of writing. They construct their understanding from concrete examples so that the learning is meaningful for them.

Create experiences that help students notice things and make their own discoveries. You might, for example, invite students to look at several nonfiction informational books carefully chosen to illustrate the minilesson principle. The students will know these books because they have heard them read aloud and have talked about them. Often, you can use the same books in several writing minilessons to make your teaching efficient. Invite students to talk about what they notice across all the books.

As fourth graders explore the mentor text examples using your questions and supportive comments as a guide, make the anchor chart with your students' input. From this exploration and the discussion, students come to the minilesson principle. Learning is more powerful and enjoyable for students when they actively search for the meaning, find patterns, talk about

A Closer Look at the Umbrella Overview

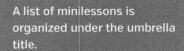
A list of minilessons is organized under the umbrella title.

Writing with Voice in Fiction and Nonfiction | Umbrella 11

Minilessons in This Umbrella

WML1 Speak directly to the reader.

WML2 Show your voice with punctuation and capitalization.

WML3 Show your voice with different styles of print.

WML4 Show your voice by saying things in a surprising way.

Before Teaching Umbrella 11 Minilessons

Voice is a characteristic that makes writing come alive. It is the authentic connection between talking and writing, so it is important to encourage students to read their writing aloud and listen to how it sounds. Students can learn to share their personalities through their writing by thinking about how authors do this in mentor texts. Support the link by helping them recognize that they can write in a way that is similar to talking but also understand that writing differs from talking. Before teaching, it is recommended that you teach CNV.U2: Learning About Punctuation and Capitalization so that students have an opportunity to explore using punctuation in traditional ways before trying it out as a way to show voice.

Use the books listed below from *Fountas & Pinnell Classroom™ Interactive Read-Aloud Collection* and *Shared Reading Collection*, or choose books from the classroom library. To help students see the print clearly, use enlarged texts, project a page of text, or write a sentence from the text on chart paper.

Interactive Read-Aloud Collection

Genre Study: Poetry

What Are You Glad About? What Are You Mad About? by Judith Viorst

Telling a Story with Photos

A Bear's Life by Nicholas Read

Exploring Identity

Crown: An Ode to the Fresh Cut by Derrick Barnes

Genre Study: Biography: Individuals Making a Difference

Farmer Will Allen and the Growing Table by Jacqueline Briggs Martin

Friendship

The Dunderheads by Paul Fleischman

Genre Study: Historical Fiction

Dad, Jackie, and Me by Myron Uhlberg

Shared Reading Collection

A Lifetime of Dance: A Biography of Katherine Dunham by Nnéka Nnolim

If Rivers Could Speak by Sherry Howard

A Spark of Genius: A Biography of Richard Turere by Myra Faye Turner

As you read and enjoy these texts together, help students notice techniques that authors use to infuse their writing with voice.

Interactive Read-Aloud
Poetry

Photos

A Bear's Life by Nicholas Read

Exploring Identity

Biography

Farmer Will Allen and the Growing Table by Jacqueline Briggs Martin

Friendship

Historical Fiction

Shared Reading

Writer's Notebook

Writer's Notebook

Section 3: Craft

Umbrella 11: Writing with Voice in Fiction and Nonfiction

■ 419

Prepare for teaching the minilessons in this umbrella with these suggestions.

Use these suggested mentor texts as examples in the minilessons in this umbrella, or use books that have similar characteristics.

Figure 2-5: Each umbrella is introduced by a page that offers an overview of the umbrella.

A Closer Look at a Writing Minilesson

The **Writing Minilesson Principle** is a brief statement that describes what students will be invited to learn and apply.

This code identifies this lesson as the fourth writing minilesson in the eleventh umbrella of the Craft section.

Look for these specific behaviors and understandings as you **assess** students' learning after presenting the lesson.

Important vocabulary used in the minilesson is listed.

Precise language is suggested for teaching the lesson.

Figure 2-6: All the parts of a single writing minilesson are contained on a two-page spread.

WML4
CFT.U11.WML4

Writing Minilesson Principle
Show your voice by saying things in a surprising way.

Writing with Voice in Fiction and Nonfiction

You Will Need

- several mentor texts with examples of surprising writing, such as the following:
  - *A Spark of Genius* by Myra Faye Turner and *If Rivers Could Speak* by Sherry Howard, from *Shared Reading Collection*.
  - *Dad, Jackie, and Me* by Myron Uhlberg, from Text Set: Genre Study: Historical Fiction
- chart paper and markers
- document camera (optional)
- writer's notebooks and/or writing folders
- To download the following online resource for this lesson, visit **fp.pub/resources**:
  - chart art (optional)

Academic Language / Important Vocabulary

- voice
- surprising

Continuum Connection

- Use memorable words or phrases

GOAL

Use surprise in writing to convey voice.

RATIONALE

When students learn to use an element of surprise in their writing, their personality and voice shine through and their writing is elevated. Helping students notice how writers use surprise adds to their enjoyment of both reading and writing.

WRITER'S NOTEBOOK/WRITING FOLDER

Make sure students have their writing folders or writer's notebooks so that during independent writing they can try out using surprising language.

ASSESS LEARNING

- Observe whether students sometimes use elements of surprise in their writing.
- Look for evidence that students can use vocabulary such as *voice* and *surprising*.

MINILESSON

To help students think about the minilesson principle, use mentor text examples that have an element of surprise and provide an interactive lesson. Here is an example.

> Listen as I read from *A Spark of Genius*.

- Show and read a few pages.

  > What are your thoughts about how the author, Myra Faye Turner, has written this biography?

  > What choices have been made that are surprising for the reader?

- Support a conversation about how it is surprising to hear figurative and rhythmic language in a biography. Begin a list on chart paper of the different ways surprise has been used, using general terms.

- Repeat with pages 9–10 in *Dad, Jackie, and Me*.

  > Let's take a look at how the author, Myron Uhlberg, has written in a surprising way.

- Show and read pages 9–10.

  > What do you notice?

- Add to chart.

  > Including something surprising is one way that voice can be used to show personality in your writing. These authors have written about a person (biography) and about a time in history (historical fiction) in an interesting way that the reader might not expect.

426

The Writing Minilessons Book, Grade 4

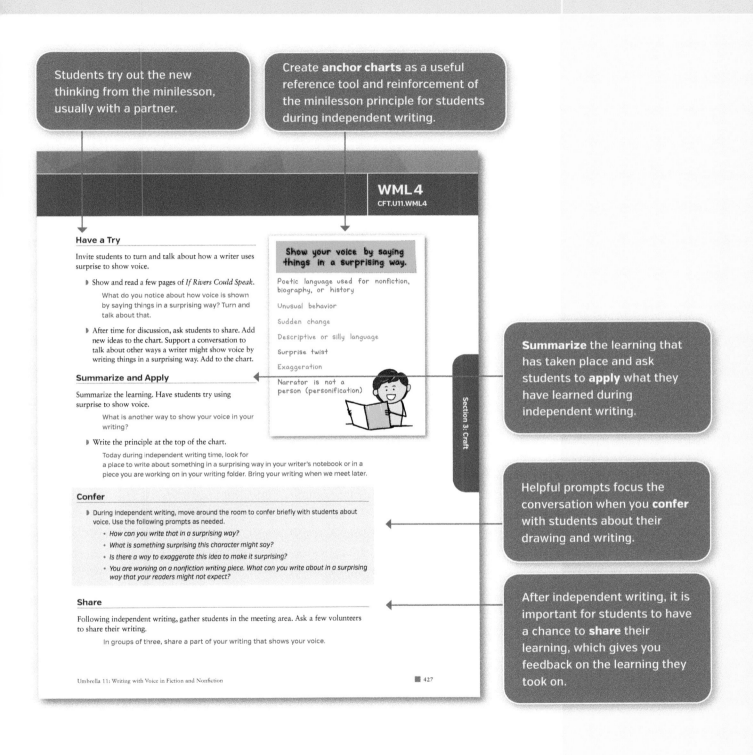

Students try out the new thinking from the minilesson, usually with a partner.

Create **anchor charts** as a useful reference tool and reinforcement of the minilesson principle for students during independent writing.

WML4

CFT.U11.WML4

Have a Try

Invite students to turn and talk about how a writer uses surprise to show voice.

▶ Show and read a few pages of *If Rivers Could Speak*.

What do you notice about how voice is shown by saying things in a surprising way? Turn and talk about that.

▶ After time for discussion, ask students to share. Add new ideas to the chart. Support a conversation to talk about other ways a writer might show voice by writing things in a surprising way. Add to the chart.

Summarize and Apply

Summarize the learning. Have students try using surprise to show voice.

What is another way to show your voice in your writing?

▶ Write the principle at the top of the chart.

Today during independent writing time, look for a place to write about something in a surprising way in your writer's notebook or in a piece you are working on in your writing folder. Bring your writing when we meet later.

> Show your voice by saying things in a surprising way.
>
> Poetic language used for nonfiction, biography, or history
>
> Unusual behavior
>
> Sudden change
>
> Descriptive or silly language
>
> Surprise twist
>
> Exaggeration
>
> Narrator is not a person (personification)

Section 3: Craft

Summarize the learning that has taken place and ask students to **apply** what they have learned during independent writing.

Confer

▶ During independent writing, move around the room to confer briefly with students about voice. Use the following prompts as needed.

• How can you write that in a surprising way?

• What is something surprising this character might say?

• Is there a way to exaggerate this idea to make it surprising?

• You are working on a nonfiction writing piece. What can you write about in a surprising way that your readers might not expect?

Helpful prompts focus the conversation when you **confer** with students about their drawing and writing.

Share

Following independent writing, gather students in the meeting area. Ask a few volunteers to share their writing.

In groups of three, share a part of your writing that shows your voice.

After independent writing, it is important for students to have a chance to **share** their learning, which gives you feedback on the learning they took on.

Umbrella 11: Writing with Voice in Fiction and Nonfiction

■ 427

their understandings, and share in making the charts. Students need to form networks of understanding around the concepts related to literacy and to be constantly looking for connections for themselves.

Writing minilessons provide many opportunities for them to express their thoughts in language, both oral and written, and to communicate with others. Students learn more about language when they have opportunities to talk. The inquiry approach found in these lessons invites more student talk than teacher talk, and that can be both a challenge and an opportunity for you as you work with multilingual learners. However, building talk routines, such as turn and talk, into your writing minilessons can be very helpful in providing opportunities for multilingual learners to talk in a safe and supportive way.

When you ask students to think about the minilesson principle across several fiction and/or nonfiction texts that they have previously heard read aloud and discussed, they are more engaged and able to participate because they know the texts and begin to notice important things about writing through them. Using familiar texts, including some writing that you and your students have created together, is particularly important for multilingual learners. When you select examples for a writing minilesson, choose books and other examples that you know were particularly engaging for the multilingual learners in your classroom. Besides choosing accessible, familiar texts, it is important to provide plenty of wait-and-think time. For example, you might say, "Let's think about that for a minute" before calling for responses.

When working with multilingual learners, look for what the students know about the concept instead of focusing on faulty grammar or language errors. Model appropriate language use in your responses, but avoid publicly correcting a student who is attempting to use language to learn it. Instead, offer alternatives. You might also provide an oral sentence frame to get the student response started, for example, "The illustrator chose _____ because _____." Accept variety in pronunciation and intonation, remembering that the more students speak, read, and write, the more they will take on the understanding of grammatical patterns and the complex intonation patterns that reflect meaning in English.

Keep the minilesson brief. If students show evidence of understanding the concept after one or two examples, move on. You do not have to use every example listed in the Minilesson section.

Have a Try

Before students leave the whole group to apply the new thinking during independent writing, give them a chance to try it out with a partner or a small group. **Have a Try** is designed to be brief, but it offers you an opportunity to gather information on how well students understand the minilesson goal. In Management lessons, students might quickly practice the new routine that they will be asked to do independently. In the other lessons, students might verbalize how they plan to apply the new understanding to their writing. Add further thinking to the chart after the students have had the chance to try out or talk about their new learning. Have a Try is an important step in reinforcing the minilesson principle and moving the students toward independence.

The Have a Try part of the writing minilesson is particularly important for multilingual learners. Besides providing repetition, it gives multilingual learners a safe place to try out the new idea before sharing it with the whole group. These are a few suggestions for how you might support students during this portion of the lesson:

 **ML CONNECTION**

- Pair students with partners that you know will take turns talking.

- Spend time teaching your students how to turn and talk (MGT.U1.WML7). Teach them how to provide wait time for one another, invite the other partner into the conversation, and take turns.

- Provide concrete examples to discuss so that students are clear about what they need to think and talk about. Multilingual learners will feel more confident if they are able to talk about a mentor text that they know very well.

- When necessary, provide the oral language structure or language stem for how you want the students to share their ideas. For example, ask them to start with the sentence frame "I noticed the writer _____" and to rehearse the language structure a few times before turning and talking.

- Provide students with some examples of how something might sound if they were to try something out in their own writing. You might say something like this: "Marco, you are writing about when you fell off your bike. You could start with dialogue. For example, you could write, 'OW! Help me!'"

- Observe partnerships involving multilingual learners and provide support as needed.

Summarize and Apply

This part of the lesson includes two parts: summarizing the learning and applying the learning to independent writing.

The **summary** is a brief but essential part of the lesson. It brings together the learning that has taken place through the inquiry and helps students think about its application and relevance to their own learning. Ask your students to think about the anchor chart and talk about what they have learned. Involve them in stating the minilesson principle. Then write it on the chart. Use simple, clear language to shape the suggestions. Sometimes, you may decide to summarize the new learning yourself to keep the lesson short and allow enough time for the students to apply it independently. Whether you state the principle or share its construction with the students, summarize the learning in a way that they understand and can remember.

After the summary, students apply their new understandings to their independent writing. The invitation to try out the new idea must be explicit but flexible enough to allow room for students to have their own ideas for their writing. The application of the minilesson principle should not be thought of as an exercise or task that needs to be forced to fit their writing but instead as an invitation for deeper, more meaningful writing. Certain craft techniques may apply only to particular genres. If students are not currently working on something to which they can apply their new learning, encourage them to revisit an old piece of writing or to experiment with the new idea in their writer's notebooks.

We know that when students first take on new learning, they often want to try out the new learning to the exclusion of some of the other things they have learned. When you teach dialogue, for example, expect to see long stretches of dialogue in their writing. Encourage them to try out new techniques while reminding them about the other things they have learned.

Before students begin independent writing, let them know that they will have an opportunity to share what they have done with the class after independent writing. Fourth graders love to share!

Confer

ML CONNECTION

While students are busy writing independently, move around the room to observe and confer briefly with individuals. Sit side by side with them and invite them to talk about what they are doing. In each minilesson, we offer prompts focused on the umbrella concept and worded in clear, direct language. Using direct language can be particularly supportive for multilingual learners because it allows them to focus on the meaning without having to work through the extra talk that we often use in our everyday conversations.

If a student is working on something that does not fit with the minilesson principle, do not feel limited to the language in this section. Respond to the student in a sincere and enthusiastic way. Remember that the invitation to apply the new learning can be extended another time. This will not be the only opportunity.

General prompts, such as the following, are provided to get students talking so that you can listen carefully to the thinking behind the writing (in using the word *writing* we include drawing). Be sure to let students do most of the talking. The one who does the talking does the learning!

> ▶ *How is your writing going?*

> ▶ *How can I help you with your writing?*

> ▶ *What do you think about this piece of writing?*

▶ What do you want to do next in your writing?

▶ What is the best part of your writing so far?

▶ Is any part of your writing confusing for the reader?

▶ What would you like to do with this writing when it is finished?

Observational notes will help you understand how each writer is progressing individually and identify common areas in which several students need further support (Figure 2-7). Use your notes to customize conversations with individual students, form guided writing groups with a few students, and plan the content of future minilessons for the class.

Teacher **Ms. DeHaven**   Grade **4**   Week of **October 17–21**

Conferring Record 1

Minilesson Focus **GEN.U6: Writing Picture Book Biographies**

Student	Monday	Tuesday	Wednesday	Thursday	Friday
Sybil	10/17: Made a list of people she's interested in researching.				10/21: Tried out leads in her writer's notebook.
Anaira					
Charlie		10/18: Reread draft to make sure made sense and was clear.			
Mateo	10/17: Talked with a partner about possible subjects.				
Colette		10/18: Decided to write about Abby Wambach.			

Teacher **Ms. DeHaven**   Grade **4**   Week of **April 3–7**

Conferring Record 2

Minilesson Focus **CFT.U12: Using Text Features in Nonfiction Writing**

Student	Comments/Observations
Sybil	4/3: Read draft and made notes about where to put headings, subheadings, photos, and captions.
Anaira	4/4: Worked on writing content for two separate sidebars.
Charlie	4/7: Reread draft, checking for accurate spelling and punctuation.
Mateo	4/3: Reread draft to find places to add sensory details.
Colette	4/3: Used sticky notes to mark places where she could add headings and subheadings.
Sebastian	4/4: Added sentences to show comparisons to make information clearer.
Kavi	4/7: Sketched a timeline in his writer's notebook to show the impact of deforestation in the Amazon rain forest.
Sophia	4/5: Printed photographs from an online resource and worked on captions.
Syed	4/7: Talked about his goal to incorporate more humor into his writing.
Andre	4/3: Researched more information about his topic and made notes in his writer's notebook.
Naomi	4/5: Talked about changing the organization of her text from categories to cause and effect to communicate her message better.
Marlena	4/5: Read draft to a partner to find places to add information and delete unnecessary information.

Share

At the end of independent writing, gather your students together for the opportunity to **share** their learning with the entire group. During group share, you can revisit, expand, and deepen understanding of the minilesson's goal as well as assess learning. Often, students are invited to bring their drawing and writing to share with the class and to explain how they tried out the minilesson principle. As you observe and talk to students during independent writing time, plan how to share by assessing how many students tried the new learning in their writing. If only a few students were able to apply the minilesson principle to their writing, you might ask those students to share with the whole group. However, if you observe most of the class applying the principle, you might have them share in pairs or small groups.

You might also consider inviting students to choose what to share about their writing instead of connecting back to the minilesson principle. For example, one student might share a detail added to make an illustration more interesting. Another might share a letter to the newspaper. Another might read part of a memoir to the class.

Share time is a wonderful way to bring the community of learners back together to expand their understandings of writing and of each other as well as to celebrate their new attempts at writing. There are some particular accommodations to support multilingual learners during the time for sharing:

ML CONNECTION

- ▶ Have students share in pairs before sharing with the group.
- ▶ While conferring, help them rehearse the language structure they might use to share their drawing and writing with the class.

Teach the entire class respectful ways to listen to their peers, and model how to give them time to express their thoughts. Many of the minilessons in the Management section will be useful for developing a peaceful, safe, and supportive community of writers.

A Closer Look at the Umbrella Wrap-Up

Following the minilessons in each umbrella, you will see the final umbrella page, which includes a section for assessing what students have learned and a section for extending the learning.

Assessment

The last page of each umbrella, shown in Figure 2-8, provides questions to help you **assess** the learning that has taken place through the entire umbrella. The information you gain from observing what the students can already do, almost do, and not yet do will help inform the selection of the next umbrella

A Closer Look at the Umbrella Wrap-Up

Umbrella 11	Writing with Voice in Fiction and Nonfiction

Assessment

After you have taught the minilessons in this umbrella, observe students in a variety of classroom activities. Use *The Fountas & Pinnell Literacy Continuum* to notice, teach for, and support students' learning as you observe their attempts at writing.

▷ What evidence do you have of students' new understandings related to voice?

- Can students articulate what it means to write with voice?
- Are they trying ways to write with voice—speaking directly to the reader, using punctuation and capitalization in specific ways, using different print styles, and writing in a surprising way?
- Do they read their own writing aloud to hear how it sounds and revise if necessary?
- Are they using vocabulary such as *voice*, *speak*, *writing*, *directly*, *punctuation*, *style*, *capitalization*, *font*, *italics*, *bold*, and *surprising*?

▷ In what ways, beyond the scope of this umbrella, are students' reading and writing behaviors showing an understanding of voice?

- Are students looking for ways to make powerful word choices?
- Do they try out different points of view in their writing?

Use your observations to determine the next umbrella you will teach. You may also consult Suggested Sequence of Lessons (pp. 665–682) for guidance.

EXTENSIONS FOR WRITING WITH VOICE IN FICTION AND NONFICTION

- ▷ Encourage students to select different fonts and font sizes when they write on a computer. Encourage creative use of fonts and print styles but also caution against their overuse.

- ▷ Pull together a temporary guided writing group of a few students who need further support in understanding and using voice in their writing.

- ▷ Use shared writing to create a class story. Experiment with different capitalization, punctuation, or print styles on one or more sentences from the story. Talk about how changing the punctuation or print style affects how the words are to be read.

- ▷ Find ways to encourage students to listen to their inner voice so that they can use writing as a way to explore and give it value.

- ▷ If you are using *The Reading Minilessons Book, Grade 4* [Fountas and Pinnell 2020] you may choose to teach LA.U10: Reading Like a Writer: Analyzing the Writer's Craft.

428

The Writing Minilessons Book, Grade 4

Gain important information by **assessing** what students have learned as they apply and share their learning of the minilesson principles. Observe and then follow up with individuals in conferences or in small groups in guided writing.

Optional suggestions are provided for **extending** the learning of the umbrella over time or in other contexts.

Figure 2-8: The final page of each umbrella offers suggestions for assessing the learning and ideas for extending the learning.

you teach (see Chapter 6 for more information about assessment and the selection of umbrellas).

Extensions for the Umbrella

Each umbrella ends with several suggestions for **extending** the learning of the umbrella. Sometimes the suggestion is to repeat a minilesson with different examples. Fourth graders will need to experience some of the concepts more than once before they are able to transfer actions to their independent writing. Other times, students will be able to extend the learning beyond the scope of the umbrella.

Effective Writing Minilessons

Figure 2-9: Characteristics of effective minilessons

The goal of all writing minilessons is to help students think and act like writers and illustrators as they build their capacity for independent writing

Effective Writing Minilessons . . .

- are based on a **writing principle** that is important to teach to fourth graders
- are based on a **goal** that makes the teaching meaningful
- are **relevant to the specific needs of students** so that your teaching connects with the learners
- are very **brief, concise, and to the point**
- use **clear and specific language** to avoid talk that clutters learning
- stay **focused on a single idea** so students can apply the learning and build on it day after day
- use an **inquiry approach** whenever possible to support active, constructive learning
- often include **shared, high-quality mentor texts** that can be used as examples
- are **well paced** to engage and hold students' interest
- are **grouped into umbrellas** to foster depth in thinking and coherence across lessons
- **usually build one understanding on another** across several days instead of single isolated lessons
- provide time for students to **"try out" the new concept** before they are invited to try it independently
- engage students in **summarizing the new learning and applying it to their own writing**
- build **important vocabulary** appropriate for fourth graders
- help students **become better artists and writers**
- **foster community** through the development of shared language
- **can be assessed** as you observe students engaged in authentic writing
- **help students understand and assess what they are learning** how to do as artists and writers

and drawing across the year. Whether you are teaching lessons about routines, genre, craft, conventions, or the writing process, the characteristics of effective minilessons, listed in Figure 2-9, apply.

Writing minilessons can be used to teach anything from a new routine to a new genre to a new craft move and more. Teach a writing minilesson whenever you see an opportunity to nudge students forward as writers and illustrators.

Chapter 3 | Minilessons for Building a Community: Management

We need a caring classroom community in which multiple perspectives are developed and used to think critically and expand learning. We need a community in which children come to appreciate the value of different perspectives for their own development, in which they recognize changes in their own and others' thinking, and that difference is the source of the change.

—Peter Johnston et al.

INDIVIDUALS LEARN BETTER AND HAVE more fun when they have some routines for working safely and responsibly. The lessons in Section 1: Management establish these routines. Students learn how to

 ⬧ listen,

 ⬧ take turns,

 ⬧ show kindness to one another,

 ⬧ include and value the uniqueness of others,

 ⬧ agree on how to work together,

 ⬧ draw and write independently,

- share their writing,
- take care of classroom materials,
- use and return materials,
- use their writing folder resources,
- record their writing projects, and
- reflect on what they have learned as writers.

They become independent problem-solvers who can work and play as members of a community.

Building a Community of Writers

Writers need to feel valued and included in a community whose members have learned to trust one another with their stories. The minilessons in the Management section are designed to help students build this trust and learn to include one another in discussions and activities. The first lesson in MGT.U1: Being a Respectful Member of the Classroom Community (WML1: Get to know your classmates) sets the tone for building this community. As students share stories about who they are, where their families come from, what languages they speak, what foods they eat, and what activities they enjoy, they begin to explore their identities and learn about the identities of others. Self-identity influences the way an individual reads and writes; it impacts the perspective one brings to these literacy experiences. When we celebrate students' unique identities and perspectives, we teach students to value and include one another. This is one of the reasons the share time at the end of independent writing is so important. This time of sharing inspires writing ideas, but it does so much more. It provides a time to celebrate writing and carves out space to celebrate each writer in the classroom community.

Create a Peaceful Atmosphere

The minilessons in the Management section will help you establish a classroom environment in which students are confident, self-determined, and kind and in which every person's identity is valued. The lessons are designed to contribute to peaceful activity and shared responsibility. Through the minilessons in MGT.U1: Being a Respectful Member of the Classroom Community, students learn how to use their words and actions to show respect to one another. They also learn to keep supplies in order, help others, use the appropriate voice level for an activity, and problem-solve independently (Figure 3-1).

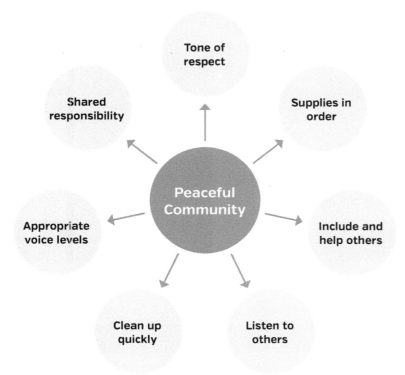

Figure 3-1: Characteristics of a peaceful atmosphere for the community of readers and writers

All of these minilessons contribute to an overall tone of respect in every classroom activity. They are designed to help you establish the atmosphere you want. Everything in the classroom reflects the students who work there; it is their home for the year.

Teach the minilessons in MGT.U1 in the order that fits your class needs, or consult the Suggested Sequence of Lessons (pp. 665–682). You may need to reteach some of these lessons because as the year goes on you will be working in a more complex way. A schedule change or other disruption in classroom operations might prompt a refresher minilesson. Any problem in your classroom should be addressed through minilessons that focus on building a community of learners.

Design the Physical Space

In addition to creating a peaceful atmosphere, prepare the physical space in a way to provide the best support for learning (Figure 3-2). Each umbrella in Section 1: Management will help your fourth graders become acquainted with the routines of the classroom and help them feel secure and at home. Make sure that the classroom has the following qualities.

Figure 3-2: In this meeting area, the teacher has access to everything she needs for interactive read-aloud, shared reading, and minilessons, and the students have plenty of room to sit comfortably.

▶ **Welcoming and Inviting.** Pleasing colors and a variety of furniture will help. There is no need for commercially published posters or slogans. The room can be filled with the work that the students have produced beginning on day one, some of it in languages other than English. They should see signs of their learning everywhere—shared writing, charts, drawings of various kinds, and their names. Be sure that your students' names are at various places in the room—on desks or tables, on a jobs chart, and on some of the charts that you will make in the minilessons. A wall of framed students' photographs and self-portraits sends the clear message that this classroom belongs to them and celebrates their unique identities. The classroom library should be as inviting as a bookstore or a library. Place books in baskets and tubs on shelves to make the front covers of books visible and accessible for easy browsing. Clearly label the supplies in the writing center so students can see the materials that are available and can access them and return them independently (Figure 3-3). Better yet, have students make labels independently or with you during shared or independent writing. Fourth graders also love to be involved in the naming of the different classroom areas so they truly feel like they have ownership of the classroom.

▶ **Organized for Easy Use.** The first thing you might want to do is to take out everything you do not need. Clutter increases stress and noise. Using scattered and hard-to-find materials increases the students' dependence on you. Consider keeping supplies for reading, writing, and word study in designated areas. The writing center might be used to store paper, highlighters, drawing materials, staplers, etc. Over the course of the year, introduce different kinds of media into this space so students can experiment with collage, 3D objects, and materials that have different textures.

Figure 3-3: Writing materials are organized and nearby for students to use.

In the first few days of school, students learn how to get supplies and return supplies. Some teachers choose to have caddies at tables instead of keeping supplies on a shelf in the writing center so that students can spread out and get started right away. Work areas are clearly organized with necessary, labeled materials and nothing else. (Figure 3-4).

▶ **Designed for Whole-Group, Small-Group, and Individual Instruction.** Writing minilessons are generally provided as whole-class instruction and typically take place at an easel in a meeting space. The space is comfortable and large enough for all students to sit as a group or in a circle. It will be helpful to have a colorful rug that helps students find an individual space to sit without crowding one another. The meeting space is next to the classroom library so that books are displayed and handy. The teacher usually has a larger chair or seat next to an easel or two to make it easy to display the mentor texts, make anchor charts, do shared or interactive writing, or place big books for shared reading. This space is available for all whole-group instruction; for example, the students come back to it for group share. In addition to the group meeting space, assign tables and spaces in the classroom for small-group

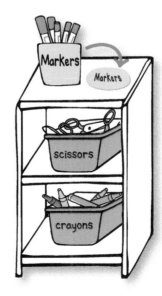

Figure 3-4: A label on the shelf helps students know where to return materials.

writing instruction. Use shelving and furniture to define and separate learning areas and to create storage opportunities. Fourth graders need tables and spaces throughout the classroom where they can work independently and where you can easily set a chair next to a student for a brief writing conference.

▶ **Respectful of personal space.** Fourth-grade students need a place to keep a personal box, including items such as a writer's notebook, writing folder, independent reading book, and reader's notebook. Students can keep these boxes on their individual desks, or you can distribute them around the room to avoid traffic jams when students retrieve them. If students make their own poetry anthologies (see GEN.U13: Making Poetry Anthologies), they decorate them and place them face out on a rack for easy retrieval. Artifacts like these add considerably to the aesthetic quality of the classroom.

Establish Independent Writing

The umbrellas MGT.U2: Establishing Independent Writing will help you set up a productive and constructive independent writing time with your fourth graders. The minilessons in these umbrellas will help them learn what to do and what tools to use during independent writing time.

At the beginning of the year, keep the writing time short (you may even start with just fifteen minutes of independent writing time) so they can feel successful right away. Add a few minutes every day until they are able to sustain writing for thirty to forty minutes. Involve students in setting goals for stretching their writing time, and celebrate each time you reach them as a class. You will soon have them asking for more time to do this important work. Fourth graders also begin to see the value of working on a piece of writing over time. Through this umbrella, they also learn that writers receive feedback and guidance from other writers. They learn the routines for talking productively with a teacher and their classmates about their writing.

Independent Writing Time

Through the minilessons in MGT.U2: Establishing Independent Writing, students create and agree on a set of guidelines for independent writing—the routines needed to be independent and productive. They learn to get started with their writing quickly and quietly, to increase their stamina, and to become efficient in storing their writing and materials at the end of writing time. They learn how to use various writing tools to support their writing, such as a writer's notebook, a writing folder, and various kinds of paper.

Students also learn that writers are never finished. They learn that when they finish a writing project, they can start another, work in their writer's notebooks, or revisit a different writing project in their writing folders.

Writing Tools

Students will use three main tools during independent writing: a writer's notebook, a writing folder, and a hanging file. The writer's notebook and the writing folder are the primary tools.

- ◗ Writer's notebook—a place to collect ideas for writing and try out new learning about the craft of writing and drawing each day
- ◗ Writing folder—a two-pocket folder with brads in the middle for fastening resources; a place to store writing that is in progress
- ◗ Hanging file in a box or crate—a place to keep finished writing projects (Figure 3-5)

Writer's Notebook Lessons in the Management section establish the routines for when to use and how to manage writer's notebooks. Because the writer's notebook is used throughout the writing process, minilessons about introducing and using it are in Section 5: Writing Process. In-depth information about writer's notebooks as well as a description of the minilessons that support using writer's notebooks with fourth graders begin on page 87 of this book.

Writing Folder The writing folder is a place to keep writing projects—drafts of books and other writing pieces on which students are working outside of their writer's notebooks. When students learn about writing memoirs, for

Figure 3-5: The main writing tools for students to use during independent writing time are a writer's notebook and a writing folder. A hanging file is used to store finished writing projects.

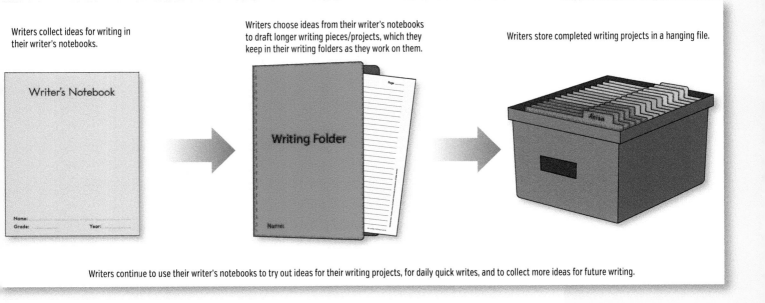

Writers collect ideas for writing in their writer's notebooks.

Writers choose ideas from their writer's notebooks to draft longer writing pieces/projects, which they keep in their writing folders as they work on them.

Writers store completed writing projects in a hanging file.

Writers continue to use their writer's notebooks to try out ideas for their writing projects, for daily quick writes, and to collect more ideas for future writing.

example, they will take an idea out of the writer's notebook, begin a draft of a memoir, and keep the draft in the writing folder. As they develop this writing piece, they will use the writer's notebook to try out ideas and craft moves that they may or may not use in the draft.

We suggest using folders with a pocket on each side and fasteners in the middle so you can secure resources for students to use during independent writing. For efficiency, fasten all the writing folder resources inside students' writing folders, and then they will be ready for you to teach the minilesson for how to use each one. The writing folders can be stored in students' personal boxes along with other literacy resources, such as an independent reading book, a reader's notebook, a writer's notebook, and a word study folder.

Hanging File As students finish a writing project, have them move it to the hanging file kept in a filing cabinet or in crates placed in the four corners of the room to minimize traffic. Using files in four colors will help students locate their files more easily, as will making sure students' names are visible on file tabs. This process allows students to have their finished writing in one place for periodic reflection on their growth as writers. Occasionally, you might want to ask them to write a reflection about their writing and staple the reflection to the piece of writing. The collection of finished writing will help you and your students see their growth over time and will help you communicate that growth during conferences and writing celebrations with students and with their parents or caregivers.

Paper Choices

Having a choice of paper gives students a chance to envision how they want their writing to look. Fourth graders often use draft paper, which provides space for revising and editing, and then choose other types of paper when publishing. The minilesson MGT.U2.WML2 (Use writing tools to help with your writing) introduces some of the paper choices students might consider when working on a writing project. We suggest offering a wide variety of paper, which might include some of the following choices (available as templates in the online resources) throughout the year.

- Draft paper with dots in the margin to encourage writing on every other line
- Paper with picture boxes and lines in varying formats (e.g., picture box on the top with lines on the bottom or picture box on the side with wrapping lines)
- Paper in landscape and portrait layouts that can be stapled into booklets

- Paper formatted for text features (e.g., sidebar, table of contents, and materials list)
- Author page
- Dedication page
- Letter format

When you give students the ability to choose from a variety of paper for their writing projects, you teach them to make important decisions as writers and illustrators.

Writing Folder Resources

Besides providing a place for students to keep ongoing writing projects, writing folders include important resources for revising and proofreading and for helping students view themselves as writers. MGT.U3: Introducing the Writing Folder addresses these resources. Available for downloading from the online resources, the writing folder resources are the following:

- Genres and Forms at a Glance (types of writing for fourth grade)
- My Writing Projects (a document to record writing projects)
- What I Have Learned How to Do as a Writer and Illustrator (a place for students to record what they have learned as writers)
- My Writing Goals (a place for students to write how they will stretch themselves as writers)
- Writing Goals for Genres and Forms
- Commonly Misspelled Words
- Revising Checklist
- Editing and Proofreading Checklist

The resources give students agency and promote their independence by giving them tools for sustaining their own writing and for helping them develop a writing identity. Introduce the resources over time so that students learn how to best use each one. For example, you might choose to introduce the two checklists after teaching minilessons in the Writing Process section about revising and editing.

The writing folder resource titled My Writing Projects (Figure 3-6) helps students reflect on their writing lives. The record of finished writing pieces gives individual writers a sense of accomplishment and provides a way for you and your students to notice patterns in their writing choices. Use this record to help your writers reflect during writing conferences: Are there

My Writing Projects

Name _____

Project #	Title	Kind of Writing (write code)	Date Completed

Figure 3-6: Students use this template to record the title, genre, and completion date of their writing projects. All writing folder resources are available from **fp.pub/resources**.

different kinds of writing they would like to try? Are they choosing topics they care about? Is there a way to write about the same topic in a different way? It can help them think about what they have learned as writers and set goals for future writing.

Management minilessons help students navigate these resources, manage the tools of writing, and understand the routines that create a productive community of writers. Use the structure of these lessons to support any routine you think would benefit the writers in your classroom.

Chapter 4

Minilessons for Studying Genres and Forms of Writing

*Genre study is where we put all of our reading-like-a-writer
skills together. When we read like writers for genre, we read across a set of
mentor texts and notice many categories of writerly moves including ideas
(what writers generally write about in that genre) and
also craft and structure (how they write about it).*

—Allison Marchetti and Rebekah O'Dell

EXPOSING STUDENTS TO DIFFERENT GENRES, forms, and modes of writing broadens their vision for what writing can be. The minilessons in the Genres and Forms section use inquiry and mentor texts to help students understand the characteristics of different genres and how to use that knowledge when they write. Through the umbrellas in this section, students are also exposed to various forms of writing and composition. Besides learning how to write in the genres of memoir, realistic fiction, opinion writing, persuasive essay, informational text (e.g., feature articles), and procedural text, students also learn how to write in various forms and modes. They learn to make picture book biographies, write poems, design multimedia presentations, write letters, and use digital writing to communicate their ideas.

It is always helpful for students to read and study a genre either before or while writing in it. If you have *Fountas & Pinnell Classroom™ Interactive Read-Aloud Collection* and/or *The Reading Minilessons Book, Grade 4*, use the genre study text sets and the minilesson umbrellas that address genre study to immerse students within a genre and to help them define the genre in their own words. The genre study process, outlined in both the *Interactive Read-Aloud Collection* lessons and *The Reading Minilessons Book, Grade 4*, is designed to help students develop a deep understanding of the characteristics of genres as readers. We have written extensively about this topic and process in our book *Genre Study: Teaching with Fiction and Nonfiction Books* (Fountas and Pinnell 2012).

It is important for students to be exposed to a variety of genres as both readers and writers, and we hope the writing minilesson umbrellas in the Genres and Forms section will further extend their genre understandings. However, we caution you to avoid jumping directly from one genre study to another. Students need time to experiment with different forms of writing. They also need time to choose their own genres based on their purpose and audience. As Ralph Fletcher points out in his book *Joy Write: Cultivating High-Impact, Low-Stakes Writing* (2017), writers need time to play with writing. The lessons in the genre umbrellas are designed to expose students to different characteristics of a genre and offer ways for them to think about writing in them. They are not meant to take students through a rigid sequence of steps for writing in that genre. Writers each have their individual ways of working on writing. You will want to make sure you respect students' own writing processes and topic choices while helping them develop new genre understandings.

Fourth Graders Love to Make Books

Bookmaking is a powerful way for students to explore different genres and to bring together all their important literacy experiences. As students begin to write longer, more complex texts, it is important for them to continue to learn how to engage in forms of composition that include a visual element. Visual composition and the combination of graphics and print have become increasingly important over time as people engage in social media—looking at memes, gaining information from infographics, and telling stories through pictures. Picture books, including comic books, are an excellent way for fourth graders to think deeply about how print and graphics work together because they are so familiar with them. Matt Glover (2009) said it well:

> The reason for making books is simple. Books are what children have the greatest vision for, and having a clear vision for what you are making is important in any act of composition. (13)

Invite your students to make their own books, just like the authors of the books they love (Figure 4-1). The act of making picture books benefits you and the students in lots of ways.

- Fourth graders see themselves as authors, illustrators, and readers.
- They develop feelings of independence and accomplishment at having created something that is uniquely theirs.
- They try out a larger range of craft techniques, such as adding meaning through illustrations, incorporating text features (e.g., sidebars and diagrams), and organizing their ideas across pages or sections.
- They develop deeper understandings of how illustrations and print work together to communicate a message.
- Writing and reading reinforce one another, so as students make their own books, they become more aware of the decisions that authors and illustrators make in their books.
- Students expand their understanding about text structure and layout.

Cover

"Leah, how was gymnastics?" asked Mealony, Leah's mom. They were having dinner.

"Great, you will never guess what happened," said Leah. "I was on the vault making sure that it was the right height. Then I got down and was running up to the vault so I could do my 'double twist,'" Leah started.

Figure 4-1: Bookmaking invites students to experiment creatively with their writing. Inspired by another student's work, Bailey experimented with making a fantasy book of her own. She applied elements of what she has learned about writing realistic fiction stories (e.g., crafting dialogue and writing interesting endings) to writing in this new genre.

> "Mrs. Catline was watching and then I landed it in the pit. Mrs. Catline cheered and said I could have a break. I knew just what to do!" Leah took a drink of her milk. "I was going to go swimming in the pit."

> "I was at the bottom, and I realized a small hole that I could fit in. I hopped in and realized I was in a new part of the world. I walked around and found little animals working on building a star." Then Leah caught her breath and went on.

> ▸ The books they write show evidence of what they know about drawing and writing, and you can use that information to decide what they need to learn next.

> ▸ They learn to use book and print features such as author pages, dedications, and acknowledgments.

The minilessons in the Genres and Forms umbrella GEN.U6: Writing Picture Book Biographies invites students to study the qualities of picture books before they make their own. This umbrella builds a foundation for making picture books that can be applied to other genres. When you teach or revisit GEN.U2: Writing Procedural Texts, GEN.U5: Writing Memoirs, and GEN.U7: Writing Realistic Fiction Stories, offer students the choice to make these genres in the form of a picture book.

"I asked them what they were doing and who owend this land. One brave animal stoped what he was doing and said we are building a stautue of the north star because this place is called Starstrike and the owner is a troll named Roylee. I headed to a big Catle where I thought the troll might life. I was so nervous most likly

"I asked them what they were doing and who owned this land. One brave animal stopped what he was doing and said, 'We are building a statue of the North Star because this place is called Starstrike, and the owner is a troll named Roylee.' I headed to a big castle where I thought the troll might live. I was so nervous. Most likely

he was a mean troll, that would eat me.

he was a mean troll that would eat me."

Once I made it too the Catle I knocked on the door! Roylee came and opened the door Roylee had blue hair and a pink body. I said I cant get back to gymnastics Can you come and help me! leah got up to get dessert. Then leah got back

"Once I made it to the castle, I knocked on the door! Roylee came and opened the door. Roylee had blue hair and a pink body. I said, 'I can't get back to gymnastics. Can you come and help me?'" Leah got up to get dessert. Then, Leah got back

to the story Roylee said sure he got his Pravite Jet to fly me back to gymnastics. By the time I got back to gymnastics they had only moved to the next staidtion.

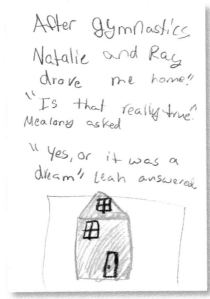

to the story. "Roylee said, 'Sure.' He got his private jet to fly me back to gymnastics. By the time I got back to gymnastics, they had only moved to the next station.'"

After Gymnastics Natalie and Ray drove me home!! " Is that really true." Mealony asked " Yes, or it was a dream" leah answered

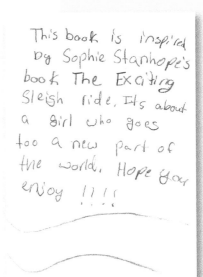

"After gymnastics, Natalie and Ray drove me home."
"Is that really true?" Mealony asked.
"Yes, or it was a dream," Leah answered.

This book is inspired by Sophie Stanhope's book The Exciting Sleigh ride. Its about a girl who goes too a new part of the world. Hope you enjoy !!!!

This book is inspired by Sophie Stanhope's book The Exciting Sleigh Ride. *It's about a girl who goes to a new part of the world. Hope you enjoy!!*

Fourth Graders Learn All About Writing Craft Through Poetry

When you teach students to read and write poetry, they learn craft moves that cross over all genres and forms. They learn how to be precise and efficient in their language, how to create sensory images, how to use figurative language, and how to evoke emotion in a reader. We have written previously that, in a way, everything writers need to know about reading and writing exists within a poem. Fourth graders benefit from learning to write poetry because they

▶ become aware of and appreciate the sound and imagery of language,

▶ reflect on themselves and the world in new ways,

▶ learn to use words, sounds, and rhythm in unique, creative ways,

▶ become able to capture the essence of a message or image with a sparse amount of language.

We recommend that you integrate poetry throughout the school year instead of teaching poetry for just a few weeks as part of a unit. Some teachers reserve one day a week or one week a month during writers' or readers' workshop time to hold a poetry workshop (Figure 4-2). During this time, students focus on reading poetry, responding to poetry in words or images, and writing and illustrating their own poetry.

Figure 4-2: Structure of poetry workshop

Structure of Poetry Workshop	
Poet Talk	• Offer advice from a poet or tell about a poet's life.
Poetry Read-Aloud and Writing Minilesson	• Read a poem aloud and teach a minilesson that can be applied to poetry. • Besides the minilessons dedicated to poetry, there are several lessons in the Craft and Writing Process sections that can be taught or retaught with poetry as the focus.
Poetry Projects and Poetry Centers	• Confer with students as they participate in reading, writing, and responding to poems.
Poetry Share	• Allow time for students to share poems they have written or memorized.

We also recommend that you help your students develop personal poetry books or anthologies. In them, they collect poems they love, respond to poetry through drawing and writing, and write their own poetry. Use the first minilesson in GEN.U13: Making Poetry Anthologies to introduce the idea to students and invite them to decorate the front cover and begin a table of contents. Providing students with multiple ways to respond, including with art, makes the poetry experience more meaningful and joyful. Fourth graders love making watercolor paintings or collages in response to poems they have read or to ones they have written. Encourage them to perform poems using movement and their voices. When they have opportunities to respond to poetry authentically, they learn more about the characteristics of poetry as well as how to write poems.

Whether students work on poetry during poetry workshop or writers' workshop, they are involved in the same writing process they go through when writing prose (Figure 4-3):

- They look at mentor texts (poems).
- They apply what they learn in minilessons.
- They collect ideas for poetry topics in a writer's notebook.
- They draft, revise, and edit their poems.
- They create art to accompany their poems.

Figure 4-3: Tyra experimented with different types of poetry in her writer's notebook, including free verse and a poem for two voices. Notice how she revised her word choice in her poem "river." The writer's notebook is a place to experiment with poems before publishing them in a poetry anthology.

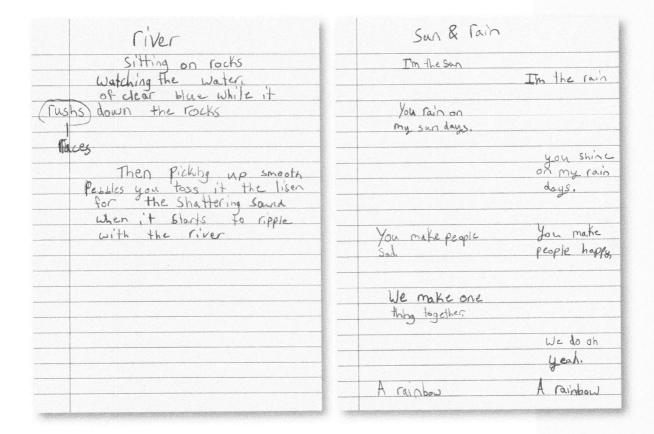

Some teachers choose to create poetry centers for their poetry workshop.

▶ Consider setting up a center to explore memorable words and phrases from books and poems. Encourage students to write their own poems using the words and phrases as inspiration. Invite them to cut out words from magazines or newspapers and make poems out of them by gluing them in a poetry book or writer's notebook.

▶ Set up a poetry window with clipboards, colored pencils, etc. Outline a portion of the window so students can look through and describe or sketch what they see. Invite them to write poems about the things they see through the poetry window.

▶ Create an illustration or art center where students have access to a variety of art media to illustrate poems they have read or written.

For more ideas, we highly recommend *Awakening the Heart: Exploring Poetry in Elementary and Middle School* (Heard 1999), *A Place for Wonder: Reading and Writing Nonfiction in the Primary Grades* (Heard and McDonough 2009), and *Poems Are Teachers: How Studying Poetry Strengthens Writing in All Genres* (VanDerwater 2018). Create a culture of poetry in your school: post poems meaningfully on the walls of the school (e.g., poems about food around the cafeteria doors or poems about water around sinks and water fountains), designate a poetry gallery where you invite students to add mentor poems as well as their own poems, create schoolwide poetry readings, or share a poem of the day as part of morning announcements. When you immerse students in poetry, you will see the results in their writing across genres.

Fourth Graders Enjoy Sharing Their Opinions

Fourth graders have strong opinions about the books they read, their hobbies and interests, their school, and their world. The umbrellas dedicated to opinion and persuasive writing provide students with the tools to express these opinions in a variety of ways.

Opinion writing is embedded in writing across the curriculum. Writing about reading, in particular, is an accessible way for students to start writing about their opinions in the early grades. They share books they love and list reasons for why they love them. They write letters stating their opinions about characters, messages, illustrations, and writing styles. They create their own book talks, sharing why the audience might be interested in reading certain books. Several minilessons in *The Reading Minilessons Books, Grade 4*, are designed to support students in writing their opinions about their reading.

Writing minilessons build on experiences students have had writing their opinions about books. In GEN.U11: Exploring Opinion Writing, students learn how to choose topics they have genuine opinions about, how to effectively introduce and state their opinions, how to provide supportive examples for their opinions, and how to conclude their opinion writing in meaningful ways.

Opinion writing sets the stage for persuasive writing but is slightly different. In opinion writing, the ultimate goal is not always to convince someone to agree with an opinion or to take action, as it is in persuasive writing. The purpose is simply to share a point of view and the reasons for it and leave it up to the audience to use this information any way they want. Think about movie or book reviews—critics write what they think about a piece, and the audience decides whether to watch the movie or read the book. Letters to the editor and online reviews are similar. The writers offer opinions to inform the audience about an issue or about something they have experienced or purchased but don't necessarily try to convince the readers to think the same way (Figure 4-4). In some cases, the purpose of an opinion piece is simply to start a conversation. That being said, we have all read reviews that shout, "Do not buy this product!" or letters to the editor that call for citizens to take action. It is important to note that while opinion writing does not have to have this persuasive quality, it sometimes does.

The lines between opinion writing and persuasive writing are often blurred, and it is our job to help students understand that people write about their opinions in many different ways. It is not productive to create strict boundaries between opinion and persuasive writing. There may be times that a writer includes some persuasive techniques in an opinion piece.

Figure 4-4: Jun wrote an opinion piece about why instrument lessons are important in school. Though it has elements of persuasion, her piece mostly just communicates her opinion on the topic.

> Learning something different is very important. It makes kids want to learn. Also it gives kids something fun to do after school. That is why I think we should keep instrument lessons.
>
> I think we should keep them because it gets kids a good hard working habbit. It said "It teaches kids responsibility and about hard work can pay off." I do instrument lessons and I have learned so much. But to get better at all the things I learned I need to have hard working habbits and I have got better hard working habbits out of instruments.
>
> Instrament lessons give kids a different and fun way of learning. It says "I have learned so much and love playing it." But also I play and love going to lessons because I get to learn and do things.
>
> We get to do things when we learn which makes it alot of fun to learn how to play a instrument.
>
> In conclustion instrument lessons are important. It helps alot of kids learn new things. Also it teaches a new way of learning. That is all my reasons I know we should have instrument lessons.

It *is* important for fourth graders to understand that they can share their opinions and provide reasons for their thinking to an audience. As they hone the purpose for writing an opinion, they may decide to use language and strong evidence to persuade an audience. Their writing might be anywhere along the continuum between opinion and persuasive writing. In GEN.U12: Writing Persuasive Essays, students will transfer their knowledge of opinion writing to learning to write persuasive essays, learning techniques for how to convince or persuade the audience to embrace an opinion or to move to action. Their experiences with opinion and persuasive writing establish a foundation for learning argumentative writing. In argumentative writing, students learn how to consider both sides of a debated topic, to address counterpoints, and to use craft techniques that persuade people on the opposing side of an issue. They learn to use well-researched evidence. Figure 4-5 shows the delineation between these different forms of writing and the blurred lines between them.

These different forms of writing, particularly opinion writing, often appear on state exams. Learning to write about their own opinions will help students write opinions to satisfy certain test prompts. GEN.U3: Writing to a Prompt: Getting Ready for Test Writing and GEN.U4: Writing to a Prompt: Extended Responses help students learn how to respond to a prompt but certainly overlap with opinion writing in terms of teaching students to state a claim and provide evidence for their thinking. Giving students time and space to develop authentic opinions about topics they care about prepares them to not only share their opinions in writing but also to engage in thoughtful and meaningful discussion across the curriculum.

Figure 4-5: These three types of writing have both similarities and differences. There is no hard line between them.

Opinion Writing	Persuasive Writing	Argumentative Writing
A writer states an opinion for the purpose of informing others of a particular perspective. The writer supports the opinion with reasons for a point of view and may include supporting details or facts. An opinion piece may serve the purpose of beginning a conversation.	A writer states an opinion for the purpose of convincing others to take a particular point of view. The writer attempts to provide compelling reasons for the point of view and includes details or facts to support it. The writer might also include an emotional appeal to persuade the reader.	A writer takes one side of a clearly debatable issue with the purpose of convincing others to join a side. The writer demonstrates a strong knowledge of a topic or issue and selects compelling points, based on evidence from research, to support the point of view. The writer also provides counterpoints to knock down reasons and points on the other side of the argument.

Test Writing: Writing to a Prompt

Students are often asked to state an opinion and provide reasons for that opinion to answer a prompt on state tests. Depending on the prompt, test-writing may include some of the characteristics of opinion, persuasive, and in rare cases, argumentative writing.

Fourth Graders Learn to Experiment with Writing in New Ways

Fourth graders get excited about trying writing that they see in the world. Engagement always increases with authenticity. When you give them multiple ways to compose and offer them new ways to play with their writing, they become more motivated to write, especially when you approach the writing with a spirit of inquiry. In GEN.U8: Writing Fairy Tales, students study the characteristics and qualities of fairy tales before writing their own. Through this engaging umbrella, students are invited to use a storyboard to plan the plot of their own fairy tales, a technique they can apply to any type of narrative writing.

In addition to experimenting with new genres for narrative writing, students also learn about new genres for writing expository text. In GEN.U10: Writing Feature Articles, they begin with a study of the genre and learn ways of engaging readers by writing interesting introductions and incorporating voice in expository texts. They also learn to share information with digital writing, photo essays, and multimedia presentations (Figure 4-6).

How to Hula Dance

All you need to do the hula is grace and confidence. Now let's get started:
Stand with your feet separated and step about 8 inches and bring the other foot over. (No sliding your foot.)

Do that again and the one that you bring over second, tap your foot on the ground.

Sway your hips and move your arms so one is farther than the other and move them like waves and don't forget to smile.

Click <u>here</u> to watch a video.

Figure 4-6: Julia wrote about hula dancing in a multimedia presentation about Hawaii. This slide, for example, links to a hula lesson video she found through her research.

Act 1 scene 1

Leya: Em can we go to are room I got a tots cool idea.(said Leya as she ran up the stairs she was jumping and then runs across the stage to the room.)

Emily: Sure(she quickly ran up the stairs feeling excited to know the new idea. So run across the stage)

Emily: So what is your idea(act excited jump up and down.)

Leya: So since tomorrow is april fools day I thought we could trick people by you wearing a dress and I wear all that gross stuff you wear.(she was hoping that Emily would do it.)

Emily: All that gross stuff is called sweat pants and tee shirts.Sounds great but we both have big things tomorrow you have your play and I have my game. But I still think it will work.(Said Emily as she drifted off to sleep try to act like you are going to sleep)

Act 2 Scene 2

Leya: Wake Up,what should I wear to look like you.(she shouted getting a little mad she was waving her hand to make it look like she did not like the clothes that she wears.)

Emily: Well I would wear sweatpants and a tee shirt, what should I wear?(she was hoping not something like a dress act worried)

Figure 4-7: After reading several plays, LaShonda wrote her own play called, "Twin Mix-Up." She demonstrates her beginning understanding of some of the characteristics of plays, including acts, scenes, and stage directions.

Once students learn a process for using mentor texts to study a genre, they can apply this process to other genres that they want to try out. For example, LaShonda learned to write her own play by reading plays and readers' theater scripts. Notice how she incorporates the characteristics of a play, including stage directions, into her writing (Figure 4-7). When you teach the minilessons in the Genres and Forms section, you teach students a generative process for learning to write in whichever genres and forms serve their purpose and audience.

Chapter 5

Minilessons for the Study of Craft, Conventions, and Writing Process

One of our primary goals is for children to be self-directed writers who have the ability to follow their own intentions. We want children to be engaged for reasons beyond the fact that they are required to write. We want them to choose projects because they want to entertain their friends or share what they know about a topic or convince someone to do something. Without the ability and opportunity to find authentic writing projects, it will be more difficult for them to become truly self-directed.

— Matt Glover

FOR STUDENTS TO BECOME ENGAGED in the writing process, they have to care about their writing. Teachers of writing know that their students are more engaged when they are able to make choices about their writing. Choice comes in many forms. Writers choose the length of their writing, their topic, their purpose, their audience, the kind of writing they will do, and how they will craft it. They make choices about where to put things on the page, how to punctuate a sentence, what to revise and edit, and whether to ultimately publish a piece of writing. If we want to develop authentic writers in our classrooms, we have to provide time, space, and instruction for students to engage in these decisions. The umbrellas and minilessons in the last three sections of this book—Craft, Conventions, and Writing Process—set the stage for you to develop writers who make these decisions, have a sense of agency, and care deeply about their writing work.

Applying Craft, Conventions, and Writing Process Minilessons

The umbrellas in the Craft, Conventions, and Writing Process sections can be used in several ways. They are perfect for selecting when you notice that your students are ready for or in need of a certain lesson. Let's say you have noticed that several of your students are starting to organize similar types of information together in their nonfiction books, and you know they would benefit from learning about headings. So you decide to teach the Craft minilesson on headings and subheadings or the entire Craft umbrella CFT.U12: Using Text Features in Nonfiction Writing.

Alternatively, you might choose to simply follow the Suggested Sequence of Lessons (pp. 665–682), which weaves the umbrellas from these three sections across the year. Students can apply their new learning about craft to writing in a single genre they are all working on (e.g., memoirs) or to writing in whatever genres individuals have chosen to work on. Whichever way you decide to use these lessons, be thoughtful about whether your students are writing something that will allow them to try out the minilessons. Some umbrellas in the Craft section are quite easy to apply to any kind of writing, while others are more easily applied to specific types of writing. For example, you might want to introduce CFT.U4: Using Dialogue in Writing when students are writing memoirs because they can probably imagine what was said at the time of the memoir's events. If they have difficulty applying new learning to their current writing, consider inviting them to revisit finished work in their writing files or folders. They also can apply the new learning to something they have started in their writer's notebooks. Sometimes, you might ask all students to finish or lay aside what they are currently writing in order to try out a principle or genre and return to their unfinished piece later. The writer's notebook is the perfect place to try out these new ideas. There are several umbrellas in the Craft, Conventions, and Writing Process sections that can be applied across all kinds of writing (e.g., CNV.U2: Learning About Punctuation and Capitalization and WPS.U8: Adding Information to Your Writing).

When deciding which minilessons from these three sections to teach, you will also want to consider where most students are in the writing process. If most students are just starting a new informational piece, you might teach WPS.U4: Writer's Notebook: Becoming an Expert, which helps them explore and research topics of interest. If many students are working on revising their work, you might teach a Craft lesson or a lesson from the drafting and revising part of the Writing Process section. If you want to engage students in editing their work, choose an umbrella from the Conventions section or one of the editing umbrellas in the Writing Process section. Whenever you decide to teach these minilessons, think of it as adding tools to your writers' toolboxes. For many students, you will hand them the right tool at exactly the right time. But others will tuck that tool away and use it when they are ready.

Studying the Craft of Writing

What do we mean when we talk about the craft of writing with fourth graders? Fourth graders appreciate writer's craft even before they know what it is. They comment on the details of the setting in Allen Say's illustrations, they are entertained by Patricia McKissack's description of characters, or they notice how Douglas Florian uses word play in his poems about the natural world. Through the talk that surrounds interactive read-aloud and shared reading, fourth graders know a lot about the craft of writing. Craft minilessons take this budding knowledge and pull back the curtain on the decisions authors make to create books that are interesting and exciting to read.

The minilessons in the Craft section are based on the behaviors and understandings in the Craft section of the grade 4 Writing continuum in *The Fountas & Pinnell Literacy Continuum*. It is important to note that minilessons that teach these behaviors and understandings are not limited to the Craft section of this book. There are minilessons that address aspects of craft built into the Genres and Forms section because craft is part of writing in any genre (e.g., creating believable characters in realistic fiction or organizing a feature article). Even minilessons in the Conventions section have an aspect of craft to them. For example, capitalization and punctuation have to do with the conventions of writing, but writers also use punctuation and capitalization to communicate their ideas and voice (e.g., using ellipses to build suspense and excitement or using all caps to indicate yelling). Whenever writers make decisions about their writing, they are making craft moves. The first umbrella in the Craft section, U1: Learning from Writers and Illustrators, sets the stage for noticing the writer's and illustrator's craft decisions whenever a book is read. The minilessons in the Craft section allow you to focus specifically on the following aspects of craft, each of which can be applied across a variety of genres.

Organization

This aspect of craft includes the structure of the whole text—the beginning, the arrangement of ideas, and the ending. In CFT.U5: Crafting Powerful Leads and Endings, you lead the students through an inquiry process using mentor texts to discover how they might try different beginnings and endings in their own writing. As fourth graders engage with more complex texts, they begin to notice the variety of ways authors organize and structure their texts. In CFT.U6: Exploring Text Structures in Nonfiction Writing and CFT.U7: Exploring Plot Structures, students look closely at different text structures and learn to apply them to their own expository and narrative writing. For example, they learn that they might present information in categories or in a way that highlights cause and effect or problem and solution. In stories or narrative writing, they might try writing a flashback or developing a circular plot. They also learn how to use specific text features to help readers navigate and understand information in a text. In CFT.U12: Using Text Features in Nonfiction Writing, they learn that they can use headings, captions, timelines, sidebars, and tables of contents to organize information. All these minilessons help students learn how to organize and arrange their ideas as writers while also contributing to their understandings as readers.

Idea Development

Idea development is how writers present and support their ideas with examples and details. For fourth graders, this means thinking about the details they can add to describe what their characters are like and where their stories take place (e.g., CFT.U2: Describing Characters and CFT.U3: Crafting a Setting). In Figure 5-1, Zamir wrote the character traits of his mom and how he can show them with actions and words. Students also learn to provide more specific and interesting examples to support their ideas in nonfiction writing. In CFT.U13: Making Nonfiction Writing Interesting, they learn how to use personal anecdotes and comparisons to further develop their ideas (Figure 5-2). Though they may have learned about some of these craft ideas in previous grades (e.g., crafting a setting or describing a character), the examples they encounter in mentor texts grow in complexity as they listen to and read more sophisticated texts. As they model their own writing after these mentor texts, idea development in their own writing becomes more complex.

Language Use

This aspect of craft addresses the way writers use sentences, phrases, expressions, and point of view to describe events, actions, or information. As fourth

Figure 5-1: Zamir worked in his writer's notebook to describe the character traits of his mom for a memoir he was writing. He has learned that you show what characters are like through their actions and words.

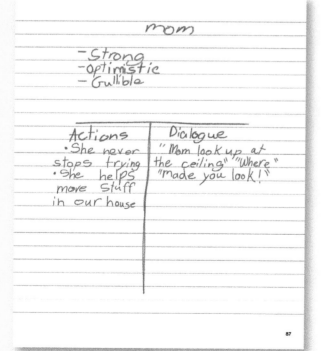

graders grow as readers, their writing begins to reflect the language in books. For example, students learn to use dialogue in more sophisticated ways. Notice how Lilly interweaves dialogue with the inner thoughts of her character to set up the problem in the story—whether she should go meet her new neighbor (Figure 5-3). CFT.U4: Using Dialogue in Writing teaches students how to avoid long strings of continuous conversation by using dialogue to meaningfully and judiciously move along the plot. Lilly would benefit from continued instruction in using dialogue judiciously.

Besides learning to vary action and dialogue, fourth graders also learn to use a variety of sentence structures and lengths in their writing. In CFT.U9: Writing Clear and Interesting Sentences, your writers learn not only how to vary their sentences but also how to use connecting words and phrases to increase sentence fluency and flow.

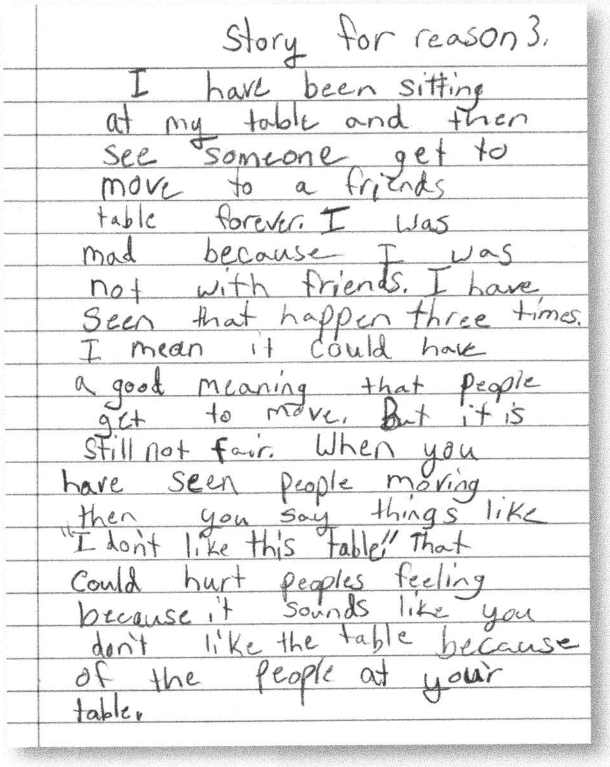

Word Choice

Word choice matters. A writer's choice of a specific word can change the whole meaning of a sentence. Consider the difference between writing *the woman strolled down the road* and *the woman sprinted down the road*. In the first sentence, we understand that the woman must have felt pretty relaxed to be strolling along. The latter conveys much more urgency; we wonder what caused her to hurry. Fourth graders quickly pick up on the importance of word choice once they are taught to pay attention to it. You can begin planting the seeds for this in your interactive read-aloud and shared reading lessons. As you read, linger on a few important words, think

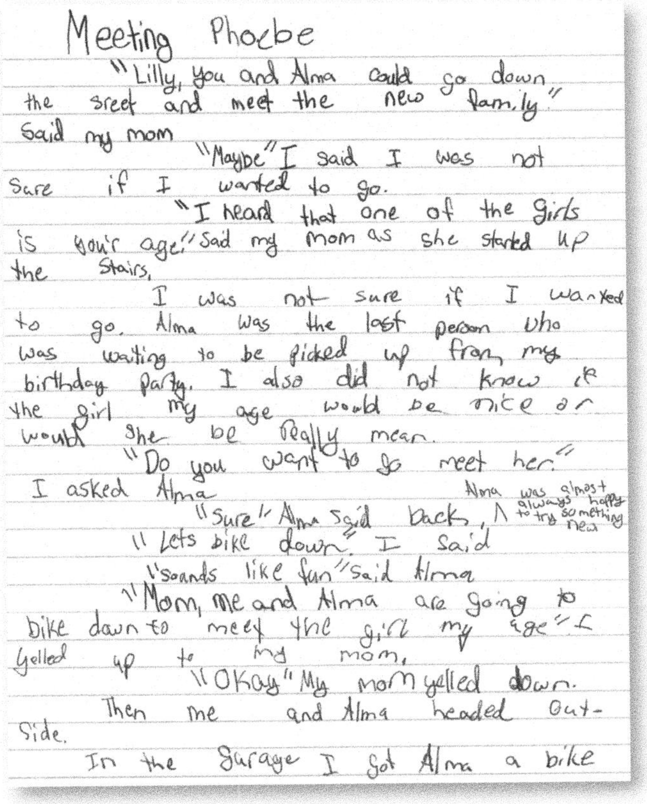

Figure 5-2: Reika wrote a short personal anecdote to support the third reason in her persuasive essay about not assigning seats at lunch. She experimented with this idea in her writer's notebook before including it in her essay.

Figure 5-3: Lilly has learned to interweave dialogue, action, and the inner thoughts of a character. She still needs to learn more about punctuating dialogue, which is addressed in both the Craft and Conventions sections (CFT.U4 and CNV.U2).

aloud about why the author chose them, repeat a word, and simply comment how much you love the author's choice of words. When you heighten your students' awareness of how carefully writers choose words, they begin to think about their own word choices (Figure 5-4). CFT.U8: Making Powerful Word Choices supports students in looking closely at their own choice of words, particularly how to select strong and specific verbs and to choose words appropriate for a particular audience.

Figure 5-4: Fourth graders Gael and Ruben have learned to use strong verbs to communicate feelings and emotions.

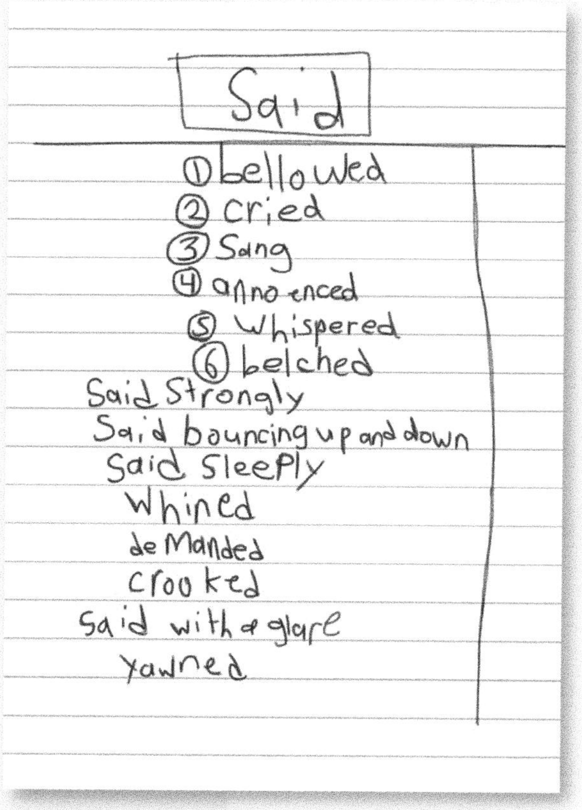

Said

① bellowed
② cried
③ Sang
④ annoenced
⑤ whispered
⑥ belched
Said Strongly
Said bouncing up and down
Said Sleeply
whined
demanded
crooked
Said with a glare
yawned

Gael brainstormed a list of verbs and adverbs in his writer's notebook to replace the word *said* and to communicate different emotions in his writing.

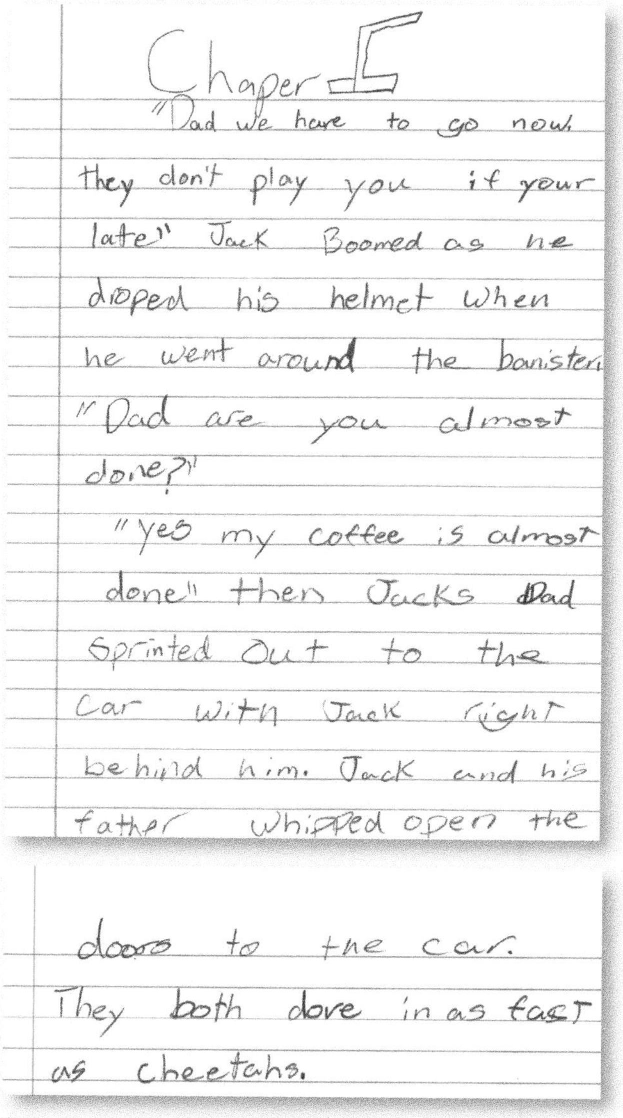

Chaper 5
"Dad we have to go now, they don't play you if your late" Jack Boomed as he droped his helmet when he went around the banister "Dad are you almost done?"
"yes my coffee is almost done" then Jacks dad Sprinted out to the car with Jack right behind him. Jack and his father whipped open the

doors to the car. They both dove in as fast as cheetahs.

Notice Ruben's use of the word *boomed* in the first paragraph to indicate that the character is loudly trying get his dad's attention. Later in the piece, he wrote, "Jack and his father whipped open the doors to the car" and "They both dove in as fast as cheetahs."

Voice

It is through the writer's voice that readers get a sense of the author's feelings and passion for a story or topic. Voice is a writer's unique style. The voices of fourth graders often naturally shine through in their writing pieces. They have unique ways of seeing the world, and the way they use words conveys this perspective. When students are encouraged to share their feelings in a story or to write the way they talk, they learn important lessons about voice. Voice is also very closely linked to the conventions of writing. When students learn to use punctuation in more sophisticated ways, their voices become even stronger. In CFT.U11: Writing with Voice in Fiction and Nonfiction, students learn how to talk directly to the reader, use punctuation and different styles of print, and integrate humor as other ways to infuse voice into a piece of writing (Figure 5-5).

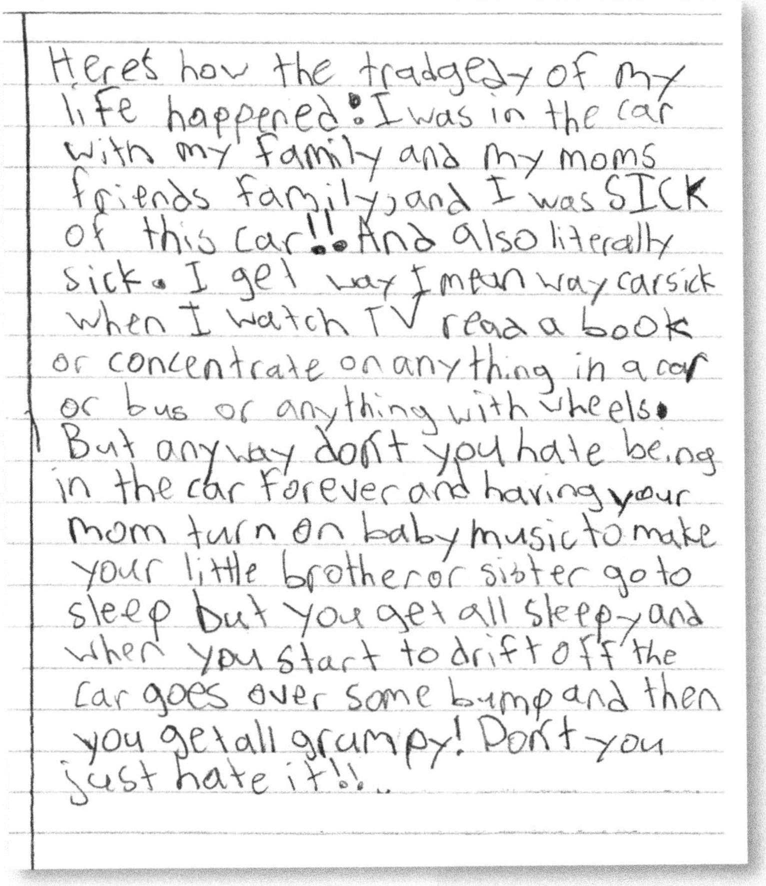

Here's how the tradgedy of my life happened: I was in the car with my family and my moms friends family, and I was SICK of this car!! And also literally sick. I get way I mean way carsick when I watch TV read a book or concentrate on anything in a car or bus or anything with wheels. But anyway don't you hate being in the car forever and having your mom turn on baby music to make your little brother or sister go to sleep but you get all sleepy and when you start to drift off the car goes over some bump and then you get all grumpy! Don't you just hate it!!

Figure 5-5: Notice how Gael had the narrator speak directly to his readers ("Don't you just hate it!!") and used both capitalization and punctuation ("I was SICK of this car!!") to show his voice and to communicate the narrator's frustration.

Drawing

Drawing is important and is used at every stage of the writing process. There are several minilessons in the Craft section to help you and your students take a close look at illustrators' craft moves—the decisions illustrators make to communicate their ideas.

Drawing in fourth grade is used in multiple ways—as a tool for idea generation and planning, as a mode of composition (e.g., making picture books and poetry anthologies), and as a way to add meaning or information to a piece of writing. Through careful examination of mentor texts in the drawing minilessons, students learn how to look at the illustrations in books with an illustrator's eye. In CFT.U14: Adding Meaning Through Illustrations, the minilessons focus on many of the craft moves illustrators make, such as using color to create a feeling or mood; using light, weather, and other details to show the seasons and the passage of time; and using layout and perspective to draw attention to important information. Making picture books is a wonderful way for students to apply the minilessons in this umbrella. Students learn how to use illustrations to add meaning

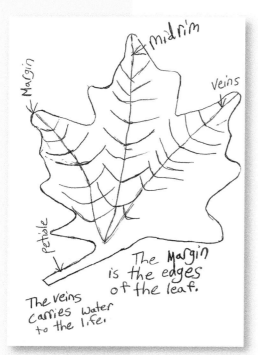

beyond the words they write. The more students learn about drawing, the more they learn about the process of revising their writing. They get excited to add new details to their pictures after talking about their stories and learning new illustration techniques. This in turn impacts the details they add to theirwriting.

The minilessons in CFT.U15: Illustrating and Using Graphics in Nonfiction Writing help students expand their understanding of how to show factual information through detailed drawings, diagrams, maps and legends, close-ups, and photographs (Figure 5-6).

Through CFT.U16: Exploring Design Features and Text Layout, students learn that they can use scenes, a mix of materials, and text layouts to make their pictures interesting (Figure 5-7). When you teach students to draw and use media in interesting ways, they become inspired to use art in their own ways to communicate their messages and ideas.

Teaching the Conventions of Writing

Conventions and craft go hand in hand. They work together to communicate meaning. A writer can have great ideas, understand how to organize them, and even make interesting word choices. But the ideas can get lost if the writer doesn't spell words in recognizable ways or use conventional grammar and punctuation. For writing to be valued and understood, writers need to understand the conventions of writing. Sophisticated writers might play with these conventions and sometimes break the rules for their use, but they are aware that they are making an intentional decision to do so.

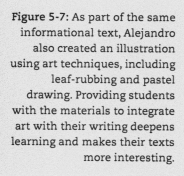

Figure 5-6: Alejandro created a diagram for an informational text about leaves and photosynthesis.

Figure 5-7: As part of the same informational text, Alejandro also created an illustration using art techniques, including leaf-rubbing and pastel drawing. Providing students with the materials to integrate art with their writing deepens learning and makes their texts more interesting.

Teaching conventions to fourth graders can be tricky. Approach it with a spirit of inquiry and discovery. Students are more motivated to use conventions when they see the rewards of others being able to read and understand their writing. Avoid being so rigid in your teaching of conventions that students are afraid to take risks. Fourth graders should celebrate their efforts to spell a new multisyllable word. How limited and boring their writing would be if they used only the words they knew how to spell! The minilessons in the Conventions section are designed to strike a balance between teaching students to write clearly while making them comfortable taking risks with their new learning. The minilessons in this section are based on the behaviors and understandings in the Conventions section of the grade 4 Writing continuum in *The Fountas & Pinnell Literacy Continuum*; however, just like craft, the conventions of writing are not limited to this section. There are aspects of conventions woven into the writing minilessons in every section. The Conventions section, in conjunction with these other sections, addresses the following conventions of writing.

Text Layout

For fourth graders, learning about text layout involves learning about where to place print and pictures on a page, including placement of headings and titles. Many of the conventions related to text layout are taught within the Craft section, particularly in CFT.U16: Exploring Design Features and Text Layout. This umbrella is a perfect example of the close relationship between craft and conventions in writing. When you introduce a variety of paper templates (available in the online resources) that show different ways to lay out a page, you teach students that writers make important choices about where they place print and pictures.

In CFT.U12: Using Text Features in Nonfiction Writing, students learn to use text features in their nonfiction writing, which influences how they lay out their text. For example, they might decide to place a sidebar beside a paragraph to enhance the meaning of the text or use headings and subheadings to organize a section. Students also learn that when they use a computer, they can select different font styles and sizes to convey meaning so that readers can follow how the information is organized.

In WPS.U11: Adding Book and Print Features, students learn to underline titles as they discuss choosing titles for books. They learn how to add other print features, like an author page, acknowledgments, and a dedication. Each decision about text layout requires that students consider how their readers will take in information and the writer's meaning or message.

Grammar and Usage

For fourth graders, grammar and usage are learned and applied in the context of writing. For example, students experience how to use past, present, and future tenses as they participate in shared and independent writing. They learn how to use adjectives, adverbs, prepositions, and conjunctions in the act of writing. The more students engage in writing and translating their talk into writing, the more experience they will have in using grammar. Before students can name the parts of speech or identify a verb tense as past, present, or future, they have an internal sense of how the language works because they have used it to converse with and communicate to others. Oral storytelling, classroom conversation, interactive read-aloud, and shared reading experiences further immerse students in how the language sounds and works. These oral experiences are especially important for multilingual learners. When students write their thoughts and ideas, their oral language experiences will influence what and how they write.

The lessons in *The Writing Minilessons Book, Grade 4*, prepare students to write in various genres and forms, to craft their writing in ways they have seen authors and illustrators do in their books, and to use the writing process. Students' writing that is produced from these minilessons presents opportunities for you to teach specifics of English grammar and usage through the curriculum and activities that are part of your classroom instruction.

Use writing conferences and guided writing to differentiate your focus on grammar based on the student in front of you. However, be judicious in pointing out grammatical errors in students' work. Focus on one thing that they can look for and make a goal for future writing. The more ownership students have over the editing process, the better they will internalize their understanding of grammar. WPS.U10: Editing and Proofreading Writing supports students in learning how to edit for grammar. For example, the first lesson in this umbrella focuses on rereading writing to make sure the ideas are clearly communicated.

In addition to editing their work on a sentence and word level, students learn more about paragraphing their writing so that readers can navigate their texts. The minilessons in CNV.U3: Learning to Paragraph engage students in an inquiry about how authors use paragraphs so they can use them appropriately in their own writing.

Capitalization

Most fourth graders are at a stage in which they begin to solidify and expand their understanding of when to capitalize words. The first minilesson in CNV.U2: Learning About Punctuation and Capitalization uses inquiry to help students engage in a study of when writers use capitals, including for proper nouns, the first letter of the first word in a sentence, for most words in a title, and for the first letter in names of days, months, and holidays. The minilessons in CFT.U4: Using Dialogue in Writing support students in learning how to properly capitalize and punctuate dialogue.

Punctuation

Fourth graders have a beginning understanding that punctuation makes their writing readable for others. CNV.U2: Learning About Punctuation and Capitalization helps students further develop their understanding that punctuation also communicates how the reader should read a sentence (e.g., an ellipsis signals the reader to pause). When students understand the role of punctuation in writing, they begin to see punctuation as a way to craft their messages. Writers communicate voice with punctuation. They communicate emotions—excitement, fear, sadness, confusion. Punctuation is inextricably linked with the craft of writing. When fourth graders learn the conventions of punctuation, they begin to notice how authors use and sometimes play with them in their books. The second minilesson in CNV.U2 engages students in an inquiry-based study of punctuation in which students have the opportunity to discover for themselves how writers use punctuation. You can continue this study over several days, adding their noticings about different kinds of punctuation to an anchor chart. Writing minilessons make students curious about what writers do and eager to imitate what they notice in their own writing.

Spelling

As fourth graders grow in their knowledge of the way words work, they transition to using mostly conventional spelling in their writing. Encourage students to write the words they know quickly and accurately and to use a range of strategies to make their best attempts at words they do not know. In CNV.U1: Writing Words, students learn to break words into syllables to write them and to use what they know about words to help them spell other words. Because fourth graders encounter and use more sophisticated vocabulary in both their reading and writing, these lessons focus on writing multisyllable words. There are also specific lessons on homophones and plurals as these are commonly misused or misspelled in fourth-grade writing. In MGT.U3: Introducing the Writing Folder, students are taught how to refer to a list of commonly misspelled words to support their use of conventional spelling. Consider using the format of these lessons to also teach students to check their spelling using digital tools like spell-check when writing on a computer.

These minilessons should accompany a strong phonics, spelling, and word study component in your classroom. The minilessons in the Conventions section are meant to *reinforce* and *supplement* what you are teaching in your phonics, spelling, and word study instruction and to help students transfer what they are learning to their writing.

Handwriting and Word Processing

Though handwriting is not specifically addressed in fourth-grade writing minilessons, it is important to recognize it as an important part of writing mechanics. If students need support with proper letter formation, use the Verbal Path for Letter Formation for both print and cursive (Figure 5-8), downloadable from the online resources. Use this resource during individual conferences or during guided writing to support specific individuals or groups of students who need to work on their handwriting.

The resources related to handwriting are not intended to replace any handwriting curriculum you already have in place. Avoid confusing students with conflicting ways of directing the formation of letters. Though you have paper choices available in the online resources, feel free to use the paper that is consistent with your school's handwriting program.

Fourth graders will also need to learn keyboarding skills to increase their writing fluency. One way to support your students' development of keyboarding skills is to on occasion offer the option of "publishing" a piece of writing on a computer. Figure 5-9 shows typed paragraphs from an informational piece Oren wrote on Greek mythology. Notice that the teacher decided not to edit the student's work to perfect this final copy. The published piece reflects Oren's current understanding of how to edit and proofread his writing. A few times a year, Oren's teacher will work with students to polish a piece in the same way an editor would help the author of a published work. In most cases, fourth-grade published pieces are edited by the student and are not necessarily perfect. In the next section, on the writing process, we discuss other ways you might choose to publish a text.

Figure 5-8: Use the language of the Verbal Path for Letter Formation for both print and cursive consistently to support students in making letters.

Verbal Path for Uppercase Cursive Formation

Sometimes it helps students to say aloud the directions for making a letter. This verbal path helps them to understand the directional movement that is essential. In addition, it gives the teacher and student a language to talk through the letter and its features. Here, we suggest language for creating a verbal path to the distinctive features of letters.

Uppercase Cursive Formation

A — pull back, around, up, down, swing up

B — swing up, pull down, up, over, in, back in and swing out

C — pull back, around, and swing up

D — curve down, loop, back around and loop up

E — pull back, in, back, and swing up

F — swing over and up, pull down, over, swing back and up

G — swing up, loop, swing up, down, swing up and swing back

H — pull over and down, pull down, up, over, loop and swing up

I — swing up, loop over, down, swing up, swing back

J — swing up, back, pull down, and swing up and cross

K — pull over and down, pull in, pull out, and swing up

L — swing up, loop, pull down, loop, swing over and up

M — pull over, down, up, over and down, up over and down, swing up

N — pull over, down, up, over and down, swing up

O — pull back, around, loop up

P — swing up, down, up, and in

Q — Pull back, around and close, swing over

R — swing up, down, up, over and around, in, swing down and up

S — swing up, loop and back, around, swing up, back, and swing up

T — swing over, pull down, over, swing back, swing in, and swing up

U — curve down, way up, down and swing up

V — pull over, down, swing up, and swing up

W — pull over, down, up, down, up, and swing up

X — pull over, down and swing up, and cross down

Y — pull over, down, way up, down, loop in and swing up

Z — pull back, in, back, loop in and swing up

Verbal Path for the Formation of Cursive Letters: Uppercase

© 2019 by Irene C. Fountas and Gay Su Pinnell. Portsmouth, NH: Heinemann. All rights reserved.

Learning About the Writing Process

The umbrellas in the Writing Process section introduce and immerse students in the phases of the writing process from planning to publishing as addressed in Chapter 1 (Figure 1-9). They are based on the behaviors and understandings in the Writing Process section of the grade 4 Writing continuum in *The Fountas & Pinnell Literacy Continuum*. The umbrellas in the Writing Process section introduce students to the following phases of the writing process.

Stories and Beliefs

One of the stories from Greek mythology is the myth of the Labyrinth. Here's the myth: A guy named Daedalus was employed by the King Minos of Crete to design and build a labyrinth that was almost impossible to escape from. He made it impossible to escape from because he was hiding the Minotaur in the labyrinth! In case you don't know what a Minotaur is, it is a creature that is half bull and half man. And in case you don't know what a labyrinth is, it is a really big maze but in this case the maze is underground.

Another story that the Greeks believed in was the legend of King Midas. Here's the legend: One day Silenus the tutor of Dionysus (see The Gods) drank too much wine and became separated from his friends. He walked around lost until he fell into a drunken sleep. Silenus was discovered by some of King Midas's servants. King Midas took care of Silenus for a couple of days and when he found Dionysus again Dionysus thanked King Midas for taking care of his friend by giving King Midas one wish. King Midas wished that everything he touched turned to gold!

Figure 5-9: Occasionally, fourth graders can type their writing as one way to publish their pieces. Here, Oren has published an informational book about Greek mythology. Notice how he used his knowledge of paragraphing and word processing to format paragraphs.

Planning and Rehearsing

For fourth graders, talk is an important part of planning and rehearsing their writing. Some of the talk is about their ideas—*what* they are writing. Some of the talk is about *why* they are writing and for *whom*—the purpose and the audience. Knowing the purpose for writing often leads to discussions about what type of writing to do and what kind of paper is best for that purpose. For example, if writers want to

- ▶ say thank you, they might write a note or a letter,
- ▶ teach others how to do something, they might write a recipe, a set of directions, or a how-to video,
- ▶ create a public service announcement, they might make a poster or a sign, or
- ▶ remember an experience or entertain their audience, they might write a memoir or a story.

In all of these cases, the writer thinks about the purpose, determines what kind of writing will serve that purpose, and then begins to write a message. WPS.U6: Thinking About Purpose, Audience, and Genre/Form helps students think and talk about their purpose and audience and how they affect the choice of a genre and form. Revisit this umbrella several times a year so students have the opportunity to thoughtfully choose not only the topic they will write about but also the genre they will write in.

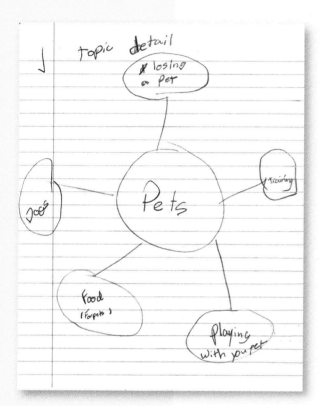

Figure 5-10: Dylan made a plan in his writer's notebook to write about a topic from his own life experience— owning a pet.

In addition to learning how to choose their own purpose, topic, and genre, students need explicit opportunities to generate and collect ideas for writing during the planning process. From discussions during interactive read-aloud, fourth graders understand that writers get their ideas from their own experiences and from what they have learned. Minilessons in the Writing Process section support students in further developing this understanding through the use of a writer's notebook. Students learn how to gather ideas from their own lives, from writers and artists, and from what they have learned about topics they are interested in. They discover stories by making webs of their favorite memories, drawing maps of special places, and sketching memories of spending time with people they care about. Webs are also useful for gathering ideas for nonfiction writing (Figure 5-10). Another way students learn to gather ideas for writing is by making lists. You can read more about using writer's notebooks with fourth graders on pages 87–91.

Drafting and Revising

Most fourth graders are enthusiastic about drafting ideas that excite them. When they choose their own topics and have a vision for the type of writing they want to do, they are often deeply engaged in getting their ideas down on paper. They also often revise while drafting, changing things as they go. However, these same students may be initially reluctant to revise their writing once it is drafted; it is indeed hard to change something you have written and care about. For other writers, the task of drafting sometimes feels daunting. It can be helpful for those students to know that they can revise and change their writing. Whether students are enthusiastic or reluctant to draft their ideas, there are several things you can put into place to make it an inviting process.

▶ Invite them to tell their stories or talk about the information they are going to write about to a partner or small group.

▶ Introduce the idea of a discovery draft—a very quick draft to get ideas down on paper and "discover" what you really want to say. The discovery draft can be very freeing for some students who think their first draft has to be perfect.

▶ Share the advice of authors. When students understand that even published authors sometimes struggle to get their ideas down on paper, they become more open to the process.

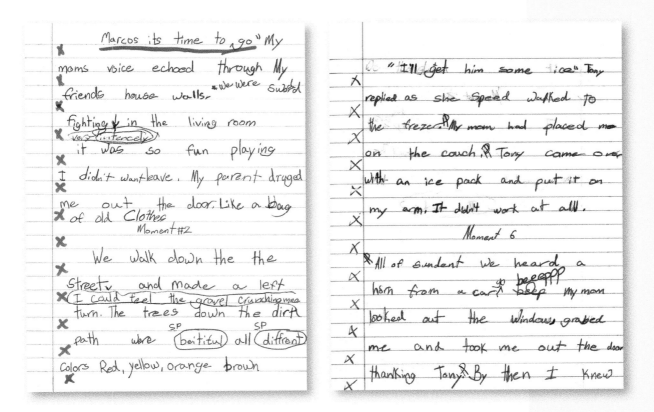

Figure 5-11: Marcos worked on revising and editing a memoir.

▶ Allow students choice in what they are writing about and often what types of genres/forms they are writing in. When students are engaged in authentic writing, they are more open to revision work.

As students learn new crafting techniques from authors they love and are explicitly taught ways to revise their writing, they become invested in the revision process. Revising becomes contagious when students have opportunities to share and celebrate their changes with one another. Minilessons in WPS.U8: Adding Information to Your Writing and WPS.U9: Revising to Focus and Organize Writing offer different ways to revise. Students learn to reread their writing to make sure it makes sense and to add new information for more detail or clarification. In Figure 5-11, Marcos skipped every other line of his notebook (each marked with an X) so that he had room for revisions. Notice how he underlined dialogue, strong verbs, and figurative language as he reviewed his writing for some of the things he learned through writing minilessons. He made decisions for how to revise his work to make it stronger. He added the words *very intensely* to describe his play "sword fighting" and incorporated more sensory language, adding the line "I could feel the gravel crunching under my feet." In addition to revising, Marcos started editing his piece, circling words he wants to check for spelling. Later in the piece, he experimented with paragraphing as well as intentionally changing the spelling of the word *beep* to express the sound.

When students revise, you gain insight into what they understand about craft. They learn that writing is an ongoing process and that you can always change it and make it better.

Proofreading and Editing

In fourth grade, your primary goal is guiding students to reread and revisit their work to help them notice what they can do to make their writing clearer for their readers. Fourth graders are learning more and more about writing conventions, print, and the way words work every day. You can teach them how to proofread to make sure the words they know are spelled correctly, have them check their writing for punctuation and capitalization, and help them think about how they have grouped similar ideas into paragraphs. The minilessons in WPS.U10: Editing and Proofreading Writing teach students how to proofread and edit, beginning with rereading their writing pieces to make sure they make sense. When students do their own proofreading and editing, it gives you a window into what they understand about conventions and what they might need to learn next. When you teach your students how to edit their own work, they feel more ownership over the piece and develop a sense of agency.

You may also want to consider creating writing groups or partners to help students with both revising and editing (Figure 5-12). It is helpful to involve your students in creating these writing partnerships and groups because writers must trust one another. Engaging students in the process of selecting a peer can help build this foundation of trust. Ask your students with whom they work well and from whose writing they can learn something. Students quickly discover that they can learn different things from different writers. Involving them in the process of developing peer mentors strengthens their writing identity and helps them be reflective about what they need as a writer.

Publishing

When we say "publish" in fourth grade, we really mean "share it with others." Students are invited to share their independent drawing and writing daily as they experiment with new ideas taught through the lessons in this book.

Figure 5-12: Peer revising and editing can be helpful with a trusted writing partner or group. Notice the comments fellow classmate and writer Luna offered Bailey on her persuasive essay.

The Writing Minilessons Book, Grade 4

Figure 5-13: Students can publish books in a variety of ways. *Fashion vs. Inner Sport* is on 8 1/2" x 11" blank paper folded in half to resemble the size of a chapter book and is bound with yarn. *The Greek Gods* has been typed, printed, and bound simply on the left by three staples. Spiral bindings, like for *Soccer*, are also durable options.

However, publishing takes this sharing a step further by having students prepare their writing for an audience to read. Publishing might mean having students type or bind their writing with cardboard or other materials to resemble a book. Published books can go into your classroom library for others to check out and read (Figure 5-13). Publishing can also take the form of framing a piece of writing or drawing, displaying it, posting it on a bulletin board, or holding informal writing celebrations. For example, you can have students share their writing with another class or with a teacher or administrator, or you can invite families and guests to look at published writing.

Fourth grade is a good time to continue thinking about broadening students' understanding of audience. The minilessons in WPS.U6: Thinking About Purpose, Audience, and Genre/Form help you and the students think about potential audiences both within the school and in the greater community. Consider asking local government officials, community organizations, or university professors and other experts in a field to listen to your students' writing and provide feedback.

By sharing their writing and celebrating risks taken and new techniques tried with a range of audiences, students have the opportunity to see how different audiences react to their writing and how they might approach their writing differently in the future. When we give students the opportunity to share their writing with authentic audiences, their engagement and motivation for writing increase. The widespread use of virtual meetings helps make the world even smaller. Your students can connect with an audience from their local community or from across the world.

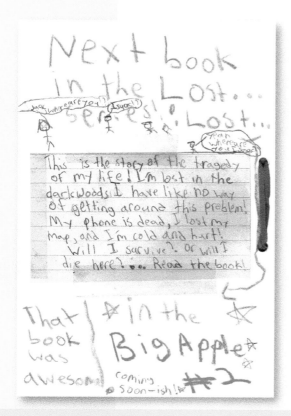

Next book in the Lost . . . series! Lost . . . in the Big Apple #2

This is the story of the tragedy of my life! I'm lost in the dark woods. I have like no way of getting around this problem! My phone is dead, I lost my map, and I'm cold and hurt! Will I survive? Or will I die here? . . . Read the book!

Preview of: Lost . . . in the Big Apple

We were going to New York City, and it was going to be awesome!

When we get there . . . I step out of the hotel to go get an apple at the store! So I walk down to the store but I don't find a store, I find an empty alley way! I wonder where the store went? I walked back to the hotel or I thought I did because I ended up on some abandoned street! And then, I realized I was lost. Again, but this time in a giant city.

Figure 5-14: As part of the publishing process, Gael wrote a summary for the back of his current book, *Lost in the Woods*, and a preview for the next book.

You can also teach your students how to add book and print features like covers, an author page, a dedication, and endpapers as part of the publishing process (WPS.U11: Adding Book and Print Features). In Figure 5-14, Gael wrote a summary and a teaser for the back of his realistic fiction book *Lost in the Woods* after becoming aware of different book and print features through minilessons and mentor texts. He extended this learning by creating a preview of the next book in his series.

Lastly, in WPS.U12: Publishing and Self-Assessing Your Writing, students learn not only how to publish their writing but also how to reflect on their growth as a writer through self-assessment. In WML2, students learn how to use a rubric to self-assess their writing. This lesson can be repeated to demonstrate how to use a rubric for any genre that your students have selected. In WML3, they participate in the development of a rubric, a process that helps them review key characteristics of writing within a genre. WML4 asks students to look over their writing pieces and select ones that show their growth as a writer. Ask students to write about their growth on the sheet What I Have Learned How to Do as a Writer and Illustrator, downloadable from the online resources and kept in the writing folder. Other teachers ask students to write on an index card or a piece of paper and attach it directly to the piece to be kept in a portfolio.

Another effective way to encourage students to reflect on their growth is to ask them to collect artifacts from throughout the writing process, including examples from drafts that show revision and editing. When you involve students in this collection of artifacts, they begin to value the writing process and the steps they took to get to a final piece of writing. Some teachers ask students to write a letter of reflection to their readers explaining each artifact and how it shows their growth.

Using a Writer's Notebook with Fourth Graders

Author Ralph Fletcher writes, "Keeping a writer's notebook can help you be more alive to the world. It can help you develop the habit of paying attention to the little pictures and images of the world you might otherwise ignore" (Fletcher 2003).

Writers notice, listen, and observe every day, all the time. They notice everything in their world—what they see, hear, and smell. They use writer's notebooks to collect these observations plus their thinking, their memories, lists, artifacts, and sketches so they can use them as sparks for writing. Writers read and reread their notebooks and add more and more ideas. It is a place for them to experiment with writing and try things out. It is a tool you can offer your students to help them expand and grow as writers.

We recommend introducing a writer's notebook to fourth graders at the very beginning of the year so they have a place to write daily and generate ideas from the start. A writer's notebook gives students a place to jot down ideas, explore different techniques, and experiment with quick writes. We provide a series of minilessons in the Writing Process section to help you introduce and use the writer's notebook. If you do not have access to the *Writer's Notebook, Intermediate* (Fountas and Pinnell 2023) for each of your students, use a simple composition book and glue in sections and insert tabs yourself to make it a neat, professional notebook that can be cherished.

WPS.U1: Introducing and Using a Writer's Notebook introduces students to the idea of using a writer's notebook. The first thing they are asked to do is to personalize the cover. The idea is to make the notebook a treasured possession for many years. In fact, at the end of the school year, you might want to help students put a protective layer over the cover to preserve the notebook. The lessons go on to establish the routine of writing in the notebook for ten minutes a day, ideally outside of writers' workshop (see pages 15–16 for more information). The rest of the umbrellas addressing the writer's notebook provide specific ways to engage students in writing daily and generating ideas. The sections of the *Writer's Notebook, Intermediate* are organized to match the teaching in these umbrellas. If your students will use plain notebooks, create the sections that you think best meets their needs. However, we encourage you to leave a substantial amount of space in the writer's notebook for free writing and drawing where writers can repeat any of the different ways they have learned to generate ideas through quick writes, experiment with new craft techniques, try out ideas for a writing project, or even start a writing piece. Students can turn anything they write in the writer's notebook into a longer piece outside of the notebook, or they can use the notebook as a source of ideas for any of their writing.

Helping Your Fourth Graders Build Their Writer's Notebooks

Showing your students how to build their writer's notebooks can lead to a joyful, robust, and truly independent writing time in your classroom. When you establish the habit of daily quick writing in the writer's notebook, you help students develop ways to generate ideas that they can repeat independently across the school year. Through quick writes, students learn that they can get ideas from their lives, from writers and artists, and from researching topics they find interesting.

Getting Ideas from Your Life

In WPS.U2: Writer's Notebook: Getting Ideas from Your Life, students learn a variety of ways to mine their own lives for writing ideas. The first minilesson invites students to make their own heart maps as a way of discovering what is important in their lives (Heard 2016). This map can be used throughout the year for writing topics across genres. Students learn that maps of places can also be a resource for writing ideas. They are taught how to make their own maps of a place and to think about the stories that are hidden in the different spaces on that map. Besides thinking about places, students also learn that sketching and writing about special people can be a source of writing ideas. Through the rest of the umbrella, students learn they can use lists, artifacts, and their observations of the world around them to get ideas and write quickly in their writer's notebooks (Figure 5-15). If you are using *Writer's Notebook, Intermediate*, this umbrella can be used with Section 1: Ideas from My Life. The last lesson in WPS.U1 teaches students that they can continue to build their notebooks in Section 4: More Writing and Sketching by revisiting any of these ways of writing about their own lives.

Getting Ideas from Writers and Artists

WPS.U3: Writer's Notebook: Getting Inspiration from Writers and Artists is designed to teach students that other people's work can be a source of inspiration for their own writing ideas. Through these minilessons, they respond in a variety of ways to books, poems, songs, and pieces of artwork. For example, in WML3, students learn that they can use books or parts of books to get writing ideas. They learn that they can write quickly about a memory triggered by a book, tell about a time that they felt like the character, or use the opening line of a book as a story starter. Other lessons invite them to make a sketch inspired by song lyrics or to write in response to a work of art. Through these minilessons, they learn that when they don't know what to write about, they can turn to the creations of others for inspiration. The writing inspired this way does not need to be connected in any way to the original piece of art; it is simply a jumping-off point for their own ideas. If you are using *Writer's Notebook, Intermediate*, this umbrella can be used with Section 2: Inspiration from Writers and Artists.

Using the Writer's Notebook to Become an Expert

Though nonfiction writing can come out of any of the ideas that writers collect in their writer's notebooks, you might find it helpful to dedicate a section of the notebook to the development of nonfiction writing. In WPS.U4: Writer's Notebook: Becoming an Expert, students learn to make lists to generate topic ideas, to use webs to focus their ideas, and to brainstorm their questions and wonderings about a topic. They also use the notebook to take notes on their topics and to prepare to interview experts on their topics

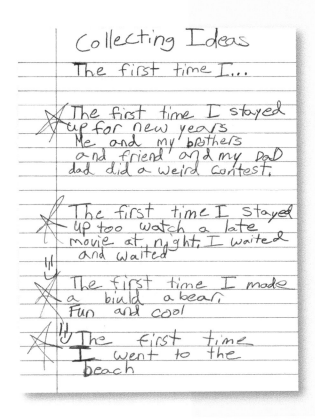

Figure 5-15: Becky made a list of first-time experiences in her writer's notebook as a way to collect writing ideas.

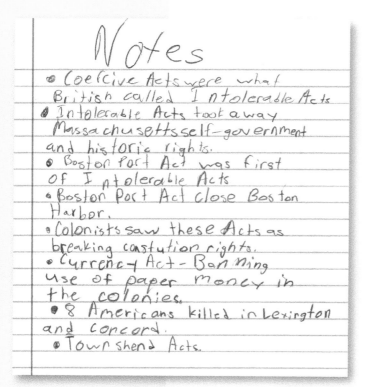

Notes
- Coercive Acts were what British called Intolerable Acts
- Intolerable Acts took away Massachusetts self-government and historic rights.
- Boston Port Act was first of Intolerable Acts
- Boston Port Act close Boston Harbor.
- Colonists saw these Acts as breaking constution rights.
- Currency Act - Banning use of paper money in the colonies.
- 8 Americans killed in Lexington and Concord.
- Townshend Acts.

Figure 5-16: Students learn to use their writer's notebooks to take notes from their research, including identifying and defining important topic-related vocabulary.

Figure 5-17: Courtney used her writer's notebook to try different leads for her story.

(Figure 5-16). The minilessons in this umbrella can be used with Section 3: Becoming an Expert if you are using the *Writer's Notebook, Intermediate*.

The minilessons focused on the writer's notebook are meant to be generative. Once students learn how to use lists, webs, sketches, maps, research questions, etc., they can continue to build their notebooks using these ideas. They learn that a writer's notebook is a place to write quickly and exercise their writing muscles. They learn that it is a place to experiment with ideas, try things out, and have fun with writing.

Using the Writer's Notebook Throughout the Writing Process

The writer's notebook is used throughout the writing process. Writers use it to collect ideas as they plan for writing, to begin a draft to see if an idea works, and to try out craft moves as they revise their writing (Figure 5-17). The writer's notebook can also be used as a tool to support editing. For example, you might encourage or invite students to try writing a word a few different ways in their notebooks to figure out the spelling. As students publish, they can use their notebooks to develop different book and print features, such as an author page, a dedication, or acknowledgments.

As shown in Figure 3-5, a writer's notebook is typically used alongside a writing folder in which students keep ongoing writing projects. Students often begin a writing project, such as a story

Leads for R. fiction
1. "Hey, Katy this is Taylor" said Emma Katy's best friend. "Cool, Hi my name is Katy" "Hi,
2. As I walked out for recess I saw my best friend Emma with that new girl I think her name was Taylor but who knows.
3. As I walked slowly out for recess I saw my best friend Emma rushing over to me with that new girl Taylor. "Why was she with her" I thought.

I want to use the #2

or an informational book, by rereading their writer's notebooks for topic ideas. Other times, students will start an idea in their writer's notebooks and discover that they want to expand it into a longer project. They take the idea out of the notebook and choose paper that makes sense for the type of writing they are doing. Students continually use their writer's notebooks as they work on their writing projects to try out different crafting techniques and to continue to collect ideas, especially as peers share their own writing project ideas. Ideas are contagious. Hearing one person's memoir often triggers a related memory for someone else. When students share their writing, encourage them to bring their writer's notebooks so they can capture ideas inspired by their classmates' writing on a writing ideas list (Figure 5-18).

My Writing Ideas

- Use this space to list ideas whenever you get them.

Video games
Getting ready for a trip
Niagra Falls
Ellis Island
Volcanoes
Mythology
Time I had to talk in assembly
Trying to find my room on the first day of school
When my dog died
My sleepover Losing my first tooth

Figure 5-18: Students use their writer's notebooks to collect ideas for writing.

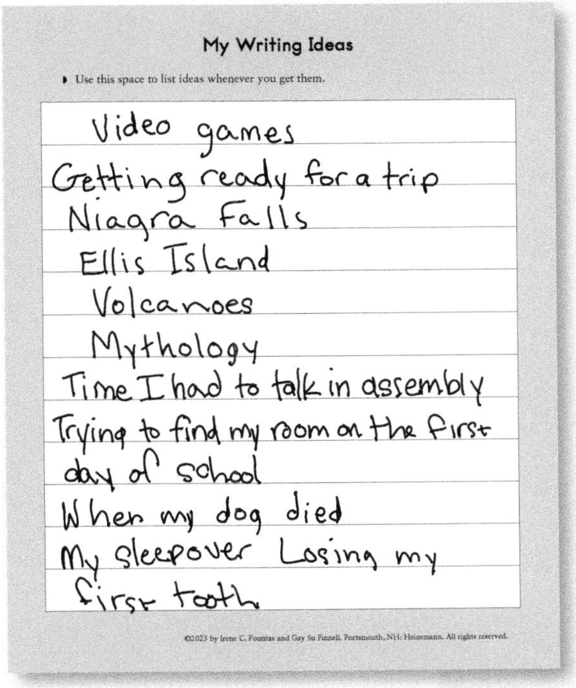

Once the writer feels a writing project is complete, we recommend that the finished product (whether published or not) be moved to a storage file somewhere in your classroom. As described earlier, sometimes teachers ask students to write a reflection about what they learned from the writing project in their writing folder. After completing a writing project, they return to their writer's notebooks to continue gathering ideas or to find another idea they want to explore for a writing project.

So many things contribute to your students' development in writing. When you surround students with literacy activities, help them notice what other writers and illustrators do, provide them with time to write, encourage their efforts with enthusiasm, and gently guide them through writing minilessons, you create the right conditions for fourth graders to grow into confident, engaged writers.

With a choice of so many writing minilessons, how do you decide which lesson to teach when? Most of your decisions will be based on your close observations of your students as they write. What do you see them doing on their own? What might they be able to do with your help? What are they ready to learn? Chapter 6 offers guidance and support for making those decisions.

Chapter 6

Putting Minilessons into Action: Assessing and Planning

With assessment, you learn what students know; the literacy continuum will help you think about what they need to know next.

—Irene Fountas and Gay Su Pinnell

WRITING MINILESSONS ARE EXAMPLES OF explicit, systematic teaching that address the specific behaviors and understandings to notice, teach for, and support in *The Fountas & Pinnell Literacy Continuum*. Goals for each lesson are drawn from the sections on Writing; Writing About Reading; Phonics, Spelling, and Word Study; Oral and Visual Communication; and Digital Communication. Taken together, the goals provide a comprehensive vision of what students need to become aware of, understand, and apply to their own literacy and learning about writing. Each minilesson lists Continuum Connections, which are the exact behaviors from *The Fountas & Pinnell Literacy Continuum* that are addressed in the lesson.

Figure 6-1 provides an overview of the processes that take place when a proficient writer creates a text and represents what students will work toward across the years. Writers must decide the purpose of a text, their audience, and their message. They think about the kind of writing that will help them communicate the message. They make important craft decisions, such as how to organize the piece, what words to use, and how they want the writing to sound. While keeping the message in their heads, writers must also consider the conventions of writing, such as letter formation, capitalization, punctuation, and grammar. They work through a writing process from planning and rehearsing to publishing. All lessons in this book are directed to helping writers expand their processing systems as they write increasingly complex texts.

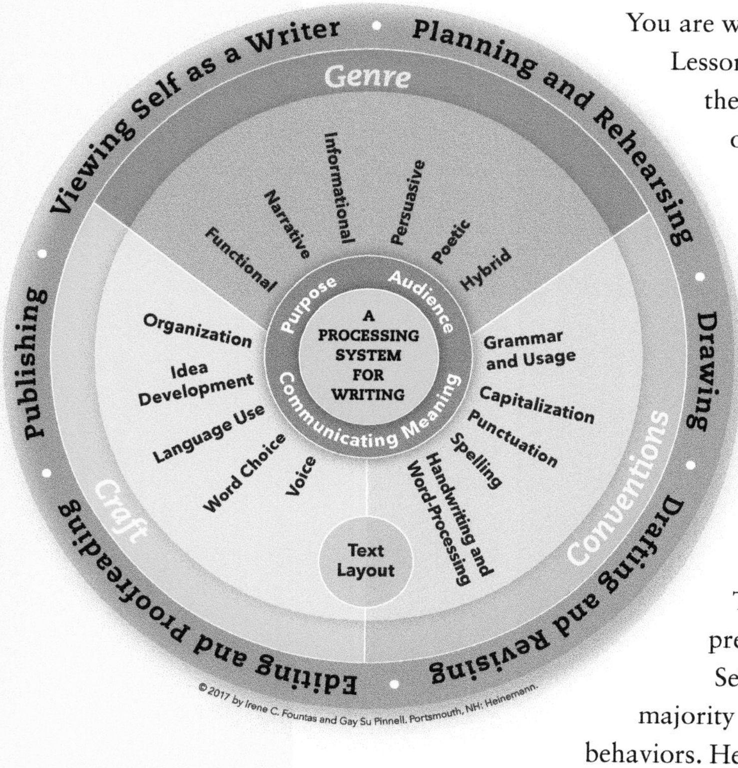

Decide Which Writing Minilessons to Teach

Figure 6-1: The writing wheel diagram, shown full size on the inside back cover, illustrates how the writing process encompasses all aspects of writing.

Figure 6-1: The writing wheel diagram, shown full size on the inside back cover, illustrates how the writing process encompasses all aspects of writing.

You are welcome to follow the Suggested Sequence of Lessons discussed later in this chapter (located in the appendix and available as a downloadable online resource). You will notice that there are more writing minilessons than days in the year. Because learners are on a continuum of understanding and development in writing, the writing minilessons in this book are designed to give you choices about what you can teach based on the writers in front of you. Teach within what Vygotsky (1979) called the "zone of proximal development"— the zone between what they can do independently and what they can do with the support of a more expert other (Figure 6-2). Teach on the cutting edge of your students' present competencies.

Select minilessons based on what you notice the majority of your class needs to learn to develop writing behaviors. Here are some suggestions and tools to help you think about the students in your classroom, the main resource being *The Fountas & Pinnell Literacy Continuum*:

▶ **Use the Writing continuum** to help you observe how students are thinking, talking, and writing/drawing. Think about what they can already do, almost do, and not yet do to select the emphasis for your teaching. Think about the ways you have noticed students initiate and sustain writing. Observe students' contributions and participation during writing minilessons, writing conferences, and guided writing. Use the Writing Process section to assess how they are developing their own independent writing process.

• Are they volunteering ideas when you talk about what to write?

The Learning Zone

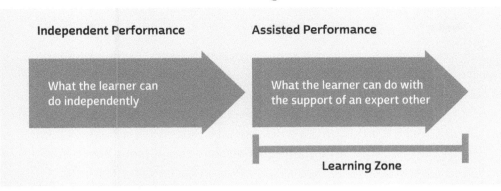

Figure 6-2: Learning zone from *Guided Reading: Responsive Teaching Across the Grades* (Fountas and Pinnell 2017)

- Do they demonstrate confidence in trying to write words they don't yet know how to spell?

- How are students applying some of the things they are learning during writing minilessons to independent writing?

▶ **Scan the Writing About Reading continuum** to analyze students' drawing and writing in response to the books you have read aloud. This analysis will help you determine next steps for having them respond to the books and poems you read together.

▶ **Review the Phonics, Spelling, and Word Study continuum** to evaluate students' knowledge of letter-sound relationships, word structure, and word meaning. These insights will help you make important choices about how to support students using writing minilessons as well as phonics, spelling, and word study lessons.

▶ **Consult the Oral and Visual Communication continuum** to help you think about some of the routines students might need for better communication between peers, especially as they share their writing with one another. You will find essential listening and speaking competencies to observe and teach for.

▶ **Review the Digital Communication continuum** to help you evaluate your students' understanding of digital literacy and citizenship. The behaviors in this section will help you integrate technology and make it an integral part of your students' writing work.

▶ **Record informal notes** about the interactions you have while conferring or the interactions you see between students as they write and share their writing. Look for patterns in these notes to notice trends in their drawing and writing. Use *The Fountas & Pinnell Literacy Continuum* to help you analyze your notes and determine strengths and areas for growth across the classroom. Your observations will reveal what students know and what they need to learn next as they build knowledge about writing over time. Each goal becomes a possible topic for a minilesson (see Conferring Record 1 and Conferring Record 2 in Figure 2-7).

▶ **Establish routines for reading your students' writing regularly.**
It is helpful to create a system for reading through a few writing folders every day. Some teachers divide the number of writing folders across five days and read through one set each day. As you read your students' writing, make notes about the patterns you see across student writing. What writing principles would the whole group benefit from learning in a writing minilesson? Which principles might be better addressed in a small guided writing group? And, which goals might you want to address in individual conferences?

▶ **Consult district, state, and/or accreditation standards.**
Analyze the suggested skills and areas of knowledge specified in your local and state standards. Align these standards with the minilessons suggested in this book to determine which might be applicable within your classroom.

▶ **Use the Assess Learning and Assessment sections** within each lesson and at the end of each umbrella. Take time to assess the students' learning after the completion of each lesson and umbrella.

The guiding questions on the last page of each umbrella will help you to determine strengths and next steps for your fourth graders. Your notes on the online resources shown in the next two sections will also help you make a plan for your teaching.

Use Online Resources for Planning and Teaching

The writing minilessons in this book are examples of how to engage fourth graders in developing the behaviors and understandings of competent writers as described in *The Fountas & Pinnell Literacy Continuum*. Use any of the planning forms in the online resources (fp.pub/resources) to help you plan your teaching.

The form shown in Figure 6-3 will help you plan each part of a new writing minilesson. You can design a lesson that uses a different set of example texts from the ones suggested in this book, or you can teach a concept in a way that fits

Figure 6-3: Use the downloadable form to plan your own writing minilessons.

| Teacher | Mr. Yavorsky | Grade | 4 | Year | |

Planning a Writing Minilesson

Umbrella: CFT.U2: Describing Characters

Minilesson Principle: WML2: Show what characters are like through their actions and words.

Continuum Goal(s):
· Describe characters by how they look, what they do, say, and think, and what other characters say about them.
· Use descriptive language and dialogue to present characters who appear in narratives.

Minilesson	Examples:	Chart:		
Revisit *Goin' Someplace Special* (pp. 1, 5, 13). Have students raise a hand when they notice a character's actions. · What does the author want you to know about 'Tricia Ann from these words and actions?	*Goin' Someplace Special* by Patricia C. McKissack *Follow the Moon Home* by Philippe Cousteau and Deborah Hopkinson	Character	Action	What it shows
		'Tricia Ann		
		Vivienne		
Have a Try	Read pages 4, 15, and 19 of *Follow the Moon Home*. Ask students to think about Vivienne's actions as you read.			
Summarize and Apply	· Today, check your writing to see if you have actions that reveal your characters. Make notes about places where you can add actions.			
Confer	Meet with Owen, Tyson, and Sammy. · What are your characters like? · What will they do and say to show what they are like or what they are feeling?			
Share	Ask the class to share actions and words they added to reveal what characters are like.			

The Writing Minilessons Book

Teacher Ms. Marquardt Grade 4 Year

Curriculum Plan: Writing Minilessons

Month February	Writing Minilessons	Comments/Observations	✓ or Date
Week 1	GEN.U14: Writing Poetry, WML1-2 GEN.U7: Writing Realistic Fiction Stories, WML1-3	Revisit GEN.U14.WML2 throughout the year. Collected additional realistic fiction stories from the library to use as examples.	2/1 2/2 2/3 2/4 2/5
Week 2	GEN.U7: Writing Realistic Fiction Stories, WML4 CFT.U3: Crafting a Setting, WML1-3 WPS.U11: Adding Book and Print Features, WML2	Use Crow Call and Goin' Someplace Special for additional examples for setting. Pulled a guided writing group for WPS.U11.WML2.	2/8 2/9 2/10 2/11 2/12
Week 3	GEN.U14: Writing Poetry, WML3 CFT.U8: Making Powerful Word Choices, WML1-3 CFT.U2: Describing Characters, WML1	Spend several more days on GEN.U14.WML3. GEN.U14 and CFT.U8 support each other nicely. Teach these together again next time.	2/16 2/17 2/18 2/19 2/22
Week 4	CFT.U2: Describing Characters, WML2-3, 5 WPS.U8: Adding Information to Your Writing, WML3	Wait to teach WML4.	2/23 2/24 2/25 2/26

Figure 6-4: Use this downloadable form to plan your teaching and to make notes about specific writing minilessons for future planning.

the current needs of your students. The form shown in Figure 6-4 will help you plan which lessons to teach over a period of time to address the goals that are important for the students.

The minilessons are here for you to teach according to the instructional needs of your class. You may not be able to use all 225 lessons in a year, so select lessons based on assessment of the needs of your students. Record or check off the lessons you have taught so that you can reflect on the work of the semester and year. You can do this with the Writing Minilessons Record (Figure 6-5).

Teacher Mrs. Daly Year

Writing Minilessons Record for Grade 4

Writing Minilesson Number	Writing Minilesson Principle	Notes	✓ or Date
SECTION 1: MANAGEMENT			
Umbrella 1: Being a Respectful Member of the Classroom Community			
MGT.U1.WML1	Get to know your classmates.	MGT.U1.WML1: Allow time for students to present slides/posters to the class.	9/2
MGT.U1.WML2	Agree on how to work together.		9/3
MGT.U1.WML3	Use an appropriate voice level.	MGT.U1.WML3: Post voice level chart.	9/7
MGT.U1.WML4	Find ways to solve problems.		9/8
MGT.U1.WML5	Make everyone feel included.	MGT.U1.WML5: Engaging conversation on inclusion!	9/9
MGT.U1.WML6	Think about how your words and actions make others feel.		9/10
MGT.U1.WML7	Turn and talk to share your thinking.		9/13
Umbrella 2: Establishing Independent Writing			
MGT.U2.WML1	Agree on guidelines for independent writing.		9/20
MGT.U2.WML2	Use writing tools to help with your writing.	MGT.U2.WML2: Have students make labels for the marker containers- green for revising and red for editing.	9/21
MGT.U2.WML3	Share your writing with others.		9/22
Umbrella 3: Introducing the Writing Folder			
MGT.U3.WML1	Keep a list of your finished writing projects.	MGT.U3.WML1: Meet with small groups to get started on writing project lists.	10/19
MGT.U3.WML2	Write what you have learned how to do as a writer and illustrator.		10/20
MGT.U3.WML3	Make writing goals to grow as a writer and illustrator.	MGT.U3.WML3: Talk about goals in individual conferences. Follow up in two weeks.	10/21

 The Writing Minilessons Book, Grade 4 **Page 1**

The Writing Minilessons Book, Grade 4 **Page 2**

Figure 6-5: Writing Minilessons Record for Grade 4

Meet Students' Needs and Build on Their Strengths

If you are new to writing minilessons, you may want to adhere closely to the suggested sequence, but remember to use the lessons flexibly to meet the needs of the students you teach and to build upon their strengths. Base your decisions about when or whether to use certain lessons on what you notice that they can already do, almost do, and not yet do.

▶ Omit lessons that you think are not necessary.

▶ Repeat lessons that you think need more time and instructional attention. Or, repeat lessons using different examples for a particularly rich experience.

▶ Move lessons around to be consistent with the curriculum that is adopted in your school or district.

Consider using the analysis tool in Figure 6-6 along with *The Fountas & Pinnell Literacy Continuum* after you have taught the minilessons in a few umbrellas. We suggest using this tool, or one of the other assessment tools offered in the online resources, to focus on one or two pieces of a student's writing. Set aside time to analyze the writing of five students a day. By the end of the week, you will have a snapshot of what the students understand and what they do not yet understand. Use Guide to Observing and Noting Writing Behaviors (Figure 6-7) quarterly as an interim assessment. This observation form comes in two versions, one for individuals and one for the whole class.

Patterns and trends across students' writing will help you plan what to address through whole-group minilessons, small-group guided writing lessons, or individual conferences. Not only will this allow you to be responsive in your teaching, but it will also give you a sense of how to build upon each student's strengths. Consult the Suggested Sequence of Lessons when necessary to decide if you want to wait to teach a particular umbrella, but don't be afraid to be responsive to your learners. You can always repeat or skip lessons if you have decided to teach them before they come up in the sequence.

Figure 6-6: Use this form to analyze student writing to make a plan for future teaching.

Analyzing Student Writing for Planning

Use *The Literacy Continuum* and the Assessment section at the end of each umbrella you have taught to analyze a student's writing for evidence of writing behaviors and understandings.

Name: Drew   Grade: 4   Genre: Memoir   Date: October

Umbrellas Taught: GEN.U5: Writing Memoirs; WPS.U3: Writer's Notebook: Getting Inspiration from Writers and Artists; CFT.U1: Learning from Writers and Illustrators

	Strengths	Next Steps	Plan (WML, GW, IC)
Genre	• Selects a meaningful topic. • Uses words to show the passage of time. • Describes the setting.	• Communicate the bigger message.	• GW: Review lesson on message (see GEN. U5.WML4) with Sam, Deja, and Marielle.
Craft	• Uses figurative language (simile/metaphor). • Uses strong verbs and modifiers. • Builds suspense leading up to the big event/moment.	• Learn a variety of ways to show the passage of time. • Expand use of figurative language to other forms (personification).	• WML: CFT.U9: Writing Clear and Interesting Sentences, WML1 • IC: Possible topic—when and why to use figurative language.
Conventions	• Understands and uses paragraph structure. • Beginning to place phrases in sentences.	• Use colons to introduce a list of items. • Spell complex plurals correctly (leaf, leaves). • Learn to punctuate dialogue.	• GW: CNV.U1: Writing Words, WML3 • WML: Teach CNV.U2: Learning About Punctuation and Capitalization, WML3.
Writing Process	• Maintains central idea or focus across paragraphs.	• Learn to identify information that does not contribute to the central message. • Use commas to separate parts of sentences.	• IC: Focus on message. • GW: Identify and correct run-on sentences.

WML: Writing Minilesson   GW: Guided Writing   IC: Individual Conference

Guide to Observing and Noting Writing Behaviors—Whole Class, Grade 4

Guide to Observing and Noting Writing Behaviors—Individual Student, Grade 4

Student's Name: Tika   Date: 3/22

Behaviors and Understandings	C P N	My Plan What are the priorities for this writer? What is my plan for support?	How will I teach this? (SW, GW, WML, IC)
Genre			
Write different types of letters (both friendly and formal) and emails.	C		
Write memory stories (both small-moment and a series of vignettes) that have a message.	P	Needs support with idea of writing vignettes.	GW
Write a variety of procedural texts that include steps/instructions.	C		
Experiment with writing a variety of poems, including free verse, lyrical, concrete, haiku, and informational, as well as poems for two voices.	P	Still needs to learn about informational poems.	WML: GEN.U15
Write informational texts, such as feature articles, that are engaging and ordered by logic (e.g., related ideas, categories, sequence).	C	Needs support with researching a subject.	IC
Write picture book biographies that include the important events and turning points in a subject's life.	P		
Write realistic fiction stories with a logical plot (problem, series of events, and solution) and that include a lesson learned by the main character.	N		
Write opinion pieces and persuasive essays with supportive reasons and examples.	N		
Use technology to write digital pieces, such as informational multimedia presentations, photo essays, and other digital texts.	N		
Craft			
Choose a title that fits the content of the piece.	C		
Write engaging leads and endings.	C		
Write from a first- or third-person point of view.	C		

SW: Shared Writing • GW: Guided Writing • WML: Writing Minilesson • IC: Individual Conference • C: Consistent • P: Partial • N: Not evident yet

The Writing Minilessons Book, Grade 4 **Page 1**

Figure 6-7: Use the observation forms about every quarter. One form helps you focus on an individual child. The other form offers a snapshot of the whole class.

Understand the Suggested Sequence of Lessons

The Suggested Sequence of Lessons (pp. 665–682 and also in online resources) is intended to establish a strong classroom community early in the year, work toward more sophisticated concepts across the year, and bring together the instructional pieces of your classroom. The learning that takes place during writing minilessons is applied in many situations in the classroom and so is reinforced daily across the curriculum and across the year.

Because many writing minilessons use mentor texts as a starting point, the lessons are sequenced so that they occur after students have had sufficient opportunities to build some clear understandings of aspects of writing through interactive read-aloud and shared reading. From these experiences, you and your students will have a rich set of mentor texts to pull into writing minilessons. If you are using shared and/or interactive writing regularly in your classroom to write together with the class, bring those texts into lessons as other mentor texts. They will be extremely meaningful since you will have developed them collaboratively. Your own modeled writing is another extremely powerful source for a mentor text.

The Suggested Sequence of Lessons follows the suggested sequence of text sets in *Fountas & Pinnell Classroom™ Interactive Read-Aloud Collection* and books in *Shared Reading Collection.* If you are using either or both of these collections, you are invited to follow this sequence of texts. If you are not using them, the kinds of books with which students will need to be familiar are described on the first page of each umbrella in this book.

The text sets in the *Interactive Read-Aloud Collection* are grouped together by theme, topic, author, or genre, not by skill or concept. That's why in many minilessons, we use mentor texts from several different text sets and why the same books are used in more than one umbrella.

We have selected the most concrete and clear examples from the recommended books. In most cases, the minilessons draw on mentor texts that have been introduced within the same month. However, in some cases, minilessons taught later in the year might draw on books you read much earlier in the year. Most of the time, students will have no problem remembering these early books because you have read and talked about them. Sometimes students have responded through art, dramatic play, or writing. Once in a while, you might need to quickly reread a book or a portion of it before teaching the umbrella so it is fresh in the students' minds, but this is not usually necessary. Looking at some of the pictures and talking about the book is enough.

Use the Suggested Sequence to Connect the Pieces

To understand how the Suggested Sequence of Lessons can help you bring these instructional pieces together, let's look at a brief example from the suggested sequence. In month 2, we suggest reading the text set Genre Study: Memoir from the *Interactive Read-Aloud Collection*. (You do not need any specific books in this text set; use any set of similar books available.) Later, the books from the *Interactive Read-Aloud Collection* become mentor texts in both reading and writing minilessons. In reading minilessons, students are engaged in understanding the characteristics of memoir, including first-person point of view, the presence of a turning point for the characters, and the reflective quality of the message. The writing minilessons in GEN.U5: Writing Memoirs introduce students to particular aspects of writing in this genre, including how to choose a small moment or a series of vignettes for their memoirs, how to add details to important scenes, and how to communicate a message through the story. You may also choose to write a memoir as a class using shared writing or in small groups using interactive writing for students who need extra support. A class-made memoir can also serve as one of the mentor texts. These mentor texts help students learn specific understandings about writing a memoir. The first minilesson in GEN.U5 engages students in an immersive study of the genre. They spend

Connecting All the Pieces

Read aloud and enjoy memoirs with the class.

Use shared or interactive writing to write about a memoir.

Study mentor texts using writing minilessons.

Teach writing minilessons on specific aspects of memoirs.

Have students write their own memoirs.

Figure 6-8: The Suggested Sequence of Lessons helps you connect all the pieces of your classroom instruction and leads to students' own independent writing.

time with a partner or small group studying memoirs and noticing the qualities of good memoir writing.

Studying the genre and engaging in shared writing experiences give students the background that helps them go deeper when they experience minilessons on specific topics. They are able to draw on their previous experiences with texts to fully understand the concepts in the minilessons. They can then apply this learning to their own independent writing. The Suggested Sequence of Lessons is one way to organize your teaching across the year to make these connections (Figure 6-8).

Schedule Writers' Workshop During the Day

After deciding which minilessons to teach and in what order to teach them, the next decision is when. In *Fountas & Pinnell Classroom™ System Guide, Grade 4* (2020), you will find frameworks for teaching and learning across a day. Using the schedules and the information there as guides, think about when you might incorporate writers' workshop as a regular part of the day in fourth grade. Ideally, the workshop would last for 45–75 minutes (see

Figure 1-4). However, not everyone has that amount of time each day to devote to writing. Some teachers substitute writers' workshop for readers' workshop a couple of times a week. It's not an ideal solution, but it does provide both reading and writing experiences for students. Of course, the more time students have for writing, the better.

Fourth graders thrive on the structure, organization, and predictability of a daily writers' workshop. When you set routines and a consistent time for writing minilessons and independent writing, you teach students what to expect. They find comfort in the reliability of the structure. Students write joyfully when they know they can count on time to experiment with and explore drawing and writing. They delight in knowing that what they have to say is valued. Writing minilessons build on the joy and enthusiasm students bring to all that they do in the classroom setting.

Section 1 | Management

Management minilessons will help you set up routines for building a community of learners in the classroom. They allow you to teach effectively and efficiently and are directed toward the creation of an orderly, busy classroom in which students know what is expected and how to act responsibly and respectfully in a community of learners. A class that has a strong feeling of community is a safe place for all students to do their best work and enjoy learning. Most of the minilessons at the beginning of the school year will come from this section.

1 Management

Minilessons in This Umbrella

WML1 Get to know your classmates.

WML2 Agree on how to work together.

WML3 Use an appropriate voice level.

WML4 Find ways to solve problems.

WML5 Make everyone feel included.

WML6 Think about how your words and actions make others feel.

WML7 Turn and talk to share your thinking.

Before Teaching Umbrella 1 Minilessons

These minilessons are designed to communicate to students that they are a community of writers who work and learn together. You can support this concept by creating a warm, inviting, well-organized, and uncluttered classroom.

Students will work on two activities across these minilessons that will help them explore who they are as a class and provide a context in which to apply the concepts in this umbrella. One is an interview slide or poster to introduce a student to the class. The other is a public service announcement (PSA), in any form that students choose, to share their classroom values with the school community. Throughout the umbrella, students will be asked to turn and talk to a partner. Specific instruction about this routine is in WML7.

If you are using *The Reading Minilessons Book, Grade 4* (Fountas and Pinnell 2020) and have already taught the first umbrella in the Management section, you may not need to teach every lesson in this umbrella. To support both classroom management and an atmosphere for getting to know one another, read books together that foster kindness and empathy and provide time each day for students to share. Use the books listed below from *Fountas & Pinnell Classroom*™ *Interactive Read-Aloud Collection* or other books related to what it means to be part of a caring community.

Interactive Read-Aloud Collection
Friendship

The Other Side by Jacqueline Woodson

Better Than You by Trudy Ludwig

Snook Alone by Marilyn Nelson

Mangoes, Mischief, and Tales of Friendship: Stories from India by Chitra Soundar

As you read and enjoy these texts together, help students

- think about different ways that people work together, and
- talk about different ways to solve problems.

Interactive Read-Aloud
Friendship

Section 1: Management

WML1

MGT.U1.WML1

Writing Minilesson Principle
Get to know your classmates.

Being a Respectful Member of the Classroom Community

You Will Need

▸ chart paper and markers

Academic Language / Important Vocabulary

▸ classroom community
▸ talent

Continuum Connection

▸ Use conventions of respectful conversation
▸ Actively participate in conversation by listening and looking at the person speaking
▸ Refrain from speaking over others
▸ Ask questions for clarification or to gain information
▸ Relate or compare one's own knowledge and experience with information from others

GOAL

Learn to value one another's unique identities.

RATIONALE

When you encourage students to get to know one another, value the unique identities of others, and embrace diversity, you create a rich classroom community in which students are comfortable sharing and learning together. Asking and answering questions of each other also allows students to practice conversational skills.

ASSESS LEARNING

▸ Observe students to notice whether they ask questions and listen carefully to the responses.
▸ Look for evidence that students are interested in learning about and talking with classmates.
▸ Look for evidence that students can use vocabulary such as *classroom community* and *talent*.

MINILESSON

To help students think about the minilesson principle, engage them in conversation to get them thinking about questions they can ask to get to know one another. Here is an example.

> We are building a community in our classroom. A community is a group of people who know each other and support each other. The first thing to do is get to know one another. First, I'll tell you a little bit about me.
>
> I was the first person in my family to go to college. Also, I'm very good at baking bread.
>
> I told you some information about myself, but what if you wanted to learn something about a classmate? What could you do?
>
> You could ask questions. What kinds of questions might you ask? What would interest you to know about your classmates?

▸ As students respond, record their questions on the chart paper. Prompt their questions as needed.

> Today, you will start the process of making an interview slide. First, you will interview a classmate. Then, you will make a slide about the person so that we can all get to know one another. When the slides are finished, I'll put together a presentation.

Have a Try

Invite pairs of students to think of more questions that would help them get to know each other.

> Turn and talk to your partner about other questions to add to the list.

▶ After time for discussion, ask volunteers to share. Add new questions to the chart.

Summarize and Apply

Summarize the lesson. Invite students to get to know one another by asking questions and jotting notes.

▶ Make sure each student has a partner. You might need to assign one or more groups of three. Assure students that they can pass on questions that cause them discomfort.

> Today, start the process of making your interview slide by asking your partner(s) some of the questions on the chart. Write some notes about what you learn. Bring your notes when we meet later.

▶ Save students' notes for WML5.

Questions for Getting to Know Each Other

- What are your three favorite foods?
- Where are you from?
- What do you like to do when you're not at school?
- What are your talents (for example, in sports, music, languages, cooking)?
- How many people are in your family?
- What pets do you have?
- What are you favorite TV shows, movies, or songs?
- What is a favorite memory of yours?
- What is your earliest memory?

Confer

▶ While students are working, move around the room to confer briefly with pairs or small groups of students about what they are asking and learning. Use the following prompts as needed.

- *What could you write to remember what your partner said?*
- *What did you learn about a classmate that you did not know before?*
- *Why is it important to get to know classmates and to share information about yourself?*

Share

After students have had time to talk with one another, gather them in the meeting area. Have two sets of partners share with each other what they learned about their classmates. Then select several students to share with the whole group.

> Share one thing you learned about a classmate that you did not know before today.

Being a Respectful Member of the Classroom Community

You Will Need

▸ chart paper and markers

Academic Language / Important Vocabulary

▸ classroom community
▸ respectful
▸ agreement

Continuum Connection

▸ Use conventions of respectful conversation

▸ Use respectful turn-taking conventions

▸ Actively participate in conversation during whole- and small-group discussion

▸ Listen and respond to a partner by agreeing, disagreeing, or adding on, and explaining reasons

▸ Express and reflect on their own feelings and recognize the feelings of others

▸ Refrain from speaking over others

▸ Ask questions for clarification or to gain information

▸ Relate or compare one's own knowledge and experience with information from others

GOAL

Understand that members of a community agree on how to work together.

RATIONALE

A community that works well means that the members must agree on how they want to work together. Making an agreement of classroom norms is one way for students to take ownership of their classroom and their behaviors so that a positive classroom environment can be established and maintained.

ASSESS LEARNING

▸ Look for evidence that students understand that they are valued as part of the classroom community.

▸ Notice whether students contribute ideas for ways they can work and learn together.

▸ Look for evidence that students can use vocabulary such as *classroom community*, *respectful*, and *agreement*.

MINILESSON

To help students think about the minilesson principle, engage them in a discussion about classroom norms that leads to creating a community agreement. Here is an example.

> In our classroom, understanding how to be a respectful member of the community will make it possible for all members of the classroom community to do their best work and enjoy working and learning together. What are some things we can agree upon to make that happen?

▸ As needed, offer the following prompts:

- *How should class members behave toward one another?*
- *When you are writing, how can you do your best work?*
- *What is something you can do to make the classroom a place where everyone can learn?*
- *How should the classroom materials be used and stored?*

▸ Make a list on chart paper with students' ideas. For each one, ask students to discuss how it will help build and maintain a positive classroom community.

> How will this idea help you work together, support each other, and enjoy learning?

Have a Try

Invite students to turn and talk about the community agreement.

> Turn and talk to your partner about other ideas for the agreement. You might also choose one of the ideas on the chart and talk about why it is important.

▶ After time for discussion, ask a few volunteers to share. Add new ideas to the chart. Have students sign the agreement now or during writing time.

Summarize and Apply

Summarize the lesson. Remind students to think about the community agreement.

▶ Assign students to work with a partner or in a small group.

> Today, you will start to work on a public service announcement, or PSA, about the values in this classroom. A PSA gives important information. Your PSA will let students and teachers in the school know what is important to us. First, decide which value you want to tell people about. Then, decide what you will do to get the word out. Be creative! For example, you could make a poster, record a video, create an advertisement, or write a short play. Start your planning today, and save your notes for later.

Our Classroom Agreement

- Be kind and respectful to each other.
- Be inclusive of others.
- Use a quiet voice when people are working.
- Take turns.
- Focus on your work.
- Help each other feel safe taking risks.
- Keep the classroom organized.
- Take good care of materials.
- Help each other learn.

Mia   Ruby   Jade   Sage
Aiden   Alejandro   Landon   Lily
Joseph   Ang   Braylin   Padma   Hiram
Emiliano   Luci   Kali   Henry
Piper   Nora   Andee   Gabriella
Maarish   Jackie   Hudson   Li

Confer

▶ While students are working, move around the room to confer briefly with pairs or small groups of students about their PSAs. Use the following prompts as needed.

- *Which idea will you focus on in your PSA? Why did you choose that idea?*
- *What form will you use for your PSA? Will it be a poster, play, video, slide presentation, or something else?*
- *Consider deciding who will do what on the PSA.*

Share

After students have had time to plan their PSAs, gather them in the meeting area. Ask each pair of students or small group to talk about plans for their PSAs.

> What are you planning for your PSA?

Writing Minilesson Principle
Use an appropriate voice level.

Being a Respectful Member of the Classroom Community

You Will Need

▸ chart paper and markers

Academic Language / Important Vocabulary

▸ classroom community
▸ voice level
▸ appropriate

Continuum Connection

▸ Speak at an appropriate volume
▸ Refrain from speaking over others
▸ Adjust speaking volume for different contexts

GOAL

Learn to use an appropriate voice level.

RATIONALE

When students identify different voice levels that are appropriate for different settings, they can independently determine the appropriate level and modulate their voices accordingly.

ASSESS LEARNING

▸ Observe whether students can identify the appropriate voice level for a particular situation.

▸ Listen to students' voices throughout the day. Do they adjust their voice levels to different situations?

▸ Look for evidence that students can use vocabulary such as *classroom community*, *voice level*, and *appropriate*.

MINILESSON

To help students think about the minilesson principle, engage them in discussing voice levels and in creating an anchor chart. Here is an example.

> When we made our classroom agreement chart, one of the things we discussed was voice level. Why are appropriate voice levels important at school?

▸ Encourage students to talk about the variety of voice levels they use at school. On chart paper, create a chart with four columns numbered 0 to 3, explaining that 0 is a silent voice and 3 is an outside voice.

> Show what a silent voice sounds like.
>
> What are some activities you do with a 0 voice level?

▸ As students make suggestions, add them under the 0 voice level column.

> Now think about the next type of voice level. When you are sharing your writing with a partner, how does your voice sound?
>
> How would you describe this voice level?
>
> What are some other times you might use a 1 voice level?

▸ Add students' examples to the chart.

▸ Repeat the activity for each remaining voice level. On the chart, indicate that 2 means using a normal voice and 3 means using a loud voice.

Have a Try

Invite students to talk to a partner about using appropriate voice levels.

> Turn and talk to your partner about paying attention to the kind of voice you use.

▶ After a brief time for discussion, ask students to share new ideas and add to the chart.

Summarize and Apply

Summarize the lesson. Remind students to use a voice level that is appropriate for the situation.

> What voice levels will you be using today? Why?

▶ Write the principle at the top of the chart.

> Today, continue working with your partner (small group) on the PSA. Save your work so that you can work on it more later.

Use an appropriate voice level.			
0	1	2	3
Silent	Soft	Normal	Loud
• Writing time	• Small-group work	• Whole-group work	• Outside recess
• Independent work	• Partner work	• Class meetings	• Physical education class (sometimes)
• Hallways	• Working with teacher	• Shared reading	
• Taking tests		• Giving a presentation	
		• Speaking to the whole class	

Confer

▶ While students are working, move around the room to confer briefly with pairs or small groups of students about their work on their PSAs. Use the following prompts as needed.

- *Look at the chart. Which voice level is appropriate for what you are doing?*
- *Talk about the work each of you is doing on the PSA.*
- *What voice level will you use when you present your PSA?*

Share

After students have had time to work on their PSAs, gather them in the meeting area to talk about their progress.

> How is your PSA coming along? What voice level did you use while you worked?

Writing Minilesson Principle
Find ways to solve problems.

Being a Respectful Member of the Classroom Community

You Will Need

- two-column chart prepared with the heads *Problem* and *Solution*
- markers

Academic Language / Important Vocabulary

- classroom community
- problem
- solution

Continuum Connection

- Write with independent initiative and investment
- Enter a conversation appropriately
- Listen with attention during instruction, and respond with statements and questions
- Listen to, remember, and follow directions with multiple steps

GOAL

Find ways to solve problems independently.

RATIONALE

Students who learn problem-solving strategies become independent and confident, which allows time for you to work with small groups or confer with individual students.

ASSESS LEARNING

- Notice whether students are trying to solve problems independently.
- Look for evidence that students can use vocabulary such as *classroom community*, *problem*, and *solution*.

MINILESSON

To help students think about the minilesson principle, engage them in a discussion of how to solve problems independently. Here is an example.

- Show the prepared chart.

  Sometimes when you are working on your own, you run into a problem or have a question that keeps you from continuing your work. What are some examples of problems you might have?

- Prompt the conversation as needed. As students provide ideas, add their ideas to the *Problem* column using general terms.

  You might need my help with a problem once in a while, but most of the time you can solve problems on your own. Think about some solutions to these problems. Turn and talk about your ideas.

- After time for discussion, ask volunteers to share. As students provide solutions, record their ideas on the chart, choosing generalized language.

  Why is it important for you to solve problems on your own?

- Encourage a conversation about the importance of independent problem solving. Support their thinking as needed (e.g., it allows the teacher time to work with small groups or individual students; it makes each student responsible for the classroom community).

- Briefly explain that it is OK to interrupt the teacher if there is an emergency.

Have a Try

Invite students to turn and talk about solving problems.

> What is another problem you might have in class? How might you solve it? Turn and talk about that.

▶ After time for discussion, ask a few volunteers to share. Add new ideas to the chart.

Summarize and Apply

Summarize the lesson. Remind students to try to solve problems independently.

> How can you solve any problems that come up while you are doing your work?

▶ Write the principle at the top of the chart.

> Continue working with your partner or in your small group on your PSAs. If you have a problem, try to solve it on your own first before you ask for help, unless it is an emergency. Look at the chart for ways to solve your problem.

Find ways to solve problems.

Problem	Solution
Finish work early	• Review your work. • Finish other work. • Write or read.
Have a problem with another student	• Talk politely and kindly to the person and try to find a solution together. • Compromise.
Don't understand directions	• Reread directions. • Think about how you have done a similar assignment. • Ask someone in the class.
Can't find or run out of something	• Look for a basket with the right label. • Look in the writing area. • Ask if you can borrow an extra.
Questions about the writing you are working on	• Reread your writing. • Begin another piece of writing.
Emergency (bleeding, sick, injury)	• Tell the teacher immediately.

Confer

▶ While students are working, move around the room to confer briefly with pairs or small groups of students about their PSAs. Use the following prompts as needed.

- *How is your PSA coming along?*
- *If you can't figure something out, what can you do?*
- *Is there anything preventing you from doing your work today? What can you do to help yourself and your group solve that problem?*

Share

After students have had time to work on their PSAs, gather them in the meeting area to talk about problem solving and their PSAs.

▶ Each pair or group can choose a representative to talk about their progress.

> How does it help our classroom community when you try to solve problems on your own?

Being a Respectful Member of the Classroom Community

You Will Need

- a fiction book that emphasizes friendship and inclusion, such as *The Other Side* by Jacqueline Woodson, from Text Set: Friendship
- chart paper and markers
- sticky notes

Academic Language / Important Vocabulary

- classroom community
- inclusive

Continuum Connection

- Learn from vicarious experiences with characters in stories
- Use conventions of respectful conversation
- Use nonpejorative and inclusive language: e.g., nonsexist, nonracist, nonbiased
- Actively participate in conversation during whole- and small-group discussion
- Use conventional techniques that encourage others to talk: e.g., "What do you think?" "Do you agree? Why or why not?"
- Express and reflect on their own feelings and recognize the feelings of others
- Refrain from speaking over others
- Ask questions for clarification or to gain information

GOAL

Lean to use language and take actions to make others feel included.

RATIONALE

When students learn to use words and actions that invite others to join in, they create an environment in which all classroom community members feel included and valued.

ASSESS LEARNING

- Look for evidence that students understand why it is important to include others.
- Notice inclusive language that students use in the classroom.
- Look for evidence that students can use vocabulary such as *classroom community* and *inclusive*.

MINILESSON

If you haven't already read *The Other Side* with the class, read it or another book in which one character feels left out at first. To help students think about the minilesson principle, encourage a discussion about the effect of words and actions that show acceptance and inclusiveness. Here is an example.

- Revisit pages 5–6 of *The Other Side*.

    Think about when the girl on the fence asks if she can play and another girl says no. How do you think the girl is feeling when that happens?

- Revisit pages 25–28.

    Have you ever felt like Annie?

    How do you think Annie feels now with Clover and the other kids?

    Using words and actions that invite others to join in is called being inclusive. What are some things you could say or do in the classroom to be sure everyone feels included?

- As students share ideas, make a list on chart paper using generalized terms.

    What are some inclusive things you could say or do outside the classroom?

- Add to the list.

Have a Try

Invite students to turn and talk with a partner about being inclusive.

> Turn and talk to your partner about a time that someone included you in an activity. What did that person say or do? How did you feel?

▶ After time for discussion, ask a few volunteers to share.

Summarize and Apply

Summarize the lesson. Invite students to work on their PSAs or interview slides. Write the principle on the chart.

> Today, we talked about making sure that everyone feels included.

▶ Write the principle at the top of the chart.

> Today, work some more on your PSA. You should be just about finished with it. As you work, notice any examples of others in the class being inclusive and write them on sticky notes or on paper. You can also continue working on your interview slide. Be prepared to share when we meet later.

Make everyone feel included.

In the Classroom

What do you think about that?

What is your opinion?

Can I help you with anything?

Make space for someone in the circle.

Outside the Classroom

Would you like to join us?

Make room at your lunch table.

Do you want to play this game with us?

Confer

▶ While students are working, move around the room to confer briefly with pairs or small groups of students about their PSAs or their interview slides from WML1 and also about being inclusive. Use the following prompts as needed.

- *What did each of you do to help prepare your PSA?*
- *Have you noticed someone saying or doing something to include another person? What did you notice?*
- *How does being inclusive help our classroom community?*

Share

After students have had time to work independently, gather them in the meeting area to talk about their progress as well as inclusive words and actions.

> Who would like to share what you worked on today?

Section 1: Management

Writing Minilesson Principle
Think about how your words and actions make others feel.

Being a Respectful Member of the Classroom Community

You Will Need

- a familiar text that encourages thinking about empathy, such as *Better Than You* by Trudy Ludwig, from Text Set: Friendship
- prepared two-column chart with the headings *What Someone Said or Did* and *How That Made Others Feel*
- markers

Academic Language / Important Vocabulary

- classroom community
- empathy

Continuum Connection

- Learn from vicarious experiences with characters in stories
- Use conventions of respectful conversation
- Actively participate in conversation during whole- and small-group discussion
- Listen and respond to a partner by agreeing, disagreeing, or adding on, and explaining reasons
- Express and reflect on their own feelings and recognize the feelings of others
- Ask questions for clarification or to gain information
- Relate or compare one's own knowledge and experience with information from others

GOAL

Learn how to show empathy toward others.

RATIONALE

When students reflect on how their words and actions affect classmates, they develop empathy and concern for others, which contributes to a positive classroom community.

ASSESS LEARNING

- Notice whether students are able to infer how their own words and actions make others feel.
- Look for evidence that students can use vocabulary such as *classroom community* and *empathy*.

MINILESSON

If you haven't already read *Better Than You* with the class, read it or another book about friendship in which one character shows empathy to another character. To help students think about the minilesson principle, lead a discussion about empathy based on that text. Here is an example.

- Revisit pages 4–8 in *Better Than You*.

    What do you notice about how Jake's words and actions make Tyler feel?

- Display the prepared chart. As students share ideas, fill in the columns with examples.

- Revisit pages 9–12.

    How do Uncle Kevin's words and actions make Tyler feel?

- Continue filling in the chart.

    The feeling that you understand how others feel is called empathy. Thinking about how your words and actions make others feel is one part of empathy.

Have a Try

Invite students to turn and talk about empathy.

> Turn and talk to your partner about a time when someone's words or actions made you feel good or bad.

▶ After time for discussion, ask a few volunteers to share. Add ideas to the chart.

Summarize and Apply

Summarize the lesson. As students finish their PSAs, remind them to think about how their words and actions make others feel.

> Throughout the day, think about the different ways you can make others feel good through your words and actions.

▶ Write the principle at the top of the chart.

> Today, you should finish your PSA so that it will be ready soon to share with the school community. If you are finished with your PSA, you can work more on your interview slide.

Think about how your words and actions make others feel.	
What Someone Said or Did	How That Made Others Feel
Jake bragged and had to be better than Tyler.	Tyler felt like he was not good enough.
Uncle Kevin asked Tyler to play the guitar.	Tyler felt a little better.
Some people asked me to sit at their lunch table.	I felt happy and included.
I didn't have anyone to play with at recess on my first day.	I felt lonely and sad.

Confer

▶ While students are working, move around the room to confer briefly with pairs or small groups of students about showing empathy toward others and the project they are working on. Use the following prompts as needed.

- *Tell a time when someone's actions or words made you feel good (bad).*
- *What is one way you can show empathy toward your classmates?*
- *How are you doing with your PSA and your interview slide?*

Share

After students have finished working independently, gather them in the meeting area to talk about examples of empathy.

> Tell about an example of empathy that you have seen, experienced, or read about.

Writing Minilesson Principle
Turn and talk to share your thinking.

Being a Respectful Member of the Classroom Community

You Will Need

- a student prepared to model turn and talk
- two texts that you have read aloud recently, such as the following from Text Set: Friendship:
  - *Snook Alone* by Marilyn Nelson
  - *Mangoes, Mischief, and Tales of Friendship* by Chitra Soundar
- chart paper and markers

Academic Language / Important Vocabulary

- turn and talk
- listen
- signal
- evidence

Continuum Connection

- Use respectful turn-taking conventions
- Actively participate in conversation during whole-and small-group discussion
- Refrain from speaking over others
- Enter a conversation appropriately
- Use turn-taking with courtesy in small-group discussion
- Engage actively in conversational routines: e.g., turn and talk
- Listen to and speak to a partner about a given idea, and make a connection to the partner's idea

GOAL

Develop guidelines for turn and talk.

RATIONALE

Engaging in the turn and talk routine allows students to express themselves verbally, to engage in conversation with others, and to share opinions. The routine also offers a chance for students to rehearse their oral language in a safe way before sharing with the class. When students learn and follow guidelines for turn and talk, they develop conversational skills that can be applied to speaking with a larger group and in situations outside the classroom.

ASSESS LEARNING

- Watch and listen to students as they turn and talk and notice if they follow the guidelines.
- Observe to determine whether both students in a pair have a chance to talk.
- Look for evidence that students can use vocabulary such as *turn and talk*, *listen*, *signal*, and *evidence*.

MINILESSON

To help students think about the minilesson principle, choose familiar texts, the ones listed on this page or any other book familiar to the class, to use for modeling the turn and talk routine. Then engage students in an interactive discussion about what they noticed. Here is an example.

- Ahead of time, decide on a transition signal that you will use each time to indicate that students should end turn and talk and return to the whole-group conversation.

- Show the cover of a book you have recently read, such as *Snook Alone*.

  > Sometimes when you write something or read a book, you turn and talk to a partner about your thinking. Today, _____ is my partner, and we are going to turn and talk about some interesting things that the writer, Marilyn Nelson, has done in *Snook Alone*.

  > While we turn and talk, watch and listen carefully.

- Briefly model the turn and talk procedure, offering an opinion about the writer's craft. Prompt the student to respond in agreement or disagreement with you and why. Use the transition signal when you finish.

  > What did you notice when you watched and listened to the turn and talk?

- As students respond, begin a list on chart paper to create turn and talk guidelines.

  > When you turn and talk, remember to always give evidence for your thinking.

Have a Try

Invite students to apply what they learned about turn and talk with a partner.

▶ Revisit a page of any book you have read recently with the students, such as *Mangoes, Mischief, and Tales of Friendship*.

> Turn and talk to your partner to share your thinking about the writing in this part of the story. You can look at the chart to remember the guidelines.

Summarize and Apply

Summarize the lesson. Remind students to follow the turn and talk guidelines as they finish their PSAs and interview slides.

> Today, when you work with a partner or in your small group, you will have an opportunity to practice some of what we just talked about, for example, using a soft voice and listening carefully. Finish your interview slide today so that it will be ready for the class presentation. Also, make sure your PSAs are finished.

> ### Turn and Talk
>
> Turn your body toward your partner.
>
> Use a 1 voice level.
>
> Take turns telling your thinking.
>
> Listen carefully.
>
> Ask questions to clarify.
>
> Politely say whether you agree or disagree with your partner or add on to what was said.
>
> Give evidence for your thinking.

Confer

▶ While students are working, move around the room to confer briefly with pairs or small groups of students about the work they are doing and how they will share their thinking during turn and talk. Use the following prompts as needed.

- *Are you thinking about what you want to say?*
- *Look at the chart. What is one thing you will do when you turn and talk?*
- *Why is it important that you know what to do when you turn and talk to a partner?*

Share

After students have finished their PSAs and interview slides, gather them in the meeting area to turn and talk with someone they have not yet worked with.

> Turn and talk to your partner about the PSA you worked on.

▶ After a few minutes, give the signal for students to turn back to you and reflect on their experience of the turn and talk routine.

Section 1: Management

Assessment

After you have taught the minilessons in this umbrella, observe students in a variety of classroom activities. Use *The Fountas & Pinnell Literacy Continuum* to notice, teach for, and support students' learning as you observe their attempts at building a classroom community and working together.

▶ What evidence do you have of students' new understandings related to working together in the classroom?

- Do they ask good questions to get to know one another?
- Do they participate in establishing and honoring classroom agreements?
- How well do students adjust their voice levels to the situation?
- Do they use a variety of problem-solving strategies?
- In what ways are they including others in conversations or activities?
- Do they think about how their words and actions make others feel?
- Do they follow turn and talk procedures?
- Are they using vocabulary such as *classroom community, respectful, agreement, voice level, appropriate, problem, solution, inclusive, empathy, turn and talk*, and *listen*?

▶ In what ways, beyond the scope of this umbrella, are students building a classroom community of members who work well together?

- Are they learning to respect and value one another by sharing their stories?
- Are they ready to learn routines for independent writing time?

Use your observations to determine the next umbrella you will teach. You may also consult Suggested Sequence of Lessons (pp. 665–682) for guidance.

EXTENSIONS FOR BEING A RESPECTFUL MEMBER OF THE CLASSROOM COMMUNITY

▶ If the technology is available, create a slide presentation of students' interview slides. Have students present their interview slides or posters to the class so that everyone can learn something about someone else.

▶ Have each pair or small group of students present their PSA announcements to the class. Then have students share PSAs with the school community, whether it's hanging posters in a common area such as the school lobby or hallway, playing a recording during morning announcements, or presenting a short play in other classrooms.

▶ When reading aloud, note examples of characters displaying inclusive and empathic behaviors.

Minilessons in This Umbrella

WML1 Agree on guidelines for independent writing.

WML2 Use writing tools to help with your writing.

WML3 Share your writing with others.

Writer's Notebook

Before Teaching Umbrella 2 Minilessons

We recommend that students have the opportunity for independent writing time every day as part of a writer's workshop. Learning guidelines and routines for independent writing time will help students build self-confidence by achieving a sense of agency and responsibility for their own work while also allowing time for you to work with individual students or small guided writing groups.

Before teaching the minilessons in this umbrella, we recommend that you teach WPS.U1: Introducing and Using a Writer's Notebook so that students will have some things to work on during the time for independent writing. Also, you will want to organize an area of the classroom to facilitate easy access to materials. Materials may include but are not limited to different kinds of paper (including the selection of paper templates in the online resources), pens, pencils, markers, scissors, tape, glue sticks, and staplers. Have students keep their writer's notebooks and writing folders in a personal box (e.g., a magazine storage box). The writing folders (see MGT.U3: Introducing the Writing Folder) will contain longer pieces of writing in process plus resources (e.g., revising checklist, editing and proofreading checklist) fastened inside. Use folders in several colors so that students can identify their own folders easily. Finished pieces of writing can be stored in hanging files (see pp. 53–54 for more information).

Establishing Independent Writing

You Will Need

- chart paper and markers
- writer's notebooks and writing folders

Academic Language / Important Vocabulary

- independent writing
- writing folder
- writer's notebook
- guidelines

Continuum Connection

- Produce a reasonable quantity of writing within the time available
- Write with independent initiative and investment
- Listen to, remember, and follow directions with multiple steps

GOAL

Agree on a set of guidelines for what to do during independent writing time.

RATIONALE

Helping students create and follow a set of guidelines for independent writing promotes independence and a sense of responsibility, allows the class to function efficiently, and gives you time to confer with individual students or small groups. Reminding students to use all the time at their disposal allows them to build their stamina for and interest in writing.

WRITER'S NOTEBOOK/WRITING FOLDER

Students will work in their writer's notebooks or on an ongoing piece of writing in their writing folders.

ASSESS LEARNING

- Notice whether students get ready for independent writing quickly, quietly, and independently.
- Look for evidence that they can use vocabulary such as *independent writing*, *writing folder*, *writer's notebook*, and *guidelines*.

MINILESSON

To help students think about the minilesson principle, work with them to create a set of guidelines for independent writing. Here is an example.

> Every day in our classroom, you will have independent writing time. During independent writing, you will spend some time writing on your own. Today, we're going to work together to create guidelines for independent writing. Does anyone know what guidelines are?

> Guidelines are rules or instructions that tell how something should be done. Let's think about what you should do and remember during independent writing time so you and your classmates are all able to do your best work.

- Guide students' thinking, as needed, using questions such as the following:
  - *How should you get started when it's time for independent writing?*
  - *What helps you do your best writing work?*
  - *What should the noise level of the classroom be during independent writing?*
  - *How can you make sure that you are writing a good amount and doing a variety of writing?*
  - *What are some things you can do if you get stuck during independent writing time and you're not sure what to do?*
- Use students' responses to write a set of guidelines for independent writing on chart paper.

Have a Try

Invite students to talk to a partner about the guidelines for independent writing.

> Is there anything else you think we should add to our guidelines for independent writing? Turn and talk to your partner about this.

▶ After students turn and talk, invite a few pairs to share their responses. Add to the guidelines as appropriate.

Summarize and Apply

Summarize the learning and remind students to follow the guidelines for independent writing.

> Today, you created guidelines for independent writing time. Today and every day during independent writing, remember to follow these guidelines. Get your writer's notebook or writing folder, get started quickly and quietly, and work on your writing for the entire writing time. Look at our guidelines if you need help remembering what to do.

Guidelines for Independent Writing Time

Getting started . . .
- Get started quickly.
- Work quietly.
- Keep your writing materials organized.

Keep writing . . .
- Write for the entire writing time.
- Work on a writing project or write in your writer's notebook.
- Try out different types of writing.

If you get stuck . . .
- Collect ideas in your writer's notebook.
- Reread your writer's notebook and add ideas.
- Reread a writing project and add to it.
- Try out what you learned from a minilesson.
- Ask for a conference with a teacher.

Confer

▶ During independent writing, move around the room to confer briefly with students about what to do during independent writing. Use prompts such as the following as needed.

- *What would you like to work on today?*

- *What materials do you need for your writing today?*

- *Are you ready to start a new writing project, or do you want to explore ideas in your writer's notebook?*

- *Remember to write for the entire writing time. What could you work on now?*

Share

Following independent writing, gather students in the meeting area. Give all students a turn to say what they worked on.

> What did you work on today during independent writing?

> How did our guidelines help you do your best work?

WML2

Writing Minilesson Principle

Use writing tools to help with your writing.

Establishing Independent Writing

You Will Need

- for each student and yourself, a writer's notebook, writing folder, and hanging file folder
- a variety of writing materials (e.g., different types of paper, pencils, pens, markers)
- chart paper and markers
- To download the following online resource for this lesson, visit **fp.pub/resources**:
  - chart art (optional)

Academic Language / Important Vocabulary

- independent writing
- writing tools
- writer's notebook
- writing folder
- hanging folder

Continuum Connection

- Listen to, remember, and follow directions with multiple steps

---

GOAL

Learn routines for finding, using, and returning writing tools during independent writing.

RATIONALE

When students understand where to find and how to use various writing materials and tools, they will be better prepared to work independently and efficiently during independent writing.

WRITER'S NOTEBOOK/WRITING FOLDER

Students will write in their writer's notebooks or work on a longer piece of writing in their writing folders.

ASSESS LEARNING

- Observe students to make sure they retrieve, use, and put back writing tools appropriately.
- Look for evidence that they can use vocabulary such as *independent writing*, *writing tools*, *writer's notebook*, *writing folder*, and *hanging folder*.

MINILESSON

To help students learn how to find and use writing tools during independent writing, engage them in a short demonstration and discussion. Here is an example.

- Show students your writer's notebook, writing folder, and hanging file and engage them in a brief discussion or explanation about each item.

  > This is my writer's notebook. Talk about how you can use a writer's notebook.

  > This is my writing folder. What do you think I will put in it?

  > This is my hanging file. When I'm completely finished with a writing project, I will put it in here for safekeeping.

- Record notes about each item on chart paper.
- Direct students' attention to the classroom writing materials.

  > At the beginning of independent writing, you will get the materials you need. What materials might you use during independent writing time?

- Briefly engage students in a discussion about each type of material. Explain that you can use different colored markers for revising (green) and editing (red). Add notes to the chart.

  > How could you use each type of paper? Think about what paper would be right for what you are writing now.

- Show and discuss the different types of paper available. Explain that it is sometimes helpful to use draft paper before deciding on a specific type of paper because it provides space to think about what to write and for revising and editing. Show students how to write on the lines that have dots. Add notes to the chart.

Have a Try

Invite students to summarize the learning with a partner.

> What did you learn today about using writing tools?

▶ After time for discussion, invite several students to share their responses.

Summarize and Apply

Write the principle at the top of the chart. Summarize the learning and remind students how to use writing tools to help with their writing.

> Today during independent writing time, get your writing tools and materials quickly and quietly. Remember to treat your writing tools with care and put them back where they belong. Choose a page in Section 1 of your writer's notebook to do some writing, or turn to an empty page in Section 4 to write or draw. Bring your notebook to share when we meet later.

Use writing tools to help with your writing.

Writer's Notebook	• Collect ideas • Try out writing ideas • Collect research • Keep writing inspirations • Try out ideas from minilessons
Writing Folder	• Use resources • Store your writing projects while in progress
Hanging Folder	• Store finished writing
Materials	• Pencil or pen: writing • Green pen: revising • Red pen: editing • Markers or colored pencils: drawing • Cardboard, textured paper, etc.: for covers and artwork
Paper	• Draft paper • Paper with picture boxes • Paper with text features • Stationery

Confer

▶ During independent writing, move around the room to confer briefly with students about using writing tools. Use prompts such as the following as needed.

- *What are you going to work on today?*
- *Which writing tools or materials would help you do your best work today?*
- *What should you do at the end of independent writing?*

Share

Following independent writing, gather students in the meeting area to share with partners and then with the whole class.

> Turn and talk to your partner about what you wrote today.

> Who would like to share with the class what you wrote today?

Establishing Independent Writing

You Will Need

- a piece of your own writing to use as an example
- a couple of students prepared to share their writing with the class
- chart paper and markers
- writing folders

Academic Language / Important Vocabulary

- audience
- feedback

Continuum Connection

- Change writing in response to peer or teacher feedback
- Show confidence when presenting
- Listen actively to others read or talk about their writing, and give feedback
- Speak directly to the audience, making eye contact with individuals

GOAL

Learn that other people can provide feedback and new ideas.

RATIONALE

Help students understand that sharing their writing with their classmates and with you can be a source of feedback that they can use to improve and expand their writing. As they talk productively with one another, they not only build their writing skills but also strengthen their conversational skills.

WRITER'S NOTEBOOK/WRITING FOLDER

Students use audience feedback to improve pieces of writing in their writing folders.

ASSESS LEARNING

- Observe whether students use feedback to develop their writing.
- Notice whether students listen respectfully and give constructive feedback.
- Look for evidence that they can use vocabulary such as *audience* and *feedback.*

MINILESSON

To help students understand and appreciate the value of feedback on their writing, model how to ask for and receive feedback. Coach students ahead of time about which part of their writing to read, what they would like the audience to listen for, and how they will respond to the audience. Here is an example.

> Today, you will be my audience as I read aloud a piece of my writing. I would like your feedback on my characters. Do they seem realistic?

- Read aloud the prepared piece of writing, modeling effective presentation skills. After reading, ask the audience for feedback about a specific aspect of your writing (e.g., character development). Then invite the audience to ask questions.

> What did you notice about how I shared my writing with you?

- As needed, ask questions such as the following to prompt discussion:
  - *What did I tell you about my writing?*
  - *How did I ask you for feedback on my writing?*
  - *What did we do after I finished sharing?*
- Record students' responses on chart paper.

> I asked for feedback on a specific thing that I've been working on, but you might have something else that you want the audience to help you with or to celebrate. For example, you can read your whole writing piece to get more ideas, read a part that you changed in some way, share a goal that you accomplished, or share something you did that helped you with your writing.

Have a Try

Invite the students you have prepared to share their writing with the class.

> _____, before you start to read your writing, please tell us about what you're working on and if you'd like feedback on anything specific.
>
> What did you notice about what _____ said? What might you say when you share?

▶ Add students' responses to the chart as appropriate.

Summarize and Apply

Summarize the learning and remind students to share their writing with an audience.

> Sometimes you will share your writing with a partner. Often, you will share it with me when we have a writing conference.

▶ Write the principle at the top of the chart.

> While you are writing today, think about how your classmates or I can help you make your writing even better. What would you like feedback on? Bring your writing to share when we come back together.

Share your writing with others.	
What You Can Do to Share	**What You Can Say**
• Read a part of your writing or the whole piece of writing.	• I've been working on . . .
• Ask for feedback on something specific.	• I would like feedback on . . .
• Answer the audience's questions.	• Can you tell me what you think about . . .
• Share a goal that you accomplished.	• Can you help me with . . .
• Share something you did that helped you with your writing.	• Was this part clear?
	• I want to . . . What do you suggest?

Section 1: Management

Confer

▶ During independent writing, move around the room to confer briefly with students about sharing their writing. Use prompts such as the following as needed.

   • *What would you like to say about your writing?*

   • *Is there anything specific you would like feedback on?*

   • *What will you tell or ask the audience about your writing?*

Share

Following independent writing, gather students in the meeting area to share their writing with a partner.

> Turn and talk to a partner about the writing you are working on. Let your partner know if there is something about which you would like feedback.

Assessment

After you have taught the minilessons in this umbrella, observe students as they prepare for, progress through, and conclude independent writing time each day. Use *The Fountas & Pinnell Literacy Continuum* to notice, teach for, and support students' learning as you observe their attempts at reading and writing.

▶ What evidence do you have of students' new understandings related to the routines for independent writing time?

- Are students able to sustain working for the whole independent writing time?

- Do students use writing tools appropriately and put them back where they belong?

- Are they using feedback from others to improve their writing?

- Do they understand and use vocabulary such as *independent writing*, *feedback*, *audience*, and *guidelines*?

▶ In what other ways, beyond the scope of this umbrella, are students getting started with independent writing?

- How are they using their writer's notebooks?

- Are they ready to write stories?

Use your observations to determine the next umbrella you will teach. You may also consult Suggested Sequence of Lessons (pp. 665–682) for guidance.

EXTENSIONS FOR ESTABLISHING INDEPENDENT WRITING

▶ Teach students how to use resources in their writing folders, such as a list of writing goals, a list of finished writing pieces, a revising checklist, and an editing and proofreading checklist (see MGT.U3: Introducing the Writing Folder).

▶ Help students with the organization of the hanging files in which they will keep finished writing pieces. Show them where to place their finished pieces of writing. For select pieces of writing, you might want to have students attach a short reflection about the writing. Using hanging files in several colors, each color stored separately, will help students find their files more quickly and efficiently. Material in the files can be used when you hold conferences with students and parents or caregivers.

Minilessons in This Umbrella

WML1 Keep a list of your finished writing projects.

WML2 Write what you have learned how to do as a writer and illustrator.

WML3 Make writing goals to grow as a writer and illustrator.

WML4 Use the word list to help with your writing.

WML5 Use checklists to help you revise and edit your writing.

Writer's Notebook

Before Teaching Umbrella 3 Minilessons

Before teaching the minilessons in this umbrella, prepare a writing folder for each student. A writing folder is a place for students to keep a record of their writing and reflections, record their writing goals, and refer to important resources for their writing. We recommend using a two-pocket folder with brads in the middle for fastening the resources inside and inserting the resources before teaching the lessons.

- Genres and Forms at a Glance
- My Writing Projects
- What I Have Learned How to Do as a Writer and Illustrator
- My Writing Goals
- Writing Goals for Genres and Forms
- Commonly Misspelled Words
- Revising Checklist
- Editing and Proofreading Checklist

Students should also keep writing projects (e.g., books, poems, or other longer pieces of writing) they are working on in their writing folders, so you will want to teach these minilessons when students have some writing to place in their folders. When they finish a writing project, they should take it out of the writing folder and put it in a permanent hanging file in a crate or file cabinet. Use several colors of pocket folders for easier identification. Ideally, the folders will be placed throughout the room (e.g., four corners) to avoid too many students trying to access the same space at once. The resources in the writing folder can be refreshed as needed or at regular intervals (e.g., every quarter), and the old ones can be stapled together and stored in the hanging file.

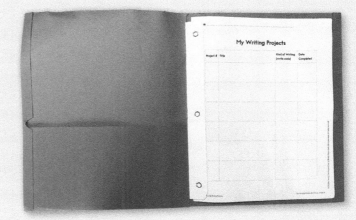

Section 1: Management

Writing Minilesson Principle
Keep a list of your finished writing projects.

Introducing the Writing Folder

You Will Need

- document camera, or chart paper made to look like the top of the My Writing Projects online resource
- writing folders
- markers
- To download the following online resources for this lesson, visit **fp.pub/resources**:
  - My Writing Projects
  - Genres and Forms at a Glance

Academic Language / Important Vocabulary

- writing folder
- record
- writing project
- title
- code
- genre

Continuum Connection

- Write in a variety of genres across the year
- Produce a reasonable quantity of writing within the time available
- Listen to, remember, and follow directions with multiple steps

---

GOAL

Learn how to keep track of finished writing to reflect on progress across the year.

RATIONALE

A log of finished writing allows students to communicate to you when they believe a piece of writing is complete so that you can plan further instruction for them. It also allows them and you to reflect on their writing across the year and provides information for you when you discuss students' progress in writing.

WRITER'S NOTEBOOK/WRITING FOLDER

Have students record a completed writing project on the My Writing Projects sheet in their writing folders.

ASSESS LEARNING

- Observe students' ability to create and maintain a log of finished writing.
- Look for evidence that they can use vocabulary such as *writing folder*, *record*, *writing project*, *title*, *code*, and *genre*.

MINILESSON

Students will need their writing folders with the online resources My Writing Projects and Genres and Forms at a Glance fastened inside. They should also have at least one piece of finished writing to record. To help students think about the minilesson principle, model filling out the writing log. Below is an example.

- Have students turn to the My Writing Projects sheet in their writing folder.

  What do you notice about this sheet? What do you think you will write on it?

  I just finished writing a book called *How to Build a Treehouse*. This will be the first project on my list. What should I write under Project Number?

- Add the numeral 1 to the chart.

  What should I write in the next column?

- Fill in the title. Model how students will record a code for the genre or form to show the type of writing (e.g., *PT* for a procedural text).

  The page called Genres and Forms at a Glance gives a description of each type of writing as well as a code, which you will use on your writing projects list. What letter should I write in this column for the genre of my book?

  What goes in the last column?

- Fill in the date you completed your writing.

Have a Try

Invite students to talk to a partner about finished writing projects they could record.

> Think about the last writing project you finished. How will you record it on your My Writing Projects page? Turn and talk to your partner about what you will write.

Summarize and Apply

Summarize the learning and remind students to record their finished writing projects on the My Writing Projects sheet in their writing folders.

> Why is it a good idea to keep a record of your finished writing projects? How could this help you as a writer?

> Before you start writing in your writer's notebook or on another writing project, take a moment to add your last finished writing project to your My Writing Projects sheet in your writing folder. Whenever you finish a new writing project, remember to record it. Bring your writing folder to share when we meet later.

My Writing Projects			
Project #	Title	Kind of Writing (write code)	Date Completed
1	How to Build a Treehouse	PT	9/18

Confer

▶ During independent writing, move around the room to confer briefly with students about recording their writing projects. Use prompts such as the following as needed.

- *What is the last writing project you finished?*
- *How will you record that project on your My Writing Projects sheet?*
- *What is the title of that piece of writing?*
- *What kind of writing is it? What is the code for that genre?*

Share

Following independent writing, gather students in the meeting area to share what they wrote on their writing logs.

> Who would like to share what you wrote on your My Writing Projects sheet in your writing folder?

Writing Minilesson Principle
Write what you have learned how to do as a writer and illustrator.

Introducing the Writing Folder

You Will Need

- document camera, or chart paper made to look like the What I Have Learned How to Do as a Writer and Illustrator online resource
- writer's notebooks and writing folders
- markers
- To download the following online resource for this lesson, visit **fp.pub/resources**:
  - What I Have Learned How to Do as a Writer and Illustrator

Academic Language / Important Vocabulary

- writing folder
- reflect
- learn

Continuum Connection

- Self-evaluate writing and talk about what is good about it and what techniques were used
- Compare previous writing to revised writing and notice and talk about the differences
- State what was learned from each piece of writing

GOAL

Reflect on what has been learned as a writer and illustrator throughout the year.

RATIONALE

When students keep a record of what they have learned from their writing, they learn to reflect on their writing. This helps them see their progress, giving them more confidence in their writing ability. They learn to view themselves as writers and think about what to work on next. Their reflections give you important information to inform your teaching.

WRITER'S NOTEBOOK/WRITING FOLDER

Have students begin to fill in the What I Have Learned How to Do as a Writer and Illustrator sheet in their writing folders. They can also continue working on a writing project or write in their writer's notebooks.

ASSESS LEARNING

- Listen carefully to what students say they have learned from their writing. Is there evidence of that learning in their writing?
- Look for evidence that they can use vocabulary such as *writing folder*, *reflect*, and *learn*.

MINILESSON

Students will need their writing folders with a copy of the online resource What I Have Learned How to Do as a Writer and Illustrator inside. Model how to reflect on what you are learning as a writer/illustrator and how to record those reflections on the form. Below is an example.

- Have students turn to the What I Have Learned How to Do as a Writer and Illustrator sheet in their writing folders.

  What do you think you will write about on this sheet in your writing folder?

  Throughout the year, you will regularly reflect on what you have learned from your writing and illustrating and write about it on this sheet in your writing folder. In my latest story, I learned more about how to include interesting dialogue to help readers get to know my characters. I'm going to write that along with today's date.

- Model recording what you have learned on the prepared chart paper or on the online resource (projected).

  What are some things you have learned how to do as a writer and illustrator? Record one thing you have learned on your What I Have Learned How to Do as a Writer and Illustrator sheet in your writing folder.

Have a Try

Invite students to share with a partner what they wrote on their What I Have Learned How to Do as a Writer and Illustrator sheet.

> Turn and talk to your partner about what you wrote on your sheet.

▶ Record a few sample entries on the chart.

Summarize and Apply

Summarize the learning and remind students to reflect on what they have learned as writers and illustrators.

> How can writing about what you have learned from your writing and illustrating help you?

> Writing what you have learned helps you think about the progress you are making as a writer and illustrator and what you want to work on next. You can use this sheet at any time to reflect on what you have learned. You may write on it after a writing lesson, after discussing your writing with me or a classmate, or after you have finished a writing project.

> During independent writing time today, reflect on what else you have learned as a writer and write about it on this sheet in your writing folder. If you have more time, continue writing in your writer's notebook or on a writing project. Bring your writing folder to share when we meet later.

What I Have Learned How to Do as a Writer and Illustrator	
Date 10/3	How to include interesting dialogue to help readers get to know my characters
Date	How to use a storyboard to plan my writing
Date	How to "show not tell" in my writing
Date	How to draw people that look realistic

Confer

▶ During independent writing, move around the room to confer briefly with students about what they have learned as a writer/illustrator. Use prompts such as the following as needed.

- *What did you learn from this writing project?*
- *Did you try any new techniques in your writing?*
- *Did you learn anything new from creating your illustrations?*

Share

Following independent writing, gather students in the meeting area to share their reflections.

> Would anyone like to share what you have learned how to do as a writer and illustrator?

Introducing the Writing Folder

You Will Need

- document camera, or chart paper made to look like the My Writing Goals and Writing Goals for Genres and Forms online resources

- markers

- writer's notebooks and writing folders

- To download the following online resources for this lesson, visit **fp.pub/resources**:

  - My Writing Goals

  - Writing Goals for Genres and Forms

Academic Language / Important Vocabulary

- writing folder

- goal

- genre

Continuum Connection

- Articulate goals as a writer

- Be willing to work at the craft of writing, incorporating new learning from instruction

GOAL

Make writing goals that include writing in different genres and using different aspects of craft and conventions.

RATIONALE

Talk with students during writing conferences about the kinds of goals that will stretch them as writers and illustrators. When you guide students to identify and record their writing goals (e.g., writing in different genres, using different aspects of craft and conventions), they learn to view themselves as writers and illustrators, and they become more invested in their writing journey.

WRITER'S NOTEBOOK/WRITING FOLDER

Have students begin a list of writing goals on the My Writing Goals sheet in their writing folders. They can also continue working on a writing project or write in their writer's notebooks.

ASSESS LEARNING

- During writing conferences, talk with students about their goals as writers.

- Look for evidence that students are working toward the goals they set.

- Look for evidence that they can use vocabulary such as *writing folder*, *goal*, and *genre*.

MINILESSON

Students will need their writing folders with the online resources My Writing Goals and Writing Goals for Genres and Forms fastened inside. To help students think about the minilesson principle, model how to record writing goals. Below is an example.

- Have students turn to the My Writing Goals sheet in their writing folders.

  What do you think you will write on this sheet in your writing folder?

  This is where you will think about and write down your writing and illustrating goals. Who can tell us what a goal is?

  A goal is something you want to do or accomplish. One of my goals this year is to write for at least forty-five minutes every day. Another goal is to use more powerful words.

- Model writing your goals on the prepared chart paper or projected resource.

  Another goal I have is to write more poetry. I will write *Write more poetry* on the My Writing Goals sheet. I will try to write six poems, so I will write the number 6 on my Writing Goals for Genres and Forms sheet in my writing folder. Whenever I write a poem, I will make a tally mark so I will have a record of how many I've written. Once I've made six marks, I will have met my goal!

- Demonstrate adding a goal to the Writing Goals for Genres and Forms sheet on the prepared chart paper or projected resource and adding a tally mark.

Have a Try

Invite students to talk to a partner about their writing goals.

> What else could you do this year to help yourself grow as a writer and illustrator? Turn and talk to your partner about another goal.

▶ After students turn and talk, invite a few students to share their goals. Record students' responses on the sample My Writing Goals sheet.

Summarize and Apply

Summarize the learning. Remind students to think about and record their writing goals.

> Why is it a good idea to record your writing goals?

> Writing down your writing goals will help you stay focused on your goals and become a better writer. Before you start writing today, write a few goals on the My Writing Goals sheet in your writing folder. If you have extra time, continue writing in your writer's notebook or writing folder.

Confer

▶ During independent writing, move around the room to confer briefly with students about their writing goals. Use prompts such as the following as needed.

- *What are your goals as a writer or illustrator?*
- *What type of writing would you most like to work on this year? How many _____ would you like to try to write?*
- *Is there anything new you would like to try in your writing or illustrating?*
- *What could you do to help yourself grow as a writer or illustrator?*

Share

Following independent writing, gather students in the meeting area to share their writing goals.

> Turn to a partner to share what you wrote on your My Writing Goals sheet.

Date	My Writing Goals
9/30	Write for at least 45 minutes every day
9/30	Make more powerful word choices
9/30	Write more poetry
9/30	Draw people that look more realistic
9/30	Make my characters more believable
9/30	Try different ways to make my illustrations more interesting
9/30	Add more details to memory stories

Writing Goals for Genres and Forms

Requirement	Genre or Form	Tally
	(FL) Friendly or Formal Letter	
	(PT) Procedural Text	
	(RF) Realistic Fiction Story	
	(FT) Fairy Tale	
	(M) Memory Story or Memoir	
	(FA) Feature Article	
	(OP) Opinion Writing	
	(PE) Persuasive Essay	
6	(P) Poem	/
	(O) Other	

WML4

Writing Minilesson Principle
Use the word list to help with your writing.

Introducing the Writing Folder

You Will Need

- chart paper and markers
- writing folders
- To download the following online resource for this lesson, visit **fp.pub/resources**:
  - Commonly Misspelled Words

Academic Language / Important Vocabulary

- writing folder
- word list
- misspelled

Continuum Connection

- Monitor own spelling by noticing when a word does not "look right" and should be checked
- Use reference tools to check on spelling when editing final draft (dictionary, digital resources)

GOAL

Use the Commonly Misspelled Words list to help with spelling during writing.

RATIONALE

When you show students how to refer to a list of commonly misspelled words, they will understand how to use resources to help with spelling and correct their own spelling independently.

WRITER'S NOTEBOOK/WRITING FOLDER

Students will try using the Commonly Misspelled Words list as they continue working on a longer project in their writing folders or write in their writer's notebooks.

ASSESS LEARNING

- Notice whether students refer to the Commonly Misspelled Words list to help with spelling.
- Look for evidence that they can use vocabulary such as *writing folder*, *word list*, and *misspelled*.

MINILESSON

Students will need their writing folders with the online resource Commonly Misspelled Words inside for this minilesson. To help students think about the principle, discuss how students can use the Commonly Misspelled Words list to help with spelling. Below is an example.

- Direct students to turn to the list of commonly misspelled words in their writing folders.

  What do you notice about this sheet in your writing folder?

  How could this list of words help you as a writer?

  How and when might you use this list?

- Record students' responses on chart paper. Ensure that students understand how they can use the list while writing, editing, and proofreading.

Have a Try

Invite students to highlight words on the Commonly Misspelled Words list that are challenging for them to spell.

> Look through the list of commonly misspelled words. Highlight any words on the list that you know are tricky for you to spell.

> ▶ Invite a few volunteers to share their tricky words. Talk with students about ways they might remember how to spell challenging words.

Summarize and Apply

Write the principle at the top of the chart. Read it to students. Summarize the learning and remind students to use the word list to help with writing.

> When you write today, try using the list of commonly misspelled words when you work on a writing project in your writing folder or when you write in your writer's notebook. You can also use it when you are editing and proofreading a piece of writing. Bring your writing to share when we meet later.

Use the word list to help with your writing.

- Use when writing to check how to spell a word.

- Learn how to spell some words.

- Use when editing or proofreading to check if you spelled a word correctly.

~~fourty~~ forty

Confer

> ▶ During independent writing, move around the room to confer briefly with students about using the word list. Use prompts such as the following as needed.
> - *What are you working on today?*
> - *Are there any words that you're not sure how to spell?*
> - *Where can you look to find out how to spell that word?*
> - *Let's see if we can find that word on the list of commonly misspelled words.*

Share

Following independent writing, gather students in the meeting area to talk about their writing.

> Did anyone use the list of commonly misspelled words today?

> How did you use it? How did it help you with your writing?

WML5

MGT.U3.WML5

Writing Minilesson Principle
Use checklists to help you revise and edit your writing.

Introducing the Writing Folder

You Will Need

- two short pieces of writing with clear errors (one unrevised, one revised and ready for editing) written on chart paper or projected
- document camera (optional)
- writing folders
- chart paper and markers
- To download the following online resources for this lesson, visit **fp.pub/resources**:
  - Revising Checklist
  - Editing and Proofreading Checklist

Academic Language / Important Vocabulary

- revising
- editing
- checklist

Continuum Connection

- Know how to use an editing and proofreading checklist
- Reread a piece asking self, "Have I made clear what I want readers to understand?"
- After reflection and rereading, add substantial pieces of text (paragraphs, pages) to provide further explanation, clarify points, add interest, or support points

GOAL

Learn how to use checklists to assist with revising and editing writing.

RATIONALE

When you show students how to use revising and editing checklists, they begin to understand the importance of revising and editing their writing. They know specific things to check for. Before teaching this lesson, we recommend teaching several craft and conventions lessons. We also recommend teaching WPS.U9 (revising) and WPS.U10 (editing). You may want to break this lesson into two lessons (revising and editing) if you feel it is too much for one lesson.

WRITER'S NOTEBOOK/WRITING FOLDER

Have students use the checklists to revise and edit a piece of writing from their writing folders.

ASSESS LEARNING

- Notice whether students use checklists to assist with revising and editing their work.
- Look for evidence that they can use vocabulary such as *revising*, *editing*, and *checklist*.

MINILESSON

Students will need their writing folders with the checklists for revising and proofreading inside. They will also need a piece of writing that is ready for revising or editing. To help students think about the principle, model using the checklists. If preferred, model how to use the checklists over two days. Here is an example.

- Have students turn to the Revising Checklist. Display the unrevised sample piece of writing.

  In your writing folder, you will find a revising checklist that will help you remember what to look for when you revise your writing. Let's use the checklist to look through this piece of writing to see what I can improve.

- Model how to use the checklist by going through some of the questions and thinking aloud about how to revise the piece of writing.

  I notice that most of my sentences are around the same length, and many of them start with the word *I*. How could I change some of my sentences to make them more varied, or different from one another?

- Show another sample piece of writing that has already been fully revised but not edited. Have students turn to the Editing and Proofreading Checklist.

  After you finish revising, proofread to see if there is anything more to fix. This checklist will help you remember what to look for.

- Use the first few questions on the checklist to model how to proofread a piece of writing. Save the paragraphing question for Have a Try.

Have a Try

Invite students to talk to a partner about how to correct the sample piece of writing.

> Let's think about this question: Have I organized my writing into paragraphs? Look carefully at my piece of writing, and turn and talk to your partner about this question.

> Are there any places where I should start a new paragraph, or where I should move a sentence from one paragraph to another?

▶ Using students' input, correct the paragraphing in the sample piece of writing as needed.

Summarize and Apply

Summarize the learning and remind students to use the revising and the editing and proofreading checklists.

> How can checklists help you with your writing?

> During independent writing today, spend some time revising and proofreading a writing project from your writing folder. Remember to use checklists to help you remember what to look for.

Confer

▶ During independent writing, move around the room to confer briefly with students about revising and/or proofreading their writing. Use prompts such as the following as needed.

- *Are you ready to start revising your writing? What do you need to look for when you revise?*

- *Let's go through the Revising Checklist together and see how you can use it to improve your writing.*

- *Have you proofread your writing? Did you use the Editing and Proofreading Checklist to help? What corrections did you make?*

Share

Following independent writing, gather students in the meeting area to share how they used the checklists.

> Turn and talk to a partner about how you used a checklist today to improve your writing.

Assessment

After you have taught the minilessons in this umbrella, observe students as they prepare for, progress through, and conclude independent writing time each day. Use *The Fountas & Pinnell Literacy Continuum* to notice, teach for, and support students' learning as you observe their writing.

▶ What evidence do you have of students' new understandings related to using a writing folder?

- Do students record each finished writing project on a list?
- Are they able to reflect and write about what they have learned from their writing and illustrating?
- Can they identify and record their goals as a writer?
- Do they use the Commonly Misspelled Words list, the Revising Checklist, and the Editing and Proofreading Checklist to help with their writing?
- Do they understand and use vocabulary such as *record*, *writing project*, *reflect*, and *goal*?

▶ In what other ways, beyond the scope of this umbrella, are students ready to expand their writing experiences?

- Are they ready to learn new craft techniques?

Use your observations to determine the next umbrella you will teach. You may also consult Suggested Sequence of Lessons (pp. 665–682) for guidance.

EXTENSIONS FOR INTRODUCING THE WRITING FOLDER

▶ Meet with students to review their writing goals and discuss their progress on them.

▶ Encourage students to write a longer reflection on a completed writing project. Attach the reflection to the writing project. Keep it handy for conferences with students or parents and caregivers.

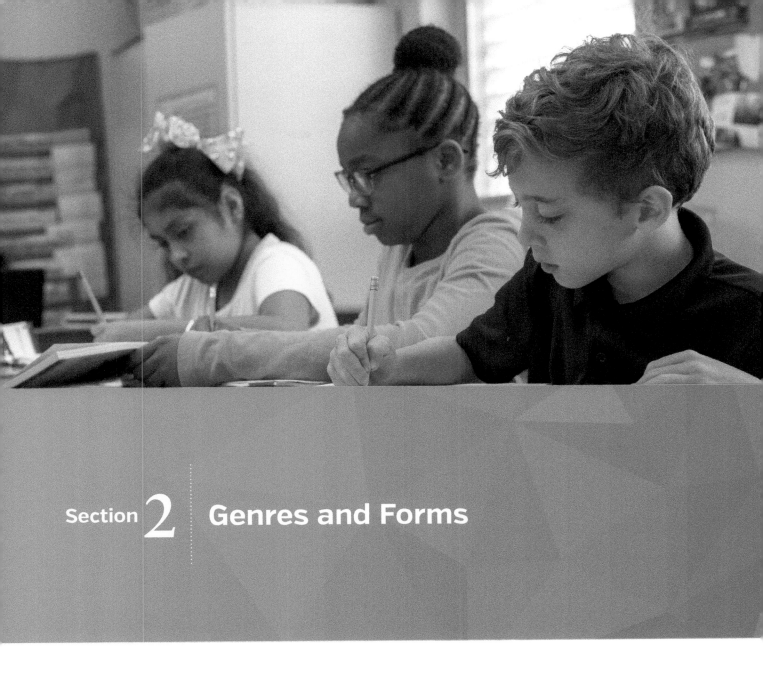

Section 2 Genres and Forms

EXPOSURE TO VARIOUS genres and forms of writing broadens students' vision for what their writing can be. The minilessons in this section support students by helping them see that they can express themselves in writing in a variety of ways. For example, they write memoirs, picture book biographies, feature articles, persuasive essays, and poetry, as well as write in other forms, such as multimedia presentations and photo essays.

Minilessons in This Umbrella

WML1 Write letters for different audiences and purposes.

WML2 Write a friendly letter.

WML3 Write a formal (business) letter.

WML4 Write emails with carefully chosen words and information.

Before Teaching Umbrella 1 Minilessons

Functional writing is practical writing, including both friendly and formal letters, invitations, emails, lists, directions, and labels. When students have experiences with functional writing, they understand that people write for practical and authentic reasons. Friendly letters (usually written to people known by the writer) are used to give information, to invite, and to thank. If you are using *The Reading Minilessons Book, Grade 4* (Fountas and Pinnell 2020), you may choose to teach WAR.U3: Writing Letters to Share Thinking About Books before or alongside this umbrella.

Teach WML1 and WML2 early in the year so that students gain experience with thinking about the purpose, audience, and types of friendly letters. Later in the year, after students have had exposure to more topics to write about in business letters and emails, teach WML3 and WML4. Use the books listed below from *Fountas & Pinnell Classroom™ Interactive Read-Aloud Collection* and *Shared Reading Collection* in addition to examples from your own collection of friendly and formal letters. If you have not yet read any of the suggested books with the class, read them now and explore them more deeply later.

Interactive Read-Aloud Collection

Genre Study: Memoir

The Scraps Book: Notes from a Colorful Life by Lois Ehlert

Genre Study: Biography: Individuals Making a Difference

Farmer Will Allen and the Growing Table by Jacqueline Briggs Martin

Friendship

The Other Side by Jacqueline Woodson

Taking Action, Making Change

Follow the Moon Home: A Tale of One Idea, Twenty Kids, and a Hundred Sea Turtles by Philippe Cousteau and Deborah Hopkinson

Perseverance

Rescue & Jessica: A Life-Changing Friendship by Jessica Kensky and Patrick Downes

Shared Reading Collection

Island Life to City Life by Sofia Martimianakis

As you read and enjoy these texts together, help students think about the purpose and content of letters.

Interactive Read-Aloud
Memoir

Genre Study:
Biography

Farmer Will Allen and the Growing Table by Jacqueline Briggs Martin

Friendship

Taking Action,
Making Change

Perseverance

Shared Reading

Writer's Notebook

Writing Minilesson Principle
Write letters for different audiences and purposes.

Writing Letters

You Will Need

- several texts with examples of types of letters, such as the following:
  - *The Scraps Book* by Lois Ehlert, from Text Set: Genre Study: Memoir
  - *Island Life to City Life* by Sofia Martimianakis, from *Shared Reading Collection*
- examples from your own collection of letters (e.g., invitations, notes, cards, business letters, emails) and/or the online resource Sample Letters
- chart paper and markers
- writer's notebooks
- To download the following online resource for this lesson, visit **fp.pub/resources**:
  - Sample Letters

Academic Language / Important Vocabulary

- friendly letter
- formal letter
- type
- audience
- purpose

Continuum Connection

- Use the terms *note, card, letter, invitation,* and *email* to describe the forms
- Use the term *business letter* to describe the form

GOAL

Understand that different types of letters serve different purposes.

RATIONALE

When students learn how to write a letter, they gain a practical life skill. When they think about why people write letters, they understand that they can write for a specific purpose and audience and with authenticity.

WRITER'S NOTEBOOK/WRITING FOLDER

Students can make notes for or draft their letters in their writer's notebooks.

ASSESS LEARNING

- Observe for evidence that students understand that there are different types of letters and that they are written for a specific purpose and audience.
- Look for evidence that students can use vocabulary such as *friendly letter, formal letter, type, audience,* and *purpose.*

MINILESSON

To help students gain independent letter writing skills, provide examples of different forms of letters (e.g., notes, invitations, cards, business letters, emails) and engage students in a conversation about different types of, audiences for, and purposes of letters. Here is an example.

- Ahead of time, gather several examples of letters from your own collection (e.g., invitations, cards, notes, emails, friendly letters, business letters) and/or the online resource.

  Notice the types of writing I share, and then we will talk about them.

- Share a few mentor text examples that show different types of letters, such as the notes at the end of *The Scraps Book* and the emails in *Island Life to City Life*.

  What did you notice?

- Guide the students to identify each type of letter.

  All of these examples are types of letters. Letters can be friendly, like a thank you note, or they can be formal, like a business letter to a company. What are some other types of letters?

- Create a three-column chart with the headings *Type, Audience,* and *Purpose.* Begin filling in the chart with students' ideas.

- Continue the conversation, guiding students to think about intended audience and purpose. Show examples of other types of letters from your own collection and/or the online resource. Add to the chart.

Section 2: Genres and Forms

Have a Try

Invite students to turn and talk about an idea they have for writing a letter.

> Turn and talk to your partner about one or more types of letters you might write and what purposes you might have for writing them.

▶ After time for discussion, ask a few volunteers to share. Guide them to identify the audience for their letter. Add new ideas to the chart.

Summarize and Apply

Summarize the lesson. Remind students to think about type, purpose, and audience when they write a letter and to begin planning their own letter.

> What does the chart show you about letters?

▶ Write the principle at the top of the chart.

> You can write different types of letters for different purposes. During independent writing time, choose a type of letter and its purpose. Begin writing some ideas in your writer's notebook. Look at the chart if you need ideas. Bring your notebook to share when we meet later.

Write letters for different audiences and purposes.

Type	Audience	Purpose
Note	To myself or to people I know well	• Plan an activity • Share some news
Invitation	Specific person	• Invite to an event
Card	Friends, family, organization	• Say hello • Birthday or holiday wish • Say thank you
Email	Friends, family, people you know, businesses	• Communicate • Show appreciation
Friendly Letter	Known reader	• Tell an opinion • Share some news • Ask how someone is doing • Share thoughts
Formal (Business) Letter	Unknown reader (individual, organization, or group)	• Ask a question • Look for a job • Learn about a product • Get information

Confer

▶ During independent writing, move around the room to confer briefly with students about writing letters. Use the following prompts as needed.

- *What type of letter do you want to write?*
- *What is your purpose for writing?*
- *Tell about the audience who will read your letter.*

Share

Following independent writing, gather students in the meeting area to talk about writing letters. Give all students a turn to tell about the type of and purpose for the letter they plan to write.

> What type of letter will you write? What is the purpose?

Write a friendly letter.

Writing Letters

You Will Need

- a mentor text with a friendly letter, such as *Farmer Will Allen and the Growing Table* by Jacqueline Briggs Martin, from Text Set: Genre Study: Biography: Individuals Making a Difference and/or the online resource from WML1

- a mentor text by an author who is popular with your students, such as *The Other Side* by Jacqueline Woodson, from Text Set: Friendship

- document camera (optional)

- sticky notes

- chart paper and markers

- writer's notebooks and writing folders

Academic Language / Important Vocabulary

- friendly letter
- invite
- thanks
- opinion
- signature
- PS

Continuum Connection

- Write a letter to an author that demonstrates appreciation for a text the individual has written

- Write a letter to an illustrator that demonstrates appreciation for the details and style of illustrations

---

GOAL

Understand how to write a friendly letter, including its tone, purpose, and components.

RATIONALE

When students learn the parts of a friendly letter and understand that important information should be included, they can write friendly letters for authentic purposes.

WRITER'S NOTEBOOK/WRITING FOLDER

Students can use the notes from their writer's notebooks to start writing a friendly letter, which they will keep in their writing folders while they work on it.

ASSESS LEARNING

- Look for evidence that students include the key parts in a friendly letter (e.g., salutation, closing, signature).

- Notice whether students include the important information in a friendly letter.

- Look for evidence that students can use vocabulary such as *friendly letter*, *invite*, *thanks*, *opinion*, *signature*, and *PS*.

MINILESSON

To help students think about the minilesson principle, share an example of a friendly letter and use shared writing to write a letter to an author. Help students name each part of the letter as you write. Here is an example.

- Project or write on chart paper the friendly letter at the end of *Farmer Will Allen and the Growing Table*.

  Listen as I read this friendly letter that Will Allen, the subject of this biography, wrote to readers.

- Read the letter and then ask students to identify the purpose, audience, important information, and parts of the letter (e.g., salutation, closing, signature).

- Show the cover of a book by an author students enjoyed, such as *The Other Side*.

  Here is one of the books you enjoyed from favorite author Jacqueline Woodson. If you wanted to write a friendly letter to her, what would be the purpose of your letter?

- Engage students in a conversation about reasons they might want to write to the author (e.g., to show appreciation, to ask about her life as a writer).

- On chart paper, use shared writing to write a letter to the author. As you write, think aloud and name the parts of the letter by labeling them each with a sticky note. Model the placement of commas, and include a PS so students gain experience with the purpose and placement of a postscript.

Have a Try

Invite students to turn and talk about writing friendly letters.

> Turn and talk about any other information you think we could include in this letter.

▶ After time for discussion, ask a few volunteers to share. Add appropriate suggestions to the letter by using a caret or an asterisk or by attaching a strip of paper (a spider leg).

Summarize and Apply

Summarize the lesson. Remind students to include each part and the important information in a friendly letter. Write the principle on the chart.

> What parts of a friendly letter are important to include?

> During independent writing time, start writing a friendly letter. You can write to a favorite author, or you can write to someone in your family. Look at the notes you wrote in your writer's notebook to see if they will help you write your letter. Bring what you have written of your letter when we meet later.

Confer

▶ During independent writing, move around the room to confer briefly with students about their friendly letters. Use the following prompts as needed.

- *Where will you place the salutation, closing, and signature in your letter?*
- *Who is the audience for the friendly letter you are writing?*
- *Show where you include commas in your letter.*

Share

Following independent writing, gather students in the meeting area to talk about their friendly letters.

> In groups of four, share the friendly letter you are in the process of writing.

Write a friendly letter.

November 5 | date

Dear Jacqueline Woodson,

We enjoyed reading The Other Side in our fourth-grade class. The friendship story of Clover and Annie taught us how important it is to be open to making new friends. We also liked that the fence was used for sitting on instead of separating Clover and Annie.

We learned from your author's note that you wanted to write a story that focused on hope. We want to do that too.

From, | closing

signature

Room 390
Handlam Elementary

PS Do you have a special place where you like to write each day? | PS

Section 2: Genres and Forms

Writing Minilesson Principle
Write a formal (business) letter.

You Will Need

- a mentor text about a topic that lends itself to writing a business letter, such as *Follow the Moon Home* by Philippe Cousteau and Deborah Hopkinson, from Text Set: Taking Action, Making Change
- document camera (optional)
- sticky notes
- chart paper and markers
- writer's notebooks and writing folders

Academic Language / Important Vocabulary

- formal letter
- business letter
- heading
- address
- salutation
- closing

Continuum Connection

- Understand that a business letter is a formal document with a particular purpose
- Understand that a business letter has parts: e.g., date, inside address, formal salutation followed by a colon, body organized into paragraphs, closing, signature and title of sender, and sometimes notification of a copy or enclosure
- Write formal letters

GOAL

Understand how to write a formal (business) letter, including its tone, purpose, and components.

RATIONALE

When students learn the parts of a formal letter and understand that important information should be included, they can write effective formal letters.

WRITER'S NOTEBOOK/WRITING FOLDER

Students may have useful notes for their letters in their writer's notebooks. Letters in progress should be kept in students' writing folders.

ASSESS LEARNING

- Observe whether students include the key parts of a formal letter (e.g., heading, address, salutation, closing, signature).
- Notice whether students clearly write important information in a formal letter.
- Look for evidence that students can use vocabulary such as *formal letter*, *business letter*, *heading*, *address*, *salutation*, and *closing*.

MINILESSON

To help students think about the minilesson principle, share an authentic business letter and then use shared writing to write a formal letter to an organization. (Use the term you prefer, *formal letter* or *business letter*.) Help students name each part of the letter as you write. Here is an example.

- Briefly review *Follow the Moon Home*. Then turn to You Can Help! at the end of the book. Project the website that is shown in the book (defenders.org/sea-turtles), or write the organization's name and mailing address ahead of time on chart paper.

    This book has a lot of information about sea turtles. At the end of the book, there are notes about a website that tells ways to help sea turtles. To learn about what you can do, you could write to this organization for information. We are going to write a business letter to ask for that information.

- Display the website and scroll to the bottom of the page to show the address.
- Model the process of writing the business letter. Think aloud as you write.

    How is this formal letter, or business letter, different from a friendly letter?

- Guide the conversation so that students notice ways that a formal letter differs from a friendly letter (e.g., in tone, in the use of formal language).

    Talk about the parts of the letter you notice.

- As students make suggestions, label the parts of the letter using sticky notes.

Have a Try

Invite students to turn and talk about formal letters.

> What type of formal (business) letter do you want to write? Turn and talk about that with a partner.

▶ After time for discussion, ask students to share. Guide the conversation to help students think of ideas, possibly connecting to something you are studying in class.

Summarize and Apply

Summarize the lesson. Remind students to include each part and the important information in a formal letter.

> What are some reasons you might write a business letter?

▶ Write the principle on the chart.

> During independent writing time, think about what type of formal letter you want to write and begin writing one. Maybe you will decide to write to a company to ask for more information or to find out about a product. Jot some notes in your writer's notebook. Start writing your letter when you are ready. Bring your writing to share when we meet later.

> ### Write a formal (business) letter.
>
> 34 Handlam Street | heading
> March 10 date
>
> Defenders of Wildlife
> 1130 17th Street NW   address
> Washington, DC 20036
> | salutation
> Dear Education Outreach Department:
>
> Our fourth-grade class enjoyed reading Follow the Moon Home. We especially liked how the people in the story worked together to make posters and to get help from neighbors in the community.
>
> We would like to learn more about ways our class might help sea turtles because we do not live near the ocean. Can you help us learn about resources or ideas?
>
> Thank you for all you do to help sea turtles and other animals and for taking time to read this letter.
>
> Sincerely,   closing
> Room 390 Handlam School   signature

Confer

▶ During independent writing, move around the room to confer briefly with students about their formal letters. Use the following prompts as needed.

• *Where will you place the heading, address, and salutation?*

• *Who will be the audience for your formal letter?*

• *What words are you using to show this is a formal letter and not a friendly letter?*

Share

Following independent writing, gather students in the meeting area to talk about their formal letters.

> In groups of three, share the formal letters you are writing.

> Who has an idea for a business letter to share?

WML4
GEN.U1.WML4

Writing Minilesson Principle
Write emails with carefully chosen words and information.

Writing Letters

You Will Need

- a mentor text with an example of an electronic message (text message, email), such as *Island Life to City Life* by Sofia Martimianakis, from *Shared Reading Collection*, and/or the online resource from WML1

- a mentor text on a topic that lends itself to writing an email, such as *Rescue & Jessica*, from Text Set: Perseverance

- chart paper prepared ahead of time with a blank email form labeled with the parts *To* and *Subject*. As an alternative, project a blank email form from your computer.

- writer's notebooks

Academic Language / Important Vocabulary

- email
- send
- receive
- inbox
- subject
- reply

Continuum Connection

- Recognize that communications within various digital tools (email, social media, discussion forums, chats, collaborative multimedia tools, and blogs) require different degrees of formality

GOAL

Understand that emails should be written with care and attention to word choice and content.

RATIONALE

Writing emails is a real-world skill that students will use for school, work, and their personal lives. Students need to learn not only the parts of an email and what information to include but also to think about who the audience is and what degree of formality is required.

WRITER'S NOTEBOOK/WRITING FOLDER

Students will write notes in their writer's notebooks as they plan their emails.

ASSESS LEARNING

- Observe for evidence that students understand the parts of an email.
- Notice whether students choose words and content that are appropriate for an email.
- Look for evidence that students can use vocabulary such as *email*, *send*, *receive*, *inbox*, *subject*, and *reply*.

MINILESSON

To help students think about the minilesson principle, use examples and modeling to guide them in how to write an email. Here is an example.

- Ahead of time, choose someone you can send email to as you model the process to students (e.g., another teacher to ask about an upcoming school picnic).

- Show page 13 in *Island Life to City Life*.

    What do you notice about this written communication?

    Emails can be friendly (for example, to a family member), or they can be formal (for example, to an organization). The emails in this book are friendly because they are to family members.

- Show and read the author's note at the end of *Rescue & Jessica*.

    Notice that the author's note at the end of *Rescue & Jessica* tells about an organization called NEADS, which helps people get service dogs.

- Display the prepared chart paper or project the blank email from your computer.

    How is an email similar to and different from a letter?

- Guide the conversation depending on the email experience level of your students. Be sure students understand *to*, *from*, *subject*, *send*, *receive*, *inbox*, and *reply*.

    One thing that's different in an email is the subject line. An email has a subject line so that the receiver knows right away what you are writing about. Think of the subject line the way you do a book title.

Have a Try

Invite students to turn and talk about writing emails.

> Often, I write emails to other teachers at the school. We can write an email to Ms. Bowhart to ask about the school picnic she is planning. What are some things we should include? We are writing to a teacher, so should our email sound formal or friendly? Turn and talk about that.

▶ After time for discussion, ask a few volunteers to share. Use shared writing to model how to compose an email, either on chart paper or on a computer.

Summarize and Apply

Summarize the lesson. Remind students to think about word choice and content for emails.

> What should you remember about how you word your email?

▶ Write the principle at the top of the chart paper (if using) or state it.

> During independent writing time, think about a family member or teacher to whom you want to send an email and what you want to include. I will be sitting with you to write and send your emails in the upcoming days. You can make some notes about your email in your writer's notebook while you are waiting for your turn on the computer. Bring your notes when we meet later.

Confer

▶ During independent writing, move around the room to confer briefly with students about writing emails. Use the following prompts as needed.

- *Who will the audience be for your email?*
- *What information will you include in your email?*
- *On the computer, show me the steps you will take when writing an email.*

Share

Following independent writing, gather students in the meeting area to talk about emails.

> Share a time when you have sent an email.

> What are some important things to think about when writing an email?

> **Write emails with carefully chosen words and information.**

TO: Ms.Bowhart@school.edu
FROM: Mr.Jans@school.edu
SUBJECT: School Picnic

Hi, Ms. Bowhart,

We are wondering what time the upcoming school picnic will start. Also, do you know when the sign-up sheets will be posted?

Thank you,
Mr. Jans and Students in Room 390

Assessment

After you have taught the minilessons in this umbrella, observe students in a variety of classroom activities. Use *The Fountas & Pinnell Literacy Continuum* to notice, teach for, and support students' learning as you observe their attempts at writing letters.

▶ What evidence do you have of students' new understandings related to writing letters?

- Do students understand that they can write letters for different purposes?
- Do they change the tone of their writing depending on the audience?
- Do their letters include the important information that students wish to convey?
- Are they including the date, greeting, closing, signature, and PS when appropriate?
- Are they using vocabulary such *friendly letter, formal letter, type, audience, purpose, invite, thanks, opinion, salutation, closing, signature, PS, heading, address, email, inbox, subject, send, receive,* and *reply*?

▶ In what ways, beyond the scope of this umbrella, are students engaged in functional writing?

- Are students writing procedural texts, such as lists or sequential directions?
- Do students show evidence of understanding that test writing serves the purpose of showing what a person can do as a writer?

Use your observations to determine the next umbrella you will teach. You may also consult Suggested Sequence of Lessons (665–682) for guidance.

EXTENSIONS FOR WRITING LETTERS

▶ Have students make cards or invitations for authentic purposes, such as a get-well card for a student who is ill or an invitation for a classroom activity.

▶ Provide opportunities for students to write business letters to local community partners.

▶ Talk about the different between Reply, Reply all, and Forward in email communications.

▶ Download rubrics from the online resources to help you and your students evaluate how well they are able to apply the concepts in these lessons.

Minilessons in This Umbrella

WML1 Notice the qualities of good procedural texts.

WML2 Choose what you want to teach and how you will teach it.

WML3 Write and/or draw the steps or instructions.

Before Teaching Umbrella 2 Minilessons

Across the minilessons in this umbrella, students will study the characteristics and forms of procedural texts for the purpose of writing their own procedural texts.

Gather a variety of different types of procedural texts—texts that teach how to make or do something, such as recipes, instruction manuals, how-to books, game instructions, and how-to video scripts or posters—to use as mentor texts. The following books from *Fountas & Pinnell Classroom™ Interactive Read-Aloud Collection* and *Shared Reading Collection* have examples of procedural texts within them. Rubrics for evaluating the students' procedural texts are available in the online resources.

Interactive Read-Aloud Collection
What It Means to Be a Family

Jalapeño Bagels by Natasha Wing

Shared Reading Collection

Get the Scoop! Plans and Poems for Making Compost by Jennifer Boudart

As you read and enjoy these texts together, help students

- identify what readers can learn from the text,
- notice the characteristics and different types of procedural texts, and
- discuss how the illustrations can support the written directions.

Interactive Read-Aloud
What It Means to Be a Family

Shared Reading

Writer's Notebook

Section 2: Genres and Forms

Writing Minilesson Principle
Notice the qualities of good procedural texts.

Writing Procedural Texts

You Will Need

- a few examples of procedural texts, such as the following:
  - *Get the Scoop!* by Jennifer Boudart, from *Shared Reading Collection*
  - *Jalapeño Bagels* by Natasha Wing, from Text Set: What It Means to Be a Family
- chart paper and markers
- a procedural text (recipe, instruction manual, how-to book, game instruction, or how-to video script or poster) for each small group
- chart paper and markers
- writer's notebooks

Academic Language / Important Vocabulary

- procedural text
- quality
- recipe
- instructions

Continuum Connection

- Understand that procedural text helps people know how to do something
- Understand that a procedural text can be written in various forms: e.g., list, sequential directions (how-to)
- Understand how to craft procedural writing from mentor texts

GOAL

Understand that there are different types of procedural texts and notice the qualities of effective ones.

RATIONALE

To be able to write in a genre, it is helpful to study examples of that genre to notice and name its characteristics. Looking at procedural texts as readers will help students create clear procedural texts of their own as writers.

WRITER'S NOTEBOOK/WRITING FOLDER

Have students make notes in their writer's notebooks about the qualities of procedural texts.

ASSESS LEARNING

- Observe for evidence of what students know about the forms and qualities of good procedural texts.
- Look for evidence that they can use vocabulary such as *procedural text*, *quality*, *recipe*, and *instructions*.

MINILESSON

To help students think about the minilesson principle, lead an inquiry-based lesson to help them notice and name the qualities of good procedural texts. Here is an example.

- Show the cover of *Get the Scoop!* and read the title. Turn to pages 14–15 (How to Compost).

  What can you learn from this part of the book?

  How does the author make it easy for you to understand how to compost?

  How does she make the instructions clear?

- Record the students' noticings on chart paper.

  The instructions about how to compost are a type of text called a procedural text. A procedural text tells readers how to make or do something.

- Show the cover of *Jalapeño Bagels* and read the title. Show the recipe for jalapeño bagels near the end of the book.

  This is also a procedural text. What is this type of procedural text called?

  A recipe is a type of procedural text. What do you notice about this recipe?

  What are the different parts of the recipe?

  How does the author make the parts you have to follow clear?

- Add students' responses to the chart, generalizing them as necessary.

Have a Try

Invite students to talk to a partner about types of procedural texts.

▶ Write the forms of procedural texts just discussed (instructions and recipe) on the chart.

Turn and talk to your partner about how else you could show someone how to make or do something. Can you think of ways other than writing?

▶ After students turn and talk, invite several students to share their thinking. Write their responses on the chart. Save the chart for WML3.

Summarize and Apply

Write the principle at the top of the chart. Summarize the learning and invite students to study procedural texts with a small group.

▶ Give each pair or group at least one procedural text.

During independent writing time today, meet with your group to study the procedural text I gave you. Discuss what you notice about it and write your observations in your writer's notebook on a page titled "Procedural Texts." Bring your notes when we come back together.

> ### Notice the qualities of good procedural texts.
>
> | Qualities of Procedural Texts | Forms of Procedural Texts |
> |---|---|
> | • The steps are written in order. | • Instructions |
> | • The steps are usually written in a list. Sometimes they are numbered. | • Recipe |
> | • Sentences are usually short and to the point. | • Instruction manual |
> | • Most sentences start with an action word (add, mix, stir). | • Directions to play a game |
> | • The pictures show what to do. | • Poster |
> | • There is often a list of the materials or ingredients. | • Video script |

Confer

▶ During independent writing, move around the room to confer with students about what they notice. Use prompts such as the following as needed.

- *What do you notice about this procedural text?*
- *What type of procedural text is this?*
- *How does the writer make the steps clear?*
- *What else does the writer do to make the instructions easy to follow?*

Share

Following independent writing, gather students in the meeting area. Ask a volunteer from each group to share the group's noticings. Add any new observations to the chart.

What type of procedural text did you study?

What qualities did you notice in it?

Writing Procedural Texts

You Will Need

- chart paper divided into quadrants labeled *Things I Have Learned, Things I Have Made, Things I Can Teach, Things I Want to Learn*
- chart paper prepared with two columns titled *Topic* and *Form*
- markers
- writer's notebooks

Academic Language / Important Vocabulary

- procedural text
- procedure
- topic
- form
- purpose
- audience

Continuum Connection

- Understand that a procedural text helps people know how to do something
- Understand that a procedural text can be written in various forms: e.g., list, sequential directions (how-to)
- Understand that a list is a functional way to organize information and can be used as a planning tool

GOAL

Use purpose and audience to help choose the topic and form of the procedural text.

RATIONALE

When you guide students to think about purpose and audience, they have to think about how their readers will experience their writing. This should help them choose the form of procedural text that will be most appropriate for communicating the information effectively.

WRITER'S NOTEBOOK/WRITING FOLDER

Students can reread their writer's notebooks to find ideas for their procedural texts and/or write new ideas to consider.

ASSESS LEARNING

- Notice whether students consider their purpose and audience when choosing what they will teach and how they will teach it.
- Look for evidence that they can use vocabulary such as *procedural text, procedure, topic, form, purpose,* and *audience.*

MINILESSON

Students will need their writer's notebooks for this lesson. To help students think about the minilesson principle, guide them to explore ideas for a procedural text. Here is an example.

- Display the first sheet of prepared chart paper.

  You can get ideas for writing a procedural text by making lists of things you have learned, have made, can teach, or want to learn. For example, one thing that I can teach is how to knit a hat. I will write that on my list of things I can teach.

- Have students list ideas for procedural texts in their writer's notebooks (page 28 in *Writer's Notebook, Intermediate*).

  Start to fill out this page in your writer's notebook. While you are making your lists, I will continue working on mine.

- Give students 5–10 minutes to make lists in their writer's notebooks. Then invite several volunteers to share what they wrote, and record their responses on the chart.

  If you listed something that you want to learn how to do, think about what would help you learn how to do it.

Have a Try

Invite students to talk to a partner about their ideas for procedural texts.

> Think about your audience and what you want to teach. What form is most appropriate? Turn and talk to your partner about what you want to teach and how you might teach it.

▶ After time for discussion, invite several students to share their ideas. Record them on the second prepared sheet of chart paper.

Summarize and Apply

Summarize the learning. Guide students to state a principle for the lesson.

> What do you need to do before you write your procedural text?

▶ Write the principle at the top of the second chart.

> Today during independent writing time, spend some more time thinking about what you would like to teach and the best way to teach your audience. Reread the lists you have made in your writer's notebook. You can add more ideas. When you're ready, circle one idea you would like to use. Write some notes about how you could teach it, and be ready to share your ideas when we meet later.

Confer

▶ During independent writing, move around the room to confer briefly with students about their plans for writing procedural texts. Use prompts such as the following as needed.

- *Let's look at the lists you made in your writer's notebook. Which ideas are you most excited about?*
- *Who is your audience?*
- *What do you think is the best way to teach that to your audience? Why?*

Share

Following independent writing, gather students in the meeting area to share their ideas.

> Who would like to share what you are going to write a procedural text about?

> How are you going to teach that? Why is that the best way to teach _____?

Things I Have Learned	Things I Have Made
• How to ride a bike	• Granola bars
• How to play chess	• Samosas
• How to draw people	• Molded figures out of foil

Things I Can Teach	Things I Want to Learn
• How to knit a hat	• How to play guitar
• How to play soccer	• How to knit
• How to do long division	• How to fold origami shapes

Choose what you want to teach and how you will teach it.

Topic	Form
How to make granola bars	Recipe
How to play chess	Instruction manual
How to save energy at home	Poster
How to play the guitar	Video script
How to fold origami shapes	How-to book
How to play soccer	Directions

Section 2: Genres and Forms

WML3

Writing Minilesson Principle

Write and/or draw the steps or instructions.

Writing Procedural Texts

You Will Need

- a familiar procedural text, such as the bagel recipe in *Jalapeño Bagels* by Natasha Wing, from Text Set: What It Means to Be a Family
- the chart from WML1
- an idea for a class procedural text
- chart paper and markers
- writer's notebooks and writing folders
- To download the following online resource for this lesson, visit **fp.pub/resources**:
  - chart art (optional)

Academic Language / Important Vocabulary

- procedural text
- steps
- instructions

Continuum Connection

- Write steps of a procedure with appropriate sequence and explicitness, using number words or transition words
- Understand that a procedural text often includes a list of what is needed to do a procedure
- Understand that a procedural text often shows one item under another item and may include a number or letter for each item
- Write clear directions, guides, and "how-to" texts with illustrations (drawings or graphics)

GOAL

Write and/or draw clear steps in a procedure.

RATIONALE

Writing a procedural text requires careful attention to detail. If writers skip a step or omit important information, the readers will not be successful. Such attention to detail is not only important in procedural writing but in other types of writing as well.

WRITER'S NOTEBOOK/WRITING FOLDER

Have students use the notes in their writer's notebooks to write their procedural texts. Drafts of the procedural texts should be stored in their writing folders.

ASSESS LEARNING

- Notice whether students write and/or draw the steps or instructions completely and clearly.
- Look for evidence that they can use vocabulary such as *procedural text*, *steps*, and *instructions*.

MINILESSON

To help students think about the minilesson principle, use shared writing to model writing a procedural text. In the example below, students will write a procedural text about how to write a procedural text. However, you may choose any activity with which students are familiar.

- Show the recipe for jalapeño bagels in *Jalapeño Bagels*.

  What did you notice about how the author wrote the instructions for making jalapeño bagels?

  The author clearly showed the ingredients you need and what you need to do.

- Show the chart from WML1 and help students recall what they have learned about writing a procedural text.

  Think about how you would write directions that teach your audience how to write a procedural text. What materials would you need?

  What should you do before you even start to write?

  How could you show that this is the first step?

  What do you need to do after you've noted some ideas for a procedural text?

  What do you think about when you are writing a procedural text?

- Use shared writing to write the instructions on chart paper.

Have a Try

Invite students to talk to a partner about the procedure they will write.

> Think about the topic that you chose for your own procedural text. What steps or instructions will readers need to follow? Turn and talk to your partner about this.

Summarize and Apply

Summarize the learning and remind students to think about the qualities of good procedural texts when they write their own.

> During independent writing time today, start to write your procedural text. Look at the notes you made in your writer's notebook to help you know what to write. Add illustrations if you think they will help your readers know what to do. Put your draft in your writing folder and bring it to share when we meet later.

How to Write a Good Procedural Text

Materials:
- Ideas
- Writer's notebook
- Pen or pencil
- Paper

Instructions:
1. Write ideas for a procedural text in your writer's notebook.
2. Decide what to teach. Circle an idea that excites you.
3. Decide how to teach it. Think about your purpose and audience.
4. Write clear steps or instructions. Make sure they are in the right order. You may want to number them.
5. Add illustrations if you want.
6. Reread your writing. Make sure the steps are complete. Revise and edit your work.

Confer

▶ During independent writing, move around the room to confer briefly with students about writing procedural texts. Use prompts such as the following as needed.

- *What is your procedural text designed to teach?*
- *What materials will readers need?*
- *What is the first step?*
- *How can you make the order of the steps clear?*

Share

Following independent writing, gather students in the meeting area to share their writing.

> Who would like to read aloud your procedural text?

> What did you think about when you were writing your procedural text?

Assessment

After you have taught the minilessons in this umbrella, observe students as they explore writing procedural texts. Use *The Fountas & Pinnell Literacy Continuum* to notice, teach for, and support students' learning as you observe their attempts at writing.

▶ What evidence do you have of students' new understandings related to writing procedural texts?

- Can students identify various types and characteristics of procedural texts?
- Do they consider purpose and audience when they choose what to write and in what form to write it?
- Are their procedural texts written clearly, sequentially, and completely?
- Do students understand and use vocabulary such as *procedural text*, *quality*, *steps*, and *instructions*?

▶ In what other ways, beyond the scope of this umbrella, are students exploring genre?

- Are they showing an interest in writing fairy tales?
- Is their opinion writing leaning more toward persuasive?

Use your observations to determine the next umbrella you will teach. You may also consult Suggested Sequence of Lessons (pp. 665–682) for guidance.

EXTENSIONS FOR WRITING PROCEDURAL TEXTS

▶ After students engage in social studies and science projects, encourage them to write procedural texts for activities, such as creating a historical timeline or making a tornado in a jar.

▶ Have students trade procedural texts with a partner and follow the directions in each other's texts. Encourage students to make revisions based on their partner's feedback.

▶ Teach students how to give an oral presentation or make a video to demonstrate how to do something.

▶ Use the teacher and student rubrics available in the online resources to evaluate students' procedural texts or to guide them to evaluate their own texts. You might also consider having students co-create rubrics with you.

Minilessons in This Umbrella

WML1 Read the directions carefully to make sure you understand what is being asked.

WML2 Write a statement that answers the prompt.

WML3 Provide evidence and details that support your response.

WML4 Write a strong concluding sentence.

WML5 Write a response that compares and contrasts two things.

Before Teaching Umbrella 3 Minilessons

This umbrella provides exploration of and practice in test writing, or writing to a prompt. The basic structure of a test response is presented here but with a focus on short responses (see also GEN.U4: Writing to a Prompt: Extended Responses). When students write to a test prompt, they will rely on the writing instruction they have had. Therefore, provide opportunities for them to continue writing independently in the genres they have explored and working in their writer's notebooks.

Before teaching this umbrella, spend time with your teaching team to examine your state's English Language Arts (ELA) tests from prior years, often accessible through a state testing website. Make note of the types of passages, writing prompts, and question or command words used in the prompts. Use this analysis to collect sample prompts or to construct similar prompts to inform your teaching of these minilessons. Modify the instruction and examples in these minilessons as needed to teach to your state's test. To read more about writing to a prompt and preparing for tests, refer to page 66.

For mentor texts, use prior years' state tests and the following books from *Fountas & Pinnell Classroom™ Interactive Read Aloud Collection,* or choose books from the classroom library that students know well.

Interactive Read-Aloud Collection

Exploring Identity

Be Water, My Friend: The Early Years of Bruce Lee by Ken Mochizuki

Imagine by Juan Felipe Herrera

The Royal Bee by Frances Park and Ginger Park

Perseverance

Razia's Ray of Hope: One Girl's Dream of an Education by Elizabeth Suneby

As you read and enjoy these texts together, help students

- notice story elements in realistic fiction books,
- discuss themes or main ideas and the details that support them, and
- explain how two texts are similar and different.

Interactive Read-Aloud
Exploring Identity

Perseverance

Writer's Notebook

WML1

GEN.U3.WML1

Writing Minilesson Principle
Read the directions carefully to make sure you understand what is being asked.

Writing to a Prompt: Getting Ready for Test Writing

You Will Need

- the book the sample prompt is about, such as *Be Water, My Friend* by Ken Mochizuki, from Text Set: Exploring Identity
- sample ELA prompts, requiring both short and long responses, written on strips of paper
- chart paper and markers
- prompts to distribute to each student pair
- writer's notebooks and writing folders

Academic Language / Important Vocabulary

- short response
- extended response
- question words
- passage
- prompt
- key words

Continuum Connection

- Understand that test writing can take various forms: e.g., short constructed response (sometimes called *short answer*), extended constructed response (or *essay*)
- Understand that test writing involves analyzing what is expected of the writer and then planning and writing a response that fits the criteria
- Understand test writing as a response carefully tailored to meet precise instructions

GOAL

Read and understand the assigned prompt.

RATIONALE

In order to write an effective response to a test prompt, students must learn to read the prompt carefully, noticing key words. Discussing a variety of prompts will help students learn the skills they will need to respond to prompts independently. When you teach this minilesson, use the terminology (e.g., *short answer, essay*) that matches your state's test.

WRITER'S NOTEBOOK/WRITING FOLDER

If students have extra time, they can write in their writer's notebooks or work on a longer piece of writing in their writing folders.

ASSESS LEARNING

- Notice whether students can identify question words and key words in a prompt.
- Look for evidence that they can use vocabulary such as *short response, extended response, question words, passage, prompt,* and *key words.*

MINILESSON

To help students think about the minilesson principle, use ELA prompts you have collected or written to model how to respond to a prompt. Here is an example.

> Sometimes you will take tests that ask you to respond in writing to a question or some directions. These are called prompts.

- Attach a prompt to chart paper.

> Reading a prompt twice will help you understand what it asks you to do.

- Guide students to analyze the prompt by asking questions such as "What is this prompt asking you to do?" "How long should the answer be?" Using students' responses, underline key words in the prompt.

> The prompt tells me how much I need to write—just one paragraph. It asks me to explain, or clearly tell about, what Bruce learns from Yip Man. It also tells me to use evidence from the book to support my response. What do you think using evidence means here?

> It means to provide specific examples, words, or sentences from the book that help show why your response is correct.

- Continue in a similar manner with a few more prompts.
- Help students notice that prompts can require short or long answers.

> This prompt says to write an essay. What is an essay?

> An essay has several paragraphs. It may be one page or even a few pages.

Have a Try

Invite students to talk to a partner about another prompt.

▶ Add another prompt to the chart or another piece of chart paper.

> What is this prompt asking you to do? What are the important key words or phrases? Turn and talk to your partner about what you notice.

▶ After time for discussion, invite a few students to share their thinking. Underline key words or phrases on the chart, and ensure that students understand what the prompt is asking.

Summarize and Apply

Summarize the learning and remind students to read test prompts carefully to make sure they understand what is being asked.

> What do you need to think about when you are asked to write to a prompt?

▶ Write the principle at the top of the chart.
Distribute one or more prompts to each pair of students.

> During independent writing time today, work with a partner to read and discuss some other test prompts. Remember to carefully read each prompt twice, underline key words or phrases, and make sure you understand what the prompt is asking you to do.

> Read the directions carefully to make sure you understand what is being asked.

Short Response

• Write a paragraph to explain what Bruce learns from Yip Man in Be Water, My Friend. Use evidence from the book to support your response.

• What is the author's message in Imagine by Juan Felipe Herrera? Write a paragraph explaining what you think Herrera wants readers to learn from his book. Be sure to use details from the book to develop your response.

Extended Response

• In The Royal Bee, Song-ho goes to great lengths to get an education. Write an essay analyzing why education is important to Song-ho. Use evidence from the book to support your response.

Confer

▶ During independent writing, move around the room to confer briefly with pairs of students about test prompts. Use prompts such as the following as needed.

- *Remember to read the prompt at least twice.*
- *What is this prompt asking you to do?*
- *What are some important words or phrases in this prompt? Underline them.*
- *How much is this prompt asking you to write?*

Share

Following independent writing, gather students in the meeting area to share their work.

> Read your prompt aloud. Then share how you and your partner thought about it.

Writing Minilesson Principle
Write a statement that answers the prompt.

Writing to a Prompt: Getting Ready for Test Writing

You Will Need

- the books the sample prompts are about, such as these from Text Set: Exploring Identity:
  - *The Royal Bee* by Frances Park and Ginger Park
  - *Imagine* by Juan Felipe Herrera
- chart paper prepared with two test prompts about familiar books
- markers
- writer's notebooks and writing folders
- prompts prepared in advance to distribute to each pair of students

Academic Language / Important Vocabulary

- main idea
- statement
- prompt

Continuum Connection

- Write focused responses to questions and to prompts
- Write concisely and to the direction of the question or prompt
- Use a variety of beginnings and endings to engage the reader

GOAL

Use the words from a prompt to generate a main idea sentence that responds to the question posed in the prompt.

RATIONALE

Once students understand what a prompt is asking of them, they can start to think about writing a response. Beginning by writing a single sentence that answers the prompt will help students focus their thinking around a main idea and craft a clear, cohesive, and focused response.

WRITER'S NOTEBOOK/WRITING FOLDER

Students will try out writing a statement in response to a test prompt in their writer's notebooks. If they have extra time, they can work on a longer piece of writing in their writing folders.

ASSESS LEARNING

- Notice whether students can write a sentence that states their main idea and succinctly answers the prompt.
- Look for evidence that they can use vocabulary such as *main idea*, *statement*, and *prompt*.

MINILESSON

Students will need their writer's notebooks for this lesson. To help students think about the minilesson principle, remind them to use what they already know about writing engaging and thoughtful beginnings. Use sample ELA prompts to discuss crafting a main idea sentence. Here is an example.

- Read the first prompt on the prepared chart paper aloud.

  This prompt is asking you to write one paragraph explaining why Song-ho wants to go to school. Think about how you would answer this prompt. Why do you think Song-ho is determined to go to school?

- Write on the chart a main idea sentence summarizing students' responses.

  To start your response to a prompt, think about how you would answer the prompt and then write a single sentence that sums up your answer. This statement should briefly tell the main idea, or the most important idea, that you are going to write about. You will write more details later on. What do you notice about the sentence that I wrote?

- Guide students to notice that your sentence repeats key words from the prompt. Highlight those words.

Have a Try

Invite students to talk to a partner about writing a main idea sentence for another prompt.

▶ Read the second prompt aloud.

> How would you answer this prompt? Turn and talk to your partner about your ideas. Then write a sentence that answers the prompt in your writer's notebook.

▶ Ask a few students to share what they wrote. Add one strong example to the chart. Highlight any key words the writer repeated from the prompt.

Summarize and Apply

Summarize the learning and remind students to write a single sentence that states their main idea and succinctly answers the prompt.

> What did you learn today about how to begin your response to a test prompt?

▶ Write the principle at the top of the chart.
Distribute one or more prompts to each pair (or small group) of students.

> During independent writing time today, work with your partner (group) to write a statement that answers the prompt(s) I gave you in your writer's notebook. Remember to briefly and clearly state the main idea you are going to write about.

▶ Save the chart for WML3.

Write a statement that answers the prompt.

Why is Song-ho in The Royal Bee determined to go to school? Write a paragraph explaining his motivations, using evidence from the book to support your response.

Song-ho is determined to go to school because getting an education will help him lift his family out of poverty.

What is the author's message in Imagine by Juan Felipe Herrera? Write a paragraph explaining what you think Herrera wants readers to learn from his book. Be sure to use details from the book to develop your response.

In Imagine by Juan Felipe Herrera, the author's message is that you can overcome any obstacle and achieve anything you set your mind to.

Confer

▶ During independent writing, move around the room to confer briefly with pairs (small groups) of students about answering test prompts. Use prompts such as the following as needed.

- *What is the prompt asking you to write about?*
- *Which words from the prompt might you repeat in your statement? Underline them.*
- *How would you answer this prompt? How can you write that idea in a single sentence?*

Share

Following independent writing, gather students in the meeting area to share their work.

> Who would like to read aloud your prompt and the statement that answers it?

Provide evidence and details that support your response.

Writing to a Prompt: Getting Ready for Test Writing

You Will Need

▸ a sample prompt and a main idea sentence written in response to it (e.g., from the chart in WML2)

▸ the book the sample prompt is about, such as *The Royal Bee* by Frances Park and Ginger Park, from Text Set: Exploring Identity

▸ chart paper and markers

▸ a copy of a sample prompt for each pair of students

▸ writer's notebooks

Academic Language / Important Vocabulary

▸ prompt

▸ evidence

▸ detail

▸ response

Continuum Connection

▸ Write focused responses to questions and to prompts

▸ Write concisely and to the direction of the question or prompt

▸ Incorporate one's knowledge of craft in shaping responses

▸ State a point of view and provide evidence

GOAL

Provide evidence to support the main idea in order to answer the question posed in the prompt.

RATIONALE

When you model how to provide evidence to support a main idea, students will be better prepared not only for test writing but also for supporting their ideas orally and in writing more generally.

WRITER'S NOTEBOOK/WRITING FOLDER

Students can practice responding to test prompts in their writer's notebooks.

ASSESS LEARNING

▸ Notice whether students can support a main idea with convincing evidence and details.

▸ Look for evidence that they can use vocabulary such as *prompt*, *evidence*, *detail*, and *response*.

MINILESSON

To help students think about the minilesson principle, use shared writing to model how to find and use evidence and details to support a response. Refer to a text students have read and enjoyed. Here is an example.

▸ Display a sample ELA prompt and main idea sentence (e.g., the chart from WML2).

> You started to respond to this prompt by writing a single sentence that answers the prompt. Now you need to add evidence and details to support the response or to prove that the response is correct. What details from the book would support the response? How do you know that Song-ho wants to lift his family out of poverty, or help them have more money?

▸ As needed, reread relevant pages of *The Royal Bee* (e.g., pages 3 and 7) and draw students' attention to details that answer the prompt. Use shared writing to write a few sentences that support the main idea sentence.

> What do you think—does the response answer the prompt? How?

> To support your response with evidence and details, you can write about specific things that happen in the story or specific things that a character says. When you write the exact words that a character says, remember to use quotation marks.

Have a Try

Invite students to talk to a partner about providing evidence and details to support a response.

> What else could we write? What other evidence and details might we provide? Turn and talk to your partner about your ideas.

▶ After students turn and talk, invite a few pairs to share their thinking. Add to the chart.

Summarize and Apply

Help students summarize the learning and remind them to provide evidence and details that support their responses to test prompts.

> What did you learn today about how to write a response to a test prompt?

▶ Write the principle at the top of the chart. Distribute a sample prompt to each pair of students.

> Today during independent writing time, work with your partner to write in your writer's notebook a response to the test prompt I gave you. Remember to write a statement that answers the prompt and then to provide evidence and details to support your response. Bring your notebook to share when we come back together.

▶ Save the chart for WML4.

Provide evidence and details that support your response.

Why is Song-ho in The Royal Bee determined to go to school? Write a paragraph explaining his motivations, using evidence from the book to support your response.

Song-ho is determined to go to school because getting an education will help him lift his family out of poverty. It makes Song-ho sad to see his mother work so hard to feed the family. When he tries to go to The Sodang School, he asks Master Min, "How can I grow up to earn a good living for my mother when I cannot read or write?" This shows that he wants to go to school so he can provide for his family. After Song-ho learns to read and write, and he speaks at The Royal Bee, he says, "The gift of hope has now been won for my poor mother and me."

Confer

▶ During independent writing, move around the room to confer briefly with pairs of students about responding to test prompts. Use prompts such as the following as needed.

- *What is the prompt asking you to write about?*
- *What could you write in a single sentence that answers the prompt?*
- *What evidence and details could you provide to support your response?*
- *What does [character] say that shows _____?*

Share

Following independent writing, gather students in the meeting area to share their writing. Ask a student from each pair to read their response.

> What evidence and details did _____ and _____ provide to support their response?

Writing Minilesson Principle
Write a strong concluding sentence.

Writing to a Prompt: Getting Ready for Test Writing

You Will Need

- the chart from WML3
- marker
- writer's notebooks

Academic Language / Important Vocabulary

- concluding sentence
- summarize

Continuum Connection

- Incorporate one's knowledge of craft in shaping responses
- Use a variety of beginnings and endings to engage the reader

GOAL

Write a concluding sentence that summarizes the big idea and leaves the reader satisfied.

RATIONALE

When you teach students how to craft an ending to a test prompt response, they learn to bring together what they have learned about writing test prompt responses and about writing endings that satisfy the readers and remain focused on the prompt.

WRITER'S NOTEBOOK/WRITING FOLDER

Have students add a concluding sentence to their test prompt response (written in their writer's notebooks during WML3) or revise a concluding sentence they have already written.

ASSESS LEARNING

- Look at students' test prompt responses. Do they include a concluding sentence that summarizes the big idea and leaves the reader satisfied?
- Look for evidence that they can use vocabulary such as *concluding sentence* and *summarize.*

MINILESSON

To help students think about the minilesson principle, use shared writing to model how to write a strong concluding sentence to end a test prompt response. Here is an example.

- Display the chart from WML3.

  You have been practicing how to write a response to a test prompt, and you started to write one. What do you know about how to finish a piece of writing? What do you need to think about?

  When you write a concluding, or final, sentence for your response, think about how to summarize the big idea you're writing about while at the same time satisfying your readers. Listen carefully as I reread the prompt and the response we wrote together.

  What could we write in our concluding sentence? How could we sum up the big idea in a satisfying way?

- Use students' responses to write a concluding sentence. Read it aloud and ask students if the sentence does what it should or if it needs to be revised.

Have a Try

Invite students to talk to a partner about writing a strong concluding sentence.

> How can you write a strong concluding sentence for a test prompt response? What will you remember to do? Turn and talk to your partner about this.

> ◗ After time for discussion, invite a few students to share their thinking.

Summarize and Apply

Write the principle at the top of the chart. Summarize the learning and remind students to end their test prompt responses with a strong concluding sentence.

> During independent writing time today, work with the same partner you worked with to write the test prompt response. Reread what you wrote together, and then work together to write a strong concluding sentence. If you have already written a concluding sentence, think about how to revise it to make it more effective. Bring your writing to share when we meet later.

Write a strong concluding sentence.

Why is Song-ho in The Royal Bee determined to go to school? Write a paragraph explaining his motivations, using evidence from the book to support your response.

Song-ho is determined to go to school because getting an education will help him lift his family out of poverty. It makes Song-ho sad to see his mother work so hard to feed the family. When he tries to go to The Sodang School, he asks Master Min, "How can I grow up to earn a good living for my mother when I cannot read or write?" This shows that he wants to go to school so he can provide for his family. After Song-ho learns to read and write, and he speaks at The Royal Bee, he says, "The gift of hope has now been won for my poor mother and me." Now that he is getting an education, Song-ho has hope that he can provide a better future for himself and his mother.

Confer

> ◗ During independent writing, move around the room to confer briefly with pairs of students about responding to test prompts. Use prompts such as the following as needed.

> - *Let's reread what you've already written.*
> - *What is the big idea that you wrote about?*
> - *How can you sum up that idea in a single sentence?*

Share

Following independent writing, gather students in the meeting area to share their writing. Have each pair of students share their concluding sentence with another pair.

> What did you notice about how your classmates ended their test prompt responses? What made their concluding sentences strong and effective?

Section 2: Genres and Forms

Write a response that compares and contrasts two things.

Writing to a Prompt: Getting Ready for Test Writing

You Will Need

- chart paper prepared with a sample ELA prompt that asks students to compare and contrast two things
- a book or books to be used to answer the prompt, such as the following:
  - *Razia's Ray of Hope* by Elizabeth Suneby, from Text Set: Perseverance
  - *The Royal Bee* by Frances Park and Ginger Park, from Text Set: Exploring Identity
- markers
- a copy of a sample compare/contrast prompt for each pair of students
- writer's notebooks

Academic Language / Important Vocabulary

- prompt
- compare
- contrast
- response

Continuum Connection

- Incorporate one's knowledge of craft in shaping responses
- Write concisely and to the direction of the question or prompt
- Respond to a text in a way that reflects analytic or aesthetic thinking

GOAL

Write a response to a prompt that compares and contrasts two things.

RATIONALE

You have likely discussed comparison and contrast with the students. Now they can blend that knowledge with what they have learned about writing a response to a test prompt. The chart you create with students will be a resource as they learn more about the genre of test writing.

WRITER'S NOTEBOOK/WRITING FOLDER

Students can use their writer's notebooks to practice writing responses to compare-and-contrast prompts.

ASSESS LEARNING

- Observe for evidence that students understand how to compare and contrast two things.
- Look for evidence that they can use vocabulary such as *prompt*, *compare*, *contrast*, and *response*.

MINILESSON

To help students think about the minilesson principle, use shared writing to model writing a compare-and-contrast response. Refer to texts that students have read and enjoyed for evidence to support the lesson. Here is an example.

- Display a sample ELA prompt that asks students to compare and contrast two things. Read it aloud.

  What is this prompt asking you to do?

  This prompt is asking you to write how two stories are similar and different.

- Display *Razia's Ray of Hope* and *The Royal Bee*. Guide students to talk about how the two stories are similar and different.

  How are these stories similar? What do Razia and Song-ho both want?

  How are Razia and Song-ho different? Where does Razia live? Where does Song-ho live?

  Why can't Razia go to school? Why can't Song-ho go to school?

- Use shared writing to write the response.

  What is the main idea we are going to write about? How can we write a single sentence that answers the prompt?

  What details can we add about how Razia and Song-ho are different?

  What details can we add about how they are alike?

Have a Try

Invite students to talk to a partner about how to write a concluding sentence for a compare-and-contrast prompt.

> What could we write in our concluding sentence to summarize our big idea and satisfy our readers? Turn and talk to your partner about your ideas.

▶ After students turn and talk, invite several pairs to share their ideas. Use their responses to write a concluding sentence.

Summarize and Apply

Write the principle at the top of the chart. Summarize the learning and invite students to practicing writing responses that compare and contrast two things.

> Today, work with a partner on a response that compares and contrasts two things. Remember what you already know about writing a response to a test prompt. Do your writing on a clean page in your writer's notebook. Bring your writing to share when we come back together.

> **Write a response that compares and contrasts two things.**
>
> Think about Razia in <u>Razia's Ray of Hope</u> and Song-ho in <u>The Royal Bee</u>. How are Razia's story and Song-ho's story similar and different? Write a paragraph comparing and contrasting the two stories.
>
> <u>Razia's Ray of Hope</u> and <u>The Royal Bee</u> are two very different stories about two children who are both determined to get an education. Razia is a girl living in Afghanistan in the 2000s. Song-ho is a boy living in Korea in the 1800s. Both children really want to go to school, but for different reasons neither one is allowed. Razia can't go to school because she is a girl, while Song-ho can't go to school because he is poor. Both have to convince someone to let them go to school, and both are successful in the end. Although the details of their stories are very different, these stories show that the desire and need for an education are universal.

Confer

▶ During independent writing, move around the room to confer briefly with pairs of students about responding to test prompts. Use prompts such as the following as needed.

- *What is your prompt asking you to compare and contrast?*
- *How are _____ and _____ similar? How are they different?*
- *What big idea are you going to focus on? How can you write that in a single sentence?*
- *What details and evidence can you provide to support your response?*

Share

Following independent writing, gather students in the meeting area to share their writing.

> Who would like to read aloud the response you wrote today?

> What two things did _____ and _____ write about? How are those two things similar and different?

Assessment

After you have taught the minilessons in this umbrella, observe students in a variety of classroom activities. Use *The Fountas & Pinnell Literacy Continuum* to notice, teach for, and support students' learning as you observe their attempts at writing.

▶ What evidence do you have of students' new understandings related to test writing?

- Are students able to explain what a prompt is asking them to write?

- Do their responses start with a statement that answers the prompt, include supporting evidence and details, and finish with a strong concluding sentence?

- Can they write a response that compares and contrasts two things?

- Do they understand and use vocabulary such as *prompt*, *response*, *evidence*, *detail*, and *concluding sentence*?

▶ In what other ways, beyond the scope of this umbrella, are students exploring writing in different genres?

- Have students tried writing like a scientist?

- Are they showing an interest in writing poetry?

Use your observations to determine the next umbrella you will teach. You may also consult Suggested Sequence of Lessons (pp. 665–682) for guidance.

EXTENSIONS FOR WRITING TO A PROMPT: GETTING READY FOR TEST WRITING

▶ Work with students to reread, revise, and edit their writing. If you have already worked on the umbrellas that discuss this part of the writing process, connect back to that work. Help students understand that they will use everything they have learned about revising and editing on the day of the test because they won't have a chance to go back on another day to revise or edit.

▶ Use the rubrics used by your state to help students understand how they will be assessed.

▶ Provide time for students to practice writing within a limited amount of time.

▶ If your state's test requires extended (long) responses, teach the minilessons in GEN.U4: Writing to a Prompt: Extended Responses. If your state's test is administered via computer, help students understand how they are to enter their responses.

Minilessons in This Umbrella

WML1 Write an introductory paragraph to respond to a prompt.

WML2 Write a paragraph for each of your reasons.

WML3 Summarize your thinking in a concluding paragraph.

Before Teaching Umbrella 4 Minilessons

This umbrella builds on GEN.U3: Writing to a Prompt: Getting Ready for Test Writing. As with that umbrella, students will rely on the writing instruction they have had, so continue to provide opportunities for them to write independently in the genres they have explored and work in their writer's notebooks. In these minilessons, students will also draw on what they have learned already about writing to a prompt and expand that knowledge to encompass knowing how to write a longer response. Because they are learning how to respond to a test prompt, which is a certain kind of writing, the structure will be more formulaic than other writing structures they use.

Because so many constructed response tests focus on writing about reading, that will be the focus of this umbrella, but consult with your own state tests to modify as needed to teach students how to achieve on your state's test.

For mentor texts, use prior years' state tests, state practice prompts, and Exemplary Extended Responses from fp.pub/resources, which are based on the following books from *Fountas & Pinnell Classroom™ Shared Reading Collection*.

Shared Reading Collection

A Spark of Genius: A Biography of Richard Turere by Myra Faye Turner

A Lifetime of Dance: A Biography of Katherine Dunham by Nnéka Nnolim

Migrate! Epic Animal Excursions by Michelle Garcia Andersen

More Than Sleeping: A Hibernation Journey Through Poems by Sona Minnetyan

As you read and enjoy these texts together, help students

- notice similarities and differences between books, and

- discuss themes or main ideas and the details that support them.

Shared Reading

Writer's Notebook

Section 2: Genres and Forms

Writing to a Prompt: Extended Responses

You Will Need

- mentor texts to use as excerpts, such as the following from *Shared Reading Collection*:
  - *A Spark of Genius* by Myra Faye Turner
  - *A Lifetime of Dance* by Nnéka Nnolim
  - *More Than Sleeping* by Sona Minnetyan
  - *Migrate!* by Michelle Garcia Andersen
- chart paper and markers
- writer's notebooks
- several practice prompts that align with the state writing assessment
- To download the following online resource for this lesson, visit **fp.pub/resources**:
  - Exemplary Extended Responses

Academic Language / Important Vocabulary

- extended response
- introductory paragraph
- prompt
- respond

Continuum Connection

- Learn how to write on tests by studying examples of short constructed responses and extended constructed responses

GOAL

Write an introductory paragraph for an extended response.

RATIONALE

When students understand that an extended response should include an idea, respond to the prompt, and give reasons to support the idea, they are better able to focus their thinking around a main idea and craft a clear, cohesive, and focused response.

WRITER'S NOTEBOOK/WRITING FOLDER

Students will use their writer's notebooks to practice an extended response to a prompt.

ASSESS LEARNING

- Notice whether students can include all the elements in their extended responses.
- Look for evidence that they can use vocabulary such as *extended response*, *introductory paragraph*, *prompt*, and *respond*.

MINILESSON

To help students think about the minilesson principle, remind them to use what they know about writing engaging and thoughtful beginnings. Display or make copies for students of the online resource Exemplary Extended Responses to engage them in a discussion about how to write an introductory paragraph. Here is an example.

- Briefly revisit *A Spark of Genius*.
- Direct students' attention to the prompt in Sample A from the online resource Exemplary Extended Responses. Read the prompt.

  What is the prompt asking you to do?

- Engage students in a discussion, ensuring that they understand that the prompt asks them to write an article about creativity and goals using the text examples. As needed, define the term *extended response*.

  You know how to write a short response to a test prompt. This prompt asks you to write a longer response. Let's look at the introductory paragraph.

- Read the introductory paragraph from Sample A.

  What do you notice?

- Guide the conversation to help students notice that the introductory paragraph introduces the idea, responds to the prompt, and gives reasons.

- Use students' responses to begin a list on chart paper with the heading *What to Think About When You Write an Extended Response*. Leave room to add to the chart in the following minilessons.

Have a Try

Invite students to talk to a partner about writing another introductory paragraph.

▶ Display pages 12–13 of *More Than Sleeping* and pages 6–7 of *Migrate!*

▶ Direct students' attention to Sample B from Exemplary Extended Responses. Read the prompt and introductory paragraph aloud.

> Turn and talk to your partner about what you notice about the introductory paragraph.

▶ After time for discussion, ask volunteers to share.

Summarize and Apply

Summarize the learning and remind students to write an introductory paragraph that answers a practice prompt.

▶ Review the chart with students. Save the chart for WML2. Distribute one or more prompts to each pair (or small group) of students.

> During independent writing time today, talk with your partner about a response to the prompt(s) you were given. Together, decide what an introductory paragraph for the prompt could say, and write the paragraph in your writer's notebooks. You'll add to your response later.

Confer

▶ During independent writing, move around the room to confer briefly with pairs (small groups) of students about answering test prompts. Use prompts such as the following as needed.

- *What is the prompt asking you to write about?*
- *Read your introductory paragraph. Does it prepare the reader to read the response?*

Share

Following independent writing, gather students in the meeting area to share their work.

> Share the introductory paragraph that you wrote with your partner.

> What do you notice about what _____ and _____ wrote?

What to Think About When You Write an Extended Response

Introductory Paragraph
- Have a clear main idea.
- Be well organized.
- Stay on topic.
- Respond to the prompt.

Writing Minilesson Principle
Write a paragraph for each of your reasons.

You Will Need

- mentor texts to use as excerpts, such as the following from *Shared Reading Collection*:
  - *A Spark of Genius* by Myra Faye Turner
  - *A Lifetime of Dance* by Nnéka Nnolim
  - *Migrate!* by Michelle Garcia Andersen
  - *More Than Sleeping* by Sona Minnetyan
- chart from WML1
- Exemplary Extended Responses [online resource from WML1]
- markers
- writer's notebooks and writing folders
- several practice prompts that align with the state writing assessment

Academic Language / Important Vocabulary

- body
- details
- evidence
- response

Continuum Connection

- Understand that test writing often requires writing about something real
- Respond to text in a way that reflects analytic or aesthetic thinking
- Restate a claim with further evidence

GOAL

Write a paragraph about each reason and include examples.

RATIONALE

When students understand that an extended response should include paragraphs with reasons, they will be better prepared not only for test writing but also for supporting their ideas using text examples when writing more generally.

WRITER'S NOTEBOOK/WRITING FOLDER

Have students add paragraphs with reasons to the test prompt response [written in their writer's notebooks during WML1] or revise the paragraphs in a piece they have already written in their writing folders.

ASSESS LEARNING

- Notice whether students can write an extended response that includes a paragraph with examples for each reason.
- Look for evidence that they can use vocabulary such as *body*, *evidence*, *details*, and *response*.

MINILESSON

To help students think about the minilesson principle, use mentor test prompt responses and practice prompts to engage in a discussion about how to write paragraphs with reasons. Here is an example.

- Draw students' attention to the prompt and response in Sample A from the WML1 online resource Exemplary Extended Responses. If possible, hide the concluding paragraph, which will be the focus of WML3. Refer to the texts as necessary when discussing the sample response.

- Display the chart from WML1.

  You have been learning about how to write a response to a test prompt, and you have written an introductory paragraph. Let's look at the body paragraphs in the writing sample and think about how those were written.

- Guide the conversation to help students notice that the paragraphs in the body give reasons and provide examples with supporting evidence from whatever text or texts are mentioned in the prompt. Make sure students understand the word *body* as used in this lesson. Pause before you talk about the concluding paragraph, which will be covered in WML3.

- Use students' responses to add to the list on the chart.

  When you write an extended response to a test prompt, give reasons, and use evidence and examples from the reading.

Have a Try

Invite students to talk to a partner about writing paragraphs that include evidence to support a response.

▶ Draw students' attention to Sample B from Exemplary Extended Responses. If possible, hide the concluding paragraph.

Turn and talk to your partner about what you notice about the paragraphs.

▶ After time for discussion, ask volunteers to share.

Summarize and Apply

Help students summarize the learning and remind them to provide evidence and details that support their responses to test prompts.

▶ Review the chart. Save the chart for WML3.

Today during independent writing time, work with the same partner (small group) to add several body paragraphs to the introductory paragraph you wrote last time. Bring your notebook to share when we meet later.

> **What to Think About When You Write an Extended Response**
>
> Introductory Paragraph
> - Have a clear main idea.
> - Be well organized.
> - Stay on topic.
> - Respond to the prompt.
>
> Body Paragraphs
> - Use examples to support your main ideas.
> - Find evidence (specific details) from the passage(s) to support the examples.
> - Write a paragraph for each of your reasons.

Confer

▶ During independent writing, move around the room to confer briefly with pairs (small groups) of students about responding to test prompts. Use prompts such as the following as needed.

- *What is the prompt asking you to do?*
- *What details from the passage provide evidence to support your reasons?*
- *Let's talk about the reading and find an example that might work here.*

Share

Following independent writing, gather students in the meeting area to share their writing. Ask a student from each pair (small group) to read their response.

What evidence and details did _____ and _____ provide to support their response?

WML3

GEN.U4.WML3

Writing Minilesson Principle
Summarize your thinking in a concluding paragraph.

Writing to a Prompt: Extended Responses

You Will Need

- mentor texts to use as excerpts, such as the following from *Shared Reading Collection*:
  - *A Spark of Genius* by Myra Faye Turner
  - *A Lifetime of Dance* by Nnéka Nnolim
  - *Migrate!* by Michelle Garcia Andersen
  - *More Than Sleeping* by Sona Minnetyan
- chart from WML2
- Exemplary Extended Responses (online resource from WML1)
- markers
- writer's notebooks and writing folders
- several practice prompts that align with the state writing assessment

Academic Language / Important Vocabulary

- extended response
- concluding paragraph
- summarize

Continuum Connection

- Understand that test writing may involve creating expository texts or persuasive texts
- Understand that test writing can take various forms: e.g., short constructed response (sometimes called *short answer*), extended constructed response (or *essay*)

GOAL

Write a concluding paragraph that summarizes the response.

RATIONALE

When you teach students how to craft a concluding paragraph to an extended response test prompt, they learn to bring together what they have learned about writing test prompt responses and about writing endings that satisfy the readers and remain focused on the prompt.

WRITER'S NOTEBOOK/WRITING FOLDER

Have students add a concluding paragraph to the test prompt response (written in their writer's notebooks across this umbrella) or revise a concluding paragraph they have already written from a piece in their writing folders.

ASSESS LEARNING

- Look for evidence that students can write a concluding paragraph that summarizes the ideas in their extended responses.
- Look for evidence that they can use vocabulary such as *extended response*, *concluding paragraph*, and *summarize*.

MINILESSON

To help students think about the minilesson principle, use mentor test prompt responses and practice prompts to engage them in a discussion about how to end an extended response test question. Here is an example.

- Draw students' attention to the prompt in Sample A from the WML1 online resource Exemplary Extended Responses. Refer to the texts as necessary when discussing the sample response.

- Display the chart from WML2.

  You have been practicing how to write a response to a test prompt, and you have written an introductory paragraph and added body paragraphs with reasons. Let's look at the concluding paragraph in the writing sample and think about how it was written.

- Guide the conversation to help students notice that the concluding paragraph summarizes the main idea of the response and gives readers something to think about. As needed, explain what it means to summarize.

  What do you notice?

- Use students' responses to add to the chart.

  When you write a concluding paragraph, think about how to summarize the big idea you're writing about and wrap it up. You can also give your readers something to think about.

Have a Try

Invite students to talk to a partner about writing the concluding paragraph for an extended response test prompt.

> ▶ Draw students' attention to Sample B from Exemplary Extended Responses.
>
>> Turn and talk to your partner about what you notice about the concluding paragraph.
>
> ▶ After time for discussion, ask volunteers to share. Add new ideas to the chart.

Summarize and Apply

Summarize the learning and remind students to end their test prompt responses with a strong concluding paragraph.

> During independent writing time today, work with the same partner (small group). Reread what you wrote together, and then work together to write a strong concluding paragraph. If you have already written a concluding paragraph, think about how to revise it to make it more effective. Bring your writing to share when we meet later.

> **What to Think About When You Write an Extended Response**
>
> Introductory Paragraph
> - Have a clear main idea.
> - Be well organized.
> - Stay on topic.
> - Respond to the prompt.
>
> Body Paragraphs
> - Use examples to support your main ideas.
> - Find evidence (specific details) from the passage(s) to support the examples.
> - Write a paragraph for each of your reasons.
>
> Concluding Paragraph
> - Wrap it up.
> - Summarize your thinking in a concluding paragraph.
> - Give the reader something to think about.

Confer

> ▶ During independent writing, move around the room to confer briefly with pairs (small groups) of students about responding to test prompts. Use prompts such as the following as needed.
>
> - *Read what you have already written.*
> - *What is the main idea in what you wrote?*
> - *How can you summarize your response?*

Share

Following independent writing, gather students in the meeting area to share their writing.

> Share the concluding paragraph you wrote.
>
> What did you notice about the concluding paragraph written by _____ and _____ ?

Assessment

After you have taught the minilessons in this umbrella, observe students in a variety of classroom activities. Use *The Fountas & Pinnell Literacy Continuum* to notice, teach for, and support students' learning as you observe their attempts at writing.

▶ What evidence do you have of students' new understandings related to test writing?

- Are students understanding what a prompt asks them to write?
- Do students' introductory paragraphs state the main idea clearly?
- Are they writing paragraphs for each of their reasons?
- Do their concluding paragraphs summarize their response?
- Do they understand and use vocabulary such as *extended response, prompt, respond, introductory paragraph, summarize,* and *concluding paragraph*?

▶ In what other ways, beyond the scope of this umbrella, are students exploring writing in different genres?

- Are students choosing to write poetry?
- Are they showing an interest in writing both fiction and nonfiction?

Use your observations to determine the next umbrella you will teach. You may also consult Suggested Sequence of Lessons (pp. 665–682) for guidance.

EXTENSIONS FOR WRITING TO A PROMPT: EXTENDED RESPONSES

▶ Spend time side-by-side with individual students to talk about their practice extended responses.

▶ Have students work in groups with copies of your state's standardized writing test rubrics to ensure they understand what will be asked of them on the test and to evaluate the extended responses they wrote across the minilessons in this umbrella.

▶ From time to time, give opportunities for students to write under a time constraint.

Minilessons in This Umbrella

WML1 Notice the qualities of good memoirs.

WML2 Write a memoir about one small moment.

WML3 Write a memoir using a series of short vignettes.

WML4 Think about the message you want to communicate.

WML5 Write details about the most important moments.

Before Teaching Umbrella 5 Minilessons

The purpose of this umbrella is to show students how to write memoirs about meaningful times and events in their own lives. Guide students to to make a choice of writing about a small moment in time or writing a series of memories (vignettes). Writing about smaller periods of time enables them to write in more depth than if they cover events over a long period of time. Decide whether to have students create picture books about their memories or write memory stories.

Prior to teaching these minilessons, we recommend teaching at least some of the minilessons in WPS.U1: Introducing and Using a Writer's Notebook and WPS.U2: Writer's Notebook: Getting Ideas from Your Life. Minilessons in the latter umbrella support students in using their writer's notebooks to plan their memoirs. To provide models of memory writing, read aloud a variety of engaging memoirs that reflect diverse cultures and experiences. Use the following texts from *Fountas & Pinnell Classroom™ Interactive Read-Aloud Collection* as well as any other books from the text set Genre Study: Memoir, or choose memoirs from your classroom library. A rubric for evaluating the students' memoirs is available in online resources.

Interactive Read-Aloud Collection

Figuring Out Who You Are

A Boy and a Jaguar by Alan Rabinowitz

Genre Study: Memoir

Play Ball! by Jorge Posada with Robert Burleigh

Twelve Kinds of Ice by Ellen Bryan Obed

As you read and enjoy these and other memoirs together, help students

- identify the characteristics of memoirs,
- notice the sequence of events,
- notice the use of first person, and
- discuss the author's message.

Interactive Read-Aloud
Figuring Out Who You Are

Genre Study: Memoir

Writer's Notebook

Writing Minilesson Principle
Notice the qualities of good memoirs.

Writing Memoirs

You Will Need

- a familiar memoir, such as *Play Ball!* by Jorge Posada with Robert Burleigh, from Text Set: Genre Study: Memoir
- chart paper and markers
- at least one familiar memoir story for each small group (see p. 181 for titles)
- writer's notebooks

Academic Language / Important Vocabulary

- memoir
- quality
- author
- organize

Continuum Connection

- Understand memoir or personal narrative as a brief, often intense, memory of or reflection on a person, time, or event
- Understand that a memoir can be composed of a series of vignettes
- Write various kinds of biographical texts by studying mentor texts

GOAL

Study the qualities of good mentor texts for the purpose of learning how to craft them.

RATIONALE

Conducting an inquiry around memoirs and having students name the qualities of them is an effective way to prepare and equip students to begin writing their own memoirs. They will model their memoirs on those they have read.

WRITER'S NOTEBOOK/WRITING FOLDER

Students can write about the qualities of good memoirs in their writer's notebooks.

ASSESS LEARNING

- Observe for evidence of what students know about memoirs.
- Look for evidence that they can use vocabulary such as *memoir*, *quality*, *author*, and *organize*.

MINILESSON

To help students think about the principle, engage them in an inquiry-based lesson to notice and name the qualities of effective memoirs. Here is an example.

- Show the cover of a memoir, such as *Play Ball!*

    Where did the authors of this book get the idea to write about baseball?

    This type of story is called a memoir because it is based on a memory or experience from the life of the main author.

- Show the covers of several other memoirs.

    Here are some other memoirs we have read. What have you noticed about memoirs?

- Record students' responses on chart paper, generalizing them as necessary.
- As needed, prompt students' thinking about memoirs with questions such as the following:
    - *Did the authors write about long periods of time or small moments?*
    - *Is each story about one memory or more than one memory?*
    - *What do you notice about how the authors told their stories?*
    - *In what order did they tell their stories?*
    - *What did the authors do to help you picture what is happening in their stories?*
    - *What do you notice about the endings of memoirs?*

Have a Try

Invite students to talk to a partner about the qualities of memoirs.

> Is there anything else you have noticed about memoirs that you think we should add to our chart? Turn and talk to your partner about this.

▶ After students turn and talk, invite a few pairs to share their thinking. Add any new ideas to the chart as appropriate.

Summarize and Apply

Summarize the learning and invite students to further discuss the qualities of memoirs in small groups.

▶ Divide students into small groups, and give each group at least one familiar memoir to study in detail.

> During independent writing time today, meet with your group to study the memoir I gave you. Discuss what you notice about the memoir.
> On a clean page in your writer's notebook, write the title "Memoirs" and write notes about what you notice. Bring your notebooks when we come back together.

Memoirs . . .

- are about an <u>important memory</u> from the author's life.
- are about <u>one small moment</u> in time or a <u>series of small moments</u> (vignettes) that are related in some way.
- are often about <u>family and childhood</u>.
- are usually told from the <u>author's point of view</u>, using pronouns such as <u>I</u>, <u>me</u>, and <u>my</u>.
- are told in the <u>order that the story happened</u>.
- use <u>descriptive words and details</u> to help readers picture the characters, setting, and events.
- tell the author's personal <u>thoughts and feelings</u> about the memory.
- often communicate a <u>message</u>—something the author wants readers to learn.

Confer

▶ During independent writing, move around the room to confer briefly with groups about what they notice about memoirs. Use prompts such as the following as needed.

- *Is this memoir about one small moment or several?*
- *How did the author make the story interesting? How did the author make it seem real?*
- *How did the author help you get to know the people in the story?*
- *What do you think the author wants you to learn from reading the memoir?*

Share

Following independent writing, gather students in the meeting area. Invite each group to share the qualities they noticed in the memoir they studied. Add any new qualities to the chart.

> What qualities did you notice in the memoir you studied?

WML2
GEN.U5.WML2

Writing Minilesson Principle
Write a memoir about one small moment.

Writing Memoirs

You Will Need

- a familiar small moment story, such as *Twelve Kinds of Ice* by Ellen Bryan Obed, from Text Set: Genre Study: Memoir
- your writer's notebook with a list of ideas for memoirs
- chart paper and markers
- writer's notebooks

Academic Language / Important Vocabulary

- memoir
- small moment

Continuum Connection

- Select and write personal experiences as "small moments" and share thinking and feelings about them

GOAL

Understand that when writing memoirs writers often focus on a small moment that is important to them.

RATIONALE

Authors of memoirs choose to write about a small moment in depth rather than writing shallowly about lengthy periods of time. When students learn to do this, their writing is more meaningful and engaging for their readers.

WRITER'S NOTEBOOK/WRITING FOLDER

Have students record in their writer's notebooks ideas for small moments that could be developed into a memoir.

ASSESS LEARNING

- Notice whether students are able to choose a small but significant moment to write about.
- Look for evidence that they can use vocabulary such as *memoir* and *small moment*.

MINILESSON

To help students think about the minilesson principle, use a familiar memoir to help them notice how authors choose memories to write about. Then model how to choose a topic for a memoir. Here is an example.

- Show the cover of *Twelve Kinds of Ice*. Review the chapter called "Flooding" (pp. 32–35).

    What is this chapter about?

    This chapter is about one thing: Dad flooding the rink. The action that the author described takes place in one evening. Why do you think the author chose this memory to write about?

- Think aloud about deciding how to write about at least one of your ideas.

    One of the ideas I wrote down is "Immigrating to America." That's too much to write about in one story, but I could write about one event: the first time my family went to a grocery store in the US. What does my idea for a memoir have in common with what Ellen Bryan Obed wrote in "Flooding"?

- Students should understand that each is about just a single event over a short period of time.

    When you write about a small moment, like flooding an ice rink or going grocery shopping for the first time, you are able to write about that moment with lots of detail. That helps your readers feel as if they were there with you.

Have a Try

Invite students to talk to a partner about their own ideas for memoirs.

> Think about small memories or moments from your own life. What could you write a memoir about? Turn and talk to your partner about your ideas.

▶ After time for discussion, invite several students to share their ideas. Record them on chart paper.

Summarize and Apply

Help students summarize the learning, and invite them to choose a memory to write about.

> What did you learn today about choosing a topic for a memoir?

▶ Write the principle at the top of the chart.

> During independent writing time today, spend some more time thinking about ideas for a memoir. Write your ideas in your writer's notebook. You might even start writing some details about one of your ideas. Bring your notebook to share when we meet later.

> ### Write a memoir about one small moment.
>
> ### One Small Moment
>
> • Going to the grocery store for the first time in the US
>
> • Going fishing with my grandmother
>
> • Riding a bus for the first time
>
> • The day my family adopted a puppy
>
> • Making naan with my mother

Confer

▶ During independent writing, move around the room to confer briefly with students about their ideas for memoirs. Use prompts such as the following as needed.

- *What special people, places, or events can you remember from when you were younger?*
- *That's a big idea. What small piece of that, or small moment, could you write about?*
- *What details could you write about your small moment?*

Share

Following independent writing, gather students in the meeting area to share their ideas for memoirs.

> Who would like to share your idea for a memoir?

Writing Minilesson Principle
Write a memoir using a series of short vignettes.

Writing Memoirs

You Will Need

- a familiar memoir written as a series of vignettes, such as *Twelve Kinds of Ice* by Ellen Bryan Obed, from Text Set: Genre Study: Memoir
- your writer's notebook with a list of ideas for memoirs
- chart paper and markers
- writer's notebooks

Academic Language / Important Vocabulary

- memoir
- moment
- vignette

Continuum Connection

- Create a series of vignettes that together communicate a bigger message

GOAL

Understand that writers sometimes construct a memoir with a series of related memories that together have a message.

RATIONALE

Authors of memoirs sometimes choose to write in depth about a series of small moments–vignettes–related to a central theme rather than writing about a single memory. Taken together, the vignettes communicate a message or idea important to the author.

WRITER'S NOTEBOOK/WRITING FOLDER

Have students record in their writer's notebooks ideas for vignettes that could be developed into a memoir.

ASSESS LEARNING

- Notice whether students write about a series of related small moments (vignettes).
- Look for evidence that they can use vocabulary such as *memoir*, *moment*, and *vignette*.

MINILESSON

To help students think about the minilesson principle, use a familiar memoir to help them notice that a memoir can consist of a series of vignettes. Then model how to choose a topic for a memoir. Here is an example.

- Show the cover of *Twelve Kinds of Ice* and read the title.

  How is this story different from many of the stories you read and write?

  This book is made up of several small moments, or vignettes. Why do you think the author decided to put several small moments together in one book?

  Each vignette is about a special memory from the author's childhood that relates to ice in some way. This book is made up of a series of vignettes, or short scenes, that together show how important the author's memories of her family and winter are to her.

  I wrote some ideas for memoirs in my writer's notebook.

- Read aloud your list of ideas for memoirs. Think aloud about how to focus at least one of your ideas.

  One of the ideas I wrote down is "Nana Sara." She was my great-grandmother. I met her only a few times, but each time was memorable. Because each memory relates to Nana Sara and the amazing person she was, I could use each meeting as a vignette and put all of them together for a memoir.

- Record a definition for *vignette* and your idea for a memoir on chart paper.

Have a Try

Invite students to talk to a partner about their own ideas for memoirs.

> Think about memories from your own life that are short and related in some way. Turn and talk to your partner about your ideas.

▶ After time for discussion, invite several students to share their ideas. Record them on the chart.

Summarize and Apply

Help students summarize the learning and invite them to choose a series of related memories to write about.

> What did you learn today about writing a memoir?

▶ Write the principle at the top of the chart.

> When you write today, spend some more time thinking about your ideas for memoirs. Write your ideas for vignettes in your writer's notebook. You might even start writing some details about one of your ideas. Bring your notebook to share when we meet later.

Write a memoir using a series of short vignettes.

Vignette—a short description of an event

Ideas for Vignettes **in a Memoir**

• Memories of my amazing great-grandmother

• Challenges of moving to a new city (starting a new school, remembering to get off at the right bus stop, making a new friend)

• Memories of getting through bad storms (lost power, flooding, tree coming down)

• Memorable times in third grade (bird flew into the classroom, teacher had to go to the hospital, pet guinea pig got out of the cage)

Confer

▶ During independent writing, move around the room to confer briefly with students about their ideas for memoirs. Use prompts such as the following as needed.

- *Let's talk about the ideas for memoirs you wrote in your writer's notebook.*

- *Talk about how these vignettes fit together.*

- *What do you want your readers to learn about you from your memoir?*

Share

Following independent writing, gather students in small groups in the meeting area to share their ideas for memoirs before sharing with the class.

> In groups of three, share the vignettes you want to write about.

> How do _____'s vignettes relate to one big idea?

WML 4
GEN.U5.WML4

Writing Minilesson Principle
Think about the message you want to communicate.

Writing Memoirs

You Will Need

- a few familiar memoirs with a clear author's message, such as the following:
  - *A Boy and a Jaguar* by Alan Rabinowitz, from Text Set: Figuring Out Who You Are
  - *Play Ball!* by Jorge Posada with Robert Burleigh, from Text Set: Genre Study: Memoir
- chart paper and markers
- writer's notebooks and writing folders

Academic Language / Important Vocabulary

- memoir
- message
- communicate

Continuum Connection

- Reveal something important about self or about life
- Create a series of vignettes that together communicate a bigger message
- Show the significance of the subject

GOAL

Write in a way that shows the importance of the story and communicates the big idea or message.

RATIONALE

When students notice how authors of memoirs communicate the big idea or message, they learn how to reveal the significance of the memories that they themselves write about. They begin to write richer and more insightful memoirs.

WRITER'S NOTEBOOK/WRITING FOLDER

Students will explore ideas in their writer's notebooks and/or start writing their memoirs, the drafts of which they will keep in their writing folders.

ASSESS LEARNING

- Notice whether students clearly communicate a big idea or message in their memoirs.
- Look for evidence that they can use vocabulary such as *memoir*, *message*, and *communicate*.

MINILESSON

To help students think about the minilesson principle, use familiar memoirs to help them notice how authors communicate a big idea or message. Here is an example.

- Show the cover of *A Boy and a Jaguar* and read the title. Read page 7.

  What do you think is Alan Rabinowitz's message, or the big idea the author wants you to understand from reading this book?

- Record responses on chart paper.

- Show the cover of *Play Ball!* and read the title. Read pages 1–2.

  How does Jorge feel about batting left-handed for the first time? How can you tell?

- Read pages 24–28.

  What message is the author trying to communicate, or teach readers? How do you know?

- Record responses on the chart.

Have a Try

Invite students to talk to a partner about the message they want to communicate.

> Think about the memory or memories you decided to write about. What did you learn from your experience? What do you want other people to learn from reading your memoir? Turn and talk to your partner about this.

▶ After students turn and talk, invite several students to share their responses. Add the two questions to the bottom of the chart.

Summarize and Apply

Write the principle at the top of the chart. Summarize the learning and invite students to continue working on their memoirs.

> During independent writing time today, spend some more time thinking about the message you want to communicate in your memoir. Write the message in your writer's notebook, along with a few notes about how you might make the message clear to readers. When you're ready, start writing your memoir on draft paper and keep it in your writing folder.

Think about the message you want to communicate.

Memory Story	Author's Message
A Boy and a Jaguar	You can find your voice and use it to speak up for those who can't speak for themselves.
Play Ball!	You can do anything you set your mind to if you work hard.

Questions to Ask Yourself
- What did you learn from your experience?
- What do you want other people to learn from reading your memoir?

Confer

▶ During independent writing, move around the room to confer briefly with students about their memoirs. Use prompts such as the following as needed.

- *Talk about why that memory is important to you.*
- *What did you learn from that experience?*
- *How can you make that lesson clear to your readers?*

Share

Following independent writing, gather students in the meeting area to talk about their memoirs.

> Turn to your partner and share the message you want to communicate in your memoir. Tell how you plan to do that.

Writing Minilesson Principle
Write details about the most important moments.

Writing Memoirs

You Will Need

- a familiar memoir that is rich with details and descriptive language, such as *Play Ball!* by Jorge Posada with Robert Burleigh, from Text Set: Genre Study: Memoir
- chart paper and markers
- writer's notebooks and writing folders

Academic Language / Important Vocabulary

- memoir
- detail
- moment
- specific
- description

Continuum Connection

- Describe and develop a setting and explain how it is related to the writer's experiences
- Describe the subject's important decisions and a turning point in the narrative
- Describe people by how they look, what they do, say, and think, and what others say about them
- Experiment with literary language (powerful nouns and verbs, figurative language)

GOAL

Understand that writers describe the most important parts of their memoirs in the most detail.

RATIONALE

Not all parts of a narrative are equal. To write an engaging memoir, students must learn to identify the most important parts and describe them in enough detail that the readers can recognize these parts as important. Vivid images of people, places, and events emphasize their importance.

WRITER'S NOTEBOOK/WRITING FOLDER

Have students refer to their writer's notebooks for ideas for their memoirs and keep their drafts in their writing folders.

ASSESS LEARNING

- Observe whether students emphasize the most important moments in their memoirs by including more detail than in the less important parts.
- Look for evidence that students can use vocabulary such as *memoir*, *detail*, *moment*, *specific*, and *description*.

MINILESSON

To help students think about the minilesson principle, engage them in an inquiry-based lesson on the details in a familiar memoir. Here is an example.

- Show the cover of *Play Ball!* and read the title. Read the first four paragraphs of page 18.

   How much did the authors write about the sights in New York City?

- Continue reading until the end of page 24. Pause regularly to draw students' attention to different types of details. Ask questions such as the following:

   - *How would you compare the description of the baseball field at Yankee Stadium to the description of New York City?*
   - *How did the authors show you how Jorge is feeling?*
   - *What did the authors do to help you picture what Jorge is doing?*

- Help students understand that the authors described the important moments in greater detail than they described the less important parts of the story.

   What do you notice about the amount of detail the authors used to describe baseball games compared with earlier in the book when Jorge was visiting places in the city?

   What can you do to show which moments are important in your memoir?

- Record students' responses on chart paper, generalizing them as necessary.

Have a Try

Invite students to talk to a partner about their ideas for writing.

> Think about the most important moment in the memoir you are writing. If you're working on a series of vignettes, think about the most important moment in just one of the vignettes you're writing. What details could you include to help readers understand that moment? Turn and talk to your partner about your ideas.

Summarize and Apply

Summarize the learning and remind students to write details to emphasize the most important moments in their memoirs.

> How can you help your readers understand the most important moments in your memoir?

▶ Write the principle at the top of the chart.

> Today during independent writing time, continue working on your memoir. Remember to include interesting details about the most important moments. Look at the chart for types of details you might include.

> ### Write details about the most important moments.
>
> #### Details
>
> - Help readers picture the setting
>
> - Use sensory words to describe what the characters see, hear, smell, feel, or taste
>
> - Tell what the characters say, do, think, and feel
>
> - Use specific and powerful words

Confer

▶ During independent writing, move around the room to confer briefly with students about their memoirs. Use prompts such as the following as needed.

- *What are you writing about in this part of your memoir?*

- *Is this part very important? Why or why not?*

- *What details could you include to help readers picture what is happening in this part of the memoir?*

- *What were you feeling or thinking when _____ happened? How can you show that?*

Share

Following independent writing, gather students in the meeting area to share their writing.

> Who would like to read aloud an important part of your memoir?

> What details in _____'s story stood out to you?

Assessment

After you have taught the minilessons in this umbrella, observe students as they write and talk about writing memoirs. Use *The Fountas & Pinnell Literacy Continuum* to notice, teach for, and support students' learning as you observe their attempts at writing memoirs.

▶ What evidence do you have of students' new understandings related to writing memoirs?

- Can students identify the characteristics of good memoirs?
- Do they understand what it means to write about a small moment or a series of small moments (vignettes)?
- Do their stories clearly communicate a message?
- Are the most important moments described in enough detail to make them stand out as important?
- Do students understand and use vocabulary such as *memoir, small moment, vignette, detail,* and *message*?

▶ In what other ways, beyond the scope of this umbrella, are students ready to explore genres and forms?

- Are they writing realistic fiction?
- Are they showing an interest in adding dialogue to their memoirs?

Use your observations to determine the next umbrella you will teach. You may also consult Suggested Sequence of Lessons (pp. 665–682) for guidance.

EXTENSIONS FOR WRITING MEMOIRS

▶ As you read memoirs, engage students in conversations about how the authors told the stories, showed emotion, and revealed important information about themselves.

▶ Download rubrics from the online resources (fp.pub/resources) to help you and your students evaluate how well they are able to apply the concepts in these lessons. You might also consider having students co-create a rubric with you.

▶ Show students how to "skip time" to focus their memoirs on the most important events (see WPS.U9: Revising to Focus and Organize Writing).

▶ When they start writing memoirs, some students might find that their chosen memory is too big. Pull together a few students in a guided writing group to help them narrow a too-large memory down to a small moment or series of related small moments so they can write in detail.

Minilessons in This Umbrella

WML1 Notice the qualities of good picture book biographies.

WML2 Choose a subject for your biography, do research, and take notes.

WML3 Select and tell about the most important events or turning points in the person's life.

WML4 Show your ideas with pictures and words.

WML5 Show how the setting is important in the life of the subject.

WML6 Use quotes from real people to show something about the subject.

Before Teaching Umbrella 6 Minilessons

Across the minilessons in this umbrella, students will study the characteristics of picture book biographies and then apply those characteristics to their own picture book biographies. Students will use a writer's notebook—*Writer's Notebook, Intermediate* (Fountas and Pinnell 2023), a composition book, or a spiral-bound notebook—to take notes and try out aspects of their writing before working on a draft, which they will keep in a writing folder. We recommend that you teach the minilessons in WPS.U4: Writer's Notebook: Becoming an Expert prior to these minilessons.

Use books from *Fountas & Pinnell Classroom™ Interactive Read-Aloud Collection* text sets Genre Study: Biography: Individuals Making a Difference and Biography: Artists (including the specific titles below) or biographies from the class or school library.

Interactive Read-Aloud Collection
Genre Study: Biography: Individuals Making a Difference

Farmer Will Allen and the Growing Table by Jacqueline Briggs Martin

Fly High! The Story of Bessie Coleman by Louise Borden and Mary Kay Kroeger

Six Dots: A Story of Young Louis Braille by Jen Bryant

Biography: Artists

Action Jackson by Jan Greenberg and Sandra Jordan

Mary Cassatt: Extraordinary Impressionist Painter by Barbara Herkert

As you read and enjoy picture book biographies together, help students

- notice the characteristics of picture book biographies,

- discuss how and why writers include certain information about a subject (e.g., setting, challenges, motivations, turning points, accomplishments), and

- think about how authors engage their readers.

Interactive Read-Aloud Genre Study:
Biography

Farmer Will Allen and the Growing Table by Jacqueline Briggs Martin

Biography: Artists

Writer's Notebook

Writing Minilesson Principle
Notice the qualities of good picture book biographies.

You Will Need

- familiar picture book biographies, such as those from Text Set: Genre Study: Biography: Individuals Making a Difference and Text Set: Biography: Artists, for the minilesson plus enough for each pair or small group
- chart paper and markers
- writer's notebooks

Academic Language / Important Vocabulary

- biography
- writer's notebook
- subject
- qualities

Continuum Connection

- Understand biography as a true account of a person's life
- Understand that a biography or an autobiography can be about the person's whole life or a part of it
- Understand that the writer of a biography or autobiography needs to select the most important events in a person's life
- Write various kinds of biographical texts by studying mentor texts

GOAL

Notice and name the characteristics of picture book biographies.

RATIONALE

When students read and study picture book biographies, they notice the characteristics of this type of writing. This will give them confidence to write their own picture book biographies, modeling them on those they have read.

WRITER'S NOTEBOOK/WRITING FOLDER

Have students make notes in their writer's notebooks about the qualities of good picture book biographies.

ASSESS LEARNING

- Observe for evidence of what students know about good picture book biographies.
- Look for evidence that students use the terms *biography*, *writer's notebook*, *subject*, and *qualities*.

MINILESSON

To help students think about the minilesson principle and how it applies to their own writing, engage them in an inquiry-based lesson around the qualities of good picture book biographies. Here is an example.

- Show the covers of several familiar picture book biographies.

  All of these books are biographies—books about someone's life written by someone else. How are these books alike? What do you notice about what the authors did to make these picture book biographies interesting to read?

- Record students' noticings on chart paper, generalizing them as necessary. You may need to prompt them with questions such as the following:

  - *How do you think the author decided on a subject—a person—to write about?*
  - *How did the author decide which events to include in the biography?*
  - *How did the author organize information about the subject?*
  - *How did the author show the importance of the setting?*
  - *Besides the words, how else do you get information from a biography?*

Have a Try

Invite students to talk to a partner about the qualities of good picture book biographies.

> What else have you noticed about picture book biographies that we can add to our chart? Turn and talk to your partner about this.

▶ After students turn and talk, invite several students to share. Write their responses on the chart.

Summarize and Apply

Summarize the learning and invite students to continue studying picture book biographies.

▶ Give each pair or group a picture book biography to study.

> During independent writing time, meet with your partner (group) to study the picture book biography I gave you. Discuss what you notice. Write "Good Picture Book Biographies" at the top of the next empty page in the last section of your writer's notebook so you can make a list of your observations. If you have time you can exchange books with other groups. Bring your notes when we come back together.

▶ Save the chart for WML5.

Picture book biographies ...

- tell the story of another person's life, or a part of it.
- include important things a person did and tell why that person is interesting.
- tell events from a person's life.
- usually tell events in the order they happened.
- use both words and pictures to share information about the time and place (setting).
- show what the person looks or looked like.
- tell about a person's challenges, motivations, and accomplishments.
- are about a person that is interesting to the author.
- sometimes include extra information at the end, like a bibliography or author's note.

Confer

▶ During independent writing, move around the room to confer briefly with pairs (groups) of students about picture book biographies. Use prompts such as the following as needed.

- *Who is the subject of this biography?*
- *How does the author make this person seem interesting?*
- *How does the author organize information about the person?*
- *How do the pictures help you better understand the person?*

Share

Following independent writing, gather students in the meeting area to share what they noticed.

> Turn to a new partner. Share the notes that you took about picture book biographies you studied.

Writing Minilesson Principle
Choose a subject for your biography, do research, and take notes.

Writing Picture Book Biographies

You Will Need

- a few familiar picture book biographies, such as the following from Text Set: Genre Study: Biography: Individuals Making a Difference:
  - *Fly High!* by Louise Borden and Mary Kay Kroeger
  - *Six Dots* by Jen Bryant
- a reference book or website about the subject of a biography you are researching
- chart paper and markers
- writer's notebooks

Academic Language / Important Vocabulary

- subject
- research
- notes
- bibliography

Continuum Connection

- Choose a subject and state a reason for the selection
- Use resources (print and online) to get information on a topic
- Use notes to record and organize information
- Search for appropriate information from multiple sources: e.g., books and other print materials, websites, interview

---

GOAL

Decide whom to write about and begin researching and taking notes.

RATIONALE

When you guide students to think about why authors choose to write about a subject and how they decide what information to include, they can consider whom they might want to write about and what part of the subject's life they will research.

WRITER'S NOTEBOOK/WRITING FOLDER

Have students make notes in their writer's notebooks about the subject of their picture book biographies.

ASSESS LEARNING

- Look for evidence that students understand how to research a subject and take notes.
- Look for evidence that students can use the terms *subject*, *notes*, *research*, and *bibliography*.

MINILESSON

Engage students in an inquiry-based lesson about how authors choose a subject for a picture book biography, decide what events are important to include, and select resources to research their subject. Here is an example.

- Show the covers of several familiar picture book biographies such as *Fly High!* and *Six Dots*.

  Why do you think the author chose this subject?

  What part of the subject's life did the author write about? Why do you think the author chose that part?

- As the conversation progresses, read and show author's notes and bibliographies.

  Notice the author's note and bibliography. What do these help you understand about how the author found information about the subject?

- Record the students' responses on chart paper. Then have students talk with a partner about ideas for the subject of a biography.

  Turn and talk to your partner about ideas you have for a person you'd like to make the subject of a picture book biography.

- Ask several students to share their ideas.

Have a Try

Invite students to talk to a partner about how they will research the subjects of their own biographies.

> As I learn about my subject, I won't write everything—just the important ideas. What is the most important information to take notes on about Bessie Coleman at a young age and her ambition? Turn and talk to your partner about this.

▶ After students turn and talk, invite a few pairs to share. Add notes to a new piece of chart paper.

> As I jot down important ideas, I close the book. I want the ideas to be written in my own words.

Summarize and Apply

Write the principle at the top of the first chart. Summarize the learning and invite students to discuss how they will research the subjects of their own biographies. They should take notes in their writer's notebooks.

> During independent writing time, begin to research a person that you find interesting. Jot down quick notes about what you are learning.

Confer

▶ During independent writing, move around the room to confer briefly with students about the information they have found so far. Use prompts such as the following as needed.

- *What makes your subject seem worth writing about?*
- *What parts of this person's life do you think you will include?*
- *What would be important to jot down in your writer's notebook?*

Share

Following independent writing, gather students in the meeting area.

> Turn and talk to your partner about the notes you took in your writer's notebook. Share who the subject is and the important events you jotted down.

Choose a subject for your biography, do research, and take notes.

The subject	Bessie Coleman	Louis Braille
The author may have chosen this subject because . . .	Bessie overcame an obstacle and fulfilled her dream of becoming a pilot.	Louis accomplished something important that helps blind people.
The author decided to include important moments like . . .	Bessie as a young girl in Texas events when Bessie was a young adult Bessie's early death (age 34)	Louis's early life: birth until age 15
The author found information about the subject by . . .	talking with Bessie's family members and researching at the library	reading books and researching on websites

Notes about Bessie Coleman at a young age

- Born in Texas
- Wanted to be in school
- Was a walker, counter, and dreamer

Notes about Young Bessie as a dreamer

- Moved to Chicago
- Got a job
- Heard stories of the women pilots in France

Umbrella 6: Writing Picture Book Biographies

Writing Minilesson Principle
Select and tell about the most important events or turning points in the person's life.

You Will Need

- a familiar picture book biography, such as *Mary Cassatt* by Barbara Herkert, from Text Set: Biography: Artists
- chart paper prepared with a few events from the first half of the book
- markers
- sticky notes in several colors
- writer's notebooks

Academic Language / Important Vocabulary

- biography
- motivation
- challenge
- turning point
- timeline

Continuum Connection

- Establish the significance of events and personal decisions made by the subject of a biography or autobiography
- Select important events and turning points to include and exclude extraneous events and details
- Describe the subject's important decisions and a turning point in the narrative
- When writing a biography, memoir, or fiction story, establish important decisions (made by the central character or subject) and the outcomes of those decisions

GOAL

Decide on, plan, and write about the most important events in the person's life.

RATIONALE

Authors decide which events from a subject's life to write about in a biography. Creating a chronological list of events from the subject's life that includes a subject's obstacles, motivations, turning points, and accomplishments will help student writers decide what to write about in their biographies.

WRITER'S NOTEBOOK/WRITING FOLDER

Have students list important events from the subject's life in their writer's notebooks. They can recreate the chart from the minilesson.

ASSESS LEARNING

- Notice whether students write about the most important events from a subject's life.
- Look for evidence that students can use the terms *biography*, *motivation*, *challenge*, *turning point*, and *timeline*.

MINILESSON

To help students understand how authors make decisions about which events from a subject's life to include in a biography, share and discuss a partial list of events from a familiar picture book biography. Engage students in a discussion about why the author included those events. Here is an example.

- Show the cover of a familiar picture book biography, such as *Mary Cassatt*.
- Display and review the prepared chart paper.

  Here are some events from Mary Cassatt's life in her biography. Why are they important?

  Would you say this event is a motivation, a challenge, a turning point, or an accomplishment in Mary Cassatt's life?

- Record students' responses on color-coded sticky notes on the chart.

  Notice that this biography is specifically about Mary Cassatt's desire to be an artist and what it took for her to become one, so the author didn't tell about her birth or death.

Have a Try

Invite students to talk to a partner about additional important events from the biography to add to the chart.

> Turn and talk to your partner about what from the second half of the biography we might add to the chart and why.

▸ After students turn and talk, invite several students to share their thinking. Add to the chart.

Summarize and Apply

Summarize the learning and invite students to list the important events in the life of their picture book biography subject in their writer's notebooks.

> What should you think about when you choose the events for your picture book biography?

▸ Write the principle at the top of the chart.

> Today, look at the notes you already have about your subject. Use them to create a list of important events in your writer's notebook. You could write the events to look like the ones on the chart, or you could put the events along a timeline. Then continue doing research and taking notes. Bring your work when we come back together.

Select and tell about the most important events or turning points in the person's life.		
Childhood Years	Mary Cassatt knew she would be an artist.	A motivation
	Girls were not encouraged to be artists.	A challenge
Teenage Years	She enrolled in art school.	A turning point
Young Adult Years	Mary went to Paris to study art. She dreamed her art would be in museums. Others said "Impossible."	A motivation
	Judges did not like her art.	A challenge
Adult Years	The artist Degas invited her to paint with him.	A turning point
	Mary's family went to live in Paris.	A turning point
Now	Her art hangs in museums. She proved that women can be artists.	An accomplishment

Confer

▸ During independent writing, move around the room to confer with students about the events for their picture book biographies. Use prompts such as the following as needed.

- *What challenges did the person face? Where will you put that in your biography?*
- *When did things begin to change for the person? What was the turning point? Where in the biography will that go?*
- *What did the person accomplish? Where will you write about that?*

Share

Following independent writing, gather students in pairs in the meeting area to share the work they have done so far on their picture book biographies.

> Turn to a partner. Share the events you listed in your writer's notebook. As the listener, share why you think your partner wrote down those ideas.

Writing Minilesson Principle
Show your ideas with pictures and words.

Writing Picture Book Biographies

You Will Need

- a familiar picture book biography, such as *Fly High!* by Louise Borden and Mary Kay Kroeger, from Text Set: Genre Study: Biography: Individuals Making a Difference
- document camera (optional)
- several sticky notes prepared in advance, some with a *W* (for words) and some with a *P* (for pictures)
- chart paper and markers
- writer's notebooks

Academic Language / Important Vocabulary

- subject
- pictures
- words
- decisions

Continuum Connection

- Use drawings to add information to, elaborate on, or increase readers' enjoyment and understanding
- Create drawings that are related to the written text and increase readers' understanding and enjoyment
- Understand that when both writing and drawing are on a page, they are mutually supportive, with each extending the other
- Provide important information in the illustrations

GOAL

Make decisions about which ideas to communicate in pictures and which to communicate in words.

RATIONALE

When students look at the decisions authors make about what to say in the words and what to show in the illustrations of picture book biographies, they can start to apply this kind of thinking to their own biography writing.

WRITER'S NOTEBOOK/WRITING FOLDER

Have students review the notes they've taken in their writer's notebooks to decide what to express through illustrations and what through words.

ASSESS LEARNING

- Observe for evidence that students make thoughtful decisions about what to include in the words and pictures of their picture book biographies.
- Look for evidence that students can use the terms *subject*, *words*, *pictures*, and *decisions*.

MINILESSON

Students will need their writer's notebooks for this lesson. Help students notice authors' decisions about what information to include in words and what to show in illustrations. Engage them in an inquiry-based lesson around how authors make these decisions. Here is an example.

- Show and read pages 7–8 in *Fly High!* where Bessie and her family are picking cotton.

  Listen carefully and study the pictures as I read these two pages.

  What did you learn about Bessie Coleman from these pages?

- Record on the chart information that students notice in the words and in the pictures.

  How did you learn that information?

  Notice that some of the information is in the words, some is in the pictures, and some is in both.

- Invite volunteers to come up and place the appropriate sticky note or notes (*W* for words, *P* for pictures, or both) on the chart.

  Turn and talk to a partner. How do you think authors make decisions about what to include in the words and what to include in the pictures?

- After students turn and talk, invite several students to share their thinking.

Have a Try

Invite students to talk to a partner about what information they will tell in the words or show in the pictures and why.

Look at the notes you wrote about your subject in your writer's notebook. Choose one or two ideas to talk about with your partner. Explain whether you will use words, pictures, or both to convey that information to your readers. Write a *W*, a *P*, or both *W* and *P* next to your notes.

Summarize and Apply

Summarize the learning and invite students to continue discussing making decisions about what to include in the words and pictures in a picture book biography.

How can you give information to the readers of your picture book biographies?

▷ Write the principle at the top of the chart.

Today during independent writing time, continue working through your notes, deciding what to include in the pictures and words of your biography. You can always change your mind later. If you have more time, do more research and add notes to your writer's notebook. Bring your notebook when we meet later.

Show your ideas with pictures and words.

W	Bessie had to miss school to pick cotton.
W	The cotton fields were in Texas.
P	Women and girls picked cotton together.
P	They put the cotton into bags hanging on their shoulders.
P W	Bessie wrote down how much each bag weighed.
W P	Bessie checked the white foreman's numbers.
W	Picking cotton was more important to the town than going to school.

Words
What is important to understand about the subject, what happens in the story

Pictures
General information about the setting—what the reader needs to understand about the time and the place—and how the characters look.

Confer

▷ During independent writing, move around the room to confer with students about their decisions about words and pictures. Use prompts such as the following as needed.

- *Will that piece of information help your readers understand your subject? Would that information best be shared in the words or the pictures?*

- *Does that information help your readers understand the setting of the subject's life? Would that information best be shared in the words or the pictures?*

Share

Following independent writing, gather students in the meeting area. Assign them to small groups, possibly organized by the time period of their picture book biographies.

Take turns talking about the notes you have taken about your subject and the decisions you have made about what to include in the words and pictures.

Writing Minilesson Principle

Show how the setting is important in the life of the subject.

Writing Picture Book Biographies

You Will Need

- a familiar picture book biography, such as *Fly High!* by Louise Borden and Mary Kay Kroeger, from Text Set: Genre Study: Biography: Individuals Making a Difference
- chart paper and markers
- writer's notebooks
- chart from WML1
- To download the following online resource for this lesson, visit **fp.pub/resources**:
  - chart art (optional)

Academic Language / Important Vocabulary

- biography
- subject
- setting
- details

Continuum Connection

- Understand that the setting may be important in a narrative nonfiction text
- Use concrete sensory details and descriptive language to develop plot (tension and problem resolution) and setting in memoir, biography, and fiction
- Try out titles, different headings and endings, and develop setting and characters in a writer's notebook

GOAL

Understand that writers of biographies include important details of the setting.

RATIONALE

When student writers explore how published authors include the time and place of the life of the subject in a biography, they can begin to think about how the setting impacted the subject's motivations, challenges, and accomplishments. This will help students learn how to make decisions about what details of the setting to include in their own picture book biographies and how to include those details.

WRITER'S NOTEBOOK/WRITING FOLDER

Have students use their writer's notebooks to try out and sketch ideas they will include about the setting that are important to the subject of their picture book biographies.

ASSESS LEARNING

- Confer with students to hear how they are thinking about the impact of the setting on a subject's motivations and accomplishments and how they plan to portray this.
- Look for evidence that students use the terms *biography*, *subject*, *setting*, and *details*.

MINILESSON

Guide students to study the words and illustrations of picture book biographies, focusing on the details of the setting that the authors chose to include. Engage students in an inquiry-based lesson about why and how the authors portrayed those details. Here is an example.

- Show the cover and read a few pages from *Fly High!* that describe the setting.

  What do you notice about the details of the setting that the authors included in this biography?

- Record the students' noticings on chart paper. Sort them into two columns, depending on how the information is given (in words or in pictures). Do not label the columns yet.

  How did the authors share those details?

- Add the labels *Words* and *Pictures* to the chart.

  What kind of information is better conveyed in words? in pictures?

- Record ideas next to *Words* and *Pictures*.

  How do the details help you understand Bessie Coleman?

- Record ideas on the chart and label that section *Why is the setting important?*

The Writing Minilessons Book, Grade 4

Have a Try

Invite students to talk to a partner about how the setting is important in their own picture book biographies.

> How is the setting of your subject's life important? What details will you include in the words and pictures in your book? Turn and talk to your partner about this.

Summarize and Apply

Summarize the learning. Invite students to begin taking notes on setting in their writer's notebooks.

> Why is it important to know about the setting in a biography?

▶ Write the principle at the top of the chart. Display the WML1 chart of qualities of picture book biographies as students begin writing.

> Today during independent writing time, think about the setting as you gather more notes about the subject of your biography. If time allows and you are ready, use your notes to start writing your biography. Remember that the subject's life is usually told in time order. Refer to the list of the qualities of good picture book biographies as you write.

Show how the setting is important in the life of the subject.

Fly High! The Story of Bessie Coleman

Words—specific information related to the subject	Pictures—general information related to the time and place
• A hundred years ago	• Log cabins with smoke coming from chimneys
• Texas, Chicago, France	• Cotton fields
• Fall of 1919	• Record player
• Walked 4 miles to school	• Old-time phone
• Streetcars, trains	• Old-fashioned clothes and cars
• Sailed to France	

Why is the setting important?
- The setting was a long time ago before the modern conveniences we know now.
- The setting was a time and place where life was challenging for girls, especially for Black girls.
- The author helped us understand how Bessie overcame these challenges.

Confer

▶ During independent writing, move around the room to confer briefly with students about the setting of their picture book biographies. Use prompts such as the following as needed.

- *What details of the setting are important to include in your biography?*
- *What words will you use to describe the setting? Will you include that in your pictures?*
- *How does the setting impact the subject? How will you explain that?*

Share

Following independent writing, gather students in pairs in the meeting area. Try to pair students who have begun writing their biography with students still working on notes. Ask a few pairs to share how and what they decided to include about setting.

> If you have started writing, read your work to your partner. Your partner will listen for information about the setting. If you are still working on your notes, talk to your partner about some of the details you plan to include about the setting and why.

Section 2: Genres and Forms

Writing Minilesson Principle
Use quotes from real people to show something about the subject.

You Will Need

▶ several familiar picture book biographies, such as the following:

- *Farmer Will Allen and the Growing Table* by Jacqueline Briggs Martin, from Text Set: Genre Study: Biography: Individuals Making a Difference

- *Action Jackson* by Jan Greenberg and Sandra Jordan, from Text Set: Biography: Artists

▶ chart paper prepared in advance with text excerpts

▶ highlighters and markers

▶ writer's notebooks and writing folders

▶ document camera (optional)

Academic Language / Important Vocabulary

▶ biography

▶ subject

▶ quotes

Continuum Connection

▶ Use commas and quotation marks correctly in writing interrupted and uninterrupted dialogue as well as to show a verbatim quote

▶ Understand the concept of plagiarism

▶ Understand that a writer gains ideas from other writers but should credit the other writers and/or put those ideas into one's own words

GOAL

Decide which quotes from an author could be included to show something about the subject.

RATIONALE

Authors think carefully about the words they choose to describe the subject of a biography. Studying authors' words and utilizing some exact quotes from their books support student writers in understanding that the words of others can help create an understanding of the challenges and accomplishments of the subject of their own picture book biography.

WRITER'S NOTEBOOK/WRITING FOLDER

Students can add a quote to the draft of their writing, or they might decide to record a quote in their writer's notebooks to save for later.

ASSESS LEARNING

▶ Notice if students correctly write direct quotes in their own writing.

▶ Look for evidence that students use the terms *biography*, *subject*, and *quotes*.

MINILESSON

To help students think about the minilesson principle and how it applies to their own writing, engage them in an inquiry-based lesson and demonstration of researching and selecting a quote that tells more about the subject of a biography. Here is an example.

> When you research the subject of a picture book biography, you make decisions about which important information to include in your writing.

▶ Show the cover of a familiar picture book biography, such as *Farmer Will Allen and the Growing Table*. Read the prepared excerpt aloud. Guide students to select a quote. Highlight the chosen words.

> Listen as I read. What exact words would help a reader understand Will Allen better? What do those words show you about him?

▶ Discuss using proper punctuation and quotation marks when using a direct quote in one's own writing. Remind students that the period at the end of the quotation goes inside the closing quotation mark.

> Sometimes writers borrow words from other writers to show something important about the subject. This is called a quote. When writers use quotes, they need to copy the words and punctuation exactly and let readers know that these are the words of another author. To do that they put quotation marks around the exact words they are borrowing and also show where they found them.

> Sometimes you will write your own words to introduce the quote.

Have a Try

Invite students to repeat this process with a partner using another text, such as *Action Jackson*. Read a page aloud.

> Which part of this page might you borrow as a quote for a biography about Jackson Pollock? Why? How would you write that in your own book? Turn and talk to your partner about this.

▶ After students turn and talk, invite a few pairs to share their thinking, highlighting the words on the chart. Next, demonstrate writing your own words and then the quote.

Summarize and Apply

Summarize the learning and invite students to begin researching quotes.

> What are you thinking about using quotes?

▶ Write the principle at the top of the chart.

> Today as you read about the subject of your biography, think about which words you might borrow. Be sure to correctly punctuate the quote. If you are not sure where to put it, write it in your writer's notebook to use later. Be sure to write where you found the quote—the book title and page number. Bring your work when we meet later.

Use quotes from real people to show something about the subject.

What could you quote to tell more about the subject?	How will the quote look in your book?
Will is always looking for new ways to make the table bigger—more schoolyard plots, a vertical farm that's five stories high, farms in empty factories or warehouses. Will Allen dreams of a day when city farms are as common as streetlights, and every table is covered with good food.	Will Allen had big hopes for farming. "Will Allen dreams of a day when city farms are as common as streetlights, and every table is covered with good food."
Some artists put a canvas on an easel or hang it on a wall. Not Jackson. He spreads his out like a sheet, smoothing it flat with his large hands. He wants his paintings to be big, big as the sky out West where he grew up, flat as the marshland behind the house.	Jackson didn't use an easel. He put his canvas on the floor because he wanted "his paintings to be big, big as the sky out West where he grew up, flat as the marshland behind the house."

Confer

▶ During independent writing, move around the room to confer briefly with students about using direct quotes. Use prompts such as the following as needed.

- *What are you learning about the subject of your biography? What words might you borrow from another author to show that?*

- *How would you write the quote in your own book?*

- *Let's look at the chart we made to remember how to write a quote.*

Share

Following independent writing, gather students in the meeting area. Share the writing of one or two students who used quotes in their writing. Use a document camera, if available.

> Turn to your partner. Why did this writer decide to borrow another author's (or the subject's) words? Notice how the writer punctuated the quote.

Assessment

After you have taught the minilessons in this umbrella, observe students as they explore making books. Use *The Fountas & Pinnell Literacy Continuum* to notice, teach for, and support students' learning as you observe their attempts at writing picture book biographies.

▶ What evidence do you have of students' new understandings related to writing picture book biographies?

- Can students identify qualities of good picture book biographies?
- Did they understand how to choose a subject for a biography, do research, and take notes?
- Were students able to choose the most important events and turning points in the subject's life?
- Do they understand how the setting is important in understanding the life of a person?
- Are students confident deciding what information to share in the words and what to share in the pictures of their picture book biographies?
- Do students understand how to use quotes?
- Do students understand and use vocabulary such as *biography*, *subject*, *notes*, *research*, *setting*, and *quotes*?

▶ In what other ways, beyond the scope of this umbrella, are students ready to explore writing picture book biographies?

- Do they need support in drawing people?
- Are they showing an interest in creating multimedia presentations?

Use your observations to determine the next umbrella you will teach. You may also consult Suggested Sequence of Lessons (pp. 665–682) for guidance.

EXTENSIONS FOR WRITING PICTURE BOOK BIOGRAPHIES

▶ Teach students how to list their sources in a bibliography.

▶ Some students may be ready to research the subject of a biography using school-approved websites.

▶ Video interviews with subjects of biographies might be of interest to some writers. Support students in finding and listening to an interview and taking notes on the interview (see p. 68 in *Writer's Notebook, Intermediate*).

Minilessons in This Umbrella

WML1   Notice the qualities of good realistic fiction stories.

WML2   Use a story arc to plan the plot of your story.

WML3   Make your characters believable.

WML4   Think about what the main character learns.

Before Teaching Umbrella 7 Minilessons

Students stretch their imaginations when they have opportunities to experiment with writing both realistic fiction and fantasy stories. Students love to write fantasy stories, and we should make time and space to listen to and honor those stories to build students' engagement, writing identities, and stamina for writing. However, we recommend spending instructional time in minilessons on teaching realistic fiction because the students will be able to build on their experiences of writing other narrative texts, such as memoirs. Students can use some of the lessons from this umbrella to support them in writing fantasy stories as well as realistic fiction stories.

We want the process of writing realistic fiction to be authentic and individual for each writer, but it is helpful to offer students planning tools for their writing. Some students may find a story arc helpful in planning their stories (WML2). Any idea on a list or web in students' writer's notebooks can serve as a spark for a story idea. Students should be encouraged to use their writer's notebooks as a place to try out elements of their stories.

Read and discuss a variety of realistic fiction stories with students. Use the following texts from *Fountas & Pinnell Classroom™ Interactive Read-Aloud Collection* or any other realistic fiction stories.

Interactive Read-Aloud Collection

Figuring Out Who You Are

The Junkyard Wonders by Patricia Polacco

Empathy

The Boy and the Whale by Mordicai Gerstein

Author/Illustrator Study: Allen Say

The Lost Lake

As you read and enjoy these and other realistic fiction texts together, help students

- notice the characteristics of realistic fiction stories,
- discuss how the author describes the characters, and
- explain what the main character learns.

Interactive Read-Aloud
Figuring Out Who You Are

Empathy

Allen Say

Writer's Notebook

Writing Minilesson Principle
Notice the qualities of good realistic fiction stories.

Writing Realistic Fiction Stories

You Will Need

- a familiar realistic fiction book for each small group
- a familiar realistic fiction book inspired by real events, such as *The Junkyard Wonders* by Patricia Polacco, from Text Set: Figuring Out Who You Are
- chart paper and markers
- writer's notebooks

Academic Language / Important Vocabulary

- realistic fiction
- quality
- character
- setting
- problem

Continuum Connection

- Understand that an additional purpose of a fiction text is to explore a theme or teach a lesson
- Understand that a fiction text may involve one or more events in the life of a main character
- Understand that a writer uses various elements of fiction (e.g., setting, plot with problem and solution, characters) in a fiction text
- Understand that writers can learn to craft fiction by using mentor texts as models

GOAL

Study mentor texts to notice the qualities of good realistic fiction.

RATIONALE

Writers learn from other writers. By studying realistic fiction, students will be better prepared and equipped to begin writing their own realistic fiction. They will model their own stories on those they have read.

WRITER'S NOTEBOOK/WRITING FOLDER

Have students look through their writer's notebooks to choose an idea for a story.

ASSESS LEARNING

- Notice whether students can identify and name the qualities of good realistic fiction.
- Look for evidence that they can use vocabulary such as *realistic fiction, quality, character, setting, and problem.*

MINILESSON

To help students think about the principle, engage them in an inquiry-based lesson on the qualities of realistic fiction stories. Here is an example.

- Show the covers of several familiar realistic fiction books.

    We have read and talked about these realistic fiction books together. Why do you think they're called realistic fiction?

- Divide students into small groups, and give each group one realistic fiction book. Direct students to look through their book and discuss what they notice about it.

    What did you notice about your book? What makes a good realistic fiction story?

- Record students' responses on chart paper, generalizing them as necessary. As needed, prompt students' thinking with questions such as the following:
    - *What did you notice about the characters in your book?*
    - *What did you notice about the setting, or where the story takes place?*
    - *What did you notice about the kinds of problems the characters in your realistic fiction book faced?*
    - *How did the author of your book make the story seem real?*
    - *How does your book end? Do the characters learn anything?*

Have a Try

Invite students to talk to a partner about their ideas for realistic fiction.

▶ Read the back flap of *The Junkyard Wonders*.

> Where did Patricia Polacco get the idea to write this book?

> This is a fiction book, so the author made up many of the characters and events in the story, but she was inspired by her own childhood experiences. Can you think of anything that has happened in your life or the life of someone you know that would make a good idea for a realistic fiction story? Turn and talk to your partner about your ideas.

▶ After students turn and talk, invite several students to share their ideas.

Summarize and Apply

Write the principle at the top of the chart. Summarize the learning and invite students to think further about their own experiences for ideas.

> During independent writing time today, look through your writer's notebook to find an idea that you could turn into a realistic fiction story. Remember that realistic fiction stories usually have a problem and a solution. Circle ideas you could use. Bring your ideas to share when we come back together.

Confer

▶ During independent writing, move around the room to confer briefly with students about their ideas for realistic fiction. Use prompts such as the following as needed.

- *What could you write a realistic fiction story about? Who would be the main character?*
- *What problem will the main character face? What will happen in the story? How will the problem be solved?*

Share

Following independent writing, gather students in the meeting area to share their ideas.

> Did anyone think of an experience that you could turn into a realistic fiction story?

> What will be the problem and solution in your story?

Notice the qualities of good realistic fiction stories.

- The author makes up the characters and settings, but they seem like they could be real.
- The main character usually faces a problem that is similar to problems people have in real life.
- The author uses powerful, descriptive words and phrases to help you picture the characters, settings, and events.
- The problem is usually solved by the end of the story.
- The main character often learns an important lesson by the end of the story.

Section 2: Genres and Forms

Writing Minilesson Principle
Use a story arc to plan the plot of your story.

You Will Need

- a familiar realistic fiction book with a traditional plot structure, such as *The Boy and the Whale* by Mordicai Gerstein, from Text Set: Empathy

- chart paper prepared with a blank story arc

- markers

- writer's notebooks and writing folders

- To download the following online resource for this lesson, visit **fp.pub/resources**:
  - Story Arc

Academic Language / Important Vocabulary

- plot
- story arc

Continuum Connection

- Understand the structure of narrative, including lead or beginning, introduction of characters, setting, problem, series of events

- Develop a plot that includes tension and one or more scenes

- Write fiction and nonfiction narratives that are ordered chronologically

- Develop a logical plot by creating a story problem and addressing it over multiple events until it is resolved

- Use sketching, webs, lists, and freewriting to think about, plan for, and try out writing

GOAL

Use a story arc to plan the plot of a realistic fiction story.

RATIONALE

Using a story arc to plan a realistic fiction story can help students develop a well-structured plot including a clearly stated problem, rising action, a climax, falling action, and a conclusion. When students learn that writers often use tools, such as a story arc, to help with planning, they begin to try out different tools and learn which ones work best for them.

WRITER'S NOTEBOOK/WRITING FOLDER

Have students glue a story arc graphic organizer into their writer's notebooks. Students can do their planning in their writer's notebooks before writing a draft on draft paper, which will be kept in their writing folders.

ASSESS LEARNING

- Observe whether students try out using a story arc to plan their realistic fiction writing.
- Look for evidence that they can use vocabulary such as *plot* and *story arc*.

MINILESSON

Before teaching this lesson, be sure that students know what they will write about. To help students think about the minilesson principle, use a familiar realistic fiction book to model how to use a story arc to plan a realistic fiction story. Here is an example.

▶ Show the prepared blank story arc.

> A story arc is a tool that you can use to plan your realistic fiction writing. What do you notice about the shape of this diagram?

> The first part shows the main character, the setting, and the problem, which are introduced early in a story. The next part shows events as they rise toward the high point, where the character solves the problem. The last part falls as the story wraps up.

▶ Show the cover of *The Boy and the Whale*. With students' input, model filling in the story arc with details of the book's plot. Ask questions such as the following:

- *Who is the main character in this story? What is the setting?*
- *What problem does Abelardo have?*
- *What happens early in the story? What happens next? What happens after that?*
- *What do you think is the most exciting moment in this story?*
- *What happens right after that? What events help wrap up the story?*
- *How does the story end? What do the characters learn or realize?*

Have a Try

Invite students to start filling in a story arc to plan a realistic fiction story.

▶ Hand out copies of the story arc graphic organizer for students to glue into their writer's notebooks.

> You can use a story arc to plan your own realistic fiction stories. What is the problem in your story? What will be the most exciting moment? Fill out these boxes in your story arc. Then turn and talk to share what you wrote with your partner. You will fill out the rest of the story arc later.

Summarize and Apply

Help students summarize the learning and invite them to finish filling in their story arcs.

> How do you think a story arc could help you plan the plot of a story?

> During independent writing time, think about the problem in your story, how the events will build up to the most exciting moment, what will happen after that, and how the story will end. Finish filling out your story arc. When you finish it, begin writing your story. Put your draft in your writing folder. Bring your story arc when we meet later.

Story Arc

Events
- Abelardo and Papa argue about saving the whale or the net.
- Abelardo decides to save whale.

High Point
Abelardo frees the whale.

Wrap Up
The whale does a celebratory dance.

Problem
A whale is stuck in a net, and Abelardo wants to save it.

Ending
Papa says Abelardo was both foolish and brave.

Main character:
Abelardo
Setting:
Beach/ocean

Confer

▶ During independent writing, move around the room to confer briefly with students about their realistic fiction stories. Use prompts such as the following as needed.

- *What information will you put at the beginning of your story?*
- *What problem does your main character have?*
- *What events will happen when the main character tries to solve the problem?*
- *How will your story end? Does the main character learn anything?*

Share

Following independent writing, gather students in the meeting area to share their story arcs.

> Who would like to share your story arc?

> Did you find it helpful to use a story arc to plan your story? Why or why not?

Writing Realistic Fiction Stories

You Will Need

- a familiar realistic fiction book, such as *The Junkyard Wonders* by Patricia Polacco, from Text Set: Figuring Out Who You Are
- chart paper and markers
- writer's notebooks and writing folders

Academic Language / Important Vocabulary

- realistic fiction
- character
- believable

Continuum Connection

- Show the problem of the story and how one or more characters respond to it
- Describe characters by how they look, what they do, say, and think, and what others say about them
- Show rather than tell how characters feel

GOAL

Describe characters in a way that makes them seem real.

RATIONALE

When students notice how authors of realistic fiction develop and describe characters, they begin to understand how to create believable characters in their own stories, and they are more likely to write stories with consistent, well-developed characters.

WRITER'S NOTEBOOK/WRITING FOLDER

Students will work on their drafts from their writing folders. They may find it helpful to sketch or jot notes about their characters in their writer's notebooks before writing about them.

ASSESS LEARNING

- Notice whether students are creating believable characters in their realistic fiction writing.
- Look for evidence that they can use vocabulary such as *realistic fiction*, *character*, and *believable.*

MINILESSON

To help students think about the principle, use mentor texts to engage them in an inquiry-based lesson on how authors make characters seem believable. Here is an example.

- Show the cover of *The Junkyard Wonders* and read the title. Reread the first few pages of the book.

  Who is the main character in this book?

  What do you know about Trisha?

  What does she look like?

  What is she like on the inside? What kind of a person is she?

  What does she think about or feel?

- Using students' responses, sketch the main character and write some notes about her on chart paper.

  Does Trisha seem like a real person? Why or why not?

  How does the author make her seem real?

- Record responses on the chart, generalizing them as necessary.

Have a Try

Invite students to talk to a partner about their own main characters.

> Think about the main character in the realistic fiction story you're working on. What is the character like? How will you make the character seem like a real person? Turn and talk to your partner about your ideas.

▶ After students turn and talk, invite a few students to share their ideas with the class.

Summarize and Apply

Write the principle at the top of the chart. Help students summarize the learning, and remind them to make their characters believable.

> Why is it important for realistic fiction authors to make their characters believable?

> Today during independent writing time, continue working on your realistic fiction story. Remember to use what you learned today about making your characters believable. You may find it helpful to sketch and write some notes about your main character in your writer's notebook.

Make your characters believable.

Trisha

Usually lives in California with Mom

Likes to dance and draw

Moves to Michigan to live with Dad and Gramma

Worries about what others think about her

Worries about making friends at new school

Is sad when classmate dies

Believable characters . . .
- do things that real people do.
- talk like real people.
- look like real people.
- have the same thoughts, feelings, worries, and fears as real people.

Confer

▶ During independent writing, move around the room to confer briefly with students about writing realistic fiction. Use prompts such as the following as needed.

- *Who is the main character in your story?*
- *How does the character look?*
- *What is the character like on the inside?*
- *How can you make the character seem like a real person?*

Share

Following independent writing, gather students in the meeting area to talk about their main characters.

> Turn and talk to a partner about the main character in your story. Describe what your character is like on the inside and the outside.

Writing Minilesson Principle
Think about what the main character learns.

Writing Realistic Fiction Stories

You Will Need

- a couple of familiar realistic fiction books in which the main character learns something, such as the following:
  - *The Junkyard Wonders* by Patricia Polacco, from Text Set: Figuring Out Who You Are
  - *The Lost Lake*, from Text Set: Author/Illustrator Study: Allen Say
- chart paper and markers
- writing folders

Academic Language / Important Vocabulary

- realistic fiction
- main character

Continuum Connection

- Understand that an additional purpose of a fiction text is to explore a theme or teach a lesson
- Show rather than tell how characters feel

GOAL

Understand how to show that a character learns a lesson in a realistic fiction story.

RATIONALE

When you help students to notice that main characters in realistic fiction often learn a lesson and to understand how authors show that learning through thoughts, dialogue, and action, students will begin to create characters that show personal growth in their own realistic fiction stories. As a result, their characters will be richer and more believable.

WRITER'S NOTEBOOK/WRITING FOLDER

Students will work on the drafts of realistic fiction stories that are in their writing folders.

ASSESS LEARNING

- Notice how well students create characters that learn a lesson and how well they convey that change clearly.
- Look for evidence that they can use vocabulary such as *realistic fiction* and *main character*.

MINILESSON

To help students think about the principle, use mentor texts to engage them in an inquiry-based lesson around how authors of realistic fiction show that a character learns something. Here is an example.

- Show the cover of *The Junkyard Wonders* and read the title. Read the last few pages of the story and the author's note.

  What does Trisha learn by the end of the story?

  How does the author show that Trisha has learned something?

- Record responses on chart paper, generalizing as necessary.
- Show the cover of *The Lost Lake*. Read pages 28–32.

  What does Luke learn in this story?

  How does the author show this?

- Record responses on the chart.

Have a Try

Invite students to talk to a partner about their own characters.

> Think about the story you're working on. Does the main character in your story learn something? If so, what? How will you show this in your writing? Turn and talk to your partner about your ideas.

Summarize and Apply

Write the principle at the top of the chart. Summarize the learning and remind students to think about whether their main character learns something.

> During independent writing time today, continue working on your realistic fiction story. Remember to think about whether your main character learns something and, if so, how you can show that. Bring your writing to share when we meet later.

Think about what the main character learns.		
Book	What the Main Character Learns	How the Author Shows This
The Junkyard Wonders	• Being "normal" does not make you smarter or better than others. • Everyone can achieve greatness.	• The main character's thoughts • What the other characters say • The author's note
The Lost Lake	• Spending time with family makes you feel close. • Sometimes silence is best.	• The main character's thoughts

Confer

▶ During independent writing, move around the room to confer briefly with students about their realistic fiction stories. Use prompts such as the following as needed.

- *Does the main character in your story learn something? What is it?*
- *How will your readers know that the character learns something?*
- *What might other characters say that show that the main character learns something?*

Share

Following independent writing, gather students in the meeting area to talk about their writing.

> Who would like to share what the main character learns in your story?

> How did you show that the character has learned that? Would you like to read aloud what you wrote?

Assessment

After you have taught the minilessons in this umbrella, observe students as they write and talk about their writing. Use *The Fountas & Pinnell Literacy Continuum* to notice, teach for, and support students' learning as you observe their writing development.

▶ What evidence do you have of students' new understandings related to writing realistic fiction stories?

- Can students identify the characteristics of good realistic fiction stories?
- Have they tried using a story arc to plan their writing?
- Do they write about characters that are believable?
- Do their main characters show evidence of personal growth?
- Do they understand and use vocabulary such as *realistic fiction*, *quality*, *character*, and *believable*?

▶ In what other ways, beyond the scope of this umbrella, are students exploring writing fiction?

- Would they benefit from learning more about describing characters or settings?
- Are they experimenting with interesting word choices?

Use your observations to determine the next umbrella you will teach. You may also consult Suggested Sequence of Lessons (pp. 665–682) for guidance.

EXTENSIONS FOR WRITING REALISTIC FICTION STORIES

▶ Pull together a small, temporary guided writing group of students who need support in a similar area of their writing, such as planning and writing a realistic fiction story.

▶ Use umbrellas in the Craft section, such as CFT.U2: Describing Characters and CFT.U3: Crafting a Setting, to help students explore different aspects of writing fiction in greater depth.

▶ Use shared writing to help students explore various aspects of writing fiction collaboratively before doing so independently.

▶ Suggest that students write alternative versions of their favorite stories (for example, by changing the ending of a familiar story, writing a sequel, or placing the main character in a different situation).

▶ Download rubrics from the online resources (fp.pub/resources) to help you and your students evaluate how well they are able to apply the concepts in these lessons.

Minilessons in This Umbrella

WML1	Notice the qualities of good fairy tales.
WML2	Think about the elements of magic you will include in your fairy tale.
WML3	Make character sketches to determine character traits.
WML4	Use a storyboard to plan the plot of your story.

Before Teaching Umbrella 8 Minilessons

For this umbrella, you might have students write their own original fairy tales or a new version of a traditional tale (e.g., Cinderella). Although we want students to develop and follow their own individual ways of writing, some might find it helpful to use planning tools such as a storyboard (WML4) to plan their fairy tales. Students should be encouraged to use their writer's notebooks as a place to try out ideas for and elements of their fairy tales.

Read and discuss with students a variety of fairy tales reflecting different cultures, traditions, and time periods, including different versions of the same tale. Use the following texts from *Fountas & Pinnell Classroom™ Interactive Read-Aloud Collection* or any other fairy tales that your students may enjoy.

Interactive Read-Aloud Collection

Genre Study: Fairy Tales

Rumpelstiltskin by Paul O. Zelinsky

Beauty and the Beast by Jan Brett

The Dragon Prince: A Chinese Beauty and the Beast Tale by Laurence Yep

Brave Red, Smart Frog: A New Book of Old Tales by Emily Jenkins

The Twelve Dancing Princesses by Rachel Isadora

Cinderella Stories

Yeh-Shen: A Cinderella Story from China by Ai-Ling Louie

Sootface: An Ojibwa Cinderella Story by Robert D. San Souci

Cendrillon: A Caribbean Cinderella by Robert D. San Souci

The Persian Cinderella by Shirley Climo

Domitíla: A Cinderella Tale from the Mexican Tradition by Jewell Reinhart Coburn

The Rough-Face Girl by Rafe Martin

As you read and enjoy these texts together, help students notice common elements of fairy tales.

Interactive Read-Aloud Fairy Tales

Cinderella

Writer's Notebook

Section 2: Genres and Forms

Writing Minilesson Principle
Notice the qualities of good fairy tales.

Writing Fairy Tales

You Will Need

- several familiar fairy tales, such as those in Text Set: Genre Study: Fairy Tales and Text Set: Cinderella Stories
- a familiar fairy tale book for each small group
- chart paper and markers
- writer's notebooks

Academic Language / Important Vocabulary

- fairy tale
- quality
- character
- magic

Continuum Connection

- Understand that a writer uses various elements of fiction (e.g., setting, plot with problem and solution, characters) in a fiction text
- Use the terms *realistic fiction, historical fiction, folktale, tall tale, fairy tale, fable, myth, legend, fantasy,* and *science fiction* to describe the genre
- Understand that writers can learn to craft fiction by using mentor texts as models

GOAL

Study mentor texts to notice the qualities of fairy tales and to learn how to craft them.

RATIONALE

By studying and identifying the shared characteristics of familiar fairy tales, students will be better prepared and equipped to begin writing their own fairy tales. They will model their own tales on those they have read.

WRITER'S NOTEBOOK/WRITING FOLDER

Have students begin exploring ideas for fairy tales in their writer's notebooks.

ASSESS LEARNING

- Notice whether students can identify and name the qualities of fairy tales.
- Look for evidence that they can use vocabulary such as *fairy tale, quality, character,* and *magic.*

MINILESSON

To help students think about the principle, engage them in an inquiry-based lesson on the qualities of fairy tales. Here is an example.

- Show the covers of several familiar fairy tales.

  What kind of stories are these?

  These stories are all fairy tales. What is a fairy tale?

- Divide students into small groups, giving each group one fairy tale to study. Direct students to look through their fairy tale and discuss what they notice.

  What did you notice about your book? What makes it a fairy tale?

- Record students' responses on chart paper, generalizing them as necessary. As needed, prompt students' thinking with questions such as the following:

  - *How are fairy tales different from realistic fiction stories?*
  - *What are fairy tales often about?*
  - *What happens in fairy tales that could not happen in real life?*
  - *Do the characters in fairy tales seem like real people? Why or why not?*
  - *How do fairy tales usually end?*
  - *What have you noticed about the language used in fairy tales? Do the authors use any similar words or phrases?*
  - *We have read different versions of the same fairy tale. How are they different?*

Have a Try

Invite students to talk to a partner about their ideas for fairy tales.

> Sometimes authors write an entirely new fairy tale. Other times they might write a new version of an old fairy tale. What could you write a fairy tale about? You could write a new version of your favorite fairy tale or make up a new fairy tale. Turn and talk to your partner about your ideas.

Summarize and Apply

Write the principle at the top of the chart. Summarize the learning and invite students to explore ideas for fairy tales.

> During independent writing time today, think about what you noticed when you have read and enjoyed fairy tales. Then think about your own ideas for fairy tales. Write your ideas for fairy tales in your writer's notebook, and bring them to share when we come back together.

> ### Notice the qualities of good fairy tales.
>
> - Fairy tales are stories about people and things that could not happen in real life.
> - They have simple characters that are either good or bad and seldom change.
> - They include elements of magic or the supernatural.
> - They often include romance or adventure.
> - Good usually triumphs over evil.
> - They reflect the values and traditions of the author's culture.
> - They often include similar language, such as "once upon a time."

Confer

▶ During independent writing, move around the room to confer briefly with students about their ideas for fairy tales. Use prompts such as the following as needed.

- *What could you write a fairy tale about?*
- *What is your favorite fairy tale? What would you change to write a new version of it?*
- *How will your readers know that your story is a fairy tale?*

Share

Following independent writing, gather students in the meeting area. Ask each student to briefly share an idea for a fairy tale. Allow students to pass if they have not thought of an idea yet.

> Let's go around the circle so that each of you can share an idea for a fairy tale.

Writing Minilesson Principle

Think about the elements of magic you will include in your fairy tale.

You Will Need

- a couple of familiar fairy tales with elements of magic, such as the following from Text Set: Genre Study: Fairy Tales:
  - *Rumpelstiltskin* by Paul O. Zelinsky
  - *Beauty and the Beast* by Jan Brett
- chart paper and markers
- writer's notebooks

Academic Language / Important Vocabulary

- fairy tale
- magic

Continuum Connection

- Write a fiction story, either realistic or fantasy
- With fantasy, include imaginative character, setting, and plot elements
- Use a writer's notebook or booklet as a tool for collecting ideas, experimenting, planning, sketching, or drafting
- Use sketching, webs, lists, and freewriting to think about, plan for, and try out writing

GOAL

Understand the importance of magic in fairy tales and how to integrate it into writing.

RATIONALE

When students analyze the importance of magic in fairy tales and notice how authors of fairy tales integrate it into their stories, they will be better prepared to effectively use magic in their own fairy tales.

WRITER'S NOTEBOOK/WRITING FOLDER

Encourage students to explore ideas for including magic in their fairy tales in their writer's notebooks.

ASSESS LEARNING

- Notice whether students effectively integrate elements of magic into their fairy tales.
- Look for evidence that they can use vocabulary such as *fairy tale* and *magic*.

MINILESSON

To help students think about the principle, use familiar mentor texts to guide students in an inquiry-based lesson on the use of magic in fairy tales. Here is an example.

- Show the cover of *Rumpelstiltskin* and read the title.

  You noticed that fairy tales usually include magic. Is there magic in *Rumpelstiltskin*?

  What happens in this fairy tale that is magical?

  Can all the characters do magical things? Who has the power to do magic?

  Why is the magic in this fairy tale important to the story?

- Record students' responses on chart paper.
- Show the cover of *Beauty and the Beast* and read the title.

  What magical things happen in this fairy tale?

  Who or what has the power to do magic in this story?

  Why is the magic in this story important? What does it help you understand?

- Record responses on the chart.

Have a Try

Invite students to talk to a partner about their ideas for including magic in their own fairy tales.

> Think about the fairy tale that you're going to write. How might you include magic in your fairy tale? What magical things will happen, and why will they be important to your story? Turn and talk to your partner about your ideas.

Summarize and Apply

Write the principle at the top of the chart. Summarize the learning and remind students to include magic when they write fairy tales.

> What did you notice today about how and why authors include magic in fairy tales?

> During independent writing time today, spend some more time thinking about how you will include magic in your own fairy tale. Make some notes in your writer's notebook about who or what has the power to do magic and why the magic is important to the story. If you have time, you can begin to write your story. Bring your notes to share when we come back together.

Think about the elements of magic you will include in your fairy tale.

Book	What magical things happen?	Who or what has the magic?	Why is the magic important?
	Rumpelstiltskin spins straw into gold.	Rumpelstiltskin	It solves the girl's original problem, while also giving her a new problem that she has to solve herself.
	The golden ring transports Beauty to the palace of the Beast.	The golden ring	It helps communicate the author's message (do not judge a book by its cover).
	The Beast transforms into a prince.	The fairy who set the spell	

Confer

▶ During independent writing, move around the room to confer briefly with students about their ideas for including magic in their fairy tales. Use prompts such as the following as needed.

- *What is your fairy tale about?*
- *How will you include magic in your fairy tale?*
- *Who or what will have the power to do magic?*
- *Why is the magic important? Will it help move the plot of your story along? Will it help readers understand something important?*

Share

Following independent writing, gather students in the meeting area to share their ideas for including magic in their fairy tales. Invite other students to ask questions or offer feedback and suggestions.

> Who would like to share your ideas for including magic in your fairy tale?

WML3

GEN.U8.WML3

Writing Minilesson Principle
Make character sketches to determine character traits.

Writing Fairy Tales

You Will Need

▸ a familiar fairy tale with clear examples of good and evil characters, such as *Rumpelstiltskin* by Paul O. Zelinsky, from Text Set: Genre Study: Fairy Tales

▸ chart paper prepared to look like the Fairy Tale Character Sketch

▸ markers

▸ a Fairy Tale Character Sketch for each student

▸ writer's notebooks

▸ To download the following online resource for this lesson, visit **fp.pub/resources**:

  ▪ Fairy Tale Character Sketch

Academic Language / Important Vocabulary

▸ fairy tale   ▸ trait
▸ character sketch

Continuum Connection

▸ Write a fiction story, either realistic or fantasy

▸ With fantasy, include imaginative character, setting, and plot elements

▸ Describe characters by how they look, what they do, say, and think, and what others say about them

▸ Use a writer's notebook or booklet as a tool for collecting ideas, experimenting, planning, sketching, or drafting

GOAL

Make a character sketch as a tool for determining character traits, particularly including concepts of good and evil.

RATIONALE

When you guide students to create a character sketch for a familiar fairy-tale character, they will gain a better understanding of the types of characters that generally appear in fairy tales (simple, unchanging characters that are either good or evil). They will also be able to use character sketches to plan their own fairy-tale characters.

WRITER'S NOTEBOOK/WRITING FOLDER

Students may find it helpful to create character sketches before writing their fairy tales. They can glue their character sketches into their writer's notebooks.

ASSESS LEARNING

▸ Notice whether students create character sketches to plan their fairy-tale characters.

▸ Look for evidence that they can understand and use vocabulary such as *fairy tale*, *character sketch*, and *trait*.

MINILESSON

To help students think about the principle, use shared writing to model how to make a character sketch for a fairy-tale character. Here is an example.

▸ Show the cover of *Rumpelstiltskin* and read the title.

  Who are the main characters in this story?

  Let's think about the character Rumpelstiltskin. Describe how the character looks.

  What does he do in the story?

  What are his character traits, or what he is like on the inside?

  What does this character want?

  You noticed that characters in fairy tales are usually either good or evil. Would you say that Rumpelstiltskin is good or evil? Why?

▸ Using students' responses, create a character sketch of Rumpelstiltskin on chart paper.

  We can make a character sketch of Rumpelstiltskin. When you make a character sketch, you think and write about the character's traits, or what the character is like. You can use character sketches to think about characters in stories you have read or to create characters for your own fairy tales.

Have a Try

Invite students to talk to a partner about making a character sketch of another character.

> Think about the miller's daughter in Rumpelstiltskin. If you made a character sketch about her, what would you write? Turn and talk to your partner about this.

▸ After time for discussion, invite several pairs to share their thinking.

Summarize and Apply

Write the principle at the top of the chart. Summarize the learning and remind students to use a character sketch to think through character traits. Have students glue their character sketches into their writer's notebooks.

> How can making character sketches help you when you are writing your own fairy tales?

> During independent writing time today, fill in a character sketch for at least one character. Think about how the character will look and act to help you know how to write about the character in your story. Bring your character sketch to share when we meet later.

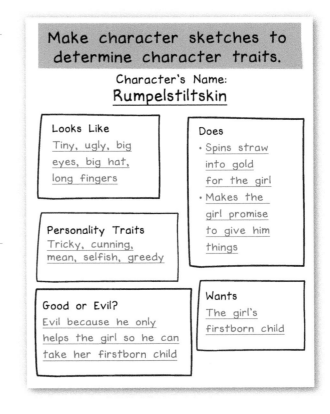

Confer

▸ During independent writing, move around the room to confer briefly with students about their characters. Use prompts such as the following as needed.

- *Who is the main character in the fairy tale you're working on?*
- *What does that character look like?*
- *What are the character's personality traits? What is the character like on the inside?*
- *Is the character good or evil? How will your readers know?*

Share

Following independent writing, gather students in the meeting area to talk about their characters.

> Who would like to tell about the main character in your fairy tale?

> Was making a character sketch helpful? Why or why not?

Section 2: Genres and Forms

WML4
GEN.U8.WML4

Writing Minilesson Principle
Use a storyboard to plan the plot of your story.

Writing Fairy Tales

You Will Need

- a blank storyboard prepared on chart paper
- markers
- writer's notebooks and writing folders
- To download the following resource for this lesson, visit **fp.pub/resources**:
  - chart art (optional)

Academic Language / Important Vocabulary

- fairy tale
- storyboard
- plot

Continuum Connection

- Write a fiction story, either realistic or fantasy
- With fantasy, include imaginative character, setting, and plot elements
- Write fiction and nonfiction narratives that are ordered chronologically
- Develop a plot that includes tension and one or more scenes
- Use a writer's notebook or booklet as a tool for collecting ideas, experimenting, planning, sketching, or drafting
- Use sketching, webs, lists, and freewriting to think about, plan for, and try out writing

GOAL

Use a storyboard for planning the plot of a fairy tale.

RATIONALE

Using a storyboard to plan a fairy tale can help students identify which events are significant and in what order they should be presented before they start writing. When students learn that some writers use tools, such as a storyboard, to help with planning, they begin to try out different tools and learn which ones work best for them.

WRITER'S NOTEBOOK/WRITING FOLDER

Students can make a storyboard in their writer's notebooks before writing a draft on draft paper, which will be kept in their writing folders.

ASSESS LEARNING

- Observe whether students try out using a storyboard to plan their fairy tales.
- Look for evidence that they can use vocabulary such as *fairy tale*, *storyboard*, and *plot*.

MINILESSON

To help students think about the minilesson principle, model how to use a storyboard to plan a fairy tale. Here is an example.

- Model the process of using a storyboard to plan a fairy tale.

  I am writing a fairy tale about a princess whose father, the king, wants her to marry a prince from a neighboring kingdom. But she doesn't want to marry the prince. Will she be able to get out of being married to the prince? To help me plan what to write, I am going to use a storyboard.

- Show the prepared blank storyboard.

  A storyboard shows the significant, or main, events in a story and the order in which they happen. Watch how I make my plan. Then we will talk about it.

- Make quick sketches in the storyboard boxes as you think aloud. Add short notes that state what is going to happen in each part of the story. Support students' understanding of the elements of a fairy tale by including the characters, setting, problem, and major events on the storyboard.

  What do you notice about how I made a storyboard?

- Emphasize that these should be quick sketches with short notes and that the events in the boxes are in chronological order.

  You can use a storyboard to plan the events you will include in your story and in what order you will present them. You can make sketches, describe the scene in words, or both.

Have a Try

Invite students to talk to a partner about using a storyboard to plan a fairy tale.

> Think about the fairy tale you're working on. Turn and talk about what you might place in the boxes of a storyboard.

Summarize and Apply

Write the principle at the top of the chart. Read it to students. Summarize the learning and invite students to try using a storyboard to plan their fairy tales.

> How can making a storyboard help you when you're working on a fairy tale?

> During independent writing time today, try using a storyboard to plan your fairy tale. You can make as many boxes as you need to show the important events in your story. Check your writer's notebook for notes that you made about the characters and magic in your story. Use those notes in your storyboard. Bring your storyboard when we meet later.

Use a storyboard to plan the plot of your story.

①
Characters: Princess Petunia, the king, Prince Peredur, fairy godmother, evil wizard

Setting: Windrush Castle

②
Problem: The king wants Princess Petunia to marry Prince Peredur, but she doesn't want to marry him.

③
Event: A fairy godmother tells the princess she won't have to marry Prince Peredur if she finds a golden compass, a vase made of ice, and a purple feather.

④
Event: The princess packs her bags at midnight and sneaks out to set off on an adventure.

Confer

▶ During independent writing, move around the room to confer briefly with students about their fairy tales. Use prompts such as the following as needed.

- *Where does your fairy tale take place, and who are the characters?*
- *What problem does the main character have?*
- *What will happen first in your fairy tale?*
- *Tell what will go in each box of your storyboard.*

Share

Following independent writing, gather students in pairs in the meeting area to share their storyboards.

> Share your storyboard with your partner.

▶ After partners share, invite a few volunteers to share their storyboards with the class.

Assessment

After you have taught the minilessons in this umbrella, observe students as they write and talk about their writing. Use *The Fountas & Pinnell Literacy Continuum* to notice, teach for, and support students' learning as you observe their writing development.

▶ What evidence do you have of students' new understandings related to writing fairy tales?

- Can students identify and name the characteristics of fairy tales?
- Do they effectively integrate elements of magic into their fairy tales?
- Have they tried making character sketches to determine character traits?
- Have they tried using a storyboard to plan their writing?
- Do students understand and use vocabulary such as *fairy tale*, *quality*, *magic*, *character*, *trait*, *storyboard*, and *plot*?

▶ In what other ways, beyond the scope of this umbrella, are students exploring writing fiction?

- Are they ready to learn more about describing characters and settings?
- Are they ready to publish any of their writing?

Use your observations to determine the next umbrella you will teach. You may also consult Suggested Sequence of Lessons (pp. 665–682) for guidance.

EXTENSIONS FOR WRITING FAIRY TALES

▶ Help students think of other ways they could present their fairy tales, for example, as a readers' theater or play, in a slideshow format, in a video, or as a picture book.

▶ Help students notice and use the language of fairy tales (common phrases, language techniques, etc.) in their writing.

▶ Teach a lesson on how the students might reflect their own culture and values in their fairy tales.

▶ Support students in writing other types of traditional tales (e.g., legends, folktales, myths) and/or other types of fantasy.

▶ Download rubrics from the online resources (fp.pub/resources) to help you and your students evaluate how well they are able to apply the concepts in these lessons.

Minilessons in This Umbrella

WML1 Notice the qualities of good multimedia presentations.

WML2 Organize and write the words for your slides.

WML3 Make strong introductory and ending slides.

WML4 Make important design decisions.

WML5 Present or narrate your multimedia presentation.

Writer's Notebook

Before Teaching Umbrella 9 Minilessons

A multimedia presentation allows for multimodal composition because it can include any combination of words, images, video, and audio. In the minilessons in this umbrella, you will use a model multimedia presentation that you have created and guide students to notice the choices you made. During independent writing time, students will have the opportunity to create their own informational multimedia presentations about topics they choose.

Depending on the technology available in your classroom, you may choose to have students make their presentations directly in slideshow software or on paper or poster board (using one page per slide). You might also have students create rough drafts of their presentations on paper and later convert them to digital presentations. Consider engaging the help of faculty in charge of the technology in your school to assist students in using a slideshow program.

Before teaching this umbrella, gather recordings of one or more strong multimedia presentations to use as mentor texts (for example, from ted.com). You will also want to read aloud a variety of informational books to provide ideas for presentation topics.

As you view and enjoy informational multimedia presentations together, help students

- notice how the authors structure and present information, and

- talk about which topics they find most interesting and why.

Section 2: Genres and Forms

<table>
</table>

WML1
GEN.U9.WML1

Writing Minilesson Principle
Notice the qualities of good multimedia presentations.

Making Informational Multimedia Presentations

You Will Need

- a video recording of a strong, age-appropriate multimedia presentation (e.g., from ted.com)
- audio/visual equipment
- chart paper and markers
- writer's notebooks

Academic Language / Important Vocabulary

- multimedia presentation
- quality
- bullet point
- topic
- informational

Continuum Connection

- Choose topics that one knows about, cares about, or wants to learn about

GOAL

Notice the qualities of multimedia presentations for the purpose of creating one.

RATIONALE

"Writing" encompasses more than putting pen to paper. With so much technology available in school, in the workplace, and at home, students need to learn how to blend written words, spoken words, and visual images to communicate information effectively.

WRITER'S NOTEBOOK/WRITING FOLDER

Have students look through their writer's notebooks to choose a topic for an informational multimedia presentation.

ASSESS LEARNING

- Notice whether students can identify the qualities of good multimedia presentations.
- Look for evidence that they can use vocabulary such as *multimedia presentation*, *quality*, *bullet point*, *topic*, and *informational*.

MINILESSON

To help students think about the minilesson principle, engage them in an inquiry-based lesson on the qualities of effective multimedia presentations. Here is an example.

> Today, we're going to start to learn how to make an informational multimedia presentation. The word *informational* tells you that you will give information about something. What do you think a multimedia presentation is?

> A multimedia presentation presents, or gives, information in more than one way. It uses some combination of pictures, video, sound, and written words.

▶ Play a video of a speaker presenting an effective multimedia presentation (e.g., from ted.com) that includes slides.

> In what ways did the presenter give you information?

> What did you notice about the multimedia presentation?

▶ Record students' responses on chart paper, generalizing them as necessary. As needed, prompt students' thinking with questions such as these:

- *What did you notice about the words on the slides?*
- *How did the slides relate to what the speaker was saying?*
- *Did the speaker give more information through the words or through the slides?*
- *What made the slides interesting to look at?*
- *What did you notice about the first slide? What did you notice about the last slide?*

Have a Try

Invite students to talk to a partner about their ideas for a multimedia presentation.

▶ Model looking in your writer's notebook to choose an idea for a multimedia presentation.

> Sloths are one of my favorite animals, and I've written a lot of facts about sloths in my writer's notebook. I could make a multimedia presentation about them. What could you make a multimedia presentation about? Turn and talk to your partner about your ideas.

▶ After students turn and talk, invite several students to share their ideas.

Summarize and Apply

Write the principle at the top of the chart. Summarize the learning and invite students to choose a topic for an informational multimedia presentation.

> Why is it important to notice the qualities of a good multimedia presentation?

> During independent writing time today, spend some time looking through your writer's notebook and thinking about your ideas for a multimedia presentation. Decide what you would like to make a multimedia presentation about. Bring your ideas to share when we come back together.

> ### Notice the qualities of good multimedia presentations.
>
> - Most of the information is spoken aloud. The slides support what the speaker is saying.
>
> - The slides are simple and have few words—just a few key points.
>
> - The slides sometimes have bullet points.
>
> - Many slides have pictures, such as photographs, illustrations, diagrams, or maps.
>
> - Some slides have audio or video.
>
> - The introductory slide tells what the presentation is about and tries to hook the audience.
>
> - The ending slide summarizes the presentation in an interesting way.

Section 2: Genres and Forms

Confer

▶ During independent writing, move around the room to confer briefly with students about their ideas for multimedia presentations. Use prompts such as the following as needed.

- *What topic would make an interesting multimedia presentation?*
- *What topics have you written about often?*
- *You could make a presentation about your favorite animal (science topic, period in history).*

Share

Following independent writing, gather students in the meeting area. Ask each student to share an idea for a multimedia presentation.

> Share one idea for a multimedia presentation. If you haven't yet decided on a topic, you can pass. You might get an idea from one of your classmates.

Writing Minilesson Principle
Organize and write the words for your slides.

You Will Need

- a chosen subject for an informational multimedia presentation
- a computer with slideshow software or several sheets of paper
- chart paper and markers
- writer's notebooks

Academic Language / Important Vocabulary

- multimedia presentation
- organize
- information
- subject
- example
- bullet

Continuum Connection

- Present ideas and information in a logical sequence
- Maintain a clear focus on the important or main ideas
- Choose clear examples that are related to the topic

GOAL

Plan how to organize information across the slides.

RATIONALE

As students begin to make their slides, they need to think about how best to present the information to the audience in a logical way. They also need to be aware of the conventions of slideshow writing. Using fewer words on slides makes it easier for the audience to focus on the meaning, so incomplete sentences and brief bulleted lists are used frequently.

WRITER'S NOTEBOOK/WRITING FOLDER

Students can plan their multimedia presentations by making a storyboard in their writer's notebooks.

ASSESS LEARNING

- Notice whether students organize information in a logical sequence, focus on the main ideas, support their ideas with examples, use content vocabulary, and follow the conventions for using print on slides.
- Look for evidence that they can use vocabulary such as *multimedia presentation*, *organize*, *information*, *subject*, *example*, and *bullet*.

MINILESSON

To help students think about the minilesson principle, model the first steps of organizing and writing a multimedia presentation. Below is an example that focuses on sloths, but select a topic that students know about and are interested in. Use slideshow software for this lesson, or plan the presentation on sheets of paper attached to chart paper.

> Today, I'm going to start to write the words on my slides for my presentation on sloths. First, I need to think about how to organize my information. Two common ways to organize information are by time order or in categories. If I were making a presentation about somebody's life or a period in history, I might use time order. But since I'm writing about an animal, I think it would make sense to put my information into categories. I could have categories about types of sloths, how they spend their time, what they eat, and fun facts about them. I'll write headings on each slide so I'll remember what I want to write about.

- Write headings on the slides.

> How should I write the information so that it will be easy for my audience to read the slides?

> It's a good idea to write a heading, use as few words as possible, and make a bulleted list. Later, I'll give more details when I talk about this slide.

Have a Try

Invite students to talk to a partner about how to organize and write a multimedia presentation.

> What did you notice about how I organized and wrote the words for my slides? Turn and talk to your partner about this.

▶ After students turn and talk, invite several pairs to share what they noticed. Summarize the learning on chart paper.

Summarize and Apply

Write the principle at the top of the chart, and invite students to start planning and writing their slides.

> During independent writing time today, start to organize and write the words for your slides. You might draw a storyboard in your writer's notebook and write your plans for the slides in the boxes. Look at my plans if you need help remembering how to plan your multimedia presentation.

Confer

▶ During independent writing, move around the room to confer briefly with students about their multimedia presentations. Use prompts such as the following as needed.

- *How will you organize the information for your multimedia presentation?*
- *What heading will you write for this slide?*
- *How can you share your main idea and examples in just a few words?*
- *Remember to focus on the main ideas and key examples. You will give more details when you talk about your slides.*

Share

Following independent writing, gather students in the meeting area to talk about their slides.

> How is writing a multimedia presentation different from other kinds of writing you have done?

Two Families of Sloth	Life in the Slow Lane
Choloepus Bradypus	Sloth hobbies:
Two Three fingers fingers	• Hanging in trees • Sleeping • Hugging
Dinner Time	More Fun Facts About Sloths

Organize and write the words for your slides.

- Think about how you want to organize the information—in time order or in categories?
- Decide what to write about on each slide.
- Use words that are appropriate for your subject.
- Support your ideas with examples.
- Use as few words as possible, but keep the meaning clear.
- Write lists with bullets.

Section 2: Genres and Forms

Writing Minilesson Principle
Make strong introductory and ending slides.

Making Informational Multimedia Presentations

You Will Need

- a prepared introductory and concluding slide for the sample presentation started in WML2
- chart paper and markers
- writer's notebooks

Academic Language / Important Vocabulary

- multimedia presentation
- introductory
- ending

Continuum Connection

- Have a clear introduction, body, and conclusion to your topic

GOAL

Understand that the introductory slide tries to hook the audience and that the concluding slide summarizes the information about the topic in an interesting way.

RATIONALE

When students study examples of strong introductory and concluding slides, they will model their own introductory and concluding slides on them. They will begin and end their presentations in engaging, meaningful, and memorable ways.

WRITER'S NOTEBOOK/WRITING FOLDER

Students can plan their introductory and concluding slides in their writer's notebooks.

ASSESS LEARNING

- Notice whether students create engaging and interesting introductory and ending slides for their presentations.
- Look for evidence that they can use vocabulary such as *multimedia presentation, introductory*, and *ending*.

MINILESSON

To help students think about the minilesson principle, use prepared slides to engage students in an inquiry-based lesson on writing strong introductory and concluding slides. Here is an example.

- Display the introductory slide you prepared for your presentation. Read it aloud.

    This will be the first slide in my presentation, also known as the introductory slide. What do you notice about my introductory slide?

    How did I make my introductory slide interesting?

    What do you think is the purpose of the introductory slide for a presentation?

- Record students' responses on chart paper.
- Display the ending slide you prepared and read it aloud.

    This is my last slide, or my ending or concluding slide. What do you notice about it?

    What do you think is the purpose of the ending slide for a presentation?

- Record responses on the chart.

    Your introductory slide should try to hook the audience, or get them interested in your topic. You might use words, an image, or maybe even some music. Your ending slide should summarize information about the topic in an interesting way. Remember to make your slides easy for your audience to read. Think about using few words and maybe a bulleted list.

Have a Try

Invite students to talk to a partner about their ideas for introductory and ending slides.

> Think about your own multimedia presentation. How could you begin and end your presentation in an interesting way? What might you write on your beginning and ending slides? Turn and talk to your partner about your ideas.

▶ After time for discussion, invite a few students to share their ideas with the class.

Summarize and Apply

Write the principle at the top of the chart. Summarize the learning and invite students to write their introductory and ending slides.

> What will you think about when you make your introductory and ending slides?

> During independent writing time today, continue working on your multimedia presentation. Remember to write a strong introductory and ending slide. You can use your writer's notebook to try out what you want to write before you make a slide.

Confer

▶ During independent writing, move around the room to confer briefly with students about their multimedia presentations. Use prompts such as the following as needed.

- *What could you put on your introductory slide to hook your audience?*
- *How could you summarize the information in an interesting way on your ending slide?*

Share

Following independent writing, gather students in the meeting area to talk about their slides.

> Who would like to share what you wrote on your introductory or ending slide?

It can take me a month to digest a meal, but then again, I'm not known for being in a hurry.

What am I?

Why Sloths Are the Best

- They are cuddly.
- They are great climbers.
- They know how to take it easy.

Make strong introductory and ending slides.

Introductory Slide	Ending Slide
• Introduce the topic.	• Summarize the information.
• Hook the audience— make them want to learn more!	• End in an interesting way.
• Could be a picture or video.	• Leave your audience with something to think about.

Writing Minilesson Principle
Make important design decisions.

You Will Need

- a couple of example slides from the presentation started in WML2 and WML3, fully designed and with media added
- chart paper and markers
- writer's notebooks

Academic Language / Important Vocabulary

- multimedia presentation
- sound
- video
- design

Continuum Connection

- Use graphics (e.g., diagrams, illustrations, slideshows, other digital media) to communicate meaning or to enhance a presentation
- Integrate technology tools (e.g., slideshows, video, audio) into multimedia presentations

GOAL

Enhance presentations with a variety of media (illustrations, images, or digital media).

RATIONALE

When students design and add media to their slides, they begin to understand how writers make choices about how best to engage the audience with their presentations.

WRITER'S NOTEBOOK/WRITING FOLDER

Students can continue to use their writer's notebooks to plan their multimedia presentations.

ASSESS LEARNING

- Notice whether students make effective design decisions and choose appropriate media to enhance and/or clarify their written and spoken content.
- Look for evidence that they can use vocabulary such as *multimedia presentation*, *sound*, *video*, and *design*.

MINILESSON

Before this lesson, add a variety of media to your model presentation. Also, make sure you are familiar with how students can search for media safely, and decide how you will facilitate the process of helping them add media to their presentations. If students are preparing slides on paper or poster board, they could consider adding photos or playing a recording during the presentation. To help students think about the minilesson principle, display the prepared presentation and engage them in a discussion about the media you chose and why. Here is an example.

- Display one of the finished slides you have prepared.

    What do you notice about this slide? What have I changed since the last time you saw it?

    I added photographs to this slide. Why do you think I added photographs?

    What do you notice about where I put the photographs?

    What else have I changed on this slide?

    I thought about how I wanted this slide to look. I changed the size, color, and position of the words.

- Display a slide to which you added audio or video. Play the audio or video.

    What did I add to this slide?

    Why do you think I added video (sound) to this slide?

    What will the video (sound) help my audience understand?

Have a Try

Invite students to talk to a partner about their ideas for adding multimedia.

> Think about your own multimedia presentation. What kinds of pictures, sounds, or videos could you add to your presentation? How will you make your slides attractive and easy to read? Turn and talk to your partner about your ideas.

Summarize and Apply

Write the principle at the top of a sheet of chart paper. Help students summarize the learning and invite them to design their presentations.

> What design decisions do you need to think about when you make a multimedia presentation?

▶ Summarize the learning on the chart.

▶ The amount of time necessary for students to add media to their presentations will depend on the technology available in your classroom and whether they have started making slides on a computer.

> During independent writing time today, think about how you will design your slides and what media you will include. Make notes of your ideas in your writer's notebook.

Confer

▶ During independent writing, move around the room to confer briefly with students about their multimedia presentations. Use prompts such as the following as needed.

- *What media could you add to this slide to help your audience better understand _____?*
- *Would a picture, sound, or video work better on this slide? Why?*
- *Where on the slide will you place that photograph? Why?*
- *What could you do to make your slides attractive and easy to read?*

Share

Following independent writing, gather students in the meeting area to talk about their multimedia presentations.

> Talk to your partner about how you made a design decision.

Two Families of Sloth

Choloepus
Two fingers

Bradypus
Three fingers

Sloth Hugs!

Make important design decisions.

- Add a background color or image.
- Add pictures, videos, or sound to help the audience learn more.
- Think about where to place the media.
- Decide on the color, size, font, and placement of your words.

WML5

GEN.U9.WML5

Present or narrate your multimedia presentation.

Making Informational Multimedia Presentations

You Will Need

- a completed digital multimedia presentation
- index cards with notes or a script for the presentation
- an example of a multimedia presentation with recorded voice narration (optional)
- a digital tool for adding voice narration to slideshows (optional)
- chart paper and markers
- index cards
- writing folders

Academic Language / Important Vocabulary

- multimedia presentation
- present
- narrate

Continuum Connection

- Have a plan or notes to support the presentation
- Show confidence when presenting
- Communicate interest in and enthusiasm about a topic
- Present information in ways that engage listeners' attention
- Make oral reports that demonstrate understanding of a topic

---

GOAL

Prepare notes and make a presentation with enthusiasm, confidence, and a strong voice.

RATIONALE

When students prepare notes for and practice giving their multimedia presentations, they are better able to communicate their ideas effectively and engage an audience.

WRITER'S NOTEBOOK/WRITING FOLDER

Students can keep printouts of their slides or their index cards in their writing folders.

ASSESS LEARNING

- Notice whether students refer to notes, speak with enthusiasm and confidence, and vary their speaking voice for emphasis.
- Look for evidence that they can use vocabulary such as *multimedia presentation*, *present*, and *narrate*.

MINILESSON

To help students think about the minilesson principle, model giving a multimedia presentation. As an option, you may also want to show students an example of a presentation with recorded voice narration. Here is an example.

- Display the completed multimedia presentation.

   Before class, I practiced giving my multimedia presentation on sloths, and now I'm going to present it to you. Watch what I do.

- Give the presentation. Model speaking with confidence and enthusiasm, referring to notes or a script, and varying your speaking voice for interest and emphasis.

- If you have a presentation with recorded voice narration, play it now.

   You can either give your presentation live or record yourself narrating your multimedia presentation. Why might you choose to present live or make a recording?

- Record students' responses on chart paper.

   What do you notice about how to give a presentation?

- Record responses on the chart. As needed, guide students to think about voice volume, rate, enthusiasm, and (for a live presentation) body language. If students mention looking at the audience, take into consideration that some students are not comfortable with establishing or able to establish eye contact because of cultural conventions or for other reasons.

Have a Try

Invite students to talk to a partner about presenting a multimedia presentation.

> How would you like to present your presentation—live or recorded? Why? What will you remember to do when you are presenting? Turn and talk to your partner about this.

▶ After time for discussion, invite several students to share their responses.

Summarize and Apply

Write the principle at the top of the chart. Summarize the learning and invite students to practice and prepare for their presentations.

> During independent writing time today, get ready to present or narrate your multimedia presentation. Make notes on index cards so that you remember what to say. Then practice your presentation with a partner or with me. I can help you record your voice if you want to narrate your presentation. When we meet later, some of you will have the chance to show your presentation to the whole class.

> **Present or narrate your multimedia presentation.**
>
> • Decide if you want to present live to an audience or record yourself narrating.
>   • Live: if you want to interact with your audience
>   • Narrate: if you want your audience to be able to view your presentation whenever they want
> • Look at your notes or script to help you remember what to say.
> • Speak clearly.
> • Speak loudly enough for people to hear you but not too loudly.
> • Speak at the right speed—not too fast or too slow.
> • Change your voice to show that an idea is important.
> • Sound excited and interested!
> • Look at your audience.

Confer

▶ During independent writing, move around the room to confer briefly with students. Invite them to talk about and practice their multimedia presentations. Use prompts such as the following as needed.

- *Will you present live or record yourself narrating your presentation? Why?*
- *What will you say at the beginning of your presentation?*
- *What can you write so that you remember what to say?*

Share

Following independent writing, gather students in the meeting area to start sharing their multimedia presentations. Set aside a block of time for students to present, or have a few students present or show their presentation each day for several days.

> Does anyone have any questions or comments for _____?

> What did you notice about how _____ gave the presentation?

Assessment

After you have taught the minilessons in this umbrella, observe students as they create and present their multimedia presentations. Use *The Fountas & Pinnell Literacy Continuum* to notice, teach for, and support students' learning as you observe their written and oral communication skills.

▶ What evidence do you have of students' new understandings related to making an informational multimedia presentation?

- Is the information on the slides presented in a logical sequence?
- Are the ideas written in clear language with powerful examples and vocabulary appropriate to the subject?
- Do students create strong introductory and concluding slides?
- How effective is their use of images, video, and sound?
- Do they practice their presentations and prepare notes?
- Do they present with enthusiasm, confidence, and a strong voice?
- Do they understand and use vocabulary such as *multimedia presentation*, *informational*, *organize*, and *present*?

▶ In what other ways, beyond the scope of this umbrella, are students experimenting with different genres and forms of composition?

- Do they show an interest in opinion writing?
- What other kinds of nonfiction are they writing?

Use your observations to determine the next umbrella you will teach. You may also consult Suggested Sequence of Lessons (pp. 665–682) for guidance.

EXTENSIONS FOR MAKING INFORMATIONAL MULTIMEDIA PRESENTATIONS

▶ Invite a guest speaker to present to the class using a multimedia presentation. Afterward, ask students what they noticed about the presentation.

▶ Regularly include multimedia presentations as part of your lessons in various subjects (e.g., math, science, social studies). Help students notice other ways you can present information in a multimedia presentation (e.g., graphs, maps, tables).

▶ Give students regular opportunities to create and present multimedia presentations on a variety of topics. Teach them how to cite their sources.

▶ Download rubrics from the online resources (fp.pub/resources) to help you and your students evaluate how well they are able to apply the concepts in these lessons.

Minilessons in This Umbrella

WML1   Notice the qualities of good feature articles.

WML2   Choose a topic and think about your point of view.

WML3   Find and collect information about your topic.

WML4   Hook your readers from the beginning.

WML5   Write with a strong voice.

Before Teaching Umbrella 10 Minilessons

A feature article is an engaging informational article with a strong voice. Feature articles can be about a wide variety of high-interest topics, including but not limited to current or historical events, significant individuals or groups, and scientific topics. Depending on the topic, the writer may conduct research using primary sources (e.g., interviews, original photographs or videos, journals, artifacts) and/or secondary sources (e.g., books, encyclopedias).

Before teaching the minilessons in this umbrella, read and discuss a variety of feature articles on topics that are of interest to your students. You may use the sample feature articles provided in the online resources for this umbrella, copies of which students can keep in their writing folders, as well as other age-appropriate feature articles you have gathered from magazines, newspapers, or websites. We also strongly recommend teaching CFT.U11: Writing with Voice in Fiction and Nonfiction before this umbrella.

As you read and enjoy feature articles together, help students

- talk about the content of each article,
- identify the writer's point of view, or perspective,
- discuss the writer's use of literary techniques, and
- notice the qualities of feature articles.

Writing Minilesson Principle
Notice the qualities of good feature articles.

Writing Feature Articles

You Will Need

- a copy of a feature article for each student (see online resources)
- chart paper and markers
- writer's notebooks and writing folders
- To download the following online resource for this lesson, visit **fp.pub/resources**:
  - Feature Articles

Academic Language / Important Vocabulary

- feature article
- quality
- topic
- voice
- quotation

Continuum Connection

- Understand that a feature article usually focuses on one aspect of a topic
- Understand that a feature article begins with a lead paragraph, with more detailed information in subsequent paragraphs, and a conclusion

GOAL

Study mentor texts to notice the qualities of feature articles and to learn how to craft them.

RATIONALE

When students study examples of feature articles and identify characteristics of the genre, they are better prepared to begin writing their own feature articles. They will model their feature articles on those they have read.

WRITER'S NOTEBOOK/WRITING FOLDER

Have students begin exploring ideas for feature articles in their writer's notebooks. Students can store copies of the feature articles in their writing folders.

ASSESS LEARNING

- Notice whether students can identify the qualities of good feature articles.
- Look for evidence that they can use vocabulary such as *feature article*, *quality*, *topic*, *voice*, and *quotation*.

MINILESSON

To help students think about the minilesson principle, use mentor texts (such as those from Feature Articles in the online resources) to engage them in an inquiry-based lesson on the qualities of feature articles. Here is an example.

- Divide students into small groups. Give each group copies of one feature article. Circulate among the groups as students read and discuss their article to be sure that they understand it.

  After you have read the article, talk with your group about what you notice.

- Invite each group to share what they noticed. Help them identify the characteristics of feature articles, and record them on chart paper, generalizing them as necessary.

  You just read a feature article. Based on what you read and what you heard your classmates say, how would you describe a feature article?

- As needed, prompt students' thinking about feature articles with questions such as the following:
  - *What topics do writers write about in feature articles?*
  - *What makes feature articles interesting to read?*
  - *How does the writer help you learn about the topic?*
  - *How are feature articles different from a regular article in a newspaper?*
  - *Do the writers share their point of view? How so?*

Have a Try

Invite students to talk to a partner about feature articles.

> Is there anything else you've noticed about feature articles? Turn and talk to your partner about your ideas.

▶ After time for discussion, invite volunteers to share what else they have noticed. Add any new characteristics to the chart, as appropriate.

Summarize and Apply

Summarize the learning and invite students to begin thinking about ideas for feature articles.

> What did you notice about feature articles?

> You are going to write your own feature articles. During independent writing time today, look through your writer's notebook for topics that you are interested in and might enjoy writing about in a feature article. Make a list of topics that you might want to write about. Bring your ideas to share when we come back together.

Qualities of Feature Articles

- Feature articles can be about any topic.
- The writer writes in detail about a topic of personal interest.
- The writer writes about the topic in an interesting or surprising way.
- Unlike in a regular news article, the writer does more than just give facts about the topic.
- You can hear the writer's voice in the writing.
- The writer sometimes tells a story.
- The writer often uses quotations.
- The writer often uses descriptive language and interesting word choices.
- You can usually figure out the writer's opinion about the topic.

Confer

▶ During independent writing, move around the room to confer briefly with students and invite them to talk about their ideas for feature articles. Use prompts such as the following as needed.

- *What are some topics that you would be interested in writing about?*
- *What topics would you like to learn more about?*
- *What interests you about that topic?*

Share

Following independent writing, gather students in the meeting area. Ask each student to share an idea for a feature article.

> Tell one idea you have for a feature article. If you haven't decided yet, you can say "pass." You might hear an idea from a classmate.

Writing Minilesson Principle
Choose a topic and think about your point of view.

Writing Feature Articles

You Will Need

- a copy of any feature articles discussed for each student [see the online resource for WML1]
- document camera [optional]
- chart paper and markers
- writer's notebooks and writing folders

Academic Language / Important Vocabulary

- feature article
- topic
- point of view

Continuum Connection

- Understand that a feature article usually focuses on one aspect of a topic
- Understand that a feature article reveals the writer's point of view about the topic or subject

GOAL

Select a topic of interest and think about your perspective or point of view.

RATIONALE

Feature articles are normally not written in a completely objective manner. Although the writer may not state an opinion explicitly (as in an opinion or persuasive piece), readers can often infer the writer's point of view, or perspective, from clues in the text. When students notice how writers of feature articles communicate their point of view, they will begin to think about how to convey their own point of view in their own feature articles.

WRITER'S NOTEBOOK/WRITING FOLDER

Have students continue exploring ideas for feature articles in their writer's notebooks. Students can keep copies of sample feature articles in their writing folders.

ASSESS LEARNING

- Notice how students choose topics for feature articles and think about their point of view.
- Look for evidence that they can use vocabulary such as *feature article*, *topic*, and *point of view*.

MINILESSON

To help students think about the minilesson principle, use mentor texts (such as those from Feature Articles in the online resources for WML1) to engage them in an inquiry-based lesson on thinking about point of view. Here is an example.

- Review or read aloud "The Gray Wolf: An Endangered Species . . . or Not?" from the online resource.

    What is this feature article about?

    This article is not about what gray wolves eat or where they live. It's about gray wolves becoming an endangered species and the fight to save them. The writer chose a specific subtopic to focus on instead of writing everything about gray wolves. How do you think the writer feels about gray wolves? How can you tell?

    The writer seems to like gray wolves and thinks they are worth saving. That is the writer's point of view. A point of view is how someone thinks about a topic.

- Show or project "Hop on Board the Bike Bus!"

    What subtopic related to bikes did the writer choose to write about?

    The writer wrote about something specific that was happening related to bikes in a specific town. What do you think is the writer's point of view on the Bike Bus? How can you tell?

Have a Try

Invite students to talk to a partner about another feature article.

▶ Show or project "She Said She Could and She Did: The Story of Nellie Bly." Read it aloud.

> What do you notice about the topic of this feature article? How can you tell the writer's point of view? Turn and talk to your partner about this.

▶ After students turn and talk, invite several pairs to share their thinking.

Summarize and Apply

Help students summarize the learning, and invite them to choose a topic for their feature article.

> What did you learn today about preparing to write a feature article?

▶ Summarize the learning on chart paper. Write the principle at the top of the chart.

> You started to make a list of topics in your writer's notebook that you might want to write about. Today, choose a topic for your first feature article. Decide what small idea or subtopic you want to focus on. Then think about your point of view on, or way of looking at, your topic. You may want to make some notes in your writer's notebook about your ideas—for example, what you already know or where you can look for information. Bring your ideas to share when we come back together.

> [!NOTE]
> **Choose a topic and think about your point of view.**
>
> • Choose a topic that interests you.
>   - a scientific topic
>   - a current event
>   - a historical event
>   - an important person
>   - something in nature
>
> • Choose a subtopic or a small idea to focus on.
>
> • Think about your point of view.
>
> Point of view is how the writer looks at or thinks about a topic.

Confer

▶ During independent writing, move around the room to confer briefly with students about choosing a topic. Use prompts such as the following as needed.

- *Let's look at your list of topic ideas. What topic are you most excited about?*
- *What small idea or subtopic related to that topic could you focus on?*
- *What is your point of view on the topic? What do you think or feel about it?*

Share

Following independent writing, gather students in the meeting area to share their topics.

> Turn and talk to a partner about the topic you chose for your feature article.

WML3

GEN.U10.WML3

Writing Minilesson Principle
Find and collect information about your topic.

Writing Feature Articles

You Will Need

- a copy of any feature articles discussed for each student (see the online resource for WML1)
- document camera (optional)
- chart paper prepared with the title *Where to Find Information About Your Topic*
- writer's notebooks and writing folders

Academic Language / Important Vocabulary

- research
- information

Continuum Connection

- Understand that an expository text may require research and will require organization
- Understand that to write an expository text, the writer needs to become very knowledgeable about a topic

---

GOAL

Use a variety of sources from which to collect information about a topic.

RATIONALE

A well-researched feature article contains information from a variety of primary and/or secondary sources. When students think about how writers of familiar feature articles found information, they will understand that they must similarly conduct research for their topics.

WRITER'S NOTEBOOK/WRITING FOLDER

As students conduct research for their feature articles, have them take notes in their writer's notebooks. Students can keep/use copies of the feature articles in their writing folders.

ASSESS LEARNING

- Notice whether students use a variety of sources and take notes about their findings.
- Look for evidence that they can use vocabulary such as *research* and *information*.

MINILESSON

To help students think about the minilesson principle, use mentor texts (see Feature Articles in the online resources for WML1) to engage them in an inquiry-based lesson on conducting research for feature articles. Here is an example.

- Show or project "She Said She Could and She Did: The Story of Nellie Bly" from the online resource. Read it aloud if students are not familiar with it.

  Nellie Bly was a newspaper reporter who wrote feature articles herself! How did Nellie Bly find information for her articles?

- Write *Personal experiences* on the prepared chart paper.

  Sometimes writers write from personal experience, but this is not always possible if you can't travel to a particular location. Or, you might be writing about something that happened long ago or far away. How do you think the writer of this article found information about Nellie Bly?

  The writer might have read books or online articles about Nellie Bly or newspaper articles that Nellie Bly wrote.

- Record each type of source discussed on the chart.

- Show or project "The Gray Wolf: An Endangered Species . . . or Not?"

  How do you think the writer learned how wolves sound when they howl?

  The writer might have gone to the Wolf Conservation Center and listened to the wolves howl in person, talked to someone at the center, or searched online for a video of wolves howling. When writers find information, they take notes to use when they write their articles.

Have a Try

Invite students to talk to a partner about another feature article.

▷ Show or project "Hop on Board the Bike Bus!"

How do you think the writer of this article collected information about the Bike Bus in Highwater? Turn and talk to your partner.

▷ After time for discussion, invite several pairs to share their ideas.

When a writer writes about a local event, it may be possible to interview people who are involved in the event and record them or take notes.

▷ Add new ideas to the chart.

Summarize and Apply

Summarize the learning and invite students to begin conducting research for their feature articles.

How will you collect information about your topic?

During independent writing time today, think about where you will find information about your topic for your feature article. You can begin doing research using the resources in our classroom. Remember to collect notes about what you learn in your writer's notebook.

> **Where to Find Information About Your Topic**
>
> • Personal experiences
>
> • Books
>
> • Websites
>
> • Newspaper articles
>
> • Online videos
>
> • Interviews

Confer

▷ During independent writing, move around the room to confer briefly with students about their research. Use prompts such as the following as needed.

• *What do you need to find out before you write your feature article?*

• *Where could you look to find that information?*

• *Is there anyone you could interview or a video you could watch about _____?*

Share

Following independent writing, gather students in the meeting area to share their research.

Talk about how you found and collected information about your topic.

Writing Minilesson Principle
Hook your readers from the beginning.

Writing Feature Articles

You Will Need

- a copy of any feature articles discussed for each student (see the online resource for WML1)
- document camera (optional)
- chart paper and markers
- writer's notebooks and writing folders

Academic Language / Important Vocabulary

- feature article
- hook
- introduction

Continuum Connection

- Understand that a factual text may use literary language and literary techniques to engage and entertain readers as it gives them factual information
- Include facts, figures, statistics, examples, and anecdotes when appropriate

GOAL

Experiment with different ways to hook readers from the beginning.

RATIONALE

When students notice and think about how writers of feature articles hook readers in the introduction, they will try some of the same techniques in their own writing. They will begin to write feature articles with engaging and interesting introductions.

WRITER'S NOTEBOOK/WRITING FOLDER

Students may experiment in their writer's notebooks with different techniques for hooking their readers and/or begin writing their feature article on draft paper to be kept in their writing folders.

ASSESS LEARNING

- Notice whether students write feature articles with engaging introductions that hook the readers.
- Look for evidence that they can use vocabulary such as *feature article*, *hook*, and *introduction*.

MINILESSON

To help students think about the minilesson principle, use mentor texts (see Feature Articles in the online resources for WML1) to engage them in an inquiry-based lesson on hooking the readers in the introduction. Here is an example.

- Show or project "The Gray Wolf: An Endangered Species . . . or Not?" Read the first paragraph aloud.

  What do you notice about how the writer used the introduction, or beginning, to make you want to keep reading?

- Record students' responses on chart paper.
- Show or project "She Said She Could and She Did: The Story of Nellie Bly" and read the first paragraph aloud.

  How did this writer hook readers, or make them want to keep reading?

- Record students' responses on the chart.

  Why do you think the writer asked questions?

- Show or project "Hop on Board the Bike Bus!" and read the first paragraph aloud.

  What do you notice about the introduction of this article? What makes it interesting to read?

- Record responses on the chart.

Have a Try

Invite students to talk to a partner about their own feature article.

> Think about the feature article you're working on. How might you hook readers from the beginning? Turn and talk to your partner about your ideas.

▶ After students turn and talk, invite several students to share their ideas.

Summarize and Apply

Write the principle at the top of the chart. Summarize the learning and invite students to start writing their feature articles.

> What did you learn today about how you can hook your readers?

> During independent writing time today, think about how you will hook your readers. You may want to try out different ideas in your writer's notebook. When you're ready, start writing your feature article on draft paper, and keep it in your writing folder.

> ### Hook your readers from the beginning.
>
> Ways to Start a Feature Article
> - Tell a story.
> - Create a picture in the reader's mind.
> - Use descriptive language.
> - Ask readers questions to make them think about or imagine something.
> - Give hints about what the article is going to be about.
> - Introduce the main "characters" (people or animals) of the article.

Confer

▶ During independent writing, move around the room to confer briefly with students about their introductions. Use prompts such as the following as needed.

- *How could you start your feature article?*
- *What could you do to hook your readers, or make them want to keep reading?*
- *Would you like to begin by telling a story?*
- *How could you create a picture for your readers?*

Share

Following independent writing, gather students in pairs in the meeting area to share their introductions.

> Listen to your partner read the introduction aloud. Then share what you like about the beginning, and ask any questions you have.

Writing Feature Articles

You Will Need

- a copy of any feature articles discussed for each student (see the online resource for WML1)
- document camera (optional)
- chart paper and markers
- writing folders

Academic Language / Important Vocabulary

- feature article
- voice

Continuum Connection

- Use literary language to make topic interesting to readers
- Include details that add to the voice
- Show enthusiasm and energy for the topic
- Write in a way that speaks directly to the reader
- Write in a way that shows care and commitment to the topic
- Produce expository writing that reveals the stance of the writer toward the topic

GOAL

Use different techniques to show a strong voice to make the article interesting.

RATIONALE

When you help students notice different ways writers show their voice in feature writing, they will try some of the same techniques in their own writing. By developing their own writing voices, they will write more engaging, interesting feature articles.

WRITER'S NOTEBOOK/WRITING FOLDER

Encourage students to use different techniques to show a strong voice as they work on their feature articles in their writing folders.

ASSESS LEARNING

- Notice whether students' personalities come through in their writing.
- Look for evidence that they can use vocabulary such as *feature article* and *voice*.

MINILESSON

To help students think about the minilesson principle, use mentor texts (see Feature Articles in the online resources for WML1) to engage them in an inquiry-based lesson on writing with a strong voice. Here is an example.

> One way you can show your personality to the world is through the choices you make in your writing. The way you show your personality through your writing is called your writing voice. Let's look at how the writers of feature articles show their writing voices.

- Show or project "Hop on Board the Bike Bus!" and read the second paragraph.

  > How does the writer's voice sound? What did the writer do to create a writing voice?

- If needed, draw students' attention to the first sentence. Point out that one way to show voice is to write in a conversational manner, as if speaking directly to the readers. Record this idea and example on chart paper.

- Show or project "She Said She Could and She Did: The Story of Nellie Bly" and read the fourth paragraph.

  > What do you notice about how the writer created voice in this paragraph?

- Record students' responses on the chart.

Have a Try

Invite students to talk to a partner about other ways a writer shows a writing voice.

> Turn and talk to your partner about what you notice about how the writer shows a writing voice and also makes the writing interesting.

▶ After time for discussion, invite several pairs to share their thinking. Add any new ideas to the chart, as appropriate.

Summarize and Apply

Write the principle at the top of the chart. Summarize the learning and remind students to show a strong voice in their writing.

> How can you write a feature article with a strong voice?

> During independent writing time today, continue working on your feature article. Remember to write with a strong voice. You may want to try some of the techniques we talked about today. Look at the feature articles in your writing folder to get ideas if you need to. Bring your writing to share when we come back together.

Write with a strong voice.

Speak directly to the reader.	"You're probably thinking, What on Earth is the Bike Bus?"
Use punctuation in interesting ways (to emphasize certain words, to show what you think).	"The article writer—a man—called the working woman 'a monstrosity!'"
Use powerful word choices.	"a fiery letter" "Nellie was horrified"
Say things in a surprising way.	"She showed the world that women could do anything that men could do. And, sometimes, they could do it better."

Confer

▶ During independent writing, move around the room to confer briefly with students about writing with a strong voice. Use prompts such as the following as needed.

- *How can you show your voice in your writing?*
- *How can you make your writing sound like the way you talk?*
- *Could you use a more powerful word here to show how you really feel about _____?*

Share

Following independent writing, gather students in the meeting area to share their writing. Choose several students to read aloud what they have written.

> What do you notice about how _____ shows a strong writing voice?

Assessment

After you have taught the minilessons in this umbrella, observe students as they write and talk about their writing. Use *The Fountas & Pinnell Literacy Continuum* to notice, teach for, and support students' learning as you observe their attempts at writing.

▶ What evidence do you have of students' new understandings related to writing feature articles?

- Can students identify and discuss the qualities of good feature articles?
- Do they write feature articles about topics that interest them?
- Is a particular point of view, or perspective, evident in their feature articles?
- Do they use a variety of primary and/or secondary sources to gather information for their feature articles?
- Do their feature articles hook readers with an engaging introduction?
- Do they write with a strong voice?
- Do students understand and use vocabulary such as *feature article*, *topic*, *point of view*, *hook*, and *voice*?

▶ In what other ways, beyond the scope of this umbrella, are students ready to explore nonfiction writing?

- Are they showing an interest in opinion writing?
- Are they ready to begin writing persuasive essays?

Use your observations to determine the next umbrella you will teach. You may also consult Suggested Sequence of Lessons (pp. 665–682) for guidance.

EXTENSIONS FOR WRITING FEATURE ARTICLES

▶ Encourage students to add illustrations or photographs, graphics, and text features (e.g., headings, sidebars) to their feature articles.

▶ Show students how to type and design their feature articles on a computer.

▶ Help students publish their feature articles in a class magazine, and/or encourage students to submit their best feature articles to magazines that accept submissions from children.

▶ Download rubrics from the online resources (fp.pub/resources) to help you and your students evaluate how well they are able to apply the concepts in these lessons.

Minilessons in This Umbrella

WML1 Notice the qualities of good opinion writing.

WML2 Write an introduction that states your opinion clearly.

WML3 Provide reasons and evidence for your opinion.

WML4 Write a strong concluding paragraph.

Before Teaching Umbrella 11 Minilessons

For the purposes of this umbrella, the term *opinion writing* refers to a piece of writing in which the writer shares an opinion for a variety of reasons but not necessarily with the goal of changing readers' minds or actions. An opinion piece might influence readers' thinking; however, the main purpose is to inform readers so they can make their own decisions. In opinion writing, the writer gives reasons for an opinion, to inform rather than to persuade. Opinion writing sets the stage for persuasive and argumentative writing.

In addition to the examples provided in the online resources, you may want to collect other examples of opinion writing from everyday life (e.g., product reviews, recipe reviews, book reviews, movie reviews, letters to the editor in children's magazines, appropriate newspaper editorials).

For students to write effective opinions, they should write about topics they care about. Encourage them to look through their writer's notebooks to find topics they feel strongly about. Ahead of these lessons, you may also want to teach WPS.U2: Writer's Notebook: Getting Ideas from Your Life (especially WML 7) and WPS.U4: Writer's Notebook: Becoming an Expert (especially WML1). These lessons will help students compile valuable thinking about topics they have genuine opinions about.

As you read and discuss opinion writing together, help students

- notice the characteristics of opinion writing,
- identify the author's opinion,
- explain how the author supports the opinion, and
- share their own opinions about the topic.

WML1

GEN.U11.WML1

Writing Minilesson Principle
Notice the qualities of good opinion writing.

Exploring Opinion Writing

You Will Need

- several examples of opinion writing in different forms (e.g., the online resource Opinion Writing)
- sticky notes
- chart paper and markers
- writer's notebooks
- To download the following online resource for this lesson, visit **fp.pub/resources**:
  - Opinion Writing

Academic Language / Important Vocabulary

- opinion writing
- quality
- reason
- connecting word

Continuum Connection

- Notice what makes writing effective and name the craft or technique

---

GOAL

Notice the characteristics of an effective opinion piece and learn how to choose a topic.

RATIONALE

Writers learn from other writers. By studying examples of opinion writing, students will be better prepared and equipped to begin writing their own opinion pieces. They will model their own opinion pieces on those they have read.

WRITER'S NOTEBOOK/WRITING FOLDER

Have students look through their writer's notebooks to choose a topic for an opinion piece.

ASSESS LEARNING

- Notice whether students can identify the qualities of good opinion writing.
- Look for evidence that they can use vocabulary such as *opinion writing*, *quality*, *reason*, and *connecting word*.

MINILESSON

Students will need their writer's notebooks for this lesson. To help students think about the minilesson principle, engage them in an inquiry-based lesson on the types and qualities of opinion writing. Here is an example.

- Divide students into small groups, and give each group at least one piece of opinion writing to study and discuss (see the online resource).

  In your group, discuss the piece of writing I gave you. In your writer's notebook, make some notes to record what you notice about the writing.

  The pieces of writing you discussed are a type of writing called opinion writing. Why do you think they're called that?

  What did you notice about opinion writing?

- Have students share what they wrote in their writer's notebooks, and write their noticings on chart paper. Help students identify the types and characteristics of the opinion pieces they studied.

- As needed, prompt students' thinking about opinion writing with questions such as the following:

  - *How do opinion pieces usually begin?*
  - *How do the writers support, or tell more about, their opinions?*
  - *What do you notice about how they provide reasons for their opinions?*
  - *How do the writers connect different ideas, or move from one idea to another?*
  - *How do opinion pieces usually end?*

Have a Try

Invite students to talk to a partner about their ideas for opinion writing.

▶ Model looking through your writer's notebook to find an idea for opinion writing.

> I've written a lot about my favorite foods, so I will write a review of my favorite restaurant. Turn and talk to your partner about your ideas for opinion writing.

▶ After time for discussion, invite several students to share their ideas.

Summarize and Apply

Summarize the learning and invite students to choose a topic for opinion writing.

> What did you notice about opinion writing today?

> During independent writing time today, spend some time looking through your writer's notebook and thinking about your ideas for opinion writing. Decide what you would like to write an opinion piece about. Bring your ideas to share when we meet later.

▶ Note that the chart from this lesson is referenced in WPS.U12.WML3.

Opinion Writing

Types of Opinion Writing

- Review (restaurant, book, product)
- Essay
- Letter

In opinion writing, the writer—
- states the opinion clearly, usually at the beginning.
- engages readers so they want to read the opinion.
- supports the opinion with reasons and evidence.
- uses personal experience to support the opinion.
- uses connecting words to show how ideas are related.
- summarizes the opinion at the end.

Confer

▶ During independent writing, move around the room to confer briefly with students about their ideas for opinion writing. Use prompts such as the following as needed.

- *What topics have you written about often?*
- *Would you like to write a review of your favorite book, movie, or restaurant? What will your opinion be?*
- *What is your favorite _____? What is the best _____? What are some reasons that _____ is your favorite?*

Share

Following independent writing, gather students in the meeting area to share their ideas.

> Each of you will share your idea for opinion writing. If you don't have an idea yet, you can pass. You might hear an idea from a classmate.

WML2

Writing Minilesson Principle
Write an introduction that states your opinion clearly.

Exploring Opinion Writing

You Will Need

- several examples of opinion writing in different forms (e.g., the online resource for WML1)
- chart paper and markers
- writer's notebooks and writing folders

Academic Language / Important Vocabulary

- opinion writing
- introduction

Continuum Connection

- Use a variety of beginnings and endings to engage the reader
- Understand the importance of the lead in a story or nonfiction piece

GOAL

Write an introduction that states an opinion clearly.

RATIONALE

As with any piece of writing, opinion writing should start by engaging readers. When students notice how authors of opinion pieces craft their introductions—engaging their readers and stating the opinion—they will be better prepared to write clear and engaging introductions for their own opinion pieces.

WRITER'S NOTEBOOK/WRITING FOLDER

Students can experiment with different ways to start their opinion pieces in their writer's notebooks before writing an introduction on draft paper to be kept in their writing folders.

ASSESS LEARNING

- Notice whether students begin their opinion pieces with an engaging introduction that states their opinion clearly and summarizes the reasons for their opinion.
- Look for evidence that they can use vocabulary such as *opinion writing* and *introduction*.

MINILESSON

To help students think about the minilesson principle, use mentor texts to engage students in an inquiry-based lesson on how to write a clear and engaging introduction to an opinion piece. You might want to give a copy of each opinion piece you plan to discuss in this lesson to each student. Here is an example.

- Display and read aloud the introductions to several opinion pieces (see WML1 for the online resource).

  What do you notice about how the writers began their opinion pieces?

- Use any of the following prompts as necessary to guide students' observations.
  - *Did the writers give any reasons for their opinions?*
  - *How much detail did they give about those reasons?*
  - *How did the writers grab your attention and make you want to keep reading their writing?*

- Record students' responses on chart paper, generalizing them as necessary.

  The beginning of an opinion piece is called the introduction. When you write the introduction for your opinion piece, you'll want to think about these ideas.

- If you have distributed copies of opinion pieces to students, have them store the copies in their writing folders.

Have a Try

Invite students to talk to a partner about writing an introduction to an opinion piece.

> Think about the topic that you decided to write about for your opinion piece. How might you start your opinion piece? What will you include in your introduction? Turn and talk to your partner about your ideas.

Summarize and Apply

Help students summarize the learning and remind them to clearly state their opinion in their introduction to an opinion piece.

> What is the main purpose of the introduction to an opinion piece?

▶ Write the principle at the top of the chart.

> Today during independent writing time, think about how to introduce your opinion piece. Remember to clearly state your opinion and briefly mention the reasons for your opinion. Experiment with how you will write the introduction in your writer's notebook. When you are satisfied with what you have written, write the introduction on draft paper and continue writing about your opinion. Bring your writing to share when we meet later.

> **Write an introduction that states your opinion clearly.**
>
> - State your opinion clearly.
>
> - Briefly mention the reasons for your opinion.
>
> - Hook the readers so they want to keep reading:
>
>   - Ask a question.
>
>   - Give the reader something to think about.
>
>   - Start with a strong emotion.

Confer

▶ During independent writing, move around the room to confer briefly with students about their introductions. Use prompts such as the following as needed.

- *What are you writing about for your opinion piece?*
- *How could you start your introduction?*
- *What do you need to remember to include in your introduction?*
- *How will you make readers want to keep reading?*

Share

Following independent writing, gather students in the meeting area to share their introductions.

> Who would like to share the introduction to your opinion piece?

Writing Minilesson Principle
Provide reasons and evidence for your opinion.

Exploring Opinion Writing

You Will Need

- a sample opinion piece displayed or a copy for each student (e.g., "Review of Sunshine Diner" from the online resource for WML1)
- chart paper and markers
- writer's notebooks and writing folders

Academic Language / Important Vocabulary

- opinion writing
- connecting word
- reason
- evidence
- fact
- support

Continuum Connection

- Introduce ideas followed by supportive details and examples
- Use common (simple) connectives and some sophisticated connectives (words that link ideas and clarify meaning) that are used in written texts but do not appear often in everyday oral language: e.g., *although, however, therefore, though, unless, whenever*

GOAL

Write reasons to support an opinion and use connectives to link the opinion and reasons clearly.

RATIONALE

When students notice how authors of opinion pieces support their opinions with reasons and evidence, they will be better equipped to write clearly stated and connected reasons in their own opinion pieces.

WRITER'S NOTEBOOK/WRITING FOLDER

Students will continue working on their opinion pieces in their writing folders. They can use their writer's notebooks to make a list of reasons.

ASSESS LEARNING

- Notice whether students provide clearly stated and well-supported reasons for the opinion and use connecting words to transition between ideas.
- Look for evidence that they can use vocabulary such as *opinion writing, connecting word, reason, evidence, fact,* and *support.*

MINILESSON

To help students think about the minilesson principle, use a mentor text to demonstrate how to provide reasons and evidence for an opinion. Here is an example.

- Display "Review of Sunshine Diner" (see WML1 for the online resource) or another opinion piece. If students each have a copy of the opinion piece, have them follow along as you read the body paragraphs aloud. Then focus the discussion on the opinion and the supporting reasons.

  Here's an opinion piece about the writer's favorite restaurant. The writer wrote a few paragraphs to explain the reasons for the opinion. What do you notice about how the writer provided reasons for the opinion?

  What kind of evidence did the writer use to support the reasons?

  What do you notice about how the writer separated the writing into paragraphs?

  What do you notice about how the writer connected different ideas? What kinds of words help readers move from one idea to another?

  What other connecting words might you use in an opinion piece?

- Record students' responses on chart paper, generalizing them as necessary.

Have a Try

Invite students to talk to a partner about providing reasons for an opinion.

> Think about the opinion piece that you're working on. What reasons and evidence could you give to support your opinion? Turn and talk to your partner about your ideas.

Summarize and Apply

Help students summarize the learning and remind them to provide reasons and evidence for their opinion when they write opinion pieces.

> How can you help readers understand your opinion?

▶ Write the principle at the top of the chart.

> During independent writing time today, continue working on an opinion piece that you've already started or start a new one. Remember to write reasons and evidence to support your opinion. You might list reasons and evidence in your writer's notebook before working on the draft of your opinion piece. Bring your writing to share when we come back together.

> ### Provide reasons and evidence for your opinion.
>
> • State your reasons for your opinion clearly.
>
> • Support your reasons with evidence:
>   • Facts
>   • Examples
>   • Personal experiences
>   • Details
>
> • Write about one big reason in each paragraph.
>
> • Use connecting words to connect different ideas. For example:
>   • In fact
>   • Also
>   • In addition
>   • Although
>   • Nevertheless

Confer

▶ During independent writing, move around the room to confer briefly with students about their opinion writing. Use prompts such as the following as needed.

- *What are you writing an opinion about today?*
- *What are some reasons for why you have your opinion?*
- *How could you support, or tell more about, a reason? Do you know any facts about that? Could you describe a personal experience related to that?*
- *What connecting word could you use to connect those two ideas?*

Share

Following independent writing, gather students in the meeting area to share their writing.

> Who would like to read aloud the reasons and evidence you wrote in your opinion piece?

> Does anyone have any comments or questions for _____ ?

You Will Need

- several examples of opinion pieces with strong conclusions displayed or a copy for each student (e.g., "Review of Sunshine Diner" from the online resource for WML1)
- chart paper and markers
- writer's notebooks and writing folders

Academic Language / Important Vocabulary

- opinion writing
- concluding

Continuum Connection

- Use a variety of beginnings and endings to engage the reader
- Bring the piece to closure with an effective summary, parting idea, or satisfying ending

GOAL

Write a paragraph that summarizes the opinion and satisfies the readers.

RATIONALE

When you help students notice different ways that authors conclude opinion pieces, they will be better equipped to finish their opinion pieces with a strong conclusion that summarizes their opinion and satisfies the readers.

WRITER'S NOTEBOOK/WRITING FOLDER

Students can try out their conclusions in their writer's notebooks before working on the draft of their opinion pieces in their writing folders.

ASSESS LEARNING

- Notice whether students finish the opinion piece with a strong concluding paragraph.
- Look for evidence that they can use vocabulary such as *opinion writing* and *concluding*.

MINILESSON

To help students think about the minilesson principle, use mentor texts to engage them in an inquiry-based lesson on how to write a strong concluding paragraph. Here is an example.

- Display the conclusion to "Review of Sunshine Diner" (see WML1 for the online resource Opinion Writing) or another opinion piece. If students each have a copy of the opinion piece, have them follow along as you read it aloud.

  What do you notice about how this opinion piece ends?

- Record students' responses on chart paper.

  The final paragraph is called the concluding paragraph, or the conclusion.

- Read aloud a few other examples of concluding paragraphs.

  What do you notice about these concluding paragraphs? How are they similar to each other? How are they different?

  How do writers make their concluding paragraphs interesting to read?

- Add responses to the chart, generalizing them as necessary. Help students notice different ways writers can conclude opinion pieces.

Have a Try

Invite students to talk to a partner about writing a strong concluding paragraph.

> Think about the opinion piece you're working on. How might you conclude your writing? Turn and talk to your partner about your ideas.

Summarize and Apply

Write the principle at the top of the chart. Help students summarize the learning and remind them to write a strong concluding paragraph.

> How can you make a concluding paragraph strong?

> During independent writing time today, continue working on an opinion piece that you've already started or start a new one. Remember to write a strong concluding paragraph. You might want to experiment with writing a few different conclusions in your writer's notebook. Bring your writing to share when we come back together.

> ### Write a strong concluding paragraph.
>
> - Summarize your opinion and reasons.
>
> - Make your ending interesting to read:
>   - End with a question.
>   - End with an emotion.
>   - End with a personal experience.
>   - Give the reader something to think about.

Confer

▷ During independent writing, move around the room to confer briefly with students about their concluding paragraphs. Use prompts such as the following as needed.

- *How could you end your opinion piece?*
- *What could you write that would summarize your opinion and reasons?*
- *How could you make your conclusion interesting for your readers?*
- *What question could you ask your readers?*

Share

Following independent writing, gather students in pairs in the meeting area to share their writing.

> Share your conclusion with your partner.

▷ After students share with a partner, invite a few students to share their conclusions with the whole class.

Assessment

After you have taught the minilessons in this umbrella, observe students as they write and talk about their writing. Use *The Fountas & Pinnell Literacy Continuum* to notice, teach for, and support students' learning as you observe their attempts at opinion writing.

▮ What evidence do you have of students' new understandings related to opinion writing?

- Can students identify the characteristics of good opinion writing?

- Do their opinion pieces start with an introduction that clearly states an opinion and engages their readers?

- Do they provide reasons and evidence to support their opinions?

- Do their opinion pieces end with a strong conclusion?

- Do students understand and use vocabulary such as *quality*, *opinion writing*, *introduction*, *reason*, and *concluding*?

▮ In what other ways, beyond the scope of this umbrella, are students ready to share their opinions?

- Are they ready to begin writing persuasive essays?

Use your observations to determine the next umbrella you will teach. You may also consult Suggested Sequence of Lessons (pp. 665–682) for guidance.

EXTENSIONS FOR EXPLORING OPINION WRITING

▶ Encourage students to write opinion pieces in different forms (e.g., poems, songs, posters, letters, speeches).

▶ Invite students to write opinion pieces about more sophisticated subjects (e.g., current events).

▶ Help students make video reviews of their favorite books, movies, foods, etc.

▶ Download rubrics from the online resources (fp.pub/resources) to help you and your students evaluate how well they are able to apply the concepts in these lessons.

Minilessons in This Umbrella

WML1   Choose a topic for a persuasive essay.

WML2   Use what you know about opinion writing to help you write a persuasive essay.

WML3   Convince your audience to agree with your opinion or to take action.

WML4   Address the counterargument.

Writer's Notebook

Before Teaching Umbrella 12 Minilessons

We strongly recommend teaching GEN.U11: Exploring Opinion Writing before teaching the lessons in this umbrella. Ideally, students will already have written several opinion pieces. In this umbrella, students will build on their understanding of opinion writing to learn how to write a persuasive essay. Persuasive writing is similar to opinion writing, but it involves more robust argumentation and appealing to the audience for support.

In addition to the examples provided in the online resources, you may want to collect other examples of persuasive writing from former students or age-appropriate magazines, newspapers, or websites.

It is important for students to write persuasive essays about topics they genuinely care about. If you have already taught WPS.U2: Writer's Notebook: Getting Ideas from Your Life (especially WML7) and WPS.U4: Writer's Notebook: Becoming an Expert (especially WML1), students will have collected plenty of ideas to choose from for a persuasive essay.

Section 2: Genres and Forms

Writing Minilesson Principle
Choose a topic for a persuasive essay.

You Will Need

- a sample persuasive essay, such as "Adopt a Cat Today" from the online resources
- document camera (optional)
- chart paper and markers
- writer's notebooks
- To download the following online resource for this lesson, visit **fp.pub/resources**:
  - Persuasive Essays

Academic Language / Important Vocabulary

- persuasive essay
- topic
- opinion
- convince

Continuum Connection

- Understand that the purpose of persuasion or argument may be to convince the reader to take the writer's point of view, take some action, or improve some aspect of the world

GOAL

Select a topic to convince someone of an opinion, to take action on an issue, or to improve the world in some way.

RATIONALE

By studying mentor texts, students will understand that the purpose of a persuasive essay is to convince others to think or act in a particular way. They will write their own persuasive essays about ideas that they care deeply about and want to convey to others.

WRITER'S NOTEBOOK/WRITING FOLDER

Have students make lists of possible topics for a persuasive essay in their writer's notebooks.

ASSESS LEARNING

- Notice whether students select a topic to convince someone of an idea, to take action on an issue, or to improve the world in some way.
- Look for evidence that they can use vocabulary such as *persuasive essay*, *topic*, *opinion*, and *convince*.

MINILESSON

To help students think about the minilesson principle, engage them in an inquiry-based lesson on choosing a topic for a persuasive essay. Here is an example.

- Display and read aloud a sample persuasive essay, such as "Adopt a Cat Today" from the online resource.

  This piece of writing is called a persuasive essay. What do you notice about this type of writing? What do you think a persuasive essay is?

  In a persuasive essay, you try to persuade, or convince, readers to agree with your opinion or to take action, perhaps to improve the world in some way. What is the topic of this persuasive essay?

  This persuasive essay is about pet cats. Who is the audience for this essay?

  What is the writer's purpose, or reason for writing? What is the writer trying to convince the audience to do?

- Record students' responses on chart paper.

  Think about what you would like to change at school, at home, in our town, in our country, or in the whole world. For example, on my way to school today, I noticed some trash on the sidewalk. I would like to convince people in our community to stop littering. Who would be my audience?

  What would be the purpose of my essay?

- Record students' responses on the chart.

Have a Try

Invite students to talk to a partner about their ideas for persuasive essays.

> What could you write a persuasive essay about? Think about what you want to change in your life, the school, the town, or the world and what you want people to do about it. Turn and talk to your partner about your ideas.

▶ After time for discussion, invite several students to share their ideas for topics for persuasive essays. Ask them to identify the audience and purpose. Add their ideas to the chart.

Summarize and Apply

Write the principle at the top of the chart. Summarize the learning and invite students to further explore topics for persuasive essays.

> During independent writing time today, look through your writer's notebook for topics you've written about before and that you could write a persuasive essay about. Make a list of all your ideas in your writer's notebook. Circle the ones that interest you. Bring your ideas to share when we meet later.

Choose a topic for a persuasive essay.

Topic	Audience	Purpose
Pet cats	People who are thinking of adopting a pet	To convince people to adopt a cat instead of a dog
Littering	People who live in our town	To convince people to stop littering
Recess	The school principal	To convince the principal to make recess longer
Bedtime	My parents	To convince my parents to let me stay up half an hour later
Voting	Government leaders	To convince the government to lower the voting age to 10

Confer

▶ During independent writing, move around the room to confer briefly with students about their ideas for persuasive essays. Use prompts such as the following as needed.

- *What is something that you think is unfair and should be changed?*
- *What is one thing that you think should be done to make our school (town, country, or world) a better place?*
- *If you wrote an essay about _____, who would be your audience? What would be your purpose?*

Share

Following independent writing, gather students in the meeting area to share their ideas for persuasive essays.

> Tell one idea you have for a persuasive essay. If you haven't decided yet, you can say "pass." You might hear an idea from a classmate.

Writing Minilesson Principle
Use what you know about opinion writing to help you write a persuasive essay.

Writing Persuasive Essays

You Will Need

- a sample persuasive essay, such as "Meatless Monday" [see the online resource for WML1]
- document camera [optional]
- chart paper and markers
- writer's notebooks and writing folders

Academic Language / Important Vocabulary

- persuasive essay
- opinion
- convince
- claim
- evidence

Continuum Connection

- Understand the importance of supporting each idea or argument with facts, reasons, or examples
- Begin with a title or opening that tells the reader what is being argued or explained and end with a conclusion
- Use opinions supported by facts
- Organize the body of the text into paragraphs
- Provide a series of clear arguments with reasons to support the argument

GOAL

Understand that writing a persuasive essay is similar to opinion writing in that you introduce the topic, provide reasons and evidence, and write a conclusion.

RATIONALE

When you help students notice the similarities and differences between opinion writing and persuasive writing, they will build on what they already know about opinion writing to write an effective persuasive essay.

WRITER'S NOTEBOOK/WRITING FOLDER

Invite students to try out ideas in their writer's notebooks or start writing their persuasive essays on draft paper to be kept in their writing folders.

ASSESS LEARNING

- Notice whether students build on their understanding of opinion writing to write a persuasive essay.
- Look for evidence that they can use vocabulary such as *persuasive essay*, *opinion*, *convince*, *claim*, and *evidence*.

MINILESSON

To help students think about the minilesson principle, use a mentor text (such as those from Persuasive Essays in the online resources for WML1) to engage students in an inquiry-based lesson on the qualities of a persuasive essay. Here is an example.

- Display and read aloud a sample persuasive essay, such as "Meatless Monday" from the online resource.

   This writer thinks that the school cafeteria should start doing Meatless Monday. This is the writer's opinion. You've learned about how to use opinion writing to share your opinion with other people. A persuasive essay is similar to opinion writing, but it's also a bit different. Think about what you've learned about opinion writing. How is a persuasive essay like opinion writing?

- Record students' responses on chart paper. Help students understand that, as in an opinion piece, the writer of a persuasive essay states a claim and provides reasons and evidence to support that claim. Guide students to identify the claim and the main reasons and evidence in the mentor text.

   What do you notice about how a persuasive essay is different from opinion writing?

- Add responses to the chart. Help students understand that the writer of a persuasive essay directs the writing to a particular audience and works hard to convince the audience to do or think something.

Have a Try

Invite students to talk to a partner about their plans for their own persuasive essays.

> Think about the topic that you chose for your persuasive essay. Who is your audience? What is your purpose for writing? What will you try to convince your audience to do or think? Turn and talk about the reasons and evidence you can give to support your claim.

Summarize and Apply

Write the principle at the top of the chart. Summarize the learning and remind students to use what they know about opinion writing to write a persuasive essay.

> What did you learn today about how to write a persuasive essay?

> During independent writing time today, start working on your persuasive essay. You may want to make a note of your claim, reasons, and evidence in your writer's notebook. When you're ready, start writing your persuasive essay on draft paper, which you will keep in your writing folder. Remember to state your claim clearly near the beginning of your essay. Bring your writing to share when we come back together.

> Use what you know about opinion writing to help you write a persuasive essay.
>
> How is a persuasive essay _like_ opinion writing?
> - The writer gives and supports an opinion about a topic.
> - The writer clearly states a claim at the beginning (introduction) of the piece.
> - The writer provides reasons and evidence to support the claim.
> - The writer uses connecting words to show how ideas are related.
> - The writer ends the piece by summarizing the opinion (conclusion).
>
> How is a persuasive essay _different_ from opinion writing?
> - The writer writes for a particular audience.
> - The writer works hard to convince the audience to do or think something.

Confer

▶ During independent writing, move around the room to confer briefly with students about their persuasive essays. Use prompts such as the following as needed.

- *How will you use what you know about opinion writing to write a persuasive essay?*
- *What claim will you make in your essay?*
- *Who are you writing your essay for? Who is your audience?*
- *What reasons and evidence might convince your audience to do or think _____?*

Share

Following independent writing, gather students in the meeting area to share their writing.

> Who would like to share the claim you are making in your persuasive essay?

> How is what you know about opinion writing helping you write your essay?

Writing Minilesson Principle
Convince your audience to agree with your opinion or to take action.

You Will Need

- several sample persuasive essays (see the online resource for WML1)
- document camera (optional)
- writer's notebooks and writing folders
- chart paper and markers

Academic Language / Important Vocabulary

- persuasive essay
- convince
- audience
- fact
- example
- emotion

Continuum Connection

- Understand that a writer can learn to write various forms of argument and persuasion by studying the characteristics of examples in mentor texts

GOAL

Use different craft moves to convince an audience of an idea.

RATIONALE

When students notice how writers of persuasive essays use persuasive techniques (e.g., appealing to emotions or providing factual evidence), they will begin to use the same techniques in their own persuasive writing.

WRITER'S NOTEBOOK/WRITING FOLDER

As students work on persuasive essays in their writing folders, they may want to try out ideas in their writer's notebooks.

ASSESS LEARNING

- Notice whether students use simple persuasive techniques to support their arguments.
- Look for evidence that they can use vocabulary such as *persuasive essay*, *convince*, *audience*, *fact*, *example*, and *emotion*.

MINILESSON

To help students think about the minilesson principle, use mentor texts (see those in Persuasive Essays in the online resources for WML1) to engage students in an inquiry-based lesson on persuasive techniques used. Here is an example.

- Divide students into small groups. Give each group one sample persuasive essay to study and discuss.

  In a persuasive essay, the writer tries to convince the audience to think or do something. Read the persuasive essay I gave you. Think about *how* exactly the writer tries to convince the audience. Discuss this with your group.

- After time for the groups to talk, ask each group to share their thinking.

  What are some sentences that you found convincing?

- As students share convincing sentences from the essay, give a name to each one (fact, emotion, example). Then create a chart that lists those three ways to convince an audience and record students' examples..

Have a Try

Invite students to talk to a partner about how they will convince their audience.

> Think about the persuasive essay you're working on. How will you convince your audience to do or think something? How might you use facts, emotions, or examples to convince them? Turn and talk to your partner about your ideas.

Summarize and Apply

Write the principle at the top of the chart. Read it to students. Summarize the learning and remind students to use different techniques to convince their audience.

> What did you learn today about how you can convince your audience when you're writing a persuasive essay?

> Continue working on your persuasive essay during independent writing time today. Remember to try to convince your audience to do or think something. Try convincing them in different ways, for example, by using facts, examples, and emotions. Bring your writing to share when we come back together.

Convince your audience to agree with your opinion or to take action.

With Facts

"Cats like to spend a lot of time on their own. In fact, they spend around 12-20 hours a day sleeping!"

"The meat industry also creates gases that cause air pollution."

With Emotions

"There are millions of cute, lonely cats in animal shelters waiting for their special person to take them home."

"Mom, sometimes you work late and don't get home until 7. On those days, we only get to spend an hour together before I have to go to bed. This makes me feel sad."

With Examples

"For one thing, cats are so cute. It's hard to resist their tiny pink noses, perfect little paws, and gentle purrs."

"However, there are many other ways to learn besides doing homework. For example, we learn when we talk to a grandparent, go for a walk outside, or practice the piano."

Confer

▶ During independent writing, move around the room to confer briefly with students about their persuasive essays. Use prompts such as the following as needed.

- *What claim are you making in your persuasive essay?*
- *How could you convince your audience to _____?*
- *What facts or examples could you share?*
- *What emotion do you want your audience to feel? How could you make them feel that?*

Share

Following independent writing, gather students in the meeting area to share their writing.

> Who would like to share one way you tried to convince your audience in your persuasive essay?

Writing Persuasive Essays

You Will Need

- two sample persuasive essays (see the online resource for WML1)
- document camera (optional)
- writer's notebooks and writing folders
- chart paper and markers

Academic Language / Important Vocabulary

- persuasive essay
- address
- concern

Continuum Connection

- Produce persuasive writing including argument with logical evidence to support ideas and to counter opposing argument

GOAL

Address some of the counterarguments to strengthen the persuasive essay.

RATIONALE

A persuasive essay is more convincing when the writer addresses counterarguments—concerns the audience might have about the writer's position. When students notice how writers of mentor texts have done this, they will start to do the same in their own persuasive essays, thus producing more effective and persuasive arguments.

WRITER'S NOTEBOOK/WRITING FOLDER

As students work on persuasive essays in their writing folders, they may want to try out ideas in their writer's notebooks.

ASSESS LEARNING

- Notice whether students effectively address concerns readers might have.
- Look for evidence that they can use vocabulary such as *persuasive essay*, *address*, and *concern*.

MINILESSON

To help students think about the minilesson principle, use mentor texts (see those from Persuasive Essays in the online resources for WML1) to engage students in an inquiry-based lesson on addressing counterarguments. Here is an example.

- Display "Why I Should Have a Later Bedtime" from the online resource or another sample persuasive essay. Read the sixth paragraph.

  What do you notice about how the writer attempted to convince the audience in this paragraph?

  In this paragraph, the writer addressed a concern that readers, his parents, might have about his idea—that he will wake up his brother. To address the concern, he explained why this won't be a problem. How did he do that?

- On chart paper, write the counterargument in one column and how the writer addresses it in a second column.

- Display another persuasive essay, such as "Meatless Monday" from the online resource, or give a copy to each student (or pair of students).

  How did the writer of this persuasive essay address, or respond to, readers' possible concerns? Turn and talk about this with your partner.

- After time for discussion, invite students to share their thinking. As needed, help them identify examples of how the writer addressed readers' concerns. Add them to the chart.

Have a Try

Invite students to talk to a partner about how they will address readers' concerns in their own persuasive essays.

> Think about the persuasive essay you're working on. What concerns might your readers have about your idea? How will you address these concerns? Turn and talk to your partner about this.

Summarize and Apply

Help students summarize the learning and invite them to continue working on their persuasive essays.

> What is something you can do to convince your readers when you're writing a persuasive essay?

▶ Lead students to state the principle. Write it at the top of the chart.

> During independent writing time today, continue working on your persuasive essay. Remember to think about concerns that your readers might have about your idea and address them in your essay. Bring your writing to share when we come back together.

Address the counterargument.

Counterargument	How the Writer Addresses the Counterargument
Might wake up little brother	Will do something quiet, like read a book or write in journal
Children won't get enough protein	Plant-based foods such as beans, nuts, and vegetables provide plenty of protein
Too hard for people to give up favorite foods	Eat many of the same foods in a different way, like pizza with vegetables

Confer

▶ During independent writing, move around the room to confer briefly with students about their persuasive essays. Use prompts such as the following as needed.

- *What concerns might your readers have about your idea?*
- *If you were having a conversation with your readers, what might they say in response to _____?*
- *How can you show your readers that they should not be worried about _____?*
- *What could you say to your readers to prove that you're right about _____?*

Share

Following independent writing, gather students in the meeting area to share their writing.

> Share with a partner how you addressed a counterargument.

Assessment

After you have taught the minilessons in this umbrella, observe students as they write and talk about writing persuasive essays. Use *The Fountas & Pinnell Literacy Continuum* to notice, teach for, and support students' learning as you observe their attempts at persuasive writing.

▶ What evidence do you have of students' new understandings related to writing persuasive essays?

- Do students choose topics they feel strongly about for their persuasive essays?
- Do they clearly state a claim and provide evidence to support that claim?
- Do they effectively use some simple persuasive techniques?
- Do they address counterarguments?
- Do students understand and use vocabulary such as *persuasive essay*, *evidence*, and *convince*?

▶ In what other ways, beyond the scope of this umbrella, are students exploring writing in different genres?

- Are they showing an interest in writing fairy tales?
- Are they interested in adding text features to their nonfiction writing?

Use your observations to determine the next umbrella you will teach. You may also consult Suggested Sequence of Lessons (pp. 665–682) for guidance.

EXTENSIONS FOR WRITING PERSUASIVE ESSAYS

▶ Teach students other forms of persuasive writing, such as letters to the editor, speeches, or advertisements.

▶ Regularly give students opportunities to read and discuss persuasive writing about pertinent current events and issues (e.g., in your local newspaper).

▶ Help students publish their completed persuasive essays in a class or school newspaper or in a class blog.

▶ Download rubrics from the online resources (fp.pub/resources) to help you and your students evaluate how well they are able to apply the concepts in these lessons.

Minilessons in This Umbrella

WML1 Make your own poetry anthology.

WML2 Respond to poems you collect.

WML3 Write a poem that connects to another poem.

WML4 Write poems from your life.

Before Teaching Umbrella 13 Minilessons

This umbrella guides students to create a poetry anthology over time. Each minilesson focuses on a different section of the poetry anthology, so allow time for students to work in a section before moving to the next minilesson. It is recommended that you start your own poetry anthology before teaching these lessons so you can model what to do in each section.

Provide blank notebooks for students to use for their poetry anthologies. WML1 and WML2 build the foundation for creating a poetry anthology. Students will create a table of contents, which will be built across the lessons, for four sections: "Poems That Tell About Me, Responses to Poems, Poem Connections," and "Poetry in My Life." Students will not write poems or responses until WML3 and WML4, so you may wish to spend several days reading, talking about, and collecting poems after teaching WML2. Have students place poems on the left-hand side of a two-page spread in their anthologies so that they can respond or draw on the right-hand side.

Creating a poetry anthology is one way to introduce a poetry workshop, an important element of the language and literacy framework, into your schedule. Substitute poetry workshop for readers' workshop or writers' workshop for one day a week or one week every month. For more information about poetry workshop, see pages 62–64.

Before teaching this umbrella, students will benefit from hearing about different poets (through poet talks), listening to poetry read aloud, reading and discussing poems with different styles, and writing their own poems. Collect as many poetry books as possible, such as those below from *Fountas & Pinnell Classroom™ Shared Reading Collection*, or choose poetry books from the classroom library.

Shared Reading Collection

A Whirling Swirl of Poems by Mike Downs

Grannie's Coal Pot by Summer Edward

Mosaic Master: Antoni Gaudí by Susan B. Katz

Stinky, Slimy, Sludgy Poems by Mike Downs

Writing Minilesson Principle
Make your own poetry anthology.

Making Poetry Anthologies

You Will Need

- your own poetry anthology that includes a decorated cover and table of contents

- a poem that you connect with written in the first section of your anthology (e.g., "The Basketball" from *A Whirling Swirl of Poems* by Mike Downs, from *Shared Reading Collection*)

- a diverse collection of poetry books and poems in which your students can see themselves

- a blank poetry anthology for each student (e.g., a blank notebook)

- markers, colored pencils, crayons, glue

- document camera (optional)

Academic Language / Important Vocabulary

- anthology
- poetry
- poet
- table of contents

Continuum Connection

- Understand poetry as a unique way to communicate about and describe feelings, sensory images, ideas, or stories

- Understand the way print works in poems and demonstrate the use in reading and writing them on a page using white space and line breaks

- Put several stories or poems together in a book

- Add cover spread with title and author information

GOAL

Understand the purpose of a poetry anthology.

RATIONALE

When you read poetry with students and help them find and respond to poems that are meaningful to them, it builds an appreciation for the art of language and the decisions poets make. The anthology becomes a useful reference for each student as a reader and as a writer across the year.

ASSESS LEARNING

- Notice whether students create a poetry anthology and make it their own.

- Look for evidence that they can use vocabulary such as *anthology*, *poetry*, *poet*, and *table of contents*.

MINILESSON

To guide students in creating a poetry anthology and making it their own, model your own poetry anthology and then have students think about poems they might include in theirs that connect to their lives. Here is an example.

- Show the poetry anthology that you have started that includes a decorated cover and a table of contents with the first section ("Poems That Tell About Me") and page number entered. Leave space for the other sections that will be added throughout this umbrella.

  A poetry anthology is a place where you can collect all types of poems. What do you notice about mine?

- Guide students to notice the decorated cover and the table of contents, including the title of the first section.

- Show and read the poem you have selected (e.g., "The Basketball" from *A Whirling Swirl of Poems*).

  I included this poem in the first section titled "Poems That Tell About Me." What do you think my choice shows about me?

- After students have made a few predictions, share the connection you feel with the poem. Then read aloud other poems that you think students can connect to their own experiences. Display them if possible so that students can join in reading aloud with you. Then discuss the poems, providing discussion prompts as needed (e.g., what they notice about the poets' choices, what the poems make them think about, what mental image the poems create).

  When we read poems, we connect with some more than others. Often, we connect to poems that make us think about something in our own lives.

Have a Try

Provide poems and poetry books for pairs of students to look through. Invite students to talk to their partner about what poem they will include in their poetry anthologies.

> With your partner, look through some poems and talk about a poem to which you feel a connection. Think about the title of this section to help you remember that the poem you select should make you think about something in your life.

▶ After students turn and talk, invite a few students to share ideas.

Summarize and Apply

Summarize the learning and remind students that they will begin a poetry anthology by creating a decorated cover and table of contents. They will title the first section "Poems That Tell About Me" and add the poem they have selected.

> Today, create the cover for your poetry anthology. Then begin a table of contents on the page after the cover. Add the first section, "Poems That Tell About Me." When you select a poem, copy the poem into your anthology. Also add an illustration. If you finish early, read more poems to see if there is another that could go in this section. If so, add it in. Bring your anthology to share when we meet later.

Make your own poetry anthology.

My Poetry Anthology

Mrs. Anders

Table of Contents

Poems That Tell About Me 3

Confer

▶ During independent writing, move around the room to confer briefly with students about their plans for making a poetry anthology. Use the following prompts as needed.

- *What are you going to put on the cover?*
- *How will the table of contents help you as you create this anthology?*
- *Tell why you selected this poem.*

Share

Following independent writing, gather students in the meeting area to share their poetry anthologies in groups of three.

> In groups of three, share your poetry anthologies. Show the cover and table of contents and share the poem that you selected for the first section.

Writing Minilesson Principle
Respond to poems you collect.

Making Poetry Anthologies

You Will Need

▸ a diverse collection of poetry books and poems, including one poem written on chart paper, such as the following from *Shared Reading Collection*:

- "Coal Pot Cook-Off" from *Grannie's Coal Pot* by Summer Edward

- *Mosaic Master* by Susan B. Katz

▸ students' poetry anthologies

▸ markers, colored pencils, crayons, and glue

Academic Language / Important Vocabulary

▸ anthology

▸ poetry

▸ poet

▸ respond

Continuum Connection

▸ Form and express opinions about a text in writing and support those opinions with rationales and evidence

▸ Notice and write about elements of the writer's craft: word choice, use of literary elements

▸ Understand that a writer can learn to write a variety of poems from studying mentor texts

GOAL

Create art and write in response to poems.

RATIONALE

Reading and discussing poems helps students develop an appreciation for the artistic language poets use. Each student will respond to an individual poem differently. Encouraging students to respond authentically to poetry through art or written words helps them show their own understanding of a poet's language.

ASSESS LEARNING

▸ Observe students as they write and create art in response to the poems they collect.

▸ Look for evidence that they can use vocabulary such as *anthology*, *poetry*, *poet*, and *respond*.

MINILESSON

To help students think about the minilesson principle, display a poem you have chosen, either in your anthology or on chart paper with space for a response. Guide students in a discussion about the poem and use shared writing to craft responses. Here is an example.

▸ Show and read "Coal Pot Cook-Off" on pages 22–23 in *Grannie's Coal Pot*.

> Talking about poems helps you notice things about the way the poet wrote the poem and helps you think about what the poem means to you. What do you notice about the way the poet wrote this poem? What does this poem say to you?

▸ Write responses to the questions next to the poem on the prepared chart paper.

▸ Model how to add the section titled "Reponses to Poems" in your table of contents.

> Writing is one way you could respond to this poem. In your anthology, you will make a new section titled "Responses to Poems" and add the section to your table of contents. The response will be on the page that faces the poem.

> Another way to respond to a poem is to use art. What are some ways you could respond to this poem with a drawing or an image that you create or find to show how you feel or what you think about the poem?

▸ After students share, use one of their ideas to make a drawing that responds to the poem in some way. Your students may need additional guidance in thinking about how to respond using art in ways that differ from making an illustration of the poem.

Have a Try

Using another poem, invite students to turn and talk about how they might respond to the poem with words and art.

▷ Show and read another poem that students can respond to, such as the poem on page 10 in *Mosaic Master*.

> Turn and talk about some ways you might respond to this poem using words and art.

▷ After time for discussion, ask a few pairs to share ideas.

Summarize and Apply

Summarize the learning and remind students that they will make a new section and add to their poetry anthology by adding a poem and responding to it with writing and art. Write the principle at the top of the chart.

> During independent writing time, read several poems to find one that you connect with in some way. You can also choose one of the poems we talked about. Copy the poem into your poetry anthology exactly as you see it on the page. You will also add this new section called "Responses to Poems" to the table of contents. Finally, write and draw a response. Bring your poetry anthology to share when we meet later.

Respond to poems you collect.

Today,
in First Capital Park,
everyone comes
to watch the coal pot chefs
whip up tasty dishes.

Stews and soups bubble.
Baked, fried and roasted
treats smell like heaven.

I stand tall with Grannie,
proud of my pelau.

from Grannie's Coal Pot
by Summer Edward

• What do you notice about the way the author wrote the poem?

The author used poetry to tell the story of special times with Grannie. A simile describes how good the food smelled at the cooking competition.

• What does the poem say to you?

I think about cooking with my family, especially my grandpa, because his cooking always smelled so good. If I close my eyes, I can hear the sounds of cooking, just like the sound of the bubbling soups in the poem.

Confer

▷ During independent writing, move around the room to confer briefly with students about the poems they have chosen. Use prompts such as the following as needed.

- *Share the poem you will be responding to.*
- *What are your thoughts about the choices the poet made?*
- *Let's look through these poems together and choose a poem you like.*
- *What does this poem make you think about?*

Share

Following independent writing, gather students in the meeting area in pairs to share their poems and responses.

> Share the poem you chose and why you chose it.

Writing Minilesson Principle
Write a poem that connects to another poem.

Making Poetry Anthologies

You Will Need

- a poem written on chart paper, such as an excerpt from p. 5 of *A Whirling Swirl of Poems* by Mike Downs, from *Shared Reading Collection*
- chart paper or your poetry anthology
- students' poetry anthologies
- a diverse collection of poetry books and poems
- markers, colored pencils, crayons, tape, and glue

Academic Language / Important Vocabulary

- anthology
- poetry
- poet
- response
- connect

Continuum Connection

- Borrow the style or some words or expressions from a writer in writing about a text
- Understand that a writer can learn to write a variety of poems from studying mentor texts
- Write a poetic text in response to another poem, reflecting the same style, topic, mood, or voice
- Write a variety of types of poems
- Shape words on a page to look like a poem

GOAL

Choose a poem and craft a poem in response.

RATIONALE

Reading and discussing poems helps students develop an appreciation for the artistic language of poets. Encouraging students to respond authentically to poetry by writing their own poem in response provides support for students as they develop their voices as writers.

ASSESS LEARNING

- Notice whether students are able to craft a response to the poems they collect.
- Look for evidence that they can use vocabulary such as *anthology*, *poetry*, *poet*, *response*, and *connect*.

MINILESSON

To help students think about the minilesson principle, use modeling and shared writing to craft responses to several poems. Here is an example.

- Show the chart paper prepared with a poem. Model how to add a new section titled "Poem Connections" to the table of contents.
- Read the poem aloud twice and talk about your connection to it. Then demonstrate writing a poem on the right-hand side of the chart.

  I connect with this poem because I enjoy poems written about nature. I want to write a poem in response to this one, and I want it to be similar in some ways. I will choose the topic of the ocean because it is another nature theme that I like. I will write my poem in the same format as this one.

- Think aloud as you demonstrate crafting a poem using the same theme and format as the example.

  What did you notice about how I wrote my poem?

- As needed, guide the conversation so that students notice that your poem uses the same theme (nature) and format and that you have added your name because you are the poet.

Have a Try

Work with students to write a poem with a different connection to the first poem (e.g., repetition, topic, favorite phrase, word).

> The poet's phrase "wrapped in clouds and gentle breeze" has stuck in my mind. Let's write a short poem that includes this phrase.

▶ Invite students to make illustrations for either of the poems at a later time and attach them to the chart.

Summarize and Apply

Summarize the learning and remind students that they will choose a poem and craft a poem in response.

> Today, choose a poem with which you feel a connection. Then write a poem in response, as I did and then we did. You will also add this new section called "Poem Connections" to the table of contents.

▶ Write the principle at the top of the chart.

> Copy the poem onto the left-hand page of your poetry anthology. Write the poet's name, the poem's title, and the book it came from. You can illustrate the poem. Then write your own poem in response on the right-hand side of your anthology and illustrate it. You might use the same repetition, a phrase, or something else. Bring your anthology to share when we meet later.

> ### Write a poem that connects to another poem.
>
> Filled with mountains,
>   oceans, trees,
>   wrapped in clouds
>   and gentle breeze.
>   To precious life
>   it's given birth,
>   our spinning home,
>   the planet Earth.
>   The Earth spins.
>
> Mike Downs
>
> Filled with starfish,
>   sharks, whales,
>   wrapped in kelp
>   and rolling sand.
>   Such wonders
>   lurk beneath,
>   our deep ocean,
>   the planet's water.
>   The ocean blue.
> Mrs. Anders
>
> The sky looks down at me.
> Wrapped in clouds
> and gentle breeze,
> sometimes shimmers,
> sometimes cries,
> always there to see.

Confer

▶ During independent writing, move around the room to confer briefly with students about their poetry anthologies. Use prompts such as the following as needed.

- *What can you do that the poet did?*
- *What does the poet make you think about?*
- *Will your poem look the same way on the page, or will you choose a different format?*

Share

Following independent writing, gather students in the meeting area to share the poems they selected and the response poems they crafted.

> In threes, share the poem that you selected and the poem you wrote in response.

Writing Minilesson Principle
Write poems from your life.

You Will Need

▶ a poem about a topic that comes from the poet's life, such as "My White-Striped Cat" from *Stinky, Slimy, Sludgy Poems* by Mike Downs, from *Shared Reading Collection*

▶ writer's notebooks (including your own)

▶ students' poetry anthologies

▶ chart paper or your poetry anthology

▶ markers

Academic Language / Important Vocabulary

▶ anthology

▶ poetry

▶ poet

▶ life

Continuum Connection

▶ Write a variety of types of poems

▶ Shape words on a page to look like a poem

▶ Understand poetry as a unique way to communicate about and describe feelings, sensory images, ideas, or stories

▶ Reread a writer's notebook to select topics: e.g., select small moments that can be expanded

GOAL

Understand that topics for poems can come from the poet's life.

RATIONALE

When students write poems in a poetry anthology that are personal to their lives, they learn that their voices have value. They are encouraged to use resources such as their writer's notebooks and life experiences for gaining poetry ideas.

ASSESS LEARNING

▶ Notice whether students use topics from their own lives to craft poems.

▶ Look for evidence that they can use vocabulary such as *anthology*, *poetry*, *poet*, and *life*.

MINILESSON

Students will need their writer's notebooks for this lesson. To help students think about the principle, model the process of choosing a poem idea from your writer's notebook and then writing a poem in your poetry anthology. Here is an example.

▶ Show and read a poem that relates to the poet's life, such as "My White-Striped Cat" on page 2 of *Stinky, Slimy, Sludgy Poems*.

> Where do you think the poet might have gotten the idea for this poem?

▶ Guide the conversation to help students recognize that the poet likely has a cat that might be similar to the one described in the poem.

> Poets often get ideas for poems from their own lives and experiences because those are most important to them.

▶ Model the process of rereading a few sections in your writer's notebook. Think aloud as you generate an idea for a poem that relates to your life. Here is an example.

> As I look back through my notebook, I notice one of the words on my heart map is *celebrations*. That gives me an idea for a poem about a family celebration when my grandmother visited from India. We made traditional foods from India in the clay pot that she brought all the way from her home.

▶ On chart paper or in your poetry anthology, write a short poem about the topic from your own life. Add a quick illustration.

> What did you notice?

▶ Point out that you are writing the poem in a new section called "Poetry in My Life." Add the section to your table of contents.

Have a Try

Have students turn and talk about using ideas from their lives for writing poetry.

> Turn and talk about poetry topics that relate to your own life. Look through your writer's notebook for ideas.

> ▶ Encourage students to look at ideas they have collected in Section 1: Getting Ideas from My Life. After time for discussion, ask a few students to share their ideas.

Summarize and Apply

Summarize the learning and remind students that they will write a poem that relates to something in their lives. Write the principle at the top of the chart.

> During independent writing time, look through your writer's notebook to get ideas for a poem topic that is meaningful to you. Turn to the place in your poetry anthology where you will create a new section called "Poetry in My Life" for the poems you write, and add the page number to the table of contents. Begin writing your poem, and bring your poetry anthology when we meet so you can share.

Write poems from your life.

Now arriving from New Delhi!

I am the first to spot Nani

in her blue embroidered sari.

Chutney   Parathas   Biryani

My mouth waters thinking about the earthen pot

that will be the first thing she pulls from her suitcase.

—Mr. Chopra

Confer

> ▶ During independent writing, move around the room to confer briefly with students about their poetry anthologies. Use prompts such as the following as needed.
> - *Tell me about the poem you are writing.*
> - *What words can you use to show how you were feeling?*
> - *In what way does the poem you are writing connect to your life?*
> - *Let's look through your writer's notebook to look for poem ideas.*

Share

Following independent writing, gather students in the meeting area to share the poems they are working on in their poetry anthologies.

> In pairs, share the poem you are working on in your poetry anthology.

Assessment

After you have taught the minilessons in this umbrella, observe students as they explore making a poetry anthology. Use *The Fountas & Pinnell Literacy Continuum* to notice, teach for, and support student's learning as you observe their attempts at reading, writing, and responding to poetry.

▶ What evidence do you have of students' new understandings related to making a poetry anthology?

- Are students choosing poems with which they have a connection?
- Do students tell through writing and drawing why they connect to poems?
- Do students write poems using a feature from a published poem?
- Do they include ideas from their own lives when they write poems?
- Do they understand and use vocabulary such as *anthology, poetry, poet, table of contents, connect,* and *respond*?

▶ In what other ways, beyond the scope of this umbrella, are students showing an interest in writing poetry?

- Are they thinking about different elements of poetry (e.g., simile, metaphor, personification, hyperbole)?
- Are they noticing different types of poems and trying some out (haiku, cinquain, limerick, concrete)?

Use your observations to determine the next umbrella you will teach. You may also consult Suggested Sequence of Lessons (pp. 665–682) for guidance.

EXTENSIONS FOR MAKING POETRY ANTHOLOGIES

▶ Introduce poets with diverse voices to students and support them in finding poets who write about topics that connect to their lives.

▶ Provide a variety of ways to get students thinking about poetry ideas (nature, music, paintings).

▶ Make poetry an integral part of the classroom community throughout the entire year.

▶ Create a poetry corner where students can display and share their poems.

Minilessons in This Umbrella

WML1　Notice the qualities of good poems.

WML2　Use line breaks and white space to communicate the meaning, rhythm, and tone of the poem.

WML3　Remove words to make your poem more powerful.

WML4　Use a metaphor or a simile to describe something.

WML5　Use personification to make your writing interesting.

WML6　Choose a meaningful title for your poem.

Before Teaching Umbrella 14 Minilessons

These minilessons can be taught as part of poetry workshop (see pp. 62–64). Allow time between lessons so students have time to think about each new poetry concept.

　The text set Genre Study: Poetry does not fall until later in the year in the suggested *Interactive Read-Aloud Collection* sequence, but there are individual poems within those books that can be shared now and read in more depth later. Use the books listed below from *Fountas & Pinnell Classroom™ Interactive Read-Aloud Collection* and *Shared Reading Collection*, or choose poetry books from the classroom library.

Interactive Read-Aloud Collection
Genre Study: Poetry

Shape Me a Rhyme: Nature's Forms in Poetry by Jane Yolen

A Place to Start a Family: Poems About Creatures That Build by David L. Harrison

On the Wing by David Elliott

Author Study: Patricia McKissack

Stitchin' and Pullin': A Gee's Bend Quilt

Author/Illustrator Study: Douglas Florian

Mammalabilia

In the Swim

Illustrator Study: Floyd Cooper

Meet Danitra Brown by Nikki Grimes

Shared Reading Collection

A Spark of Genius: A Biography of Richard Turere by Myra Faye Turner

More Than Sleeping: A Hibernation Journey Through Poems by Sona Minnetyan

My Typhoon by Mike Downs

Stinky, Slimy, Sludgy Poems by Mike Downs

As you read and enjoy poetry together, help students notice qualities that make it the unique type of writing that it is.

Interactive Read-Aloud Poetry

Patricia McKissack

Douglas Florian

Floyd Cooper

Shared Reading

Writer's Notebook

Writing Minilesson Principle
Notice the qualities of good poems.

Writing Poetry

You Will Need

- several mentor texts with poems, such as the following:
  - *Shape Me a Rhyme* by Jane Yolen and *A Place to Start a Family* by David L. Harrison, from Text Set: Poetry
  - *A Spark of Genius* by Myra Faye Turner and *More Than Sleeping* by Sona Minnetyan, from *Shared Reading Collection*
- poetry books for Have a Try
- chart paper and markers
- writer's notebooks

Academic Language / Important Vocabulary

- poem
- poet
- quality
- characteristic
- effective
- unique

Continuum Connection

- Understand poetry as a unique way to communicate about and describe feelings, sensory images, ideas, or stories
- Understand that a writer can create different types of poems (e.g., limerick, haiku, concrete poem)
- Understand the difference between poetic language and ordinary language
- Understand that poems do not have to rhyme
- Understand that a writer can learn to write a variety of poems from studying mentor texts

GOAL

Notice and understand the characteristics of poetry.

RATIONALE

When students learn to notice the qualities of good poetry, they can begin to try out new poetry moves in their own writing.

WRITER'S NOTEBOOK/WRITING FOLDER

Students will record qualities of good poems in their writer's notebooks.

ASSESS LEARNING

- Notice whether students can identify and discuss the qualities of poetry.
- Observe for evidence that students try out new poetry moves as they write their own poems.
- Look for evidence that students can use vocabulary such as *poem*, *poet*, *quality*, *characteristic*, *effective*, and *unique*.

MINILESSON

To help students think about the minilesson principle, use mentor texts to help them notice some characteristics of poetry through inquiry. Here is an example.

- Show and read pages from a variety of poetry books. Include examples that show different characteristics of poetry. Some suggestions are listed below.
  - *Shape Me a Rhyme,* pages 14–15
  - *A Place to Start a Family,* pages 6–7
  - *A Spark of Genius,* page 14
  - *More Than Sleeping,* pages 2, 16
- Encourage students to notice how poems differ from other kinds of writing they have seen.

  Think about how these poems are different from the writing you see in a chapter book or an informational book. What are some qualities, or characteristics, that you noticed?

- Support the conversation to help students notice some characteristics of poetry. Begin a list of the qualities of good poetry on chart paper, using general terms. Encourage students to also draw on their previous experiences with poetry to list characteristics.

Have a Try

Invite students to turn and talk about the qualities of good poetry.

▶ Have students sit in groups of three. Give each group at least one book of poems.

> Take a look at some poems and notice their characteristics. You might notice qualities that we have already written on the list, but you might also find some new ones.

▶ After time for students to engage in an inquiry of characteristics of poems, ask volunteers to share their noticings. Add new ideas to the chart.

Summarize and Apply

Summarize the lesson. Remind students to think about the qualities of good poems. Write the principle on the chart.

> During independent writing time, work individually or with a partner to notice qualities of good poetry. You can choose any poems to look at. You can even study poems you have written. Write what you notice in your writer's notebook on a page titled "Qualities of Good Poems." You can also start writing a poem and think about including one or more of these characteristics.

Notice the qualities of good poems.

- Strong words that show feelings
- Descriptive language that creates images
- Meaningful topics
- Help reader see something in a new way
- Words that show not tell
- Rhythm
- Sometimes rhyme or repetition, sometimes no rhyme or repetition
- Sensory language
- Careful word placement on the page
- White space
- Line breaks to show how to read the poem
- Punctuation used in different ways
- Language that compares
- A few carefully chosen words

Confer

▶ During independent writing, move around the room to confer briefly with students about characteristics of good poetry. Use the following prompts as needed.

- *What ideas from the chart will you use in your poem?*
- *What topic are you thinking of writing about in a poem?*
- *What new ways of writing poems are you thinking of trying out?*

Share

Following independent writing, gather students in the meeting area in a circle. Go around the circle so that each student has a chance to share.

> Share something new you learned about poetry today.

> Now, look at the list. Is there anything that should be added? Is there something on the list that you would like to try in a poem you are working on?

Writing Minilesson Principle
Use line breaks and white space to communicate the meaning, rhythm, and tone of the poem.

You Will Need

- several examples of poetry books with poems that utilize line breaks and white space to convey meaning, such as the following:
  - *Shape Me a Rhyme* by Jane Yolen and *A Place to Start a Family* by David L. Harrison, from Text Set: Genre Study: Poetry
  - *Stitchin' and Pullin'* by Patricia C. McKissack, from Text Set: Author Study: Patricia McKissack
- chart paper prepared with a poem that uses no line breaks or white space
- chart paper and markers
- writer's notebooks

Academic Language / Important Vocabulary

- shape
- line breaks
- white space
- meaning
- rhythm
- tone

Continuum Connection

- Use white space and line breaks to communicate the meaning and tone of the poem
- Understand the role of line breaks, white space for pause, breath, or emphasis
- Shape words on a page to look like a poem

GOAL

Think about where to place the words on a page when writing a poem.

RATIONALE

When students learn to notice the way poets use line breaks and white space to convey meaning, create rhythm, and show readers how to read a poem, they learn to think about how they can arrange words and lines for effect.

WRITER'S NOTEBOOK/WRITING FOLDER

Students can use their writer's notebooks to try out ideas for their poems.

ASSESS LEARNING

- Look for evidence that students are using line breaks and white space effectively in their poems.
- Look for evidence that students can use vocabulary such as *shape*, *line breaks*, *white space*, *meaning*, *rhythm*, and *tone*.

MINILESSON

To help students think about the minilesson principle, share poetry examples and use shared writing to show how line breaks and white space can be used effectively in poems. Here is an example.

- Show and read "Circle" on pages 8–9 in *Shape Me a Rhyme*.

  What do you notice about the way the words are placed on the page?

  Listen as I read the poem again and then share your ideas about why the poet placed the words this way.

- Reread the poem. Guide the conversation to help students notice the use of line breaks and white space and how it affects meaning, rhythm, and tone. As students share ideas, begin a list on chart paper.

  Poets use line breaks and white space to show how to read the poem with rhythm and to communicate meaning. The white space, or silent space, often has meaning, too. Poets also use line breaks and white space to create a tone by the way you read the poem.

  Think about how and why the poets arranged the words in these poems.

- Show and read a variety of poems. Some suggestions are listed below. For each poem, ask students to share ideas and add to the chart.

  - *Shape Me a Rhyme*, pages 12–13, 22–23
  - *A Place to Start a Family*, page 8
  - *Stitchin' and Pullin'*, pages 15–16, 19

Have a Try

Invite students to turn and talk about using line breaks and white space in a poem.

▶ Show the prepared poem. Read it as prose.

> Turn and talk about some ways this poem could be written on the page so that the line breaks and white space communicate meaning, rhythm, or tone.

▶ After time for discussion, have students share ideas, and use shared writing to rewrite the poem using line breaks and white space.

Summarize and Apply

Summarize the lesson. Remind students to think about how to use line breaks and white space effectively when writing poems. Write the principle on the chart.

> Today you looked at examples of poems that use line breaks and white space to show how the poet wants the poem to be read.

> During independent writing time, think about how to use line breaks and white space in a poem you are working on or on a new poem. Try out ideas in your writer's notebook. Bring the poem to share when we meet later.

Confer

▶ During independent writing, move around the room to confer briefly with students about using line breaks and white space in their poems. Use the following prompts as needed.

- *Read the poem you are working on the way you want your readers to read it.*
- *How will you place the words on the page?*
- *Where will this line end and where will the next line begin?*

Share

Following independent writing, gather students in the meeting area to share their poems.

> Share the poem you are working on with a partner and talk about your ideas for using line breaks and white space.

	Use line breaks and white space to communicate the meaning, rhythm, and tone of the poem.	
Poem	**How do line breaks and white space affect the poem?**	
"Circle"	Rhythm—line breaks show where to pause Tone—playful	
"Coil"	Meaning—line breaks emphasize important words Tone—white space creates suspense, anticipation	
"Wave"	Meaning—shaped like a wave Rhythm—line breaks show where to take a breath and think	
"King Corbra"	Meaning—shaped like a snake	
"Progress?"	Rhythm—white space makes readers think about the words Tone—ironic, solemn	
"Stereotypes"	Rhythm—line breaks show to read the poem (including talking) Tone—critical, pensive	

Summer Storm

A thick blanket of clouds covers the sky. The light dims. The trees grow still. Splat! The first drops fall. The skies open and pour water on the thirsty earth. Gradually, the roar of the water fades. The light brightens. A breeze ruffles the trees. The clouds slide away, and the sun shines.

WML3
GEN.U14.WML3

Writing Minilesson Principle
Remove words to make your poem more powerful.

You Will Need

- several poetry books with examples of poems that exhibit sparsity of words, such as the following:
  - *On the Wing* by David Elliott, from Text Set: Genre Study: Poetry
  - *Mammalabilia* by Douglas Florian, from Text Set: Author/Illustrator Study: Douglas Florian
- chart paper prepared with a poem that has some unnecessary and bland words
- chart paper and markers
- writer's notebooks and writing folders

Academic Language / Important Vocabulary

- poem
- powerful
- descriptive
- remove
- replace

Continuum Connection

- Understand the importance of specific word choice in poetry
- Remove extra words to clarify the meaning and make the writing more powerful
- Use words to show not tell
- Use words to convey images

GOAL

Use only words that are necessary when writing poems.

RATIONALE

Sometimes a poem of a few carefully chosen words can have a greater effect than a poem with more words. When students learn that poets select each word carefully, they learn how to make their own poems more powerful by selecting words thoughtfully.

WRITER'S NOTEBOOK/WRITING FOLDER

Students will continue to write poems either in their writer's notebooks or on draft paper to be kept in their writing folders.

ASSESS LEARNING

- Notice whether students understand that poets select words carefully when they write poems.
- Observe whether students are using only necessary words in the poems they write.
- Look for evidence that students can use vocabulary such as *poem*, *powerful*, *descriptive*, *remove*, and *replace*.

MINILESSON

To help students think about the minilesson principle, share poetry examples from mentor texts that show the poets' selective word choice. Then engage students in shared writing. Here is an example.

> As I read a poem, think about the words that the poet decided to use.

- Show and read "The Oriole and the Woodpecker" from page 6 in *On the Wing*.

  > What do you notice about the number of words?

- Guide students to notice that the poem is powerful, yet the poet uses just a few carefully chosen words.

- Repeat with several poems from *Mammalabilia*, such as "The Fox" on page 10 and "The Beaver" on page 17.

  > What do you notice about the words?

- Show and read the poem "Scared at Bedtime" on the prepared chart paper.

  > What do you notice about this poem?

- Help students recognize that the poem would be stronger with fewer words.

  > Poets often make their point by creating an image or idea using the fewest number of words. They remove or replace words so that only the most descriptive and most powerful words remain in the poem.

Have a Try

Invite students to turn and talk about how to make a poem more powerful.

> Turn and talk about how to make "Scared at Bedtime" stronger.

▶ After time for discussion, use shared writing to write a new version of the poem that uses fewer and more descriptive words.

Summarize and Apply

Summarize the lesson, guiding students to the principle. Remind students to think about how to make their poems more powerful.

> What did you learn today about how to make poems more powerful?

▶ Write the principle at the top of the chart.

> During independent writing time, look at the poem you are working on and think about words you could remove or replace to make the poem more powerful. If you are starting on a new poem today, choose your words carefully. Bring a poem you would like to share when we meet later.

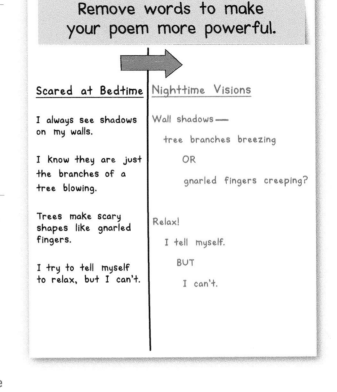

Remove words to make your poem more powerful.

Scared at Bedtime	Nighttime Visions
I always see shadows on my walls.	Wall shadows— tree branches breezing
I know they are just the branches of a tree blowing.	OR gnarled fingers creeping?
Trees make scary shapes like gnarled fingers.	Relax! I tell myself.
I try to tell myself to relax, but I can't.	BUT I can't.

Confer

▶ During independent writing, move around the room to confer briefly with students about selecting words carefully in poems. Use the following prompts as needed.

- *Share the poem you are working on.*
- *How does removing (replacing) some words change your poem?*
- *How else could you say that?*
- *Are there some words that you could replace with stronger ones?*

Share

Following independent writing, gather students in the meeting area in groups of four to share their poetry.

> Share a poem you are working on. Did you improve it by removing or replacing some words?

Writing Minilesson Principle
Use a metaphor or a simile to describe something.

Writing Poetry

You Will Need

- several poetry books that have examples of poems with metaphors and similes, such as the following:
  - *In the Swim* and *Mammalabilia* by Douglas Florian, from Text Set: Author/Illustrator Study: Douglas Florian
  - *More Than Sleeping* by Sona Minnetyan and *My Typhoon* by Mike Downs, from *Shared Reading Collection*
- chart paper prepared with a poem that has no figurative language
- chart paper and markers
- writer's notebooks and writing folders

Academic Language / Important Vocabulary

- poem
- simile
- metaphor
- compare
- senses
- describe

Continuum Connection

- Understand the importance of specific word choice in poetry
- Understand the difference between poetic language and ordinary language
- Use figurative language (e.g., simile, metaphor, personification) to make comparisons
- Select words to make meanings memorable

GOAL

Understand and use metaphors and similes to create imagery and convey emotion.

RATIONALE

Poets use metaphors and similes to achieve maximum description with a minimum number of words. When students understand reasons to use metaphors and similes, they learn to think about using them in their own poetry.

WRITER'S NOTEBOOK/WRITING FOLDER

Students will continue to write poems either in their writer's notebooks or on draft paper to be kept in their writing folders.

ASSESS LEARNING

- Look for evidence that students are using some metaphors and similes in their poems.
- Look for evidence that students can use vocabulary such as *poem*, *simile*, *metaphor*, *compare*, *senses*, and *describe*.

MINILESSON

To help students think about the minilesson principle, provide an inquiry-based lesson to help them identify metaphors and similes. Then use shared writing to help them add figurative language to a poem. Here is an example.

- Read and show "The Flounders" on page 25 of *In the Swim*.

  How does the poet describe flounders?

- Guide the conversation to help students notice the comparative language.

  When a poet compares two things without using the words *like* or *as*, it is called a metaphor. Saying flounders are "living dishes" is using a metaphor. When a poet compares two things using the words *like* or *as*, it is called a simile. As I read the poem again, listen for metaphors and similes.

- Reread the poem and guide the conversation to help students identify the similes and metaphors. Begin a two-column list on chart paper with the headings *Metaphor* and *Simile* and list the examples in the appropriate column.

- Show and read poems from a variety of poetry books. Include examples of both metaphors and similes and have students identify them. Add each example to the chart. Some suggestions are listed below.

  - *In the Swim*, page 41
  - *More Than Sleeping*, pages 6–7
  - *My Typhoon*, pages 14, 16
  - *Mammalabilia*, page 46

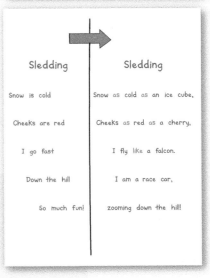

Have a Try

Invite students to turn and talk about using metaphors and similes in their poems.

▶ Show and read the prepared poem.

> Turn and talk about some ideas you have for adding metaphors and similes to make the poem more descriptive.

▶ After time for discussion, use students' suggestions and shared writing to rewrite the poem using metaphors and similes.

Summarize and Apply

Summarize the lesson and guide students to the principle. Remind students to think about using metaphors and similes to make poems more interesting.

> How can you add interest and description to your poems?

▶ Write the principle at the top of the first chart.

> During independent writing time, work on a poem you have started or begin a new poem. Think about how you could compare one thing to another using metaphors and similes. Bring your poem to share when we meet later.

Confer

▶ During independent writing, move around the room to confer briefly with students about their poems. Use the following prompts as needed.

- *How can you describe that using just a few words?*
- *What is something you could compare that to?*
- *Let's talk about a metaphor or a simile that you could use here.*

Share

Following independent writing, gather students in the meeting area in pairs to share their poems.

> Share a poem of yours in which you used a metaphor or a simile, or share a poem and talk about where you could add a metaphor or a simile.

Writing Poetry

You Will Need

- several poetry books containing poems with examples of personification, such as the following from *Shared Reading Collection*:
  - *Stinky, Slimy, Sludgy Poems* by Mike Downs
  - *More Than Sleeping*, by Sona Minnetyan
  - *A Spark of Genius* by Myra Faye Turner
- chart paper and markers
- writer's notebooks and writing folders

Academic Language / Important Vocabulary

- poem
- personification
- describe

Continuum Connection

- Understand the importance of specific word choice in poetry
- Understand the difference between poetic language and ordinary language
- Use words to convey images
- Use words to show not tell
- Use language to create sensory images
- Use figurative language (e.g., simile, metaphor, personification) to make comparisons
- Select words to make meanings memorable

GOAL

Understand how to use personification in poetry.

RATIONALE

Personification, representing an animal or inanimate object as human, is a way that poets not only bring interest to their poems but also are able to use fewer words to convey meaning or an image to their readers.

WRITER'S NOTEBOOK/WRITING FOLDER

Students will continue to write poems either in their writer's notebooks or on draft paper to be kept in their writing folders.

ASSESS LEARNING

- Observe whether students recognize that writers use personification in poetry.
- Look for evidence that students are experimenting with personification in their poems.
- Look for evidence that students can use vocabulary such as *poem*, *personification*, and *describe*.

MINILESSON

To help students think about the minilesson principle, provide an inquiry-based lesson to help them identify and understand personification. Then use shared writing to help them write a poem using personification. Here is an example.

- Read and show "The Ravenous Garbage Can" on pages 12–16 of *Stinky, Slimy, Sludgy Poems*.

  What do you notice about how the poet described the garbage can?

- Guide the conversation to help students notice personification.

  When a poet uses language that treats a thing or an animal as if it were a person, it is called personification.

  What human qualities did the poet give to the garbage can?

- Begin a list on chart paper of examples.

- Show and read poems from a variety of poetry books that include examples of personification, and have students identify them. Add each example to the chart. Some suggestions are listed below.

  - *More Than Sleeping*, page 12
  - *A Spark of Genius*, page 4

  Why do you think a poet would use personification in a poem?

Have a Try

Invite students to turn and talk about writing a poem that uses personification to make the poem interesting.

▶ Choose a topic that is interesting to the students, perhaps something they have been studying in science or social studies. Use shared writing to write a poem using personification.

> Let's choose a topic that we have been thinking about, such as clouds. Turn and talk about some ideas you have for writing a poem about clouds that uses personification.

▶ After time for discussion, use students' suggestions and shared writing to write a poem using personification. If students have had limited experience using personification, you may have to use modeling to get them started.

Summarize and Apply

Summarize the lesson and guide students to the principle. Remind students to think about using personification to make poems more interesting.

> How can you make your writing interesting?

▶ Write the principle at the top of the first chart.

> During independent writing time, work on a poem you have started or begin a new poem. Think about how you could use personification in your poem. Bring your poem to share when we meet later.

Use personification to make your writing interesting.

	Examples of Personification
garbage can	Walking 'cross the floor Beneath the table yowling It quickly grunts for more It waddles off
frog	I freeze, I thaw, then freeze again I alone am the sleeping one
afternoon	Blinks

Mr. Nimbus blows out smoke

From his big, wide mouth.

He billows, he blows,

then suddenly he knows.

Rain is in the forecast tonight!

Confer

▶ During independent writing, move around the room to confer briefly with students about their poems. Use the following prompts as needed.

- *What words can you use to describe that?*
- *How might you use personification to make this object seem like it is alive?*
- *Let's talk about an example of personification that could be used here.*

Share

Following independent writing, gather students in the meeting area to share their poems.

> Who has an example of personification to share? Talk about how you decided to use personification.

Writing Minilesson Principle

Choose a meaningful title for your poem.

Writing Poetry

You Will Need

- several poetry books with poems that have interesting titles, such as the following:
  - *Meet Danitra Brown* by Nikki Grimes, from Text Set: Illustrator Study: Floyd Cooper
  - *Stitchin' and Pullin'* by Patricia McKissack, from Text Set: Author Study: Patricia McKissack
- two poems without titles written on chart paper
- chart paper and markers
- writer's notebooks and writing folders

Academic Language / Important Vocabulary

- poem
- title
- meaningful
- message

Continuum Connection

- Choose a title that communicates the meaning of a poem
- Select an appropriate title for a poem, story, or informational book

GOAL

Understand that the title of a poem can reveal a lot about the poem's message.

RATIONALE

A poem's title is important. When students notice and think about the titles that poets choose, they realize that they need to think carefully about selecting titles for their poems.

WRITER'S NOTEBOOK/WRITING FOLDER

Students will look in their writer's notebooks or writing folders to assess the titles of poems they have written.

ASSESS LEARNING

- Look for evidence that students are putting thought into the titles of their poems.
- Look for evidence that students can use vocabulary such as *poem*, *title*, *meaningful*, and *message*.

MINILESSON

To help students think about the minilesson principle, use mentor texts and an interactive lesson. Here is an example.

> Poets choose titles for their poems for a variety of reasons. Think about the titles as you listen to several poems today.

- Show and read "Mom and Me Only" on pages 13–14 of *Meet Danitra Brown*, including the title.

> Why do you think the poet, Nikki Grimes, chose to call this poem "Mom and Me Only"?

- Guide the conversation to help students recognize that the title helps readers understand the message of the poem better.

> The title shows the message of the poem and helps readers understand that this poem is about the subject's feelings about having one parent when some kids have two.

- Show and read "Sweet Blackberry" on pages 15–16.

> What are your thoughts about the title of this poem?

- Repeat with several poems from *Stitchin' and Pullin'*, such as the following:
  - "Nothing Wasted," pages 9–10
  - "Puzzling the Pieces," page 11
  - "Colors," page 18
- Lead students to notice that all the titles are meaningful in some way.

Have a Try

Invite students to turn and talk about choosing titles for poems.

▶ Show and read the prepared poems.

> Here are two poems without titles. What titles would you give them? You might think of a title that tells the message of the poem, reveals what the poem is about, or helps readers understand the poem better. Turn and talk about that.

▶ After time for discussion, ask students to share ideas. Write the suggested titles on chart paper next to the poems.

Summarize and Apply

Summarize the lesson. Remind students to think about the titles for poems they write.

> Poets sometimes choose a title that reveals exactly what the poem is about or adds meaning.

▶ Write the principle on the chart.

> Today during independent writing time, look at some poems you have written and think about the titles. You might want to add a new title to one or more of your poems. Or if you begin writing a new poem, think about the title and what you want your readers to know about your poem. Bring your poem when we meet.

Choose a meaningful title for your poem.	
Poem	Possible Titles
I have a ....rope, rope, rope But no one to ....turn, turn, turn. Please, could you ... join, join, join So I can .... jump, jump, jump?	"Alone" "A Rope That Jumps" "Skipping Rope" "I Want a Friend"
Beetle, black as darkness lay, Upon my red rain boot. Until brown mud washed it away, And the beetle went *KERPLOOT*.	"Rainy Day Colors" "Unwanted Visitor" "Journey of a Beetle" "Thanks, Mud!"

Confer

▶ During independent writing, move around the room to confer briefly with students about using meaningful titles for their poems. Use the following prompts as needed.

- *What message do you want your readers to know from your title?*
- *Read your poem aloud, and then we can talk about some possible titles.*
- *This title helps your readers understand your poem better because _____.*

Share

Following independent writing, gather students in the meeting area to share their poems.

> As you share your poem title, tell why you chose it.

Assessment

After you have taught the minilessons in this umbrella, observe students in a variety of classroom activities. Use *The Fountas & Pinnell Literacy Continuum* to notice, teach for, and support students' learning as you observe their attempts at writing poetry.

▶ What evidence do you have of students' new understandings related to writing poetry?

- Do students recognize that poems look and sound different from other types of writing?

- Do they use line breaks and white space effectively when they write poems?

- Do they think about using fewer or different words in their poetry?

- Are they including figurative language, such as metaphors, similes, and personification?

- Do they choose meaningful titles for their poems?

- Are they using vocabulary such as *poem*, *poet*, *quality*, *effective*, *unique*, *line breaks*, *white space*, *meaning*, *rhythm*, *tone*, *simile*, *metaphor*, *compare*, *senses*, *describe*, *powerful*, *descriptive*, *title*, and *message*?

▶ In what ways, beyond the scope of this umbrella, are students engaged in writing poetry?

- Are students keeping a poetry anthology?

- Do students get ideas for writing from their writer's notebooks?

Use your observations to determine the next umbrella you will teach. You may also consult Suggested Sequence of Lessons (pp. 665–682) for guidance.

EXTENSIONS FOR WRITING POETRY

▶ Provide outdoor and virtual field trip experiences so students can make observations and get inspired to write poetry.

▶ Make poetry a consistent part of students' lives by scheduling regular poetry workshop time (see pp. 62–64).

▶ If you are using *The Reading Minilessons Book, Grade 4* (Fountas and Pinnell 2020) you may choose to teach LA.U6: Studying Poetry and LA.U7: Exploring Different Kinds of Poetry.

Minilessons in This Umbrella

WML1 Write a free verse poem.

WML2 Write a concrete (shape) poem.

WML3 Write a lyrical poem.

WML4 Write a poem for two voices.

WML5 Write a haiku.

WML6 Write a poem that gives information about a topic.

Before Teaching Umbrella 15 Minilessons

Prior to teaching these minilessons, immerse students in reading, writing, and talking about poems. We also recommend that you first teach GEN.U14: Writing Poetry.

You do not need to teach these lessons consecutively or even at the same time of the year. Consider teaching each minilesson during a poetry workshop (see pp. 62–64). Students can use their writer's notebooks as a source for poem topics, for experimenting with craft ideas, and for drafting poems. (Students can also write on draft paper to be kept in their writing folders.) Finished poems can be added to their poetry anthologies; the poems do not have to be perfect to go into an anthology (see GEN.U13: Making Poetry Anthologies). Use the books listed below from *Fountas & Pinnell Classroom™ Interactive Read-Aloud Collection* and *Shared Reading Collection*, or choose a variety of poetry books from the classroom library.

Interactive Read-Aloud Collection

Author/Illustrator Study: Douglas Florian

Insectlopedia

Lizards, Frogs, and Polliwogs

Exploring Identity

Imagine by Juan Felipe Herrera

Illustrator Study: Floyd Cooper

Meet Danitra Brown by Nikki Grimes

Genre Study: Poetry

Shape Me a Rhyme: Nature's Forms in Poetry by Jane Yolen

Shared Reading Collection

A Spark of Genius: A Biography of Richard Turere by Myra Faye Turner

My Typhoon by Mike Downs

Grannie's Coal Pot by Summer Edward

More Than Sleeping: A Hibernation Journey Through Poems by Sona Minnetyan

Get the Scoop! Plans and Poems for Making Compost by Jennifer Boudart

Mosaic Master: Antoni Gaudí by Susan B. Katz

Interactive Read-Aloud
Douglas Florian

Exploring Identity

Floyd Cooper

Poetry

Shape Me a Rhyme by Jane Yolen

Shared Reading

Writer's Notebook

Section 2: Genres and Forms

Writing Minilesson Principle
Write a free verse poem.

You Will Need

- several free verse poems, such as those found in the following from *Shared Reading Collection*:
  - *A Spark of Genius* by Myra Faye Turner
  - *My Typhoon* by Mike Downs
  - *Grannie's Coal Pot* by Summer Edward
- writer's notebooks

Academic Language / Important Vocabulary

- poem
- free verse
- emotion
- mental image
- pattern
- rhythm

Continuum Connection

- Understand poetry as a unique way to communicate about and describe feelings, sensory images, ideas, or stories
- Understand the difference between poetic language and ordinary language
- Use words to convey images
- Use words to convey strong feelings
- Understand that poems do not have to rhyme
- Notice the beat or rhythm of a poem and its relation to line breaks

GOAL

Understand that free verse poems do not have a defined rhythm and usually do not rhyme.

RATIONALE

When students recognize the characteristics of free verse poetry, they begin to think about the poetry writing choices they want to make and about what they want their readers to feel when reading their poems.

WRITER'S NOTEBOOK/WRITING FOLDER

Have students reread their writer's notebooks for poem ideas and try out their poems in their writer's notebooks.

ASSESS LEARNING

- Observe whether students choose words that engage readers' feelings or create a mental image.
- Look for evidence that students can use vocabulary such as *poem*, *free verse*, *emotion*, *mental image*, *pattern*, and *rhythm*.

MINILESSON

Before teaching, read and enjoy poems with students. To prepare students to write free verse poems, use mentor texts and shared writing. Here is an example.

- Show and read the poems on pages 10 and 14 in *A Spark of Genius*.

  What do you notice as you listen to these poems?

  What feelings do you have?

- Engage students in noticing characteristics of free verse poetry. As students make observations, begin a list on chart paper using general terms.

- Show and read page 8 in in *My Typhoon*.

  What words make a picture in your mind as you listen to this poem?

- Read "The Laundress" on pages 10–11 in *Grannie's Coal Pot*.

  Look at the chart. Turn and talk about whether this poem has any of the same characteristics as the other poems.

- After time for discussion, ask students to share ideas. Guide the conversation to help them recognize the similarities between the poems. Add new ideas to the chart.

  These poems are all written in free verse. In free verse poems, you get to make your own rules. The poems are meant to have readers make a mental image and to feel an emotion. They might follow a language pattern and they do use poetic language, but they do not have to rhyme.

Have a Try

Invite students to turn and talk about writing free verse poems. Then engage them in shared writing of a free verse poem.

> Spend a moment looking in your writer's notebook for poem ideas. Then turn and talk about some ideas you found.

> ▶ After time for a brief discussion, ask a few students to share their ideas. Using shared writing, write one or more free verse poems on chart paper.

Summarize and Apply

Summarize the learning. Have students write a free verse poem in their writer's notebooks. Write the principle at the top of the chart.

> During independent writing time, start writing a poem. It can be about anything. Think about the feelings or images you want to show. You might use your senses to create an image—write about what you see, hear, smell, touch, or taste. Use your writer's notebook to find more ideas and to try out ideas for a poem. Bring your poem, even if it's not finished, to share when we meet later.

Write a free verse poem.

- Rhythm
- Does not have to rhyme
- Some language patterns
- Poetic language
- Mental image
- About any topic
- Short or long
- Poet makes the rules

Confer

> ▶ During independent writing, move around the room to confer briefly with students about their free verse poems. Use the following prompts as needed.

> - *What do you want your readers to feel when reading your poem?*
> - *What image will your readers picture in their minds?*
> - *What poetic language have you included in your free verse poem?*

Share

Following independent writing, gather students in small groups in the meeting area to share their poems. Then select a few students to share with the class.

> Turn and talk to your group about the free verse poem you are working on.

> What are some things you learned about writing free verse poetry?

Writing Minilesson Principle
Write a concrete (shape) poem.

You Will Need

- several concrete poems, such as those found in the following from Text Set: Author/Illustrator Study: Douglas Florian:
  - *Insectlopedia*
  - *Lizards, Frogs, and Polliwogs*
- chart paper and markers
- writer's notebooks
- To download the following online resource for this lesson, visit **fp.pub/resources**:
  - chart art (optional)

Academic Language / Important Vocabulary

- concrete poem
- white space
- line break

Continuum Connection

- Understand that a writer can create different types of poems (e.g., limerick, haiku, concrete poem)
- Use the terms *poem*, *limerick*, *haiku*, and *concrete poem* to describe poetry
- Understand that poems take a variety of shapes
- Use white space and line breaks to communicate the meaning and tone of the poem
- Shape words on a page to look like a poem

GOAL

Think about where to place the words on the page when writing a poem.

RATIONALE

Poems look different from prose, some more than others. The words of a concrete, or shape, poem are arranged in the shape of the topic of the poem. When students notice the shape of a poem, they begin to think about how layout and white space can be used to add meaning. Use the term you prefer, either *shape poem* or *concrete poem*.

WRITER'S NOTEBOOK/WRITING FOLDER

Have students reread their writer's notebooks for poem ideas and try out their poems in their writer's notebooks.

ASSESS LEARNING

- Notice whether students use line breaks, spacing, and word placement to add meaning to their poems.
- Look for evidence that students can use vocabulary such as *concrete poem*, *line break*, and *white space*.

MINILESSON

Before teaching, read and enjoy a variety of poetry with the students. Use mentor texts and shared writing to talk about concrete poems to draw students' attention to how the placement of print and the space in a poem can convey meaning. Here is an example.

- Choose several concrete poems, such as the following in *Insectlopedia* and *Lizards, Frogs, and Polliwogs*. As you show and read each poem, engage students in a conversation about the line breaks, white space, and how the shape and placement of the words add meaning to the poem. As you show each poem, ask students what they notice about how it looks.
  - "The Inchworm," *Insectlopedia,* pages 14–15
  - "The Whirligig Beetles," *Insectlopedia,* pages 22–23
  - "The Termites," *Insectlopedia,* pages 38–39
  - "The Skink," *Lizards, Frogs, and Polliwogs,* pages 6–7
  - "The Python," *Lizards, Frogs, and Polliwogs,* pages 24–25
- Prompt the discussion as needed. For each poem, encourage students to notice the shape of the poem, how the choice of writing connects to the topic, the poet's choices about line breaks and white space, and how word choice connects to the poet's message.

  A concrete poem shows meaning through both the words and the shape of the poem.

Have a Try

Invite students to turn and talk about writing concrete poems.

> A concrete poem can be about anything. Turn and talk about an idea you have for writing a concrete poem. Tell your partner how you could arrange the words on the page.

▶ After time for discussion, use shared writing to craft a concrete poem or two on chart paper.

Summarize and Apply

Write the principle at the top of the chart. Summarize the learning. Have students try writing a concrete poem in their writer's notebooks.

> During independent writing time, think of some ideas for a concrete poem. Use the idea you talked about with your partner, find an idea in your writer's notebook, or come up with a new idea. When you have an idea, start writing your concrete poem. Think how you will place the words on the page. Bring your poem to share when we meet later.

Write a concrete (shape) poem.

Following the sun, heliotropism in place. I will be over six feet tall. Hard to believe that I'm just a.... SUNFLOWER. Up I go, stretching my long stem. Reaching and climbing, warmth on my face.

Confer

▶ During independent writing, move around the room to confer briefly with students about their concrete poems. Use the following prompts as needed.

- *What will your poem look like on the page?*
- *Talk about how you decided to arrange the words.*
- *How does the white space add to the meaning of your poem?*
- *In what ways will the poem's shape relate to the poem's topic?*

Share

Following independent writing, gather students in the meeting area to share their poems.

> In groups of four, share a concrete poem that you have written or that you are working on.

> How does the shape of _____'s poem add to the meaning of the poem?

WML3

Writing Minilesson Principle
Write a lyrical poem.

Writing Different Kinds of Poems

You Will Need

- several lyrical poems, such as the following:
  - *Imagine* by Juan Felipe Herrera, from Text Set: Exploring Identity
  - *Meet Danitra Brown* by Nikki Grimes, from Text Set: Illustrator Study: Floyd Cooper
- chart paper and markers
- writer's notebooks

Academic Language / Important Vocabulary

- lyrical poem
- rhythm
- rhyme
- description

Continuum Connection

- Notice the beat or rhythm of a poem in its relation to line breaks
- Understand the importance of specific word choice in poetry
- Understand the difference between poetic language and ordinary language
- Use words to convey images

GOAL

Understand that poems can be songlike and have rhythm and sometimes rhyme.

RATIONALE

When students understand that poets can use rhythm in a way that makes a poem sound like a song, they are able to try out writing lyrical poetry on their own.

WRITER'S NOTEBOOK/WRITING FOLDER

Have students reread their writer's notebooks for lyrical poem ideas and try out their poems in their writer's notebooks.

ASSESS LEARNING

- Observe whether students are using rhythm and sometimes rhyme in their poems.
- Look for evidence that students can use vocabulary such as *lyrical poem, rhythm, rhyme,* and *description*.

MINILESSON

Before teaching, read and enjoy poetry with the students. Use mentor texts and shared writing to help them think about writing lyrical poems. Consider selecting a topic from content that students are learning in social studies or science. Here is an example.

- Show and read the first few pages of *Imagine.* Use rhythm as you read so students can hear the lyrical, songlike quality of the words.

  What do you notice about the sound of this poetry by Juan Felipe Herrera?

- Engage students in a conversation about the way the words sound like a song, have rhythm, and use description.

- Repeat with another example, such as "The Secret" on pages 17–18 in *Meet Danitra Brown.*

  Poems like this are called lyrical poems. Lyrical poems have a steady rhythm, and sometimes they rhyme. They are written in a way that reminds you of a song. They usually express the feelings of the poet or perhaps describe something the poet has observed. Let's write a lyrical poem.

- Choose a familiar topic and use shared writing to write a song or lyrical poem.

  In social studies, you have learned about covered wagons. Describing a journey might make a good topic for a lyrical poem or a song. What might people traveling in covered wagons have seen and heard?

- As students share ideas, model how to begin a song or lyrical poem by choosing descriptive words and then using them in a rhythmic way. Clapping the beats in a line can help with the rhythm of the words.

Have a Try

Invite students to turn and talk about writing lyrical poems.

> Think about an idea you have for writing a poem that sounds like a song. Tell your partner about your idea and talk about some descriptive words you might include.

▶ After time for a discussion, ask a few students to share ideas.

Summarize and Apply

Summarize the learning. Have students try writing a lyrical poem in their writer's notebooks. Write the principle at the top of the chart.

> During independent writing time, start to write a lyrical poem, which can be a song if you wish. It can be about anything. Think about the rhythm, descriptive words, and figurative language you will use and how you will arrange the words so readers will know how the poem should sound. Choose language that helps your readers form a mental image. Bring your poem to share when we meet later.

Write a lyrical poem.

Prairie Trails

Clip-clop, Clip-clop
Hooves on dirt.
Breathe-in, Breathe-out
Choking on dusty air.
Bump-bounce, bump-bounce
Me on seat
Click-clack, rattle-rap
Wheels need repair!

Confer

▶ During independent writing, move around the room to confer briefly with students about their lyrical poems. Use the following prompts as needed.

- *Describe the rhythm your poem will have. Will it also rhyme?*
- *Read this page aloud so you can hear the rhythm.*
- *How does this description help your readers make an image?*
- *Compare your poem to a song. In what ways are they similar?*

Share

Following independent writing, gather students in the meeting area to share their poems.

> Read one of your lyrical poems to a partner. Read it in a way that your partner can hear the rhythm and songlike quality.

Section 2: Genres and Forms

Writing Minilesson Principle
Write a poem for two voices.

You Will Need

- chart paper prepared with a poem for two voices
- two students prepared to read the poem
- chart paper and markers
- writer's notebooks
- To download the following online resource for this lesson, visit **fp.pub/resources**:
  - chart art (optional)

Academic Language / Important Vocabulary

- point of view

Continuum Connection

- Understand the difference between poetic language and ordinary language
- Understand the way print works in poems and demonstrate the use in reading and writing them on a page using white space and line breaks
- Understand that poems take a variety of shapes
- Understand the role of line breaks, white space for pause, breath, or emphasis
- Write a variety of types of poems

GOAL

Notice that a poem can be written in a way that is intended for two voices.

RATIONALE

When students learn that there are different kinds of poems and that they can choose to write a poem for two voices, they begin to think about and try out writing poetry from multiple perspectives.

WRITER'S NOTEBOOK/WRITING FOLDER

Have students jot down ideas for a poem for two voices and then try writing the poem in their writer's notebooks.

ASSESS LEARNING

- Observe for evidence that students understand what it means to write a poem for two voices.
- Look for evidence that students can use vocabulary such as *point of view*.

MINILESSON

Students will need their writer's notebooks for this lesson. To help students think about the minilesson principle, use a mentor text and modeling to support them as they write a poem for two voices with a partner. Here is an example.

- Show a poem for two voices on the prepared chart paper.

  What do you notice about this poem that is different from other poems you have seen?

  The print is placed so that one reader, or voice, reads the lines on the left and a second reader reads the lines on the right. When the print lines up, both readers read at the same time. Listen to how the poem sounds as two students read it.

- Have the prepared students read the poem.

  When you write a poem for two voices, you can show how two people might notice things in a different way or say things a little differently. You might even think of writing a poem about something you have learned in science or social studies.

Have a Try

Invite students to turn and talk about writing poems for two voices.

▶ Have students sit by the partner they will work with to write a poem for two voices.

> In your writer's notebook, jot down some ideas for topics you might like to write about. Then share them with your partner.

▶ After time for discussion, ask partners to share their ideas. Support the conversation so each pair has an idea for a poem.

Summarize and Apply

Summarize the learning. Have students write a poem for two voices in their writer's notebooks. Write the principle at the top of the chart.

> During independent writing time, you and your partner will start writing a poem for two voices. It can be about anything. Decide on the topic you will write about and how you will place the words on the page. Bring your poem to share when we meet later.

Write a poem for two voices.

Seventy pounds and two feet high	Seven pounds, not one-foot high
Sweet as can be.	Sweet as can be.
Strong as Hercules but ever so friendly	Weak as a kitten but feisty and fierce
We love cuddles!	We love cuddles!
What am I? I am a golden retriever.	What am I? I am a Yorkshire terrier
What are we? Dogs that aim to please!	What are we? Dogs that aim to please!

Confer

▶ During independent writing, move around the room to confer briefly with pairs of students about their poems. Use the following prompts as needed.

- *What topic will you write about?*
- *Where will you place the words on the page?*
- *Are there words that both readers will say at the same time? How will you show that?*

Share

Following independent writing, gather students in the meeting area to share their poems.

> In groups of four, share the poem for two voices you have written or that you are working on.

Writing Minilesson Principle
Write a haiku.

Writing Different Kinds of Poems

You Will Need

- several haiku poems, such as from the following:
  - *More Than Sleeping* by Sona Minnetyan, from *Shared Reading Collection*
  - *Shape Me a Rhyme* by Jane Yolen, from Text Set: Genre Study: Poetry
- chart paper and markers

Academic Language / Important Vocabulary

- haiku
- rhyme
- syllable
- mental image
- mood
- feeling

Continuum Connection

- Understand that a writer can create different types of poems (e.g., limerick, haiku, concrete poem)
- Use the terms *poem, limerick, haiku,* and *concrete poem* to describe poetry
- Understand that poems do not have to rhyme

GOAL

Learn about and write haiku poetry.

RATIONALE

Exposing students to different kinds of poems gives them choices for writing poetry, which may increase their motivation. Haiku may appeal to students who enjoy writing about nature because nature is often the focus of the form.

WRITER'S NOTEBOOK/WRITING FOLDER

Have students use their writer's notebooks to find poem ideas and to try out their poems.

ASSESS LEARNING

- Observe whether students understand how to write haiku poetry.
- Look for evidence that students can use vocabulary such as *haiku, rhyme, syllable, mental image, mood,* and *feeling.*

MINILESSON

Before teaching, read and enjoy a variety of poetry with the students. Use mentor texts and shared writing to think about haiku poems so they can think about and plan for writing haiku. Here is an example.

- Choose several haiku poems such as those listed below. As you show and read each poem, engage students by having them clap to the syllables as you read. Have a conversation about the line breaks, white space, topic, and feeling of each poem.
  - "Hibernation," *More Than Sleeping,* page 2
  - "Arch: A Haiku," *Shape Me a Rhyme,* pages 20–21

  Turn and talk about what you notice about the poem.

- After time for discussion, have students share their thinking.

  Haiku poetry is about a meaningful topic that is often related to nature. It has three lines. The first and third lines have five syllables, and the second line has seven syllables. Because there are so few words, choosing just the right words is very important.

  Listen as I reread the poem, and think carefully about the words.

- Reread each poem several times. While it is important that students understand the syllable count, extend their thinking to help them understand that haiku is an ancient form of Japanese poetry that conveys truths about the natural world. Haiku poems focus on a brief moment in time and evoke a mood or a feeling. The meaning of some haiku may not be obvious on the first reading.

Have a Try

Invite students to turn and talk about writing a haiku.

> Think about an idea you have for writing a haiku poem. Tell your partner about your idea and how you want your readers to feel.

▶ After time for a discussion, ask a few students to share ideas. Using their ideas, use shared writing to write a haiku, thinking aloud as you do. You may decide to write several more haiku poems together if your students need more practice before writing them independently.

Summarize and Apply

▶ Summarize the learning. Have students try writing a haiku in their writer's notebooks. Write the principle at the top of the chart.

> During independent writing time, write a haiku in your writer's notebook. Remember that it is three lines and that the first and third lines have five syllables and the second line has seven syllables. The topic should be connected to nature and the world around you. Haiku poems do not have to rhyme. Bring your poem to share when we meet later.

Write a haiku.

A Place to Sit and Think

Soft, gentle whispers
Swaying with each breath of wind
Peaceful, calm palm tree

Confer

▶ During independent writing, move around the room to confer briefly with students about their haiku poems. Use the following prompts as needed.

- *Describe the topic you want to write about.*
- *Let's read your poem together and clap the syllables.*
- *What mood or feeling will your haiku poem express?*

Share

Following independent writing, gather students in the meeting area to share their poems.

> Who would like to share the haiku you are writing?

> What are some things you noticed about _____'s haiku?

Writing Minilesson Principle
Write a poem that gives information about a topic.

You Will Need

- several poems that teach about a topic, such as those found in the following texts from *Shared Reading Collection*:
  - *Get the Scoop!* by Jennifer Boudart
  - *Mosaic Master* by Susan B. Katz
  - *More Than Sleeping* by Sona Minnetyan
- chart paper and markers
- writer's notebooks

Academic Language / Important Vocabulary

- poem
- topic
- teach

Continuum Connection

- Understand poetry as a unique way to communicate about and describe feelings, sensory images, ideas, or stories
- Understand that a writer can learn to write a variety of poems from studying mentor texts
- Understand the difference between poetic language and ordinary language
- Select topics that are significant and help readers see in a new way

GOAL

Understand that you can use poetry to teach about a topic, often in a new or interesting way.

RATIONALE

When students understand that poems can teach about something in an interesting way, they are able to try out writing this type of poetry on their own.

WRITER'S NOTEBOOK/WRITING FOLDER

Have students use their writer's notebooks to find ideas for poems and to try out their poems in their writer's notebooks.

ASSESS LEARNING

- Observe whether students are sometimes writing poems that teach something.
- Look for evidence that students can use vocabulary such as *poem*, *teach*, and *topic*.

MINILESSON

Before teaching, read and enjoy poetry with the students. Use mentor texts and modeling to help them think about writing poems that teach something. Here is an example.

- Show and read the titles of the books and several poems from *Get the Scoop!* and from *Mosaic Master*.

  What do you notice about these poems?

- Guide the conversation to help students notice the topic of the poems and the way the poems teach about making compost and about the life of a famous artist.

- Show and read "Queen Bee" on page 10–11 in *More Than Sleeping*.

  What do you think the poet's goal was in writing this poem?

  Why do you think the poet included these facts about queen bees on the next page?

- Choose a topic that students have recently learned about.

  We have learned about wants and needs, and we noticed that the basic needs people have are food, clothing, and shelter. We have studied the Powhatan Native American people in social studies and thought about how they met their basic needs. I could teach this information in a poem.

- Model the process of writing a poem to teach something about the topic, thinking aloud as you do.

  Writing or reading a poem about a topic might help you think about the topic in a different way.

Have a Try

Invite students to turn and talk about writing a poem that teaches about a topic.

> Think about a topic for a poem that teaches about the topic. Turn and talk about your idea.

▶ After time for a discussion, ask several students to share ideas. Guide the conversation to be sure all students have a poetry topic.

Summarize and Apply

Summarize the learning. Have students use writer's notebooks to try writing a poem that teaches about a topic. Write the principle at the top of the chart.

> During independent writing time, use your writer's notebook to start writing a poem that gives information about a topic. It can be about anything you have learned about. Decide what facts you want to include and how you will arrange the words on the page. Bring your poem to share when we meet later.

Write a poem that gives information about a topic.

POWHATAN

On the land near their homes,
They grew beans, pumpkins, squash, corn.
Nearby waters provided fish, clams, and oysters.
In the forests they found roots, nuts, berries, and game.
Speaking Algonquian, the Powhatans conversed about
the current season—summer planting, spring fishing, winter hunting.
Homes of saplings, woven reeds, and bark kept them safe from weather.
The fire at the lodge center burning bright day and night.
Aprons of deerskin, fur cloaks, moccasins, and leggings,
decorated with beads and bones and fringe and shells.
Everything they needed, everything they made
They harvested, fished, or hunted from
THE EARTH.

Confer

▶ During independent writing, move around the room to confer briefly with students about their poems that teach about a topic. Use the following prompts as needed.

- *Share the topic you will write a poem about. What is one fact you will include?*
- *How will you place the words on the page?*
- *What do you want your readers to learn or think about in an interesting way?*

Share

Following independent writing, gather students in the meeting area to share their poems with a partner. Then select several students to share their poems with the class.

> Share your poem by reading it aloud.

> Who has another topic you might like to write a poem about? Share your idea.

Assessment

After you have taught the minilessons in this umbrella, observe students in a variety of classroom activities. Use *The Fountas & Pinnell Literacy Continuum* to notice, teach for, and support students' learning as you observe their attempts at writing poetry.

▶ What evidence do you have of students' new understandings related to writing different kinds of poems?

- Are students writing poems that show feelings or that create a mental image?
- How well do they use elements of poetry, such as line breaks, white space, rhythm, and rhyme?
- Are they writing different types of poems (e.g., concrete, lyrical, for two voices, haiku)?
- Can they use poetry to teach about a topic in an interesting way?
- Are they using vocabulary such as *poem, free verse, emotion, mental image, pattern, rhythm, concrete poem, line break, white space, lyrical poem, rhyme, description, point of view, haiku, syllable, mood, feeling, teach,* and *topic*?

▶ In what ways, beyond the scope of this umbrella, are students experiencing poetry?

- Do they show an interest in using powerful words?
- Have they made a poetry anthology?

Use your observations to determine the next umbrella you will teach. You may also consult Suggested Sequence of Lessons (pp. 665–682) for guidance.

EXTENSIONS FOR WRITING DIFFERENT KINDS OF POEMS

▶ Encourage students to write a poem inspired by a book they enjoyed reading.

▶ Use the format of these lessons to teach other types of poems (e.g., cinquain, diamante, acrostic, limerick).

▶ As students engage with new topics in science and social studies, encourage them to use poetry as a way to share their learning.

Minilessons in This Umbrella

WML1 Notice the qualities of photo essays.

WML2 Decide what the photos should show and how to order and place them on the pages.

WML3 Add information that explains the photos.

WML4 Write an introduction or conclusion to explain the photo essay.

Before Teaching Umbrella 16 Minilessons

One way to tell a story is through photographs. Photo essays, which can be either print or digital, are a mode of storytelling with photos and accompanying information that can be oral or written. Students might create a strictly pictorial photo essay with added narration, or they might write text alongside the photos. Depending on your class and the available resources, students might take and print the photos, find them online, or find them in magazines.

Prior to beginning this umbrella, engage students in examining several photo essays. This umbrella aims to guide students through the process of creating a photo essay and learning how to tell a story through pictures by selecting a topic, choosing photos, and adding information. Teach these minilessons several days apart to provide time for students to work on each step in the process. Use the books listed below from *Fountas & Pinnell Classroom™ Interactive Read-Aloud Collection*, or choose books from the classroom library.

Interactive Read-Aloud Collection

Telling a Story with Photos

Wolf Island by Nicholas Read

A Bear's Life by Nicholas Read

The Seal Garden by Nicholas Read

A Little Book of Sloth by Lucy Cooke

Face to Face with Whales by Flip and Linda Nicklin

Series: Vanishing Cultures

Sahara by Jan Reynolds

Himalaya by Jan Reynolds

Amazon Basin by Jan Reynolds

Frozen Land by Jan Reynolds

Far North by Jan Reynolds

As you read and enjoy these texts together, help students

- notice how photographs are used to tell a story, and

- observe the way that many photo essay writers include text alongside the photos.

Section 2: Genres and Forms

Writing Minilesson Principle
Notice the qualities of photo essays.

You Will Need

- multiple photo essays, such as those in Text Set: Telling a Story with Photos and Text Set: Series: Vanishing Cultures
- chart paper and markers
- pencils for each group
- writer's notebooks

Academic Language / Important Vocabulary

- photo essay
- topic
- qualities
- perspective
- characteristics

Continuum Connection

- Learn ways of using language and constructing texts from other writers (reading books and hearing them read aloud) and apply understandings to one's own writing
- Attend to the nuances of illustrations and how they enhance a text in order to try them out for oneself

GOAL

Identify characteristics of photo essays and think about a topic for a photo essay.

RATIONALE

Photo essays are another form of storytelling. Learning about them opens students up to new possibilities and ideas for them for expressing themselves and telling stories. Because photo essays are mainly visual, they tend to be highly motivational for students who prefer sharing information visually.

WRITER'S NOTEBOOK/WRITING FOLDER

Students will use their writer's notebooks to record characteristics of and list topics for photo essays.

ASSESS LEARNING

- Look for evidence that students recognize characteristics of photo essays.
- Listen for evidence that students are engaged in thinking and talking about photo essay topics.
- Look for evidence that students can use vocabulary such as *photo essay*, *topic*, *qualities*, *perspective*, and *characteristics*.

MINILESSON

Students will need their writer's notebooks for this lesson. To help students think about the minilesson principle, use mentor texts to engage them in studying photo essays to notice common characteristics. Here is an example.

- Have the class sit in groups of 3–5 students. Provide one or more photo essay books for each group. Make sure each student has a writer's notebook and a pencil.

  Open your notebook to a clean page. Write "Photo Essays" and today's date at the top. Then, in your group, talk about the characteristics, or qualities, you notice in the photo essays. Write what you notice in your writer's notebook.

- As students talk about the characteristics of photos essays in their groups, check in with each group and prompt their thinking if necessary.

- When groups are finished, write the minilesson principle on chart paper. Begin the conversation by asking a group member to share what they have written about photo essays. Begin a list on chart paper.

  As you notice characteristics in other photos essays, you can add new noticings to the chart.

Have a Try

Invite students to turn and talk about topic ideas for photo essays.

> Think about some ideas you have for photo essays. Turn and talk about some possible topics you could use for a photo essay.

▶ After time for discussion, ask volunteers to share. As they do, use their ideas to make a list of topic ideas on a new sheet of chart paper.

Summarize and Apply

Summarize the learning. Have students gather ideas for photo essays during independent writing.

> You talked about characteristics of photo essays and thought about some topic ideas for making your own. During independent writing time, make notes in your writer's notebook about ideas for topics and about photos you might like to take or find. Bring your notes to share when we meet later.

Confer

▶ During independent writing, move around the room to confer briefly with students about their photo essay ideas. Use the following prompts as needed.

- *Would you like to give information, tell a story, or both?*
- *What are some topics you are interested in for your photo essay?*
- *Let's look at the topics list we made as a class. What ideas do you see that you might be interested in?*

Share

Following independent writing, gather students in the meeting area to share their ideas for photo essay topics.

> In pairs, share the notes you made about photo essay topic ideas.

> Share a topic idea that you heard from your partner, and I will add it to the chart.

Notice the qualities of photo essays.

- Have a theme or tell a story
- Photos are related to each other
- Photos are taken from different perspectives
- Words go with each photo
- Show emotions
- Photos show more than words tell
- Give information
- Teach how to do something
- Identify a problem in the world

Photo Essay Topic Ideas

- Seasons
- Transportation in the city
- Things my family does together
- Games I play at home
- Bulletin boards around the school
- Tools used in the art room
- Science experiment: before, during, after photos
- Flowers and vegetables in the school garden

Writing Minilesson Principle

Decide what the photos should show and how to order and place them on the pages.

Making Photo Essays

You Will Need

- several mentor texts with photo essays, such as the following:
  - *A Bear's Life* by Nicholas Read and *A Little Book of Sloth* by Lucy Cooke, from Text Set: Telling a Story with Photos
  - *Himalaya* by Jan Reynolds, from Text Set: Series: Vanishing Cultures
- chart paper and markers
- writer's notebooks

Academic Language / Important Vocabulary

- photo essay
- organization
- layout

Continuum Connection

- Present ideas clearly and in a logical sequence
- Use layout of print and illustrations to convey the meaning of a text
- Get ideas from other books and writers about how to approach a topic: e.g., organization, point of view, layout
- Reorder the information in a text to make the meaning clearer by cutting apart, cutting and pasting, laying out pages, using word-processing

GOAL

Make decisions about what the photos should show, how to order them, and where to place them on the pages.

RATIONALE

To create an effective photo essay, students must think about what they want their readers to see in the photos. Doing this thinking helps students realize that writers have many decisions to make when creating a photo essay, and they begin to take ownership of each step in the process.

WRITER'S NOTEBOOK/WRITING FOLDER

Students will use their writer's notebooks to sketch a plan and make notes for their photo essays.

ASSESS LEARNING

- Talk with students about their decisions about what to show in their photos.
- Notice evidence that students are thoughtful about placing their photos.
- Look for evidence that students can use vocabulary such as *photo essay*, *organization*, and *layout*.

MINILESSON

Before this minilesson, students should have a photo essay topic selected. To help students in planning and organizing photos for their photo essays, use mentor texts to engage them in talking about the process of making a photo essay. Here is an example.

- Show the cover and revisit a few pages in *A Bear's Life*.

  What are things the writer and photographer probably thought about before creating this photo essay book?

- Prompt the conversation as needed to help students think about choices in photography, organization, and layout. For example:
  - *Why do you think the photographer took this photo?*
  - *Why do you think the author included this photo in this photo essay?*
  - *What do you notice about the organization of the photos?*
  - *What do you notice about the layout of the photos on the pages?*

- Repeat with *A Little Book of Sloth* and *Himalaya*.

- As needed, guide the conversation so students recognize that they need to think about what photos to include and then plan how to order and place them on a pages. As students provide ideas, write questions to think about on chart paper in two sections: *Taking (Finding) Photos* and *Organization and Layout*.

Have a Try

Invite students to turn and talk about planning a photo essay.

Look at the questions on the chart. Turn and talk to a partner about how you might answer some of these questions for the photo essay you are planning to create.

▶ After time for discussion, ask a few students to share. If students share any new questions, add them to the chart.

Summarize and Apply

Summarize the learning. Have students plan their photo essays during independent writing. Write the principle at the top of the chart.

During independent writing time, use your writer's notebook to plan your photo essay. Think about what to show in the photos, the order you want the photos to be placed in, and how you might place them on the pages. You might want to draw boxes and plan one photo essay page in each box, showing where you might put the photos and where you might put any words. Bring your plan to share when we meet later.

> **Decide what the photos should show and how to order and place them on the pages.**
>
> <u>Taking (Finding) Photos</u>
> - What photos will you want to take (find)?
> - What perspectives will you take the photos from?
> - What content will be in each photo?
> - What emotion do you want to show?
> - What information or story do you want to share?
>
> <u>Organization and Layout</u>
> - Which photos are the most powerful for your purpose?
> - In what order will you place your photos?
> - What page layout will be best?
> - How many photos will be on each page?
> - Will there be any words? If so, where will they go?

Confer

▶ During independent writing, move around the room to confer briefly with students about planning their photo essays. Use the following prompts as needed.

- *What photos do you want to include in your photo essay?*
- *What information (story, emotion) do you want to share with your readers?*
- *Let's talk about where you will place the photos on the pages.*

Share

Following independent writing, gather students in the meeting area. Ask a few volunteers to share their photo essay plans.

In groups of three, share your plan for your photo essay.

Look at the chart. Is there a question you have not yet been able to answer?

Making Photo Essays

You Will Need

- several mentor texts with photo essays, such as the following:
  - *Face to Face with Whales* by Flip and Linda Nicklin and *A Little Book of Sloth* by Lucy Cooke, from Text Set: Telling a Story with Photos
  - *Far North* by Jan Reynolds, from Text Set: Series: Vanishing Cultures
- prepared narrated photo essay (video or slideshow (optional))
- chart paper and markers
- students' photos for their photo essays
- writer's notebooks and writing folders

Academic Language / Important Vocabulary

- photo essay
- digital
- written
- audience
- narrated
- purpose

Continuum Connection

- Create illustrations and writing that work together to express the meaning
- Integrate technology tools (e.g., slideshows, video, audio) into multimedia presentations
- Use digital tools to express ideas and opinions, tell stories, write poems, craft persuasive arguments using text and other digital media

GOAL

Add information (handwritten, digital, or oral) to go along with the photos.

RATIONALE

Photos tell part of the story, but sometimes words are helpful for further detailed explanation. Words can be added in handwritten or oral form or entered digitally if students are making online photo essays (e.g., in a slideshow format). When thinking of what to say about the photos, students should think about their purpose and audience.

WRITER'S NOTEBOOK/WRITING FOLDER

Students will use their writer's notebooks to jot notes about the words they will add to their photo essays. If students are making physical copies of their photo essays, they should store the drafts in their writing folders.

ASSESS LEARNING

- Look for evidence that students think about purpose and audience when deciding what information to add and how to add it
- Look for evidence that students can use vocabulary such as *photo essay*, *written*, *narrated*, *digital*, *audience*, and *purpose*.

MINILESSON

Before teaching this lesson, students should have taken or found photos they will use for their photo essays. To model text that could accompany a photo essay, use mentor texts and create your own photo essay as a narrated slideshow or as a video. Here is an example.

- Show (or project) a page from *Face to Face with Whales*. Read the words and point to the corresponding photo.

  Think about the purpose of and audience for this photo essay.

- Prompt the conversation as needed to help students think about whether the purpose is storytelling, procedural, or informational/expository and who the intended audience is.

  What do you notice about the words that go with the photo(s)?

- Make sure students recognize that the words support the photos.
- Repeat with several pages in *A Little Book of Sloth* and *Far North*.

  Authors choose the words they use in their photo essays. They also choose whether to use written words or narrated words.

- Display the narrated photo essay video or slideshow you have prepared. Share the decisions you made that connect purpose, audience, and format.

Have a Try

Invite students to turn and talk about the content and form of the text that accompanies photos in a photo essay.

> What words will you use to explain your photos? Will you have written descriptions, or will you talk about them to your audience? Turn and talk about that.

▶ After time for discussion, ask several students to share. As they do, create a chart with students' names, the purpose and intended audience of their photo essay, and notes about how they will add information to support the photos.

Summarize and Apply

Summarize the learning. During independent writing, have students plan the words for their photo essays.

> How can you give your readers more information in your photo essay?

▶ Add the principle to the top of the chart.

> During independent writing time, take a look at your photos. In your writer's notebook, jot down notes about your purpose, audience, and what you want to explain about each photo. Also make notes about whether your photo essay will have handwritten, digital, or narrated words. Bring your photo essay to share when we meet later.

Add information that explains the photos.			
Name	Purpose	Audience	Ways to Add Information
Tommie	Tell a story about my mom and aunt when they were kids	My family	Add words to a slideshow (in Spanish and English)
Ziggy	Show the steps in my science experiment	Fourth grade students at my school	Narrate the photos in a slideshow to explain each step
Francine	Share close-ups of things I see on my street	Students or neighbors	Write a caption about each object and what it makes me think about
Sequoia	Tell a story about a day in the life of my kitten	Classmates	Narrate a video that tells what my kitten is doing
Blair	Give information about different animals at a shelter	Families	Write captions that give facts about each animal

Confer

▶ During independent writing, move around the room to confer briefly with students about their photo essays. Use the following prompts as needed.

- *What is the purpose of your photo essay (e.g., storytelling, procedural, informative)?*
- *What do you want your audience to know about your photos?*
- *Will the words be written or narrated?*

Share

Following independent writing, gather students in the meeting area. Ask a few volunteers to share their ideas for the words they will use in their photo essays.

> Talk about your purpose, audience, and writing form for your photo essay.

Writing Minilesson Principle

Write an introduction or conclusion to explain the photo essay.

Making Photo Essays

You Will Need

- multiple photo essays with introductions and/or conclusions, such those in Text Set: Telling a Story with Photos and Text Set: Series: Vanishing Cultures

- chart paper prepared with a two-column chart with the heads *Introduction* and *Conclusion*

- writer's notebooks

- markers

- document camera (optional)

- chart paper and markers

Academic Language / Important Vocabulary

- photo essay

- explain

- introduction

- conclusion

Continuum Connection

- Use a variety of beginnings and endings to engage the reader

- Bring a piece to closure with a concluding statement

- Introduce, develop, and conclude the topic or story

- Bring the piece to closure with an effective summary, parting idea, or satisfying ending

GOAL

Understand the function of an introduction and a conclusion in a photo essay.

RATIONALE

When students recognize that authors often include an introduction and/or conclusion to explain their photo essays, they begin to think about what readers might need to know before looking at a photo essay and what they might want to know after they look at it.

WRITER'S NOTEBOOK/WRITING FOLDER

Students will use their writer's notebooks to draft ideas for an introduction and conclusion for their photo essays.

ASSESS LEARNING

- Talk with students about their photo essays. What do they understand about introductions and conclusions?

- Look for evidence that students can use vocabulary such as *photo essay*, *explain*, *introduction*, and *conclusion*.

MINILESSON

Students will need their writer's notebooks for this lesson. To help students think about the minilesson principle, share mentor texts and talk with them about why authors often include an introduction and/or conclusion in their photo essays. Here is an example.

- Show and read the introduction in one of the photos essays you have gathered.

  What are your thoughts about the introduction that the author included in this photo essay?

- Guide students to talk about the type of information that is provided. As they do, use general language to write their ideas on the chart under *Introduction*.

- Show and read the conclusion.

  What do you notice about how the author chose to end the photo essay?

- Using general language, add student suggestions to the *Conclusion* column.

- Have the class sit in groups of 3–5 students. Give one or more photo essays to each group.

  In your group, look at the introduction and conclusion in several photo essays and write what you notice in your writer's notebook.

- After the groups finish with their photo essay book(s), encourage them to exchange books with other groups to explore more examples.

Have a Try

Invite students to turn and talk about having an introduction or conclusion in their photo essays.

> Think about whether you will have an introduction, a conclusion, or both in your photo essay. What information will the introduction or conclusion provide? Turn and talk to your partner about that.

> ▶ After time for a brief discussion, ask several volunteers to share.

Summarize and Apply

Summarize the learning. Have students write or record introductions or conclusions during independent writing.

> How can you provide further information for your photo essay?

> ▶ Write the principle at the top of the chart.

> Today you learned that in photo essays, writers often include an introduction, a conclusion, or both. During independent writing time, write, enter, or record your introduction and/or conclusion. Use your writer's notebook to draft some ideas.

Write an introduction or conclusion to explain the photo essay.

Introduction	Conclusion
• Facts about the topic	• Other important facts
• Why the author chose this topic	• Where to learn more
• How the author took the photos	• How people can help
• How the author decided to organize the photos	• Wraps up the big idea
• Note from the photographer	• Summarizes the photos
• How the author became interested in the topic	• Important notes about the photos
• Why the photo essay is important	• Details about how the photos were taken

Confer

> ▶ During independent writing, move around the room to confer briefly with students about having an introduction and/or conclusion in their photo essays. Use the following prompts as needed.

> • *Will you have an introduction, a conclusion, or both?*
> • *Talk about the introduction (conclusion) you are working on.*
> • *What information would your readers want to see in the introduction (conclusion)?*
> • *What do you want to leave your readers thinking about in your conclusion?*

Share

Following independent writing, gather students in the meeting area. Ask a few volunteers to discuss their ideas about introductions and conclusions.

> Will your photo essay include an introduction, a conclusion, or both? Share how you made that decision.

Assessment

After you have taught the minilessons in this umbrella, observe students in a variety of classroom activities. Use *The Fountas & Pinnell Literacy Continuum* to notice, teach for, and support students' learning as you observe their attempts at making photo essays.

▶ What evidence do you have of students' new understandings related to making photo essays?

- Are students noticing and talking about the qualities of photo essays?
- Do they think about their purpose and audience when they decide on the content and organization of the photos in their photo essays?
- How are they deciding whether to write or narrate text to accompany their photos?
- How helpful are the introduction and/or conclusion to students' photo essays?
- Are they using vocabulary such as *photo essay, topic, characteristics, qualities, organization, layout, written, audience, purpose, narrated, digital, introduction,* and *conclusion*?

▶ In what ways, beyond the scope of this umbrella, are students writing in different genres?

- Do they show an interest in writing poetry?
- Are they paying attention to word choice?

Use your observations to determine the next umbrella you will teach. You may also consult Suggested Sequence of Lessons (pp. 665–682) for guidance.

EXTENSIONS FOR MAKING PHOTO ESSAYS

▶ Plan time for students to present their photo essays to each other in the classroom. They might also want to share them with another class or with invited guests (e.g., school staff, family).

▶ Pull together a few students who need support in the same aspect of writing in a guided writing group.

▶ Have students engage in a photo tour around the school or neighborhood. Encourage them to take photos from varying perspectives (e.g., close up, from above, from below, from a variety of distances, with background, without background).

Minilessons in This Umbrella

WML1 Notice the qualities of digital texts.

WML2 Find and organize the information for your audience.

WML3 Include links, images, or videos to enhance digital writing.

WML4 Design your digital text and images to capture the audience's attention.

Before Teaching Umbrella 17 Minilessons

Students are immersed in digital texts, both inside and outside of the classroom. Writing their own digital texts draws on all of the writing skills they have acquired and requires additional thought and decision-making. When you support students in writing digital texts (e.g., blogs, websites, news, nonfiction/fiction), they view themselves as writers in any type of media.

The goal of these minilessons is to guide students through the process of creating a digital text on an informational topic they care about. Students will benefit from having previous experience with note-taking (WPS.U4: Writer's Notebook: Becoming an Expert). When students are researching a topic for this umbrella they can use nonfiction books, printed articles, or student-friendly websites. Students may need direction beyond these minilessons on the mechanics of embedding links, videos, or images in their digital texts. Consider enlisting the help of a technology support person at your school.

To prepare for this umbrella, choose a digital tool that allows students to write digital texts and share them with others, perhaps on a class blog or website. You'll want to create a list of student-friendly, school-district-approved search engines and websites to share with your students to ensure they access safe, reputable sources. You'll also want to determine how and when your students will have access to digital devices during the school day and put procedures in place for appropriate use.

As you teach the minilessons in this umbrella, immerse students in digital texts—including several examples of digital texts that include links, images, and videos. Help them notice and think about the difference between creating digital texts out of convenience and creating digital texts for a purpose (i.e., to enhance meaning).

Exploring Digital Writing

You Will Need

- a computer or tablet with internet access (connected to a projector, if possible), bookmarked to a digital text on a topic familiar to students
- chart paper and markers
- writer's notebooks

Academic Language / Important Vocabulary

- digital text
- topic
- characteristics
- qualities
- give information

Continuum Connection

- Show familiarity with computer and word-processing terminology
- Understand audience as all readers rather than just the teacher
- Use digital tools to express ideas and opinions, tell stories, write poems, craft persuasive arguments using text and other digital media
- Understand different digital publishing environments (on apps, computers, and mobile devices) such as school or classroom websites, blogs, wikis, message boards, social media, gaming platforms, and e-books

GOAL

Understand the characteristics of digital texts and think about a topic for a digital text.

RATIONALE

Developing content for a digital text is similar to developing content for comparable writing pieces in that students will apply what they have learned about genre, craft, conventions, and writing process. However, noticing the qualities of digital texts and understanding how writers use this medium opens possibilities beyond the static page for how students might inform readers about a topic they care about.

WRITER'S NOTEBOOK/WRITING FOLDER

Students will make notes in their writer's notebooks of ideas for topics and subtopics.

ASSESS LEARNING

- Look for evidence that students can identify and name characteristics of digital texts.
- Look for evidence that students can use vocabulary such as *digital text*, *topic*, *characteristics*, *qualities*, and *give information*.

MINILESSON

Engage students in an interactive discussion to help them notice the characteristics of digital texts. Here is an example.

- Display a digital text on a familiar topic.

  With your partner, talk about the characteristics, or qualities, you notice in this [blog post, website, online story].

- As students talk about the characteristics of digital texts with a partner, listen to conversations and prompt their thinking as necessary. For example:

  - *What type of information does the writer share? Is this text telling a story, giving information, or both?*

  - *What enhancements or tools does the writer use to share information with readers? How do those tools capture your attention?*

  - *What do you notice about how the text is organized?*

  - *What do you notice about colors, fonts, and placement of text? Why do you think the writer made those choices?*

  - *Why might the writer have used that image, link, or video?*

- Write the minilesson principle on chart paper. Ask students to share what they noticed. Write the noticings (in a generalized way) on the chart.

  As you learn about digital writing, we can add new ideas to the chart.

Have a Try

Invite students to turn and talk about topic ideas for their own digital text.

> Think about some ideas you have for an informational digital text. Turn and talk about some possible topics you might want to write about.

▶ After time for discussion, ask volunteers to share. As they do, use their ideas to make a list of topics and some related subtopics on a clean sheet of chart paper.

Summarize and Apply

Summarize the learning. Have students gather more ideas for digital text topics during independent writing, and add them to the chart. Remind students of ways they can take notes (see Section 3 in *Writer's Notebook, Intermediate*).

> You talked about characteristics of digital texts and thought about some topics for making your own. During independent writing time, make notes in your writer's notebook about your ideas for a topic that you care about. Use what you know about researching topics for informational writing and taking notes. Bring your notes to share when we meet later.

Confer

▶ During independent writing, move around the room to confer briefly with students about their informational digital-text ideas. Use the following prompts as needed.

- *What would you like to give information about?*
- *What are some topics you are interested in for your digital text? What are some subtopics?*
- *Let's look at the chart (in your writer's notebook). What ideas do you see that you might be interested in?*

Share

Following independent writing, gather students in the meeting area to share their ideas for informational digital-text topics.

> In pairs, share the notes you made about informational digital-text topic ideas.

> Share a topic idea that you heard from your partner, and I will add it to the chart.

Notice the qualities of digital texts.

- Visually appealing
- Easy to navigate
- Include images or photos
- Include links to other digital texts
- Include videos
- Use images to link to subtopics
- Organized by subtopic
- Link certain words to a glossary or dictionary (hyperlinks)
- Give information
- Teach how to do something
- Tell a story

Digital Text Topic Ideas

- Fishing
  - fly fishing
  - deep-sea fishing
- Gymnastics
- Playing baseball
- Babysitting
- Skateboards
- Soccer
- Singing in the choir
- A country (Brazil, Ecuador)
  - geographic features
  - climate
  - economy

WML2

GEN.U17.WML2

Writing Minilesson Principle
Find and organize the information for your audience.

Exploring Digital Writing

You Will Need

- a computer or tablet with internet access (connected to a projector, if possible), bookmarked to a digital text on a topic familiar to students
- chart paper and markers
- a chart prepared in advance with notes for your own informational digital text (see Have a Try)
- writer's notebooks

Academic Language / Important Vocabulary

- audience
- groups
- categories
- topics
- subtopics

Continuum Connection

- Understand that a writer creates an expository text for readers to learn about a topic
- Plan and organize information for the intended readers
- Create categories of information
- Locate, evaluate, and analyze literary and informational content using approved digital resources such as websites, public and subscription-based databases, e-books, and apps
- Communicate and share ideas with an audience through blogs, video, learning management systems, podcasts, and other digital tools

GOAL

Think about the audience when selecting and organizing information for digital writing.

RATIONALE

When students learn to plan out their informational digital texts by considering what they want the reader to understand and organizing notes into categories or subtopics, they realize that writers have many decisions to make when creating a digital text.

WRITER'S NOTEBOOK/WRITING FOLDER

Students will reread and reorganize the notes they have taken about a topic in their writer's notebooks.

ASSESS LEARNING

- Observe for evidence that students think about their audience when finding and organizing information for a digital text.
- Look for evidence that students can use vocabulary such as *audience*, *groups*, *categories*, *topics*, and *subtopics*.

MINILESSON

Before this minilesson, students should have a topic selected for an informational digital text (see WML1). To help students think about the minilesson principle, share a student-friendly digital text to engage them in an interactive discussion around intended audience, purpose for writing, and organization of information into categories. Here is an example.

- Display a digital text on a familiar topic, perhaps the one you used in WML1, to engage students in a conversation about audience, purpose, and organization. Prompt the conversation as needed.
  - *Who is the audience for this? What makes you think that?*
  - *What are things the author probably thought about when choosing what information to share and how to organize it?*
  - *What can you do to organize your digital text for your audience?*
- Scroll through the digital text. If there are headings, read them to students.

  What do you notice about how the author organized the information? How is this similar to other texts you have read?

- Guide students through the steps they would take to find and organize information for an audience of a digital text. Record students' responses on chart paper.

  These strategies are similar to how you would organize your writing whether you are writing on paper or on a device.

Have a Try

Display your notes about a familiar topic. Read them aloud and invite students to turn and talk to a partner about how they might organize the notes.

> My topic is giant squid. These are my research notes. I will use my notes to create a digital text to teach about giant squid. How might I organize my notes into subtopics? What other questions might my audience have about giant squid? Turn and talk about that.
>
> After time for discussion, ask a few students to share, writing ideas on the chart.

Summarize and Apply

Help students summarize the learning. Invite students to organize research for their informational digital texts during independent writing.

> How can you organize your writing for your audience?

▶ Write the principle at the top of the first chart.

> During independent writing time, use your writer's notebook to organize your research into subtopics. Think about questions your audience might have. Use the chart to help you remember what to do. Bring your work to share when we meet later.

Confer

▶ During independent writing, move around the room to confer briefly with students about what they want their readers to learn. Use the following prompts as needed.

- *What types of facts do you want to share with your readers?*
- *What information have you already collected? How can these facts be organized into categories or subtopics?*
- *What other questions might your readers have? Where will you find that information? In what category will you put that information?*

Share

Following independent writing, gather students in the meeting area. Ask a few volunteers to share their digital text plans.

> With a partner, share how you organized the information for your digital text. What subtopics did you choose? What questions do you still want to research?

Find and organize the information for your audience.

Take notes.
- What do you already know about the topic?
- What does your research tell you about the topic?

Reread your research notes.
- Does anything not belong?
- Is anything missing?

Make subtopics.
- Which notes are similar / go together?
- What can you title that category or subtopic?

Write questions.
- What might the audience want to understand about the topic?

Research more to find answers to the questions.

My Research Notes on Giant Squid	Giant Squid
• Tentacles can be 30 feet long.	Tentacles
	• Tentacles can be 30 feet long.
• Giant squid have large eyes that help them to see bits of light in the dark.	• Tentacles squeeze the prey.
	Adaptations for survival
• Tentacles squeeze the prey.	• Giant squid have large eyes that help them to see bits of light in the dark.
• Jet propulsion helps giant squid escape quickly.	• Jet propulsion helps giant squid escape quickly.

Questions My Audience Might Have About Giant Squid
- What do giant squid eat?
- How long do giant squid usually live?

Exploring Digital Writing

You Will Need

- a computer or tablet with internet access (connected to a projector, if possible), bookmarked to a digital text on a topic familiar to students that include links, images, or videos
- chart paper and markers
- writer's notebooks

Academic Language / Important Vocabulary

- links
- images
- navigate
- enhance

Continuum Connection

- Integrate technology tools (e.g., slideshows, video, audio) into multimedia presentations
- Show familiarity with computer and word-processing terminology
- Create website entries and articles with appropriate text layout, graphics, and access to information through searching
- Add details or examples to make the piece clearer or more interesting
- Use a variety of methods to manage digital artifacts such as copying and pasting text and images, downloading and saving files, and citing sources
- Use digital tools to create simple documents, multimedia products, presentations, and e-books and to share resources

GOAL

Understand how links, images, and videos can enhance a digital text.

RATIONALE

Helping students to think critically about links, images, and videos in digital texts assists them in getting the most out of digital texts and can bring their digital writing to the next level of sophistication. When you teach students to think about the purpose of digital tools and which to use in different instances—and why—it helps them think about digital texts in new ways, both as readers and writers.

WRITER'S NOTEBOOK/WRITING FOLDER

Students will make notes in their writer's notebooks about which links, images, or videos might complement their digital texts.

ASSESS LEARNING

- Observe students as they consider the links, images, or videos that will enhance their digital texts.
- Look for evidence that students can use vocabulary such as *links*, *images*, *navigate*, and *enhance*.

MINILESSON

Students will need their writer's notebooks for this lesson. Before this minilesson, students should have researched their topics for their informational digital texts (see WML2). Share student-friendly digital texts to help students think critically about how and why links, videos, and images are used and to help them understand how these tools assist readers. Here is an example.

- Display a digital text to engage students in a conversation about the writer's use of and purpose for embedded links. Add ideas to chart paper.

  Do you see a link in this text? Let's see where it goes. Why do you think the author included the link? How does linking to another place help the readers? How might you include links in your digital text?

- Repeat this process, examining images and videos in a digital text.

  Why do you think the author has placed this image in the middle of this page?

  Why did the author include this video within the digital text? How does that enhance the readers' experience? How does the video provide more or different information from the text?

- Help students understand that too many digital enhancements might clutter the text and that they need to think critically about the quality and validity of any digital sources they link to.

Have a Try

Invite students to turn and talk about using links, images, and videos in their digital texts.

> Think about your topic and the links, images, or videos you might include in your informational digital text. Why will those tools be helpful? Turn and talk about that, and jot ideas in your writer's notebook.

▶ After time for discussion, ask several students to share. As they do, add new ideas to the chart.

Summarize and Apply

Help students summarize the learning. If devices are available, invite students to find links, images, and videos for their digital texts. If not, students may indicate in their writer's notebooks the kinds of links, images, or videos that would enhance their digital texts.

> What are you thinking about the use of digital tools in your digital text?

▶ Write the principle at the top of the chart.

> During independent writing time, find two or three links, images, or videos to enhance your readers' experience and help them to know more. These should be from trustworthy sources. When we come back together, be prepared to share what you plan to use and why these tools will be helpful to your audience.

Include links, images, or videos to enhance digital writing.

Digital Tool	Purpose/Why?
Links	Define a word
	Navigate to another digital text that provides more information
	Information on something related to the topic of the digital text
Images	Capture the reader's attention
	Maps to show where things are
	Photos to help the reader see what you are writing about
	Link to videos
Videos	Explain something visually
	Show how to do something
	Teach the reader more

Confer

▶ During independent writing, move around the room to confer briefly with students about enhancing their digital writing. Use the following prompts as needed.

- *How will that image (video, link) help readers understand more?*
- *Why is linking to that other site helpful to your readers?*
- *Which word would your readers need to understand? How might you help them learn what that word means?*

Share

Following independent writing, gather students in pairs in the meeting area.

> Show your partner the link, video, or image you want to include in your digital text. The listening partner can then tell how those tools might add to the digital text.

WML4

GEN.U17.WML4

Writing Minilesson Principle
Design your digital text and images to capture the audience's attention.

You Will Need

- a computer or tablet with internet access (connected to a projector, if possible), bookmarked to a digital text on a topic familiar to students
- a two-column chart prepared in advance with column heads (see chart)
- markers and sticky notes
- writer's notebooks
- document camera (optional)

Academic Language / Important Vocabulary

- design
- audience
- font
- capture
- placement

Continuum Connection

- Make decisions about where in a text to place features such as photographs with legends, insets, sidebars, and graphics
- Arrange print on the page to support the text's meaning and to help the reader notice important information
- Use layout of print and illustrations to convey the meaning of a text
- Use layout of print and illustrations (e.g., drawings, photos, maps, diagrams) to convey the meaning in a nonfiction text
- Use layout, spacing, and size of print to create titles, headings, and subheadings

GOAL

Consider how color, font, and placement of text and images capture the audience's attention.

RATIONALE

The digital landscape is busy. Students need to understand that to capture the audience's attention their digital content needs to be visually appealing but not overwhelming with respect to color, font, and placement of text and images. This is important, as it will help engage the audience in learning more about the writer's topic. Learning to engage readers of digital content is a skill students will apply throughout their educational and professional careers.

WRITER'S NOTEBOOK/WRITING FOLDER

Students will sketch a design for their digital text in their writer's notebooks.

ASSESS LEARNING

- Look for evidence that students are considering what makes a digital text appealing to the audience.
- Notice whether students are making choices about their own introductions and conclusions.
- Look for evidence that students can use vocabulary such as *design*, *font*, *placement*, *audience*, and *capture*.

MINILESSON

Students will need their writer's notebooks for this lesson. Share student-friendly digital texts to engage students in an interactive discussion about how design decisions capture the audience's attention. Help students think about how to apply this to their own digital texts. Here is an example.

- Display a digital text on a familiar topic to engage students in a conversation about making design decisions. Prompt and generalize their comments to develop a list of features and questions to ask themselves as they create their own digital texts. Use questions such as the following:
  - *What did the writer of this digital text do to capture your attention?*
  - *What do you think the writer thought about when choosing images?*
  - *What do you notice about where the writer placed the headings?*
  - *What do you notice about the background or the color the writer used as the background?*
  - *What do you notice about the font or the type of lettering the writer used? How are the headings similar to or different from the main paragraphs?*
- Write design features (e.g., *Color*, *Font and Spacing*, *Images*) on sticky notes added to the first column of the chart, with examples of each listed below the sticky notes. Add questions to the second column.

Have a Try

Invite students to turn and talk about the design choices they will make in their own digital texts.

▶ Refer students to the chart.

> Think about your topic and the information you have already gathered. Use the questions we generated to talk with your partner about the choices you will make for your digital text to capture your readers' attention. Start a quick sketch in your writer's notebook as you talk.

▶ After time for a brief discussion, ask several students to share.

Summarize and Apply

Summarize the learning. Have students continue to design their digital texts during independent writing.

> What did you learn about how writers capture readers' attention when designing a digital text?

▶ Write the principle at the top of the chart.

> Today during independent writing time, spend some time designing your digital text in your writer's notebook. Think about color, font, and the placement of images. Ask yourself the questions on the chart as you make your decisions.

Design your digital text and images to capture the audience's attention.	
What should you consider?	What questions can you ask yourself as you design your digital text?
Color • Background • Headings • Text below the headings	What color background will work? What color text will capture readers' attention? Should the color of the headings be the same as the color of the text written below?
Font and Spacing • Font size • Style of font • Spacing between lines • Space around text	What font style and size will be easy to read? What font style is appealing? How much space should be between the lines? Should I center the headings?
Images • Size • Quality • Placement	What images will show the information? How big should the images be? Where should the images be placed?

Confer

▶ During independent writing, move around the room to confer briefly with students about the design of their digital texts. Use the following prompts as needed.

- *What type of font might capture the audience's attention?*
- *What color might you use for the headings to capture the audience's attention?*
- *What images might you look for to encourage your readers to read more?*
- *What color background will catch the audience's attention?*

Share

Following independent writing, gather students in the meeting area. Ask a few volunteers to share their designs using a document camera (if available).

> Why did you make that design choice of color (font, image)? How does that help the readers?

Section 2: Genres and Forms

Assessment

After you have taught the minilessons in this umbrella, observe students in a variety of classroom activities. Use *The Fountas & Pinnell Literacy Continuum* to notice, teach for, and support students' learning as you observe their attempts at making digital texts.

▸ What evidence do you have of students' new understandings related to making digital texts?

- Are students noticing and talking about the qualities of digital texts?
- Are they thinking about what an audience might want to know about the topic?
- Are they using what they have previously learned about informational writing, researching, and taking notes?
- How are they deciding which digital tools to include? Are they considering how these tools enhance a reader's experience?
- How are students considering the audience as they design their digital text?
- Are they using vocabulary such as *digital text*, *topics*, *characteristics*, *qualities*, *give information*, *subtopics*, *categories*, *groups*, *audience*, *enhance*, *images*, *links*, *design*, *font*, *placement*, *audience*, and *capture*?

▸ In what ways, beyond the scope of this umbrella, are students engaged in working with digital texts?

- Do they show an interest in creating a digital text in a different genre?
- Are they interested in writing a variety of digital texts?

Use your observations to determine the next umbrella you will teach. You may also consult Suggested Sequence of Lessons (pp. 665–682) for guidance.

EXTENSIONS FOR EXPLORING DIGITAL WRITING

▸ Guide students to think about these questions to evaluate a website or any digital text: Is the organization or author well known and trustworthy? Does the website have a legitimate purpose? Is the content accurate (can it be verified elsewhere)? Has the content been recently updated? Is the information relevant to their needs?

▸ Explore fiction digital texts with students and encourage students to create their own. Using a "choose your own adventure" format may be particularly engaging for students.

▸ Discuss how students might create their own blog to write and collect the digital texts they have created. Consider engaging the help of the technology specialist at your school.

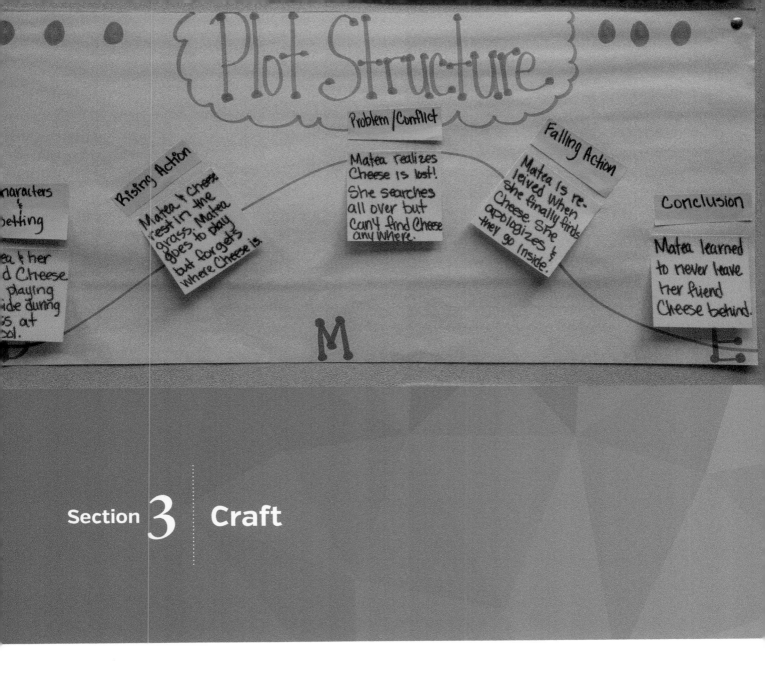

Section **3** | **Craft**

THROUGH THE TALK that surrounds interactive read-aloud
and shared reading, fourth graders learn much about the craft
of writing. The minilessons in this section take this growing
knowledge and pull back the curtain on the decisions authors
and illustrators make (e.g., choosing powerful words, using
dialogue, crafting leads and endings, incorporating text
features, choosing a structure for fiction and nonfiction writing)
to create writing that is interesting and exciting to read.

Minilessons in This Umbrella

WML1 Notice the decisions writers make.

WML2 Notice the decisions illustrators make.

WML3 Learn from writer and illustrator talks.

Before Teaching Umbrella 1 Minilessons

The minilessons in this umbrella are designed to help students notice elements of author's craft and illustrator's craft that they can try in their own writing. Consider teaching each lesson and then following it with a few days for students to immerse themselves in noticing and naming writing and illustrating techniques before they begin to try them on their own. Repeat lessons throughout the year as students get to know different authors and illustrators, tailoring the lessons to the authors and illustrators you are studying.

Read and discuss engaging books with a variety of writing and illustration styles. Use familiar texts so students can focus on craft decisions and begin to think about how these techniques might be useful in their own writing. Consider using the following books from *Fountas & Pinnell Classroom™ Interactive Read-Aloud Collection*, or choose books from your classroom library.

Interactive Read-Aloud Collection

Friendship

The Other Side by Jacqueline Woodson

Better Than You by Trudy Ludwig

The Dunderheads by Paul Fleischman

Figuring Out Who You Are

A Boy and a Jaguar by Alan Rabinowitz

The Junkyard Wonders by Patricia Polacco

As you read and enjoy these texts together, help students

- notice and discuss interesting examples of author's and illustrator's craft, and

- discuss how the decisions writers and illustrators make can help with their own writing and illustrating.

Interactive Read-Aloud
Friendship

Figuring Out Who You Are

Writer's Notebook

Section 3: Craft

Writing Minilesson Principle
Notice the decisions writers make.

You Will Need

- several familiar books that exemplify author's craft, such as the following:
  - *Better Than You* by Trudy Ludwig and *The Dunderheads* by Paul Fleischman, from Text Set: Friendship
  - *A Boy and a Jaguar* by Alan Rabinowitz and *The Junkyard Wonders* by Patricia Polacco, from Text Set: Figuring Out Who You Are
- several books for each pair of students
- chart paper prepared with three questions (see chart)
- sticky notes
- chart paper and markers
- writer's notebooks

Academic Language/ Important Vocabulary

- craft
- technique
- decisions

Continuum Connection

- Notice what makes writing effective and name the craft or technique
- Show interest in and work at crafting good writing, incorporating new learning from instruction
- Be willing to work at the craft of writing, incorporating new learning from instruction

GOAL

Study familiar books and notice crafting decisions writers make.

RATIONALE

Once students become aware of and can name the ways that authors craft their books, they can begin to apply some of the same crafting decisions and techniques to their own writing. This reinforces the practice of learning from other writers.

WRITER'S NOTEBOOK/WRITING FOLDER

Students can use their writer's notebooks to record notes about writer's craft.

ASSESS LEARNING

- Listen to students as they talk about books. Can they identify examples of author's craft?
- Look at students' writing. Are students using craft techniques they have noticed from other authors?
- Look for evidence that students can use vocabulary such as *craft*, *technique*, and *decisions*.

MINILESSON

To help students think about the minilesson principle, use mentor texts, samples of your own writing, or students' writing to guide them to notice the authors' craft decisions. Here is an example.

- Show *Better Than You* and read the first page.

  What do you notice about the sentences that the author, Trudy Ludwig, wrote?

  Why do you think she decided to write the sentences the way she did?

- Record students' responses on chart paper.
- Think aloud about how you might use this in your own writing.

  I might try Trudy Ludwig's technique in my own writing about a cake baking that went all wrong. I could start with a surprising sentence that talks directly to my readers like "It looked like cake, but it sure didn't taste like cake!" Would that sentence draw you into my story? Why?

- Discuss other decisions in the same manner with a couple of familiar books, such as *A Boy and a Jaguar* (one-word sentence on page 9, arrangement of words on pages 12–13) and *The Junkyard Wonders* (language).

Have a Try

Use a book that has a good example of author's craft to have students think more about reading like an author.

▶ Review a few pages of *The Dunderheads*.

> Turn and talk to your partner about something Paul Fleischman did to make his book interesting or something he did that helps you understand the story.

▶ After students turn and talk, invite a few students to share their thinking. Add their responses to the chart.

Summarize and Apply

Write the principle at the top of the chart. Summarize the learning. Provide books for each pair of students to find and discuss authors' decisions. Display the chart paper prepared with the three questions.

> Today, you will work with a partner to look in books to notice more examples of authors' decisions. Ask each other the questions on the chart. Mark the author's decisions with sticky notes. If you keep the sticky notes, add them to your writer's notebook after sharing with the class. If your partner keeps the sticky notes, copy their content into your writer's notebook. Bring your books and notes when we meet later.

Confer

▶ During independent writing, move around the room to confer with students about writers' decisions. Use prompts such as those below if needed. Follow each with "Why might the writer have done that?" and/or "How might you try that in your own writing?"

- *What interesting language did the writer use?*
- *How did the writer decide to place the words [sentences] on the page?*
- *How did the writer decide to begin [end] this book?*

Share

Gather students in the meeting area for partners to share their noticings with the whole group.

> What did you hear from your classmates that you might try in your writing?

Notice the decisions writers make.

Writer's Decision	Why?
Surprising first sentence	• Grabs the reader's attention • Shows character's feelings
Talk directly to the reader	• Draws the reader into the story • Builds a relationship between readers and the character
One word sentences	• Makes the word have a strong impact
Memorable language	• Shows how the character feels • Helps readers imagine the characters and the scene
Font grows as character speaks	• Shows the character's voice getting louder
Colons	• Sets words apart for dramatic effect
Characters with interesting and humorous nicknames	• Sets tone and creates mood • Shows the narrator's sense of humor and personality

Questions to ask each other:

- What did the writer do to make the writing interesting?

- What did the writer do to help you understand more?

- What might you do that is similar?

WML2

CFT.U1.WML2

Writing Minilesson Principle
Notice the decisions illustrators make.

Learning from Writers and Illustrators

You Will Need

- several familiar books that exemplify illustrator's craft, such as the following:
  - *The Dunderheads* by Paul Fleischman and *The Other Side* by Jacqueline Woodson, from Text Set: Friendship
  - *A Boy and a Jaguar* by Alan Rabinowitz, from Text Set: Figuring Out Who You Are
- several books for each pair of students
- chart paper prepared with three questions [see chart]
- chart paper and markers
- sticky notes
- writer's notebooks

Academic Language/ Important Vocabulary

- decisions
- craft
- illustrations

Continuum Connection

- Understand that when both writing and drawing are on a page, they are mutually supportive, with each extending the other
- Attend to the nuances of illustrations and how they enhance a text in order to try them out for oneself

GOAL

Study illustrations from familiar books and notice the craft decisions that illustrators make.

RATIONALE

Once students become aware of and can name the ways that illustrators craft their illustrations, they can begin to apply some of the same crafting decisions to their own drawings. This reinforces the practice of learning from other illustrators.

WRITER'S NOTEBOOK/WRITING FOLDER

Students can use their writer's notebooks to record notes about illustrator's craft.

ASSESS LEARNING

- Listen to students as they talk about books. Can they identify examples of illustrator's craft?
- Look for evidence that students can use vocabulary such as *decisions*, *craft* and *illustrations*.

MINILESSON

To help students think about the minilesson principle, use mentor texts to guide them to notice illustrators' craft decisions in books they know. Here is an example.

- Show the cover of *The Dunderheads*. Show the illustration on page 10.

  Why do you think the illustrator, David Roberts, decided to use both color and black-and-white illustrations on the same page?

- Record students' responses on chart paper. Think aloud about how you might try this in your own writing.

  In my own writing, I can use black-and-white and color illustrations to draw attention to certain characters and add layers to scenes, just like David Roberts did.

- Repeat this process, showing the illustration on pages 20–21.

  What do you notice about the layout on these pages? Why do you think David Roberts chose to do this? How does the layout help the story?

- Add responses to the chart.

  In my story, I could place more than one illustration on a page to show what is happening. I could put them in different shapes, too, to add interest. This will help move the story along in just one page.

- Continue in a similar manner with E. B. Lewis's illustrations in *The Other Side* (multiple pages of the fence, watercolor paintings, two-page spreads at the beginning and end).

Have a Try

Use a book that has a good example of illustrator's craft, such as *A Boy and a Jaguar*, to have students think more about reading like an illustrator.

▶ Show the illustrations on pages 2–3 in *A Boy and a Jaguar*. After time for discussion, show the illustrations from pages 4–5.

> What do you notice about the decisions the illustrator, Cátia Chien, made? Turn and talk to your partner. How are the pages different from each other?

▶ After students turn and talk, invite a few students to share their thinking. Add responses to the chart.

Summarize and Apply

Write the principle at the top of the chart. Summarize the learning. Provide books for pairs of students to look in for decisions the illustrators made in their illustrations. Display the chart with the questions.

> Today, look at books with a partner to notice more examples of decisions made by illustrators. Ask each other the questions on the chart. Mark the illustrator's decisions you notice with sticky notes. If you keep the sticky notes, add them to your writer's notebook after you share with the class. If your partner keeps the sticky notes, copy their content onto a page in your writer's notebook. Bring your books and notes when we meet later.

Notice the decisions illustrators make.	
Illustrator's Decision	**Why?**
Combination of color and black-and-white illustrations	• Draws attention to certain characters • Illustrations can overlap without being confusing
Multiple layouts of text and illustrations on some pages	• Helps the reader understand more detailed parts of the story • Moves the story along
Fence appears in many illustrations	• Shows the impact of the fence throughout the story
Watercolor paintings	• Creates a softness and an innocence that is reminiscent of childhood
Full page spreads only at the beginning and end of the book	• Highlights that the fence brings them together • Creates a change in perspective and mood from beginning to end
Background colors	• Shows changes in character's feelings and how they change

Questions to ask each other:

- What did the illustrator do to make the illustrations more interesting?

- How did the illustrator use the picture to tell more of the story?

- What similar thing could you do in your own books?

Confer

▶ During independent writing, move around the room to confer with students about illustrators' crafting decisions. Use prompts such as those below if needed. Follow each with "Why might the illustrator have done that?" and/or "How might you try that in your own books?"

- *What decisions did the illustrator make to give readers more information or to make the book more interesting?*
- *What do you notice about how the illustrations are placed on the page?*

Share

Gather students in the meeting area for partners to share what they noticed.

> What decisions by the illustrator did you notice in your books?

Learning from Writers and Illustrators

You Will Need

- quotes from Advice from Writers and Illustrators [online resource] and *Writer's Notebook, Intermediate* [Fountas and Pinnell 2023]
- chart paper and markers
- sticky notes
- writer's notebooks
- To download the following online resource for this lesson, visit **fp.pub/resources**:
  - Advice from Writers and Illustrators

Academic Language/ Important Vocabulary

- decisions
- craft
- technique
- advice
- quote

Continuum Connection

- Show interest in and work at crafting good writing, incorporating new learning from instruction

GOAL

Learn about writing from writer and illustrator talks.

RATIONALE

In writer and illustrator talks, the speaker offers a glimpse into the process of authors and illustrators. When students listen to the talks, they understand that they can learn about writing not just by reading the words and studying the illustrations but also from what the authors and illustrators say about themselves as writers and illustrators.

WRITER'S NOTEBOOK/WRITING FOLDER

Invite students to write in their writer's notebook inspiration from authors and illustrators.

ASSESS LEARNING

- Look for evidence that students apply what they learn from writer and illustrator talks to their own writing.
- Notice evidence they can use vocabulary such as *decisions*, *craft*, *technique*, *advice*, and *quote*.

MINILESSON

To help students think about the minilesson principle, have quotes prepared to read on chart paper, note cards, or a device (e.g., phone or tablet). Use the online resource Advice from Writers and Illustrators, or if you are using *Writer's Notebook, Intermediate*, see the Section 2 tab. This lesson uses a writer talk.

- Give a short writer talk.

  Author Jacqueline Woodson said this about writing: "The advice I'd give is to read. You learn to write by reading and studying the way other writers have done it. . . . If you read slowly, you'll understand stuff like how writers get dialogue on the page, how they make setting, how they get you to feel certain ways. . . . I wouldn't be here writing if it wasn't for the writers who had come before me, who I copied and then eventually found my own voice." How could this quote from Jacqueline Woodson help you with your own writing?

- Record students' responses on chart paper. Give another writer talk.

  Author Chitra Soundar also has advice for writers. "Write, write, write every day in a little notebook." What can you learn from this quote?

- Add responses to the chart.

  A few times a week, I will give a writer or illustrator talk. It might be advice, something about the author's or illustrator's life, or something about the way authors and illustrators think about writing.

Have a Try

Invite students to talk to a partner about the importance of writer and illustrator talks.

> Turn and talk to your partner about what you can learn by listening to talks about the work of authors and illustrators and how you might apply that knowledge to your own writing.

▶ After time for discussion, invite several students to share their thinking.

Summarize and Apply

Summarize the learning. Invite students to use writer and illustrator talks to help with their own writing.

> What is a way to learn about how you can improve your writing?

▶ Write the principle at the top of the chart.

> During independent writing time today, jot down in your writer's notebook anything you want to remember from the writer talks I gave today. As you write today and every day, keep in mind what you learn from the authors and illustrators you know and love. If you ever find useful advice or something about an author's or illustrator's life that might be helpful for all of us to know, share it with the class by giving your own writer or illustrator talk.

Learn from writer and illustrator talks.	
Author's Quote	**What I Learn from the Quote**
"The advice I'd give is to read. You learn to write by reading and studying the way other writers have done it. . . . If you read slowly, you'll understand stuff like how writers get dialogue on the page, how they make setting, how they get you to feel certain ways. . . . I wouldn't be here writing if it wasn't for the writers who had come before me, who I copied and then eventually found my own voice." —Jacqueline Woodson	• Study and learn from other writers by reading and thinking about their words • Try out in my own writing what I notice other writers do • Think about how to make my writing sound like me
"Write, write, write every day in a little notebook." —Chitra Soundar	• Make time to write every day • The importance of always having a notebook with me

Confer

▶ During independent writing, move around the room to confer with students about learning from authors and illustrators. Use prompts such as the following as needed.

- *How is your writing going today? Is there anything you need help with?*
- *What have you learned from other authors (illustrators) that could help?*
- *Let's see how some of the authors (illustrators) we know would handle this.*

Share

Following independent writing, gather students in the meeting area to share their notes.

> With a partner, share what you worked on today during independent writing. What advice did you find yourself thinking about while you were writing?

Assessment

After you have taught the minilessons in this umbrella, observe students as they write and draw. Use the behaviors and understandings in *The Fountas & Pinnell Literacy Continuum* to notice, teach for, and support students' learning as you observe their attempts at writing and drawing.

▶ What evidence do you have of students' new understandings related to learning from writers and illustrators?

- Can students notice and talk about the craft decisions that writers and illustrators made?
- What craft decisions are they trying in their own writing and illustrations?
- Do they apply lessons they've learned from writer and illustrator talks?
- Do they understand and use vocabulary such as *craft*, *technique*, *decisions*, *quote*, *advice*, and *illustrations*?

▶ In what other ways, beyond the scope of this umbrella, are students ready to expand their writing?

- Are they beginning to share their writing with others?
- Are they adding dialogue to their writing?

Use your observations to determine the next umbrella you will teach. You may also consult Suggested Sequence of Lessons (pp. 665–682) for guidance.

EXTENSIONS FOR LEARNING FROM WRITERS AND ILLUSTRATORS

▶ Continue adding to the charts created during these minilessons as students notice more examples of crafting decisions that authors and illustrators make. Refer to these charts across the year as you explore similar ideas in different minilessons.

▶ Repeat the first two minilessons in this umbrella with nonfiction writing, such as informational texts, and other genres you teach throughout the year. Use the online resource Planning a Minilesson to help you plan the books and examples for new minilessons.

▶ Repeat the third minilesson with illustrator talks.

▶ When you notice a student trying out an interesting craft decision, use it as a sample for other students to look at with an eye toward learning from each other as writers and illustrators.

▶ If you are using *The Reading Minilessons Book, Grade 4* [Fountas and Pinnell 2020], LA.U11: Studying Illustrators and Analyzing an Illustrator's Craft complements the concepts in this umbrella.

Minilessons in This Umbrella

WML1   Describe how characters look.

WML2   Show what characters are like through their actions and words.

WML3   Describe the character's feelings, thoughts, and dreams.

WML4   Describe a character through another character's thoughts, words, and actions.

WML5   Think about what to name your character.

Before Teaching Umbrella 2 Minilessons

Before teaching, provide opportunities for students to read and discuss books with detailed character descriptions as well as for students to independently write narratives. While this umbrella focuses on realistic fiction, the minilessons can apply to real people in any narrative writing, such as a memoir or biography. If you use these lessons for narrative nonfiction, such as biography, you may want to change the language from *character* to *subject*.

Make sure students are working on writing to which they can apply the lessons. For mentor texts, choose fiction books with well-developed characters. Use the books listed below from *Fountas & Pinnell Classroom™ Interactive Read-Aloud Collection*, or choose books from the classroom library.

Interactive Read-Aloud Collection

The Idea of Home

> *Red Butterfly: How a Princess Smuggled the Secret of Silk Out of China* by Deborah Noyes

Friendship

> *The Dunderheads* by Paul Fleischman
>
> *Better Than You* by Trudy Ludwig

Empathy

> *A Symphony of Whales* by Steve Schuch

Figuring Out Who You Are

> *A Boy and a Jaguar* by Alan Rabinowitz
>
> *The Junkyard Wonders* by Patricia Polacco

As you read and enjoy these texts together, help students

- notice how characters are portrayed, and
- talk about what actions, thoughts, and dialogue reveal about characters.

Interactive Read-Aloud
The Idea of Home

Friendship

Empathy

Figuring Out Who You Are

Writer's Notebook

Writing Minilesson Principle
Describe how characters look.

Describing Characters

You Will Need

- a mentor text with physical descriptions of a character, such as *Red Butterfly* by Deborah Noyes, from Text Set: The Idea of Home
- chart paper and markers
- writer's notebooks and writing folders

Academic Language / Important Vocabulary

- character
- describe
- descriptive
- physical features

Continuum Connection

- Describe characters by how they look, what they do, say, and think, and what others say about them
- Use descriptive language and dialogue to present characters/subjects who appear in narratives (memoir, biography, and fiction) and informational writing

GOAL

Use language that helps readers picture a character.

RATIONALE

Writers describe how characters look so that readers can visualize them and become more engaged in the stories. When students recognize this, they think about how to use physical descriptions of the characters in their own writing.

WRITER'S NOTEBOOK/WRITING FOLDER

Students can use their writer's notebooks to try out descriptions of the characters as they work on story drafts from their writing folders.

ASSESS LEARNING

- Look at students' writing. How clearly do students describe the characters, especially the main character?
- Look for evidence that students can use vocabulary such as *character*, *describe*, *descriptive*, and *physical features*.

MINILESSON

To help students learn about the minilesson principle, use a mentor text to show how writers describe how a character looks. (It's best if students have not read or seen the mentor text.) Below is an example. Teach this lesson when students are writing fiction stories or memory stories.

- Read pages 1 and 4 of *Red Butterfly* without showing the illustrations.

    How do you know how the princess looks?

- Guide the students to recognize the detailed descriptions that help the readers know how the princess looks. Show the illustrations.

    The writer describes the princess because what she looks like is important to the story. What words does the author use?

- Write the descriptive words on chart paper along with the character and the book title.

    Think about the characters you are writing about. What do they look like?

    What physical features of your characters are important to the story?

- As students share ideas, guide the conversation to help them be more descriptive.

    What picture do you form in your mind when _____ describes the character?

- Add the descriptions to the chart, along with the students' names.

Have a Try

Invite students to turn and talk about describing a character in their own stories.

> Turn and talk about how a character looks in the story you are writing.

▶ After time for a brief discussion, ask a few students to share their ideas. Add to the chart.

Summarize and Apply

Summarize the learning. Remind students to use descriptive words for the characters they write about. Write the principle at the top of the chart.

> During independent writing time today, look at a piece of fiction writing or of a memoir to see if you have given readers enough information to picture how a character or person looks. You might need to add some descriptive details. If you are getting ready to write a new story, you can make some notes in your writer's notebook about how the characters look. Bring your writing to share when we meet later.

Describe how characters look.	
The Princess in Red Butterfly	"careful eyebrows" "silver pins" "my hair spills into my gentle maidservant's hands" "I am a child with my hair yet cut across my forehead." "combing my black hair back"
Mason	"skin the color of the setting sun"
Anna	"wrinkled fingers" "I can hear her feet dragging on the ground with each step."
Dhruv	"jeans so full of dirt from exploring the mountain that they looked brown instead of blue"
Amelia	"so tall he could almost touch the bottom of the basketball hoop" "red and black sneakers"

Confer

▶ During independent writing, move around the room to confer briefly with students about how they are describing their characters. Use the following prompts as needed.

- *What does the character's face look like?*
- *Describe the character's hair (hands, feet, body).*
- *What is the character wearing?*

Share

Following independent writing, gather students in groups of four in the meeting area.

> Describe a character so the members of your group can picture what your character looks like.

> What description from a classmate stood out to you as being very helpful in picturing a character?

Writing Minilesson Principle

Show what characters are like through their actions and words.

Describing Characters

You Will Need

- a mentor text that describes the actions and words of a character, such as *Better Than You* by Trudy Ludwig, from Text Set: Friendship:
- chart paper and markers
- writer's notebooks and writing folders

Academic Language / Important Vocabulary

- character
- describe
- words
- actions
- gestures

Continuum Connection

- Describe characters by how they look, what they do, say, and think, and what others say about them
- Use descriptive language and dialogue to present characters/subjects who appear in narratives (memoir, biography, and fiction) and informational writing

GOAL

Describe characters through their actions and dialogue.

RATIONALE

Sometimes writers describe a character's behavior or use a character's words to help readers know more about the character. When students realize this, they understand that they have different ways to share information about the characters in their own writing.

WRITER'S NOTEBOOK/WRITING FOLDER

Students can use their writer's notebooks to try out descriptions of the characters as they work on story drafts from their writing folders.

ASSESS LEARNING

- Notice whether students include a character's actions and words to reveal something about the character.
- Look for evidence that students can use vocabulary such as *character*, *describe*, *words*, *actions*, and *gestures*.

MINILESSON

To help students think about the minilesson principle, use familiar texts to provide an interactive lesson and model how a writer reveals what a character is like through actions and words. Here is an example.

> Let's think about the way the author of *Better Than You* describes Tyler and Jake. As I read, raise your hand when you notice something that shows what the characters are like. I will pause so we can talk about it.

▶ Revisit pages 1–8 of *Better Than You*. Pause when a student raises a hand to talk about the characters' traits as shown through words and actions.

> What does the author want you to know about Tyler (Jake) by including those words or that action?

▶ Guide the conversation as needed. Begin a chart to list the words or actions and what they show about the character.

> Writers include words and actions that help make characters come to life. The words and actions might show what kind of a person the character is, or they may show how the character is feeling at that moment.

Have a Try

Invite students to turn and talk about describing a character.

▶ Read page 9.

> On this page, how does the author help you understand how Tyler is feeling? Turn and talk about this with your partner.

▶ After time for a brief discussion, ask a few students to share their ideas. Support the conversation as needed. Add to the chart.

Summarize and Apply

Summarize the learning. Remind students to write about a character's actions and words.

> How can you show what a character is like?

▶ Write the principle at the top of the chart.

> During independent writing time today, check the story you are working on to see if you have included a character's actions and/or words. Make some notes in your writer's notebook about what a character might say or do. Bring your writing to share when we meet later.

Show what characters are like through their actions and words.			
Tyler		**Jake**	
Actions and Words	What It Shows	Actions and Words	What It Shows
Spends weeks practicing basketball moves	Hard-working Determined to do well	Says, "Yeah, well, I bet you can't do this."	Arrogant
He couldn't just say, "Cool, Tyler!"	Wants approval from others	Goes on and on about all the things his music player can do	Show off
"My hands get all sweaty"	Lacks confidence about math tests	"I must be, like, five times smarter than you in math."	Mean

Confer

▶ During independent writing, move around the room to confer briefly with students about how they are describing their characters. Use the following prompts as needed.

- *What is your character like?*
- *How will you show what kind of person your character is? What actions can you add?*
- *How can you show how your character is feeling?*

Share

Following independent writing, gather students in the meeting area to share their writing.

> Who would like to read your description of your character?

> What do the words and actions of _____'s character show about the character?

Section 3: Craft

Writing Minilesson Principle
Describe the character's feelings, thoughts, and dreams.

Describing Characters

You Will Need

- several mentor texts that describe the feelings, thoughts, or dreams of a character, such as the following from Text Set: Figuring Out Who You Are:
  - *A Boy and a Jaguar* by Alan Rabinowitz
  - *The Junkyard Wonders* by Patricia Polacco
- chart paper and markers
- writer's notebooks and writing folders

Academic Language / Important Vocabulary

- character
- feelings
- thoughts
- dreams
- inner life

Continuum Connection

- Describe characters by how they look, what they do, say, and think, and what others say about them
- Show rather than tell how characters feel
- Use descriptive language and dialogue to present characters/subjects who appear in narratives (memoir, biography, and fiction) and informational writing

GOAL

Reveal characters by showing their feelings, thoughts, and dreams.

RATIONALE

When students understand that writers reveal things about a character by sharing the character's inner thoughts and feelings, they realize that they can use words to convey a character's inner life and to reveal information in their own writing.

WRITER'S NOTEBOOK/WRITING FOLDER

Students can use their writer's notebooks to try out descriptions of the characters as they work on story drafts from their writing folders.

ASSESS LEARNING

- Look at students' writing. Do they sometimes write about a character's feelings, thoughts, and dreams?
- Look for evidence that students can use vocabulary such as *character*, *feelings*, *thoughts*, *dreams*, and *inner life*.

MINILESSON

To help students think about the minilesson principle, use familiar texts to provide an interactive lesson and model how a writer reveals a character's feelings, thoughts, and dreams. Here is an example.

- Show the cover of *A Boy and a Jaguar*.

  As I revisit *A Boy and a Jaguar*, I am going to think aloud about what the author, Alan Rabinowitz, did to show what Alan is like.

- Begin reading and pause to point out when Alan's feelings, thoughts, or dreams are revealed.

- Continue reading, encouraging students to raise a hand when they notice that the author reveals something about the character.

  What does the author show about Alan's inner life, or about his feelings, thoughts, and dreams?

- Begin a chart, writing in general terms what the author shows and what the information reveals about the character.

  Turn and talk about why the author probably included the information about what Alan feels or thinks.

- After time for a brief discussion, ask volunteers to share. Add any new examples to the chart.

- Repeat with *The Junkyard Wonders*.

Have a Try

Invite students to turn and talk about describing a character's feelings, thoughts, and dreams.

> Think about a character in the story you are writing. Turn to your partner and describe what feelings, thoughts, and dreams you could include to show something important about the character.

▶ After time for a brief discussion, ask a few students to share their ideas. Support the conversation as needed.

Summarize and Apply

Summarize the learning. Remind students to reveal a character's (or person's) inner life.

> How can you show your readers what a character is like?

▶ Write the principle at the top of the chart.

> During independent writing time today, check the story you are working on to see if you can describe a character's feelings, thoughts, or dreams so that your readers learn about the character's inner life. Write some notes in your writer's notebook about what a character might think or say that you can add to your story. Bring your notebook to share when we meet later.

Describe the character's feelings, thoughts, and dreams.	
Alan	Trisha
The writer shows what Alan is thinking about when he cannot speak and how he sees similarities between his animals and himself.	The writer shows how Trisha's thoughts and feelings about her new school change as she realizes that she has been put in a special class.
This shows that even though he cannot speak well, he wants to speak well and he is just as smart and thoughtful as anyone else. He has a lot of empathy for animals.	This shows that Trisha worries a lot about what other people think of her. She really wants to be seen as normal.

Confer

▶ During independent writing, move around the room to confer briefly with students about how they are describing their characters. Use the following prompts as needed.

- *What is your character thinking?*
- *What will your character say?*
- *What could this character think or say to help your readers learn more?*

Share

Following independent writing, gather students in the meeting area to share their writing.

> Who would like to share the notes in your writer's notebook about ways to show a character's feelings, thoughts, and dreams? Share what you wrote.

WML4
CFT.U2.WML4

Writing Minilesson Principle
Describe a character through another character's thoughts, words, and actions.

Describing Characters

You Will Need

- a mentor text that reveals a character through the thoughts, words, and actions of other characters, such as *A Symphony of Whales* by Steve Schuch, from Text Set: Empathy
- chart paper and markers
- writer's notebooks and writing folders

Academic Language / Important Vocabulary

- character
- describe
- thoughts
- words
- actions

Continuum Connection

- Describe characters by how they look, what they do, say, and think, and what others say about them
- Use descriptive language and dialogue to present characters/subjects who appear in narratives (memoir, biography, and fiction) and informational writing

---

GOAL

Describe characters by what others think, say, and do.

RATIONALE

When students understand that writers reveal something about a character by sharing the thoughts, words, and actions of another character, they realize that they can use the same technique to convey information in their own writing.

WRITER'S NOTEBOOK/WRITING FOLDER

Students can use their writer's notebooks to try out describing characters through other characters as they work on story drafts from their writing folders.

ASSESS LEARNING

- Look at students' writing. Do they sometimes reveal something about a character through another character's thoughts, words, and actions?
- Look for evidence that students can use vocabulary such as *character*, *describe*, *thoughts*, *words*, and *actions*.

MINILESSON

To help students think about the minilesson principle, use a familiar text to provide an interactive lesson and model how a writer reveals something about a character through the thoughts, words, and actions of other characters. Here is an example.

- Show the cover of *A Symphony of Whales*.

  As I read some pages from *A Symphony of Whales*, think about what the author, Steve Schuch, did to give information about Glashka. Put your hand up when you hear something about Glashka.

- Read pages 1–5, and look for students' raised hands when they notice something another character thinks, does, or says that reveals Glashka's character. Begin a chart of how the text reveals Glashka's character.

  The author wrote about the thoughts, words, and actions of other characters to help you know more about Glashka. What do the other characters' thoughts, words, or actions show about Glashka?

- Guide the conversation to help students think about what the writer reveals. As they provide ideas, write them in a new column on the chart.

Have a Try

Invite students to turn and talk about showing something about a character through other characters' thoughts, words, and actions.

> Think about the main character in the story you are writing. Turn to your partner and describe thoughts, words, and actions of another character you could use to show something important about the main character.

▶ After time for a brief discussion, ask a few students to share their ideas. Support the conversation as needed.

Summarize and Apply

Summarize the learning. Remind students to use other characters to show something about the main character.

> How can you show your readers what a character is like?

▶ Write the principle at the top of the chart.

> During independent writing time today, check the story you are working on to see if you included the thoughts, words, or actions of other characters so that your readers learn more about the main character. If you can, add that to your writing. Write some notes in your writer's notebook about what characters might think, do, or say about another character. Bring your writing to share when we meet later.

Describe a character through another character's thoughts, words, and actions.

Character: Glashka

What Other Characters Think, Say, or Do	What That Shows About the Main Character
• "It is a great gift you have."	• The elders know Glashka has a special gift.
• But you will know the way home.	• Her parents know that Glashka is wise and capable.
• Glashka's parents let her lead the dogs.	• Her parents trust her.

Confer

▶ During independent writing, move around the room to confer briefly with students about how they are describing their characters. Use the following prompts as needed.

  • *What do you want to show about your main character?*
  • *What will your characters think, do, or say?*
  • *Share the notes you have made in your writer's notebook.*

Share

Following independent writing, gather students in the meeting area to share their writing.

> What do the thoughts, words, and actions of other characters show about your main character? Share your writing in groups of three and talk about that.

WML5

Writing Minilesson Principle
Think about what to name your character.

Describing Characters

You Will Need

- several mentor texts that have meaningful character names, such as the following:
  - *A Symphony of Whales* by Steve Schuch, from Text Set: Empathy
  - *The Dunderheads* by Paul Fleischman, from Text Set: Friendship
- chart paper and markers
- document camera (optional)
- writer's notebooks and writing folders

Academic Language / Important Vocabulary

- character
- name

Continuum Connection

- Learn ways of using language and constructing texts from other writers (reading books and hearing them read aloud) and apply understandings to one's own writing

GOAL

Understand that a name can sometimes reveal something about a character.

RATIONALE

Writers think carefully and intentionally about naming their characters. Sometimes there is meaning in the character's name. When students understand that writers reveal something about a character by the name they choose, they realize the importance of a character's name.

WRITER'S NOTEBOOK/WRITING FOLDER

Students can use their writer's notebooks to try out character names as they work on story drafts from their writing folders.

ASSESS LEARNING

- Look at students' writing. Do they name their characters with intention?
- Look for evidence that students can use vocabulary such as *character* and *name*.

MINILESSON

To help students think about the minilesson principle, use familiar texts to provide an interactive lesson and to help them notice that writers purposefully choose character names. Below is an example. Teach this lesson when students are writing fiction stories.

- Show the cover of *A Symphony of Whales*.

  Glashka is the main character. What do you think about the name that the writer, Steve Schuch, chose for the main character?

- Guide the conversation so students recognize that the writer has chosen a name that might be a typical name in the Chukchi Peninsula of Siberia, where the main character lives.

  This book is based on events that are real, but the writer made up the characters. How does the name Glashka make you feel that the main character is a real person?

- Show the cover of *The Dunderheads* and read the first page.

  Turn and talk about why the author might have chosen the name "Miss Breakbone" for this character.

- After time for discussion, ask volunteers to share ideas. Guide the conversation to help students recognize that the author chose this name to be humorous and to show what the character's personality is like.

  What might you expect a character named Happy to be like?

  You might think about naming a character to show a character trait or the time period in which the character lives.

Have a Try

Invite students to turn and talk about naming characters.

> Think about a character in the story you are writing. Turn to your partner and talk about some ways the character's name could be important to your story.

> ▶ After time for a brief discussion, ask a few students to share their ideas. Add to the chart using general terms.

Summarize and Apply

Summarize the learning. Remind students to think about what names to choose for their characters.

> During independent writing time today, look at the story you are working on and think about the names you have chosen for your characters. If you decide you want to change a name, write some ideas in your writer's notebook. Decide on a name and add it to your writing. Bring your writing to share when we meet later.

> ### What to Think About When You Name a Character
>
> • Being authentic to the place where the character lives
>
> • Connecting to the character's heritage or culture
>
> • Showing the time period the character lives in
>
> • Using playful language (if appropriate)
>
> • Relating to what the character acts like

Section 3: Craft

Confer

> ▶ During independent writing, move around the room to confer briefly with students about character names. Use the following prompts as needed.
>
> - *How did you choose this character's name?*
> - *Talk about how the names you have chosen will help readers know something about the characters.*
> - *Share a character's name and tell why you chose that name.*

Share

Following independent writing, gather students in pairs in the meeting area to share their writing.

> Share the name of a character in the story you are working on and tell how you chose the name.

Assessment

After you have taught the minilessons in this umbrella, observe students in a variety of classroom activities. Use *The Fountas & Pinnell Literacy Continuum* to notice, teach for, and support students' learning as you observe their attempts at writing.

▶ What evidence do you have of students' new understandings related to describing characters?

- Do students use physical descriptions of characters in a way that helps readers know more about them?

- Are they using actions, thoughts, and dialogue to describe characters?

- Do they try to reveal something about the characters when they choose names?

- Are they using vocabulary such as *character*, *describe*, *physical features*, *actions*, *gestures*, *thoughts*, *feelings*, and *dreams*?

▶ In what ways, beyond the scope of this umbrella, are students showing an interest in writing fiction?

- Do they show an interest in including detailed illustrations that support the text descriptions?

- Are they using dialogue in their stories?

Use your observations to determine the next umbrella you will teach. You may also consult Suggested Sequence of Lessons (pp. 665–682) for guidance.

EXTENSIONS FOR DESCRIBING CHARACTERS

▶ Have students make a sketch to plan how a character looks.

▶ As you read aloud, pause to help students notice how writers use thoughts, actions, and dialogue to help readers learn more about a character.

▶ Talk about how writers keep character traits consistent through all books in a series to help students understand that once a character is established, the character should always have the same traits.

▶ If you are using *The Reading Minilessons Book, Grade 4* [Fountas and Pinnell 2020] you may choose to teach LA.U26: Understanding Characters' Feelings, Motivations, and Intentions and LA.U27: Understanding a Character's Traits and Development.

▶ Choose a character from a mentor text that does not have any physical description. Have students decide how the character looks and think of ways to describe the character's physical appearance.

Minilessons in This Umbrella

WML1   Make a sketch to show your thinking about the setting.

WML2   Use your senses to describe the setting.

WML3   Add small, real-life details to create a setting that gives important information.

Before Teaching Umbrella 3 Minilessons

Students often focus on the action or the characters when writing and do not necessarily take time to picture and describe the setting. The minilessons in this umbrella help them realize that details in the illustrations and information about time and place add meaning to their writing. Setting is important in most fiction stories, but it can also play a role in narrative nonfiction such as memoirs and biographies. As students work on crafting settings throughout this umbrella, they learn how to incorporate relevant details. Students can apply this learning right away to a writing project, or they might write about a setting in their writer's notebooks that they will revisit for an idea later when they write something new. Sometimes, working on the description of a setting can give students an idea for a book or a story, so these lessons can be used to generate ideas in addition to developing the craft of writing.

Use the books listed below from *Fountas & Pinnell Classroom™ Interactive Read-Aloud Collection*, or choose books from the classroom library in which there are clear descriptions of the settings.

Interactive Read-Aloud Collection

Genre Study: Historical Fiction

The Houdini Box by Brian Selznick

Uncle Jed's Barbershop by Margaree King Mitchell

The Buffalo Storm by Katherine Applegate

Dad, Jackie, and Me by Myron Uhlberg

Crow Call by Lois Lowry

As you read and enjoy these texts together, help students

- notice the details in the words and drawings that relate to setting, and
- make connections between the setting and students' own life experiences.

Writer's Notebook

Section 3: Craft

Writing Minilesson Principle
Make a sketch to show your thinking about the setting.

Crafting a Setting

You Will Need

- several mentor texts that show setting, such as the following from Text Set: Genre Study: Historical Fiction:
  - *The Houdini Box* by Brian Selznick
  - *Uncle Jed's Barbershop* by Margaree King Mitchell
- document camera [optional]
- chart paper and markers
- writer's notebooks

Academic Language / Important Vocabulary

- setting
- description
- sketching
- details

Continuum Connection

- Use sketching, webs, lists, and freewriting to think about, plan for, and try out writing
- Use a writer's notebook or booklet as a tool for collecting ideas, experimenting, planning, sketching, or drafting
- Use sketching to support memory and help in planning
- Use sketching to capture detail that is important to a topic
- Understand the difference between drawing and sketching and use them to support the writing process
- Use the terms *sketching* and *drawing* to refer to these processes and forms

GOAL

Use sketching to prompt details for describing the setting.

RATIONALE

Sketching the setting of a story represents the students' process of thinking and provides a concrete visual to write about. A quick sketch can help remind students of details they might not remember otherwise and can result in more effective writing.

WRITER'S NOTEBOOK/WRITING FOLDER

Students can use the blank or lined pages in their writer's notebooks for sketching.

ASSESS LEARNING

- Notice whether students are able to make a simple sketch to show a setting.
- Observe whether students write about the details that are in their sketches.
- Look for evidence that students can use vocabulary such as *setting*, *sketching*, *description*, and *details*.

MINILESSON

Students will need their writer's notebooks for this lesson. To help students think about the minilesson principle, provide an interactive lesson to help them understand how sketching can help a writer describe a setting. Here is an example.

- Show and read pages 16–17 in *The Houdini Box*.

  What do you learn about the setting from the words and the sketch?

  Suitcases and old-fashioned hats show a busy train station from long ago.

- Show the last spread.

  Turn and talk about the setting, or where and when the story takes place.

  The writer uses a simple sketch and includes just enough details to tell you important information, like the time of day and the place.

- Show pages 9–10 in *Uncle Jed's Barbershop*.

  This drawing shows the final version of the illustration of a bedroom. What might the illustrator have sketched as he was thinking about what to draw on this page? Turn and talk about that.

- Use students' suggestions to draw on chart paper a few items that the illustrator might have sketched. Then use shared writing to write a brief description of the sketch.

  Making a sketch of what you are thinking about a setting will help you write about it and draw it.

Have a Try

Invite students to make a sketch of a common setting and then turn and talk to describe the setting.

▶ Have students notice a common setting, such as a part of the classroom, the view outside the classroom window, or another location in the school.

> If you want to write a story that takes place in this setting, what details would you include? In your writer's notebook, make a quick sketch of the setting.

▶ Provide a brief time for sketching.

> Turn and talk about how you would describe the setting that you sketched.

Summarize and Apply

Summarize the learning. Have students sketch their settings.

> Making a sketch can help you think about what to write about a setting. Remember that a sketch is a quick drawing to help you with planning, not a full illustration.

▶ Write the principle at the top of the chart.

> If you are working on a story today, picture the setting in your mind and make a sketch in your writer's notebook. If you are not working on a story, sketch a setting you might use in a story someday. After you finish sketching, write a description of your setting. Bring your notebook when we meet.

Make a sketch to show your thinking about the setting.

Blue wallpaper dotted with flowers surrounds the room. The quilt is made of colorful squares.

Confer

▶ During independent writing, move around the room to confer briefly with students about crafting a setting. Use the following prompts as needed.

• *Where does your story take place? What will you sketch to show that?*

• *What details about the setting did your sketch help you think about?*

Share

Following independent writing, gather students in the meeting area to share their sketches.

> In groups of four, share your setting sketches and descriptions.

> What did _____'s sketch show you about the setting?

Writing Minilesson Principle
Use your senses to describe the setting.

Crafting a Setting

You Will Need

- several mentor texts with a clear setting, such as the following from Text Set: Genre Study: Historical Fiction:
  - *The Buffalo Storm* by Katherine Applegate
  - *Dad, Jackie, and Me* by Myron Uhlberg
- document camera (optional)
- chart paper and markers
- writer's notebooks
- To download the following online resource for this lesson, visit **fp.pub/resources**:
  - chart art (optional)

Academic Language / Important Vocabulary

- setting
- describe
- senses
- details
- sensory language
- imagine

Continuum Connection

- Describe the setting with appropriate detail
- Use language to create sensory images
- Observe carefully events, people, settings, and other aspects of the world to gather information on a topic
- Use a writer's notebook or booklet as a tool for collecting ideas, experimenting, planning, sketching, or drafting
- Choose a setting and describe details that evoke a particular mood

GOAL

Use sensory details to describe the setting.

RATIONALE

Encouraging students to use their senses when they think about how to describe the setting enables them to notice more details, resulting in a richer description.

WRITER'S NOTEBOOK/WRITING FOLDER

Have students use their writer's notebooks to record sensory details about a setting.

ASSESS LEARNING

- Notice whether students recognize that they can use their senses when they describe the setting.
- Observe whether students sometimes use sensory words to describe the setting.
- Look for evidence that students can use vocabulary such as *setting*, *senses*, *sensory language*, *describe*, *details*, and *imagine*.

MINILESSON

Students will need their writer's notebooks for this lesson. To help students include sensory details to craft their settings, use mentor texts and provide an interactive lesson. Here is an example.

- Show and read pages 12–13 of *The Buffalo Storm*.

  As I read from *The Buffalo Storm*, listen for words and notice the details that the writer, Katherine Applegate, used to help you picture the setting, or get an image of the setting in your mind. Pay close attention to the details that involve your senses–what you see, hear, smell, taste, and touch. Put your hand up when you notice details that describe where or when the story takes place.

- As students share ideas, begin a two-column chart. Write the book title on the left. On the right, jot down a few sensory details.

- Continue with pages 14, 25, and 29, pausing to add several examples to the chart as students raise a hand when they notice details about the setting.

- Repeat with pages 10–13 of *Dad, Jackie, and Me*.

  Sometimes, writers use sensory language to show the setting. Sometimes, they show the setting only in drawings. And sometimes, they do both. As a writer, you have a choice as to how you show the setting.

Have a Try

Invite students to turn and talk about using sensory details to reveal the setting.

▶ Have students bring their writer's notebooks to an area in the school and use their senses to observe.

> Use your senses to observe the area. Jot down some words in your writer's notebook that describe this setting.

▶ After a brief time to observe and make notes, ask students to turn and talk to share.

Summarize and Apply

Summarize the learning. Remind students to include sensory details in their writing to reveal the setting.

> What can you do to describe the setting in detail for your readers?

▶ Write the principle at the top of the chart.

> During independent writing time, if you are working on a story, think about how to describe the setting so that your readers can imagine it. If you are not working on a story, think of a place to write about. It could be a setting from a story you have read or written, or it could be a place you know very well. Write about it in your writer's notebook. Bring your writing when we meet later.

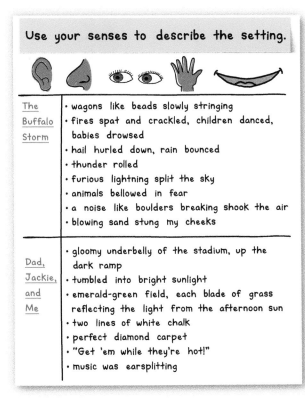

Use your senses to describe the setting.

The Buffalo Storm	• wagons like beads slowly stringing • fires spat and crackled, children danced, babies drowsed • hail hurled down, rain bounced • thunder rolled • furious lightning split the sky • animals bellowed in fear • a noise like boulders breaking shook the air • blowing sand stung my cheeks
Dad, Jackie, and Me	• gloomy underbelly of the stadium, up the dark ramp • tumbled into bright sunlight • emerald-green field, each blade of grass reflecting the light from the afternoon sun • two lines of white chalk • perfect diamond carpet • "Get 'em while they're hot!" • music was earsplitting

Confer

▶ During independent writing, move around the room to confer briefly with students about describing the setting. Use the following prompts as needed.

- *What are some sensory words you might use to describe the setting?*
- *What sensory words will you use to show where your story is happening?*
- *If you write a story using this setting, what would the people in your story notice with their senses?*

Share

Following independent writing, gather students in the meeting area to share their writing.

> In pairs, share what you wrote today to describe a setting.

Writing Minilesson Principle

Add small, real-life details to create a setting that gives important information.

Crafting a Setting

You Will Need

- several mentor texts with a clear setting, such as the following from Text Set: Genre Study: Historical Fiction:
  - *Uncle Jed's Barbershop* by Margaree King Mitchell
  - *Crow Call* by Lois Lowry
- chart paper and markers
- document camera [optional]
- writer's notebooks and writing folders

Academic Language / Important Vocabulary

- setting
- information
- real-life details

Continuum Connection

- Describe the setting with appropriate detail
- Understand that the setting of fiction may be current or historical
- Observe carefully events, people, settings, and other aspects of the world to gather information on a topic
- Use a writer's notebook or booklet as a tool for collecting ideas, experimenting, planning, sketching, or drafting
- Use notebooks to plan, gather, and rehearse for future published writing
- Add details or examples to make the piece clearer or more interesting

GOAL

Include small, real-life details to describe the setting.

RATIONALE

When students understand that writers include real-life details as a way to help readers know more about the setting, they begin to think about what setting information to include in their own writing. They learn that they can make a deliberate choice about where and when the story takes place and that the setting has to make sense within the story.

WRITER'S NOTEBOOK/WRITING FOLDER

Have students jot down real-life details or objects that reveal the setting in their writer's notebooks. They can also look through their writing folders to review settings they have written about.

ASSESS LEARNING

- Look for evidence that students recognize that writers include details in text and illustrations that show the setting and that they use similar types of details in their own writing.
- Notice whether students understand and use vocabulary such as *setting*, *real-life details*, and *information*.

MINILESSON

Students will need their writer's notebooks for this lesson. To help students think about the minilesson principle, use mentor texts and an interactive discussion about using details to reveal important information about the setting. Here is an example.

> Listen and look for details about the setting as I show and read a few pages in *Uncle Jed's Barbershop*.

- Read page 5 and then turn to show the illustration on page 27.

  > What do the words and illustration show about the setting?

  > The carefully folded towels, fancy chairs, and clean floors show a lot about the barbershop and Uncle Jed.

- As students provide ideas, use general terms to begin a list on chart paper of the types of real-life details that writers include to help readers understand the setting.

  > As I read through *Crow Call*, raise your hand when you notice a real-life detail that helps you understand where and when the story takes place.

- Begin reading and showing the illustrations in *Crow Call*, pausing when students indicate they notice a setting detail so they can share. Add to the chart.

  > Small details can show a lot about a setting, and they make it feel real. This is especially important when you write realistic fiction stories and memoirs. When you write stories, you can choose which details to include so your readers learn more about not only the setting but also the characters.

Have a Try

Invite students to make notes in their writer's notebooks and then turn and talk about how real-life details can reveal something about the setting.

> Think about a setting you know really well. What are some real-life details you could include that would give readers important information about the setting? In your writer's notebook, list or sketch details or objects that would make the setting seem real.

▶ After time for a brief discussion, ask a few students to share their ideas.

> Turn and talk about what your real-life details show about the setting.

Summarize and Apply

Summarize the learning. Have students show how real-world details can be included to reveal the setting. Write the principle at the top of the chart.

> If you are working on a story today, think about real-world details that would show something about the setting. If you are not working on a story, look at a description of a setting that you have written in your writer's notebook or in a story you finished. What real-life details could you add? Bring your writing to share when we meet later.

Add small, real-life details to create a setting that gives important information.

- building details to show how well a place is cared for

- words that show the time of day or weather

- things that show if it is the city or the country

- plant details that reveal the location or time of year

- clothing or other details to tell what year it is

- describe the way an object looks (e.g., sinks so shiny they sparkled, honey in a covered silver pitcher)

Confer

▶ During independent writing, move around the room to confer briefly with students about crafting a setting. Use the following prompts as needed.

- *What real-life objects would paint a picture of where your story takes place?*
- *What will these details help readers understand about the setting?*
- *Share some words you might use to show the time and place.*

Share

Following independent writing, gather students in groups of three in the meeting area to share their details. Then bring the groups together.

> Share a real-world detail you heard from one of your group members. What did the detail help you know about the setting?

Assessment

After you have taught the minilessons in this umbrella, observe students in a variety of classroom activities. Use *The Fountas & Pinnell Literacy Continuum* to notice, teach for, and support students' learning as you observe their attempts at writing.

▶ What evidence do you have of students' new understandings related to setting?

- Do students make a sketch to help think about the setting?

- Do they try to use their senses to describe the setting?

- Do they include real-life setting details that give information relevant to the story?

- Do they use vocabulary such as *setting*, *sketching*, *drawing*, *description*, *real-life details*, *senses*, *sensory language*, *imagine*, and *information*?

▶ In what ways, beyond the scope of this umbrella, do students show readiness for writing?

- Do they show an interest in adding illustrations that connect to the text?

- Are they open to revising their writing in order to improve it?

Use your observations to determine the next umbrella you will teach. You may also consult Suggested Sequence of Lessons (pp. 665–682) for guidance.

EXTENSIONS FOR CRAFTING A SETTING

▶ Extend these minilessons by introducing similar lessons, such as CFT.U14.WML4, that focus on adding specific details to illustrations of a setting.

▶ Encourage students to observe the background illustrations in books to get ideas from illustrators. What details do the illustrators show? What colors do the illustrators use? How do the characters look in or against the background?

▶ If you are using *The Reading Minilessons Book, Grade 4* (Fountas and Pinnell 2020) you may choose to teach LA.U24: Thinking About the Setting in Fiction Books.

Minilessons in This Umbrella

WML1   Use dialogue to make your writing interesting and meaningful.

WML2   Make it clear who is speaking when you use dialogue.

WML3   Include action with dialogue in your writing.

Before Teaching Umbrella 4 Minilessons

Prior to teaching these minilessons, make sure students have experienced a variety of fiction books with dialogue. The goal of this umbrella is to help students understand how and why writers sometimes show directly what characters say. Part of writing with dialogue is understanding not only what dialogue is and how it is punctuated but also that dialogue can be broken up with action as a way to move a story along.

Teach these lessons when students are writing fiction or memoirs. Use as mentor texts the following books from *Fountas & Pinnell Classroom™ Interactive Read-Aloud Collection*, or use other text examples of dialogue from the classroom library or from class shared writing.

Interactive Read-Aloud Collection
Figuring Out Who You Are

La Mariposa by Francisco Jiménez

Heroes by Ken Mochizuki

Genre Study: Memoir

Play Ball! by Jorge Posada

Empathy

Step Right Up: How Doc and Jim Key Taught the World About Kindness by Donna Janell Bowman

As you read and enjoy these texts together, help students notice

- the way the writers show what the characters say and think,

- how writers let readers know who is talking,

- how dialogue makes stories more interesting, and

- how dialogue and action work together to move a story along.

Interactive Read-Aloud
Figuring Out Who You Are

Genre Study: Memoir

Empathy

Writer's Notebook

Section 3: Craft

Writing Minilesson Principle

Use dialogue to make your writing interesting and meaningful.

Using Dialogue in Writing

You Will Need

- a few familiar fiction books with dialogue, such as the following:
  - *La Mariposa* by Francisco Jiménez, from Text Set: Figuring Out Who You Are
  - *Play Ball!* by Jorge Posada, from Text Set: Genre Study: Memoir
- document camera (optional)
- chart paper and markers
- sticky notes for the students
- a book with dialogue for each pair of students
- writer's notebooks and writing folders

Academic Language / Important Vocabulary

- dialogue
- interesting
- intent
- meaning

Continuum Connection

- Use dialogue as appropriate to add to the meaning of the story

GOAL

Notice why authors use dialogue and identify some techniques for crafting interesting dialogue.

RATIONALE

When you help students notice why authors use dialogue, they will begin to include meaningful dialogue in their own stories.

WRITER'S NOTEBOOK/WRITING FOLDER

Students can add dialogue to the draft of a story from their writing folders. Suggest that they try out dialogue in their writer's notebooks before adding it to a draft.

ASSESS LEARNING

- Observe whether students write dialogue that adds meaning and interest to their stories.
- Look for evidence that they can use vocabulary such as *dialogue, interesting, intent,* and *meaning.*

MINILESSON

To help students think about the minilesson principle, use mentor texts to engage students in an inquiry-based lesson on reasons authors use dialogue. Here is an example.

- Show the cover of *La Mariposa.* Show and read pages 2–3.

  What do you learn from the talking, or dialogue?

  Why do you think the author wrote dialogue as part of the story?

- Guide the students to notice that the dialogue shows that the characters speak Spanish, what they are doing, and a little bit about how the characters relate to one another. On chart paper, begin a list of how and why writers use dialogue.

- Show and read page 10 in *Play Ball!*

  How does the dialogue add to the intent or meaning of the story?

- Record students' responses on the chart.

- Show and read page 5, pausing after the first paragraph.

  The writer used the word *complained* instead of *said* to show you how the character is feeling and how the words should be read. As I continue reading, raise your hand if you notice any words the writer used instead of *said.*

- As students point out variations for *said*, write them on sticky notes and place them on a new chart.

Have a Try

Invite students to talk to a partner about dialogue.

▶ Give each pair of students a book.

> As you look through your book, think about how and why the writer used dialogue. If you notice a word instead of *said*, write it on a sticky note and add it to the chart.

▶ After time for discussion, ask volunteers to share. Add any new ideas to the chart and read the sticky notes.

Summarize and Apply

Summarize the learning and remind students to think about including dialogue when they write fiction.

> Why do writers add dialogue to their stories?

▶ Write the principle at the top of the first chart.

> During independent writing time today, take a look at the piece you are working on, and think about whether dialogue would add to the meaning or make your writing more interesting. If you begin a new writing piece, try adding some dialogue. Look at the chart for ideas. You can try out some dialogue in your writer's notebook first. Bring your writing to share when we come back together.

Confer

▶ During independent writing, move around the room to confer briefly with students about using dialogue. Use prompts such as the following as needed.

> • *What is happening in this part of your story?*
> • *What might the characters say to each other during this part of the story?*
> • *How could you use dialogue to show how the character is feeling?*

Share

Following independent writing, gather students in the meeting area to share their writing.

> In pairs, share the dialogue you added or are thinking about adding to your story. Tell your partner how you think the dialogue makes the story more interesting.

Use dialogue to make your writing interesting and meaningful.

Dialogue—
- can be in more than one language
- adds interest and meaning to the story
- shows what is happening in the story
- reveals information about the characters
  - what characters are doing
  - what characters are thinking or feeling about themselves, about other characters, about a situation
  - how characters are trying to solve a problem
- can use words instead of said to add more meaning

Words to Use in Place of Said

complained	broke in	called
grumbled	screamed	whispered
exclaimed	demanded	groaned
hissed	snarled	beamed

Writing Minilesson Principle
Make it clear who is speaking when you use dialogue.

Using Dialogue in Writing

You Will Need

- a familiar fiction book that has dialogue, such as *Heroes* by Ken Mochizuki, from Text Set: Figuring Out Who You Are
- document camera (optional)
- chart paper and markers
- highlighter
- writing folders

Academic Language / Important Vocabulary

- dialogue
- speaker tag
- quotation mark
- comma
- unassigned dialogue

Continuum Connection

- Use dialogue as appropriate to add to the meaning of the story
- Use commas and quotation marks correctly in writing interrupted and uninterrupted dialogue as well as to show a verbatim quote
- Add ideas in thought bubbles or dialogue in quotation marks or speech bubbles to provide information, provide narration, or show thoughts and feelings

GOAL

Understand how to make it clear who is speaking when using assigned and unassigned dialogue.

RATIONALE

When you teach students how to show who is speaking in a story, they will be better able to communicate their ideas clearly and effectively when writing dialogue.

WRITER'S NOTEBOOK/WRITING FOLDER

Students can add dialogue to the draft of a story from their writing folders.

ASSESS LEARNING

- Look at students' writing. Do they make it clear who is speaking in the dialogue?
- Look for evidence that they can use vocabulary such as *dialogue, speaker tag, quotation mark, comma,* and *unassigned dialogue.*

MINILESSON

To help students think about the minilesson principle, use mentor texts to engage students in an interactive lesson about how to make it clear who the speaker is when writing dialogue. Here is an example.

- Show the cover of *Heroes*.

  Remember this story about Donnie, who gets help from his father and uncle when the other kids always make him the enemy when they play war games?

  Let's look at how the writer, Ken Mochizuki, used dialogue in this story.

- Show and read page 3.

  What do you notice about the way the writer made clear who is speaking?

- On chart paper, write the example and describe the way it is written. Highlight the speaker tag.

- Repeat with pages 5 and 7, guiding students to recognize different ways dialogue is written (e.g., alternating speakers, speaker's name at the beginning of the quote). Point out the punctuation. Add to the chart.

- Show and read the middle of page 2 in *Play Ball!*

  How do you know who says "Yes, you can"?

  This is called unassigned dialogue. There is no speaker tag, but the writer makes it clear that Papa is speaking.

- Add the example to the chart.

Have a Try

Invite students to talk to a partner about how to punctuate dialogue to help the reader know who is speaking.

> Look at the chart. Turn and talk about what you notice about the punctuation.

▸ Students should notice that punctuation related to the dialogue is inside the quotation marks and that one person's sentence can be split across the speaker tag.

Summarize and Apply

Summarize the learning and remind students to make clear who is speaking when they use dialogue. Write the principle at the top of the chart.

> During independent writing time today, look at the story you are working on. Is there a place to add dialogue? Remember to make it clear to readers who is speaking and to punctuate the dialogue correctly. Bring your writing to share when we meet later.

Make it clear who is speaking when you use dialogue.	
"He was a war hero," Zach said.	Speaker tag at the end
"No way!" Zach said. "How could your dad or uncle be in *our* army?" Tori asked.	Alternating speakers
. . . he just said, "You kids should be playing something else besides war."	Speaker tag at the beginning
"I can't do it, Papa," the boy called. "I can't."	Speaker tag in the middle
"Yes, you can."	Unassigned dialogue

Confer

▸ During independent writing, move around the room to confer briefly with students about using dialogue. Use prompts such as the following as needed.

- *What do the characters say to each other in this part of the story?*
- *How can you make it clear who is speaking?*
- *Do you want to put the speaker tag before, in the middle of, or after the dialogue?*
- *What punctuation marks do you need to add to this dialogue?*

Share

Following independent writing, gather students in the meeting area to share their writing.

> Who wrote dialogue today? Show how you helped the reader know who is speaking.

WML 3
CFT.U4.WML3

Writing Minilesson Principle
Include action with dialogue in your writing.

Using Dialogue in Writing

You Will Need

- several familiar fiction books with dialogue, such as the following:
  - *Heroes* by Ken Mochizuki, from Text Set: Figuring Out Who You Are
  - *Step Right Up* by Donna Janell Bowman, from Text Set: Empathy
  - *Play Ball!* by Jorge Posada, from Text Set: Genre Study: Memoir
- chart paper prepared with examples of dialogue with action
- two colors of highlighters
- writer's notebooks and writing folders

Academic Language / Important Vocabulary

- dialogue
- action

Continuum Connection

- Use dialogue as appropriate to add to the meaning of the story
- Use commas and quotation marks correctly in writing interrupted and uninterrupted dialogue as well as to show a verbatim quote
- Add ideas in thought bubbles or dialogue in quotation marks or speech bubbles to provide information, provide narration, or show thoughts and feelings

GOAL

Break up dialogue with narration and action.

RATIONALE

When students notice how writers interweave dialogue with narration or action, they begin to see how the combination can move a story along and also begin to try this in their own writing. Combining action and dialogue infuses motion into the story and gives a clearer picture of what the characters are doing.

WRITER'S NOTEBOOK/WRITING FOLDER

Students try out blending dialogue and action in their writer's notebooks before doing it in the draft of a story from their writing folders.

ASSESS LEARNING

- ▶ Observe for evidence that students try inserting action into dialogue in meaningful ways.
- ▶ Look for evidence that they can use vocabulary such as *dialogue* and *action*.

MINILESSON

To help students think about the minilesson principle, use mentor texts to engage students in an inquiry-based lesson on interweaving dialogue and action. Here is an example.

- ▶ Show and read the first row (from page 27 of *Heroes*) on the prepared chart paper.

  What do you notice about how the writer used dialogue in this passage?

- ▶ Guide students to recognize that the passage is not just dialogue; the author also wrote about the character's actions.

- ▶ Ask one student to highlight the dialogue and the speaker tag and another student to highlight the parts that show action. Each student should use a different highlighter color.

- ▶ Repeat with the other two rows (from page 19 of *Step Right Up* and page 8 of *Play Ball!*).

Have a Try

Invite students to talk to a partner about why authors break up dialogue with action.

> Look back at the chart. Why do you think writers include both dialogue and action in their stories? Turn and talk to your partner about that.

▶ After time for discussion, invite several students to share their thinking. As needed, guide them to recognize that dialogue and action together can help move the story along.

Summarize and Apply

Summarize the learning and remind students to include action with dialogue in their writing. Write the principle at the top of the chart.

> During independent writing time today, look in your writing for a place where you can include action with the dialogue. Show what the characters are saying *and* what they are doing. This will help your story move along. You can try it out in your writer's notebook first. Bring your story to share when we meet later.

Include action with dialogue in your writing.

Uncle Yosh held my football in his hand, and when he found me in the crowd, he shouted, "Hey, Donnie, catch!" He threw a perfect spiral.

from <u>Heroes</u> by Ken Mochizuki

"Jim, do you want a piece of apple?" she asked. Jim nodded his head up and down. Mrs. Key ran back to the house calling, "Doctor, Doctor, the horse can say yes!"

from <u>Step Right Up</u> by Donna Janell Bowman

"Watch this." Jorge snared a ground ball and underhanded it to Ernesto, who spun and flipped it to Manuel.

"Qué pasa? What's up?"

Jorge walked over to where his bat lay on the ground. "Here's what's up," he said. Jorge put the bat on his left shoulder.

from <u>Play Ball!</u> by Jorge Posada

Section 3: Craft

Confer

▶ During independent writing, move around the room to confer briefly with students about using dialogue. Use prompts such as the following as needed.

- *What is happening in this part of your story?*
- *What are the characters saying?*
- *What is the character doing while speaking?*
- *Would it be better to use action or dialogue to show _____?*

Share

Following independent writing, gather students in the meeting area to share their writing.

> In groups of four, share part of your writing that includes both dialogue and action. Then choose one person from your group to share with the class.

Assessment

After you have taught the minilessons in this umbrella, observe students as they write. Use *The Fountas & Pinnell Literacy Continuum* to notice, teach for, and support students' learning as you observe their attempts at reading and writing.

▶ What evidence do you have of students' new understandings related to adding dialogue to writing?

- How do they use dialogue to make their writing more interesting?

- Do they make clear who is speaking when writing dialogue?

- Are they able to incorporate a character's actions before and/or after dialogue?

- Do they understand and use vocabulary such as *dialogue*, *interesting*, *intent*, *meaning*, *quotation mark*, *comma*, and *action*?

▶ In what other ways, beyond the scope of this umbrella, are students ready to explore fiction writing?

- Are they trying to show their voice in their writing?

- Are they experimenting with different ways of beginning and ending stories?

Use your observations to determine the next umbrella you will teach. You may also consult Suggested Sequence of Lessons (pp. 665–682) for guidance.

EXTENSIONS FOR USING DIALOGUE IN WRITING

▶ Encourage students to try adding speech bubbles and thought bubbles to their illustrations.

▶ Plays are heavily dependent on dialogue. Have students read, discuss, and act out plays and/or write their own plays.

▶ Have students note during interactive read-aloud how authors use dialogue in their stories.

Minilessons in This Umbrella

WML1 Learn from other writers different ways to write engaging leads.

WML2 Learn from other writers a variety of ways to write good endings.

Before Teaching Umbrella 5 Minilessons

These minilessons will help students talk about the decisions writers make about how to engage their readers by crafting effective beginnings and endings and support them in crafting their own. Often, students focus more on the middle of a writing piece, so by giving attention to the beginning and ending, they learn that all parts of writing should be attended to with care.

Make sure students have their writer's notebooks for the lessons so that they can try out different leads and conclusions and then select the one that best fits their writing. Students can try out the leads and endings on a new piece of writing or go back to existing writing and try out new ways to begin and end. Use the books listed below from *Fountas & Pinnell Classroom™ Interactive Read-Aloud Collection* and *Shared Reading Collection*, or choose books with strong beginnings and endings from the classroom library.

Interactive Read-Aloud Collection

Genre Study: Memoir

Play Ball! by Jorge Posada

Illustrator Study: Floyd Cooper

A Dance Like Starlight: One Ballerina's Dream by Kristy Dempsey

Ruth and the Green Book by Calvin Alexander Ramsey

Illustration Study: Craft

Eye to Eye: How Animals See the World by Steve Jenkins

Dingo by Claire Saxby

Gecko by Raymond Huber

Empathy

A Symphony of Whales by Steve Schuch

Step Right Up: How Doc and Jim Key Taught the World About Kindness by Donna Janell Bowman

Shared Reading Collection

Amazing Axolotls by Sherry Howard

The Power and Influence of Color by Michelle Garcia Andersen

The Breadfruit Bonanza by Summer Edward

As you read and enjoy these texts together, help students notice how writers begin and end their books.

Interactive Read-Aloud Genre Study: Memoir

Illustrator Study: Floyd Cooper

Illustration Study: Craft

Empathy

Shared Reading

Writer's Notebook

Section 3: Craft

WML1

Crafting Powerful Leads and Endings

You Will Need

- mentor texts with varied beginnings, such as these:
  - *Eye to Eye* by Steve Jenkins, *Dingo* by Claire Saxby, and *Gecko* by Raymond Huber, from Text Set: Illustration Study: Craft
  - *Play Ball!* by Jorge Posada, from Genre Study: Memoir
  - *A Dance Like Starlight* by Kristy Dempsey and *Ruth and the Green Book* by Calvin Alexander Ramsey, from Text Set: Illustrator Study: Floyd Cooper
- at least two books for each small group
- chart paper and markers
- writer's notebooks and writing folders

Academic Language / Important Vocabulary

- beginning
- lead
- engaging

Continuum Connection

- Begin with a purposeful and engaging lead
- Learn ways of using language and constructing texts from other writers (reading books and hearing them read aloud) and apply understandings to one's own writing

---

Writing Minilesson Principle

Learn from other writers different ways to write engaging leads.

GOAL

Study and craft leads that hook the reader.

RATIONALE

When students learn that writers make choices about how to begin their writing, they realize that they, too, can make thoughtful decisions about how best to begin their own writing.

WRITER'S NOTEBOOK/WRITING FOLDER

Students will work on story drafts from their writing folders. They can use their writer's notebooks to try out different beginnings for their writing pieces.

ASSESS LEARNING

- Observe for evidence that students recognize that writers use a variety of leads to engage their readers.
- Look at students' writing. Are they trying out different beginnings in their own writing?
- Look for evidence that students can use vocabulary such as *beginning*, *lead*, and *engaging*.

MINILESSON

To help students learn about the minilesson principle, use mentor texts to help them identify a variety of beginnings. Here is an example.

- Show and read page 1 in *Eye to Eye*.

  What do you notice about how the author, Steve Jenkins, began his book *Eye to Eye*?

- Guide students to recognize that the book begins with an interesting fact.

  This author began his book with an interesting fact. Sharing an interesting fact is one type of lead, or beginning, that engages readers, or gets them interested.

- Begin a list on chart paper of ways a writer can begin a piece of writing.

  Let's take a look at some other fiction and nonfiction books to notice how they begin.

- Show and read a variety of texts, having students talk about and identify the ways they begin. Add the information to the chart.

  Take a look at the list. Are there any other types of beginnings you have seen or used in your writing that we can add?

- Add any new ideas to the chart, leaving room for text examples to be added.

Have a Try

Invite students to turn and talk in small groups about different ways that writers begin their writing pieces.

▶ Hand each group at least two books.

Look at the books together. How did the authors start their books? What do you think about the leads?

▶ After time for a brief discussion, ask a few students to share. Guide students to notice that some types of beginnings are more suited for fiction writing and others for nonfiction writing.

Summarize and Apply

Summarize the learning. Remind students to try out different ways to begin their writing. Write the principle at the top of the chart.

During independent writing time today, try two or three leads in your writer's notebook for a piece of writing you are working on. Choose the one you like best and add it to your writing. Bring your writing to share when we meet later.

Learn from other writers different ways to write engaging leads.	
A writer can begin with . . .	Where did you see it?
an interesting fact	Eye to Eye
dialogue	Play Ball!
a question	Dingo
a description of the setting	A Dance Like Starlight Gecko
a feeling	Ruth and the Green Book
an action	Gecko
a flashback	

Confer

▶ During independent writing, move around the room to confer briefly with students about how they want to begin their writing. Use the following prompts as needed.

- *How will you engage your readers at the beginning of your story?*
- *Try out a few different leads in your writer's notebook so you can choose which one works best.*
- *Let's take a look at the list and think about which type of beginning might fit well with the fiction (nonfiction) piece you are working on.*

Share

Following independent writing, gather students in the meeting area to share their writing.

Who tried out a few different beginnings in your writer's notebook? Share what you wrote.

Writing Minilesson Principle
Learn from other writers a variety of ways to write good endings.

You Will Need

- mentor texts with strong endings, such as these:
  - *The Breadfruit Bonanza* by Summer Edward, *The Power and Influence of Color* by Michelle Garcia Andersen, and *Amazing Axolotls* by Sherry Howard, from *Shared Reading Collection*
  - *A Symphony of Whales* by Steve Schuch and *Step Right Up* by Donna Janell Bowman, from Text Set: Empathy
  - *A Dance Like Starlight* by Kristy Dempsey, from Text Set: Illustrator Study: Floyd Cooper
- at least two books for each small group
- chart paper and markers
- writer's notebooks and writing folders

Academic Language / Important Vocabulary

- ending

Continuum Connection

- Use a variety of beginnings and endings to engage the reader

GOAL

Study and craft a variety of interesting endings.

RATIONALE

When students learn that writers make choices about how to end their writing, they realize that they, too, can make thoughtful decisions about writing good endings for their pieces.

WRITER'S NOTEBOOK/WRITING FOLDER

Students will continue to work on story drafts from their writing folders. They can use their writer's notebooks to try out different endings for their writing pieces.

ASSESS LEARNING

- Do students recognize that writers end their writing pieces in a variety of ways?
- Are students thinking about the best way to end their own writing?
- Look for evidence that students can use vocabulary such as *ending*.

MINILESSON

To help students learn about the minilesson principle, use mentor texts to help them identify a variety of endings. Here is an example.

- Show and read page 16 in *The Breadfruit Bonanza*.

  How did the author, Summer Edward, choose to end *The Breadfruit Bonanza*?

- Guide students to recognize that Naaren writes in his journal about the pride he feels because he has helped other families learn about growing food.

  Summer Edward ended this story by sharing how Naaren is feeling. Sharing a feeling is one way an author can end a piece of writing.

- Begin a list of ways a writer can end a piece of writing.

  Let's take a look at some other fiction and nonfiction books and think about how the authors chose to end their books.

- Show and read a variety of texts, having students talk about and identify the ways they end. Write the information on the chart.

  Take a look at the list. Are there any other types of endings you have seen or used in your writing that we can add?

- Add any new ideas to the chart, leaving room for text examples to be added.

Have a Try

Invite students to talk in small groups about ways that writers end their writing.

▶ Hand each group at least two books.

> Look at the books together. How did the authors end their books? What makes a good ending?

▶ After time for a brief discussion, ask a few students to share their noticings.

> Which types of endings might work well for fiction writing, and which might work well for nonfiction writing? Why?

Learn from other writers a variety of ways to write good endings.	
A writer can end with...	**Where did you see it?**
a feeling	The Breadfruit Bonanza
a question	The Power and Influence of Color
a call to action	Amazing Axolotls
dialogue	A Symphony of Whales
a quote	Step Right Up
a circular ending	A Dance Like Starlight
a surprise ending	
an interesting fact	
extra information	

Summarize and Apply

Summarize the learning. Remind students to try out different ways to end their writing pieces. Write the principle at the top of the chart.

> During independent writing time today, try two or three types of endings in your writer's notebook for a piece of writing you are working on. Choose the one that works the best for your writing. Bring your writing to share when we meet later.

Confer

▶ During independent writing, move around the room to confer briefly with students about how they want to end their writing. Use the following prompts as needed.

- *What would make a good ending for your writing?*

- *Try out a few different endings in your writer's notebook so you can choose which one works best.*

- *Let's take a look at the chart and think about which type of ending might fit well with the fiction (nonfiction) piece you are working on.*

Share

Following independent writing, gather students in the meeting area to share their writing.

> In pairs, share the ending you will use for the writing piece you are working on. If you tried out different endings in your writer's notebook, share those also.

Section 3: Craft

Assessment

After you have taught the minilessons in this umbrella, observe students in a variety of classroom activities. Use *The Fountas & Pinnell Literacy Continuum* to notice, teach for, and support students' learning as you observe their attempts at writing.

▶ What evidence do you have of students' new understandings related to crafting powerful leads and endings?

- Do students vary the way they begin and end their writing?
- Are they thoughtful in choosing the best way to begin or end their writing?
- Do they understand that writers have choices to make about how to begin and end their fiction and nonfiction writing?
- Are they using vocabulary such as *beginning*, *lead*, *engaging*, and *ending*?

▶ In what ways, beyond the scope of this umbrella, are students showing an interest in applying things they learn from other writers to their own writing?

- Do they sometimes incorporate dialogue into their writing?
- Are they including details about the setting?

Use your observations to determine the next umbrella you will teach. You may also consult Suggested Sequence of Lessons (pp. 665–682) for guidance.

EXTENSIONS FOR CRAFTING POWERFUL LEADS AND ENDINGS

▶ Have students write a variety of leads or endings for the same piece of writing and then talk about which version they like best and why.

▶ As you read aloud or as you talk with students about the books they are reading independently, pause to notice how the authors begin and end the books.

▶ In groups, have students craft alternative beginnings and endings for a familiar mentor text, such as a fairy tale or a narrative nonfiction book.

▶ If you are using *The Reading Minilessons Book, Grade 4* (Fountas and Pinnell 2020), you may choose to teach LA.U28: Analyzing the Writer's Craft in Fiction Books.

Minilessons in This Umbrella

WML1 Notice different ways writers organize and present information.

WML2 Experiment with different ways to organize and present information.

WML3 Think about the overall organization of your nonfiction writing.

Before Teaching Umbrella 6 Minilessons

The goal of this umbrella is to help students understand that writers of nonfiction make decisions about how to organize information in a way that makes the topic understandable to readers. There are a variety of ways that a nonfiction text can be organized, such as chronological, categorical, descriptive, question and answer, and cause and effect. Use mentor texts to introduce each option to provide students with the understandings they need to try out some nonfiction organizational structures in their own writing. These lessons are best taught when students are preparing to write nonfiction.

Before teaching, provide multiple experiences for students to talk about nonfiction text structures, especially as readers. Spend time when you read nonfiction books talking about how the writing is organized. If you are using *The Reading Minilessons Book, Grade 4* (Fountas and Pinnell 2020), it would be helpful to teach LA.U16: Noticing How Nonfiction Authors Choose to Organize Information. For mentor texts, choose the following nonfiction books from *Fountas & Pinnell Classroom™ Interactive Read-Aloud Collection* and *Shared Reading Collection*, or choose books from the classroom library.

Interactive Read-Aloud Collection
Innovative Thinking and Creative Problem Solving

Ivan: The Remarkable True Story of the Shopping Mall Gorilla by Katherine Applegate

Parrots Over Puerto Rico by Susan L. Roth and Cindy Trumbore

Illustration Study: Craft

Magnificent Birds by Narisa Togo

Series: Vanishing Cultures

Himalaya by Jan Reynolds

Shared Reading Collection

Pangaea: The World's Biggest Puzzle by Susan B. Katz

If Rivers Could Speak by Sherry Howard

Amazing Axolotls by Sherry Howard

Swarm! When Animals Move as One by Michelle Garcia Andersen

As you read and enjoy these texts together, help students

- notice how the books are organized, and
- talk about the decisions writers make about how to present information.

Interactive Read-Aloud
Innovative Thinking

Illustration Study: Craft

Series: Vanishing Cultures

Shared Reading

Writer's Notebook

Section 3: Craft

Writing Minilesson Principle
Notice different ways writers organize and present information.

Exploring Text Structures in Nonfiction Writing

You Will Need

- nonfiction texts that have a variety of text structures, such as the following:
  - *Ivan* by Katherine Applegate, from Text Set: Innovative Thinking and Creative Problem Solving
  - *Magnificent Birds* by Narisa Togo, from Text Set: Illustration Study: Craft
  - *Himalaya* by Jan Reynolds, from Text Set: Series: Vanishing Cultures
  - *Pangaea* by Susan B. Katz, from *Shared Reading Collection*
- basket of nonfiction books
- writer's notebooks
- chart paper and markers

Academic Language / Important Vocabulary

- nonfiction
- organize
- chronological
- categories

Continuum Connection

- Use underlying structural patterns to present different kinds of information in nonfiction: e.g., description, temporal sequence, question and answer, cause and effect, chronological sequence, compare and contrast, problem and solution, categorization

GOAL

Identify different ways authors choose to organize and present information in nonfiction texts.

RATIONALE

Understanding how nonfiction is structured helps students not only when they write but also when they read. When students learn to recognize nonfiction text structures, they are better able to make decisions about how to best present information in their own writing.

WRITER'S NOTEBOOK/WRITING FOLDER

Students can use their writer's notebooks to jot down observations about different nonfiction text structures they notice.

ASSESS LEARNING

- Observe whether students can identify the text structure in a nonfiction writing piece.
- Look for evidence that students can use vocabulary such as *nonfiction*, *organize*, *chronological*, and *categories*.

MINILESSON

To help students learn about the minilesson principle, provide mentor text examples and an inquiry-based lesson. Here is an example.

- Show the cover of *Ivan* and briefly revisit the text.

  Think about the way the writer, Katherine Applegate, decided to organize and present the information in this nonfiction book. What do you notice?

- Support students in noticing that the information is told in time order, like a story, from when Ivan was a baby to when he grew old.

  When information is told in time order, it is called chronological order. You might organize your facts this way.

- On chart paper, begin a list of ways writers organize nonfiction texts. Add *Chronological* to the chart.

- Show the cover of *Magnificent Birds* and briefly revisit the text.

  The writer made a different choice about organizing information in *Magnificent Birds*. What do you notice about the way that Narisa Togo organized and presented the information in this nonfiction book?

- Guide students to notice that the writer decided to organize information into categories based on each type of bird. Add *Categories* to the chart.

- Repeat with *Himalaya* to help students identify a nonfiction text that is organized using a descriptive text structure. Add *Description* to the chart.

Have a Try

Invite students to turn and talk about nonfiction text structures.

▶ Briefly revisit a mentor text with a new text structure, such as *Pangaea*.

Turn and talk about how the writer organized and presented the information in this book.

▶ After discussion, ask volunteers to share. Add *Question and Answer* to the chart.

▶ Keep the chart for WML2 and WML3.

Summarize and Apply

Summarize the learning. Form groups of three or four students to examine how writers organize and present nonfiction texts. Write the principle at the top of the chart.

During independent writing time today, investigate the different ways that writers choose to organize and present their information. With your group, look at two or three nonfiction books and notice how the information in the books is organized and presented. In your writer's notebook, jot down your observations. Bring your notes to share when we meet later.

> Notice different ways writers organize and present information.
>
> Chronological
>
> Categories
>
> Description
>
> Question and Answer
>
> Cause and Effect
>
> Compare and Contrast

Confer

▶ During writing, move around the room to confer briefly with groups about nonfiction text structures. Use the following prompts as needed.

• *What do you notice about the way the information is organized and presented?*

• *Why do you think the writer decided to organize the information in this way?*

• *Look at the chart. Did the author organize this book in any of the ways listed?*

Share

Following writing, gather students in the meeting area. Ask a volunteer from each group to share. If students notice additional text structures, add them to the chart.

What did you notice about how the writers organized and presented the information in the books you talked about?

Writing Minilesson Principle

Experiment with different ways to organize and present information.

Exploring Text Structures in Nonfiction Writing

You Will Need

- chart from WML1
- chart paper prepared with two nonfiction writing samples that are on the same topic but that use different text structures (text structure column heads left blank)
- writer's notebooks
- markers
- To download the following online resource for this lesson, visit **fp.pub/resources**:
  - chart art (optional)

Academic Language / Important Vocabulary

- nonfiction
- organize
- information

Continuum Connection

- Use underlying structural patterns to present different kinds of information in nonfiction: e.g., description, temporal sequence, question and answer, cause and effect, chronological sequence, compare and contrast, problem and solution, categorization

GOAL

Understand why a writer might try out different text structures to present information.

RATIONALE

When students think about the reasons why a writer chooses one nonfiction organizational structure over another, they will begin to ask themselves questions about the information they are writing about in order to choose the most appropriate text structure.

WRITER'S NOTEBOOK/WRITING FOLDER

Students can reread their writer's notebooks to identify a nonfiction topic to write about and use their notebooks to try out different nonfiction text structures.

ASSESS LEARNING

- Look at students' nonfiction writing to see whether they are using different text structures.
- Look for evidence that students can use vocabulary such as *nonfiction*, *organize*, and *information*.

MINILESSON

Teach this lesson when students have chosen a topic for their nonfiction writing. To help students learn about the minilesson principle, model the process of deciding which nonfiction text structure to use. Here is an example.

- Show the chart from WML1.
- Model your thinking process of trying out two different ways to organize information. Here is an example.

  I want to write about butterflies and bees, so I looked back at the notes about them in my writer's notebook. I tried out two different ways to organize the information so I could decide which I like best. Look at what I have so far, and then share your thoughts about what I have written.

- Display and read the prepared writing samples.

  What do you notice about how the information is organized in each case?

- Support students in identifying the text structures, and fill in the column heads on the chart above each writing sample. Guide them to talk about the benefits of each choice to help you decide which works better for this writing piece, including which readers might prefer.

  Since I am the writer, I need to think about which way works better and which way my readers might enjoy more. When you write nonfiction, try out different ways to organize and present the information so that you can choose the one that works best for your readers.

Have a Try

Invite students to turn and talk about choosing a nonfiction text structure.

> Turn and talk about a nonfiction piece of writing you are working on or that you might like to start. How will you organize and present the information? Turn and talk about that.

▶ After time for discussion, ask a few volunteers to share.

Summarize and Apply

Summarize the learning. Remind students to think about the best way to organize information when they write. Write the principle at the top of the chart.

> During independent writing time today, look at your notes on nonfiction books in your writer's notebook. Think about how you could organize the information and which way might work best. Try out a few different ways of organizing the information in your writer's notebook. Bring your writing to share when we meet later.

▶ Refer students to the chart from WML1 as needed.

Experiment with different ways to organize and present information.

Question and Answer	Compare and Contrast

Bees and Butterflies
 	
Who can see red?
    Butterflies
 	
Which are the best pollinators around?
    Bees
 	
Who can see UV colors?
    Bees and Butterflies
 	
Which are important for the garden?
    Bees and Butterflies
	Two of my favorite "B's" are Bees and Butterflies. They have a lot in common. They can both see ultraviolet colors. They are both pollinators, which is important for gardens.
	    While bees are the best pollinators around, there is something important to know if you prefer butterflies to bees. You should plant red flowers! Butterflies can see the color red, and they are attracted to it, but bees cannot. Stick with red flowers and you might see more butterflies than bees.

Confer

▶ During independent writing, move around the room to confer briefly with students about how to organize information in a nonfiction writing piece. Use the following prompts as needed.

- *What are some ideas you have about how to organize this information?*
- *Tell about how you decided to organize and present your writing in this way.*
- *In what ways will this choice be helpful for your readers?*

Share

Following independent writing, gather students in the meeting area. After students share in small groups, ask a few volunteers to share their writing with the class.

> In groups of three, share the ways you tried out organizing information today.

Think about the overall organization of your nonfiction writing.

Exploring Text Structures in Nonfiction Writing

You Will Need

- nonfiction texts that have both an underlying and an overlying text structure, such as the following:

  - *If Rivers Could Speak* and *Amazing Axolotls* by Sherry Howard, and *Swarm!* by Michelle Garcia Andersen, from *Shared Reading Collection*

  - *Parrots Over Puerto Rico* by Susan L. Roth and Cindy Trumbore, from Text Set: Innovative Thinking and Creative Problem Solving

- chart from WML1

- chart paper prepared with a nonfiction writing sample that uses several text structures

- writer's notebooks

- markers

Academic Language / Important Vocabulary

- nonfiction
- organize
- information

Continuum Connection

- Use underlying structural patterns to present different kinds of information in nonfiction: e.g., description, temporal sequence, question and answer, cause and effect, chronological sequence, compare and contrast, problem and solution, categorization

GOAL

Choose overarching and underlying text structures to organize a nonfiction text.

RATIONALE

When students understand that writers sometimes use more than one organizational structure within the same text, they see how they can use multiple organizational structures within a piece of their own writing.

WRITER'S NOTEBOOK/WRITING FOLDER

Students can reread their writer's notebooks to identify a nonfiction topic to write about and use their notebooks to try out different nonfiction text structures.

ASSESS LEARNING

- Look at students' writing. Are they experimenting with using more than one text structure in a piece of nonfiction writing?

- Look for evidence that students can use vocabulary such as *nonfiction*, *organize*, and *information*.

MINILESSON

To help students learn about the minilesson principle, use mentor texts and modeled writing to inspire students to try out more than one text structure in a piece of nonfiction writing. Here is an example.

- Show the chart from WML1. Show the cover and briefly revisit *If Rivers Could Speak*.

  What do you notice about how the writer organized *If Rivers Could Speak?*

- Guide students to recognize that information is organized in several different ways.

  Sherry Howard organized the information in two different ways. She used question and answer, and within that, she used description. Let's look at a few more examples.

- Repeat with other mentor texts:

  - *Amazing Axolotls* (question and answer, description)

  - *Swarm!* (description, chronological)

  - *Parrots Over Puerto Rico* (chronological, cause/effect, problem/solution)

- Show and read the prepared writing.

  I organized information about endangered animals information in one main way and used other ways within it. Turn and talk about what you notice.

- After time for discussion, ask students to share ideas. Add responses to the chart.

Have a Try

Invite students to turn and talk about the overall organization of a nonfiction writing piece.

> Turn and talk about why writers might use more than one way to organize information in a single writing piece.

▶ After time for discussion, ask volunteers to share ideas.

Summarize and Apply

Summarize the learning. Remind students to think about the overall organization of a nonfiction piece of writing. Write the principle at the top of the chart.

> During independent writing time today, look at your notes about a nonfiction topic in your writer's notebook. Choose a topic that might work well with more than one type of organization in the same writing piece. Try out your ideas in your writer's notebook. Bring your writing to share when we meet later.

▶ Refer students to the chart from WML1 as needed.

Think about the overall organization of your nonfiction writing.	
Critically Endangered Species Many types of animals are considered endangered. A group of these are called critically endangered. This means that if they are not saved, they might become extinct.	categories
	chronological
Eastern Lowland Gorilla: Poaching, land clearing, and ongoing civil war caused near extinction. In 1970, these gorillas had 8,100 square miles to live on. In 1995, there were about 17,000 gorillas living. Today, their habitat is only 4,600 square miles and there are only about 8,500 gorillas.	cause and effect
Black Rhino: Because of illegal hunting, black rhinos almost became extinct. In 1900, about 100,000 rhinos roamed the land. By 1995, there were only 2,500. Efforts in the past 25 years have brought the numbers up to 5,600 today.	

Confer

▶ During independent writing, move around the room to confer briefly with students about the overall organization of a nonfiction writing piece. Use the following prompts as needed.

- *What is your nonfiction topic? Tell about what type of writing you might like to do on that topic.*
- *Look at the chart. Which types of organization might work well for your writing?*
- *How did you decide to choose these two ways to organize the information?*

Share

Following independent writing, gather students in the meeting area. After students share in small groups, ask a few volunteers to share their writing with the class.

> What types of organization did you use in a single writing piece today?

> Share the reasons why you decided to organize the information the way you did.

Section 3: Craft

Assessment

After you have taught the minilessons in this umbrella, observe students in a variety of classroom activities. Use *The Fountas & Pinnell Literacy Continuum* to notice, teach for, and support students' learning as you observe their attempts at writing.

▶ What evidence do you have of students' new understandings related to text structures?

- Do students think and talk about how nonfiction texts are organized?
- Are they trying out different ways to organize and present information when they write nonfiction?
- Do they recognize that writers can use multiple text structures in one writing piece?
- Are they using vocabulary such as *nonfiction*, *organize*, *chronological*, and *categories*?

▶ In what ways, beyond the scope of this umbrella, are students showing an interest in nonfiction writing?

- Do they use illustrations and graphics in their nonfiction writing?
- Are they noticing the writer's craft in nonfiction books and trying some of these ideas in their own writing?

Use your observations to determine the next umbrella you will teach. You may also consult Suggested Sequence of Lessons (pp. 665–682) for guidance.

EXTENSIONS FOR EXPLORING TEXT STRUCTURES IN NONFICTION WRITING

▶ As you read nonfiction books with the students, pause when a new text structure is noticed (e.g., compare and contrast, problem and solution) and talk about why the author chose to use that text structure.

▶ Encourage students to notice signal words that indicate the text structure (e.g., *as a result of*, *because*, *five years later*, *the problem is*) in the books they read and jot them down in their writer's notebooks to have as a reference for their own writing.

Minilessons in This Umbrella

WML1   Write stories that have a beginning, a series of events, a high point, and an ending.

WML2   Write a story with more than one problem.

WML3   Start with the high point or an important part of the story.

WML4   Use a flashback to give background information for the story.

WML5   Make the end of your story circle back to the beginning.

Before Teaching Umbrella 7 Minilessons

Before exploring these minilessons, students should have had many experiences reading fiction books that have clearly defined plots. Before they are able to write narratives that include a beginning, a series of events, a high point, and an ending, students need to understand that a plot is what happens in a story. As well, students will benefit from exposure to high-quality pieces of literature that have different plot structures.

These minilessons would be best taught over time rather than consecutively so that students have opportunities in between to try out each new text structure. They can experiment with each text structure in their writer's notebooks. Use the books listed below from *Fountas & Pinnell Classroom™ Interactive Read-Aloud Collection*, or choose other books from the classroom library to serve as models.

Interactive Read-Aloud Collection

Genre Study: Memoir

Play Ball! by Jorge Posada

Figuring Out Who You Are

A Boy and a Jaguar by Alan Rabinowitz

Author/Illustrator Study: Allen Say

Tea with Milk

Illustrator Study: Floyd Cooper

Ruth and the Green Book by Calvin Alexander Ramsey

A Dance Like Starlight: One Ballerina's Dream by Kristy Dempsey

Biography: Artists

Me, Frida by Amy Novesky

Empathy

The Crane Wife by Odds Bodkin

As you read and enjoy these texts together, help students notice

*   the beginning and end of the story,
*   the series of events, and
*   the most important part of the story.

Interactive Read-Aloud
Memoir

Figuring Out Who You Are

Allen Say

Floyd Cooper

Biography: Artists

Empathy

Writer's Notebook

Section 3: Craft

WML1

CFT.U7.WML1

Writing Minilesson Principle
Write stories that have a beginning, a series of events, a high point, and an ending.

Exploring Plot Structures

You Will Need

- a mentor text with a clear plot structure, such as *Play Ball!* by Jorge Posada from Text Set: Genre Study: Memoir
- chart paper prepared with a blank Story Arc, or document camera to display it
- markers
- Story Arc for each student
- writer's notebooks and writing folders
- To download the following online resource for this lesson, visit **fp.pub/resources**:
  - Story Arc

Academic Language / Important Vocabulary

- plot structure
- high point
- beginning
- ending
- events

Continuum Connection

- Understand the structure of narrative, including lead or beginning, introduction of characters, setting, problem, series of events, resolution of problem, and ending
- Write fiction and nonfiction narratives that are ordered chronologically
- Develop a logical plot by creating a story problem and addressing it over multiple events until it is resolved

GOAL

Use a typical plot structure by creating a problem and a subsequent series of events that lead to a high point and resolution.

RATIONALE

Most stories are told in a linear fashion with a beginning, a series of events that lead to a high point, and finally a resolution to a problem set out at the beginning. For students to write a story that their readers can follow and enjoy, they need to understand the elements to include and the order in which to arrange them.

WRITER'S NOTEBOOK/WRITING FOLDER

Students can fill in the online resource Story Arc and glue it into their writer's notebooks or draw their own story arc. They can reread the drafts in their writing folders to see whether they have included each element of plot and revise as needed.

ASSESS LEARNING

- Notice whether students include a beginning, a series of events, a high point, and an ending in the stories they write.
- Look for evidence that students can use vocabulary such as *plot structure*, *beginning*, *events*, *high point*, and *ending*.

MINILESSON

To help students think about including each element of plot structure in the narratives they write, use a mentor text and provide an interactive lesson that uses a graphic organizer. Here is an example.

- Before this lesson, students should be familiar with the terms *plot structure*, *beginning*, *events*, *high point*, and *ending*.

- Show the cover and briefly turn through the pages of *Play Ball!*

  Think about the plot, or what happens, in this story, including the beginning, events, high point, and ending. Turn and talk about that.

- After time for discussion, ask volunteers to share.

  What happens in the story?

- Guide the conversation as needed. Ensure students understand that the high point is when Jorge steps up to bat and decides to switch hands (page 24).

- On chart paper, use students' suggestions to fill in a story arc with the details from *Play Ball!*

  Writers include a beginning, a series of events, a high point, and an ending in the stories they write. Include each of these parts when you write your own stories. All together, these parts of a story are called the plot structure.

Have a Try

Invite students to turn and talk about plot structure.

> Think about a story you are working on. Where would each part of your story fit on a story arc? Turn and talk about that.

▶ After time for discussion, ask a few volunteers to share ideas.

Summarize and Apply

Summarize the lesson. Provide each student with a copy of the Story Arc, or have them draw it in their writer's notebooks. (See also the more explicit Story Arc in GEN.U7.WML2.) Add the principle to the top of the chart.

> Today you thought about plot structure by thinking about the beginning, series of events, high point, and ending of your story. During independent writing time, work on writing a story. Use a story arc to plan your story if you think it will help you. You also might look at one or more stories in your writing folders and think about the plot structure.

Write stories that have a beginning, a series of events, a high point, and an ending.

Story Arc

Play Ball!

High Point: Jorge hit a double as a lefty, and his team won the baseball game.

Events: Jorge went to a game at Yankee Stadium and said he would play there some day. Jorge's team was in a big game.

Ending: Jorge got to choose the pizza toppings.

Beginning: Jorge's dad taught him to switch hit.

Confer

▶ During independent writing, move around the room to confer briefly with students about plot structure. Use the following prompts as needed.

- *Share what you have written on your story arc so far.*
- *How will your story begin and end?*
- *What events will happen in this story?*
- *What will be the high point of the story?*

Share

Following independent writing, gather students in the meeting area to share their writing.

> In groups of three, share the story arcs you made in your writer's notebooks.

Writing Minilesson Principle
Write a story with more than one problem.

You Will Need

- several mentor texts that include more than one problem, such as the following:

  - *A Boy and a Jaguar* by Alan Rabinowitz, from Text Set: Figuring Out Who You Are

  - *Tea with Milk* by Allen Say, from Text Set: Author/ Illustrator Study: Allen Say

- document camera (optional)
- chart paper and markers
- writer's notebooks

Academic Language / Important Vocabulary

- problem
- solution

Continuum Connection

- Understand the structure of narrative, including lead or beginning, introduction of characters, setting, problem, series of events, resolution of problem, and ending

- Understand that a fiction text may involve one or more events in the life of a main character

GOAL

Develop a plot with more than one problem.

RATIONALE

When students are able to write stories with more than one problem, they increase the complexity of their writing.

WRITER'S NOTEBOOK/WRITING FOLDER

Students can use their writer's notebooks to jot down story ideas that have more than one problem.

ASSESS LEARNING

- Notice whether students sometimes include more than one problem in the stories they write.

- Look for evidence that students can use vocabulary such as *problem* and *solution*.

MINILESSON

To help students understand that they can include more than one problem in a story, use mentor texts and provide an interactive lesson. Here is an example.

- Show the cover of *A Boy and a Jaguar* and turn through a few pages.

  What is a problem that Alan faces in the story?

  What is another problem that Alan has?

- Guide the conversation so students recognize that Alan has some difficulties when he speaks, and he also feels sad when animals are kept in small cages.

- Repeat with *Tea with Milk*.

- Model the planning process of thinking about a story you might write that has more than one problem. If your students are ready, you might choose to write about two characters that have different problems. Here is an example.

  I am thinking of having two characters in my story and writing about how each character has a problem. I think I will have one character that doesn't know how to swim and one character that doesn't know how to ride a bike. They will help each other learn so they can both solve their problems.

- Begin a chart with your name and list the two problems you will include in the story.

  When you write stories, think about the problems that will occur and how they will be solved before you start writing.

Have a Try

Invite students to turn and talk about including more than one problem in a story.

> Turn and talk about ideas you have for a story with more than one problem.

▶ After time for discussion, add a few student ideas to the chart.

Summarize and Apply

Summarize the lesson. Have students use their writer's notebooks to jot down ideas for stories with more than one problem. Add the principle to the top of the chart.

> During independent writing time, use your writer's notebook to jot down some ideas for stories that have more than one problem. Be sure to write down each problem so you can remember it later. Your story idea might have two characters who both have problems. Or, you might have one main character that faces more than one problem. Bring your ideas when we meet later.

	Write a story with more than one problem.	
Writer	Problem 1	Problem 2
Ms. George	Character 1 wants to go swimming but does not know how.	Character 2 does not know how to ride a bicycle but wants to learn.
Suze	A girl gets on the wrong bus and gets lost on her way home.	The girl does not have any money left.
Enrico	The character forgot to do his science project.	The character gets in a fight with his brother.

Confer

▶ During independent writing, move around the room to confer briefly with students about stories with more than one problem. Use the following prompts as needed.

- *What problems will your character face?*
- *Talk about these two characters and the problems they have.*
- *Describe this character so that we can brainstorm ideas for another problem she might have.*

Share

Following independent writing, gather students in the meeting area to share their writing.

> In pairs, share an idea you have for a story with more than one problem.

Exploring Plot Structures

You Will Need

- several mentor texts that begin with the most important part of the story, such as the following:
  - *Ruth and the Green Book* by Calvin Alexander Ramsey, from Text Set: Illustrator Study: Floyd Cooper
  - *Me, Frida* by Amy Novesky, from Text Set: Biography: Artists
- document camera (optional)
- chart paper and markers
- writer's notebooks and writing folders
- To download the following online resource for this lesson, visit **fp.pub/resources**:
  - chart art

Academic Language / Important Vocabulary

- important
- high point

Continuum Connection

- Establish an initiating event and follow with a series of events in a narrative

GOAL

Understand that some stories begin with the high point or an important part of the story and use that to launch the rest of the story.

RATIONALE

Many stories start at the beginning and move linearly to the end. Some authors, for effect, launch a story with the high point and then proceed to tell the events that led up to that part. Other authors start with an important event without which the rest of the story would not happen. When students learn that writers can explore different ways to organize a plot, they begin to try out different plot structures in their own writing.

WRITER'S NOTEBOOK/WRITING FOLDER

Students can use their writer's notebooks to experiment with ways to begin a story. They might also look at a draft in their writing folders to try writing a new beginning.

ASSESS LEARNING

- Notice whether students understand that writers can choose to begin with the most important part of a story and that they can do the same in their own writing.
- Look for evidence that students can use vocabulary such as *important* and *high point*.

MINILESSON

To help students recognize that they can begin their narratives in a variety of ways, use mentor texts and provide an interactive lesson. Here is an example.

- Show the cover of *Ruth and the Green Book* and read pages 1–2.

  What do you notice about how the writer, Calvin Alexander Ramsey, decided to begin the story?

- Guide the conversation so students recognize that Dad buying the car was an important event in the story because it enabled Ruth and her family to take the road trip.

  When Ruth's dad bought the car, it allowed all of the other events in the story to happen, so buying the car is an important event in the story.

- Repeat with *Me, Frida*.

  Why might a writer begin a story with an important part of the story? Turn and talk to your partner.

- After a short time for discussion, ask several students to share their thoughts.

- On chart paper, model the process of beginning a story with the high point or an important part. Think aloud as you write.

Have a Try

Invite students to turn and talk about beginning a story with the most important part.

> What do you think I might write about next? Turn and talk about that.

▶ After time for discussion, ask students to share ideas. Encourage a discussion of how starting with the most important part might impact the rest of the story.

Summarize and Apply

Summarize the lesson. Have students try out beginning a story with the most important part.

> How might you start your story?

▶ Guide students to state the principle. Write it at the top of the chart.

> During independent writing time, jot down ideas in your writer's notebook about how a story you are working on might begin with the high point or an important part. Or you can look at a draft in your writing folder and think about how you might write a new beginning for it. Bring your ideas when we meet later.

Start with the high point or an important part of the story.

As I opened the mailbox, I immediately noticed a shiny envelope with bright blue writing that read, "Welcome, New Teacher." I was so excited I could hardly breathe. My mind raced through the events that got me to this place.

Confer

▶ During independent writing, move around the room to confer briefly with students about beginning a story with the high point or an important part. Use the following prompts as needed.

- *Tell about the high point (important part) of your story.*
- *How might your story change if you begin with the high point?*
- *Why does it help the reader to begin this story with _____?*

Share

Following independent writing, gather students in the meeting area to share their writing.

> Share an idea for a story you might write that begins with the high point or an important part.

Writing Minilesson Principle
Use a flashback to give background information for the story.

Exploring Plot Structures

You Will Need

- a mentor text that uses a flashback, such as the online resource Flashback
- chart paper and markers
- highlighter
- writer's notebooks and writing folders
- To download the online resource for this lesson, visit **fp.pub/resources**:
  - Flashback

Academic Language / Important Vocabulary

- flashback

Continuum Connection

- Understand that writers can learn to craft fiction by using mentor texts as models
- Understand that a writer uses various elements of fiction (e.g., setting, plot with problem and solution, characters) in a fiction text
- Use organization in writing that is related to purpose and genre e.g., letters, essays

GOAL

Understand how and why to use flashbacks in a story.

RATIONALE

When students understand that flashbacks are stories about something that happened before the events of the main story, they learn to try using flashbacks as a way to write stories in a more complex and interesting way.

WRITER'S NOTEBOOK/WRITING FOLDER

Students can try out different ideas for flashbacks in their writer's notebooks. Students can look at drafts from their writing folders and think about whether they might incorporate flashbacks.

ASSESS LEARNING

- Notice whether students sometimes use flashbacks in their own writing.
- Look for evidence that students can use vocabulary such as *flashback*.

MINILESSON

To help students try using flashbacks in their own writing, engage them in identifying and discussing a flashback. Here is an example.

- Display the online resource Flashback by writing the text on chart paper, projecting it, or giving each student a copy. Read it aloud or have students read it silently.

  What is happening in the story?

- Guide the conversation to help students recognize that the middle paragraph tells about an incident that happened about five years before the first and last paragraphs. If needed, define *flashback*.

  What is the purpose of using a flashback here?

  Authors use flashbacks to provide information to explain something in a story or to give more information about a character or a character's feelings. The flashback about Emma explains why she doesn't like rainy days. How do you know which part is the flashback?

- Explain that a flashback differs from a memory or a story that a character tells in that it is told as if it were happening in the present. It interrupts the chronological sequence.

Have a Try

Invite students to turn and talk about using flashbacks in their writing.

> Think about a story idea you have. How might you include a flashback in the story to tell it in an interesting way? Turn and talk about that.

▶ After time for discussion, ask a few students to share their ideas.

Summarize and Apply

Summarize the lesson. Have students try using a flashback in a story they are working on. Add the principle to the top of the chart.

> During independent writing time, use your writer's notebook to write down some ideas you have for including a flashback in a story you plan to write. Or you might choose a draft from your writing folder and think about including a flashback. Bring your ideas when we meet later.

Use a flashback to give background information for the story.

Eleven-year-old Emma looked out the window and saw that it was gray and rainy. She wondered why she hated rainy days.

It's Valentine's Day. All week, Emma has worked on cards for her kindergarten classmates. Her mom packs them in a box, gives her an umbrella, and sends her off to school. Once at school, Emma struggles to hold on to the box and the umbrella as she heads to the entrance. Suddenly, she stumbles, and the cards fly into a puddle. All her hard work, wasted!

Emma looked out the window again. It was raining harder. Emma was not happy.

Confer

▶ During independent writing, move around the room to confer briefly with students about using a flashback in their own writing. Use the following prompts as needed.

- *What ideas do you have for including a flashback?*
- *How does a flashback help the reader understand the story's events?*
- *Read the part of your story with the flashback.*
- *What words can you use to show your readers that this is a flashback?*

Share

Following independent writing, gather students in the meeting area to share their writing.

> Turn and talk about why a writer might include a flashback in a story.

> Share an example of a flashback you might include in a story you are writing.

Writing Minilesson Principle

Make the end of your story circle back to the beginning.

Exploring Plot Structures

You Will Need

- several mentor texts with a circular ending, such as the following:
  - *The Crane Wife* by Odds Bodkin, from Text Set: Empathy
  - *A Dance Like Starlight* by Kristy Dempsey, from Text Set: Illustration Study: Floyd Cooper
- document camera (optional)
- chart paper and markers
- writer's notebooks and writing folders

Academic Language / Important Vocabulary

- plot
- beginning
- circular ending

Continuum Connection

- Bring a piece to closure with a concluding statement
- End a narrative with a problem solution and a satisfying conclusion

GOAL

Understand and use a circular plot structure.

RATIONALE

A circular plot structure, ending the story with a connection to the beginning, can add a certain feeling to a story. Although the story begins and ends similarly, the character or characters are usually changed in some way by the end. Exploring different ways that writers end stories, including using circular endings, enables students to include variety in their stories so their writing stays fresh and interesting.

WRITER'S NOTEBOOK/WRITING FOLDER

Students can try out ideas for circular endings in their writer's notebooks. Students can look at drafts in their writing folders to think about whether a circular ending might be appropriate for one of the stories.

ASSESS LEARNING

- Look for evidence in students' writing that they understand that writers can end stories in a variety of ways.
- Look for evidence that students can use vocabulary such as *plot*, *beginning*, and *circular ending*.

MINILESSON

To help students understand that they can write stories with circular endings, provide mentor text examples and an interactive lesson. Here is an example.

- Show the covers of several examples of mentor texts with circular endings, such as *The Crane Wife* and *A Dance Like Starlight*. Briefly share the beginnings and endings of each.

  Think about these stories. In what ways are the endings alike?

- Guide the conversation to help students recognize that all of the books have endings that circle back to the beginning in some way.

  These books have circular endings. Why do you think the endings of these stories are called circular?

  Having the end of a story circle back to the beginning is one way you might decide to write a story.

  Why might an author choose to write a circular ending to a story?

- Ask volunteers to share their thoughts.

Have a Try

Invite students to turn and talk about circular endings.

> What are some ways a writer might end a story by circling back to the beginning? What could connect the end to the beginning? Turn and talk about that.

▶ After time for discussion, have students share ideas. Write students' ideas on chart paper.

Summarize and Apply

Summarize the lesson. Have students try out ideas for circular endings in a story.

> How might you decide to end your story?

▶ Guide students to state the principle. Write it at the top of the chart.

> During independent writing time, use your writer's notebook to jot down ideas for how you might use a circular ending for a story. Or, you might choose a draft from your writing folder and change the ending so that it circles back to the beginning. Bring your ideas when we meet.

> Make the end of your story circle back to the beginning.

- A character begins and ends in the same situation
- A repeating symbol at the beginning and the end
- Circle back to a similar idea
- End in same location as the story begins
- Return to the same exact moment in the story, but a lesson has been learned

Confer

▶ During independent writing, move around the room to confer briefly with students about circular endings. Use the following prompts as needed.

- *How could the end circle back to the beginning?*
- *Share the ideas you have for a circular ending.*
- *Look at the chart. Is there an idea listed that you might use to end this story?*

Share

Following independent writing, gather students in the meeting area to share their writing.

> Who would like to share an idea for a circular ending for a story you might write or that you are writing?

Assessment

After you have taught the minilessons in this umbrella, observe students in a variety of classroom activities. Use *The Fountas & Pinnell Literacy Continuum* to notice, teach for, and support students' learning as you observe their attempts at writing.

▶ What evidence do you have of students' new understandings related to narrative text structures?

- Do students understand that most narratives they write should have a beginning, a series of events, a high point, and an ending?

- Are they sometimes including more than one problem in the stories they write?

- Do they try out different formats, such as starting with the most important part of the story?

- Are they sometimes using flashbacks to help tell a story?

- Are they able to write stories with circular endings?

- Are they using vocabulary such as *beginning, events, high point, ending, plot structure, problem, solution, flashback,* and *circular ending*?

▶ In what ways, beyond the scope of this umbrella, are students showing an interest in the writing process?

- Are they crafting powerful leads and endings?

- Are they incorporating dialogue into their narratives?

Use your observations to determine the next umbrella you will teach. You may also consult Suggested Sequence of Lessons (pp. 665–682) for guidance.

EXTENSIONS FOR EXPLORING PLOT STRUCTURES

▶ If you are using *The Reading Minilessons Book, Grade 4* (Fountas and Pinnell 2020), you might complement these minilessons by teaching plot structure from the viewpoint of the reader: LA.U25: Understanding Plot.

▶ Pull together a temporary guided writing group of a few students who need support in writing stories with a clear plot structure.

▶ During interactive read-aloud, talk with students about the plot structure the author chose for the story and the effect it has on the experience of reading the story.

Minilessons in This Umbrella

WML1   Use words to show not tell.

WML2   Use strong nouns and verbs.

WML3   Choose words that fit the audience and tone of the writing.

Before Teaching Umbrella 8 Minilessons

The goal of these minilessons is to help students understand that writers are thoughtful and intentional about the words they use in their writing. By having students notice authors' use of words that show not tell, strong nouns and verbs, and formal or informal language, they learn that the words they choose matter. As students engage with making powerful word choices, you may want to teach GEN.U14: Writing Poetry for other ways to explore how writers decide what words have the best effect.

Use the books listed below from *Fountas & Pinnell Classroom™ Interactive Read-Aloud Collection*, or choose books from the classroom library that exemplify strong and varied word choice.

Interactive Read-Aloud Collection

Genre Study: Historical Fiction

> *The Buffalo Storm* by Katherine Applegate

Exploring Identity

> *Crown: An Ode to the Fresh Cut* by Derrick Barnes
>
> *The Royal Bee* by Frances Park and Ginger Park

Genre Study: Poetry

> *A Place to Start a Family: Poems About Creatures That Build* by
> David L. Harrison

Perseverance

> *Razia's Ray of Hope: One Girl's Dream of an Education* by Elizabeth Suneby
>
> *King for a Day* by Rukhsana Khan

As you read and enjoy these texts together, help students

- notice and appreciate authors' word choices, and
- become aware of how the language makes them feel.

Interactive Read-Aloud
Historical Fiction

Exploring Identity

Poetry

Perseverance

Writer's Notebook

WML1

Writing Minilesson Principle
Use words to show not tell.

Making Powerful Word Choices

You Will Need

- mentor texts with examples of language that shows instead of tells, such as the following:
  - *The Buffalo Storm* by Katherine Applegate, from Text Set: Genre Study: Historical Fiction
  - *Crown* by Derrick Barnes, from Text Set: Exploring Identity
- document camera (optional)
- chart paper prepared with a simple sentence that tells rather than shows
- markers
- writer's notebooks and writing folders

Academic Language / Important Vocabulary

- word choice
- comparing
- descriptive
- show not tell
- language

Continuum Connection

- Use language to show instead of tell
- Learn ways of using language and constructing texts from other writers (reading books and hearing them read aloud) and apply understandings to one's own writing
- Use figurative language (e.g., simile, metaphor, personification) to make comparisons
- Provide details that are accurate, relevant, interesting, and vivid

GOAL

Use language to show instead of tell.

RATIONALE

When students understand the concept of showing rather than telling, they begin to think about finding alternative ways to say things to help readers paint pictures in their minds.

WRITER'S NOTEBOOK/WRITING FOLDER

Students can try using language to show instead of tell in a writing project draft from their writing folders or in their writer's notebooks.

ASSESS LEARNING

- Look for evidence that students are using language to show instead of tell.
- Notice whether students are trying out surprising comparisons to show instead of tell.
- Look for evidence that students can use vocabulary such as *word choice*, *descriptive*, *language*, *comparing*, and *show not tell*.

MINILESSON

To help students think about the minilesson principle, use mentor text examples to demonstrate what it means to use language that shows instead of tells. Here is an example.

> Picture in your mind what is happening in the story as I read aloud from *The Buffalo Storm*.

▷ Read pages 17–18 in *The Buffalo Storm*.

> What is happening in the story? How do you know?

▷ Support the conversation to help students notice that the writer didn't just state directly what happened and how it made Hallie feel. Instead, she used sensory details to help readers use their imagination. As needed, revisit the text.

> Katherine Applegate used words that show instead of tell, like "Mud sucked at the wheels" and "The current tried to swallow me whole . . . till Papa hauled me in like a fish." How did she surprise the reader by comparing Hallie being pulled in from the water to a fish on a fishing pole?

▷ Guide students to notice how the description and figurative language paint a vivid picture in a reader's mind.

> Listen as I read a few more pages, and notice language the writer used that shows you rather than tells you what is happening.

▷ Read pages 27 and 29, pausing after each page to ask students what they notice about the language. Repeat with pages 2, 8, and 16 in *Crown*.

Have a Try

Invite students to turn and talk about how writers can choose powerful words.

▶ Display the prepared chart paper.

  This sentence tells how I was feeling and why. Turn and talk about some ways I could use words to *show* instead of *tell*. Think about surprising comparisons I could use.

▶ As needed, prompt the conversations by asking students how the experience would look, sound, and feel. After time for discussion, ask volunteers for ideas. Using their suggestions and helping them develop their thoughts further, write examples on the chart.

Summarize and Apply

Summarize the learning. Remind students to use language that shows instead of tells when they write.

  Why do writers use words that show instead of tell?

▶ Write the principle at the top of the chart.

  During independent writing time today, look at the writing you are working on. Is there a place where you can try using words that show instead of tell? If not, look for a place in another writing project or something you have written in your writer's notebook. Bring your writing to share when we meet later.

Use words to show not tell.

I felt surprised because my sister was cooking breakfast.

The aroma of frying bacon wrapped around me like a blanket. My nose tingled and my mouth started to water. As I peeked into the kitchen, my eyebrows shot all the way up to my hair. Was that my sister at the stove?

My eyes opened like a flower blooming in spring as I heard the bacon sizzling on the stove. My body lurched out of bed, but my foggy brain couldn't figure out what was happening.

I am the breakfast cook in my family. That's why, when I got to the kitchen, my eyes opened so wide I thought they might take over my whole body. Standing at the stove with a mess of eggshells and flying spoons was my little sister.

Section 3: Craft

Confer

▶ During independent writing, move around the room to confer briefly with students about using powerful words. Use the following prompts as needed.

  • *What is a way you could say this that shows instead of tells the reader?*

  • *Let's talk about some words that describe what you want your readers to know.*

  • *What surprising comparison might show the reader what is happening?*

Share

Following independent writing, gather students in the meeting area to share their writing.

  Choose a sentence from your writing that shows instead of tells. Read it aloud.

  What did you picture in your mind when you listened to _____'s sentence?

Making Powerful Word Choices

You Will Need

- mentor texts with examples of strong nouns and verbs, such as the following:
  - *A Place to Start a Family* by David L. Harrison, from Text Set: Genre Study: Poetry
  - *Razia's Ray of Hope* by Elizabeth Suneby, from Text Set: Perseverance
  - *The Royal Bee* by Frances Park and Ginger Park, from Text Set: Exploring Identity
- chart paper and markers
- sticky notes
- writer's notebooks

Academic Language / Important Vocabulary

- word choice
- specific
- noun
- detail
- verb

Continuum Connection

- Use memorable words or phrases
- Use strong nouns and verbs
- Use range of descriptive words to enhance meaning
- Select words to make meanings memorable
- Vary word choice to create interesting description and dialogue

GOAL

Write with strong nouns and verbs.

RATIONALE

By choosing strong nouns and verbs, writers help their readers get a better image of what is happening. When students understand this, they learn to do this in their own writing.

WRITER'S NOTEBOOK/WRITING FOLDER

Students can make a list of nouns and verbs in their writer's notebooks.

ASSESS LEARNING

- Observe for evidence that students understand why writers use specific nouns and verbs.
- Look at students' writing. Do they sometimes use specific nouns and verbs?
- Look for evidence that students can use vocabulary such as *word choice*, *noun*, *verb*, *specific*, and *detail*.

MINILESSON

Students will need their writer's notebooks for this lesson. To help students think about the minilesson principle, engage them in noticing that writers use strong nouns and verbs. Here is an example.

- Show and read page 8 in *A Place to Start a Family*.

  What do you notice about the words the writer, David L. Harrison, chose to name things and show action?

- As necessary, define the meanings of *noun* and *verb* as well as the meanings of unfamiliar nouns and verbs. Begin a list on chart paper of interesting nouns and verbs. Repeat with pages 12–13.

  Why do you think the writer chose these particular nouns and verbs?

  Writers choose words that are specific so that readers have a better understanding of what the writer is writing about. Sometimes writers add extra words to describe the nouns and verbs more clearly or specifically.

- Continue adding words that students notice as you show and read pages 1–2 in *Razia's Ray of Hope* and page 4 in *The Royal Bee*.

- Help students understand the difference between using vague language and stronger, more specific nouns and verbs.

  How would the picture in your mind be different if you read the word *sunlight* or *light* rather than *dawn light*?

  What about *cornfields* instead of *autumn cornfields*?

Have a Try

Invite students to turn and talk about using strong nouns and verbs.

▶ Choose a common noun and a verb that tend to be overused by the students in your class. Write the words on new chart paper.

> In your writer's notebook, write some stronger, more specific nouns that you could use instead of *bug* and some verbs that you could use instead of *see*. Then turn to your partner and share your words.

▶ After a few moments, ask a few volunteers to share their words. Choose several suggestions to add to the chart on sticky notes.

Summarize and Apply

Summarize the learning. Remind students to notice and use interesting nouns and verbs.

> When you notice an interesting noun or verb, write it on a sticky note and add it to the chart.

▶ Write the principle at the top of the second chart.

> During independent writing time today, look at your writing to see if you can use a noun or verb that is more specific or better describes something. You can also add words to the list in your writer's notebook so that you will have some words to choose from when you write. Bring your writing when we meet later.

Confer

▶ During independent writing, move around the room to confer briefly with students about their choice of words. Use the following prompts as needed.

- *Is there a more interesting way you could describe what this person is doing?*
- *What other word could you use that is more specific?*
- *Let's talk about some descriptive words you could use.*

Share

Following independent writing, gather students in the meeting area to share their writing.

> What specific noun or verb did you use in your writing today?

> Did you include any descriptive words to strengthen a noun or a verb? Share the word.

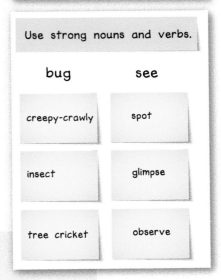

Nouns		Verbs
serpent	dry earth	twisting
silken thread	shiny papers	coiling
windowsill	dawn light	flutter
weaver	autumn cornfields	blunder
artistic trap	wilted fruits	raced
fragile moth	hut	murmured
gentle gust	rags	echoed
empty lot	mountain	
shards	stream	
clay tiles	ding dong	
ribbons		

Use strong nouns and verbs.

bug	see
creepy-crawly	spot
insect	glimpse
tree cricket	observe

WML3

CFT.U8.WML3

Writing Minilesson Principle
Choose words that fit the audience and tone of the writing.

Making Powerful Word Choices

You Will Need

- a familiar mentor text, such as *King for a Day*, by Rukhsana Khan, from Text Set: Perseverance
- examples of your own writing that are for various audiences (e.g., an email to the principal, a letter to your grandparent)
- chart paper and markers
- document camera (optional)
- writer's notebooks and/or writing folders

Academic Language / Important Vocabulary

- audience
- tone
- formal
- informal
- appropriate

Continuum Connection

- Learn ways of using language and constructing texts from other writers (reading books and hearing them read aloud) and apply understandings to one's own writing
- Choose words with the audience in mind
- Use words that convey an intended mood or effect

GOAL

Understand that writers use words to establish a tone to reach an intended audience.

RATIONALE

Word choice creates the tone of a piece of writing. Additionally, words that are appropriate for one audience may not be appropriate for another. When students recognize that writers choose more formal or less formal words depending on the audience, they begin to think about what words are appropriate for each type of writing.

WRITER'S NOTEBOOK/WRITING FOLDER

Students can try using language that matches the intended audience and desired tone in a writing project draft from their writing folders or in their writer's notebooks.

ASSESS LEARNING

- Look for evidence in students' writing that their word choice creates a tone that is right for the audience.
- Look for evidence that students can use vocabulary such as *audience*, *tone*, *formal*, *informal*, and *appropriate*.

MINILESSON

To help students think about the minilesson principle, engage them in an interactive discussion to recognize that the tone should match the intended audience. Here is an example.

- Revisit a few pages from *King for a Day*.

    Whom do you think the author, Rukhsana Kahn, wrote this book for?

    If Rukhsana Kahn had written a letter to her aunt, do you think she would have chosen these types of words, and would it sound the same?

- Guide students to recognize that writers choose words based on their audience.

    A writer's personality or attitude comes across through the words the writer chooses. This is called tone. To figure out the appropriate tone to use, writers think about their audience.

- Show and read the prepared writing samples.

    What do you notice about the tone of these different examples?

- Ensure that students recognize that you chose different words based on your audience.

    Your writing can be very formal (serious), formal, informal, or very informal (slang). Depending on how formal the writing is, a writer chooses different types of words.

Have a Try

Invite students to turn and talk about audience and tone.

▶ On chart paper, write degrees of formality in the left-hand column. Leave space to the right for examples.

> Turn and talk about examples of writing that would fit in these categories.

▶ After a few moments, ask a few volunteers to share their ideas. Choose several suggestions to add to the chart.

Summarize and Apply

Summarize the learning. Remind students to think about their audience when deciding on word choice. Write the principle at the top of the chart.

> During independent writing time today, take time to look at some of your writing. Make sure your tone matches your audience. You might decide to write something using different words so that your tone better matches your audience. If you are starting on a new piece of writing, think about your audience when you choose what words to use. Bring your writing when we meet later.

Choose words that fit the audience and tone of the writing.

Tone	Type of Writing
Very formal, serious	letter or email to someone you do not know
Formal	email to the principal
	informational writing
	news article
Informal	letter to family member
	dialogue between friends in a realistic fiction story
	advertisement
Very informal, slang	note to friends
	text message to close friends
	comic strip

Confer

▶ During independent writing, move around the room to confer briefly with students about their choice of words. Use the following prompts as needed.

• *Who will be reading this piece of writing?*

• *Point out the words you use that give a clue about your audience.*

• *Does this word match your tone? Talk about that.*

Share

Following independent writing, gather students in the meeting area to share their writing.

> In groups of three, share a piece of writing. Ask your group members to talk about whether the tone matches the audience.

Assessment

After you have taught the minilessons in this umbrella, observe students in a variety of classroom activities. Use *The Fountas & Pinnell Literacy Continuum* to notice, teach for, and support students' learning as you observe their attempts at writing.

▶ What evidence do you have of students' new understandings related to word choice?

- Do students use words that show instead of tell?

- Do they choose strong, specific nouns and verbs?

- Do they choose words that fit the audience and the tone of the writing?

- Are they using vocabulary such as *word choice, descriptive, language, comparing, noun, verb, specific, detail, audience, tone, formal, informal,* and *appropriate*?

▶ In what ways, beyond the scope of this umbrella, are students' reading and writing behaviors showing an understanding of word choice?

- Are they choosing words that create a strong writing voice?

- Do they think about word choice when writing poems?

Use your observations to determine the next umbrella you will teach. You may also consult Suggested Sequence of Lessons (pp. 665–682) for guidance.

EXTENSIONS FOR MAKING POWERFUL WORD CHOICES

▶ If you are using *The Reading Minilessons Book, Grade 4* (Fountas and Pinnell 2020) you may choose to teach LA.U10: Reading Like a Writer: Analyzing the Writer's Craft.

▶ As opportunities arise, guide students to make powerful word choices through the use of figurative language (e.g., metaphor, simile, personification, hyperbole) and strong adjectives.

▶ Encourage students to choose words to replace *said* to show how someone is speaking.

▶ If you have students who speak other languages, encourage them to include words or phrases from the language when describing characters or settings that would be best described in that language.

▶ If you are using *Writer's Notebook, Intermediate* (Fountas and Pinnell 2023), have students record memorable words and phrases on page 41.

Minilessons in This Umbrella

WML1 Start your sentences in different ways.

WML2 Vary the length and structure of your sentences.

WML3 Use connecting words and phrases to help sentences flow.

WML4 Use commas to create sentences that contain more than one idea.

Before Teaching Umbrella 9 Minilessons

The goals of these minilessons are to help students recognize the ways that authors craft sentences that read smoothly, have an easy flow, and have clear transitions from one to another, as well as to think about how to apply what they learn about crafting sentences to their own writing. Before teaching this umbrella, students should have had many opportunities to read and talk about books by writers who use varied, clear, and interesting sentences. Students also should be working on some writing to which they can apply these lessons.

Use the books listed below from *Fountas & Pinnell Classroom™ Interactive Read-Aloud Collection,* or choose books that have varied sentence structures from the classroom library. Students should be able to see the sentences clearly, so use a document camera to project a page of text or write the sentences from the text on chart paper.

Interactive Read-Aloud Collection

Telling a Story with Photos

A Little Book of Sloth by Lucy Cooke

A Bear's Life by Nicholas Read

The Seal Garden by Nicholas Read

Wolf Island by Nicholas Read

Biography: Artists

Radiant Child: The Story of Young Artist Jean-Michel Basquiat by Javaka Steptoe

As you read and enjoy these texts together, help students

- observe the way the sentences are written, and
- talk about the way the authors craft sentences.

Interactive Read-Aloud
Telling a Story with Photos

A Bear's Life
by Nicholas Read

The Seal Garden
by Nicholas Read

Wolf Island
by Nicholas Read

Biography: Artists

Writer's Notebook

Section 3: Craft

Writing Minilesson Principle
Start your sentences in different ways.

Writing Clear and Interesting Sentences

You Will Need

- a mentor text that uses varied sentence beginnings, such as *A Little Book of Sloth* by Lucy Cooke, from Text Set: Telling a Story with Photos
- chart paper and markers
- highlighter
- document camera [optional]
- writer's notebooks and writing folders

Academic Language / Important Vocabulary

- sentences
- clear

Continuum Connection

- Use variety in sentence structure and sentence length

GOAL

Understand that writers purposely vary how their sentences begin.

RATIONALE

When sentences are well crafted, they are smooth and have flow, which makes them easy and enjoyable to read. Varying the beginnings is one way to create smooth, flowing sentences. When students notice that writers pay attention to how their sentences sound, they become aware of how their own sentences sound or could sound.

WRITER'S NOTEBOOK/WRITING FOLDER

Students can try out new sentence beginnings in their writer's notebooks and revise sentence beginnings in the draft of a writing project in their writing folders.

ASSESS LEARNING

- Look at students' writing for evidence that they are varying the ways they begin their sentences.
- Look for evidence that students can use vocabulary such as *sentences* and *clear*.

MINILESSON

To help students think about the minilesson principle, use mentor texts that have examples of sentences that begin in a variety of ways. Here is an example.

- Show the cover of *A Little Book of Sloth*.

  Listen to some of the sentences that the author, Lucy Cooke, wrote for *A Little Book of Sloth*.

- Begin reading the book, pausing after each page to ask students to notice how the sentences begin.

  What do you notice about the words the author used to begin the sentences?

- As students identify the words, begin a list on chart paper.

- Continue through the book until you have a list of varied sentence beginnings.

  The author began each of these sentences in a different way. Why do you think writers start sentences in different ways?

  How might the writing sound different if the writer began each sentence with "Sloths"?

- Engage students in a conversation about how starting sentences in different ways makes their writing more interesting and fun to read. Write the principle at the top of the chart.

Have a Try

Invite students to turn and talk about ways to vary how they begin sentences.

▶ On a new sheet of chart paper, write three sentences that all begin the same way. Read them aloud and highlight the beginnings to show they are the same.

> In your writer's notebook, rewrite one or two of the sentences so that they start in a different way. When you finish writing, share your sentences with your partner.

▶ After time for discussion, ask volunteers to share how they varied the sentence beginnings. Write the new beginnings on the chart as examples. Highlight the revised beginnings.

Summarize and Apply

Summarize the learning. Have students vary the way they begin sentences in their writing pieces.

> What did you learn today about making your sentences interesting to read?

> When you are writing today, reread what you have written. Look for places where you have started sentences the same way. Use your writer's notebook to try out some different ways to start at least one of the sentences. Then revise your draft. Bring your writing to share when we meet later.

Start your sentences in different ways.	
It all started with . . .	The burgeoning brood . . .
Baby Buttercup . . .	The Choloepus . . .
Buttercup's new home . . .	Sloths' natural home . . .
Two decades later . . .	Not only do sloths . . .
Word got out . . .	Sloths aren't monkeys . . .

Koala bears aren't really bears.	⇒	Despite the name, koala bears aren't really bears.
Koala bears are picky eaters.	⇒	Finding something to eat can be challenging because koala bears are picky eaters.
Koala bears sometimes sleep many hours per day.	⇒	Sometimes, koala bears sleep many hours per day.

Confer

▶ During independent writing, move around the room to confer briefly with students about writing clear, interesting sentences. Use the following prompts as needed.

- *What are you writing about today?*
- *Read this sentence. Is there another way you might start it?*
- *Take a look at the sentences on this page. Talk about whether they all begin in the same way or in different ways.*

Share

Following independent writing, gather students in the meeting area to share their writing.

> Share with your partner any sentences you started in different ways.

Section 3: Craft

Writing Minilesson Principle
Vary the length and structure of your sentences.

Writing Clear and Interesting Sentences

You Will Need

- several mentor texts that have sentences of varied lengths and structures, such as the following from Text Set: Telling a Story with Photos:
  - *A Bear's Life* by Nicholas Read
  - *A Little Book of Sloth* by Lucy Cooke
- chart paper prepared with several short sentences all the same length
- document camera (optional)
- markers
- writing folders

Academic Language / Important Vocabulary

- sentence
- vary
- flow
- structure
- length

Continuum Connection

- Use variety in sentence structure and sentence length
- Arrange simple and complex sentences for an easy flow and sentence transition
- Vary sentence length to create feeling or mood

GOAL

Use sentences of different lengths so that they flow easily.

RATIONALE

When sentences are well crafted, they flow, which makes them easy and enjoyable to read. Writers vary their sentences by making them different lengths and using different sentence structures. When students notice that writers pay attention to how their sentences sound, they begin to think about how to do the same in their own writing.

WRITER'S NOTEBOOK/WRITING FOLDER

Students look at their drafts from their writing folders to see where they might revise some sentences by varying their length and structure.

ASSESS LEARNING

- ▶ Examine students' writing to see whether they vary their sentences.
- ▶ Look for evidence that students can use vocabulary such as *sentence*, *vary*, *flow*, *structure*, and *length*.

MINILESSON

To help students think about the minilesson principle, use mentor texts that have sentences of varying lengths and structures. Here is an example.

- ▶ Show and read pages 6–7 of *A Bear's Life*.

    What do you notice about the length of the sentences the writer, Nicholas Read, wrote?

- ▶ Help students notice that some are short, some are long, and some are structured differently (e.g., start with some introductory words, are fragments). Write some of the sentences on chart paper so that sentences are written under each other in order for students to be able to compare sentence length.

    Sometimes writers use a few words rather than a whole sentence to make an idea stand out.

- ▶ Repeat with *A Little Book of Sloth*, pages 9–10.

    The writer, Lucy Cooke, used some short sentences and some long sentences. Why do you think she may have decided to do this?

- ▶ Engage students in a conversation about how varying their sentences can give the writing rhythm and flow, make sentences stand out, and create a mood or feeling.

    When writers vary the length and structure of sentences, how does that affect the reader?

Have a Try

Invite students to turn and talk about ways to vary sentence length and structure.

▷ Show the prepared writing. Read the sentences aloud.

How does my writing sound? Turn and talk about how I could make the sentences sound better. Think about adding words to the sentences or putting two sentences together.

▷ After time for discussion, ask volunteers to share. Use students' suggestions to revise the sentences.

Summarize and Apply

Summarize the learning. Remind students to vary the length and structure of sentences in their writing.

We have been talking about how writers include some short sentences and some longer sentences so that the writing is more interesting for a reader. Varying sentence length and structure makes the writing flow.

▷ Write the principle at the top of the second chart.

When you write today, think about how you can vary sentence length and structure in the writing project you are working on. Bring your writing to share when we meet later.

Confer

▷ During independent writing, move around the room to confer briefly with students about sentences. Use the following prompts as needed.

- *What are you writing about today?*

- *Read aloud what you have written on this page. How does it sound? Are there any sentences that should be shorter or longer?*

- *These sentences all start with a noun. You could start a sentence with some introductory words, like "While they live alone."*

Share

Following independent writing, gather students in the meeting area to share their writing.

In groups of four, share several parts of your writing that show that you wrote sentences that have different lengths and structure.

A Bear's Life	For young grizzlies, the Great Bear Rainforest is a place full of wonder and surprise.
	They never know what they're going to see next.
	A deer?
	A wolf?
	An eagle?
	Maybe all three.
A Little Book of Sloth	Sloths' natural home is the jungles of South and Central America where they spend their whole lives hanging about in trees.
	Literally.

Vary the length and structure of your sentences.

I like stingrays.	I like stingrays.
They are graceful.	Stingrays are graceful swimmers.
They live alone.	While they live alone, they usually migrate in groups.
They migrate in groups.	
They have barbs.	They have barbs to protect themselves.
Sharks are predators.	Watch out for sharks!

Writing Minilesson Principle

Use connecting words and phrases to help sentences flow.

Writing Clear and Interesting Sentences

You Will Need

- a mentor text that includes a variety of connecting words and phrases, such as *The Seal Garden* by Nicholas Read, from Text Set: Telling a Story with Photos
- chart paper and markers
- document camera (optional)
- chart paper prepared with sentences for adding connecting words
- highlighter
- writing folders

Academic Language / Important Vocabulary

- sentence
- connecting
- flow

Continuum Connection

- Use well-crafted transitions to support the pace and flow of the writing
- Work on transitions to achieve better flow

GOAL

Use a variety of connecting words and phrases to help sentences transition and flow.

RATIONALE

Writers use connecting words and phrases to clarify the relationship between ideas. These words and phrases add meaning, form transitions between sentences, and add variety to the sentence structures—all of which add flow to the writing.

WRITER'S NOTEBOOK/WRITING FOLDER

Students look at their drafts from their writing folders to see where they might revise sentences to use connecting words.

ASSESS LEARNING

- Notice whether students are able to identify and use connecting words and phrases.
- Look for evidence that students can use vocabulary such as *sentence*, *connecting*, and *flow*.

MINILESSON

To help students think about the minilesson principle, use a mentor text that has sentences with connecting words. Write sentences on chart paper or project the pages so that students can see the words. Here is an example.

- Show the cover and read pages 12–13 in *The Seal Garden*.

    What do you notice about the way the writer, Nicholas Read, used words to connect ideas?

- Guide the conversation so students recognize that *and* connects the ideas within one sentence together and *meanwhile* connects the ideas from one sentence to the next. On chart paper, begin a list of connecting words and phrases that students notice in mentor text examples at the beginning or middle of a sentence.

    Listen for connecting words as I continue to read through the book. They can come at the beginning or in the middle of a sentence. Raise your hand when you notice a connecting word.

- Continue reading through the book, pausing when students notice an example of a connecting word or phrase.

    Sometimes, a writer uses several words, like "so long as" or "after an hour," to connect ideas. How do connecting words help readers?

- Talk about how connecting words not only make sentences smoother and easier to read but also clarify the relationship between ideas.

Have a Try

Invite students to turn and talk about ways to include connecting words and phrases.

▶ Show the prepared sentences and read them aloud.

> Turn and talk to you partner about using connecting words to make these sentences sound better and to make the meaning clear.

▶ After time for discussion, ask volunteers to share. Write the new sentences on the chart.

Summarize and Apply

Summarize the learning. Have students include some transition words and phrases in their writing.

> How can you make your sentences flow?

▶ Write the principle at the top of the second chart.

> We have been talking about how writers include connecting words and phrases to make their writing flow. When you write today, think about how you can do this in the piece you are working on. Bring your writing to share when we meet later.

Confer

▶ During independent writing, move around the room to confer briefly with students about connecting words and phrases. Use the following prompts as needed.

- *What are you writing about today?*
- *Let's talk about a word you could add to make your writing flow.*
- *What connecting word or phrase could you add here?*

Share

Following independent writing, gather students in the meeting area. Ask a few volunteers to share their writing.

> Share a few sentences from your writing that include a connecting word.

> How does the connecting word make _____'s writing flow?

Connecting Words and Phrases

Beginning of Sentence	Middle of Sentence
Meanwhile	and
Besides	because
Eventually	so
But	but
So as long as	
Even so	
After an hour	

Use connecting words and phrases to help sentences flow.

I know you want to go to the restaurant. Could we just eat at home?

I know you want to go to the restaurant. Instead, could we just eat at home?

If you're hungry, we can eat now. We can eat later.

If you're hungry, we can eat now. Otherwise, we can eat later.

I want to be on the team. I missed the tryouts.

I want to be on the team, but I missed the tryouts.

Section 3: Craft

WML4
CFT.U9.WML4

Writing Minilesson Principle
Use commas to create sentences that contain more than one idea.

You Will Need

- several mentor texts that include examples of sentences that use commas to combine sentences, such as the following:
  - *Radiant Child* by Javaka Steptoe, from Text Set: Biography: Artists
  - *Wolf Island* and *A Bear's Life* by Nicholas Read, from Text Set: Telling a Story with Photos
- chart paper and markers
- highlighter
- document camera (optional)
- writing folders
- To download the following online resource for this lesson, visit **fp.pub/resources**:
  - chart art (optional)

Academic Language / Important Vocabulary

- combine
- commas

Continuum Connection

- Notice the role of punctuation in the craft of writing
- Try out new ways of using punctuation
- Identify redundant words, phrases, or sentences and remove if they do not serve a purpose or enhance the voice

GOAL

Use commas and a conjunction to combine ideas to improve sentence fluency and flow.

RATIONALE

When students understand that writers use commas and a conjunction to combine ideas in a sentence to avoid unnecessary repetition and choppiness, they think about how to make their own writing more fluent.

WRITER'S NOTEBOOK/WRITING FOLDER

Students look at their drafts from their writing folders to see where they might revise sentences to use commas and a conjunction to combine ideas in a sentence.

ASSESS LEARNING

- Notice whether students are able to combine ideas with commas.
- Look for evidence that students can use vocabulary such as *combine* and *commas*.

MINILESSON

To help students think about the minilesson principle, use mentor texts that have sentences that use commas to combine ideas. Write sentences on chart paper or project the pages so that students can see the words. Here is an example.

- Show and read page 7 of *Radiant Child*.

  What do you notice about the ideas the author, Javaka Steptoe, combined?

- Guide the conversation so students recognize that the writer used commas and a conjunction to combine related ideas.

- Show and read the sentence beginning "But in another way" on page 6 in *Wolf Island*.

  How would this sentence sound if Nicholas Read had decided not to combine the ideas together?

  The writer could have written several sentences, so it would sound something like this: He knew there would be deer in the woods. He knew there would be clams in the sand. He knew there would be seals in the sea.

  Why is it a good idea to use commas to combine sentences?

- Guide the conversation to help students recognize that using commas and the word *and* to combine ideas makes the writing less repetitive, places the ideas closer together, and makes the writing flow better.

Have a Try

Invite students to turn and talk about ways to use commas to combine ideas.

▶ Show and read pages 11–12 in *A Bear's Life*.

What are some things that mother bears teach their bear cubs?

▶ On chart paper, write a sentence for each student's suggestion.

Turn and talk about how you might use commas and the word *and* to combine these ideas.

▶ After time for discussion, ask volunteers to share. Write the new sentence on the chart. Ask a student to highlight the commas and the word *and*.

Summarize and Apply

Summarize the learning. Have students use commas and a conjunction to combine ideas in their writing.

How can you make your writing sound smoother?

▶ Write the principle at the top of the chart.

Writers often use commas to combine ideas so that they don't repeat words over and over and so that the sentences are smoother to read. When you write today, think about how you can do this in the piece you are working on. Bring your writing to share when we meet later.

Use commas to create sentences that contain more than one idea.

They teach them where, when, and how to find food. → Mother bears teach their cubs how to find food, how to keep safe, and how to fish.

They teach them what is dangerous and what is safe.

In the fall they teach them to fish.

Confer

▶ During independent writing, move around the room to confer briefly with students about combining sentences with commas. Use the following prompts as needed.

- *How can you combine these ideas into one sentence?*
- *Show where you will place the commas.*
- *Read your writing aloud. Do you hear a place where you could use commas to combine ideas in a sentence?*

Share

Following independent writing, gather students in the meeting area to share their writing.

Show where in your writing you used commas to combine ideas.

Assessment

After you have taught the minilessons in this umbrella, observe students in a variety of classroom activities. Use *The Fountas & Pinnell Literacy Continuum* to notice, teach for, and support students' learning as you observe their attempts at writing.

▶ What evidence do you have of students' new understandings related to writing sentences?

- Do they understand why writers start sentences in different ways, vary sentence lengths and structures, and use connecting words?

- Do they attempt to vary sentences in their own writing?

- Are they using commas to combine sentences?

- Are they using vocabulary such as *sentences, clear, vary, structure, length, connecting, flow, combine,* and *commas*?

▶ In what ways, beyond the scope of this umbrella, are students' reading and writing behaviors showing an understanding of making writing clear and interesting?

- Are students looking for ways to show voice in their writing?

- Do they use varied word choice to make their writing more powerful?

Use your observations to determine the next umbrella you will teach. You may also consult Suggested Sequence of Lessons (pp. 665–682) for guidance.

EXTENSIONS FOR WRITING CLEAR AND INTERESTING SENTENCES

▶ During interactive read-aloud or shared reading, ask students to notice the punctuation used with connecting words and phrases. Point out that a comma often follows a connecting word or phrase when it comes at the beginning of a sentence. Use a document camera as needed.

▶ Use shared writing to create a song or a chant that uses sentences with varying lengths. Engage in conversation about how the rhythm and beat are affected by sentence length.

▶ Pull together a small, temporary guided writing group of students who need further support in understanding how to improve their sentence fluency.

▶ If you are using *The Reading Minilessons Book, Grade 4* (Fountas and Pinnell 2020) you may choose to teach LA.U28: Analyzing the Writer's Craft in Fiction Books.

Minilessons in This Umbrella

WML1 Write from a first-person point of view.

WML2 Write from a third-person point of view.

WML3 Choose the point of view that best fits your story.

Before Teaching Umbrella 10 Minilessons

Writers choose the type of narration—or point of view—for their writing to best convey the message. This decision-making applies to fiction and nonfiction, though certain genres lend themselves to a specific point of view. For example, memoir and autobiography are almost always written in first person.

The minilessons in this umbrella are designed to help students think about the purpose of first- and third-person points of view and then decide which perspective best serves their writing. As first-person point of view is the way we tell personal stories verbally, writing from this perspective may feel most natural to students, so it will be important for them to understand the purpose for each and the importance of maintaining a consistent point of view throughout a piece of writing.

Students may find it helpful to hear you think aloud about the decision-making process as you begin to write and then write along with you from a consistent perspective. These actions will provide models for students to follow as they experiment in their writer's notebooks. You will also want to collect familiar texts with clear examples of first- and third-person writing. Use the books listed below from *Fountas & Pinnell Classroom*™ *Interactive Read-Aloud Collection,* or choose books from the classroom library.

Interactive Read-Aloud Collection

Empathy

  A Symphony of Whales by Steve Schuch

Biography: Artists

  Me, Frida by Amy Novesky

Figuring Out Who You Are

  A Boy and a Jaguar by Alan Rabinowitz

Illustrator Study: Floyd Cooper

  Ruth and the Green Book by Calvin Alexander Ramsey

As you read and enjoy these texts together, help students

- notice the point of view,

- talk about the author's decision to write from a specific point of view, and

- discuss how first-person and third-person writings sound and are written.

Interactive Read-Aloud
Empathy

Biography: Artists

Figuring Out Who You Are

Illustrator Study: Floyd Cooper

Writer's Notebook

Section 3: Craft

WML1

CFT.U10.WML1

Write from a first-person point of view.

Choosing a Point of View

You Will Need

- several texts with examples of first-person point of view, such as the following:
  - *A Boy and a Jaguar* by Alan Rabinowitz, from Text Set: Figuring Out Who You Are
  - *Ruth and the Green Book* by Calvin Alexander Ramsey, from Text Set: Illustrator Study: Floyd Cooper
- chart paper and markers
- writer's notebooks and writing folders

Academic Language / Important Vocabulary

- perspective
- point of view
- narrator
- first person

Continuum Connection

- Take a point of view by writing in first or third person
- Use language to establish a point of view
- Understand the differences between first and third person

GOAL

Understand first-person point of view and how it affects the writing.

RATIONALE

When students understand first-person point of view, they can begin to use it in their own writing. If they choose to write in first person, it may help them explore a character more deeply. It also allows the reader to experience the story as the main character, which creates an intimacy and a connection between the writer, reader, and character.

WRITER'S NOTEBOOK/WRITING FOLDER

Students can select a draft from their writing folders, identify the perspective, and try writing it from an alternative perspective in their writer's notebooks.

ASSESS LEARNING

- Notice whether students write from a first-person point of view.
- Look for evidence that students can use vocabulary such as *perspective*, *point of view*, *narrator*, and *first person*.

MINILESSON

Students will need their writing folders for this lesson. To help students think about the minilesson principle, use mentor texts written in first person to engage them in a conversation about the characteristics that define the point of view and the choices the author made to achieve this. Here is an example.

- Show and read pages 1–3 of *A Boy and a Jaguar*.

  What do you notice about the way the author is telling the story?

- Record responses on the chart. Guide the students to notice first-person point of view.

  The boy, the main character, tells the story, so he is the narrator.

  This book is written from his perspective. This is called first-person point of view. What tells you this is written in the first person?

  Why do you think the author decided to tell this story from the first-person point of view?

- Record responses on the chart.
- Repeat this process with pages 7–8 of *Ruth and the Green Book*.

  When you write a memory story about yourself and you use the words *I*, *me*, and, *my*, you are writing from a first-person point of view.

Have a Try

Invite students to identify and discuss the point of view of their writing with a partner.

> Select a piece of writing from your writing folder to share with your partner. Notice the point of view. Is it first person? What tells you that? If you did not write in first person, discuss how the writing would sound if you were to write it in first person.

▶ After time for discussion, ask a few volunteers to share.

Summarize and Apply

Summarize the learning. Have students try writing from the first-person point of view in their writer's notebooks.

> What did you learn about first-person point of view?

▶ Write the principle at the top of the chart.

> During independent writing time, reread a piece of writing you are working on. Is it in first person? If so, try writing about the event in first person from a *different* character's perspective. Bring your writing to share when we meet later.

Write from a first-person point of view.

- Tells the story from the main character's perspective.
- Reader sees only what the main character sees.
- Reader knows the character's inner thoughts, worries, and fears and what the character thinks about events and other characters.

Why/Purpose	How To
• Learn a lot about the main character.	• Use I, me, myself, mine.
• Writing in this way feels natural—it's the way we tell stories to one another.	• Tell the story as if you are the main character.
• Shares main character's inner thoughts.	• Tell your inner thoughts.
• Readers experience the story alongside the main character.	• Write events as if you are experiencing them as the main character.

Confer

▶ During independent writing, move around the room to confer briefly with students about the point of view of their writing. Use the following prompts as needed.

- *What are you writing about today? What is the point of view?*
- *What words are you using to show readers that your story is written in first person?*
- *How does writing from a first-person point of view help your story?*

Share

Following independent writing, gather students in the meeting area to share their writing.

> Did anyone try some new writing from a first-person point of view? How did that affect your story? Share what you wrote.

Writing Minilesson Principle
Write from a third-person point of view.

Choosing a Point of View

You Will Need

- several texts with examples of third-person point of view, such as the following:
  - *A Symphony of Whales* by Steve Schuch, from Text Set: *Empathy*
  - *Me, Frida* by Amy Novesky, from Text Set: *Biography: Artists*
- chart paper and markers
- writer's notebooks and writing folders

Academic Language / Important Vocabulary

- perspective
- point of view
- third person

Continuum Connection

- Take a point of view by writing in first or third person
- Use language to establish a point of view
- Understand the differences between first and third person

GOAL

Understand third-person point of view and how it affects the writing.

RATIONALE

When students understand third-person point of view, they can begin to use it in their own writing. Writing in third person helps students explore a story more broadly by focusing on different characters and events and providing their readers with multiple perspectives.

WRITER'S NOTEBOOK/WRITING FOLDER

Students can select a draft from their writing folders, identify the perspective, and try writing it from an alternative perspective in their writer's notebooks.

ASSESS LEARNING

- Notice whether students write from a third-person point of view.
- Look for evidence that students can use vocabulary such as *perspective*, *point of view*, and *third person*.

MINILESSON

Students will need their writing folders for this lesson. To help students think about the minilesson principle, use mentor texts written in third person to engage them in a conversation about the characteristics that define the point of view and the choices the author made to achieve this. Here is an example.

- Show and read pages 6–8 of *A Symphony of Whales*.

  What do you notice about the way the author is telling the story?

- Record responses on the chart. Guide the students to notice third-person point of view.

  This book is written from the third-person point of view. The narrator is telling the story, not one of the characters. Why do you think the author decided to tell this story from the third-person point of view?

- Record responses on the chart.

  How did the author let you know that this is written from a third-person point of view?

  How does this perspective affect the story?

- Record responses on the chart. Repeat this process with pages 6–10 of *Me, Frida*.

Have a Try

Invite students to identify and discuss the point of view of their writing with a partner.

> Select a piece of writing from your writing folder to share with your partner. Discuss the point of view. Is it third person? What tells you that? If you did not write in third person, discuss how the story would sound if you were to write it in third person.

▶ After time for discussion, ask a few volunteers to share.

Summarize and Apply

Summarize the learning. Have students try writing from a third-person point of view in their writer's notebooks.

> What is it called when you write as the narrator instead of as one of the characters?

▶ Write the principle at the top of the chart.

> During independent writing time, reread a piece of your writing. Is it third person? If so, are there places where the narrator might add more information, or a place where you could write more about another character or event? Bring your writing to share when we meet later.

Write from a third-person point of view.

- The narrator (writer) shares what characters see and think (more than just the main character).

- The narrator is not a character in the story.

Why/Purpose	How To
• Learn about more than one character.	• Use he, him, his, she, her, hers, it, its, they, their, themselves.
• Allows you to zoom in and out of events and move around in time—an observer's point of view.	• Tell the story as if you are an onlooker.
• Helps to create suspense, because the reader knows more than the characters.	• Follow one or more characters.

Confer

▶ During independent writing, move around the room to confer briefly with students about the point of view of their writing. Use the following prompts as needed.

- *What are you writing about today? What is the point of view?*
- *What words are you using to show readers that your story is written in third person?*
- *How does writing from a third-person point of view help your story?*

Share

Following independent writing, gather students in the meeting area to share their writing.

> Did anyone try writing from a third-person point of view today? How did that affect your story? Share what you wrote.

Writing Minilesson Principle
Choose the point of view that best fits your story.

Choosing a Point of View

You Will Need

- chart paper prepared with the same story written in first person and then third person by you, the whole class, or an individual student, or a copy of the online resource Point of View (projected)
- document camera (optional)
- chart paper and markers
- writer's notebooks
- To download the following online resource for this lesson, visit **fp.pub/resources**:
  - Point of View (optional)

Academic Language / Important Vocabulary

- first person
- third person
- point of view
- perspective

Continuum Connection

- Take a point of view by writing in first or third person
- Select a point of view with which to tell a story
- Write in both first and third person and understand the differences in effect so as to choose appropriately
- Use language to establish a point of view
- Understand the differences between first and third person

GOAL

Select the point of view that best supports the story.

RATIONALE

When students understand there is more than one point of view from which to tell a story, they can think about which one best serves their writing based upon what they are trying to accomplish.

WRITER'S NOTEBOOK/WRITING FOLDER

Students can try out different points of view for their writing in their writer's notebooks.

ASSESS LEARNING

- Observe students as they write and consider point of view.
- Notice whether students write in both first and third person and how they talk about the decision to write from a particular perspective.
- Look for evidence that students can use vocabulary such as *first person*, *third person*, *point of view*, and *perspective*.

MINILESSON

To help students think about the minilesson principle, engage them in noticing how the decision to write in first person or third person affects the writing. Share the same story written in each perspective by you, a student, or the whole class (see the online resource Point of View). Here is an example.

- Display first-person and third-person writing.

  Here are some drafts of my writing. I wrote the same scene from both a first-person and third-person point of view. I did this so I could see which perspective is best for my story. This is like the work you have been doing as you write your own stories.

- Read the excerpt written in first person and invite students to share their noticings.

  What do you notice about the way I wrote this?

- Repeat with the excerpt written in third person.

  What do you notice about the way I wrote this?

  What is the same and different about these pieces of writing?

  How does the point of view affect the story?

  What questions might I consider as I choose which point of view to use in my final draft?

- Record responses on a new sheet of chart paper.

Have a Try

Invite students to talk to a partner about the point of view they are considering for their own writing.

> Share a draft of your writing with your partner. Discuss the point of view. Is it first person? third person? How does the perspective affect the story? Use the chart to help you decide which point of view to use in your final draft.

▶ After time for discussion, ask a few volunteers to share. Add new ideas to the chart.

Summarize and Apply

Summarize the learning and invite students to continue thinking about point of view as they write.

> What did you learn today about choosing a point of view for your writing?

▶ Write the principle at the top of the second chart.

> During independent writing time, think about the point of view you chose for your writing. If you decided to write in first person, think about how you might add inner thoughts to help develop your character. If you're writing in third person, think about how you might write from an onlooker's perspective. What more can you add?

Confer

▶ During independent writing, move around the room to confer briefly with students about the point of view of their writing. Use the following prompts as needed.

- *What are you writing about today? What is the point of view?*
- *How does writing from that point of view help your story?*
- *How did you decide which point of view to write from?*

Share

Following independent writing, gather students in the meeting area to share their writing.

> Who would like to share your writing today?

First-person point of view draft

This is my fourth year of surfing lessons. My instructor wants me to surf on my own. I've learned to read the waves and choose the best one.

"Are you ready, Sybil?" asked my instructor.

"Sure," I said. But I was thinking, "Not sure at all!"

Third-person point of view draft

This is Sybil's fourth year of surfing lessons. Her instructor says she is ready to surf on her own.

"Are you ready, Sybil?" asked the instructor.

"Sure," she said.

"Glad to hear it!" the instructor said as he handed Sybil a surfboard.

Choose the point of view that best fits your story.

First person	Third person
• How important is it for the reader to know inner thoughts?	• Do I want to create suspense?
• Do I want the main character to tell the story?	• Do I want the reader to know more about all the characters?
• How do I want my reader to connect to the main character?	• Which events do I want to zoom into?
• Does writing in first person help the story flow?	• Which events do I want to zoom out of?
	• Does writing in third person make my story flow?

Assessment

After you have taught the minilessons in this umbrella, observe students in a variety of classroom activities. Use *The Fountas & Pinnell Literacy Continuum* to notice, teach for, and support students' learning as you observe their attempts at writing.

▶ What evidence do you have of students' new understandings related to choosing a point of view?

- Do students demonstrate an ability to write in first and third person?
- Do they consider how the point of view of their writing affects the writing?
- Do they experiment with writing the same story in both first and then third person to decide which best serves the story?
- Are they using vocabulary such as *perspective*, *point of view*, *first person*, and *third person*?

▶ In what ways, beyond the scope of this umbrella, are students experimenting with craft decisions?

- Are students writing with voice in fiction and nonfiction?
- Do they use text features in nonfiction writing?

Use your observations to determine the next umbrella you will teach. You may also consult Suggested Sequence of Lessons (pp. 665–682) for guidance.

EXTENSIONS FOR CHOOSING A POINT OF VIEW

▶ Offer students opportunities to write from multiple perspectives in the same piece of writing.

▶ Offer students opportunities to further explore point of view by using personification. For example, they could write from the viewpoint of an animal or an object.

▶ As you read aloud both fiction and nonfiction texts, engage students in conversations about decisions the authors made regarding point of view.

Minilessons in This Umbrella

WML1 Speak directly to the reader.

WML2 Show your voice with punctuation and capitalization.

WML3 Show your voice with different styles of print.

WML4 Show your voice by saying things in a surprising way.

Before Teaching Umbrella 11 Minilessons

Voice is a characteristic that makes writing come alive. It is the authentic connection between talking and writing, so it is important to encourage students to read their writing aloud and listen to how it sounds. Students can learn to share their personalities through their writing by thinking about how authors do this in mentor texts. Support the link by helping them recognize that they can write in a way that is similar to talking but also understand that writing differs from talking. Before teaching, it is recommended that you teach CNV.U2: Learning About Punctuation and Capitalization so that students have an opportunity to explore using punctuation in traditional ways before trying it out as a way to show voice.

Use the books listed below from *Fountas & Pinnell Classroom*™ *Interactive Read-Aloud Collection* and *Shared Reading Collection*, or choose books from the classroom library. To help students see the print clearly, use enlarged texts, project a page of text, or write a sentence from the text on chart paper.

Interactive Read-Aloud Collection

Genre Study: Poetry

What Are You Glad About? What Are You Mad About? by Judith Viorst

Telling a Story with Photos

A Bear's Life by Nicholas Read

Exploring Identity

Crown: An Ode to the Fresh Cut by Derrick Barnes

Genre Study: Biography: Individuals Making a Difference

Farmer Will Allen and the Growing Table by Jacqueline Briggs Martin

Friendship

The Dunderheads by Paul Fleischman

Genre Study: Historical Fiction

Dad, Jackie, and Me by Myron Uhlberg

Shared Reading Collection

A Lifetime of Dance: A Biography of Katherine Dunham by Nnéka Nnolim

If Rivers Could Speak by Sherry Howard

A Spark of Genius: A Biography of Richard Turere by Myra Faye Turner

As you read and enjoy these texts together, help students notice techniques that authors use to infuse their writing with voice.

Interactive Read-Aloud
Poetry

Photos

A Bear's Life by Nicholas Read

Exploring Identity

Biography

Farmer Will Allen and the Growing Table by Jacqueline Briggs Martin

Friendship

Historical Fiction

Shared Reading

Writer's Notebook

Section 3: Craft

Writing Minilesson Principle
Speak directly to the reader.

Writing with Voice in Fiction and Nonfiction

You Will Need

- fiction and nonfiction mentor texts in which the author writes directly to readers, such as the following:
  - *What Are You Glad About? What Are You Mad About?* by Judith Viorst, from Text Set: Genre Study: Poetry
  - *A Bear's Life* by Nicholas Read, from Text Set: Telling a Story with Photos
  - *Crown* by Derrick Barnes, from Text Set: Exploring Identity
- chart paper prepared with a writing sample that speaks directly to readers
- writing folders
- To download the following online resource for this lesson, visit **fp.pub/resources**:
  - chart art (optional)

Academic Language / Important Vocabulary

- voice
- speak
- writing
- directly

Continuum Connection

- Write in an expressive way but also recognize how language in a book would sound
- Write in a way that speaks directly to the reader

GOAL

Write in a way that speaks directly to the reader.

RATIONALE

When students learn that writers can write in a way that speaks directly to readers, they begin to think about how their writing sounds and try to incorporate voice into their writing.

WRITER'S NOTEBOOK/WRITING FOLDER

Students will check pieces of writing in their writing folders for voice.

ASSESS LEARNING

- Notice whether students recognize that a writer can show voice by speaking directly to readers and that they can try to do the same in their own writing.
- Look for evidence that students can use vocabulary such as *voice*, *speak*, *writing*, and *directly*.

MINILESSON

To help students think about the minilesson principle, use mentor texts with writing that speaks directly to the reader. Here is an example.

- Show and read page 2 in *What Are You Glad About? What Are You Mad About?*

  How does Judith Viorst's writing sound?

- Help students notice that the writing sounds like she is speaking to her readers.

  Judith Viorst wrote these poems in a conversational way, the way you would talk to someone you know.

- Show and read pages 6 and 27 in *A Bear's Life*.

  How does this writing sound? Turn and talk to your partner about that.

- After time for discussion, ask volunteers to share their thinking. Guide the conversation to help students notice that it sounds like the writer is speaking directly to the readers.

- Show and read pages 25–26 in *Crown*.

  When the writer, Derrick Barnes, asks "You know why?," how do you know whom he is talking to?

- Guide the conversation so students recognize that the writer uses words to talk directly to the readers in the way he would talk to people he knows.

  A writer's voice is created by the words the writer chooses and the way the writer arranges the words into sentences. Voice is what makes your writing sound like you. One way you can show voice is by making your writing sound as if you were talking directly to readers.

Have a Try

Invite students to turn and talk about using voice in their writing by speaking directly to readers.

▶ Read the prepared chart paper.

> In what ways does this writing sound like it speaks directly to you, the readers? Turn and talk to your partner about that.

▶ After time for discussion, ask volunteers to come to the chart and point out parts that speak directly to the reader (questions, the word *you*).

Summarize and Apply

Summarize the learning. Have students try speaking directly to the reader as they write. Add the principle to the top of the chart.

> During independent writing time, look at pieces of writing in your writing folder. Choose one or two to quietly read aloud to yourself. Does your personality shine through? Would it work to make the writing sound like you are talking directly to your readers? If so, think about how you can revise your writing to add voice. Bring your writing to share when we meet later.

Speak directly to the reader.

Did you see those magic wheels my neighbor has? Papa says that if I work at the store this summer, I might earn enough money to buy my own board. Can't you just see me skating down the sidewalk? I would be as excited as my cat gets when she sees that red bird out the window. Nothing would be better than a new skateboard! Don't you agree?

Confer

▶ During independent writing, move around the room to confer briefly with students about voice. Use the following prompts as needed.

- *Read this sentence the way you want your readers to read it.*
- *How would you say this sentence to a friend? Try writing it that way.*
- *How are you showing your voice in this piece?*

Share

Following independent writing, gather students in the meeting area to share their writing.

> Find a part of your writing that sounds like you are speaking directly to your readers. Share what you wrote.

Writing Minilesson Principle
Show your voice with punctuation and capitalization.

Writing with Voice in Fiction and Nonfiction

You Will Need

- mentor texts with examples of punctuation and capitalization used to show voice, such as the following:
  - *Farmer Will Allen and the Growing Table* by Jacqueline Briggs Martin, from Text Set: Genre Study: Biography: Individuals Making a Difference
  - *A Lifetime of Dance* by Nnéka Nnolim, from *Shared Reading Collection*
- chart paper and markers
- writer's notebooks and/or writing folders

Academic Language / Important Vocabulary

- voice
- punctuation
- capitalization
- aloud
- sounds

Continuum Connection

- Use punctuation to make the text clear, effective, interesting, and to support voice
- Study mentor texts to learn the role of punctuation in adding voice to writing
- Notice the role of punctuation in the craft of writing

GOAL

Use punctuation and capitalization to convey meaning and support voice.

RATIONALE

When students learn they can play with punctuation and capitalization to convey meaning and support voice, they understand that writers have a variety of tools they can use to express themselves. Students might be inspired to experiment with punctuation and capitalization in their own writing.

WRITER'S NOTEBOOK/WRITING FOLDER

Make sure students have their writing folders and/or writer's notebooks so that during independent writing they can try out ways to show voice in their writing.

ASSESS LEARNING

- Examine students' writing to see whether they are experimenting with punctuation and capitalization to express voice.
- Look for evidence that students can use vocabulary such as *voice, punctuation, capitalization, aloud,* and *sounds.*

MINILESSON

To help students think about how writers use punctuation and capitalization to show voice, use mentor text examples and provide an interactive lesson. Here is an example.

- Show page 3 of *Farmer Will Allen and the Growing Table*.

  What do you notice about the words on the page?

- Support a conversation about how using capitalization for the word *laughing* conveys the idea that the word is important and should be emphasized. Talk about how the use of dashes shows emphasis. Read the page with emphasis as indicated by the punctuation and capitalization. As students talk, record text examples on chart paper.

  The use of punctuation and capitalization shows the writer's voice because the writer's personality shines through. It helps readers know how the writer wants the words to be read.

- Repeat with pages 7–8. Add examples to the chart.

- Show and read page 13.

  Talk about how the writer used punctuation and capitalization on this page.

- Support a discussion about how the writer used punctuation and capitalization to show voice. Add examples to the chart.

  Writers use punctuation and capitalization in certain ways to show their unique voices and personalities.

Have a Try

Invite students to turn and talk about how a writer uses punctuation and/or capitalization to show voice.

▶ Show and read a mentor text example, such as page 9 in *A Lifetime of Dance*.

> What do you notice about the print on this page? How does Nnéka Nnolim use it to show voice? Turn and talk about that.

▶ After time for discussion, ask students to share. Write the sentence on the chart. Have students read it aloud, emphasizing how the author uses punctuation to show voice.

Summarize and Apply

Summarize the learning. Have students remember to read their writing aloud to hear how it sounds and then try using punctuation or capitalization to show voice. Add the principle to the chart.

> Today when you write, check to see if your personality shines through. You may want to read aloud softly to yourself or to a friend. You might try using punctuation or capitalization to make the writing sound the way you want it to sound. Bring your writing to share when we meet later.

<table>
<tr><td colspan="2" align="center">Show your voice with
punctuation and capitalization.</td></tr>
<tr><td>Farmer
Will Allen</td><td>his favorite—lima beans with ham—

LAUGHING

Will believed everyone, everywhere, had a RIGHT to good food.

BUT HOW could Will farm in the middle of pavement and parking lots?

Will spotted six empty greenhouses on a plot of land about the size of a large supermarket, FOR SALE!

Will Allen bought that city lot!

Then one day - bad news: THE RED WIGGLER CREW WAS DYING.</td></tr>
<tr><td>A Lifetime
of Dance</td><td>Ah, the dancing! So different from ballet—like a new language!</td></tr>
</table>

Confer

▶ During independent writing, move around the room to confer briefly with students about voice. Use the following prompts as needed.

- *Read this page aloud. Does your writing sound the way you want it to sound?*
- *How can you use punctuation to show voice here?*
- *How should this part sound? Is there a way to show that with capitalization?*

Share

Following independent writing, gather students in the meeting area to share their writing.

> Choose a piece of your writing to read aloud to a partner. Ask your partner to listen to how it sounds. Then talk about what you did to make your voice come through in your writing.

Writing Minilesson Principle
Show your voice with different styles of print.

You Will Need

- several mentor texts with examples of different styles of print, such as the following:
  - *The Dunderheads* by Paul Fleischman, from Text Set: Friendship
  - *If Rivers Could Speak* by Sherry Howard, from *Shared Reading Collection*
- chart paper and markers
- writer's notebooks and/or writing folders

Academic Language / Important Vocabulary

- voice
- style
- font
- italics
- bold

Continuum Connection

- Use underlining, italics, and bold print to convey a specific meaning
- Use the size of print to convey meaning in printed text

GOAL

Use different styles of print to convey meaning and support voice.

RATIONALE

When students learn they can use different styles and sizes of print to convey meaning and support voice, they understand that writers have a variety of tools they can use to express themselves. Students might be inspired to use different styles of print in their own writing.

WRITER'S NOTEBOOK/WRITING FOLDER

Make sure students have their writing folders and/or writer's notebooks so that during independent writing they can try using styles of print to show voice in their writing.

ASSESS LEARNING

- Examine students' writing to see whether they are experimenting with styles of print to express voice.
- Look for evidence that students can use vocabulary such as *voice*, *style*, *font*, *italics*, and *bold*.

MINILESSON

To help students think about how writers use different styles of print to show voice, use mentor text examples and provide an interactive lesson. Here is an example.

- Show page 7 (the first spread) of *The Dunderheads*.

  What do you notice about the words on the page?

- Support a conversation about how the large size of the letters and the bold print convey the idea that these words are important and should be emphasized. Read the page with emphasis on those words. As students talk, write the word on chart paper in the font style of the word (e.g., use heavy, dark lettering to write the word *bold*).

  The type of print shows voice and helps the reader know how the writer wants the words to be read.

- Repeat as you continue revisiting the story. Add responses to the chart.

  Why do you think the writer decided to use different styles of print?

- Support a discussion about how print style affects voice. Point out that on a computer, different fonts as well as italics and underlining are available. With handwriting, underlining is most commonly used in place of italics.

Have a Try

Invite students to turn and talk about how a writer uses styles of print to show voice.

▶ Show and read page 14 in *If Rivers Could Speak*.

How does Sherry Howard use print to show voice? Turn and talk about that.

▶ After time for discussion, ask students to share. Add new ideas to the chart list. Have students read the words aloud, aiming to read them the way the writer intended.

▶ Leave the list posted and add any new print styles that students notice or use in their own writing.

Summarize and Apply

Summarize the learning. Have students try using different styles of print to show voice.

How can you add voice to your writing?

▶ Write the principle at the top of the chart.

Today during independent writing time, read your writing aloud to see if your personality shines through. You might decide to try different styles of print in your writer's notebook or in a piece from your writing folder. Bring your writing when we meet later.

Show your voice with different styles of print.
Bold
Size
Italics
Placement on page
Color
<u>Underline</u>

Confer

▶ During independent writing, move around the room to confer briefly with students about voice. Use the following prompts as needed.

- *How can you use a different style of print here?*
- *How should this part sound? Is there a way to show that with print?*
- *Can you read this part aloud?*

Share

Following independent writing, gather students in the meeting area. Ask a few volunteers to share their writing.

Who would like to share how your writing shows your voice? Share what you wrote.

Look at the chart. What print style would you like to try using in your writing next?

WML4

CFT.U11.WML4

Writing Minilesson Principle
Show your voice by saying things in a surprising way.

Writing with Voice in Fiction and Nonfiction

You Will Need

- several mentor texts with examples of surprising writing, such as the following:
  - *A Spark of Genius* by Myra Faye Turner and *If Rivers Could Speak* by Sherry Howard, from *Shared Reading Collection*.
  - *Dad, Jackie, and Me* by Myron Uhlberg, from Text Set: Genre Study: Historical Fiction
- chart paper and markers
- document camera (optional)
- writer's notebooks and/or writing folders
- To download the following online resource for this lesson, visit **fp.pub/resources**:
  - chart art (optional)

Academic Language / Important Vocabulary

- voice
- surprising

Continuum Connection

- Use memorable words or phrases

GOAL

Use surprise in writing to convey voice.

RATIONALE

When students learn to use an element of surprise in their writing, their personality and voice shine through and their writing is elevated. Helping students notice how writers use surprise adds to their enjoyment of both reading and writing.

WRITER'S NOTEBOOK/WRITING FOLDER

Make sure students have their writing folders or writer's notebooks so that during independent writing they can try out using surprising language.

ASSESS LEARNING

- Observe whether students sometimes use elements of surprise in their writing.
- Look for evidence that students can use vocabulary such as *voice* and *surprising*.

MINILESSON

To help students think about the minilesson principle, use mentor text examples that have an element of surprise and provide an interactive lesson. Here is an example.

> Listen as I read from *A Spark of Genius*.

- Show and read a few pages.

  > What are your thoughts about how the author, Myra Faye Turner, has written this biography?

  > What choices have been made that are surprising for the reader?

- Support a conversation about how it is surprising to hear figurative and rhythmic language in a biography. Begin a list on chart paper of the different ways surprise has been used, using general terms.

- Repeat with pages 9–10 in *Dad, Jackie, and Me*.

  > Let's take a look at how the author, Myron Uhlberg, has written in a surprising way.

- Show and read pages 9–10.

  > What do you notice?

- Add to chart.

  > Including something surprising is one way that voice can be used to show personality in your writing. These authors have written about a person (biography) and about a time in history (historical fiction) in an interesting way that the reader might not expect.

Have a Try

Invite students to turn and talk about how a writer uses surprise to show voice.

▶ Show and read a few pages of *If Rivers Could Speak*.

What do you notice about how voice is shown by saying things in a surprising way? Turn and talk about that.

▶ After time for discussion, ask students to share. Add new ideas to the chart. Support a conversation to talk about other ways a writer might show voice by writing things in a surprising way. Add to the chart.

Summarize and Apply

Summarize the learning. Have students try using surprise to show voice.

What is another way to show your voice in your writing?

▶ Write the principle at the top of the chart.

Today during independent writing time, look for a place to write about something in a surprising way in your writer's notebook or in a piece you are working on in your writing folder. Bring your writing when we meet later.

Show your voice by saying things in a surprising way.

Poetic language used for nonfiction, biography, or history

Unusual behavior

Sudden change

Descriptive or silly language

Surprise twist

Exaggeration

Narrator is not a person (personification)

Confer

▶ During independent writing, move around the room to confer briefly with students about voice. Use the following prompts as needed.

• *How can you write that in a surprising way?*

• *What is something surprising this character might say?*

• *Is there a way to exaggerate this idea to make it surprising?*

• *You are working on a nonfiction writing piece. What can you write about in a surprising way that your readers might not expect?*

Share

Following independent writing, gather students in the meeting area. Ask a few volunteers to share their writing.

In groups of three, share a part of your writing that shows your voice.

Assessment

After you have taught the minilessons in this umbrella, observe students in a variety of classroom activities. Use *The Fountas & Pinnell Literacy Continuum* to notice, teach for, and support students' learning as you observe their attempts at writing.

▶ What evidence do you have of students' new understandings related to voice?

- Can students articulate what it means to write with voice?

- Are they trying ways to write with voice—speaking directly to the reader, using punctuation and capitalization in specific ways, using different print styles, and writing in a surprising way?

- Do they read their own writing aloud to hear how it sounds and revise if necessary?

- Are they using vocabulary such as *voice*, *speak*, *writing*, *directly*, *punctuation*, *style*, *capitalization*, *font*, *italics*, *bold*, and *surprising*?

▶ In what ways, beyond the scope of this umbrella, are students' reading and writing behaviors showing an understanding of voice?

- Are students looking for ways to make powerful word choices?

- Do they try out different points of view in their writing?

Use your observations to determine the next umbrella you will teach. You may also consult Suggested Sequence of Lessons (pp. 665–682) for guidance.

EXTENSIONS FOR WRITING WITH VOICE IN FICTION AND NONFICTION

▶ Encourage students to select different fonts and font sizes when they write on a computer. Encourage creative use of fonts and print styles but also caution against their overuse.

▶ Pull together a temporary guided writing group of a few students who need further support in understanding and using voice in their writing.

▶ Use shared writing to create a class story. Experiment with different capitalization, punctuation, or print styles on one or more sentences from the story. Talk about how changing the punctuation or print style affects how the words are to be read.

▶ Find ways to encourage students to listen to their inner voice so that they can use writing as a way to explore and give it value.

▶ If you are using *The Reading Minilessons Book, Grade 4* (Fountas and Pinnell 2020) you may choose to teach LA.U10: Reading Like a Writer: Analyzing the Writer's Craft.

Minilessons in This Umbrella

WML1	Notice why authors use different text features.
WML2	Use headings and subheadings to tell what a part is about.
WML3	Use sidebars to give extra information.
WML4	Write captions under pictures.
WML5	Use timelines to give information in chronological order.

Before Teaching Umbrella 12 Minilessons

Consider providing a mentor text that students can relate to by writing your own informational text or by using shared writing to write one with the class. We recommend that you teach this umbrella alongside a genre study of nonfiction (e.g., feature articles or any other type of informational text) so that students have authentic opportunities to apply the learning to their current writing. However, students can also apply the techniques they learn in these minilessons by revising a piece of nonfiction they have written previously, or they can experiment with the techniques in their writer's notebooks.

Read and discuss engaging nonfiction books with a variety of text features, including headings, subheadings, sidebars, captions, and timelines. Use the following texts from *Fountas & Pinnell Classroom™ Interactive Read-Aloud Collection* and *Shared Reading Collection,* or choose nonfiction books with text features from the classroom or school library.

Interactive Read-Aloud Collection

Telling a Story with Photos

Face to Face with Whales by Flip and Linda Nicklin

Biography: Artists

Me, Frida by Amy Novesky

Illustration Study: Craft

Magnificent Birds by Narisa Togo

Innovative Thinking and Creative Problem Solving

One Plastic Bag: Isatou Ceesay and the Recycling Women of the Gambia by Miranda Paul

Shared Reading Collection

Pangaea: The World's Biggest Puzzle by Susan B. Katz

As you read and enjoy these texts together, help students

- notice headings and subheadings and talk about what each page or section is about, and

- discuss information provided in sidebars, captions, and timelines.

Interactive Read-Aloud
Telling a Story with Photos

Face to Face with Whales by Flip and Linda Nicklin

Biography: Artists

Illustration Study: Craft

Innovative Thinking

Shared Reading

Writer's Notebook

Section 3: Craft

Writing Minilesson Principle
Notice why authors use different text features.

Using Text Features in Nonfiction Writing

You Will Need

- a familiar nonfiction book with several different kinds of text features, such as *Face to Face with Whales* by Flip and Linda Nicklin, from Text Set: Telling a Story with Photos
- several other nonfiction books and magazines with a variety of text features
- chart paper and markers
- writer's notebooks

Academic Language / Important Vocabulary

- heading
- subheading
- sidebar
- caption
- timeline
- text feature

Continuum Connection

- Incorporate book and print features (e.g., labeled pictures, diagrams, table of contents, headings, subheadings, sidebars, page numbers) into nonfiction writing

GOAL

Identify a variety of text features and understand why writers choose to use them.

RATIONALE

When students notice text features in nonfiction books and think about why the author chose to include them, they will begin to use text features in their own nonfiction texts in meaningful ways. They will model their own text features on those they have seen in books they have read.

WRITER'S NOTEBOOK/WRITING FOLDER

As students study text features in nonfiction books, have them take notes on their findings in their writer's notebooks.

ASSESS LEARNING

- Observe students as they read and talk about nonfiction books.
- Notice whether students can identify common text features and explain their purpose.
- Look for evidence that they can use vocabulary such as *heading, subheading, sidebar, caption, timeline,* and *text feature.*

MINILESSON

To help students think about the principle, use a familiar nonfiction book with a variety of text features to engage students in an inquiry-based lesson on text features. Here is an example.

- Show the cover of *Face to Face with Whales* and read the title. Show pages 6–7. Point to the main text on the pages.

  This is the main text in the book. It's written in paragraphs, and it tells most of the information in the book. How else do the authors give you information?

- Draw students' attention to the sidebar on page 6.

  This is called a sidebar. This sidebar is about sea monsters.

  Why do you think the authors put a sidebar about sea monsters here?

  Why do authors sometimes include sidebars in nonfiction books?

- Record students' responses about the purpose of sidebars on chart paper.
- Point to the captions on pages 6–7.

  Does anyone know what this text feature is called?

  These are captions. Why do authors use captions?

  Where do you see captions in a book?

- Record responses on the chart.

Have a Try

Invite students to talk to a partner about another text feature.

▶ Turn to page 28 of *Face to Face with Whales*. Point to the heading and subheadings.

> What do you notice about these words? What is this text feature called, and why did the authors use it? Turn and talk to your partner about this.

▶ After time for discussion, invite a few pairs to share their thinking. Add their responses to the chart.

Summarize and Apply

Write the principle at the top of the chart. Summarize the learning and invite students to study text features in nonfiction texts.

> Today you noticed some different types of text features, like sidebars, captions, headings, and subheadings. Text features are the parts of a text that are separate from the main text and give readers more information. During independent writing time, look through a nonfiction book, magazine, or online article with a partner. See what text features you can find, and talk about what you notice about them. Take notes in your writer's notebook about what you notice. Bring your notes to share when we come back together.

▶ Give each pair of students at least one nonfiction book or magazine to study.

Notice why authors use different text features.	
Sidebar	To give extra information about the main text
	To give information on a slightly different but related topic
Caption	To explain what is shown in the picture (usually a photograph)
Heading Subheading	To organize information and to indicate the category of information that will follow
Timeline	To show the order of when important things happened
Table of Contents Index	To help readers find information quickly
Glossary	To explain the meaning of words readers might not know
Bibliography	To show the resources used to find information for the book

Confer

▶ During independent writing, move around the room to confer briefly with students about text features. Use prompts such as the following as needed.

- *What is this feature called? What does it tell you about?*
- *Why do you think the author included a _____ on this page?*

Share

Following independent writing, gather students in the meeting area and invite partners to share what they noticed about text features. Add any new features mentioned to the chart.

> What kinds of text features did you notice?

Writing Minilesson Principle
Use headings and subheadings to tell what a part is about.

You Will Need

- a familiar nonfiction book that has headings and subheadings, such as *Face to Face with Whales* by Flip and Linda Nicklin, from Text Set: Telling a Story with Photos
- chart paper prepared with text to which a heading and subheadings will be added (see chart)
- chart paper and markers
- writing folders

Academic Language / Important Vocabulary

- nonfiction
- heading
- subheading

Continuum Connection

- Use headings, subheadings, a table of contents, and other features to help the reader find information and understand how facts are related in expository writing
- Incorporate book and print features (e.g., labeled pictures, diagrams, table of contents, headings, subheadings, sidebars, page numbers) into nonfiction writing
- Use layout, spacing, and size of print to create titles, headings, and subheadings

GOAL

Understand the purpose of headings and subheadings and use them in writing.

RATIONALE

When you help students notice headings and subheadings in nonfiction books, they begin to understand that authors group together related details on a page or in a paragraph or a section. They learn to structure their own nonfiction texts in a similar way and to use headings and subheadings to help readers know what to expect.

WRITER'S NOTEBOOK/WRITING FOLDER

Students will work on adding headings and subheadings to longer pieces of nonfiction in their writing folders.

ASSESS LEARNING

- Observe students as they talk about nonfiction texts. What do they understand about headings and subheadings?
- Notice whether students use headings and subheadings in their own nonfiction texts.
- Look for evidence that they can use vocabulary such as *nonfiction*, *heading*, and *subheading*.

MINILESSON

To help students think about the minilesson principle as they write nonfiction pieces, engage them in an inquiry-based lesson on headings and subheadings. Then demonstrate how to add headings and subheadings to a piece of writing that does not already have them. Here is an example.

- Show pages 28–29 of *Face to Face with Whales*.

    Where is the heading on these pages?

    Where are the subheadings?

    How do the heading and subheadings look different?

- Point to and read aloud the heading on page 28.

    What is this part of the book about?

- Point to and read aloud one of the subheadings.

    What is this paragraph about?

    Why do authors use headings and subheadings?

    How do headings and subheadings help you when you read nonfiction?

- Record students' responses on chart paper.

Have a Try

Invite students to talk to a partner about adding headings and subheadings.

▶ Display the prepared chart paper. Read or have students read the text.

> Turn and talk to your partner about a heading and subheadings for this piece of writing.

▶ After time for discussion, invite a few pairs to share their responses. Agree on a heading and subheading(s) and add them to the chart.

Summarize and Apply

Summarize the learning and remind students to think about using headings and subheadings in nonfiction.

> Why do nonfiction authors use headings and subheadings?

▶ Write the principle at the top of the first chart.

> You can use headings and subheadings in your own nonfiction writing. During independent writing time today, try adding headings and subheadings to a nonfiction writing project that you're currently working on or have already written. Bring your writing to share when we come back together.

Confer

▶ During independent writing, move around the room to confer briefly with students about their nonfiction writing. Use prompts such as the following as needed.

- *What heading could you add to help readers know what to expect?*
- *Would it make sense to add any subheadings to this page? Where?*
- *How will you make your headings and subheadings stand out?*

Share

Following independent writing, gather students in the meeting area to share their writing.

> Tell about the headings and subheadings you wrote.

Use headings and subheadings to tell what a part is about.

What are headings and subheadings?

- <u>Headings</u> tell what a page or section is about.

- Subheadings tell what a small section or paragraph is about.

- Headings and subheadings help readers find information.

- Headings and subheadings help readers know what to expect.

- Headings and subheadings help you organize your ideas when you're writing.

- Headings give a big idea, and subheadings give smaller, related ideas.

Endangered Whales

Many species of whales are endangered. Some whales could become extinct.

North Atlantic Right Whales

The North Atlantic right whale, a baleen whale, is one of the most endangered whales in the ocean. The whales were hunted almost to extinction by the 1890s because people considered them the "right" whale to hunt.

North Pacific Right Whales

The North Pacific right whale, a toothed whale, is also endangered. Scientists think there are probably fewer than five hundred of these whales left.

Writing Minilesson Principle
Use sidebars to give extra information.

You Will Need

- a couple of familiar nonfiction books that have sidebars, such as the following:
  - *Face to Face with Whales* by Flip and Linda Nicklin, from Text Set: Telling a Story with Photos
  - *Pangaea* by Susan B. Katz, from *Shared Reading Collection*
- a page from a familiar nonfiction book without a sidebar, or a sample nonfiction book written by you or the whole class
- chart paper and markers
- writing folders

Academic Language / Important Vocabulary

- sidebar
- nonfiction
- information
- author

Continuum Connection

- Incorporate book and print features (e.g., labeled pictures, diagrams, table of contents, headings, subheadings, sidebars, page numbers) into nonfiction writing

GOAL

Understand how to use sidebars to give extra information.

RATIONALE

When you help students notice and think about sidebars in nonfiction texts, they learn that they, too, can use sidebars to give extra information in their own books. They begin to think about what other information readers might need or want to know about the topic.

WRITER'S NOTEBOOK/WRITING FOLDER

Students will work on adding sidebars to informational texts in their writing folders.

ASSESS LEARNING

- Listen to students as they talk about nonfiction books. What do they understand about sidebars?
- Notice whether students include sidebars in their own nonfiction texts.
- Look for evidence that they can use vocabulary such as *sidebar*, *nonfiction*, *information*, and *author*.

MINILESSON

To help students think about the minilesson principle, engage them in an inquiry-based lesson on sidebars in familiar nonfiction books. Then demonstrate how to create a sidebar for an existing text. Here is an example.

- Show the cover of *Face to Face with Whales* and read the title. Read aloud pages 6–7. Point to and read the sidebar on page 6.

  What do you notice about this part of the page? How do these words look different from the other words on the page?

  These words that are off to the side of the page in a different font are called a sidebar. Sometimes, sidebars are placed in boxes, though not in this book. What does this sidebar have to do with the other information?

  The main text is about the author's first experience observing whales underwater. The sidebar is about what makes whales seem like sea monsters. The sidebar information is related to but doesn't fit in the main text.

- Read aloud page 5 of *Pangaea*, including the sidebar.

  How does the information in this sidebar relate to the main text on the page?

  You can use sidebars in your own nonfiction texts. What should you think about when you make a sidebar?

- Record responses on chart paper.

Have a Try

Invite students to talk to a partner about what to write in a sidebar.

▶ Display a page from a nonfiction text without sidebars, such as page 19 of *Face to Face with Whales*.

> This page doesn't have a sidebar. If the authors wanted to add a sidebar to this page, what could they write about in it? Turn and talk to your partner about your ideas.

▶ After time for discussion, invite several pairs to share their ideas. Demonstrate writing the sidebar on a new sheet of chart paper or on a sticky note that you will attach to the book.

Summarize and Apply

Summarize the learning and remind students to think about including sidebars when they write nonfiction.

> Why do authors sometimes include sidebars in nonfiction texts?

▶ Write the principle at the top of the chart.

> Today during independent writing time, try adding a sidebar to a nonfiction writing project that you're currently working on or have already written. Think about what extra information the reader might need or want to know. Bring your writing to share when we come back together.

Confer

▶ During independent writing, move around the room to confer briefly with students about adding sidebars to their nonfiction writing. Use prompts such as the following as needed.

- *What are you writing about?*
- *What else might readers need or want to know about that? Do you know any fun facts related to that?*
- *Where on the page will you put the sidebar?*
- *How can you make the sidebar look different from the main text?*

Share

Following independent writing, gather students in the meeting area to share their writing.

> Who would like to share a sidebar you added to a nonfiction text today?

> How did you decide what to write in the sidebar and where to put it?

Sidebar charts

Use sidebars to give extra information.

- Think about what else readers might want or need to know about the topic.
- Use a sidebar to give extra facts or information.
- Make sure the sidebar relates to the topic or idea in the main text.
- Think about how you can make the sidebar look different from the main text.

> **Did You Know?**
> Sidebars can come in different shapes, sizes, and colors.

More About Krill...
Most krill are about the size of a paper clip. You may be wondering how an animal as big as a blue whale can survive by eating an animal so small. The answer: by eating tons of them. Literally. Blue whales eat up to four tons of krill every day!

Writing Minilesson Principle
Write captions under pictures.

You Will Need

- a familiar nonfiction book that has captions, such as *Face to Face with Whales* by Flip and Linda Nicklin, from Text Set: Telling a Story with Photos
- a sample nonfiction text written by you or the whole class (through shared writing) with an illustration but no caption
- chart paper and markers
- writing folders

Academic Language / Important Vocabulary

- nonfiction
- information
- caption

Continuum Connection

- Incorporate book and print features (e.g., labeled pictures, diagrams, table of contents, headings, subheadings, sidebars, page numbers) into nonfiction writing

GOAL

Write captions that enhance readers' understanding of a picture and how it relates to the text.

RATIONALE

When students notice and think about captions in nonfiction books, they learn that they can add captions to images to give additional important information that cannot be gleaned from the main text or the image itself. They develop the ability to communicate information through different types of writing.

WRITER'S NOTEBOOK/WRITING FOLDER

Students will work on adding captions to the illustrations in informational texts in their writing folders.

ASSESS LEARNING

- Look for evidence that students understand the purpose of captions and can distinguish them from other types of text.
- Notice whether students include clear and meaningful captions in their own nonfiction texts.
- Look for evidence that they can use vocabulary such as *nonfiction*, *information*, and *caption*.

MINILESSON

Students will need access to nonfiction writing that they are currently working on or have finished. To help students think about the minilesson principle, use a mentor text to engage them in a discussion about captions. Then use shared writing to model adding a caption to an image. Here is an example.

- Turn to page 7 of *Face to Face with Whales*. Point to and read aloud the caption.

  What is this text feature called?

  What is a caption?

  A caption is a group of words near an illustration or photograph that tells more about it. What does this caption help you understand?

- Continue in a similar manner with the caption on page 9.

  Why is it important to include captions in nonfiction books?

- Help students understand that captions add information that readers cannot obtain simply by looking at the illustration or reading the main text.

- Display a class-written nonfiction text or a sample text written by you. Read one page aloud. Help students compose a caption for the illustration.

  We wrote this page about how birds see. We included an illustration of a kingfisher. What could we write in the caption to help readers understand why we included this illustration? What do we want readers to know?

Have a Try

Invite students to talk to a partner about captions.

▶ Make sure students have access to a nonfiction text they are working on or have already written.

> Look through your writing and see if you can find an illustration to which you could add an interesting caption. What might you write? Turn and talk to your partner about your ideas.

▶ After students turn and talk, invite a few students to share their ideas.

Summarize and Apply

Write the principle at the top of the chart. Summarize the learning and remind students to think about including captions when they write nonfiction.

> How are captions helpful for readers?

> During independent writing time today, try adding at least one caption to a nonfiction writing project that you're currently working on or have already written. Think about what information readers might need or want to know about your illustrations. Bring your writing to share when we come back together.

Write captions under pictures.

Have you ever wondered why some birds have eyes on the sides of their head? It may seem like it would be hard for them to see where they are going. Having eyes on the side helps non-predatory birds, like parrots and pigeons, focus each eye on a different object so they can see predators. This type of vision is called monocular vision.

Predatory birds, such as owls, have eyes on the front of their head. Both of their eyes work together. This is known as binocular vision. Focusing both eyes on the same object helps makes it easier to spot and capture small prey.

The common kingfisher has both monocular and binocular vision. It uses monocular vision in the air to stay safe and binocular vision in the water to hunt fish.

Confer

▶ During independent writing, move around the room to confer briefly with students about writing captions. Use prompts such as the following as needed.

- *What does this illustration show?*
- *Why did you include this illustration on this page?*
- *What might readers need or want to know about this illustration?*
- *What could you write in the caption?*

Share

Following independent writing, gather students in the meeting area to share their writing.

> Who would like to share a caption you wrote?

> Why did you decide to include that information in your caption?

WML5
CFT.U12.WML5

Writing Minilesson Principle
Use timelines to give information in chronological order.

Using Text Features in Nonfiction Writing

You Will Need

- a familiar nonfiction book with a timeline, such as *One Plastic Bag* by Miranda Paul, from Text Set: Innovative Thinking and Creative Problem Solving

- a familiar nonfiction book that could benefit from the addition of a timeline, such as *Me, Frida* by Amy Novesky, from Text Set: Biography: Artists

- a familiar nonfiction book that would not benefit from the addition of a timeline, such as *Magnificent Birds* by Narisa Togo, from Text Set: Illustration Study: Craft

- chart paper and markers

- writing folders

Academic Language / Important Vocabulary

- nonfiction

- timeline

- information

- chronological

Continuum Connection

- Incorporate book and print features (e.g., labeled pictures, diagrams, table of contents, headings, subheadings, sidebars, page numbers) into nonfiction writing

GOAL

Understand how to use and develop timelines to give information.

RATIONALE

When students notice and think about timelines in nonfiction books, they learn that they too can include timelines in their nonfiction texts to help readers understand and remember the dates of important events as well as understand patterns and relationships between events.

WRITER'S NOTEBOOK/WRITING FOLDER

Students will work on adding a timeline to an informational text in their writing folders.

ASSESS LEARNING

- Look for evidence that students understand the purpose of timelines and can distinguish them from other types of text features.

- Notice whether students include timelines in their nonfiction texts, when appropriate.

- Look for evidence that they can use vocabulary such as *nonfiction*, *timeline*, *information*, and *chronological*.

MINILESSON

Students will need their writing folders for this lesson. To help them think about the minilesson principle, use a mentor text to engage students in a discussion about timelines. Then use shared writing to model creating a timeline. Here is an example.

- Show the cover of *One Plastic Bag* and read the title. Display the timeline near the end of the book. Read the heading and the first few entries.

  > This is a type of text feature called a timeline. What does a timeline show?

  > A timeline shows important events and the dates on which they happened. The dates are arranged in chronological order, or in time order. How is the information in this timeline different from the information in the rest of the book?

  > How does this timeline help you better understand the topic of the book?

- Show the covers of *Me, Frida* and *Magnificent Birds*.

  > Neither of these nonfiction books have timelines. Let's add a timeline to one of them. In which book would a timeline be more helpful for readers? Why?

- Help students understand that timelines are useful in books that tell the history of a person or event—something for which dates are important.

  > What could we include in a timeline about Frida Kahlo?

- Use shared writing to create a timeline on chart paper.

Have a Try

Invite students to talk to a partner about timelines.

▶ Make sure students have their writing folders.

> Look through your writing folder and see if you can find a nonfiction text you have written that would benefit from a timeline. Then turn and talk to your partner about which part of the text you could add a timeline to and why.

▶ After time for discussion, invite a few students to share their thinking.

Summarize and Apply

Summarize the learning and remind students to think about including timelines when they write nonfiction.

> Why do nonfiction authors sometimes include timelines? How are timelines helpful for readers?

▶ Write the principle at the top of the chart.

> During independent writing time today, add a timeline to a nonfiction writing project you are currently working on or have already written. Bring your writing to share when we come back together.

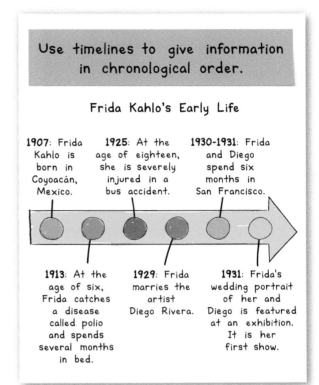

Use timelines to give information in chronological order.

Frida Kahlo's Early Life

1907: Frida Kahlo is born in Coyoacán, Mexico.

1925: At the age of eighteen, she is severely injured in a bus accident.

1930-1931: Frida and Diego spend six months in San Francisco.

1913: At the age of six, Frida catches a disease called polio and spends several months in bed.

1929: Frida marries the artist Diego Rivera.

1931: Frida's wedding portrait of her and Diego is featured at an exhibition. It is her first show.

Section 3: Craft

Confer

▶ During independent writing, move around the room to confer briefly with students about creating timelines. Use prompts such as the following as needed.

- *Which nonfiction text of yours would you like to add a timeline to? Why that one?*
- *What events could you include in the timeline?*
- *What information can you give readers that they won't get from the main text?*
- *What will the timeline help readers understand?*

Share

Following independent writing, gather students in the meeting area to share their timelines.

▶ Have students share their timelines with a partner.

Assessment

After you have taught the minilessons in this umbrella, observe students as they write and talk about their writing. Use *The Fountas & Pinnell Literacy Continuum* to notice, teach for, and support students' learning as you observe their attempts at writing.

▶ What evidence do you have of students' new understandings related to using text features in nonfiction writing?

- Do students use headings and subheadings to tell what each part of a nonfiction text is about?

- Do they use sidebars, captions, and timelines to give extra information in meaningful ways?

- Do students understand and use vocabulary such as *heading*, *subheading*, *sidebar*, *caption*, and *timeline*?

▶ In what other ways, beyond the scope of this umbrella, are students ready to develop their nonfiction writing?

- Are students experimenting with using different types of graphics in nonfiction?

- Do they need more support to make their nonfiction writing clear and interesting?

Use your observations to determine the next umbrella you will teach. You may also consult Suggested Sequence of Lessons (pp. 665–682) for guidance.

EXTENSIONS FOR USING TEXT FEATURES IN NONFICTION WRITING

▶ Guide students to notice other types of text features in nonfiction texts, such as tables of contents, glossaries, and indexes, and help them make their own.

▶ Teach students how to make headings, subheadings, sidebars, timelines, and other text features on a computer.

Minilessons in This Umbrella

WML1 Use description to give readers a picture in their minds.

WML2 Tell how two things are the same or different.

WML3 Tell about an experience from your life to teach more about a topic.

WML4 Select fascinating facts.

Before Teaching Umbrella 13 Minilessons

Before teaching the minilessons in this umbrella, it would be helpful to teach the first minilessons in WPS.U8: Adding Information to Your Writing so students understand the mechanics of revising text.

Continue to display charts created in the course of teaching umbrellas related to nonfiction writing to remind students that they will use what they have already learned about nonfiction writing alongside these new techniques. Consider writing your own nonfiction piece or writing one with the students through shared writing to use as an example in these minilessons.

Read and discuss engaging nonfiction books. Use the following texts from *Fountas & Pinnell Classroom™ Interactive Read-Aloud Collection*, or choose nonfiction books from your classroom library.

Interactive Read-Aloud Collection

Illustration Study: Craft

Magnificent Birds by Narisa Togo

Dingo by Claire Saxby

Eye to Eye: How Animals See the World by Steve Jenkins

Telling a Story with Photos

Wolf Island by Nicholas Read

Face to Face with Whales by Flip and Linda Nicklin

The Seal Garden by Nicholas Read

As you read and enjoy these texts together, help students

- notice descriptive language authors use to help readers picture more about a topic,

- notice how authors compare or contrast things,

- think about how the author chooses what information will capture readers' attention, and

- consider the breadth of ideas that authors share about one topic as a way to understand how much one can write on a topic.

Interactive Read-Aloud
Illustration Study: Craft

Telling a Story with Photos

Wolf Island by Nicholas Read

Face to Face with Whales by Flip and Linda Nicklin

The Seal Garden by Nicholas Read

Writer's Notebook

Section 3: Craft

WML1
CFT.U13.WML1

Writing Minilesson Principle
Use description to give readers a picture in their minds.

Making Nonfiction Writing Interesting

You Will Need

- several familiar nonfiction books, such as the following:
  - *Eye to Eye* by Steve Jenkins, from Text Set: Illustration Study: Craft
  - *Face to Face with Whales* by Flip and Linda Nicklin, from Text Set: Telling a Story with Photos
- writer's notebooks
- chart paper prepared with three headings and text excerpts (see first chart)
- chart paper and markers

Academic Language / Important Vocabulary

- description
- describe
- details

Continuum Connection

- Introduce ideas followed by supportive details and examples
- Use memorable words or phrases
- Use range of descriptive words to enhance meaning
- Tell about a topic in an interesting way
- Select information that will support the topic
- Select details that will support a topic or story
- Add words, phrases, or sentences to provide more information to readers

---

GOAL

Use descriptive details to create a picture for readers.

RATIONALE

The goal of a nonfiction writer is to convey information about a topic. To do this, the writer must use detailed, descriptive language to help readers picture what the writing is about.

WRITER'S NOTEBOOK/WRITING FOLDER

Have students sketch in their writer's notebooks what they picture in their minds when they hear descriptive language.

ASSESS LEARNING

- Observe students as they talk about nonfiction books. Do they understand why writers use descriptive details?
- Notice whether students add descriptive details to their own writing.
- Look for evidence that students can use vocabulary such as *description*, *describe*, and *details*.

MINILESSON

Make sure students have their writer's notebooks or paper for sketching. To help students think about the minilesson principle, engage them in noticing descriptive details in a familiar nonfiction book and sketching what they see in their minds. Here is an example.

- Show the cover of *Eye to Eye*. Read page 24. Draw attention to the excerpt on the chart.

  What do you picture in your mind? Make a quick sketch in your writer's notebook.

- After a brief time, ask several students to share their sketches, talk about how they knew what to draw, and tell what the writer described.

  Tell about your picture. How did the writer help you know what to draw?

- Record students' responses in the columns on the prepared chart paper.

- Repeat this process with *Face to Face with Whales*, using the caption at the top of page 15 and the sidebar on page 17.

- Guide students to think about using descriptive details that create a picture in their own writing.

  What are some things you can do as a writer to think about what words to use to give the reader a picture of an idea?

- Add ideas to a new sheet of chart paper.

Have a Try

Invite students to talk to a partner about using descriptive details in their nonfiction writing.

> I want to help my readers understand what it looks and sounds like when a baby giraffe calls to its mother. I will act that out for you. Watch and listen.

> What could I write to help my readers picture how the baby giraffe looks and sounds when it looks for its mother? Turn and talk about that.

▶ After students turn and talk, invite several pairs to share their ideas. Agree on a few sentences and add them to the second chart. Note that students could watch a video for ideas.

Summarize and Apply

Help students summarize the learning. Remind them that they can use description in their own books to help readers picture the topic.

> What can you do to help your readers understand more about your topic?

▶ Write the principle at the top of the second chart.

> Today as you write, think about what you can do to help your readers picture your topic. Think about how looking at a book, making a quick sketch in your writer's notebook, or acting something out can help you describe something in writing. Be prepared to share your writing with a partner.

What Flip and Linda Nicklin Wrote	What You Picture in Your Mind	What You Understand
Built-in goggles The hippopotamus... can see well underwater, where its eyes are protected by a special clear membrane.	A hippo with goggles and open eyes	How hippos see underwater
[Beluga whales] communicate with squeaks, squeals, chirps, barks, whistles, or moans, which is why they were once called "sea canaries."	A large canary singing	How a beluga whale sounds
Imagine taking a giant mouthful of cereal and milk. If you closed your teeth and squeezed the milk out, trapping the cereal inside, you would be eating like a baleen whale.	A child with a closed mouth and milk slipping out	How a baleen whale eats

Use description to give readers a picture in their minds.

Ways to Write a Good Description

- Make a quick sketch.
- Think about what it looks or sounds like.
- Look at a picture in a book.
- Act out the ideas.

When a baby giraffe is looking for its mother, it walks around. It might gallop and move in circles. As it walks it calls out. If you close your eyes, it sounds as if a young cow is mooing.

Confer

▶ During independent writing, move around the room to confer briefly with students about expanding their nonfiction writing. Use prompts such as the following as needed.

- *What do you want to help your readers understand about your topic? How could you describe that to help readers picture it?*
- *Draw a quick sketch of that idea. What words will help your readers picture it?*
- *Act out that idea. What words will help your readers picture it?*

Share

Following independent writing, gather students in the meeting area to share their writing with a partner before sharing with the class.

> Who would like to share how you used description?

Writing Minilesson Principle
Tell how two things are the same or different.

Making Nonfiction Writing Interesting

You Will Need

- several familiar nonfiction books, such as the following:
  - *Dingo* by Claire Saxby, from Text Set: Illustration Study: Craft
  - *The Seal Garden* and *Wolf Island* by Nicholas Read, from Text Set: Telling a Story with Photos
- excerpts from books written on pieces of paper to attach to chart paper
- highlighter
- a sample nonfiction book written by you, the whole class, or an individual student (optional)
- chart paper and markers
- writer's notebooks and writing folders
- To download the following online resource for this lesson, visit **fp.pub/resources**:
  - chart art (optional)

Academic Language / Important Vocabulary

- same
- different
- similar
- topic

Continuum Connection

- Introduce ideas followed by supportive details and examples
- Select information that will support the topic
- Select details that will support a topic or story

GOAL

Compare and contrast one thing with another to provide more information to the readers.

RATIONALE

Comparing and contrasting two things is a very useful way to help readers understand a new concept. When you help students notice how writers (of all genres) use comparison and contrast in their writing as a way to help readers understand a topic more deeply, they begin to try this in their own writing.

WRITER'S NOTEBOOK/WRITING FOLDER

Students can make notes in their writer's notebooks about how their topics are similar to or different from something else and add that description to a draft from their writing folders.

ASSESS LEARNING

- Listen to students as they talk about nonfiction books. Do they understand how a writer uses comparison and contrast to tell more about a topic?
- Notice whether students use comparison and contrast in their own nonfiction books.
- Look for evidence that students can use vocabulary such as *same*, *similar*, *different*, and *topic*.

MINILESSON

To help students think about the minilesson principle, engage them in noticing comparison and contrast in familiar nonfiction books and/or a piece of nonfiction writing by you, a student, or the whole class. Here is an example.

- Show the cover of *Dingo*. Read the title and the excerpt from page 14. Attach the excerpt to the chart paper.

  What did the author do to teach you more about the topic?

- Add students' responses to the chart.

  The author compared how far dingoes can travel in a day to the distance that a runner covers in a marathon so that you will understand more about dingoes.

- Have a student highlight the words in the excerpt that show comparison.

- Repeat this process with another example, such as that from page 22 of *The Seal Garden* or a piece of nonfiction shared writing that you and the class created.

Have a Try

Invite students to talk to a partner about how their topics are similar to or different from something else.

▶ Share the example from page 3 of *Wolf Island* to demonstrate how the author contrasts two things.

> Turn and talk to your partner about what the author did to teach you about how well the rainforest wolves can swim.

▶ After students turn and talk, invite a few students to share their ideas and add them to the chart.

Summarize and Apply

Help students summarize the learning. Remind them to think about using comparison and contrast as they write nonfiction.

> How can you help your readers understand more about your topic?

▶ Write the principle at the top of the chart.

> Today as you write, think about what is the same or different about your topic and something else. Write about that as a way to help your readers learn more about your topic. Be prepared to share your writing with your partner.

Tell how two things are the same or different.

Dingoes are lean and can travel up to 40 km per day. They are the marathon runners of the animal world.
—from <u>Dingo</u> by Claire Saxby

- A dingo can run long distances like a marathon runner.

Orcas are patient, and they patrol the garden like police.
—from <u>The Seal Garden</u> by Nicholas Read

- Orcas hunt by keeping watch on the seal garden the way a police officer keeps watch on a park.

Of course, [wolves] don't swim as well as seals do.
—from <u>Wolf Island</u> by Nicholas Read

- The author contrasts how well the wolf can swim with how well a seal can swim.

Confer

▶ During independent writing, move around the room to confer briefly with students about helping their readers understand a topic. Use prompts such as the following if needed.

- *What is something that is the same as your topic? How are they the same? What could you write to explain that to the reader?*
- *What is something that is different from your topic? How are they different? What could you write to explain that to the reader?*

Share

Following independent writing, gather students in the meeting area to share their writing with a partner and then with the group.

> Who would like to share your description of how two things are the same or different?

Writing Minilesson Principle
Tell about an experience from your life to teach more about a topic.

Making Nonfiction Writing Interesting

You Will Need

- chart paper prepared with an example of text that contains the writer's life experience as a way to teach more, such as from *Face to Face with Whales* by Flip and Linda Nicklin, from Text Set: Telling a Story with Photos
- highlighter
- chart paper and markers
- writing folders

Academic Language / Important Vocabulary

- experience
- explain
- topic

Continuum Connection

- Introduce ideas followed by supportive details and examples
- Select information that will support the topic
- Select details that will support a topic or story
- Add words, phrases, or sentences to provide more information to readers

GOAL

Use details from personal experience to explain more about a topic.

RATIONALE

When students notice and think about how authors (of all genres) use details from personal experience to explain more about a topic, they learn another way to engage readers and can apply this to their own writing.

WRITER'S NOTEBOOK/WRITING FOLDER

Students can apply what they learn about expanding nonfiction writing to a draft from their writing folders.

ASSESS LEARNING

- Notice whether students understand the purpose of using details from their personal experience in nonfiction texts.
- Observe whether students include personal experience to explain more about a topic in their own nonfiction books.
- Look for evidence that students can use vocabulary such as *experience*, *explain*, and *topic*.

MINILESSON

Students will need a nonfiction text from their writing folders for this lesson. To help students notice how a writer uses information from personal experience to explain more about a topic, use an excerpt from a book, a student's writing, or your own writing. Here is an example.

- Display examples from pages 9–10 of *Face to Face with Whales* on chart paper.

  This is what Flip and Linda Nicklin wrote about whales. Listen as I read it aloud. Notice what they did to provide information about the topic.

- Read the excerpt. Ask a student to highlight the part that includes Flip Nicklin's personal experience with whales and tell what was learned about the topic.

  Flip Nicklin's experience explains how we know that whales are mammals, not fish, because fish do not breathe the way mammals do.

Have a Try

Invite students to talk to a partner about an experience from their lives to explain a topic they are writing about.

▶ Make sure students have a piece of nonfiction writing they have been working on or have already written.

> What is an experience of yours that would help your readers understand your topic more? Turn and talk about that.

▶ After time for discussion, invite a few students to share their thinking. Add to the chart. Assure students that not everyone will have had experiences related to their topics.

Summarize and Apply

Summarize the learning. Remind students to think about including experiences from their lives.

> How can you teach readers more about a topic?

▶ Write the principle at the top of the chart.

> During independent writing time, reread a draft of nonfiction writing from your writing folder. Is there a place where you can add personal experience to one of the pages? Will you use a caret or a spider leg, or do you need another piece of paper? Bring your writing to share when we come back together.

> **Tell about an experience from your life to teach more about a topic.**
>
> **Meet the Whale**
> When I was a boy, my family used to watch whales from the coast near San Diego. All we saw from shore were puffs of mist in the distance. We were actually looking at their breath....
>
> —from Face to Face with Whales by Flip and Linda Nicklin

	Topic	Experience
Liam	Snakes	Used to have a pet snake
Yasmin	How to make it easier to get around the school	Had a broken leg and couldn't get around
Owen	Moving to a new place	Has moved twice

Confer

▶ During independent writing, move around the room to confer briefly with students about expanding their nonfiction writing. Use prompts such as the following if needed.

- *What are you writing about? How can you describe that to explain more to your readers?*

- *What personal experience do you have with your topic? How might that help your readers learn more? Where will you add that to your writing?*

Share

Following independent writing, gather students in the meeting area to share their writing.

> Who would like to share a personal experience you had that would teach others more about your topic?

> How did that help you, as the readers, know more about the topic?

Writing Minilesson Principle
Select fascinating facts.

Making Nonfiction Writing Interesting

You Will Need

- a variety of familiar nonfiction books, such as the following:
  - *Magnificent Birds* by Narisa Togo, from Text Set: Illustration Study: Craft
  - *Wolf Island* by Nicholas Read, from Text Set: Telling a Story with Photos
- chart paper and markers
- writer's notebooks and writing folders

Academic Language / Important Vocabulary

- audience
- purpose
- fascinating
- facts

Continuum Connection

- Write about a topic, keeping in mind the audience and their interests and likely background knowledge
- Introduce ideas followed by supportive details and examples
- Select information that will support the topic
- Select details that will support a topic or story
- Use notebooks to plan, gather, and rehearse for future published writing

GOAL

Select facts that will be interesting to the reader.

RATIONALE

There are a wide range of facts students could draw on for any particular subject. When you teach students to consider the audience and the purpose of their informational piece of writing, it helps them to choose the most intriguing facts and pares down their writing.

WRITER'S NOTEBOOK/WRITING FOLDER

Students can revisit the notes they have taken in their writer's notebooks as they choose which facts to include in a draft from their writing folders.

ASSESS LEARNING

- Observe students as they review notes they have taken about their topics. Are they choosing the most fascinating facts to share with their readers?
- Look for evidence that students can use vocabulary such as *audience*, *purpose*, *fascinating*, and *facts*.

MINILESSON

Students will need their writer's notebooks for this lesson. To help students think about the minilesson principle, engage them in an inquiry-based lesson on why writers choose facts that will be most intriguing to readers. Here is an example.

- Show the cover of *Magnificent Birds* and read the title. Read page 12.

  What did Narisa Togo teach you about this bird? There is so much information that she could have given us. How do you think she decided what information to include about the toco toucan?

- After time for discussion, prompt students to think more about how the author chose which facts to include.

  The author wanted to share what makes birds magnificent. She selected facts that would fascinate readers and that readers may not already know.

  What questions might she have asked herself as she was deciding what information to include? What would she have wondered about?

- After time for discussion, write the questions on chart paper.

  Repeat this process with *Wolf Island*.

  This book is all about a wolf in the Great Bear Rainforest. What are some of the facts the author included?

  There is so much that the author could have taught us about wolves. What questions might he have asked himself as he was choosing which facts to include?

Have a Try

Invite students to talk to a partner about which facts they might include in their nonfiction writing.

> Take turns with your partner asking yourselves and discussing the questions on the chart. Make a star by the notes in your writer's notebook that you think will fascinate your readers. If you think of other ideas that will intrigue your readers, write those in your notebook so you can explore them later.

▶ After students turn and talk, invite several pairs to share their ideas.

Summarize and Apply

Help students summarize the learning. Remind them to think about choosing fascinating facts.

> When you write informational pieces, look for facts that your readers might not already know.

▶ Write the principle at the top of the chart.

> As you continue to write your informational piece, think about the questions to ask yourself to decide which information will be the most fascinating to your readers. Think about whether the notes in your writer's notebook include fascinating facts. If you think of other ideas your readers might be interested in, jot those ideas in your writer's notebook. Be prepared to share your writing with your partner.

Select fascinating facts.

Questions to Think About When Selecting Facts

- Who is my audience? Who will read this informational piece?

- What is my purpose? Why am I writing this informational piece?

- What might my readers want to know about my topic?

- Will this fact fascinate my readers?

- Is this fact commonly known, or will it be new and interesting to my readers?

Confer

▶ During independent writing, move around the room to confer briefly with students about making their writing interesting. Use prompts such as the following if needed.

- *Talk about your purpose for writing. What fascinating facts go with that purpose?*

- *What other questions or ideas might your readers find interesting? Where can you find out that information?*

Share

Following independent writing, gather students in the meeting area to share their writing with a partner. Listen in on discussions. Then choose one pair to share with the whole class.

> Talk to your partner about the facts you selected to include in your writing and why. Also, talk about the facts from your writer's notebook you decided not to include.

Umbrella 13: Making Nonfiction Writing Interesting

Assessment

After you have taught the minilessons in this umbrella, observe students as they write and talk about their writing. Use *The Fountas & Pinnell Literacy Continuum* to notice, teach for, and support students' learning as you observe their attempts at writing.

▶ What evidence do you have of students' new understandings related to nonfiction writing?

- Do students use descriptive details to create a picture for their readers?

- Do they use both comparison and contrast to make their writing interesting? How successfully do they use these techniques?

- Do they tell about a personal experience to teach more about a topic? Do they focus on how the experience teaches the reader more about the topic (rather than just tells a story)?

- Is there evidence students can use vocabulary such as *details*, *same*, *different*, *similar*, *topic*, *experience*, *explain*, *audience*, and *purpose*?

- Are they able to select facts that their readers will find interesting?

▶ In what other ways, beyond the scope of this umbrella, are students making their nonfiction writing interesting?

- Do they show an awareness of text features, like headings or captions?

- Do they understand how to create illustrations and graphics that not only provide information but also capture the reader's attention?

Use your observations to determine the next umbrella you will teach. You may also consult Suggested Sequence of Lessons (pp. 665–682) for guidance.

EXTENSIONS FOR MAKING NONFICTION WRITING INTERESTING

▶ Gather a small guided writing group of students who need to strengthen their nonfiction writing.

▶ Encourage students to think about different text structures they might incorporate as ways to elaborate or expand on their writing (e.g., a question-and-answer section, rather than a whole question-and-answer book; a how-to section rather than a how-to book). Refer to CFT.U6: Exploring Text Structures in Nonfiction Writing as needed.

▶ Talk with students about other ways to add interest to their nonfiction writing, such as adding photographs, drawings, or diagrams; writing an engaging introduction; or writing with voice.

Minilessons in This Umbrella

WML1   Include details in the pictures to show something about a character.

WML2   Use colors to create the mood of your story.

WML3   Draw your picture so readers know what is important.

WML4   Use light, weather, and other details to show time of day, season, or passage of time.

WML5   Use perspective to make things appear close or far away.

Before Teaching Umbrella 14 Minilessons

The minilessons in this umbrella will help students notice techniques illustrators use to support readers in understanding more about a story. The minilessons can be taught in any order. They will be helpful for students as they make picture book biographies (see GEN.U6: Writing Picture Book Biographies) or any other picture books, such as realistic fiction stories or fairy tales. To further support students when they draw illustrations, teach CFT.U1.WML2, a general inquiry lesson around the decisions that illustrators make.

Give students plenty of opportunities to make their own illustrations. Read and discuss enjoyable books with detailed and informative illustrations. Use the following texts from *Fountas & Pinnell Classroom™ Interactive Read-Aloud Collection*, or choose books from the classroom library that are well illustrated.

Interactive Read-Aloud Collection

Illustrator Study: Floyd Cooper

Ruth and the Green Book by Calvin Alexander Ramsey

A Dance Like Starlight: One Ballerina's Dream by Kristy Dempsey

Ma Dear's Aprons by Patricia C. McKissack

Illustration Study: Craft

Giant Squid by Candace Fleming

Genre Study: Memoir

The Upside Down Boy by Juan Felipe Herrera

Author/Illustrator Study: Allen Say

The Lost Lake

Empathy

The Crane Wife by Odds Bodkin

Figuring Out Who You Are

The Junkyard Wonders by Patricia Polacco

As you read and enjoy these texts together, help students notice

- what the illustrations reveal about a character, and
- how illustrators use color, details, and perspective.

Interactive Read-Aloud
Floyd Cooper

Craft

Memoir

Allen Say

Empathy

Figuring Out Who You Are

Writer's Notebook

Section 3: Craft

Writing Minilesson Principle

Include details in the pictures to show something about a character.

Adding Meaning Through Illustrations

You Will Need

- several texts with detailed illustrations, such as the following from Text Set: Illustrator Study: Floyd Cooper:

  - *Ruth and the Green Book* by Calvin Alexander Ramsey
  - *A Dance Like Starlight* by Kristy Dempsey
  - *Ma Dear's Aprons* by Patricia C. McKissack

- chart prepared in advance with book titles and column headings [see chart]
- markers
- sticky notes
- writer's notebooks

Academic Language / Important Vocabulary

- details
- illustration
- traits
- feelings
- character

Continuum Connection

- Create drawings that are related to the written text and increase readers' understanding and enjoyment
- Add detail to drawings to add information or increase interest

GOAL

Draw details in pictures that reveal something about a character.

RATIONALE

Illustrators often include details in their illustrations that reveal something about a character that the words may not say. Helping students understand how these details allow them to enjoy a story more by gaining a deeper understanding of the story will support them as they begin to try this in their own illustrations.

WRITER'S NOTEBOOK/WRITING FOLDER

Students can sketch in their writer's notebooks as they think through what they will draw in their final illustrations.

ASSESS LEARNING

- Observe for evidence that students recognize that details in drawings give information about characters beyond the words themselves.
- Notice students' use of details in their own illustrations.
- Observe for evidence that students can use vocabulary such as *details*, *illustration*, *traits*, *feelings*, and *character*.

MINILESSON

Use familiar texts to engage students in noticing how details in illustrations can help readers understand more about a character than what the words say. Here is an example.

- Show the cover of *Ruth and the Green Book* and read the title. Show and read pages 7–8.

  What details do you notice in the illustration of Ruth's mother?

  What do those details help you understand about this character that you might not know from the words alone?

- Add responses to the chart paper.
- Repeat with pages 15–16.
- Repeat this process with pages 1–2 and 13–14 of *A Dance Like Starlight* and pages 5–6 and 12 of *Ma Dear's Aprons*.

Have a Try

Invite students to talk to a partner about what the details in the illustrations help them understand about the characters' traits and feelings.

> Turn and talk to your partner about each example. What do the details tell you about the characters in the story? For each example, do you learn about the character's traits or the character's feelings?

▶ After students turn and talk, ask a few to share. Add sticky notes with responses to the chart.

Summarize and Apply

Summarize the learning and remind students to include details in their illustrations that give information.

> What can you try to do in your illustrations?

▶ Write the principle at the top of the chart.

> The details in your illustrations—how people stand, what their eyes look like, where they place their arms or hands—show the reader more about the characters in your stories. What details will you include in your illustrations to show something about a character? Spend some time sketching in your writer's notebook before you draw the final illustrations. Bring your writing and your sketches to share when we meet later.

Include details in the pictures to show something about a character.			
Book Title	Details	What the Details Tell You	What You Learn About the Characters
Ruth and the Green Book	• Mama is looking away and looks sad. • The man at the Esso station has a big, welcoming smile.	• Mama is worried about what might happen. • He is glad Ruth's family stopped there.	Feelings
A Dance Like Starlight	• The young girl sits on a rooftop, hands folded, looking up at the sky. • She jumps up, arms wide, eyes closed, head high.	• She is a dreamer. • She is determined to show she can be a ballerina.	Traits
Ma Dear's Aprons	• David Earl sits on Ma Dear's lap. His hand is touching her cheek. • They stand close and Ma Dear is kissing David Earl's forehead.	• Ma Dear and David Earl love one another.	Feelings

Confer

▶ During independent writing, move around the room to confer briefly with students about their illustrations. Use prompts such as the following as needed.

- *Talk about the characters in your story. How do they look? What are they like? What details might you add to your illustrations to convey that?*
- *Talk about how the characters in your story feel about one another. What details in your illustrations help the readers understand this?*

Share

Following independent writing, gather students in the meeting area to share their writing and illustrations with a partner before sharing with the class.

> Talk about the details your partner added to the illustrations.

Writing Minilesson Principle
Use colors to create the mood of your story.

Adding Meaning Through Illustrations

You Will Need

- several texts with illustrations that convey the mood clearly, such as the following:
  - *A Dance Like Starlight* by Kristy Dempsey, from Text Set: Illustrator Study: Floyd Cooper
  - *Giant Squid* by Candace Fleming, from Text Set: Illustration Study: Craft
- strip of paper prepared in advance: *Mood is the feeling conveyed to the reader.*
- chart prepared in advance with column headings (see chart)
- markers and tape
- crayons or colored pencils that match colors in the mentor texts
- writing folders

Academic Language / Important Vocabulary

- color
- mood
- illustration
- convey

Continuum Connection

- Understand that illustrations play different roles in a text: e.g., increase readers' enjoyment, add information, show sequence
- Create drawings that employ careful attention to color or detail
- Create drawings that are related to the written text and increase readers' understanding and enjoyment

GOAL

Use different colors to convey different moods or feelings in illustrations.

RATIONALE

When students notice that illustrators carefully choose colors for illustrations that support or enhance the mood, or feeling, of a book, and that these choices help readers gain deeper understanding, they can begin to try this in their own writing and illustrations.

WRITER'S NOTEBOOK/WRITING FOLDER

Have students apply what they learn about using color to the illustrations for stories they are working on in their writing folders.

ASSESS LEARNING

- Observe for evidence that students understand how a color can create a mood in an illustration.
- Look for evidence that students can use vocabulary such as *color*, *mood*, *illustration*, and *convey*.

MINILESSON

Use familiar texts to support students in understanding what mood is (the feeling of the text created by the author and/or illustrator), how color can be used to create a mood, and how to employ this technique to develop a mood in their own illustrations. Here is an example.

- Discuss what is meant by *mood*, and then tape the prepared definition on the chart, leaving room at the top for the principle.

  The feeling an author and illustrator convey in a book is called the mood. Let's look at some illustrations from books we have read to see how the author or illustrator created the mood.

- Show the cover of *A Dance Like Starlight* and pages 1–2 with shades of brown, pages 13–14 with a pink background, and the last two two-page spreads with orange and yellow. Discuss the mood, using the following prompts as necessary. Add noticings to the chart.
  - *What kind of feeling or mood do you get from these pages?*
  - *What type of feeling does the author convey to you as a reader?*
  - *How does the illustrator create that mood?*
  - *How does the illustrator indicate a change in mood?*

- Repeat this process with *Giant Squid*, showing the pages where the ocean is dark and the ink is spreading.

Have a Try

Invite students to talk to a partner about how they might use color to create a mood.

> Think about the story or book that you are working on now. Turn and talk to your partner about the mood of your writing. What mood or feeling do you want to convey in your writing? Does the mood change as your story moves along? What colors could you use to help create that feeling?

▶ After students turn and talk, ask a few to share.

Summarize and Apply

Summarize the learning. Suggest that students think carefully about the colors they use to create the mood.

> How do authors and illustrators create mood?

▶ Write the principle at the top of the chart.

> Today as you begin to write, continue thinking about what you and your partner said. Reread the story you are working on in your writing folder. Think about the feeling you want to convey to your readers. Add some color to the illustrations to create that mood for your readers. Think about this as you begin a new piece of writing, too. Bring your writing to share when we meet later.

Use colors to create the mood of your story.

Mood is the feeling conveyed to the reader.

Colors	Where are the colors used?	What mood do the colors create?
Brown Gray	• Buildings, rooftop, sky	• Simplicity • Calm
Light blue Pink Yellow Orange	• Girl's leotard • Background of the words and illustrations	• Happiness • Hope
Black Deep blue	• In the deep ocean	• Mystery

Confer

▶ During independent writing, move around the room to confer briefly with students about their writing and illustrations. Use prompts such as the following as needed.

- *Read your story aloud. What mood do you want to convey to your readers? What color(s) might you add?*

- *What color are you thinking of adding to your illustration? Where will you use that color? What mood will that create?*

Share

Following independent writing, gather students in the meeting area to share their writing and illustrations with a partner.

> Read a page to your partner and show the illustration. Ask your partner to describe the mood of that part of the story.

Writing Minilesson Principle
Draw your picture so readers know what is important.

Adding Meaning Through Illustrations

You Will Need

- several texts with illustrations that draw readers' attention to what is important, such as the following:
  - *The Upside Down Boy* by Juan Felipe Herrera, from Text Set: Genre Study: Memoir
  - *Ruth and the Green Book* by Calvin Alexander Ramsey, from Text Set: Illustrator Study: Floyd Cooper
- chart prepared in advance with column headings (see chart)
- sticky notes
- chart paper and markers
- writer's notebooks and writing folders

Academic Language / Important Vocabulary

- illustration
- illustrator
- technique
- details

Continuum Connection

- Understand that illustrations play different roles in a text: e.g., increase readers' enjoyment, add information, show sequence
- Create drawings that employ careful attention to color or detail
- Create drawings that are related to the written text and increase readers' understanding and enjoyment
- Add detail to drawings to add information or increase interest

GOAL

Use different techniques to draw readers' attention to what is important.

RATIONALE

Illustrators make decisions about how to create illustrations that show readers what is important at a particular point in a story. When students notice the different techniques illustrators use, they can begin to try them out in their own illustrations.

WRITER'S NOTEBOOK/WRITING FOLDER

Students can practice what they learn about showing what is important in an illustration in their writer's notebooks before they illustrate the stories they are working on in their writing folders.

ASSESS LEARNING

- Observe whether students recognize that illustrators make decisions about how to draw an illustration to draw readers' attention to what is important.
- Talk with students about their illustrations. Can they describe how an illustration shows what is important?
- Look for evidence that students can use vocabulary such as *illustration*, *illustrator*, *technique*, and *details*.

MINILESSON

Use familiar texts to engage students in noticing how an illustrator draws attention to what is important. Discuss how they can apply these techniques to their own writing and illustrations. Here is an example.

- Show the cover of *The Upside Down Boy*. Show pages 8–9.

  What do you notice about how the illustrator drew Juan and his classmates?

  Why do you think the illustrator made that decision?

- Record ideas on the chart.
- Repeat this process by showing the last spread in *Ruth and the Green Book*.

  What do you notice about the details the illustrator included in this illustration?

  What does that help you understand about the story?

  What could you try in your own illustrations to show how characters have strong feelings toward each other?

Have a Try

Invite the students to talk to a partner about how they will use these techniques in their own illustrations.

> Could you try one of these illustration techniques in your own writing? Turn and talk about how you might do that.

▶ After students turn and talk, ask a few to share. Add ideas to the chart using sticky notes.

Summarize and Apply

Help students summarize the learning. Remind students to think about how they can use these techniques for their own illustrations.

> What did you learn about drawing illustrations?

▶ Write the principle at the top of the chart.

> Before you begin to write, reread your story or think about a new piece you are beginning. What do you want your readers to focus on? How will you draw your picture to help readers know that? Take some time to work on your illustrations today. You might want to sketch your ideas in your writer's notebook before you make the final illustrations. Bring your writing to share when we meet later.

Draw your picture so readers know what is important.

What details are in the illustration?	What do the details help you understand?	What can you do to try this?	
Juan's face is large, while his classmates sitting at their desks are small.	• He feels like all the attention is on him.	Think about the size of a character. Make large drawings to attract readers' attention.	Jack: Draw myself and the broken board large when I finally could break it in tae kwon do.
A full-page illustration of Ruth and her grandmother hugging. Both are smiling.	• They care very much about each other. • Their relationship is important.	Draw characters sitting close to one another. Fill the whole page with the characters.	Katey: Use a whole page to draw my sister and me to show she is important to me.

Confer

▶ During independent writing, move around the room to confer briefly with students about their illustrations. Use prompts such as the following as needed.

- *Talk about the story you are writing. What is important in this part? What do you want readers to focus on? How will you show that?*
- *You focus on _____ in your picture. That helps readers understand that _____ is important.*

Share

Following independent writing, gather students in the meeting area to share their writing with a partner. Then select several students to share with the class. Add new ideas to the chart.

> How did you draw your pictures to help your readers know what is important?

> What ideas did you hear from your classmates that you might try in your illustrations?

WML4

Writing Minilesson Principle

Use light, weather, and other details to show time of day, season, or passage of time.

Adding Meaning Through Illustrations

You Will Need

- several texts with illustrations that show time of day and/or season, such as the following:
  - *The Lost Lake* by Allen Say, from Text Set: Author/ Illustrator Study: Allen Say
  - *The Crane Wife* by Odds Bodkin, from Text Set: Empathy
- chart prepared in advance with book titles and column headings
- markers
- writer's notebooks
- To download the following online resource for this lesson, visit **fp.pub/resources**:
  - chart art (optional)

Academic Language / Important Vocabulary

- illustration
- details
- illustrator
- season
- setting

Continuum Connection

- Understand that illustrations play different roles in a text: e.g., increase readers' enjoyment, add information, show sequence
- Create drawings that employ careful attention to color or detail
- Create drawings that are related to the written text and increase readers' understanding and enjoyment
- Add detail to drawings to add information or increase interest

GOAL

Draw details in the pictures to add to information about the setting.

RATIONALE

Illustrators make decisions about how to depict the time of day or the season through their illustrations. The details they add help readers understand the passage of time across a story. Noticing the illustrator's craft gives students an opportunity to think about what details about time are important to share in their own illustrations.

WRITER'S NOTEBOOK/WRITING FOLDER

Students can plan illustrations to support their writing by creating a series of sketches with details of time and season in their writer's notebooks. Cumulatively these sketches may show the progression of time.

ASSESS LEARNING

- Observe for evidence that students recognize the time of day or season by noticing details in illustrations. Notice how they use these observations to understand the passage of time.
- Observe students' use of this technique in their own illustrations.
- Look for evidence that students can use vocabulary such as *illustration*, *illustrator*, *setting*, *details*, and *season*.

MINILESSON

Students will need their writer's notebooks or paper for sketching during Have a Try. To encourage students to think about incorporating details of light, weather, and the seasons in their own illustrations, engage them in a study of illustrations in familiar texts. Discuss how they can also apply these techniques as a way to show not only when a story takes place but also the passage of time. Here is an example.

- Show the cover of *The Lost Lake* and read the title. Then show and discuss pages 11, 13, and 18–19.

  What do you notice about how the illustrator used light and color in these illustrations?

  What does that help you understand about the setting?

  How does that help you know how much time passed?

- Add responses to the chart paper.
- Repeat this process with pages 3–4, 11–12, 15–16, and 25–26 of *The Crane Wife*.

Have a Try

Invite students to sketch as a way to plan for adding details about the time, weather, or season in their illustrations.

▶ Make sure students have a writer's notebook or paper for sketching.

> Think about the story you are writing or want to begin writing. At what time of day does your story begin? During which season? What details will you include in the illustrations to show that? Quickly draw a few details.

▶ After students turn and talk, ask a few to share.

Summarize and Apply

Help students summarize the learning. Remind them to use details to illustrate the setting.

> What did you learn about showing time of day, season, or passage of time in your illustrations?

▶ Write the principle at the top of the chart.

> As you work on your illustrations, think about what readers need to understand about the setting, and include those details. Bring your writing to share when we meet later.

Use light, weather, and other details to show time of day, season, or passage of time.		
Book Title	What details are in the illustration?	What does that help you understand?
The Lost Lake	Dark skies, headlights on, few lights in windows	They walked from early morning all the way to nighttime.
	Bright, blue sky, a few clouds	
	Gray, gloomy sky	
	Dark blue sky, tent lit from inside	
The Crane Wife	Leaves falling—fall	Osamu and Yukiko spent about one year together.
	Snow falling—winter	
	Lily pads and flowers in the water—spring	
	Leaves that fell from trees—fall	

Confer

▶ During independent writing, move around the room to confer briefly with students about their illustrations. Use prompts such as the following as needed.

- *Talk about the story you are writing. What time of day does this occur? What details will you draw so readers understand that?*

- *Talk about the story you are writing. What time of year does it take place? What details will you draw so readers understand that?*

- *You included _____ in your picture. That helps readers understand that it is _____.*

Share

Following independent writing, gather students in the meeting area to share their writing.

> How did you help your readers understand the time of day or the season?

> What ideas did you hear from your classmates that you might try?

Writing Minilesson Principle
Use perspective to make things appear close or far away.

Adding Meaning Through Illustrations

You Will Need

- several texts with illustrations that demonstrate perspective, such as the following:
  - *The Junkyard Wonders* by Patricia Polacco, from Text Set: Figuring Out Who You Are
  - *A Dance Like Starlight* by Kristy Dempsey, from Text Set: Illustrator Study: Floyd Cooper
- chart prepared in advance with column headings
- markers
- writer's notebooks and writing folders

Academic Language / Important Vocabulary

- perspective

Continuum Connection

- Understand that illustrations play different roles in a text: e.g., increase readers' enjoyment, add information, show sequence
- Create drawings that employ careful attention to color or detail
- Create drawings that are related to the written text and increase readers' understanding and enjoyment
- Add detail to drawings to add information or increase interest

GOAL

Draw things larger or smaller to make them appear closer or farther away.

RATIONALE

When students notice how perspective is used in illustrations to make something appear closer or farther away as a way to bring focus to an element, they will understand how this technique helps them to enjoy stories more and gain a deeper understanding. They can then begin to try using perspective in their own illustrations.

WRITER'S NOTEBOOK/WRITING FOLDER

Have students practice in their writer's notebooks sketching things larger or smaller to make them appear closer or farther away before applying this technique to the illustrations for stories they are working on in their writing folders.

ASSESS LEARNING

- Observe whether students recognize that perspective can be used to make things appear closer or farther away.
- Notice students' use of perspective in their illustrations.
- Look for evidence that students can use vocabulary such as *perspective*.

MINILESSON

Students will need their writer's notebooks or paper for sketching during Have a Try. To help students think about the minilesson principle, use familiar texts to engage them in noticing how perspective can be used in an illustration to help readers understand more. Here is an example.

▷ Show the cover of *The Junkyard Wonders* and the next to last spread.

> What do you notice about the illustration?
>
> What do you notice about the size of the people and buildings on the page?
>
> Why do you think the illustrator chose to do that?

▷ Add noticings to the chart.

> When illustrators think about creating things smaller as a way to make them appear farther away, or larger to appear closer, they are using perspective. Illustrators make decisions about perspective to help readers understand more about the story.

▷ Ask partners to repeat this process with *A Dance Like Starlight*. Show the illustrations on pages 21–22 and 23–24.

> What do you notice about the illustrations? What do you notice about the size of the characters on the pages? Why do you think the illustrator chose to do that? Turn and talk about that.

Have a Try

Invite students to think about using perspective in their own illustrations.

▶ Make sure each student has a writer's notebook or piece of paper for sketching.

> Think about one part of your story. What do you want your readers to notice or think about? How will you show that in your illustration? Use your writer's notebook to make a quick sketch. Then share your sketch with your partner.

▶ After students turn and talk, ask a few to share their sketches.

Summarize and Apply

Summarize the learning and remind students to think about perspective when drawing.

> How can you use perspective in your illustrations?

▶ Write the principle at the top of the chart.

> Think about the part of the story you sketched. How will that look in your final drawing? Are there other places in your story that you could use perspective to help your readers understand more? If you find a place, sketch the illustration in your writer's notebook before making your final drawing. Bring your story to share when we meet later.

Use perspective to make things appear close or far away.		
Book Title	How did the illustrator use perspective?	What does this help you, as the reader, understand?
The Junkyard Wonders	The people, the trees, the cars, and houses all look small and far away.	The Junkyard Wonder flew way up high even though others doubted it would happen.
A Dance Like Starlight	The young girl and her mom appear large, while the ballerina on stage appears small. The ballerinas appear large, while the audience appears small.	The Metropolitan is a very large theater. The girl imagines dancing onstage and far away from the audience.

Confer

▶ During independent writing, move around the room to confer briefly with students about their illustrations. Use prompts such as the following as needed.

- *What is this part of your story about? What do you want readers to think about? What will you draw large, or close up? What will you draw small, or far away?*

- *You drew _____ small [large]. That makes me think it is far away [close up].*

Share

Following independent writing, gather students in the meeting area to share their illustrations.

> Share a drawing with your partner. Talk about how you used perspective.

Assessment

After you have taught the minilessons in this umbrella, observe students as they draw, write, and talk about their writing. Use the behaviors and understandings in *The Fountas & Pinnell Literacy Continuum* to notice, teach for, and support students' learning as you observe their attempts at drawing and writing.

- ▶ What evidence do you have of students' new understandings related to adding meaning through illustrations?
  - Do students add details in the illustrations that reveal something about a character?
  - How effectively do they use color to convey the mood?
  - Do they draw pictures that show what is important?
  - How do they use light, weather, or details to indicate time of day, season, or passage of time?
  - Have they tried using perspective to make things appear closer or farther away?
  - Do they notice and use vocabulary such as *feelings, traits, character, illustration, color, mood, setting, illustrator, season, perspective,* and *details*?
- ▶ In what other ways, beyond the scope of this umbrella, are students showing an interest in adding meaning through illustrations?
  - Are they using illustrations and graphics in their nonfiction writing?
  - Do they show an interest in learning about design features or text layout?

Use your observations to determine what you will teach next. You may also consult Suggested Sequence of Lessons (pp. 665–682) for guidance.

EXTENSIONS FOR ADDING MEANING THROUGH ILLUSTRATIONS

- ▶ Spend time studying poetry books and the illustrations that accompany the poems. Talk about the techniques the illustrators used and how those techniques might help students as they write.

- ▶ Show students other illustrative ways to add information and interest to their writing, such as borders around the pages, speech or thought bubbles, and sound or motion lines.

- ▶ Gather together a guided writing group of several students who need support in a specific area of writing, such as adding details to or using color in their illustrations.

- ▶ Study graphic novels and the techniques authors and illustrators use to add meaning through illustrations. Discuss how those decisions can support students in their own writing.

Minilessons in This Umbrella

WML1 Use a variety of illustrations and graphics to teach about your topic.

WML2 Use photographs and detailed illustrations to present information.

WML3 Draw diagrams to give information.

WML4 Use a close-up to show something in greater detail.

WML5 Use maps and legends to give information.

WML6 Use comparisons to show size.

Before Teaching Umbrella 15 Minilessons

To immerse students in nonfiction writing, read aloud a variety of engaging, illustrated nonfiction books about different topics and give students plenty of opportunities to experiment with creating their own nonfiction texts. Teach these minilessons when they are relevant to the nonfiction writing that students are doing.

Use the following books from *Fountas & Pinnell Classroom™ Interactive Read-Aloud Collection* and *Shared Reading Collection*, or choose other suitable nonfiction books that include photographs, diagrams, maps with legends, and different styles of illustration.

Interactive Read-Aloud Collection

Telling a Story with Photos

The Seal Garden by Nicholas Read

Face to Face with Whales by Flip and Linda Nicklin

Illustration Study: Craft

Magnificent Birds by Narisa Togo

Giant Squid by Candace Fleming

Eye to Eye: How Animals See the World by Steve Jenkins

Shared Reading Collection

A Spark of Genius: A Biography of Richard Turere by Myra Faye Turner

Pangaea: The World's Biggest Puzzle by Susan B. Katz

Get the Scoop! Plans and Poems for Making Compost by Jennifer Boudart

As you read and enjoy these texts together, help students

- notice the use of photographs or illustrations,

- look closely at the pictures and share details that they notice,

- notice and understand maps (with and without legends) and diagrams, and

- discuss how the images help them better understand the topics.

Interactive Read-Aloud
Telling a Story with Photos

The Seal Garden by Nicholas Read

Face to Face with Whales by Flip and Linda Nicklin

Illustration Study: Craft

Shared Reading

Writer's Notebook

Writer's Notebook

Section 3: Craft

Writing Minilesson Principle

Use a variety of illustrations and graphics to teach about your topic.

Illustrating and Using Graphics in Nonfiction Writing

You Will Need

- a selection of familiar nonfiction books with various kinds of illustrations and graphics for each small group of students
- chart paper and markers
- sticky notes
- writer's notebooks and writing folders

Academic Language / Important Vocabulary

- nonfiction
- illustration
- graphic
- photograph
- diagram
- map

Continuum Connection

- Use illustrations and book and print features (e.g., labeled pictures, diagrams, table of contents, headings, subheadings, sidebars, boxes of facts set off from other text, page numbers) to guide the reader
- Use graphics (diagrams, illustrations, photos, charts) to provide information
- Provide important information in the illustrations

GOAL

Understand different kinds of illustrations and graphics that can be used in nonfiction books to give information about a topic.

RATIONALE

Making students aware of different kinds of illustrations and graphics used in nonfiction books gives them choice when it comes to illustrating their own nonfiction writing. They will learn to choose the illustration or graphic that best teaches their readers more about the topic.

WRITER'S NOTEBOOK/WRITING FOLDER

Students can record in their writer's notebooks observations of how illustrations and graphics are used in nonfiction books and apply what they have learned when they work on longer pieces of nonfiction writing in their writing folders.

ASSESS LEARNING

- Observe whether students are beginning to use different kinds of illustrations and graphics in their own nonfiction writing.
- Look for evidence that they can understand and use vocabulary such as *nonfiction*, *illustration*, *graphic*, *photograph*, *diagram*, and *map*.

MINILESSON

Students will need their writer's notebooks for this lesson. To help students think about the minilesson principle, use mentor texts to engage them in an inquiry-based lesson on different types of illustrations and graphics in nonfiction books. Here is an example.

- Form small groups of students. Give each group one familiar nonfiction book.

  With your group, take a few minutes to look through the book I gave you. Think about how the author and illustrator used pictures to help you learn more about the book's topic. What kinds of pictures do you see? How do the illustrations and graphics help you learn about the topic? Jot some notes in your writer's notebook.

- Listen in to each group as they discuss their book. Prompt each group as necessary to comment on the illustrations and graphics in the book.

- After time for discussion, invite each group to share what they noticed about the illustrations and graphics in their book. Summarize their noticings on chart paper.

Have a Try

Invite students to talk to a partner about how they might use illustrations and graphics in their own writing.

> What type of illustration or graphic do you think would help your readers understand more about your topic? Turn and talk to your partner about that. Jot down ideas and sketches in your writer's notebook.

▶ After students turn and talk, invite a few students to share their thinking. Add their examples to the chart on sticky notes.

Summarize and Apply

Write the principle at the top of the chart. Summarize the learning. Have students study a variety of illustrations and graphics in nonfiction books.

> Today, work with a partner (or group) to look at more nonfiction books to find examples of illustrations and graphics. Put sticky notes on pages with examples. Write the reasons for the illustrations on the sticky notes. If you write the sticky notes, add them to your writer's notebook after you share with the class. Otherwise, write the notes in your notebook. Bring your books and writer's notebooks when we meet later.

Use a variety of illustrations and graphics to teach about your topic.		
What did the author use?	The author used that to . . .	What might you try as a writer?
Photographs Detailed drawings	give more information about a topic	DeShaun: Photo of a forest
Diagrams	show the parts of something or how something works	Mia: Diagram of the different layers of a polar bear's skin and fur
Labels Captions	help readers understand the image	Damien: Label the life cycle of a frog
Maps Legends	teach readers about places provide information about the map	Anisa: Map of where in the world kangaroos live
Comparisons	help readers understand size	Andrew: Drawing of a big blue whale next to a school bus
Close-ups	show details of something	Jailyn: Close-up of a snake's skin

Confer

▶ During independent writing, move around the room to confer briefly with pairs or groups of students about using illustrations and graphics in their nonfiction writing. Use prompts such as the following as needed.

- *How does this illustration help you understand more about the topic?*
- *Why do you think the illustrator decided to use a _____ on this page?*
- *How might an illustration or graphic like this support your writing?*

Share

Following independent writing, gather students in the meeting area. Ask a volunteer from each pair (or group) to share their notes.

> What kinds of illustrations and graphics did you see? Why do you think the author chose that?

Writing Minilesson Principle
Use photographs and detailed illustrations to present information.

Illustrating and Using Graphics in Nonfiction Writing

You Will Need

- one familiar nonfiction book with photographs and one with detailed illustrations, such as the following:
  - *The Seal Garden* by Nicholas Read, from Text Set: Telling a Story with Photos
  - *Magnificent Birds* by Narisa Togo, from Text Set: Illustration Study: Craft
- a simple nonfiction text with an illustration, affixed to chart paper
- a collection of photographs (e.g., taken by you, printed from the internet, or cut out from magazines)
- markers
- writer's notebooks and writing folders
- To download the following online resource for this lesson, visit **fp.pub/resources**:
  - chart art (optional)

Academic Language / Important Vocabulary

- nonfiction
- illustration
- photograph
- detail
- present

Continuum Connection

- Create drawings that are related to the written text and increase readers' understanding and enjoyment
- Add detail to drawings to add information or increase interest

GOAL

Understand that photographs and illustrations make books interesting and help readers understand more about a topic.

RATIONALE

When students notice ways nonfiction authors use photographs and illustrations, they begin to think carefully about how to illustrate their own nonfiction writing.

WRITER'S NOTEBOOK/WRITING FOLDER

Students will use their writer's notebooks to sketch an idea for an illustration and then work on the longer nonfiction writing pieces in their writing folders.

ASSESS LEARNING

- Observe whether students use meaningful illustrations or photographs that enhance the information in their nonfiction writing.
- Look for evidence that they can understand and use vocabulary such as *nonfiction*, *illustration*, *photograph*, *detail*, and *present*.

MINILESSON

Students will need their writer's notebooks for this lesson. To help students think about the minilesson principle, use mentor texts to demonstrate the use of photographs and detailed illustrations in nonfiction writing. Make sure students understand the word *present* as used in this lesson. Here is an example.

- Display the cover of *The Seal Garden* and read the title. Show several pages.

  What kind of pictures do you see in this book?

  This nonfiction book has photographs. Why might a nonfiction author decide to use photographs instead of drawings?

  Photographs let readers know exactly what something looks like in real life, which is particularly helpful in a book about a science topic.

- Show page 12.

  What does this photograph in the book help you understand?

- Show the cover of *Magnificent Birds* and read the title. Show several pages.

  What kind of pictures does this book have?

  This book has drawings. How do the drawings help you learn about birds?

  In drawings, illustrators can show exactly what they want to show you. What details do you notice in these illustrations?

  The illustrator of *Magnificent Birds* includes details to help you understand what these birds and their habitats look like.

Have a Try

Invite students to talk to a partner about adding a photograph or illustration to a nonfiction text.

▶ Share a sample nonfiction text with an illustration.

> How does this drawing help readers?

> Talk with your partner about a drawing you could create to teach your readers more. Begin a quick sketch in your writer's notebook to plan for this illustration.

▶ After students turn and talk, invite a few students to share their thinking.

Summarize and Apply

Help students summarize the learning and remind them to use photographs or detailed illustrations in their own nonfiction books.

> How are photographs and detailed illustrations in nonfiction books helpful for the readers?

▶ Write the principle at the top of the chart.

> As you work on a piece of nonfiction writing today, think about including photographs or detailed illustrations to help your readers understand more about your topic. Bring your writing to share when we come back together.

Use photographs and detailed illustrations to present information.

Giraffes have unusual tongues. They are dark black, blue, or purple in color and can be 18 to 20 inches long. Giraffes love the leaves on acacia trees. Acacia trees have lots of thorns to protect the leaves. Luckily, the giraffe's tongue has a thick skin to keep it from getting cut by the thorns. If it does get cut, thick saliva helps it heal.

Section 3: Craft

Confer

▶ During independent writing, move around the room to confer briefly with students about using illustrations and photographs. Use prompts such as the following as needed.

- *What is this page about? Would a photograph or drawing help readers better understand that? What should the illustration show?*
- *What details could you include in your illustration to help readers understand _____?*

Share

Following independent writing, gather students in the meeting area to share their writing.

> Who would like to share a photograph or illustration you decided to include in your writing? Why did you choose to use that?

Writing Minilesson Principle
Draw diagrams to give information.

Illustrating and Using Graphics in Nonfiction Writing

You Will Need

- familiar nonfiction books with diagrams, such as the following:
  - *Giant Squid* by Candace Fleming, from Text Set: Illustration Study: Craft
  - *A Spark of Genius* by Myra Faye Turner and *Pangaea* by Susan B. Katz, from *Shared Reading Collection*
- markers
- writing folders

Academic Language / Important Vocabulary

- nonfiction
- diagram

Continuum Connection

- Use illustrations and book and print features (e.g., labeled pictures, diagrams, table of contents, headings, subheadings, sidebars, boxes of facts set off from other text, page numbers) to guide the reader
- Use graphics (diagrams, illustrations, photos, charts) to provide information

GOAL

Learn how to draw diagrams to give information.

RATIONALE

When students study diagrams in nonfiction books and think about why the diagrams were included, they learn that they, too, can create diagrams to give more information about a topic.

WRITER'S NOTEBOOK/WRITING FOLDER

Students will continue to work on their longer pieces of nonfiction writing in their writing folders.

ASSESS LEARNING

- Notice evidence that students understand the purpose of a diagram.
- Observe whether students try creating diagrams for their own nonfiction texts.
- Look for evidence that they can understand and use vocabulary such as *nonfiction* and *diagram*.

MINILESSON

To help students think about the minilesson principle, use mentor texts to demonstrate how diagrams can be used to communicate information. Here is an example.

- Show the diagram at the end of *Giant Squid*.

  What do you notice about this illustration? How is it different from other illustrations?

  What does the illustration help you understand?

- Show and read pages 12–13 of *A Spark of Genius*.

  What did the illustrator include to make it easier for you to understand Richard's invention?

  These are special kinds of illustrations called diagrams. The labels make it easier to understand the parts of the giant squid and Richard's "lion lights."

- Repeat this process with pages 6–7 of *Pangaea*.

  This is also a diagram. What does it help you understand?

  How does it help you understand what the author meant when she wrote "If you cut out the continents on a map, they fit back together almost perfectly"?

- Repeat with pages 8–9.

Have a Try

Invite students to talk to a partner about how to define a diagram and how diagrams are helpful to readers.

> Turn and talk to your partner about what a diagram looks like and where you might use one.

▶ After students turn and talk, invite a few pairs to share their thinking. Record ideas on chart paper.

> How does a diagram help readers?

▶ Add students' responses to the chart.

Summarize and Apply

Write the principle at the top of the chart. Summarize the learning and remind students that they can include diagrams when they write nonfiction.

> When might you choose to include a diagram in a nonfiction book?

> If you are working on a piece of nonfiction writing today, think about whether you could include a diagram to show the parts of something or how something works. If you are not writing nonfiction now, think of something for which you can draw a diagram. Draw it in your writer's notebook. Bring your diagram to share when we come back together.

> ### Draw diagrams to give information.
>
> - An illustration that shows the parts of something
>
> - Has pictures and words
>
> - An illustration that shows how something works
>
> - Has labels and arrows
>
> - Has lines and shapes
>
> ---
>
> A diagram helps readers understand something more complicated by including both pictures and words.

Confer

▶ During independent writing, move around the room to confer briefly with students about illustrations and graphics for their nonfiction writing. Use prompts such as the following as needed.

- *What are you writing about now? Would a diagram be helpful to readers?*
- *What could the diagram show? What will you write on the diagram?*
- *Will your diagram have any arrows? What will the arrows show?*

Share

Following independent writing, gather students in the meeting area to share their diagrams.

> What does your diagram show? What will it help readers learn or understand?

WML4

CFT.U15.WML4

Use a close-up to show something in greater detail.

Illustrating and Using Graphics in Nonfiction Writing

You Will Need

- familiar nonfiction books with close-up illustrations or photographs, such as the following:
  - *Get the Scoop!* by Jennifer Boudart from *Shared Reading Collection*
  - *Eye to Eye* by Steve Jenkins, from Text Set: Illustration Study: Craft
- a full-body drawing of the giraffe sketch from WML2 alongside a close-up of the giraffe's face and tongue
- markers
- writer's notebooks and writing folders
- To download the following online resources for this lesson, visit **fp.pub/resources**:
  - chart art (optional)
  - paper templates (optional)

Academic Language / Important Vocabulary

- nonfiction
- close-up
- detail
- illustration

Continuum Connection

- Use graphics (diagrams, illustrations, photos, charts) to provide information

---

GOAL

Use close-ups to magnify one part of a picture in greater detail.

RATIONALE

When students notice close-up illustrations in nonfiction books and think about why they are included, they learn that they, too, can use close-ups to show one part of an illustration in greater detail.

WRITER'S NOTEBOOK/WRITING FOLDER

Students can practice drawing close-ups in their writer's notebooks or continue to work on longer pieces of nonfiction writing in their writing folders.

ASSESS LEARNING

- Notice evidence that students understand the purpose of a close-up illustration.
- Observe whether students try creating close-up illustrations for their own nonfiction writing.
- Look for evidence that they can understand and use vocabulary such as *nonfiction*, *close-up*, *detail*, and *illustration*.

MINILESSON

To help students think about the minilesson principle, use a mentor text to demonstrate how and why close-ups are used in nonfiction. Here is an example.

- Show the cover of *Get the Scoop!* and read the title. Show pages 8–9.

  What do you notice about this small illustration?

  The small illustration is called a close-up. Why do you think it's called that?

  A close-up shows one small part of the bigger picture, as if you've moved much closer to it. How does this close-up help you understand more about microbes?

- Repeat this process with page 25 of *Eye to Eye*.

  Why might this be helpful to the readers?

  A close-up helps you see one part of the picture in more detail. What details can you see in the close-up that you can't see in the full illustration?

  When might it be helpful to include a close-up in a nonfiction book?

Have a Try

Invite students to talk to a partner about adding a close-up to their own writing.

▶ Show a full-body drawing of the giraffe sticking out its tongue along with a close-up of a the tongue and the acacia thorns.

> How does this close-up help you to know more? Turn and talk to your partner about how you might include a close-up in your own nonfiction writing.

▶ After time for discussion, invite a few pairs to share their thinking.

Summarize and Apply

Help students summarize the learning and remind them that they can use close-ups in their own nonfiction texts. If it will help students, provide the close-up paper template from the online resources.

> Why do illustrators use close-ups?

▶ Write the principle at the top of the chart.

> If you are working on nonfiction writing today, think about how you might use a close-up to show something in greater detail. If you are not working on nonfiction writing, try drawing a close-up of something in your writer's notebook. Bring your drawing to share when we come back together.

Use a close-up to show something in greater detail.

Confer

▶ During independent writing, move around the room to confer briefly with students about illustrating nonfiction. Use prompts such as the following as needed.

- *What does this illustration help readers understand?*
- *How could you show that part in more detail? Would you like to add a close-up?*
- *What details will you show in the close-up?*

Share

Following independent writing, gather students in the meeting area to share their illustrations.

> Raise your hand if you added a close-up to an illustration today.

> How does the close-up increase the readers' understanding?

Umbrella 15: Illustrating and Using Graphics in Nonfiction Writing

WML5

CFT.U15.WML5

Writing Minilesson Principle
Use maps and legends to give information.

Illustrating and Using Graphics in Nonfiction Writing

You Will Need

- familiar nonfiction books with maps and legends, such as the following:
  - *Face to Face with Whales* by Flip and Linda Nicklin, from Text Set: Telling a Story with Photos
  - *A Spark of Genius* by Myra Faye Turner, from *Shared Reading Collection*
- chart paper prepared with a simple map (with a legend) that relates to a piece of your own writing
- markers
- writing folders
- document camera (optional)

Academic Language / Important Vocabulary

- nonfiction
- legend
- map
- information

Continuum Connection

- Use illustrations and book and print features (e.g., labeled pictures, diagrams, table of contents, headings, sidebars, page numbers) to guide the reader
- Use graphics (diagrams, illustrations, photos, charts) to provide information

GOAL

Use maps and legends to provide more information for the readers.

RATIONALE

When students study maps in nonfiction books, they learn how to read maps and understand why they are helpful. They also learn that they, too, can use maps and legends to provide more information for the readers.

WRITER'S NOTEBOOK/WRITING FOLDER

Students will continue to work on longer pieces of nonfiction writing in their writing folders.

ASSESS LEARNING

- Observe for evidence that students understand maps and legends and attempt to use them in their nonfiction writing.
- Look for evidence that they can understand and use vocabulary such as *nonfiction*, *map*, *legend*, and *information*.

MINILESSON

To help students think about the minilesson principle, use mentor texts to demonstrate how to use maps and legends. Here is an example.

- Show the cover of *Face to Face with Whales* and read the title. Turn to page 29 and point to the map.

  What kind of illustration do you see on this page?

  This page has a map.

  What information does the map show you?

  It shows the countries and oceans of the world and where whales migrate.

- Help students understand that the legend gives information about what is shown on the map.

  In the legend, there are differently colored arrows. What do the arrows represent?

  The arrows show the migration routes of several types of whales.

- Continue in a similar manner with the map on page 3 of *A Spark of Genius*.

- Show the map you prepared to support your own writing.

  I am writing about giraffes. I made this map of Africa. Take a look at the legend. How does this map and the legend help you learn something about giraffes?

Have a Try

Invite students to talk to a partner about including a map in their own nonfiction writing.

> Think about a piece you are writing. How might a map help you teach your readers about your topic? What will be important to include on the map and in the legend? Turn and talk to your partner about this.

▶ After time for discussion, invite several pairs to share their ideas.

Summarize and Apply

Help students summarize the learning and remind them that they can include maps and legends in their own nonfiction texts.

> Why do nonfiction authors use maps and legends?

▶ Write the principle at the top of the chart.

> As you work on nonfiction writing today, think about whether you could include a map and legend to give your readers more information about the topic. Bring your writing to share when we come back together.

▶ Students can draw their maps if they know enough to do so, or you can assist them in finding a suitable map that they can trace or use.

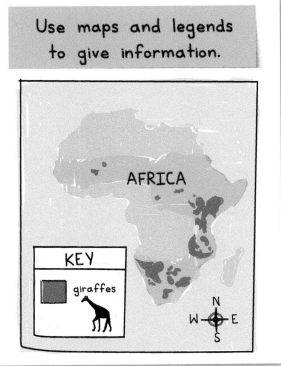

Use maps and legends to give information.

AFRICA

KEY
giraffes

N W E S

Confer

▶ During independent writing, move around the room to confer briefly with students about using maps and legends in their nonfiction writing. Use prompts such as the following as needed.

- *What place do you want your map to show? Let's look for a map of that place.*
- *Where on the page will you put the map?*
- *Do you want to add a legend to your map? What information will the legend give?*

Share

Following independent writing, gather students in the meeting area to share their writing with a partner. Then ask a few to share with the whole group.

> Turn and talk to your partner about the map and legend you created today. As the listener, talk about how the map helps you understand the topic more.

Writing Minilesson Principle
Use comparisons to show size.

Illustrating and Using Graphics in Nonfiction Writing

You Will Need

- a familiar nonfiction book that uses graphic comparisons to help readers understand size, such as *Face to Face with Whales* by Flip and Linda Nicklin, from Text Set: Telling a Story with Photos
- document camera (optional)
- chart paper prepared with a simple drawing that uses comparison to show size, related to a piece of your own writing
- writer's notebooks and writing folders
- To download the online resource for this lesson, visit **fp.pub/resources**:
  - chart art (optional)

Academic Language / Important Vocabulary

- nonfiction
- illustration
- comparison
- size

Continuum Connection

- Use illustrations and book and print features (e.g., labeled pictures, diagrams, table of contents, headings, subheadings, sidebars, boxes of facts set off from other text, page numbers) to guide the reader
- Use graphics (diagrams, illustrations, photos, charts) to provide information

GOAL

Create graphic comparisons to show size.

RATIONALE

When you help students notice graphic comparisons in nonfiction books, they think about another way illustrators can convey information in nonfiction books. They learn that they, too, can use comparisons to help readers understand size.

WRITER'S NOTEBOOK/WRITING FOLDER

Students will sketch comparisons in their writer's notebooks and then continue to work on longer pieces of nonfiction writing in their writing folders.

ASSESS LEARNING

- Notice evidence that students understand how to interpret graphic comparisons in nonfiction books.
- Observe whether students try creating graphic comparisons for their own nonfiction texts.
- Look for evidence that they can understand and use vocabulary such as *nonfiction*, *illustration*, *comparison*, and *size*.

MINILESSON

To help students think about the minilesson principle, use a mentor text to demonstrate how illustrators use comparisons to help readers understand size. Use a document camera if available. Here is an example.

- Show page 12 of *Face to Face with Whales*. Point to the photo that shows the research boat alongside the blue whale.

  Look closely at this photo. What did the photographer do to help you understand the size of the blue whale?

  Comparing the blue whale to the research boat helps you understand the size of a blue whale.

- Show the photograph on pages 24–25.
- What does this photo tell you about the size of the whale?

  The sea birds look very small compared with just the whale's tail. They would look even smaller next to the whole whale!

Have a Try

Invite students to talk to a partner about graphic comparisons.

▸ Show the chart with a graphic comparison that supports your writing.

> Turn and talk to your partner about what is being compared here. What does this comparison help you understand?

▸ Make sure students understand that the second object in the comparison should be something nearly all readers will be familiar with.

Summarize and Apply

Help students summarize the learning and remind them that they can include comparisons when they illustrate nonfiction.

> Why do illustrators use comparisons?

▸ Write the principle at the top of the chart.

> If you are working on a piece of nonfiction writing today, think about whether you could include a comparison to help readers understand the size of something. If you are not working on nonfiction writing, draw two things in your writer's notebook to show a size comparison. Bring your writing to share when we come back together.

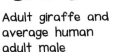

Use comparisons to show size.

Adult giraffe and average human adult male

Baby giraffe and average human toddler

Confer

▸ During independent writing, move around the room to confer briefly with students about using comparisons. Use prompts such as the following as needed.

- *How big is a _____?*
- *What could you compare a _____ to?*
- *How much bigger [smaller] should the _____ be than the _____?*

Share

Following independent writing, gather students in the meeting area to share their writing.

> What two things did you compare? How will that help your readers understand more about your topic?

Assessment

After you have taught the minilessons in this umbrella, observe students as they write, draw, and talk about their writing and drawing. Use *The Fountas & Pinnell Literacy Continuum* to notice, teach for, and support students' learning as you observe their writing and drawing.

▶ What evidence do you have of students' new understandings related to illustrating nonfiction?

- Do students include photographs and detailed illustrations in their nonfiction texts?

- Do they include diagrams and maps with legends to help their readers understand more?

- Do they use close-ups to show things in greater detail?

- Do they use graphic comparisons to help readers understand size?

- Do they experiment with a variety of illustrations and graphics to teach about a topic?

- Do they understand and use vocabulary such as *nonfiction*, *photograph*, *detail*, *diagram*, *map*, and *legend*?

▶ In what other ways, beyond the scope of this umbrella, are students working on nonfiction writing?

- Are they trying to add text and organizational features to their nonfiction writing?

- Are they trying different text structures such as comparison and contrast or question and answer?

Use your observations to determine the next umbrella you will teach. You may also consult Suggested Sequence of Lessons (pp. 665–682) for guidance.

EXTENSIONS FOR ILLUSTRATING AND USING GRAPHICS IN NONFICTION WRITING

▶ Encourage students to write captions for the photographs in their nonfiction texts.

▶ Discuss other types of graphics in nonfiction books (e.g., graphs, charts, and infographics). Invite students to include these types of graphics in their own nonfiction texts.

▶ Gather a guided writing group of several students who need support in a specific area of writing, such as deciding what kind of illustrations to add to their nonfiction texts.

Minilessons in This Umbrella

WML1 Use scenes to show action and details.

WML2 Place illustrations on the page to communicate an idea.

WML3 Use a mix of materials to create art for books.

WML4 Use size and color to add meaning to words.

Before Teaching Umbrella 16 Minilessons

The minilessons in this umbrella should be taught when they are relevant to writing that students are working on (e.g., picture book biographies), rather than consecutively, so that they can apply their new learning. In addition to the materials suggested for each lesson, students will need blank paper. Writers use the blank space to make decisions about orientation (portrait or landscape) and to visualize how and where they will place illustrations and words on the page.

Read and discuss picture books that illustrate a variety of art techniques exemplifying the minilesson principles. Use the following books from *Fountas & Pinnell Classroom™ Interactive Read-Aloud Collection,* or choose books from your classroom library that have interesting design features.

Interactive Read-Aloud Collection

Friendship

Snook Alone by Marilyn Nelson

The Dunderheads by Paul Fleischman

Empathy

The Boy and the Whale by Mordicai Gerstein

Biography: Artists

The East-West House: Noguchi's Childhood in Japan by Christy Hale

Radiant Child: The Story of Young Artist Jean-Michel Basquiat by Javaka Steptoe

Illustration Study: Craft

Giant Squid by Candace Fleming

Perseverance

King for a Day by Rukhsana Khan

Taking Action, Making Change

The Promise by Nicola Davies

Follow the Moon Home: A Tale of One Idea, Twenty Kids, and a Hundred Sea Turtles by Philippe Cousteau and Deborah Hopkinson

Emmanuel's Dream: The True Story of Emmanuel Ofosu Yeboah by Laurie Ann Thompson

As you read and enjoy these texts together, discuss why illustrators might have made their design decisions and how these decisions impact readers.

Interactive Read-Aloud
Friendship

Empathy

Biography: Artists

Illustration Study: Craft

Perseverance

Taking Action, Making Change

Writer's Notebook

WML1

CFT.U16.WML1

Writing Minilesson Principle
Use scenes to show action and details.

Exploring Design Features and Text Layout

You Will Need

- a variety of books with illustrations that use scenes, such as the following:
  - *Snook Alone* by Marilyn Nelson, from Text Set: Friendship
  - *The Boy and the Whale* by Mordicai Gerstein, from Text Set: Empathy
- a chart prepared in advance with column headings and excerpts from the books (see chart)
- markers
- writing folders

Academic Language/ Important Vocabulary

- scenes
- details
- action
- author
- illustrator

Continuum Connection

- Understand that when both writing and drawing are on a page, they are mutually supportive, with each extending the other
- Provide important information in illustrations
- Add detail to drawings to add information or increase interest
- Create drawings that employ careful attention to color or detail
- Create drawings that are related to the written text and increase readers' understanding and enjoyment

GOAL

Understand that writers and illustrators use scenes to show action and detail.

RATIONALE

Help students notice how illustrators draw scenes to add small details that show the action the writer is telling about. They can use this technique in their own writing, allowing them to convey what is happening more clearly to the readers.

WRITER'S NOTEBOOK/WRITING FOLDER

Students can apply what they learn about illustrations to the stories they are working on in their writing folders.

ASSESS LEARNING

- Notice how students use scenes in their illustrations to show action and details.
- Look for evidence that students can use vocabulary such as *scenes*, *details*, *action*, *author*, and *illustrator*.

MINILESSON

To help students think about the minilesson principle, use mentor texts and/or your own writing to discuss how authors/illustrators use scenes to show action and details. Here is an example.

- Show the cover of *Snook Alone* and read the title. Show and read page 5. What do you notice the illustrator did here?

  The illustrator drew several smaller pictures instead of one big one. Talk about what you think the illustrations show.

- Write responses on chart paper. Guide students to notice that the illustrations show what is meant by the words in the text.

- Repeat this process with *The Boy and the Whale*, showing and reading page 34.

  How do these small scenes help you understand the story?

- Write students' thoughts on the chart. Guide students to notice that the illustrations show all the different ways the whale dances in the water.

Have a Try

Invite partners to talk about why illustrators use scenes in their books to show details or action.

> Why might an illustrator choose to draw several small scenes instead of one large illustration? Turn and talk to your partner about that.

▶ After students turn and talk, invite a few students to share their ideas.

Summarize and Apply

Help students summarize the learning. Remind them that they can use scenes in their own books.

> What did you discover about authors and illustrators today?

▶ Write the principle at the top of the chart.

> You can think about drawing small scenes to illustrate your own stories. Today as you work, think about how you might draw scenes to illustrate the writing you are working on in your writing folder. Bring your illustrations to share when we meet later.

Use scenes to show action and details.	
What the Words Say	**What the Illustrations Show**
Snook Alone "Sometimes Snook routed a sleeping hare and won a high-speed race with a delicious prize."	• Snook chasing a hare
"Sometimes Snook . . . watched Abba Jacob work on the plumbing or the wiring."	• Abba Jacob fixing the toilet
The Boy and the Whale "The whale slapped its tail and leaped again and again."	• The kinds of jumps and turns the whale makes

Confer

▶ During independent writing, move around the room to confer briefly with students about design features and text layout. Use the following prompts as needed.

> • *What part of your story are you working on? How might you draw scenes to show your readers that action (those details)?*

> • *Reread parts of your story and ask yourself whether using scenes would help your readers understand more about the action or details.*

> • *What are you hoping to show in your scenes? How will that help your readers understand the action or details of your story?*

Share

Following independent writing, gather students in the meeting area to share how they used scenes to illustrate their writing.

> Who would like to share where you used scenes to illustrate your story? How did you decide to use scenes for this part of your story?

> What did you learn from your classmates' work that you might try as a writer?

Writing Minilesson Principle
Place illustrations on the page to communicate an idea.

You Will Need

- books with pages that utilize white space or have illustrations trailing off of the page, such as the following:
  - *The East-West House* by Christy Hale and *Radiant Child* by Javaka Steptoe, from Text Set: Biography: Artists
  - *Giant Squid* by Candace Fleming from Text Set: Illustration Study: Craft
- chart paper with questions prepared in advance (see chart)
- markers
- writer's notebooks and writing folders

Academic Language/ Important Vocabulary

- place
- page
- author
- illustrator

Continuum Connection

- Provide important information in illustrations
- Add detail to drawings to add information or increase interest
- Create drawings that employ careful attention to color or detail
- Create drawings that are related to the written text and increase readers' understanding and enjoyment

GOAL

Understand that illustrators communicate ideas by the way they place their illustrations.

RATIONALE

When you help students notice how illustrators communicate ideas by thoughtfully placing their illustrations, they can experiment with the same technique in their own writing.

WRITER'S NOTEBOOK/WRITING FOLDER

Students can try out ideas in their writer's notebooks for how to design their book pages, or they might decide to design illustrations directly onto the pages of their books.

ASSESS LEARNING

- Talk with students about the illustrations in their books. Do they show evidence of having thought through how and where to place the illustrations to communicate meaning?
- Look for evidence that students can use vocabulary such as *place*, *page*, *author*, and *illustrator*.

MINILESSON

To help students understand how illustrations can help authors communicate ideas to their readers, use fiction and nonfiction mentor texts that have examples of different ways to place illustrations on the page. Here is an example.

- Show the cover of *The East-West House* and read the title. Show pages 6–7.

   What do you notice about how the illustrator placed the illustration across the whole two pages?

- Make sure students understand the use of the word *place* as a verb in this lesson. If students need more guidance, ask the following questions:
  - *Why do you think the illustrator placed Isamu and his mother in that spot on the page?*
  - *What does it tell you about how Isamu and his mother felt in that crowd of people?*

- Record students' responses on chart paper.

- Show the cover of *Giant Squid* and read the title. Show the two-page spread that says "It's gone."

   What do you notice about this illustration?

   What do you notice about how the illustrator placed the squid on the page? What idea do you think the illustrator wanted to communicate?

- Add students' responses to the chart.

Have a Try

Invite students to discuss the border created by Javaka Steptoe in *Radiant Child* with a partner.

▶ Show the cover and several two-page illustrations. Then read the section titled About This Book aloud.

> Listen as I read the About This Book section. Then turn and talk to your partner. Why do you think Javaka Steptoe decided to make the illustrations like this? How could you try this in your own illustrations? What idea might that communicate to your readers?

▶ After students turn and talk, invite a few students to share. Record responses on the chart.

Summarize and Apply

Help students summarize the learning. Remind them that they can use these techniques in their own books.

> What did you discover about placing illustrations?

▶ Guide students to the principle. Write it on the chart.

> Today as you work on a book, think about how you might place your illustrations on the pages to communicate ideas to your readers. Look at the chart for some ideas. You can try out your ideas by sketching them in your writer's notebook first. Bring your book to share when we meet later.

Place illustrations on the page to communicate an idea.	
What do you notice?	**What idea might the illustration be showing you?**
• People gathered together	• The family felt alone
• Isamu and his mother alone	• Others didn't welcome the mother and son
• Deep, dark blue	• The size of the squid
• Ink behind the tail of the squid that is floating off the page	• The depth of the ocean • The mystery of the squid
• Painted wood borders around illustrations	• Honors the style of art of the subject of the biography

Confer

▶ During independent writing, move around the room to confer briefly with students about design features and text layout. Use prompts such as the following if needed.

- *What type of story are you working on today? How might you use the space on the page to communicate that idea?*
- *You created borders on the page. How do they help your readers?*
- *You drew your illustration trailing off the page. What does that show your readers?*

Share

Following independent writing, gather students in the meeting area to share their books.

> Who would like to share an illustration you made?

> What did you learn from your classmates' work that you might try as a writer?

WML3
CFT.U16.WML3

Writing Minilesson Principle
Use a mix of materials to create art for books.

You Will Need

- a variety of books with examples of collage or interesting art techniques, such as the following:
  - *The East-West House* by Christy Hale, from Text Set: Biography: Artists
  - *King for a Day* by Rukhsana Khan, from Text Set: Perseverance
  - *The Promise* by Nicola Davies, from Text Set: Taking Action, Making Change
- chart paper and markers
- writer's notebooks and writing folders
- To download the following online resource for this lesson, visit **fp.pub/resources**:
  - chart art (optional)

Academic Language/ Important Vocabulary

- materials
- collage
- author
- illustrator
- technique
- mix

Continuum Connection

- Add detail to drawings to add information or increase interest
- Create drawings that employ careful attention to color or detail
- Create drawings that are related to the written text and increase readers' understanding and enjoyment

GOAL

Understand that writers and illustrators use a mix of materials or techniques to create interest and art in books.

RATIONALE

By helping students notice that illustrators have different ways of creating illustrations, you give them a wide choice in designing their illustrations. This allows students to express their personalities and gives them ownership of their work.

WRITER'S NOTEBOOK/WRITING FOLDER

Students can make a list of art materials in their writer's notebooks and use the materials to create illustrations for a writing project in their writing folders.

ASSESS LEARNING

- Observe whether students try combining materials in their illustrations.
- Look for evidence that students can use vocabulary such as *materials*, *collage*, *author*, *illustrator*, *technique*, and *mix*.

MINILESSON

Students will need their writer's notebooks or paper for this lesson. To help students think about the minilesson principle, use mentor texts to help them notice how authors and illustrators use mixed media to create interest in their illustrations. Here is an example.

- Show the cover of *The East-West House* and read the title. Show several pages, including pages 6–7.

  > What do you notice about the illustrations in this book? How do you think the illustrator made them?

  > She made the illustrations using collage. Say it with me, *collage*. You can use collage by tearing or cutting pieces of paper into shapes and gluing them onto a sheet of paper to make a picture.

  > How might you try combining ripped paper with markers or colored pencils in your own books?

- Show the cover of *King for a Day*. Show a few pages, allowing students to study the illustrations. Guide them to notice the use of ripped paper and textured fabrics to create the artwork.

  > What do you notice about the illustrations in this book? How do you think the illustrator made them? What might you use to create art like this?

- If time allows, repeat this process with *The Promise*, guiding students to notice the use of watercolors, pastels, and crayons to create the illustrations.

Have a Try

Encourage students to discuss materials they might try to use to create art for their books.

> Make a list of materials in your writer's notebook that you could use to create art in your illustrations. Then turn to your partner and share your list.

▶ After time for conversation, ask students to share. Write their ideas on chart paper.

Summarize and Apply

Summarize the learning and remind students that they can use different art materials to create illustrations in their books.

> What did you learn today about making your books interesting to read?

▶ Write the principle at the top of the chart.

> You can use two or more art materials together to make illustrations for your own books. Today during independent writing time, try doing that for your illustrations.

▶ Provide students with a variety of art materials. You will likely want to leave these materials out to give students the opportunity to experiment.

Use a mix of materials to create art for books.

Watercolors

Torn paper

Strips of fabric

Glue stick

Colored pencils

Markers

Crayons

Pencils

Things to glue on (string, yarn, googly eyes, cotton balls)

Construction paper

Confer

▶ During independent writing, move around the room to confer briefly with students about design features and text layout. Use the following prompts as needed.

- *What are you writing about? What are you planning for the illustration?*
- *What art materials will you use to create that?*
- *Take this piece of scrap paper (provide a small piece). Try mixing watercolors and markers (or two other materials). What do you think about using these materials?*

Share

Consider asking students to leave their illustrations on top of their desks or hanging the illustrations on a clothesline to dry until the next day. Lead students on a tour of the classroom to see one another's illustrations, returning to the meeting area.

> What did you see in your classmates' work that you might try?

Writing Minilesson Principle
Use size and color to add meaning to words.

Exploring Design Features and Text Layout

You Will Need

- a variety of books with interesting placement of words on the page, such as the following:
  - *The Dunderheads* by Paul Fleischman, from Text Set: Friendship
  - *Follow the Moon Home* by Philippe Cousteau and Deborah Hopkinson and *Emmanuel's Dream* by Laurie Ann Thompson, from Text Set: Taking Action, Making Change
  - *Giant Squid* by Candace Fleming, from Text Set: Illustration Study: Craft
- chart paper and markers
- writing folders

Academic Language/ Important Vocabulary

- place
- illustrator
- placement
- author

Continuum Connection

- Use layout of print and illustrations to convey the meaning of a text
- Arrange print on the page to support the text's meaning and to help the reader notice important information
- Use underlining, italics, and bold print to convey a specific meaning
- Understand that when both writing and drawing are on a page, they are mutually supportive, with each extending the other

GOAL

Understand that writers and illustrators make decisions about the size and color of words for effect.

RATIONALE

Authors can enhance the meaning of a text and engage readers by making decisions about the size, the color, and the placement of print on the page. Helping students notice these decisions supports them in understanding more about what they are reading and leads to a use of this craft technique when writing their own books.

WRITER'S NOTEBOOK/WRITING FOLDER

Have students store their work in progress in their writing folders.

ASSESS LEARNING

- Look for evidence of students using the size and color of words in interesting ways.
- Observe for evidence that students can use vocabulary such as *place*, *placement*, *illustrator*, and *author*.

MINILESSON

To help students think about the minilesson principle, use mentor texts to show examples of decisions authors made about the size and color of certain words. Make sure all students can see the pages clearly. Here is an example.

- Show the cover of *The Dunderheads* and read the title. Show and read pages 1–2.

  What do you notice about the size of the words? Why do you think the author made this decision?

- Write students' responses on chart paper.
- Show page 8 and read the part of the text that has words in italics. Repeat with page 9.

  What do you notice about the way the author wrote these words? Why do you think he made this decision?

- Repeat this process with *Follow the Moon Home*. Show and read several pages with text in different colors.

  What do you notice about some of the words on these pages?

  What do the colors show you?

- Write students' responses on the chart.

Have a Try

Invite students to turn and talk about an author's choice to only place one or two words on a page.

▶ Show the covers of *Giant Squid* and *Emmanuel's Dream*. Read the titles and the pages where the authors placed only one or two words on a page.

> Turn and talk to your partner. What do you notice about the placement of the words on these pages? Why do you think the authors made this decision?

▶ After students turn and talk, invite a few students to share. Talk about what makes this technique interesting and meaningful. Add to the chart.

Summarize and Apply

Help students summarize the learning. Remind them that they can make decisions about the size, color, and placement of words in their own books.

> How can you add meaning to certain words?

▶ Write the principle at the top of the chart.

> Before you begin to write today, think about how you can add meaning to words and make your writing interesting by thinking about the color, size, and placement of your words. Begin with a blank page or add to a page you have already begun. Look at the chart for some ideas. Bring your book to share when we meet later.

Use size and color to add meaning to words.

What the Words Look Like	What It Shows
Small to big	• How loudly (or softly) someone is speaking
Italics	• Emphasizes/stresses the word
Different colors	• Calls out something important
Only one or two words on the page	• Excitement • Surprise

Confer

▶ During independent writing, move around the room to confer briefly with students about design features and text layout. Use the following prompts as needed.

- *Look at the illustrations you have already created. How are you thinking about placing the words on the page with those illustrations?*
- *You wrote those words in a different color (made those words larger/smaller, placed them in an interesting way). Talk about your decision to do that.*

Share

Following independent writing, gather students in the meeting area to share their writing. Choose students who have made different design decisions to share.

> Talk about the decisions you made for this page.

Assessment

After you have taught the minilessons in this umbrella, observe students as they draw, write, and talk about their drawing and writing. Use *The Fountas & Pinnell Literacy Continuum* to notice, teach for, and support students' learning as you observe their attempts at writing and illustrating.

▶ What evidence do you have of students' new understandings related to exploring design features and text layout?

- Are students using scenes to show action and details?
- Do students think carefully about how or where to place illustrations on a page to communicate an idea?
- Do they use a mix of materials and techniques to create interesting art for their books?
- Are they thoughtful about the size and color of words?
- Do they understand and use vocabulary such as *illustrator*, *placement*, *collage*, *mix*, *materials*, and *author*?

▶ In what other ways, beyond the scope of this umbrella, are students ready to expand their design and layout techniques?

- Are they creating text features (e.g., table of contents, captions) for their books?
- How are they illustrating nonfiction writing?
- Do they need support in adding meaning through illustrations?

Use your observations to determine the next umbrella you will teach. You may also consult Suggested Sequence of Lessons (pp. 665–682) for guidance.

EXTENSIONS FOR EXPLORING DESIGN FEATURES AND TEXT LAYOUT

▶ Lead the class in an illustrator study to examine the work of a single illustrator. Have students note characteristics of the illustrator's style (e.g., the colors, the art medium or media, similarities and differences across books). Illustrators might include Douglas Florian, Allen Say, and Patricia Polacco.

▶ Collaborate with the school art teacher or a local artist as you explore creating illustrations with your students.

▶ To support students in thinking more deeply about their illustrations, discuss with them their reasons for choosing different materials for their illustrations.

Section 4 · Conventions

A WRITER CAN have great ideas, understand how to organize
them, and even make interesting word choices. But the ideas
can get lost if the writer doesn't spell words in recognizable
ways, use conventional grammar and punctuation, and organize
ideas into paragraphs. For writing to be valued and understood,
writers need to understand the conventions of writing. The
minilessons in this section are designed to strike a balance
between teaching students to write clearly and making them
comfortable about taking risks with their writing. Teach these
lessons whenever you see that students are ready for them.

4   Conventions

Minilessons in This Umbrella

WML1 Break words into syllables to write them.

WML2 Use what you know about words to write new words.

WML3 Spell complex plurals correctly.

WML4 Think about the meaning of homophones to spell them correctly.

WML5 Use a phonogram list to spell single-syllable words correctly.

Writer's Notebook

Before Teaching Umbrella 1 Minilessons

The lessons in this umbrella support students in writing words fluently and accurately to help them convey their ideas. Students will continue to use known words, syllables, and their knowledge of complex plurals and homophones so that they can focus on the message of their writing and conveying the meaning to their readers with ease.

Learning to spell every word individually would be a monumental task. These lessons highlight several important, high-utility ways of helping students know how to write words. However, they are intended to supplement the phonics and word study work you are doing with your students. It is not necessary to teach these lessons consecutively, so feel free to teach them whenever students' writing indicates a readiness or the need for a reminder of a particular concept. As you introduce words to spell, use words students might not know in a sentence as a way to provide context.

WML1

CNV.U1.WML1

Writing Minilesson Principle
Break words into syllables to write them.

Writing Words

You Will Need

- a word card or whiteboard for each pair of students
- chart paper and markers
- writer's notebooks

Academic Language / Important Vocabulary

- parts
- word
- syllables
- clap

Continuum Connection

- Use a range of spelling strategies to take apart and spell multisyllable words (word parts, connections to known words, complex sound-to-letter cluster relationships)
- Spell correctly two- or three-syllable words that have vowel and *r*
- Hear, say, clap, and identify syllables in words with three or more syllables: e.g., *fish/er/man, par/a/graph, el/e/va/tor, un/u/su/al, wat/er/mel/on*

GOAL

Break multisyllable words apart to write them.

RATIONALE

Breaking a word into syllables helps students isolate the sounds. By attending to all the sounds they hear, they are more likely to represent them in spelling. Clapping syllables emphasizes the breaks in words and offers a tool to assist in writing longer, unfamiliar words.

WRITER'S NOTEBOOK/WRITING FOLDER

Students can practice writing words in their writer's notebooks.

ASSESS LEARNING

- Observe for evidence that students can say and clap syllables in multisyllable words.
- Notice if students use syllables to break apart words when writing.
- Look for evidence that students can use vocabulary such as *parts, word, syllables,* and *clap*.

MINILESSON

To help students think about the minilesson principle, select words with three or four syllables that represent a variety of syllable types (e.g., open, closed, *r*-influenced, vowel combinations, consonant-*le*). Model clapping the syllables to help isolate and listen to the sounds in each syllable. Here is an example.

- Say the word *yesterday* and demonstrate clapping the syllables.

  How many parts, or syllables, do you hear in the word yes/ter/day?

  Yesterday has three syllables, so I clapped three times.

  To write the word *yesterday*, say the first syllable slowly and write the letter for each sound you hear. What sounds do you hear?

- Record the letters for the first syllable on the chart. Then have the students clap *yesterday* again, stressing the second syllable. Record the letters for the second syllable on the chart. Repeat with the third syllable. Then write the word without the syllable breaks.

  Let's check the word. Clap as I point to each syllable.

  When you want to write a word you don't know how to spell, try clapping the syllables. Notice the sounds you hear in each syllable and think about the letters that go with the sounds to help you write the whole word.

- Repeat the process with more words, such as *develop, volcano, incomplete, terrible* and *vegetable*. Assist in adding letters that are not pronounced (e.g., silent *e* at the end of a word).

Have a Try

Invite students to work with a partner to write words with multiple syllables.

▶ Give each pair of students a blank word card or whiteboard.

With your partner, clap the syllables you hear in *congratulate*. Talk to your partner about the number of parts you hear. Say the parts slowly and talk about the sounds you hear and the letters that stand for those sounds. Write the word on your word card.

▶ Invite volunteers to clap the parts of the word and show what they have written. Add the word to the chart. Repeat with another word, such as *horrible*.

Summarize and Apply

Summarize the lesson. Remind students to say an unknown word slowly and clap the syllables to hear each sound.

▶ Write the principle at the top of the chart.

During independent writing time, find a word with several syllables in your writer's notebook you weren't sure how to spell. Give it another try by clapping out the syllables. Then continue with your writing. When you want to write an unknown word, clap the syllables to help you hear the parts and say the parts slowly to hear the sounds. Then you can write the letters for the sounds you hear.

Break words into syllables to write them.	
yes / ter / day	yesterday
de / vel / op	develop
vol / ca / no	volcano
in / com / plete	incomplete
ter / ri / ble	terrible
veg / e / ta / ble	vegetable
con / grat / u / late	congratulate
hor / ri / ble	horrible

Confer

▶ During independent writing, move around the room to confer briefly with students about their writing. Use the following prompts as needed.

• *Listen for the parts. Clap the parts you hear.*
• *Listen for the sounds you hear in the first (next, last) part.*
• *You can think about the sound and write the letter.*

Share

Following independent writing, gather students in the meeting area to share their writing.

Did anyone write a word with three or more syllables? What did you do to write it?

Writing Minilesson Principle
Use what you know about words to write new words.

Writing Words

You Will Need

- sticky notes
- chart paper and markers
- writer's notebooks

Academic Language / Important Vocabulary

- letter
- word
- ending
- beginning
- sounds

Continuum Connection

- Identify words that have the same letter pattern and use them to solve an unknown word: e.g., *hat/sat, light/night, crumb/thumb, curious/furious*
- Use known word parts (some are words) to solve unknown larger words: e.g., *in/into, can/canvas, us, crust*

GOAL

Use knowledge of known words to write unknown words.

RATIONALE

Teaching students to read and write every individual word in a language would be a huge, time-consuming, and impossible task. A more efficient approach is to teach students to use what they know (known words or parts of words, such as a letter or a cluster of letters, word patterns, or smaller words that are part of bigger words) to understand something new. This equips them with tools to solve new words when they read and write and prepares them to express increasingly sophisticated ideas in their writing.

WRITER'S NOTEBOOK/WRITING FOLDER

Students can practice writing words in their writer's notebooks.

ASSESS LEARNING

- Observe for evidence that students can use what they know to write unknown words.
- Notice if students use parts of words (e.g., a letter or a cluster of letters, word patterns, or smaller words that are part of bigger words) to help write new words.
- Look for evidence that students can use vocabulary such as *letter*, *word*, *ending*, *beginning*, and *sounds*.

MINILESSON

Students will need their writer's notebooks for this lesson. To help students think about the minilesson principle, demonstrate how to use what is known about words to write new words. Here is an example.

- Write the word *catch* on a sticky note and place on chart paper.

  This is a word you know well. Say it with me slowly: *catch*.

- Write the word *etch* on the chart directly below *catch*.

  What do you notice about these two words?

- Point under the letters as you guide the students to read the two words aloud.

  I used what I know about the sound at the end of *catch* and what I know about the sound at the beginning of *etch*.

- Invite students to use *catch* and what they know about other words to add words to the list. If time permits, repeat this process with the word *edge*.

- Model how to use a known word, such as *arm*, to write unfamiliar words.

  You can also use words that you know to write new words. You know the word *arm*. Let's think about how you can use the word *arm* to write the word *harm*. What other words can you make from *arm*?

The Writing Minilessons Book, Grade 4

Have a Try

Invite students to use the word *port* to write other words.

> This is the word *port*. In your writer's notebook, write some words you can write using the word *port*.

▶ After a few moments, invite a few volunteers to share their words. Write them on the chart.

Summarize and Apply

Summarize the lesson. Remind students to use what they know about words to write words that are unfamiliar to them.

> What is something you can do to help you write new words?

▶ Write the principle at the top of the chart.

> Whenever you are writing and you want to write a new word, say it and think whether you can use a word you already know to help you. You can try out how to write new words in your writer's notebook. Bring your writing to share when we meet later.

Use what you know about words to write new words.			
ca<u>tch</u>	e<u>dge</u>	<u>arm</u>	<u>port</u>
e<u>tch</u>	gru<u>dge</u>	h<u>arm</u>	s<u>port</u>
ma<u>tch</u>	bri<u>dge</u>	f<u>arm</u>er	rep<u>ort</u>
wi<u>tch</u>	bu<u>dge</u>t	<u>arm</u>or	exp<u>ort</u>
swi<u>tch</u>	ba<u>dge</u>r	ph<u>arm</u>acy	p<u>ort</u>al
pi<u>tch</u>er	knowle<u>dge</u>	h<u>arm</u>ony	p<u>ort</u>rait
ha<u>tch</u>ed			imp<u>ort</u>ant
bu<u>tch</u>er			opp<u>ort</u>unity

Confer

▶ During independent writing, move around the room to confer briefly with students about their writing. Use the following prompts as needed.

- *What can you do if you don't know how to write a word?*
- *Do you know a word that starts like that?*
- *Do you know a word that ends like that?*
- *Do you know a word that sounds the same in the middle of the word?*
- *What word do you know that could help you write the word?*

Share

Following independent writing, gather students in the meeting area. Invite individual students to share their writing.

> Who would like to share your writing?

> Can you point to a new word you wrote? How did you know what letters to write?

Section 4: Conventions

Writing Words

You Will Need

- chart paper prepared with singular nouns that have complex plurals (see top half of chart)
- markers
- writer's notebooks

Academic Language / Important Vocabulary

- singular
- plurals
- complex
- irregular

Continuum Connection

- Spell complex plurals correctly: e.g. *knife/knives, woman/women, sheep/sheep*
- Recognize and use plurals that add *-es* to words after changing the final *f* or *fe* to *v*: e.g., *knives, scarves, wolves*
- Recognize and use irregular plurals that change the spelling of the word: e.g., *goose/geese, mouse/mice, ox/oxen, woman/women*
- Recognize and use irregular plurals that are the same as the singular form of the word: e.g., *deer, moose, salmon, sheep*

GOAL

Use knowledge of complex plurals to write words.

RATIONALE

Irregular, or complex, plurals don't follow common plural spelling patterns. When you help students to notice these words, they begin to spell them more accurately and efficiently. This equips them with tools to solve new words when they read and write about increasingly sophisticated ideas because they are not interrupted by the unfamiliarity of a word.

WRITER'S NOTEBOOK/WRITING FOLDER

Students can make lists of complex plurals in their writer's notebooks.

ASSESS LEARNING

- Observe whether students are spelling complex plurals correctly in their writing.
- Notice evidence that students can use vocabulary such as *singular, plurals, complex,* and *irregular.*

MINILESSON

To help students think about the minilesson principle, work with them to sort the words into categories based on how the plural word is formed. Here is an example.

- Display the list of singular nouns.

    These are all singular nouns. They refer to only one thing—one knife, one deer, one fish, and so forth. If you wanted to refer to two knives, how would you write that?

- Accept students' responses and write *knives* on the chart in the first column of three.

    If we are talking about more than one knife we say *knives*. What is the word for more than one deer?

- Accept students' responses and write *deer* on the chart in the second column.
- What is the word for more than one fish? more than one goose?
- Write *fish* in the second column and *geese* in the third column.
- Repeat the process with the remaining words. If students notice the patterns, ask them to tell you in which column you should write the plural form of the word.

Have a Try

Invite students to work with a partner to notice the reason for each column.

> All the words on the list have been placed in columns. How can you describe how each column of plurals was formed? Turn and talk to your partner about that.

▶ After a brief time for discussion, ask volunteers to share. Label the three columns.

Summarize and Apply

Summarize the lesson and write the principle at the top of the chart. Remind students to notice irregular plural patterns as they read and write.

> Some plurals don't follow common patterns. These are irregular words you will have to learn and remember. During independent writing time, if you need to write one of these words, look at the chart to help you. Bring your writing when we meet later.

Spell complex plurals correctly.

knife	foot	moose
deer	woman	aircraft
fish	reindeer	sheep
goose	leaf	child
life	tooth	thief
scarf	mouse	bison

Drop -f/-fe and add -ves	No change—same word used for one or many	The spelling of the word changes
knives	deer	geese
lives	fish	feet
scarves	reindeer	women
leaves	moose	teeth
thieves	aircraft	mice
	sheep	children
	bison	

Confer

▶ During independent writing, move around the room to confer briefly with students about their writing. Use the following prompts as needed.

- *What are you writing today?*
- *When you write an unfamiliar word, what do you do to help you write it?*
- *Have you used any of these complex plurals in your writing today?*

Share

Following independent writing, gather students in the meeting area. Ask a few volunteers to share their writing.

> Are there words you would like to add to the chart?

Writing Minilesson Principle
Think about the meaning of homophones to spell them correctly.

Writing Words

You Will Need

- chart paper prepared in advance with homophone sentence examples
- markers
- writer's notebooks
- To download the following online resource for this lesson, visit **fp.pub/resources**:
  - chart art [optional]

Academic Language / Important Vocabulary

- same
- different
- homophones

Continuum Connection

- Use difficult homophones (e.g., *their,/there*) correctly
- Recognize and use homophones [words that have the same sound, different spellings, and different meanings]: e.g., *blew/blue, higher/hire*

GOAL

Use knowledge of homophones to write words.

RATIONALE

The English language has its origins in many languages, which is why there are so many irregularities in the spelling and pronunciation of words. Homophones are a good example of such irregularities. Homophones are two or more words that sound the same but have different meanings and spellings. When students learn to recognize, spell, and use these words correctly in context, they are better able to get an accurate message across to their readers.

WRITER'S NOTEBOOK/WRITING FOLDER

Students can make lists of homophones in their writer's notebooks.

ASSESS LEARNING

- Observe whether students are contextually using and spelling homophones correctly in their writing.
- Notice evidence that students can use vocabulary such as *same, different*, and *homophones*.

MINILESSON

Students will need their writer's notebooks for this lesson. To help students think about the minilesson principle, demonstrate the use of several homophones and discuss how important it is to use them correctly in writing. Here is an example.

- Display the chart prepared in advance. Read the first set of sentences containing *here* and *hear*.

  What do you notice about the underlined words in the sentences?

  They sound the same, but they are spelled differently.

  What does *here* mean in the first sentence? And what does *hear* mean in the second sentence?

- Discuss the differences in meaning and spelling and write a brief, student-generated definition for each homophone on the chart.

  Words that sound the same but are spelled differently and mean different things are called homophones. You need to use the correct homophone when you are writing so your readers understand your meaning.

- Repeat the process with *aloud* and *allowed*.

Have a Try

Invite students to work with a partner to think about the meaning of another set of homophones: *cent, sent, scent*. Read the sentences on the chart.

> These three words are homophones. They all have different meanings. Turn and talk with your partner. What does each homophone mean? Then write a sentence using each homophone in your writer's notebook.

▶ Add student definitions to the chart. Ask a few students to read their sentences aloud. For each sentence, ask another student to spell the homophone.

Summarize and Apply

Summarize the lesson. Remind students to think carefully when they use homophones in their writing.

> What did you learn today about words that sound the same but have different meanings?

▶ Write the principle at the top of the chart.

> There are many homophones in the English language. It can be confusing to your readers if you don't use them correctly in your writing. As you write today, and every day, pay careful attention to homophones to make sure you are using the correct word for the meaning you want to convey to your readers.

Confer

▶ During independent writing, move around the room to confer briefly with students about their writing. Use the following prompts as needed.

- *When you're writing a homophone, how can you make sure you are spelling it correctly?*
- *Have you used any homophones in your writing today?*

Share

Following independent writing, gather students in the meeting area. Ask a few volunteers to share their writing.

> Are there homophones you would like to add to the chart?

Writing Minilesson Principle
Use a phonogram list to spell single-syllable words correctly.

Writing Words

You Will Need

- chart paper and markers
- a copy of a phonogram list in each student's writing folder
- writing folders and writer's notebooks
- document camera (optional)
- To download the following online resources for this lesson, visit **fp.pub/resources**:
  - Phonograms
  - Common Phonograms

Academic Language / Important Vocabulary

- writing folder
- phonogram
- alphabetical order
- syllable

Continuum Connection

- Use a range of spelling strategies to take apart and spell multisyllable words: e.g., word parts, connections to known words, complex sound-to-letter cluster relationship
- Use reference tools to check on spelling when editing final draft: e.g., dictionary, digital resources

GOAL

Use a phonogram list or another resource to help with spelling.

RATIONALE

Teaching students to use what they know about a word in combination with a reference tool (e.g., a phonogram list) improves their ability to spell words independently.

WRITER'S NOTEBOOK/WRITING FOLDER

Students can work on a writing project in their writing folders or write in their writer's notebooks as they try using a phonogram list—your own or those available from the online resources.

ASSESS LEARNING

- Notice whether students refer to a phonogram list or another resource to help them spell words.
- Look for evidence that students can use vocabulary such as *writing folder*, *phonogram*, *alphabetical order*, and *syllable*.

MINILESSON

Students will need their writing folders with a copy of a phonogram list fastened inside. This lesson is based on the online resource Phonograms. Depending on your students, you might wish to use the online resource Common Phonograms or a list of your own. To help students learn about the minilesson principle, engage them in an interactive lesson on how to use a phonogram list. Here is an example.

- Have students open their writing folders to the phonogram list.

  This is a tool that can help you when you want to write a word you don't know how to spell.

- Choose a familiar word and model the process of using a phonogram list to help spell the word. Here is an example.

  If you want to spell the word *dance*, say the first part of the word, and then say the rest of the word like this: /d/ /ans/.

  At the beginning of the last part, what vowel sound do you hear? What sound do you hear next? What letters stand for the sounds?

- Show the phonogram list you are using and point as you model the process.

  The phonograms, or word parts, are in alphabetical order. Now that I know the last part begins with -*an*, I can look for a phonogram that has letters for the sounds I hear.

- Repeat the process with several more words, such as *kind*, *boat*, and *drink*.

Have a Try

Invite students to turn and talk about using a phonogram list to help spell words.

> Turn and talk about how you can use a phonogram list to help you spell the word *skate*.

▶ After time for discussion, ask volunteers to share how they used a phonogram list to spell *skate*.

> What steps did you use to spell *skate*?

▶ As students share ideas, write them in order on the chart, using general terms.

Summarize and Apply

Summarize the learning. Remind students to use a resource such as a phonogram list to help with their spelling. Write the principle on the top of the chart.

> During independent writing time today, try using the phonogram list in your writing folder to spell new words. You can use this tool when you are writing, editing, and proofreading. Bring your writing to share when we meet later.

> Use a phonogram list to spell single-syllable words correctly.
>
> • Say the new word (the word you want to write).
>
> • Say the first part and then the rest of the word.
>
> • Think about the sounds and letters at the beginning of the last part.
>
> • Find that last part on the phonogram list.
>
> • Think about the first sound of the new word.
>
> • Write the new word.

Section 4: Conventions

Confer

▶ During independent writing, move around the room to confer briefly with students about using a phonogram list. Use the following prompts as needed.

- *What writing are you working on today?*
- *How can you use a phonogram list to help spell a word you are unsure about?*
- *You can use the phonogram list to help spell that word.*

Share

Following independent writing, gather students in the meeting area. Ask a few volunteers to share their writing.

> In groups of three, share how you figured out the spelling of a word you didn't know how to spell.

Assessment

After you have taught the minilessons in this umbrella, observe students as they draw, write, and talk about their writing. Use *The Fountas & Pinnell Literacy Continuum* to notice, teach for, and support students' learning as you observe their attempts at writing.

▶ What evidence do you have that students have learned ways to write words?

- Do they break apart words into syllables and listen for sounds?
- Is there evidence that students use what they know about words to write new words?
- Are they spelling complex plurals correctly?
- Do they think about the meaning of homophones in order to spell them correctly?
- Can they use a phonogram list to spell new words?
- Do they understand and use vocabulary such as *syllables*, *parts*, *clap*, *letter*, *word*, *ending*, *beginning*, *sounds*, *plurals*, *complex*, *irregular*, *same*, *different*, and *homophones*?

▶ In what other ways, beyond the scope of this umbrella, are students developing as writers?

- Are students proofreading and editing their writing?
- Are they willing to share their writing with others?

Use your observations to determine the next umbrella you will teach. You may also consult Suggested Sequence of Lessons (pp. 665–682) for guidance.

EXTENSIONS FOR WRITING WORDS

▶ Support students in using known words to write new words. Use letter tiles or magnetic letters to interchange letters to make new words to increase flexibility with this strategy.

▶ Make a matching game to practice homophones. Write each word of a homophone pair on a word card. Students place the cards face down in a grid. They try to match the homophone pairs by turning over a card and finding its match. Suggested homophone pairs: *ate/eight, blue/blew, cheap/cheep, for/four, knew/new, lead/led, mail/male, plane/plain, read/red, right/write, root/route, weather/whether, whose/who's, your/you're.*

▶ Gather a temporary guided writing group of several students who need support in a specific area of writing.

▶ Teach students to use a phonogram list to spell multisyllable words.

Minilessons in This Umbrella

WML1 Notice how authors use capitalization.

WML2 Notice how authors use punctuation.

WML3 Use capitalization and punctuation correctly when writing dialogue.

WML4 Use a comma to separate parts of a sentence to make the meaning clear.

WML5 Use an apostrophe to show something belongs to someone or to make a contraction.

WML6 Use an ellipsis to show a pause or to build excitement.

WML7 Use colons for a variety of reasons.

WML8 Use parentheses to clarify or add extra information.

Before Teaching Umbrella 2 Minilessons

Conventions and craft are closely connected because they work together to convey meaning. Without attention to punctuation and capitalization, ideas can get lost. By teaching conventions through inquiry and with an eye to the writer's craft, students are able to use conventions in ways that deliver meaning to the readers.

These minilessons can be taught all at once, or they can be broken up over time. The open-ended inquiries in the first two minilessons are designed for students to notice not only the way punctuation and capitalization are conventionally used, but also how authors use punctuation in interesting ways to craft their writing. Use the books listed below from *Fountas & Pinnell Classroom™ Interactive Read-Aloud Collection* and *Shared Reading Collection*, or choose books from the classroom library.

Interactive Read-Aloud Collection

Illustrator Study: Floyd Cooper

Ma Dear's Aprons by Patricia C. McKissack

Meet Danitra Brown by Nikki Grimes

Biography: Artists

Action Jackson by Jan Greenberg and Sandra Jordan

Me, Frida by Amy Novesky

Shared Reading Collection

A Cuban American Familia by Laura Platas Scott

My Typhoon by Mike Downs

As you read and enjoy these texts together, help students

- notice the way that writers convey meaning through punctuation, and
- notice the impact that punctuation and capitalization have on meaning.

Interactive Read-Aloud
Floyd Cooper

Biography: Artists

Shared Reading

Writer's Notebook

Section 4: Conventions

Writing Minilesson Principle
Notice how authors use capitalization.

You Will Need

- several books that show a variety of examples of capitalization for each small group
- chart paper and markers
- sticky notes
- document camera (optional)
- writer's notebooks

Academic Language / Important Vocabulary

- capitalize
- capitalization
- title
- sentence
- uppercase (capital)
- lowercase (small)

Continuum Connection

- Use a capital letter in the first word of a sentence
- Use capital letters appropriately for the first letter in days, months, holidays, city and state names, and titles of books
- Use capitalization for specialized functions (emphasis, key information, voice)

GOAL

Notice how and why authors use a variety of capitalization.

RATIONALE

When students learn that writers use capitalization to make writing clear and engaging for their readers, they think about how to use capitalization in their own writing. Use the terms you prefer (*uppercase* or *capital; lowercase* or *small*).

WRITER'S NOTEBOOK/WRITING FOLDER

Have students record in their writer's notebooks how they see authors use capitalization.

ASSESS LEARNING

- Observe whether students are using capitalization correctly in their own writing.
- Look at students' writing to see if they try using capitalization for effect.
- Look for evidence that students can use vocabulary such as *capitalize, capitalization, title, sentence, uppercase (capital),* and *lowercase (small).*

MINILESSON

Students will need their writer's notebooks for this lesson. Use mentor texts to provide an inquiry-based lesson on how authors use capitalization. Here is an example.

> You know that writers use both uppercase and lowercase letters. Today you will work with a group to notice different ways that authors use uppercase letters, also known as capital letters.

- Have students sit in small groups. Provide each group with a basket of texts that show capitalization used for different purposes.
- Make a chart with two columns: *Words to Capitalize* and *Examples*.

> Look through these books for examples of capitalization. One of you will mark the examples with sticky notes. All of you will write the examples and reasons in your writer's notebooks.

- As student work in groups, circulate to guide the conversations as needed. After time for working, create an anchor chart that can be kept in the classroom as a reference. Give each group a chance to share what they found.

> What is an example of capitalization that you found? Show what you marked.

- Record responses on the chart.

Have a Try

Invite students to turn and talk about how writers use capitalization to convey meaning.

▶ Show a page from a mentor text that has interesting capitalization.

> Turn and talk about how the author used capitalization on this page.

▶ After time for a brief discussion, ask a few students to share their ideas. Add new ideas to the chart.

▶ If students are interested, allow them to spend more time examining ways that authors use capitalization. This will immerse students in the craft aspect of capitalization.

Summarize and Apply

Summarize the learning. Have students think about how they are using capitalization in their own writing. Add the principle to the top of the chart.

> During independent writing time today, think about how you are using capitalization in the piece you are working on or in a new one you are starting. Look at the chart to remember how you can use capitalization. Bring the writing you are working on when we meet later.

Notice how authors use capitalization.

Words to Capitalize	Examples
First word and important words in a title	• Ma Dear's Aprons • Me, Frida
First word in a sentence	• The day of the party has finally arrived. • What movie should we watch?
Cities, towns, countries	• Ely, Nevada • Mexico
Specific place	• Lone Mountain • Grand Canyon
Days, months	• Monday • March
Holidays	• Thanksgiving • Memorial Day
For emphasis	• STOP!
Important information	• NOTE: The time has been changed.
Words that should be read loudly	• CREAK!

Confer

▶ During independent writing, move around the room to confer briefly with students about capitalization. Use the following prompts as needed.

- *What do you notice about the way the writer used capitalization?*
- *Why do you think the writer decided to use uppercase letters here?*
- *Which letters will be uppercase in the writing you are working on?*

Share

Following independent writing, gather students in the meeting area. Have students talk about capitalization decisions in their writing.

> Talk about your reasons for using uppercase letters in your writing today.

WML2
CNV.U2.WML2

Writing Minilesson Principle
Notice how authors use punctuation.

You Will Need

- baskets of books that have a variety of punctuation (one set per small group)
- chart paper and markers
- sticky notes
- document camera (optional)
- writer's notebooks
- an example of punctuation used in an interesting way (e.g., an apostrophe used to shorten a word as in *jumpin'*)

Academic Language / Important Vocabulary

- punctuation
- sentence
- end mark
- period
- question mark
- exclamation point

Continuum Connection

- Consistently use periods, exclamation points, and questions marks as end marks in a conventional way
- Notice the role of punctuation in the craft of writing
- Study mentor texts to learn the role of punctuation in adding voice to writing

GOAL

Notice how and why authors use a variety of punctuation.

RATIONALE

Punctuation is important in conveying a clear message to readers. It can also be used to engage readers and make writing interesting. Once students understand that they can think about punctuation as a craft move, they are motivated to try out different techniques.

WRITER'S NOTEBOOK/WRITING FOLDER

Have students record in their writer's notebooks how they see authors using punctuation.

ASSESS LEARNING

- Notice whether students recognize that punctuation is connected to a writer's craft, especially voice.
- Observe whether students are trying out different ways to use punctuation in their writing.
- Look for evidence that students can use vocabulary such as *punctuation*, *sentence*, *end mark*, *period*, *question mark*, and *exclamation point*.

MINILESSON

Students will need their writer's notebooks for this lesson. Use mentor texts to provide an inquiry lesson about how authors use punctuation. Here is an example.

> You have learned about periods, question marks, and exclamation points, but authors use many types of punctuation in different ways. In groups, see what you notice about how authors use punctuation.

- Have students sit in small groups. Provide each group with a basket of mentor texts that show a variety of punctuation types and uses.
- Make a chart with two columns: *Punctuation Mark* and *Why Use It*.

> Look through the books to find examples of punctuation. One of you will mark the examples with sticky notes. All of you will write the examples and reasons in your writer's notebooks.

- As student work in groups, circulate to guide the conversations as needed. After time for working, create an anchor chart that can be kept in the classroom as a reference. Give each group a chance to share what they found.

> What is an example of punctuation that you found? Show what you marked in the book.

- Record responses on the chart.

Have a Try

Invite students to turn and talk about how writers use punctuation to convey meaning.

▶ Display an example of punctuation used in an interesting way.

> Turn and talk about the decision the author made about punctuation.

▶ After time for a brief discussion, ask a few students to share their ideas.

▶ If students are interested, allow them to spend more time examining ways that authors use punctuation. This will immerse students in the craft aspect of punctuation.

Summarize and Apply

Summarize the learning. Have students try some new punctuation moves.

> How can you learn ways to use punctuation?

▶ Write the principle at the top of the chart.

> During independent writing time, think about how you are using punctuation in the writing piece you are working on or in a new one you are starting. Are there new ways you might try out some punctuation marks? Bring the writing you are working on when we meet later.

Notice how authors use punctuation.	
Punctuation Mark	**Why Use It**
.	• Complete thoughts
?	• Asking questions
!	• Strong emotion • Excitement
'	• Something belongs to someone • Two words made into one
,	• Pause • List • Set off the beginning of a sentence
. . .	• Something is coming • Pause
" "	• Talking • Quotations
:	• Introduce a list of items • Introduce information
( )	• Add information • Make something clear • Talk to the reader

Confer

▶ During independent writing, move around the room to confer briefly with students about using punctuation. Use the following prompts as needed.

  • *Why do you think the writer made this punctuation choice?*

  • *What punctuation marks are you using in the writing you are working on? Why?*

Share

Following independent writing, gather students in the meeting area to talk about punctuation.

> Share with a partner how you made decisions about using punctuation.

> Look at the chart and talk about a punctuation idea you would like to try out.

Writing Minilesson Principle
Use capitalization and punctuation correctly when writing dialogue.

Learning About Punctuation and Capitalization

You Will Need

- mentor texts with examples of dialogue, such as the following:
  - *Ma Dear's Aprons* by Patricia C. McKissack, from Text Set: Illustrator Study: Floyd Cooper
  - *A Cuban American Familia* by Laura Platas Scott, from *Shared Reading Collection*
- chart paper prepared with an example of different ways to write dialogue in each of three columns
- document camera (optional)
- markers
- writer's notebooks and writing folders

Academic Language / Important Vocabulary

- punctuation
- capitalization
- dialogue
- quotation marks
- opening
- closing
- comma

Continuum Connection

- Use capital letters correctly in dialogue
- Use commas and quotation marks correctly in writing interrupted and uninterrupted dialogue as well as to show a verbatim quote

---

GOAL

Use correct capitalization and punctuation when writing dialogue.

RATIONALE

When students learn to write dialogue correctly, their writing is clear to their readers.

WRITER'S NOTEBOOK/WRITING FOLDER

Have students check how they have written dialogue in some writing in their writing folders or practice writing dialogue in their writer's notebooks.

ASSESS LEARNING

- Observe whether students are showing evidence that they know how and why to capitalize and punctuate dialogue.
- Look for evidence that students can use vocabulary such as *punctuation, capitalization, dialogue, quotation marks, opening, closing,* and *comma.*

MINILESSON

To help students understand the minilesson principle, engage them in an interactive lesson about how to capitalize and punctuate dialogue. Here is an example.

- Ahead of time, prepare the three-column chart with each example of dialogue written in separate columns. Leave space for more writing both above and below each example.

  > Turn and talk about what you notice about each example of dialogue. What is the same and what is different about the examples?

- Allow a few minutes for students to talk. Then ask volunteers to share their noticings. Introduce the word *dialogue* if it is unfamiliar to students. Be sure they notice that the spoken words can come before or after the speaker tag (uninterrupted dialogue) and both before and after the speaker tag (interrupted dialogue). Students should mention the use of quotation marks, the capitalization, and the location of other punctuation marks.

  > Quotation marks are always used as a pair—opening and closing quotation marks—so that readers know where the spoken words begin and end.

- Show or project the examples of dialogue from *Ma Dear's Aprons*, pages 17, 22, and 23, and from *A Cuban American Familia*, pages 6–7. As you show each page, have students select examples to show different ways of writing dialogue and identify where on the chart each the example should be placed. Add representative examples to the chart.

Have a Try

Invite students to turn and talk about how to punctuate dialogue.

> What could you write to explain how to punctuate each example of dialogue? Turn and talk about that.

▶ After time for discussion, have students share their ideas. Use general language to write each rule above the corresponding column of examples.

Summarize and Apply

Summarize the learning. Remind students to use correct capitalization and punctuation when writing dialogue. Write the principle at the top of the chart.

> During independent writing time, look at a piece of your writing from your writing folder to see if you have used dialogue, or practice writing dialogue in your writer's notebook. Check to see whether you need to change the punctuation to make who is speaking and what is being said clear to your readers. Bring a piece of writing that has dialogue when we meet.

Use capitalization and punctuation correctly when writing dialogue.		
RULE: Use quotation marks and a comma when the dialogue comes first.	**RULE:** Use commas and sometimes a period when there is interrupted dialogue.	**RULE:** Use a comma and then quotation marks when the dialogue comes last.
"Thank you," says Mom.	"Please," I say, "give thanks more often."	He said, "Thank you."
"Brown, so it won't show dirt," she explains.	"You're too young to stay home by yourself," she says, "so don't even ask."	Papi says, "En casa, español." Mami says, "At school, only English."
"For your schooling comes next year," she says.	"You're a big mess," Ma Dear says. "Just look at my floor!"	

Confer

▶ During independent writing, move around the room to confer briefly with students about dialogue and punctuation. Use the following prompts as needed.

- *How will your readers know that someone is speaking?*
- *Which words should be capitalized?*
- *Where will the opening (closing) quotation mark be placed?*
- *Show where you will place the comma before the quotation marks.*

Share

Following independent writing, gather students in the meeting area. Ask a few volunteers to share their writing.

> In pairs, share a piece of your writing that has dialogue. Read what you wrote and share where you placed the punctuation and which words you capitalized.

Use a comma to separate parts of a sentence to make the meaning clear.

Learning About Punctuation and Capitalization

You Will Need

- mentor texts that have commas, such as *My Typhoon* by Mike Downs and *A Cuban American Familia* by Laura Platas Scott, from *Shared Reading Collection*
- chart paper and markers
- two sentence strips, one with an example of commas that separate items in a list and one with a comma that follows introductory words
- tape
- highlighter
- writer's notebooks

Academic Language / Important Vocabulary

- punctuation
- comma
- introductory words
- series
- list

Continuum Connection

- Use commas correctly to separate an introductory clause or items in a series

GOAL

Use commas to set off introductory clauses or phrases and to separate items in a series.

RATIONALE

Commas, when used judiciously, make writing clearer for the readers. Two common and useful ways to use commas are to separate an introductory clause or phrase from the rest of the sentence and to separate each item in a list.

WRITER'S NOTEBOOK/WRITING FOLDER

Students will write in their writer's notebooks sentences that use commas to set off introductory words and to separate items in a series.

ASSESS LEARNING

- Observe whether students' writing shows evidence that they use commas correctly.
- Look for evidence that students can use vocabulary such as *punctuation*, *comma*, *introductory words*, *series*, and *list*.

MINILESSON

Students will need their writer's notebooks for this lesson. To help students understand the minilesson principle, use familiar texts to illustrate the use of commas in a series and to set off introductory words. Here is an example.

- Show and read the second sentence on page 3 of *My Typhoon*.

    What do you notice about the commas in this sentence?

    Why did the author punctuate the sentence in that way?

- Lead students to articulate that the commas separate items in a list. Begin a two-column chart. Write the noticing as the heading for the first column. Add the prepared text example, and invite a student to highlight the commas.

- Show and read page 10 of *A Cuban American Familia*.

    What do you notice about the comma in this sentence?

- Guide the conversation to help students understand that the comma indicates a pause that sets off the introductory words from the rest of the sentence.

- Use general terms to write the noticing as a heading for the second column. Add the prepared example, and invite a student to highlight the comma.

- Show and read the last sentence on page 9 of *A Cuban American Familia*.

    What do you notice about the commas in this sentence?

    This sentence has commas that separate items in a list *and* introductory words. Commas can be used for more than one reason in a single sentence.

Have a Try

Invite students to write sentences that use commas to separate items in a list or introductory words from the rest of the sentence. They can work on their own or with a partner.

> In your writer's notebook, write a sentence that uses a comma to separate introductory words from the rest of the sentence or to separate each item in a list.

▶ After time for writing, have volunteers share. Select several sentences to write on the chart. Emphasize the commas with a highlighter or a different color.

Summarize and Apply

Summarize the learning. Remind students to use commas properly in their writing pieces.

> Why does it matter where a writer places a comma?

▶ Write the principle at the top of the chart.

> During independent writing time, notice where you pause when you read a sentence. Are there words in a list? Are there words that introduce the sentence? If so, add a comma. Bring your writing when we meet later.

▶ Depending on the examples that arise naturally in students' reading and writing, you may want to use the structure of this lesson to teach other uses of commas.

Chart

Use a comma to separate parts of a sentence to make the meaning clear.

Use commas to separate items in a list.	Use a comma after introductory words.
I live here with my parents, two brothers, two sisters.	While the rest of the house sleeps, we walk to the Riviera bodega.
I like ice cream, pizza, and fries.	Someday, I want to swim in a pool.
We walked to the store, the post office, and the library.	After searching my bedroom, I found my lost homework.
Seals have whiskers, front flippers, and back flippers.	If you want healthy teeth, you should brush them before going to bed.

Confer

▶ During independent writing, move around the room to confer briefly with students about punctuation. Use the following prompts as needed.

- *Where will you put the commas to separate items in a list?*
- *In what ways are commas useful for readers?*
- *Where will you place a comma to show that the readers should pause?*

Share

Following independent writing, gather students in the meeting area to share their writing.

> Who would like to read a sentence you wrote that uses commas?

> What do you notice about the way _____ used commas on this page?

Use an apostrophe to show something belongs to someone or to make a contraction.

You Will Need

- several mentor texts with examples of possessives and contractions, such as the following:
  - *A Cuban American Familia* by Laura Platas Scott, from *Shared Reading Collection*
  - *Ma Dear's Aprons* by Patricia C. McKissack, from Text Set: Illustrator Study: Floyd Cooper
- chart paper and markers
- books from the classroom library with examples of apostrophes and contractions (1–2 books per pair of students)
- writer's notebooks

Academic Language / Important Vocabulary

- punctuation
- apostrophe
- possessive
- belongs
- contraction

Continuum Connection

- Use apostrophes correctly in contractions and possessives

GOAL

Use apostrophes to show possessives and contractions.

RATIONALE

An apostrophe can show possession, or it can represent missing letters in a contraction. Students should understand that even a small punctuation mark like an apostrophe carries important meaning to readers.

WRITER'S NOTEBOOK/WRITING FOLDER

Students will write in their writer's notebooks examples of possessives and contractions.

ASSESS LEARNING

- Look at students' writing to see if they are using apostrophes correctly.
- Look for evidence that students can use vocabulary such as *punctuation*, *apostrophe*, *possessive*, *belongs*, and *contraction*.

MINILESSON

Students need their writer's notebooks for this lesson. To help students understand the minilesson principle, use examples from mentor texts to illustrate how apostrophes are used to show possession and make contractions. Here is an example.

- Show page 16 in *A Cuban American Familia*.

  What do you notice about the way the author used apostrophes on this page?

- Guide the students to notice the apostrophe that shows possession and the ones that show contractions. Define *possessive* and *contraction* as needed.

  To make a possessive, use an apostrophe and an s. To make a contraction, use an apostrophe to show where the missing letter or letters were. The new word is called a contraction. What are the contractions on this page?

- Make a two-row chart. Label the top row *Contraction* and add *we're* and *we'll*.

  What words does *we're* stand for? How did the author make this contraction?

- Write responses on the chart.

- Label the bottom row *Possessive* and add *Abuelo's new boat*.

  What does the apostrophe tell you in this example?

- Write responses on the chart. Read pages 3 and 6 from *Ma Dear's Aprons*.

  Raise your hand when you notice a contraction or a possessive.

- As students share examples, ask them to explain how the words were made. Add them to the chart.

Section 4: Conventions

Have a Try

Invite students to turn and talk about apostrophes.

▶ Provide pairs of students with one or two books that have examples of possessives and contractions.

> With your partner, find examples of apostrophes that show possessives and contractions. In your writer's notebook, make a column for possessives and a column for contractions and write examples that you find.

▶ After a few minutes, ask volunteers to share. Add new examples to the chart.

Summarize and Apply

Summarize the learning. Remind students to use apostrophes to show possession and contractions.

> When should you use an apostrophe?

▶ Lead students to state the principle. Write it at the top of the chart.

> When you write today, remember to use an apostrophe to show possessives and contractions. Bring your writing to share when we meet later.

Use an apostrophe to show something belongs to someone or to make a contraction.		
Contraction	we're	we are
	we'll	we will
	that's	that is
	it's	it is
	I'm	I am
	she's	she is
	he's	he is
Possessive	Abuelo's new boat	the new boat that belongs to Abuelo
	Ma Dear's Aprons	the aprons that belong to Ma Dear
	day's end	the end of the day
	his mother's lap	lap that belongs to his mother

Confer

▶ During independent writing, move around the room to confer briefly with students about using apostrophes. Use the following prompts as needed.

- *Is there a place in your writing where you need to show that something belongs to someone or something else?*
- *How will this apostrophe help your readers?*
- *Point to where you will put the apostrophe when you write the contraction.*

Share

Following independent writing, gather students in the meeting area. Ask a few volunteers to share their writing.

> Share a part of your writing that uses an apostrophe.

> How do apostrophes make your writing clearer?

Use an ellipsis to show a pause or to build excitement.

Learning About Punctuation and Capitalization

You Will Need

- a mentor text that has ellipses, such as *My Typhoon* by Mike Downs, from *Shared Reading Collection*
- chart paper prepared in advance with a paragraph to which ellipses will be added
- markers
- writing folders

Academic Language / Important Vocabulary

- punctuation
- ellipsis
- pause
- build suspense
- surprise
- excitement

Continuum Connection

- Understand and use ellipses to show pause or anticipation, often before something surprising

---

GOAL

Use an ellipsis to show a pause or build excitement in writing.

RATIONALE

Learning how to use an ellipsis contributes to voice and adds interest to a piece of writing.

WRITER'S NOTEBOOK/WRITING FOLDER

Have students look at writing pieces in their writing folders to see if there is a place to insert an ellipsis.

ASSESS LEARNING

- Observe students' writing to see if they sometimes use an ellipsis to indicate a pause or to build excitement.
- Look for evidence that students can use vocabulary such as *punctuation*, *ellipsis*, *pause*, *build suspense*, *surprise*, and *excitement*.

MINILESSON

To help students understand the minilesson principle, use mentor texts and a writing sample to help them notice and talk about ellipses. Here is an example.

> Listen as I show and read several pages from *My Typhoon*.

- Read the sentence with the ellipses on pages 9, 13, 16, and 23, emphasizing the pause at the ellipses.

  > What do you notice about how I read the sentences?

- Guide the conversation to help students notice the ellipses.

  > Why do you think the writer placed an ellipsis here?

- Guide the conversation to help students recognize that the writer used the ellipses to build suspense or excitement for what was to come next.

  > When a writer uses an ellipsis, readers start to wonder what is going to happen. It builds suspense. The writer used an ellipsis here to show that readers should pause before reading the next word.

- You may want to point out that the plural of *ellipsis* is *ellipses*.

Have a Try

Invite students to turn and talk about ellipses.

▶ Show and read the prepared chart.

> Is there any place in this paragraph where I could build suspense? How might I write that with an ellipsis? Turn and talk about that.

▶ After time for discussion, ask volunteers to share ideas. Using students' suggestions, rewrite the paragraph with the ellipses. Ask the class to join in as you read the new paragraph aloud.

▶ Note that if these sentences were in a book, the ellipses might come right before a page turn.

Summarize and Apply

Summarize the learning. Have students try using ellipses to build suspense or to indicate a pause.

> What is an ellipsis and when do you use it?

▶ Write the principle at the top of the chart.

> Today, look at pieces of writing in your writing folder for a place to build suspense or show a pause. If you find one, use an ellipsis in the sentence. If you are writing a book, you might place an ellipsis before a page turn to make readers wonder what will happen next. Bring your writing to share when we meet later.

> **Use an ellipsis to show a pause or to build excitement.**
>
> One winter afternoon, I was walking home from school. Suddenly an envelope landed in front of me. What could it be? I looked around for the owner of the letter, but I didn't see anyone. Then I realized that it was addressed to me! I decided to open the letter. Inside I found a strange clue.
>
> ---
>
> One winter afternoon, I was walking home from school. Suddenly . . . an envelope landed in front of me. What could it be? I looked around for the owner of the letter, but I didn't see anyone. Then I realized that it was addressed to me! I decided to open the letter. Inside I found . . . a strange clue.

Section 4: Conventions

Confer

▶ During independent writing, move around the room to confer briefly with students about ellipses. Use the following prompts as needed.

- *Show me a place in your writing where something exciting is about to happen.*
- *How will this ellipsis help your readers?*
- *Where will you put the ellipsis?*
- *If you want to try using an ellipsis in this sentence, where might it be placed?*

Share

Following independent writing, gather students in the meeting area to share their writing.

> Who used an ellipsis in your writing today? Read the part of your writing with the ellipsis and show how you want readers to pause.

Learning About Punctuation and Capitalization

You Will Need

- several mentor texts with examples of colon usage, such as the following from Text Set: Biography: Artists
  - *Action Jackson* by Jan Greenberg and Sandra Jordan
  - *Me, Frida* by Amy Novesky
- document camera (optional)
- writing folders
- chart paper and markers

Academic Language / Important Vocabulary

- punctuation
- colon

Continuum Connection

- Use colons correctly to introduce a list of items or a long, formal statement or quotation

GOAL

Use a colon to introduce a list of items or a long formal statement or quotation.

RATIONALE

When students learn that colons can be used to introduce a list, a formal statement or a quotation, they learn another way to punctuate their own writing to make it interesting and clear.

WRITER'S NOTEBOOK/WRITING FOLDER

Have students look at writing pieces in their writing folders to see if there is a place to insert a colon.

ASSESS LEARNING

- Observe whether students' writing shows evidence that they sometimes use colons.
- Notice whether colons are used correctly in students' writing.
- Look for evidence that students can use vocabulary such as *punctuation* and *colon*.

MINILESSON

To help students understand the minilesson principle, use examples from mentor texts to illustrate the use of colons. Here is an example.

> Think about the punctuation as I read a paragraph from *Action Jackson*.

- Show page 11 from *Action Jackson* and read the first paragraph.

  > What do you notice about the punctuation in the last sentence of this paragraph?

- Ask a volunteer to come point to the colon.

  > How does the colon make the sentence clear?

- Write the sentence with the colon on chart paper, leaving space above the sentence to add the reason for the colon.

- Repeat with pages 24 and 26 in *Me, Frida*.

  > Let's read these sentences with colons together.

- Read each sentence all together, emphasizing how there is a pause after the colons.

Have a Try

Invite students to turn and talk about using colons.

> What are the reasons that the authors used these colons? Turn and talk about that.

▶ After time for discussion, ask students to share. Using generalized language, add each reason to the chart above the sentence it explains.

Summarize and Apply

Summarize the learning. Remind students to sometimes use colons in their writing pieces.

> During independent writing time, look at pieces of writing in your writing folder to see if there are places where you might use a colon. If you begin a new piece of writing, try using a colon to introduce a list, a formal statement, or a quotation. Bring your writing when we meet later.

Ways to Use a Colon

Introduce a list of items

> Sprays of color: tan, teal, yellow, and white.

Introduce a formal statement

> That night, Frida painted something great: a colorful wedding portrait of herself and Diego.

Introduce a quotation

> In the beak of a pink bird, she wrote a tiny note on violet ribbon: "Here you see us, me, Frida Kahlo, with my adored husband Diego Rivera.

Confer

▶ During independent writing, move around the room to confer briefly with students about punctuation. Use the following prompts as needed.

- *What punctuation will you use to introduce this list?*
- *How might you punctuate this statement?*
- *Show how you could introduce this statement with a colon. Where would the colon be placed?*

Share

Following independent writing, gather students in the meeting area to share their writing.

> Who used a colon today? Share what you wrote.

> What do you notice about how _____ used a colon in this sentence?

Use parentheses to clarify or add extra information.

Learning About Punctuation and Capitalization

You Will Need

- a mentor text with examples of use of parentheses, such as *Meet Danitra Brown* by Nikki Grimes, from Text Set: Illustrator Study: Floyd Cooper
- document camera (optional)
- writing folders
- chart paper and markers

Academic Language / Important Vocabulary

- punctuation
- parentheses
- clarify

Continuum Connection

- Use commas and parentheses correctly to set off parenthetical information

GOAL

Use parentheses to clarify or add extra information.

RATIONALE

When students learn that parentheses can be used to clarify or add extra information, they think about new and interesting ways to express their thoughts in writing to help readers know what they are trying to say.

WRITER'S NOTEBOOK/WRITING FOLDER

Have students look at writing pieces in their writing folders to see if there is a place to use parentheses.

ASSESS LEARNING

- Observe whether students' writing shows evidence that they are using parentheses to clarify or add extra information.
- Look for evidence that students can use vocabulary such as *punctuation*, *parentheses*, and *clarify*.

MINILESSON

To help students understand the minilesson principle, provide an inquiry-based lesson using examples from a mentor text to illustrate how parentheses can be used to clarify or add extra information. Here is an example.

- Show (or project) page 5 from *Meet Danitra Brown* and read the first paragraph, changing your voice when you read the part in parentheses.

  What do you notice about the punctuation?

  These curved lines are called parentheses. Parentheses are always used in pairs, just like quotation marks. How does the writer's use of parentheses help me know how to read this part?

- Show and read page 10.

  How do the parentheses help you know how to read this aloud?

  Let's think about how adding the parentheses helps you understand what the writer is communicating.

- Write the last two lines on chart paper in two ways: the way it is written in the book with parentheses and written without parentheses.

- Read the text two different ways, emphasizing how the parentheses impact the way it is read and the meaning. Then ask students what they notice about what parentheses do in a sentence. Begin a list on a new sheet of chart paper. Add an example for each way mentioned.

Have a Try

Invite students to turn and talk about using parentheses.

▶ Show and read page 12 in *Meet Danitra Brown*.

Turn and talk about why the author used parentheses here. How would the meaning change without the parentheses?

▶ After time for discussion, ask students to share. Add any new ideas to the chart.

Summarize and Apply

Summarize the learning. Remind students to sometimes use parentheses to clarify or add information in their writing.

During independent writing time, look at pieces of writing in your writing folder to see if there are any places where you might use parentheses. If you begin a new writing piece today, try using parentheses in it. Bring your writing when we meet later.

Confer

▶ During independent writing, move around the room to confer briefly with students about punctuation. Use the following prompts as needed.

- *Is there a place where you might use parentheses to clarify or add information?*
- *Read this part with the parentheses.*
- *Look back at your writing and check if you included both the open parenthesis and the closed parenthesis.*

Share

Following independent writing, gather students in the meeting area. Ask a few volunteers to share their writing.

In what ways did you use parentheses today?

Read part of your writing that includes parentheses.

We took soup to her mom. (I was quiet as a mouse!) It was serious work. We were the ladies of the house.

We took soup to her mom. I was quiet as a mouse! It was serious work. We were the ladies of the house.

Ways to Use Parentheses

Make information clear
 I picked up a lot of shells (mostly scallop shells) on the beach.

Add extra information
 Elephants (African bush, African forest, and Asian) are the largest living land animals.

Talk to the readers
 Some tarantulas can live up to thirty years. (That's a long time for a spider!)

Add humor
 I'm all wet because I got caught in the rain (again!) without an umbrella.

Assessment

After you have taught the minilessons in this umbrella, observe students in a variety of classroom activities. Use *The Fountas & Pinnell Literacy Continuum* to notice, teach for, and support students' learning as you observe their attempts at writing.

▶ What evidence do you have of students' new understandings related to punctuation and capitalization?

- Are students noticing ways that authors use punctuation and capitalization?
- Are they punctuating dialogue correctly?
- Do students use a comma after introductory words and between items in a list?
- Can they use apostrophes correctly for possessives and contractions?
- Are they experimenting with ellipses to show pauses or to build excitement?
- Do they sometimes use colons in their writing?
- Are they able to use parentheses to clarify or add extra information?
- Are they using vocabulary such as *punctuation, sentence, period, question mark, exclamation point, dialogue, quotation marks, comma, list, apostrophe, contraction, ellipsis, colon,* and *parentheses*?

▶ In what ways, beyond the scope of this umbrella, are students showing an understanding of conventions?

- Do they show an interest in editing and revising their work?
- Do they show voice in their writing?

Use your observations to determine the next umbrella you will teach. You may also consult Suggested Sequence of Lessons (pp. 665–682) for guidance.

EXTENSIONS FOR LEARNING ABOUT PUNCTUATION AND CAPITALIZATION

▶ Introduce students to using hyphens (to divide words correctly at the syllable break at the end of a line), brackets (to separate different ideas or kinds of information), and dashes (to indicate a longer pause, to slow down, or to emphasize particular information).

▶ Teach students that the apostrophe goes after the *s* when showing possession with a plural noun (e.g., groups' projects).

▶ Gather together a few students who need support in the same aspect of writing to form a temporary guided writing group.

Minilessons in This Umbrella

WML1 Notice how and why authors use paragraphs.

WML2 Make a new paragraph for a new idea.

WML3 Use paragraphs to show when a new speaker is talking.

Before Teaching Umbrella 3 Minilessons

The minilessons in this umbrella will help students organize their writing into paragraphs, including organizing dialogue. The minilessons discuss ways to organize information by topic (without sacrificing craft) so readers can easily understand and remember what they read. Students are ready to consider the decisions authors make about paragraphs so they can begin to apply this to the organization of their own writing.

Begin by noticing how and why authors use paragraphs. Discuss how opening a book and seeing continuous text without breaks might cause a feeling of being overwhelmed and, conversely, that breaking text into paragraphs makes it more accessible.

In the classroom, students are often writing their drafts by hand and skipping a line, so encouraging students to skip a line between paragraphs may not make much sense at this point. When to do that is a decision that you as the teacher will need to make.

Read and discuss enjoyable books with clear use of paragraphs organized by topic and paragraphs used to indicate dialogue. Use the following texts from *Fountas & Pinnell Classroom™ Interactive Read-Aloud Collection*, choose familiar books from the classroom library, or gather examples of paragraphs in articles, short stories, or passages from familiar novels.

Interactive Read-Aloud Collection

Telling a Story with Photos

Face to Face with Whales by Flip and Linda Nicklin

Figuring Out Who You Are

The Gold-Threaded Dress by Carolyn Marsden

Illustration Study: Craft

Magnificent Birds by Narisa Togo

Genre Study: Memoir

Twelve Kinds of Ice by Ellen Bryan Obed

Friendship

Mangoes, Mischief, and Tales of Friendship: Stories from India by Chitra Soundar

As you read and enjoy these texts together, help students

- notice how paragraphs look, and
- talk about the decisions writers make when organizing writing into paragraphs, such as for a new idea or for dialogue.

Interactive Read-Aloud
Telling a Story with Photos

Face to Face with Whales by Flip and Linda Nicklin

Figuring Out Who You Are

Craft

Memoir

Friendship

Writer's Notebook

Section 4: Conventions

Writing Minilesson Principle

Notice how and why authors use paragraphs.

You Will Need

- several familiar texts with clear examples of how authors use paragraphs, such as the following:

  - *Face to Face with Whales* by Flip and Linda Nicklin, from Text Set: Telling a Story with Photos

  - *The Gold-Threaded Dress* by Carolyn Marsden, from Text Set: Figuring Out Who You Are

- chart paper prepared with column headings (see chart)

- one or more texts for each pair of students and sticky notes (see Have a Try)

- document camera (optional)

- markers

- writer's notebooks and writing folders

Academic Language / Important Vocabulary

- paragraphs
- organize
- indent
- spacing

Continuum Connection

- Organize information according to purpose and genre

- Use paragraphs to organize ideas

- Learn ways of using language and constructing texts from other writers (reading books and hearing them read aloud) and apply understandings to one's own writing

GOAL

Use inquiry to notice how and why authors use paragraphs to organize their writing.

RATIONALE

As students notice and discuss the decisions writers make to organize their writing into paragraphs, they can begin to make these kinds of decisions in their own writing.

WRITER'S NOTEBOOK/WRITING FOLDER

Students will write in their writer's notebooks reasons authors use paragraphs, and they will think about how to use paragraphs as they work on longer writing pieces from their writing folders.

ASSESS LEARNING

- Observe for evidence that students recognize that writers use paragraphs to organize their writing and can articulate why they do this.

- Notice students' use of paragraphs in their own writing.

- Observe for evidence that students can use vocabulary such as *paragraphs*, *organize*, *indent*, and *spacing*.

MINILESSON

Students will need their writer's notebooks for this lesson. To help students think about the minilesson principle, use inquiry to guide them in noticing how and why writers organize their writing into paragraphs. Emphasize the style of paragraphing (indentation, space between paragraphs) used in your classroom. Here is an example.

- Show *Face to Face with Whales*. Use a document camera, if available, to show and read pages 9–10.

  What do you notice about how the authors organized their writing on these pages? How do the paragraphs look? What do they help the authors to do, and how do they help you as a reader? Turn and talk with a partner.

- After time for discussion, invite a few students to share. Record ideas in general terms on the prepared chart.

  What information do the paragraphs tell you? Why do you think the authors organized their paragraphs this way?

- Record ideas in general terms on the chart.

  The authors included their personal experiences with whales and information about whales in the same section, organized into paragraphs.

- Repeat this process with pages 1–3 from *The Gold-Threaded Dress*.

Have a Try

Invite students to discover additional, authentic ways authors use paragraphs.

▸ Provide partners with sticky notes and one or more familiar texts with good examples of text organized into paragraphs.

> As you look through these books together, notice when an author made the decision to start a new paragraph. Mark these with a sticky note and write in your writer's notebook why you think the author chose to do that.

▸ After time for discussion, invite students to share their ideas. Add new noticings to the chart.

Summarize and Apply

Help students summarize the learning. As they work on longer pieces of writing, remind them to think about where they might start a new paragraph.

> What can you do to organize your writing?

▸ Write the principle at the top of the chart.

> As you write, think about how you will group your sentences together. When you start writing about a new topic or idea, or when a character starts talking, start a new paragraph. Remember how to show where a new paragraph starts. Bring your writing to share when we meet later.

Notice how and why authors use paragraphs.	
What do you notice about the paragraphs?	**What do paragraphs help the author do?**
Tell about one idea or topic	Organize facts about one topic into categories
Separate author's experiences from information about the topic	Organize information for the reader
Separate dialogue from narration	Help the reader follow the story and the dialogue
Are indented (first line)	
Show transitions between actions, dialogue, and character's internal thoughts	Give the text a manageable layout

Confer

▸ During independent writing, move around the room to confer briefly with students about how they are using paragraphs in their writing. Use prompts such as the following as needed.

- *Where does your next idea or topic start?*
- *Is there dialogue that needs to be separated?*
- *Why did you start a new paragraph here? Do all of these sentences go together?*
- *How do you know when to start a new paragraph?*

Share

Following independent writing, gather students in the meeting area to share their writing.

> How did you decide to start a new paragraph? Why?

Writing Minilesson Principle
Make a new paragraph for a new idea.

Learning to Paragraph

You Will Need

- several familiar texts with clear examples of paragraphs organized by topic, such as the following:
  - *Face to Face with Whales* by Flip and Linda Nicklin, from Text Set: Telling a Story with Photos
  - *Magnificent Birds* by Narisa Togo, from Text Set: Illustration Study: Craft
  - *Twelve Kinds of Ice* by Ellen Bryan Obed, from Text Set: Genre Study: Memoir
- chart paper and markers
- a sample piece of nonfiction writing without paragraph breaks, such as the online resource, written on chart paper (or projected)
- document camera (optional)
- writing folders
- To download the following online resource for this lesson, visit **fp.pub/resources**:
  - Maple Trees (optional)

Academic Language / Important Vocabulary

- paragraph
- organize
- indent
- spacing

Continuum Connection

- Organize information according to purpose and genre
- Use paragraphs to organize ideas
- Create transitions between paragraphs to show the progression of ideas

---

GOAL

Understand that writers start a paragraph when they write about a new idea.

RATIONALE

Using paragraphs to organize the information in a piece of writing helps readers better understand what they are reading. As students notice how authors organize information into paragraphs, they can begin to do the same in their own writing.

WRITER'S NOTEBOOK/WRITING FOLDER

Students will think about how to use paragraphs as they work on longer writing pieces from their writing folders.

ASSESS LEARNING

- Observe for evidence that students organize their writing into meaningful paragraphs, with indentation or spacing.
- Observe for evidence that students can use vocabulary such as *paragraph*, *organize*, *indent*, and *spacing*.

MINILESSON

To help students think about the minilesson principle, use familiar texts to guide them in noticing how writers organize their writing into paragraphs when a new idea is introduced. Use a document camera, if available. Here is an example.

- Show *Face to Face with Whales* and read pages 18–21.

  What decisions do you think the authors made about how to organize the information into paragraphs?

- Repeat this process with page 6 of *Magnificent Birds* and pages 22–23 of *Twelve Kinds of Ice*.

  How do the writers of these books show you when a new paragraph begins?

  Some writers indent the first line. Other writers put extra space between the paragraphs.

- Emphasize the style of paragraphing (indented first line or space between block paragraphs) that you use in your classroom.

  What kinds of ideas did these writers group together in paragraphs? Turn and talk to your partner about that.

- After time for discussion, invite a few students to share. Record responses in general terms on chart paper.

  How does breaking sentences into paragraphs help you as a reader?

Have a Try

Display a piece of nonfiction writing (e.g., the online resource Maple Trees). Read it aloud and invite students to turn and talk to a partner about how they might organize the writing into paragraphs.

> I wrote about maple trees. How might I organize my sentences into paragraphs? When does the topic or idea change? Turn and talk about that.

▶ After time for discussion, decide with the students where to insert paragraph marks (¶).

> When you are writing or rereading drafts, think about how to organize your writing. When you come to a place where a new paragraph should begin, you can use this symbol to remind you where to start a new paragraph.

Summarize and Apply

Help students summarize the learning. Remind them to think about how they will organize their writing into paragraphs.

> What is one way you can organize your writing for your readers?

▶ Write the principle at the top of the first chart.

> As you write or reread drafts, think about how you will organize your writing so readers can better understand and remember the information. When you want to start a new paragraph, indent the first sentence by putting two fingers down on the side of the paper. Bring your writing to share when we meet later.

Make a new paragraph for a new idea.

Reasons to Start a New Paragraph

- Share information about different types of something
- Separate different pieces of information related to the same topic
- Make it easier for readers to remember what they read
- Provide general information (first paragraph), followed by more specific details (second paragraph)
- Tell readers new information is coming
- Show the progression of activities leading up to something
- Describe steps in a process
- Show time transitions
- Organize information for the readers

¶ If you live in the northern hemisphere, you've probably seen a maple tree. They grow in many parts of the United States and Canada. Canada even has a maple leaf on its flag and a hockey team named after it. ¶ The leaves of maple trees change color in the fall—orange, red, and yellow. Lots of people travel to see these magical colors. ¶ Maple syrup comes from the sap of maple trees. A little spout is put into the trunk of the tree. (It doesn't hurt the tree!) Forty to fifty gallons of sap are boiled down to make one gallon of syrup. ¶ The wood from maple trees carries sound well. It is used for instruments, like violins and cellos. Baseball bats, furniture, and paper are also made from the wood of maple trees.

Confer

▶ During independent writing, move around the room to confer briefly with students about how they are using paragraphs in their writing. Use prompts such as the following as needed.

- *Why did you start a new paragraph here?*
- *What can you do to help your readers know this is a new idea?*
- *How do you know when to start a new paragraph?*

Share

Following independent writing, gather students in the meeting area to share their writing.

> What did you think about to decide whether to start a new paragraph?

Writing Minilesson Principle
Use paragraphs to show when a new speaker is talking.

You Will Need

- several familiar texts with clear examples of dialogue in paragraphs, such as the following:
  - *The Gold-Threaded Dress* by Carolyn Marsden, from Text Set: Figuring Out Who You Are
  - *Mangoes, Mischief, and Tales of Friendship* by Chitra Soundar, from Text Set: Friendship
- document camera [optional]
- chart paper prepared with column headings [see chart]
- a writing sample with dialogue but no paragraph breaks, such as the online resource, written on chart paper [or projected]
- markers
- writing folders
- To download the following online resource for this lesson, visit **fp.pub/resources**:
  - Fishing [optional]

Academic Language / Important Vocabulary

- dialogue
- paragraphs
- unassigned dialogue
- speaker
- indent

Continuum Connection

- Understand and use paragraphs to show speaker change in dialogue

GOAL

Understand that writers use paragraphs to show when the speaker changes.

RATIONALE

Writers use a new paragraph to show a change in the speaker. This helps readers understand who is speaking. When students notice this, they can begin to do this in their own writing.

WRITER'S NOTEBOOK/WRITING FOLDER

Students will think about how to use paragraphs to show dialogue as they work on longer writing pieces from their writing folders.

ASSESS LEARNING

- Observe for evidence that students recognize that writers use paragraphs to indicate a change in speaker, including unassigned dialogue.
- Notice students' use of paragraphs in their own writing.
- Observe for evidence that students can use vocabulary such as *dialogue*, *paragraphs*, *unassigned dialogue*, *speaker*, and *indent*.

MINILESSON

To help students think about the minilesson principle, use familiar texts to guide them in noticing how writers use paragraphs to organize dialogue. Here is an example.

- Show *The Gold-Threaded Dress*. Project the text, if possible, to show and read pages 68–69.

  What do you notice about how the author organized the words the characters say—the dialogue? Turn and talk with a partner.

- After time for discussion, invite a few students to share what they noticed. Record responses in general terms in the first column of the prepared chart paper.

  What do the paragraphs help the author do?

- Record responses in general terms in the second column of the chart.

  Writers use paragraphs to separate dialogue in their writing and to show a different character is talking so that readers can keep track of who is speaking. Sometimes dialogue is unassigned. This means the writer doesn't say who is talking; a new paragraph shows the change of speaker.

- If needed, refer to the top of page 69 to show an example of unassigned dialogue.

- Repeat this process with page 50 from *Mangoes, Mischief, and Tales of Friendship*.

Have a Try

Invite students to turn and talk to a partner about how they might organize writing into paragraphs.

▶ Display a piece of writing with dialogue and without paragraph breaks (e.g., the online resource Fishing). Read it aloud.

> How can you organize this writing into paragraphs? Where does a new speaker start talking? Turn and talk about that.

▶ After time for discussion, insert (or have a student insert) the paragraph symbol to mark where a new paragraph indicates a new speaker.

Summarize and Apply

Help students summarize the learning. Remind them to start a new paragraph when a new speaker is talking. Let students know whether they should indent or leave space before their new paragraphs.

> What can you do to organize your writing for your readers?

▶ Write the principle at the top of the first chart.

> As you write, notice where you have talking in your writing. When the speaker changes, start a new paragraph. Remember to place two fingers on the side of the page to show where to indent the first sentence. Bring your writing to share when we meet later.

Confer

▶ During independent writing, move around the room to confer briefly with students about how they are using paragraphs in their writing. Use prompts such as the following as needed.

- *Where does the next speaker start talking?*
- *Why did you start a new paragraph here?*
- *Where else are you thinking of grouping your sentences into paragraphs?*
- *How do you know when to start a new paragraph?*

Share

Following independent writing, gather students in the meeting area to share their writing.

> Who would like to share where you decided to start a new paragraph to make it clear who is talking?

Use paragraphs to show when a new speaker is talking.

What do you notice about the paragraphs?	What do paragraphs help the author do?
Each time the speaker changes, the writer starts a new paragraph.	Help readers notice the talking
Some of the dialogue doesn't say who is talking (unassigned dialogue).	Tell readers that the speaker is changing
Sometimes the paragraphs have other sentences in addition to the dialogue.	Help readers keep track of who is talking when it doesn't say (unassigned dialogue)
The paragraphs are indented.	Show readers who is talking and what the person is doing

---

¶ "I think I feel a fish nibbling on the hook," Jack whispered as he leaned over, peering into the water to get a closer look. ¶ "Gently and slowly start reeling in the line," Dad said calmly. "You don't want to pull it in too fast and risk snapping the line." ¶ Jack let out a long, slow breath as he cautiously began winding the reel. "It's getting heavy, Dad. The fish is really pulling," Jack said nervously. ¶ Dad nodded as he helped Jack pull the line out of the water. "Look, you caught a branch!"

Section 4: Conventions

Assessment

After you have taught the minilessons in this umbrella, observe students as they write and talk about their writing. Use *The Fountas & Pinnell Literacy Continuum* to notice, teach for, and support students' learning as you observe their attempts at writing.

▶ What evidence do you have of students' new understandings related to organizing paragraphs?

- Are students able to articulate their decision-making process for organizing their writing into paragraphs?

- Do they start a new paragraph for a new idea?

- Do they use paragraphs to show when a new speaker is talking?

- Do they indent or use good spacing to set off paragraphs?

- Is there evidence students can use vocabulary such as *paragraphs*, *indent*, *spacing*, *dialogue*, *unassigned dialogue*, *speaker*, and *organize*?

▶ In what other ways, beyond the scope of this umbrella, are students learning about the conventions of writing?

- Are they thinking about time transitions as a way to organize paragraphs?

- Are they noticing conventions writers use?

Use your observations to determine the next umbrella you will teach. You may also consult Suggested Sequence of Lessons (pp. 665–682) for guidance.

EXTENSIONS FOR LEARNING TO PARAGRAPH

▶ Create a chart that collects students' noticings about paragraphs as they continue exploring familiar texts.

▶ Remind students to apply the lessons in this umbrella as they revise their writing, using the paragraph symbol to indicate the start of a new paragraph.

▶ Gather a small group of students who need additional support in organizing their writing into paragraphs for guided writing.

▶ If students type their final draft on a computer, show them how to indent or insert an extra return.

Section 5 | Writing Process

WRITERS LEARN TO write by writing. As they write, they engage in some aspect of the writing process. They plan what to write, write a first draft and make changes to improve it, check their work to be sure the message is clear to the readers, and publish it by sharing it with an audience. Not all aspects of the writing process will happen at one time, and they won't always happen in the same order. Writers tend to move back and forth. But over time, each will experience the full writing process. The lessons in this section will help you guide the students in your class through the writing process.

5 Writing Process

Planning and Rehearsing

Drafting and Revising

Editing and Proofreading

Publishing

Writer's Notebook

Minilessons in This Umbrella

WML1 Make your writer's notebook your own.

WML2 Write in your writer's notebook at least ten minutes every day.

WML3 Collect your thinking in your writer's notebook.

WML4 Keep your writer's notebook organized.

WML5 Keep building your writer's notebook.

Before Teaching Umbrella 1 Minilessons

A writer's notebook is a very important tool for any writer. It is a place to record seeds of ideas for writing, experiment with quick writes, and find ideas for longer writing projects. These longer writing projects will be done on separate paper and usually kept in a writing folder. As students build the content in their notebooks, they will develop a rich resource for writing inspiration.

Provide each student with *Writer's Notebook, Intermediate* (Fountas and Pinnell 2023) or guide students to create their own writer's notebooks from composition books or spiral-bound notebooks. (For suggestions on how to organize a writer's notebook if you are creating one, see pages 87–91.)

Receiving a new writer's notebook is a time of celebration for young writers. Help students develop a sense of pride in and ownership of their writer's notebook by delivering it to them in a momentous way and encouraging them to decorate the cover (WML1). Introduce the writer's notebook as you begin teaching the routines of writers' workshop. It will be helpful for you to write in a writer's notebook of your own so that you can provide authentic examples to your students.

You do not need to teach the minilessons in this umbrella consecutively. WML5 should be taught only after some or all of the lessons in WPS.U2: Writer's Notebook: Getting Ideas from Your Life and WPS.U3: Writer's Notebook: Getting Inspiration from Writers and Artists have been taught.

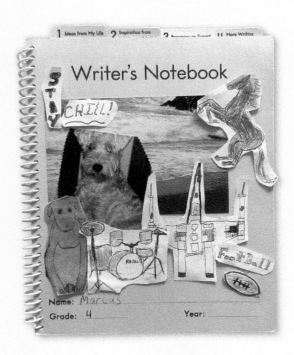

WML1

Writing Minilesson Principle

Make your writer's notebook your own.

Introducing and Using a Writer's Notebook

You Will Need

- your own writer's notebook with a decorated front cover
- a new writer's notebook for every student
- highlighters
- chart paper and markers
- art materials for decorating the notebook covers (stickers, different kinds of paper, glitter, photos from magazines, markers, etc.)
- To download the following online resource for this lesson, visit **fp.pub/resources**:
  - Writer's Notebook Letter (optional)

Academic Language / Important Vocabulary

- writer's notebook

Continuum Connection

- Use a writer's notebook or booklet as a tool for collecting ideas, experimenting, planning, sketching, or drafting

GOAL

Understand that a writer's notebook is a special place to keep ideas about yourself and your world.

RATIONALE

A writer's notebook is a special place to collect and save personal ideas for writing. The act of keeping a writer's notebook builds a foundation for a lifelong habit of writing. When students decorate the cover of a writer's notebook in a creative and personalized way, they develop a sense of ownership over it and will be more inclined to use it as intended.

WRITER'S NOTEBOOK/WRITING FOLDER

Students will start decorating the front and back covers of their writer's notebooks.

ASSESS LEARNING

- Notice what students understand about a writer's notebook.
- Get to know your students by noticing how they decorate the cover of their writer's notebooks.
- Look for evidence that students understand and use the term *writer's notebook*.

MINILESSON

Emphasize the delight and potential of a new writer's notebook as you distribute a new notebook to each student. For this lesson, use the letter printed in *Writer's Notebook, Intermediate* (also available from the online resources) or write your own and have students glue it into their notebooks. Here is an example.

> Today is a very special day in your life as a writer! I'm going to give each of you your very own writer's notebook. Don't open it yet! We all want to open our notebooks at the same time.

- Distribute the notebooks in a fun or ceremonial way.
- When all students have a notebook, direct them to open the notebooks all at once. Then have them turn to the letter at the beginning and read it to themselves. Direct them to highlight parts of the letter that stand out to them.

  > What are some ideas in the letter that stood out to you?

- Record students' responses on chart paper.

Have a Try

Engage students in a conversation about decorating the front and back covers of their writer's notebooks.

▸ Display your own writer's notebook.

> Look at the front and back covers of my writer's notebook. What do you notice about how I decorated them? How did I show something about myself?

> Turn and talk to your partner about ways you might decorate your notebook to show who you are and how you are unique.

▸ After time for discussion, invite several volunteers to share their ideas. Record ideas on the chart.

Summarize and Apply

Summarize the lesson and write the principle at the top of the chart. Invite students to decorate their writer's notebooks.

> Today, you each got your own writer's notebook, and you thought about how you can decorate it to show who you are. Now, start decorating the front and back covers of your notebook. This can take time, just like writing, so you don't need to finish today. As you work, think about whether there's anything you'd like to bring in from home to decorate your notebook. Bring your writer's notebook to share when we meet later.

Make your writer's notebook your own.

- You will have three tools—a writer's notebook, a writing folder, and a writing file.
- Write or sketch in your notebook for at least 10 minutes every day.
- Collect memories, lists, observations, artifacts, and sketches.
- Record all your ideas for writing.
- Everyone's notebook will be different.
- Decorate the cover to show something about yourself.

- Pictures of yourself or people you love
- Sketches of your favorite things or activities
- Writer's Notebook
- Favorite quotes
- Lines from favorite poems or songs
- Stickers

Confer

▸ While students are writing, move around the room to confer briefly with them about decorating their writer's notebooks. Use prompts such as the following as needed.

- *How are you going to decorate the cover of your notebook?*
- *How can you show important things about yourself?*
- *Who or what is important in your life? How can you show that on the notebook cover?*
- *Why did you decide to put _____ on the cover of your notebook?*

Share

At the end of the writing time, gather students in the meeting area. Have students show their writer's notebook covers one at a time.

> What ideas do you notice on your classmates' notebooks that you might try?

Section 5: Writing Process

Writing Minilesson Principle
Write in your writer's notebook at least ten minutes every day.

Introducing and Using a Writer's Notebook

You Will Need

▸ chart paper and markers

▸ writer's notebooks

Academic Language / Important Vocabulary

▸ writer's notebook

Continuum Connection

▸ Produce a reasonable quantity of writing within the time available

▸ Write routinely over extended timeframes and shorter timeframes from a range of discipline-specific tasks, purposes, and audiences

GOAL

Develop the routine of writing daily in a writer's notebook.

RATIONALE

It is important to provide students with many opportunities to do short quick writes every day in addition to independent writing to help them build writing fluency and stamina, add to their ideas in their writer's notebooks, and expand their ability to write in a variety of ways. Sometimes you may choose to provide a prompt for this writing time, or students can write about ideas they have already gathered in their writer's notebooks. These ten minutes of writing in the writer's notebook can happen at any time of the day outside of writers' workshop.

WRITER'S NOTEBOOK/WRITING FOLDER

Students will do a quick write in their writer's notebooks to help them develop the habit of writing in a notebook every day.

ASSESS LEARNING

▸ Notice whether students can write for ten minutes at a time.

▸ Observe for evidence that they can use the term *writer's notebook*.

MINILESSON

If you are not using *Writer's Notebook, Intermediate*, set up sections in students' notebooks ahead of time so that students will have a place to write. To help students think about the minilesson principle, invite them to write for ten minutes in a section of the writer's notebook that has plenty of blank pages (e.g., Section 4 in *Writer's Notebook, Intermediate*). Here is an example.

> Writers write every day. Setting aside time to write every day is important to help you grow as a writer. Every day, you will spend ten minutes writing or sketching in your writer's notebook outside of our normal writing time.

> One way that you can write in your writer's notebook is to do a quick write about an idea. For today's quick write, think about the word *peace.*

▸ Write the word *peace* on a sheet of chart paper.

> What does this word make you think of? What feelings do you have when you think of this word? What does this word mean to you? Turn and talk to your partner about your ideas.

▸ After students turn and talk, invite a few students to share their ideas.

> Now that you've spent a few minutes thinking about and discussing the word *peace,* let's see what it's like to write for ten minutes. You can write anything you want, as long as it has to do with the word *peace.*

▸ Set a timer for ten minutes and remind students to write for the entire time.

Have a Try

Invite students to talk to a partner about writing in a writer's notebook every day.

> Why is it a good idea to write in your writer's notebook for ten minutes every day? How could this help you grow as a writer? Turn and talk to your partner about this.

▶ After time for discussion, invite several students to share their thinking. Record their responses on chart paper.

Summarize and Apply

Summarize the learning and remind students to write for at least ten minutes a day in their writer's notebooks.

> What was it like to write in your writer's notebook for ten minutes?

▶ Write the principle at the top of the chart.

> Do some writing and sketching in your writer's notebook. Think of an idea—any idea—you want to write about. You may continue writing about the word *peace*, write about a different word that is important to you, or write about something else entirely.

> **Write in your writer's notebook at least ten minutes every day.**
>
> Why write for ten minutes a day?
>
> • To gather ideas for writing
>
> • To try out ideas for writing
>
> • To try new types of writing
>
> • To develop the habit of writing every day
>
> • To become a better writer
>
> • To collect your thinking about different ideas

Confer

▶ While students are writing, move around the room to confer briefly with them about what they are writing. Use prompts such as the following as needed.

- *How's your writing going today?*
- *What are you working on today?*
- *What else could you write about?*

Share

At the end of the writing time, gather students in the meeting area to talk about their writing.

> What did you write about in your writer's notebook today?

> What do you think you will like about writing in your writer's notebook every day?

WML 3
WPS.U1.WML3

Writing Minilesson Principle
Collect your thinking in your writer's notebook.

Introducing and Using a Writer's Notebook

You Will Need

- writer's notebooks
- chart paper and markers

Academic Language / Important Vocabulary

- writer's notebook
- section
- inspiration
- expert

Continuum Connection

- Use a writer's notebook or booklet as a tool for collecting ideas, experimenting, planning, sketching, or drafting
- Use sketching, webs, lists, and freewriting to think about, plan for, and try out writing
- Have topics and ideas for writing in a list or notebook

GOAL

Learn the organization of the writer's notebook to help with collecting and organizing ideas.

RATIONALE

Understanding the organization of their writer's notebooks (see pages 87–91 for guidance on creating sections) will help students know where to record their ideas and where to look when they reread their notebooks to find ideas to expand into longer pieces.

WRITER'S NOTEBOOK/WRITING FOLDER

Students will start collecting ideas in their writer's notebooks.

ASSESS LEARNING

- Notice whether students understand how the writer's notebook is organized and what they will write about in each section.
- Look for evidence that students can use vocabulary such as *writer's notebook*, *section*, *inspiration*, and *expert*.

MINILESSON

Students will need their writer's notebooks for this minilesson. To help students think about the minilesson principle, have them work in groups to learn about the organization of their writer's notebooks. Below is an example.

> Each of you has your own writer's notebook. You will use your notebook all year to collect your ideas for writing and to try out different ideas and types of writing. Let's explore the sections in your notebook.

- Draw students' attention to the tabs at the top of the writer's notebook. Note that the tops of the tabs need to be unfolded.

> The writer's notebook has four sections. You can use the tabs at the top to find each section. You can get ideas for writing in lots of different ways, and the sections in your writer's notebook will help you learn how to build your notebook with ideas and to keep your ideas organized.

- Divide students into four groups and direct each group to investigate one of the sections. Then invite each group to share what they noticed about their section.

> What did your group notice about Section 1: Ideas from My Life? What is this section about?

- Use students' responses to write a summary statement on chart paper.

- Continue in a similar manner with the three remaining sections (Inspiration from Writers and Artists, Becoming an Expert, More Writing and Sketching).

Have a Try

Invite students to turn and talk to a partner about the writer's notebook.

> Turn and talk to your partner about what you might write about in one of the sections of your writer's notebook.

▶ After time for discussion, ask a few volunteers to share. Confirm their understanding of the writer's notebook and clear up any misconceptions.

Summarize and Apply

Write the principle at the top of the chart. Summarize the lesson. Invite students to write down some ideas in Section 4 of their notebooks.

> How can your writer's notebook help you grow as a writer?

▶ Make sure students understand that they will reread their notebooks from time to time to find ideas for longer pieces of writing.

> Turn to the last section in your writer's notebook. Write some ideas for writing on the tabbed page. Once you have a list of ideas, you can look there any time you need an idea to write about. If you would like to write about one of your ideas today, turn to the first clean page and start writing. Bring your writer's notebook to share when we come back together.

Collect your thinking in your writer's notebook.			
Ideas from My Life	**Inspiration from Writers and Artists**	**Becoming an Expert**	**More Writing and Sketching**
Collect writing ideas from your everyday life.	Collect ideas from reading someone else's writing or from looking at art.	Collect and organize notes on topics that are interesting to you.	Write or draw about any idea in all types of ways.

Confer

▶ While students are writing, move around the room to confer briefly with students about collecting ideas in their writer's notebook. Use the following prompts as needed.

- *What ideas do you have for your writing?*
- *What are you interested in?*
- *What do you look forward to writing about?*

Share

At the end of the writing time, gather students in the meeting area. Ask each student to share one idea for writing.

> Share one idea you wrote on your list.

> Did anyone hear an idea from a classmate that you might put on your list?

Writing Minilesson Principle
Keep your writer's notebook organized.

You Will Need

▸ writer's notebooks

▸ chart paper and markers

Academic Language / Important Vocabulary

▸ guidelines

▸ organized

▸ writer's notebook

Continuum Connection

▸ Use a writer's notebook or booklet as a tool for collecting ideas, experimenting, planning, sketching, or drafting

---

GOAL

Keep the writer's notebook organized so it can be used efficiently.

RATIONALE

Teaching students ways to take care of the writer's notebook and keep it organized helps them use it more efficiently. Developing guidelines for using the writer's notebook together helps students take ownership of the guidelines and of their notebooks.

WRITER'S NOTEBOOK/WRITING FOLDER

Students will decorate and/or write in their writer's notebooks.

ASSESS LEARNING

▸ Look at students' notebooks. Are they well cared for and organized?

▸ Look for evidence that students can use vocabulary such as *guidelines*, *organized*, and *writer's notebook*.

MINILESSON

To help students understand the minilesson principle, engage them in developing guidelines for using a writer's notebook. Below is an example. If you are using *Writer's Notebook, Intermediate*, there are guidelines inside the front cover. If not, make a copy of the guidelines that students develop in this minilesson for them to glue into their notebooks.

> To do your best work in your writer's notebook, it will be helpful to have some guidelines. Let's think about what you can do to keep your writer's notebook organized.

▸ Build a list of guidelines on chart paper using questions such as the following as needed.

  • *How can the sections keep your writing organized?*

  • *What materials might you use to write or sketch in your notebook?*

  • *How can you start an entry in a way that helps keep your notebook organized?*

  • *How can you be sure you'll be able to read your writing when you reread what you have written?*

  • *What could you do if you are writing and you want to make a change or need to correct a mistake?*

Have a Try

Invite students to talk to a partner about the guidelines. If you are using *Writer's Notebook, Intermediate*, you might have students compare the guidelines they just developed with those inside the front cover.

> Are there any other guidelines that you think we should add to our chart? Turn and talk to your partner about this.

▶ After time for discussion, continue adding to the chart, as appropriate.

Summarize and Apply

Summarize the lesson and remind students to keep their writer's notebooks organized.

> What will you remember to do when you use your writer's notebook?

▶ Write the principle at the top of the chart.

> Today, you can spend some more time decorating the covers of your writer's notebook or you can open to Section 4, write today's date on the first clean page, and write about whatever you want. Bring your notebook to share when we meet later.

Keep your writer's notebook organized.

HOW	WHY
• Follow the tabs to know what to write in each section.	• It will be easier to find what you wrote when you need it.
• Write the date every time you start an entry.	• You will know when you worked on an entry.
• Write on the next clean page of the appropriate section.	• You won't waste any pages.
• Write neatly.	• You will be able to read what you wrote.
• Cross out with one line only when you make a mistake or make a change.	• You might change your mind and use the idea later.

Confer

▶ While students are writing, move around the room to confer briefly with students about using a writer's notebook. Use the following prompts as needed.

- *What will you do to keep your writer's notebook organized?*
- *What are you writing about in your writer's notebook today?*
- *What is the first thing you should write on the page before you start writing your ideas?*

Share

At the end of writing time, gather students in the meeting area to talk about their notebooks.

> Turn and talk to your partner about what you worked on in your writer's notebook.

Writing Minilesson Principle
Keep building your writer's notebook.

Introducing and Using a Writer's Notebook

You Will Need

- chart paper and markers
- writer's notebooks

Academic Language / Important Vocabulary

- writer's notebook

Continuum Connection

- Write routinely over extended timeframes and shorter timeframes from a range of discipline-specific tasks, purposes, and audiences

GOAL

Continue building a writer's notebook by writing in it in a variety of ways.

RATIONALE

Building a daily habit of writing is important for developing fluent thinkers and writers. This lesson should be taught only after students have been thoroughly introduced to all sections of the writer's notebook. Therefore, we recommend teaching either some or all of the lessons in WPS.U2: Writer's Notebook: Getting Ideas from Your Life and WPS.U3: Writer's Notebook: Getting Inspiration from Writers and Artists before teaching this lesson.

WRITER'S NOTEBOOK/WRITING FOLDER

Students will learn ways to continue building their notebooks.

ASSESS LEARNING

- Observe for evidence that students understand how to build their writer's notebooks.
- Look for evidence that they can use the term *writer's notebook*.

MINILESSON

Students will need their writer's notebooks for this minilesson. To help students think about the minilesson principle, talk about different ways to write in a writer's notebook. Below is an example. If you are using *Writer's Notebook, Intermediate*, there is a list of ways to build a writer's notebook inside the back cover. If not, make copies of the list that students develop in this minilesson for them to glue into their notebooks.

> You have been writing in your writer's notebooks in a lot of different ways and for different purposes. Spend a few minutes looking through the writing you have done in your writer's notebook.
>
> What are some of the ways you have written in your notebook? Turn and talk to your partner about this.

▶ After students turn and talk, invite several students to share their responses. Record responses on chart paper.

> Once you learn about, for example, making a list or a web, you can make your own lists and webs to gather even more ideas for your writing.

WML5
WPS.U1.WML5

Have a Try

Invite students to talk to a partner about how they would like to write in their writer's notebook.

> How would you like to write in your writer's notebook in the future? This may be something you haven't tried yet or something you would like to do more of. Turn and talk to your partner about this.

▶ After time for discussion, invite several students to share their thinking.

Summarize and Apply

Write the principle at the top of the chart. Summarize the learning and remind students to keep building their writer's notebooks.

> Today you thought about different ways you can write in your writer's notebook. You will continue to build your writer's notebook by writing in it every day. If you're not sure what to write about, look at the list we made to get ideas. Find the next clean page in Section 4 and start writing or sketching. Bring your notebook to share when we come back together.

> **Keep building your writer's notebook.**
> - Make a list.
> - Make a web.
> - Make a map.
> - Make a sketch.
> - Respond to a poem or song.
> - Write from a quote.
> - Observe and sketch the world around you.
> - Write about something on your heart map.
> - Glue in artifacts.
> - Collect memorable words and phrases.
> - Write about a book or a piece of art.

Confer

▶ While students are writing, move around the room to confer briefly with them about building their writer's notebooks. Use prompts such as the following as needed.

- *How would you like to work in your writer's notebook today?*
- *Are there any ideas on our list that you haven't tried yet? Any you would like to try again?*
- *Look at the writing you have already done in your writer's notebook. Does your writing give you any ideas for new writing?*
- *Would you like to try writing about a piece of art?*

Share

At the end of writing time, gather students in the meeting area to talk about their writing.

> How did you write in your writer's notebook today?

> What is your favorite way to use your notebook? Why?

Umbrella 1: Introducing and Using a Writer's Notebook

539

Assessment

After you have taught the minilessons in this umbrella, observe students when they use their writer's notebooks. Use *The Fountas & Pinnell Literacy Continuum* to notice, teach for, and support students' learning as you observe their attempts at writing.

▶ What evidence do you have of students' new understandings related to using the writer's notebook?

- Have students created a personalized cover for their writer's notebooks?
- Do they understand the purpose and organization of the writer's notebook?
- Are they able to write in their writer's notebooks for at least ten minutes every day?
- Are they using their writer's notebooks in a variety of ways?
- Do they understand and use the terms *writer's notebook*, *organized*, and *section*?

▶ In what ways, beyond the scope of this umbrella, are students using a writer's notebook?

- Do they reread their notebooks to get ideas for writing?
- Are they expanding upon ideas they collect in their notebooks?

Use your observations to determine the next umbrella you will teach. You may also consult Suggested Sequence of Lessons (pp. 665–682) for guidance.

EXTENSIONS FOR INTRODUCING AND USING A WRITER'S NOTEBOOK

▶ Support students in using sketches in a writer's notebook to generate ideas for writing or to revise their writing. For example, they can sketch the setting of a realistic fiction story as a way to think about words to describe it.

▶ When students share stories about their activities, weekends, families, etc., with you, remind them to note important ideas in their writer's notebooks.

▶ When students share their knowledge on a topic or an experience, encourage them to add notes to Section 3: Becoming an Expert in their writer's notebooks.

▶ Help students set individual goals for using their writer's notebooks (e.g., write in them for thirty minutes a day, experiment with different ways of using a writer's notebook).

Minilessons in This Umbrella

WML1 Make a heart map to discover what is important in your life.

WML2 Use maps to get ideas.

WML3 Make a web about yourself to get ideas.

WML4 Make webs to get ideas from memories.

WML5 Think about special places to get ideas.

WML6 Think about special people to get ideas.

WML7 Use lists to gather ideas from your life.

WML8 Collect artifacts in your writer's notebook.

WML9 Observe the world around you to get ideas.

Before Teaching Umbrella 2 Minilessons

The purpose of this umbrella is to teach students different ways to generate and gather ideas for writing from their own lives. Using a writer's notebook to gather the information, students will think about their personal observations and experiences. Throughout the lessons, students will be writing in their notebooks, and you will write alongside them, so these lessons may take longer than typical minilessons. By writing in your own writer's notebook, you will authentically model other ways of thinking. Use a document camera to project your notebook, or demonstrate the work on chart paper.

Each student will need a writer's notebook, so it is helpful to teach WPS.U1: Introducing and Using a Writer's Notebook prior to this umbrella. If you are using *Writer's Notebook, Intermediate* (Fountas and Pinnell 2023), the writing throughout this umbrella should be done in Section 1: Ideas from My Life. If not, students can create a section in their own notebooks dedicated to ideas from their own lives. See pages 87–91 for suggestions about setting up a writer's notebook. Use the books listed below from *Fountas & Pinnell Classroom™ Shared Reading Collection*, or choose books from the classroom library.

Shared Reading Collection

My Typhoon by Mike Downs

A Cuban American Familia by Laura Platas Scott

Shared Reading

Writer's Notebook

Section 5: Writing Process

Writing Minilesson Principle
Make a heart map to discover what is important in your life.

Writer's Notebook: Getting Ideas from Your Life

You Will Need

- chart paper prepared with the outline of a large heart map, or the projected first tab from *Writer's Notebook, Intermediate*
- chart paper and markers
- writer's notebooks

Academic Language / Important Vocabulary

- writer's notebook
- heart map
- matters
- ideas

Continuum Connection

- Use notebooks to plan, gather, and rehearse for future published writing
- Use a writer's notebook or booklet as a tool for collecting ideas, experimenting, planning, sketching, or drafting
- Use sketching, webs, lists, and freewriting to think about, plan for, and try out writing
- Gather a variety of entries (e.g., character map, timeline, sketches, observations, freewrites, drafts, lists) in a writer's notebook
- Have topics and ideas for writing in a list or notebook

GOAL

Use a writer's notebook to record important pieces of one's identity in a heart map to inspire writing ideas.

RATIONALE

Information about what matters to students can inspire their writing. Adding these ideas to a heart map (Heard 2016) is a strategy students can use to collect and generate ideas in a writer's notebook.

WRITER'S NOTEBOOK/WRITING FOLDER

Students will write ideas about themselves on a heart map in their writer's notebooks.

ASSESS LEARNING

- Observe whether students make and use a heart map.
- Look for evidence that they can use vocabulary such as *writer's notebook*, *heart map*, *matters*, and *ideas*.

MINILESSON

Students will need their writer's notebooks for this minilesson. To help students think about the minilesson principle, model the process of making a heart map and engage them in exploring topics from their lives. Below is an example.

- Display a heart map.

    Writers have different ways of getting ideas for writing in a writer's notebook. One way is to make a heart map. This heart map will be about me. It will show what is important to me. Watch as I add some things to my heart map.

- Think aloud as you add a few authentic things about yourself to the heart map.

    In this section of the heart map, I am going to write the words *building brick walls*. My sister and I work on Saturday mornings and in the summers building houses, and I know how to build brick walls. I will add a quick sketch to show about that. I am going to write the words *visiting family in Taiwan* over here. My family lives in Taiwan, so I want to write about my family and about visiting them there.

    I can refer to the heart map anytime I need an idea to write about and add to it whenever I think about something I might want to write about.

- Have students turn to the first tab in *Writer's Notebook, Intermediate* or draw a heart in their writer's notebooks.

    What are some parts of who you are that you could put on your heart map? Add some ideas to your heart map as I continue working on mine.

Have a Try

Invite students to turn and talk about ideas for heart maps.

> Turn and talk to your partner about something you wrote on your heart map.

▶ After time for discussion, ask volunteers to share. Encourage students to add new ideas inspired by their classmates to their heart maps.

Summarize and Apply

Summarize the learning and remind students to add authentic ideas about themselves to a heart map in their writer's notebooks.

> What are some types of things that you can add to a heart map?

▶ Write the principle at the top of a clean sheet of chart paper. Begin a list of ideas using generalized terms.

> When you write today, add on to your heart map. Or, you can choose one thing you wrote on your heart map and begin writing about it. You will not finish your heart map today because you will add to it throughout the year.

▶ Students can start to write about something on their heart maps in Section 1 or on the first clean page in Section 4.

Confer

▶ During independent writing, move around the room to confer briefly with students about their heart maps. Use prompts such as the following as needed.

- *What will you add to your heart map next?*
- *Share a few things you added to your heart map.*
- *What is one thing that is special about you or special to you?*

Share

Following independent writing, gather students in the meeting area. Give all students a turn to share something on their heart maps.

> Think about one word on your heart map. Let's go around the circle and each share a word.

> Is making a heart map hard or easy for you? Turn and talk in threes about that.

Heart Map

building brick walls

raising rabbits

visiting family in Taiwan

swimming in the ocean

Make a heart map to discover what is important in your life.

Things to Draw or Write About on a Heart Map

- Hobbies
- Sports
- Friends and family
- Special places
- Music
- Traditions
- Where I have lived
- Vacations

Writing Minilesson Principle
Use maps to get ideas.

You Will Need

- a familiar text featuring a special place, such as *My Typhoon* by Mike Downs, from *Shared Reading Collection*
- chart paper prepared with a simple map of a place that is special to you or your projected map from page 2 of *Writer's Notebook, Intermediate*
- document camera (optional)
- markers
- writer's notebooks

Academic Language / Important Vocabulary

- writer's notebook
- maps
- ideas

Continuum Connection

- Use notebooks to plan, gather, and rehearse for future published writing
- Use sketching, webs, lists, and freewriting to think about, plan for, and try out writing
- Generate and expand ideas through talk with peers and teacher
- Look for ideas and topics in personal experiences, shared through talk
- Gather a variety of entries (e.g., character map, timeline, sketches, observations, freewrites, drafts, lists) in a writer's notebook

GOAL

Create maps of special places to generate ideas for writing.

RATIONALE

When students learn to use a writer's notebook to create a memory map of a meaningful place, they learn a way to generate ideas for writing.

WRITER'S NOTEBOOK/WRITING FOLDER

In their writer's notebooks, students will draw and label a map of a place that has meaning for them.

ASSESS LEARNING

- Notice whether students understand that they can get ideas for writing by drawing and labeling a map of a special place.
- Look for evidence that they can use vocabulary such as *writer's notebook*, *maps*, and *ideas*.

MINILESSON

Students will need their writer's notebooks for this minilesson. To help students think about the minilesson principle, have them draw and label a memory map. Model the process by using your own memory map to generate ideas. Below is an example.

- Revisit pages 2–3 of *My Typhoon*.

    What place is special in *My Typhoon*?

    Notice how there is a map of the special place, too. This book makes me remember a place where I spent a lot of time when I was young.

- Display your hand-drawn map of a special place. Label the map with words to remind you of stories that happened in a few different places on the map as you think aloud. Here is an example.

    This is a map of the alley that was by my house when I was growing up. I added the tree stump because it makes me think of the time I tripped on it and broke my nose. I also added the big street at the end because we weren't allowed to go any farther than that street. I drew the hopscotch on here because it reminds me of the fun we had playing in the alley.

- Have students turn to a clean page in Section 1 of their writer's notebooks (p. 2 in *Writer's Notebook, Intermediate*).

    Draw your own map of a special place and start labeling it with words to remind you of the stories.

- After a brief time, invite volunteers to share.

Have a Try

Invite students to note ideas for stories on their maps.

> On my map, I have a lot of ideas for stories that I could write. I am going to write a few story ideas. While I do that, you can do the same thing in your notebook.

▶ Begin modeling the process as students write alongside you on the next page in their writer's notebooks. After a brief time, ask a few volunteers to share.

Summarize and Apply

Summarize the learning. Students can continue working on their maps or make a different one.

> How can you get ideas for writing?

▶ Guide students to state the principle. If you made a chart, write it at the top.

> During independent writing time, add on to what you started on your map or continue your list of story ideas. You can also make a different map and label it with how the places on the map make you feel. Bring your notebook to share when we meet later.

▶ Remind students that they can use Section 4 of their writer's notebooks if they need more room.

Confer

▶ During independent writing, move around the room to confer briefly with students about their notebook entries. Use prompts such as the following as needed.

- *Describe your special place.*
- *What is something funny (scary, sad) that happened here?*
- *What feelings do you have about your special place?*

Share

Following independent writing, gather students in the meeting area to talk about their notebook entries.

> Turn to your partner and tell a story from a place on your map.

My Alley

the stump

Tollie lived here.

I live here.

playing in the alley

big street: DON'T CROSS

Use maps to get ideas.

- the time I tripped on the stump and broke my nose
- tell funny things that happened playing in the alley
- how afraid we were to cross the big street
- memories I have with Tollie, my neighbor and best friend
- how sad I felt when Tollie moved away

Writing Minilesson Principle
Make a web about yourself to get ideas.

Writer's Notebook: Getting Ideas from Your Life

You Will Need

▸ chart paper prepared with a web, or projected page 6 from *Writer's Notebook, Intermediate*

▸ markers

▸ document camera (optional)

▸ writer's notebooks

Academic Language / Important Vocabulary

▸ writer's notebook

▸ webs

▸ identity

Continuum Connection

▸ Use notebooks to plan, gather, and rehearse for future published writing

▸ Use sketching, webs, lists, and freewriting to think about, plan for, and try out writing

▸ Generate and expand ideas through talk with peers and teacher

▸ Look for ideas and topics in personal experiences, shared through talk

▸ Gather a variety of entries (e.g., character map, timeline, sketches, observations, freewrites, drafts, lists) in a writer's notebook

GOAL

Understand that making a web can inspire writing.

RATIONALE

A web is a generative way for students to gather ideas for writing. Once they learn to make a web about one thing, they can make a web about anything.

WRITER'S NOTEBOOK/WRITING FOLDER

In their writer's notebooks, students will fill in a web about themselves that will become a source of ideas for their writing.

ASSESS LEARNING

▸ Observe whether students are creating webs in order to generate writing ideas.

▸ Look for evidence that they can use vocabulary such as *writer's notebook*, *webs*, and *identity*.

MINILESSON

Students will need their writer's notebooks for this minilesson. To help students think about the minilesson principle, model the process and engage them in creating an identity web. Below is an example.

▸ Display the prepared chart paper or project the web on page 6 in *Writer's Notebook, Intermediate*. Begin filling in the spokes with words that show your identity as you think aloud. Include both serious and playful examples. Here is an example.

> There are a lot of different ways I could finish the sentence *I am a* _____.
> One way is to write *Mandarin speaker* because I speak Mandarin with my family at home. Another way I could finish the sentence is *donut lover*. You have seen me eating donuts, so you know that is definitely true!

▸ After you write a few things about your identity, ask students to begin filling in their own webs.

> What are some ways you describe yourself that show your identity? Write your ideas on the spokes of the web.

▸ After a few minutes, ask students to share their webs in small groups, encouraging students to get other writing ideas by listening to classmates.

Have a Try

Invite students to write about one idea from their identity webs.

> I know a lot about donuts, so there are many things I could write about donuts. I could write a review of the best donut shops in the area, or I could make a list of all my favorite donuts and include sketches of each one. This time, I think I will write a review while you choose one of the ideas on your web and write about that. Write on the first clean page in Section 4 in your writer's notebook.

> ❱ After about ten minutes, ask a few volunteers to share what they wrote.

Summarize and Apply

Summarize the learning. Students can continue working on their webs or start writing from an idea on their webs.

> When you write today, continue the writing you just started or choose a new idea from your web and write about that. Bring your writing to share when we meet later.

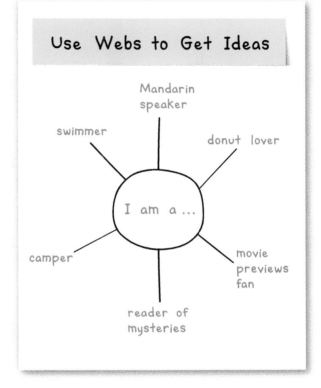

Confer

> ❱ During independent writing, move around the room to confer briefly with students about their webs. Use prompts such as the following as needed.

> • *Share some words that describe yourself. Think about the person you really are.*

> • *What is one thing that you think will surprise classmates about you? You could write about that.*

> • *Which idea will you write about?*

Share

Following independent writing, gather students in the meeting area to share their notebook entries first with a partner and then with the group.

> What is something about your identity that you are looking forward to writing about? Why?

WML4
WPS.U2.WML4

Writing Minilesson Principle
Make webs to get ideas from memories.

Writer's Notebook: Getting Ideas from Your Life

You Will Need

- two pieces of chart paper, each prepared with a web, or projected pages 8 and 9 from *Writer's Notebook, Intermediate*
- markers
- document camera (optional)
- writer's notebooks

Academic Language / Important Vocabulary

- writer's notebook
- webs
- memories
- details

Continuum Connection

- Use notebooks to plan, gather, and rehearse for future published writing
- Use sketching, webs, lists, and freewriting to think about, plan for, and try out writing
- Generate and expand ideas through talk with peers and teacher
- Look for ideas and topics in personal experiences, shared through talk
- Gather a variety of entries (e.g., character map, timeline, sketches, observations, freewrites, drafts, lists) in a writer's notebook

GOAL

Understand that making a memory web in a writer's notebook can inspire writing.

RATIONALE

When students first identify things that happened during a time or event they remember and then focus on one of those things, they can more effectively choose and write about small moments when they write memoirs. This lesson shows students how to use that technique to generate ideas for writing.

WRITER'S NOTEBOOK/WRITING FOLDER

Students will fill in a web about a memory in their writer's notebooks that will become a source of ideas for their writing.

ASSESS LEARNING

- Observe whether students are creating webs in order to generate writing ideas.
- Look for evidence that they can use vocabulary such as *writer's notebook*, *webs*, *memories*, and *details*.

MINILESSON

Students will need their writer's notebooks for this minilesson. To help students think about the minilesson principle, model the process and engage them in creating a memory web. Below is an example.

- Display the prepared chart paper or project the web on page 8 in *Writer's Notebook, Intermediate*. Fill in the center section with a big idea that students in your class will have memories about, such as celebrations. Then begin filling in the spokes as you think aloud. Here is an example.

  I would like to think about some memories that relate to special celebrations. I am going to write *Celebrations* in the center of my web. Some of my favorite celebrations are school assemblies. I remember when the school got an award for helping to clean up trash in the neighborhood. I think I could write a good memory story about that.

- After you write a few things you remember, ask students to begin filling in their webs. Have students draw a web on a clean page in their writer's notebooks (p. 8 in *Writer's Notebook, Intermediate*).

  Do you have celebrations that you remember? Write *Celebrations* in the center of the web. Or if you have another idea, then you can write that idea in the center. Then write what you remember happening on the spokes as I continue working on my web.

- After a few minutes, ask volunteers to share, encouraging students to get other writing ideas by listening to classmates.

Have a Try

Invite students to begin another web in their writer's notebooks.

▶ Display the second web. Choose one idea from the previous web and write it in the center. Think aloud as you begin to fill in one spoke. Then ask students to begin a second web.

> My first web shows some celebrations I remember. One thing I would like to write about is my birthday party last year. This time, I am going to write *My birthday party* in the center of the web. Then I will fill in details on the spokes.

▶ Ask students to begin a second web as you work on yours.

> Go to the next page in your writer's notebook. Choose an idea from the web you just made. Write it in the center. Then add some details in the spaces. I will continue working on mine, too.

Summarize and Apply

Summarize the learning. Students can continue working on their webs or start writing from them.

> Today you learned that you can make a memory web in a writer's notebook to help you think of ideas to write about.

> During independent writing time, add more details to the web you started or start writing about the memory on the first clean page in Section 4 in your writer's notebook. Bring your writing to share when we meet later.

Confer

▶ During independent writing, move around the room to confer briefly with students about their webs. Use prompts such as the following as needed.

- *Tell about your memory web.*
- *What are some memories you will include on your web?*
- *What memory will you be writing about today?*

Share

Following independent writing, gather students in the meeting area to share their notebook entries in groups of four.

> Share one idea from your memory web. If someone in your group mentions an idea that sparks your memory, write that idea in your writer's notebook.

Section 5: Writing Process

WML5
WPS.U2.WML5

Writing Minilesson Principle
Think about special places to get ideas.

Writer's Notebook: Getting Ideas from Your Life

You Will Need

- writer's notebooks
- chart paper and markers
- document camera (optional)
- chart paper prepared with a sketch of a place you want to go, or projected page 16 from *Writer's Notebook, Intermediate*

Academic Language / Important Vocabulary

- writer's notebook
- places
- ideas

Continuum Connection

- Use notebooks to plan, gather, and rehearse for future published writing
- Use a writer's notebook or booklet as a tool for collecting ideas, experimenting, planning, sketching, or drafting
- Use sketching, webs, lists, and freewriting to think about, plan for, and try out writing
- Gather a variety of entries (e.g., character map, timeline, sketches, observations, freewrites, drafts, lists) in a writer's notebook
- Have topics and ideas for writing in a list or notebook

GOAL

Use a writer's notebook to sketch and think about places to inspire writing.

RATIONALE

When students learn to use a writer's notebook to sketch and write about special places, they learn to think about places as a way of generating ideas for writing.

WRITER'S NOTEBOOK/WRITING FOLDER

Students will use their writer's notebooks to sketch and write about special places that they have been to or would like to visit.

ASSESS LEARNING

- Observe whether students are using a writer's notebook to think about places to generate writing ideas.
- Look for evidence that they can use vocabulary such as *writer's notebook*, *places*, and *ideas*.

MINILESSON

Students will need their writer's notebooks for the minilesson. To help students think about the minilesson principle, model the process and engage them in thinking, sketching, and writing about special places. Below is an example.

> Writers get ideas for writing from places they have been, places that are important to them, or places they want to visit. You can use your writer's notebook to think about and sketch places in order to get ideas for writing.

▶ Introduce the idea of making a sketch to prompt ideas for writing by sketching a special place in your writer's notebook or on chart paper.

> A place that is special to me is the pier on the rocky beach near my apartment. I go there every day to walk my dog and to think about my day.

> What is a place that is special to you? Make a sketch of your special place in your writer's notebook as I make a sketch of mine.

▶ Have students turn to a clean page in Section 1 of their writer's notebooks (p. 16 in *Writer's Notebook, Intermediate*). Provide time for sketching.

> You can use the sketch you made of your special place as inspiration for writing. Notice what I do as I start writing about mine.

▶ Begin writing about your special place, thinking aloud as you do. After you write a few sentences, invite students to write about their special place in their own notebooks.

> As I continue writing about my special place, use your sketch for inspiration and begin writing in your own notebooks.

Have a Try

Invite students to use a special place as inspiration in their writer's notebooks.

▶ Display your prepared sketch.

> Here's a sketch of a place I want to visit, a redwood forest. I also wrote a poem about the place. Think of a place that you have been or that you would like to visit. Make a sketch.

▶ Provide time for students to make their sketches.

Summarize and Apply

Summarize the learning and remind students to use places as inspiration for writing.

> You can use a sketch to get ideas for your writing. A place is one thing you can sketch and then write about. I wrote a poem about the place I want to visit.

▶ Write the principle at the top of the chart with the sketch and the poem.

> During independent writing time, try writing a poem about the place you have sketched. Bring your poem when we meet to share what you have so far.

Confer

▶ During independent writing, move around the room to confer briefly with students about their notebook entries. Use prompts such as the following as needed.

- *What special place will you sketch in your writer's notebook?*
- *What does this place make you think about?*
- *What are some special words that describe your place?*

Share

Following independent writing, gather students in the meeting area to share their writing.

> In groups of three, share the sketch you made of a special place.

> Who would like to share a poem you started in your writer's notebook?

My special place.
This is the lighthouse off the pier near the rocks on the beach.
I love this place because I can see for miles and miles. I take my dog on walks here every day after work. I love the sound of the water washing against the rocks.
The water changes color with the sky, and I like that.

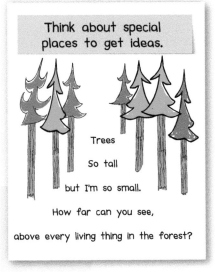

Think about special places to get ideas.

Trees
So tall
but I'm so small.
How far can you see,
above every living thing in the forest?

WML6
WPS.U2.WML6

Writing Minilesson Principle
Think about special people to get ideas.

Writer's Notebook: Getting Ideas from Your Life

You Will Need

- document camera (optional)
- writer's notebooks
- your writer's notebook or chart paper that has the beginning of some writing about a person who is special to you
- chart paper and markers

Academic Language / Important Vocabulary

- writer's notebook
- people
- ideas

Continuum Connection

- Use notebooks to plan, gather, and rehearse for future published writing
- Use a writer's notebook or booklet as a tool for collecting ideas, experimenting, planning, sketching, or drafting
- Use sketching, webs, lists, and freewriting to think about, plan for, and try out writing
- Gather a variety of entries (e.g., character map, timeline, sketches, observations, freewrites, drafts, lists) in a writer's notebook
- Have topics and ideas for writing in a list or notebook

GOAL

Use a writer's notebook to sketch and think about people to inspire writing.

RATIONALE

When students learn to use a writer's notebook to sketch and write about people, they learn to think about people as a way of generating ideas for writing.

WRITER'S NOTEBOOK/WRITING FOLDER

Students will use their writer's notebooks to sketch and write about people they know or would like to know.

ASSESS LEARNING

- Observe whether students are using a writer's notebook to think about people to generate writing ideas.
- Look for evidence that they can use vocabulary such as *writer's notebook*, *people*, and *ideas*.

MINILESSON

Students will need their writer's notebooks for this lesson. To help students think about the minilesson principle, model the process and engage them in thinking about ways to write about a special person. Below is an example.

> Writers sometimes get ideas for writing from people they know or they would like to know. You can use your writer's notebook to sketch and think about people to get ideas for writing.

▶ Display your writing about a special person.

> A special person in my life is my friend Frank, who is a geologist. We love going to a nearby stream to search for rocks. He can tell me all about the rocks. I started writing about Frank in my writer's notebook.

> Who is a special person in your life? Sketch and write about your special person in your notebook while I continue writing about mine.

▶ Have students turn to a clean page in Section 1 of their writer's notebooks (p. 18 in *Writer's Notebook, Intermediate*). Sketch and write about a special person in your life as students do the same in their notebooks.

▶ After time for writing, share your writing and ask several students to share what they sketched and wrote.

Have a Try

Invite students to turn and talk about writing about a special person in a writer's notebook.

> What are some ways you could write about a special person? Turn and talk about that.

▶ Prompt the conversation as needed. Begin a list on chart paper of what to think about when writing about a special person.

Summarize and Apply

Summarize the learning and remind students that special people in their lives can be inspirations for writing.

> Today we talked about using a person to inspire your writing ideas.

▶ Write the principle at the top of the chart.

> During independent writing time today, add on to what you started in your writer's notebook or choose a different way to write about your special person. Bring your writer's notebook to share when we meet later.

Section 5: Writing Process

Think about special people to get ideas.

- Describe what you like to do with your special person.
- Describe what makes the person special.
- Write about a memory you have of spending time together.
- Write what you would like to know about the person.
- Describe what your special person likes.
- Make a list of questions you have for your special person.
- Draw a scene that shows you and your special person doing something you both enjoy.
- Write about why you would like to meet the person.

Confer

▶ During independent writing, move around the room to confer briefly with students about using a writer's notebook to write about people in their lives or people they want to know. Use prompts such as the following as needed.

- *What makes this person special to you?*
- *What are some words that describe the special person?*
- *What details would you include in a sketch of your special person?*

Share

Following independent writing, gather students in the meeting area to talk about their writing.

> Turn and talk about other ideas you have for writing about a special person.

> What idea did you use for writing about a special person today?

Writing Minilesson Principle
Use lists to gather ideas from your life.

Writer's Notebook: Getting Ideas from Your Life

You Will Need

- a familiar book with memories, such as *A Cuban American Familia* by Laura Platas Scott, from *Shared Reading Collection*
- document camera (optional)
- writer's notebooks
- chart paper and markers

Academic Language / Important Vocabulary

- writer's notebook
- lists
- ideas

Continuum Connection

- Use notebooks to plan, gather, and rehearse for future published writing
- Use a writer's notebook or booklet as a tool for collecting ideas, experimenting, planning, sketching, or drafting
- Use sketching, webs, lists, and freewriting to think about, plan for, and try out writing
- Generate and expand ideas through talk with peers and teacher
- Look for ideas and topics in personal experiences, shared through talk
- Gather a variety of entries (e.g., character map, timeline, sketches, observations, freewrites, drafts, lists) in a writer's notebook

GOAL

Use a writer's notebook to make a list of memories in order to inspire writing.

RATIONALE

One way to generate ideas for writing is to make lists. A good starting point for students is for them to make lists of their memories. Encourage students to make many lists in their writer's notebooks so that they can refer to them when they are looking for a writing idea.

WRITER'S NOTEBOOK/WRITING FOLDER

Students will make lists of memories in their writer's notebooks.

ASSESS LEARNING

- Observe whether students are using a writer's notebook to make lists of their memories in order to generate ideas for writing.
- Look for evidence that they can use vocabulary such as *writer's notebook*, *lists*, and *ideas*.

MINILESSON

Students will need their writer's notebooks for this lesson. To help students think about the minilesson principle, engage them in an interactive lesson making lists to generate story ideas. Below is an example.

> We are going to try out three ways to make lists in order to get writing ideas.

- Show and revisit a few pages from *A Cuban American Familia*.

  > When I read this story of the author's memories of Cuba, I thought about my own memories of living in Mexico when I was young. You can create lists in your writer's notebook to collect memories so that you will have writing ideas.

- Have students turn to a clean page in Section 1 of their writer's notebooks (p. 22 in *Writer's Notebook, Intermediate*). Project the page from your writer's notebook or do your writing on chart paper.

- Model making a list of memories. As you do, have students make their own lists in their writer's notebooks.

  > Think about a memory you have, perhaps a time you did something for the first time or a time you felt excited or surprised. I am going to write *List of Memories* on the first line and write *living in Mexico* underneath. Start your list while I add another idea to mine.

- Repeat the process with one more type of list, such as a Top Ten List (p. 24 in *Writer's Notebook, Intermediate*).

  > Turn and talk about your lists with a partner. If you get any new ideas from your partner, write them in your writer's notebook.

Have a Try

Invite students to make a new list in their writer's notebooks.

> Now I'm going to list hopes that I have for myself or for the world. While I do that, make another list in your writer's notebook. You can choose the same topic as mine or choose one of your own.

▶ Begin a new list as students write in their writer's notebooks (pp. 26–27 in *Writer's Notebook, Intermediate*). After a brief time, invite volunteers to share, and add to the list based on the ideas they share.

Summarize and Apply

Summarize the learning and remind students to make lists in writer's notebooks as inspiration for writing.

> During independent writing time, choose one of your list ideas and write about it for ten minutes on the next page in your writer's notebook. Or, begin a new list of ideas you might use later. Making lots of lists will give you many ideas that you might want to write about, though not all of them will become a writing project. Bring your writing to share when we meet later.

Use Lists to Get Ideas		
List of Memories	Top Ten List	List of Hopes
1. living in Mexico	Foods 1. mac and cheese 2. chocolate 3. granola bars	I hope I run a faster mile.
2. getting a kitten		I hope people will recycle more.
	Books 1. The Other Side 2. Baseball in April	

Confer

▶ During independent writing, move around the room to confer briefly with students about their lists. Use prompts such as the following as needed.

- *Which item on your list will provide a lot of details to write about? Circle it so you can remember it later.*
- *Tell about the things you wrote on this list.*
- *Let's talk about some other ideas for lists you could make.*

Share

Following independent writing, gather students in the meeting area to talk about their lists.

> In groups of three, share the lists you made in your writer's notebook.

> Tell about an idea you learned from a classmate that you might like to write about.

WML8
WPS.U2.WML8

Writing Minilesson Principle
Collect artifacts in your writer's notebook.

Writer's Notebook: Getting Ideas from Your Life

You Will Need

- artifacts students have collected from home or class activities
- glue or drawing materials
- writer's notebooks
- your writer's notebook or chart paper prepared with an artifact or a sketch of it and the beginning of some writing about the artifact
- document camera (optional)
- chart paper and markers

Academic Language / Important Vocabulary

- writer's notebook
- artifacts
- items
- collect
- ideas

Continuum Connection

- Use notes to record and organize information
- Use notebooks to plan, gather, and rehearse for future published writing
- Conduct research to gather information in planning a writing project: e.g., life interviews, Internet, artifacts, articles, books
- Gather a variety of entries (e.g., character map, timeline, sketches, observations, freewrites, drafts, lists) in a writer's notebook
- Have topics and ideas for writing in a list or notebook

GOAL

Use a writer's notebook to collect artifacts to inspire writing ideas.

RATIONALE

Objects can inspire ideas for writing. When students use a writer's notebook to collect artifacts, they learn another way to gain inspiration for writing. In addition, you get a glimpse into the lives of your students.

WRITER'S NOTEBOOK/WRITING FOLDER

Students will glue or sketch a personal artifact in their writer's notebooks and then write about it.

ASSESS LEARNING

- Observe whether students are using a writer's notebook to collect artifacts to inspire writing.
- Look for evidence that they can use vocabulary such as *writer's notebook*, *artifacts*, *items*, *collect*, and *ideas*.

MINILESSON

Students will need their writer's notebooks and artifacts (if they have them) for this lesson. To help students think about the minilesson principle, model the process of and engage them in thinking about collecting and writing about artifacts in their notebooks. Below is an example.

- Ahead of time, have students bring items from home or gather artifacts from school activities (e.g., photos, stickers, receipts, tickets). If students don't have artifacts with them or they can't be glued into a writer's notebook, they can draw the items.

  You can use items that remind you of important moments in your life as ideas for your writing because artifacts make you think about memories.

- Show and describe how you could use personal artifacts to spark ideas for writing.

  This receipt reminds me of taking my grandpa to dinner. I could write about the food we ate and the things we talked about. This is a photo of a hamster. It was taken after we got him back in the cage after he escaped! I have so many stories I could write about the fish and the other class pets I have had.

- Have students turn to a clean left-hand page in Section 1 of their writer's notebooks (p. 30 in *Writer's Notebook, Intermediate*).

  If you have an artifact to glue in, go ahead and do that. If you don't have the artifact, sketch it. Write a label on the page, too.

- Allow a few minutes for students to either glue in or sketch their artifacts.

  Turn and talk about your artifact and the memories it makes you think about.

Have a Try

Invite students to write about an artifact in their writer's notebooks.

▶ Display and read aloud your prepared writing.

> This is the beginning of my writing about a memory I have. When I look at my artifact, it helps me remember. Choose how you want to write about your artifact and then start writing on the next page. I will finish my writing while you write.

▶ Ensure that each student has an idea for writing. Provide a few minutes for students to start writing about the artifact.

Summarize and Apply

Summarize the learning and remind students to use artifacts as inspiration for writing.

> What are some ideas for artifacts you could write about?

▶ Using students' suggestions, make a list on chart paper of ideas for artifacts. Add the principle to the top of the chart.

> During independent writing time today, add on to what you started in your writer's notebook about your artifact. Or, you can choose a different artifact to glue or sketch in your notebook and try writing about that. If you need more pages, go to the first blank page in Section 4. Bring your writing when we meet later.

The class pet, Hamilton the hamster, was very clever. Hamilton was able to open the cage even when we tried to lock it. One day, Hamilton got out of the cage, and the whole class had to search for him.

Collect artifacts in your writer's notebook.

- ticket from concert or trip
- photograph of a special person, place, or thing
- receipt from the purchase of a favorite item
- sticker
- brochure about a place you visited
- thank you note
- name tag from camp

Confer

▶ During independent writing, move around the room to confer briefly with students about their notebook entries. Use prompts such as the following as needed.

- *Which artifact are you writing about? Share what you have written so far.*
- *Tell about this artifact. Why did you choose it?*
- *What are some other memories you think about when you look at this artifact?*

Share

Following independent writing, gather students in the meeting area to share their writing about artifacts.

> What artifact did you write about today and why did you choose it?

> Share three words you used in your writing that describe your artifact.

WML 9
WPS.U2.WML9

Writing Minilesson Principle
Observe the world around you to get ideas.

Writer's Notebook: Getting Ideas from Your Life

You Will Need

- writer's notebooks
- chart paper and markers

Academic Language / Important Vocabulary

- writer's notebook
- observe
- nature
- sketch
- ideas
- senses

Continuum Connection

- Use notebooks to plan, gather, and rehearse for future published writing
- Use a writer's notebook or booklet as a tool for collecting ideas, experimenting, planning, sketching, or drafting
- Use notes to record and organize information
- Gather a variety of entries (e.g., character map, timeline, sketches, observations, freewrites, drafts, lists) in a writer's notebook
- Have topics and ideas for writing in a list or notebook

GOAL

Use a writer's notebook to observe and sketch the world around you to inspire writing.

RATIONALE

Writers get some of their ideas for writing from being close observers of the world around them. Guiding students to become good observers will help them find ideas for their own writing. Collecting notes and sketches of their observations in their writer's notebooks ensures that students will always have plenty of ideas to write about.

WRITER'S NOTEBOOK/WRITING FOLDER

Students will sketch, record, and write about their observations in their writer's notebooks.

ASSESS LEARNING

- Observe whether students are using a writer's notebook to observe and sketch the world around them to generate writing ideas.
- Look for evidence that they can use vocabulary such as *writer's notebook*, *observe*, *nature*, *sketch*, *ideas*, and *senses*.

MINILESSON

Students will need their writer's notebooks for the minilesson. To help students think about the minilesson principle, model the process of and engage them in noticing, sketching, and writing about the world around them. Below is an example. If possible, plan to take students outside the classroom, either outdoors or somewhere in the school building.

> Writers often get inspired for writing by observing the world around them. Today, we will go outside to do some close observing. When we observe, we use all our senses.

▶ Have students turn to a clean page in Section 1 of their writer's notebooks (p. 34 in *Writer's Notebook, Intermediate*).

> Today you will use your senses to observe an object in nature closely so that you notice the details. In your notebook, you will sketch the object with as much detail as possible so you can write about it later.

▶ Have students take writer's notebooks and pencils outside the classroom. Model how to make a detailed sketch of the object.

> I notice that big rock over there. It looks very heavy and has some curvy parts and a pointy part on one side. I am going to sketch it with as many details as possible. As I do, choose an object that you would like to observe closely and make a sketch of that object in your writer's notebook.

▶ Give students time to observe and sketch. Then return to the classroom.

Have a Try

Invite students to share their observations and prepare to write about them.

> Now that you have a sketch, what are some ways you could write about it? Turn and talk to your partner.

▶ Give the students time to talk briefly. Then ask for their ideas and begin a list in general terms on chart paper. Guide the conversation to prompt their thinking.

Summarize and Apply

Summarize the learning and remind students that they can use observations of the world around them as inspiration for writing.

> Use your observations to spark ideas for writing. When you write today, write about your sketch. Use one of the ideas on the chart or another idea. If you need more space to write or draw, use the first clean page in Section 4. Bring your notebooks to share later.

> ### Observe the world around you to get ideas.
>
> • Paint a picture of the object with your words.
>
> • Write anything it makes you wonder.
>
> • Tell a story about the object.
>
> • Write a poem that captures the image.
>
> • Describe what the object looks like.
>
> • Write a fantasy story about the object coming to life.

Confer

▶ During independent writing, move around the room to confer briefly with students about their observations. Use prompts such as the following as needed.

• *Talk about the details in your sketch.*

• *Describe your object using your senses. Are there other details you could add to your sketch?*

• *What ideas do you have for writing about your observation?*

Share

Following independent writing, gather students in the meeting area to talk about their observations.

> What feelings did you have when you observed and sketched things in nature?

> Tell about something you noticed when you observed an object closely.

Assessment

After you have taught the minilessons in this umbrella, observe students as they write in their notebooks and talk about their writing. Use *The Fountas & Pinnell Literacy Continuum* to notice, teach for, and support students' learning as you observe their attempts at collecting ideas from their lives.

▶ What evidence do you have of students' new understandings related to using a writer's notebook to write about ideas from their own lives?

- Do students make and use heart maps?
- Do they use maps, webs, and lists to get ideas?
- Do they think about memories to generate writing ideas?
- Do they consider places and people to get writing topics?
- Are they collecting artifacts in their writer's notebooks?
- Do they observe and sketch the world around them?
- Do they understand and use vocabulary such as *writer's notebook*, *heart map*, *matters*, *ideas*, *maps*, *webs*, *identity*, *memories*, *lists*, *collect*, *artifacts*, *observe*, and *sketch*?

▶ In what other ways, beyond the scope of this umbrella, are students using a writer's notebook?

- Are students able to write in their writer's notebooks daily for at least ten minutes?
- Are they using notebooks to plan and rehearse future writing?

Use your observations to determine the next umbrella you will teach. You may also consult Suggested Sequence of Lessons (pp. 665–682) for guidance.

EXTENSIONS FOR WRITER'S NOTEBOOK: GETTING IDEAS FROM YOUR LIFE

▶ Show maps (printed or online) to inspire students to draw detailed maps of other places they know to get writing ideas.

▶ Revisit WML6 and have students write a poem about a special person.

▶ Revisit WML7, suggesting new list ideas for students to try (e.g., things they want to learn, things they have made). Then have them do a quick write about a list item.

▶ Have students divide a notebook page into quadrants and label the quadrants: What do you hear? What do you smell? What do you see? What can you feel (touch)? Then take them to a quiet spot indoors or outdoors to write down their noticings. Later they can choose one idea for a quick write.

Minilessons in This Umbrella

WML1   Collect memorable words and phrases from authors you love.

WML2   Use poems to inspire writing ideas.

WML3   Use books or parts of books to inspire writing ideas.

WML4   Use song lyrics to inspire writing ideas.

WML5   Use art to inspire writing ideas.

Before Teaching Umbrella 3 Minilessons

Many writers find inspiration in the work of other writers and artists, and that is what Section 2 of the writer's notebook, Inspiration from Writers and Artists, guides students to do. There are opportunities for collecting ideas from books, poems, songs, and art. Teach minilessons in this umbrella after introducing students to a writer's notebook in WPS.U1: Introducing and Using a Writer's Notebook.

Throughout this umbrella, students will be getting comfortable using the writer's notebook by writing alongside you. For this reason, these minilessons may take longer than typical minilessons. This umbrella uses *Writer's Notebook, Intermediate* (Fountas and Pinnell 2023). If you are not using this notebook, be sure students have created a section in a plain notebook dedicated to inspirations from other writers and artists (see p. 89) and also a section for writing and drawing called Section 4: More Writing and Sketching.

Gather authentic samples of language, poems, books, songs, and art to use as mentor texts. Have copies of poems available for students to glue into their notebooks. To inspire writing ideas, use books with memorable language such as those listed below from *Fountas & Pinnell Classroom™ Interactive Read-Aloud Collection* and *Shared Reading Collection* or books from the classroom library.

Interactive Read-Aloud Collection

Figuring Out Who You Are

Heroes by Ken Mochizuki

A Boy and a Jaguar by Alan Rabinowitz

Shared Reading Collection

A Cuban American Familia by Laura Platas Scott

Mosaic Master: Antoni Gaudí by Susan B. Katz

As you read and enjoy these books together, help students notice

- interesting words and phrases, and
- what the story makes them think about.

Interactive Read-Aloud
Figuring Out Who You Are

Shared Reading

Writer's Notebook

Writing Minilesson Principle
Collect memorable words and phrases from authors you love.

Writer's Notebook: Getting Inspiration from Writers and Artists

You Will Need

- a mentor text with memorable language, such as *A Cuban American Familia* by Laura Platas Scott, from *Shared Reading Collection*
- chart paper prepared with the chart shown in this lesson, one entry filled in, or the projected Section 2 tab of *Writer's Notebook, Intermediate* one entry filled in
- writer's notebooks
- markers

Academic Language / Important Vocabulary

- writer's notebook
- memorable
- collect
- words
- phrases
- inspire

Continuum Connection

- Continue to learn from other writers by borrowing ways with words, phrases, and sentences
- Learn ways of using language and constructing texts from other writers (reading books and hearing them read aloud) and apply understandings to one's own writing
- Use a writer's notebook or booklet as a tool for collecting ideas, experimenting, planning, sketching, or drafting
- Have topics and ideas for writing in a list or notebook

GOAL

Use a writer's notebook to collect memorable words and phrases from authors to inspire writing.

RATIONALE

Asking students to collect memorable words and phrases will make them more aware of and appreciative of the variety of words that authors use. They will learn to savor and cherish interesting language and then think about how to use it in their own writing, resulting in richer and more inspired writing.

WRITER'S NOTEBOOK/WRITING FOLDER

Students will collect memorable words, quotes, and phrases in their writer's notebooks to use as inspiration for their writing.

ASSESS LEARNING

- Look for evidence that students collect memorable words and phrases in their writer's notebooks and use them to inspire their own writing.
- Notice evidence that they can use vocabulary such as *writer's notebook*, *memorable*, *collect*, *words*, *phrases*, and *inspire*.

MINILESSON

Students will need their writer's notebooks for the minilesson. To help students think about the minilesson principle, model how to collect memorable language in your writer's notebook and engage students in conversation and collection of their own list of memorable words and phrases. Here is an example.

- Display page 10 of *A Cuban American Familia* and the prepared chart paper or your writer's notebook entry.

    What do you notice about what I've written?

- Support students in recognizing that you have written some of the language you like and the name of the author who wrote it.

    When we read *A Cuban American Familia*, I noticed some words and phrases that I liked and wanted to remember. I wrote them down along with the author's name.

- Model the process of adding a few notes in the *Why I Love It* column, thinking aloud as you do.

    These words are special to me because they remind me of shopping with my grandma. Also, I love the sound of "clap-clop on the sidewalk."

    Turn and talk to your partner about how you think this author's writing could help you with your writing.

- After a short time for discussion, ask students to share.

Have a Try

Invite students to write a few memorable words or phrases in their writer's notebooks.

▶ Show or project page 15 from *A Cuban American Familia*.

> What memorable words or phrases do you notice?

> Turn to the back of the second tab in your writer's notebook. Write a word or phrase that caught your attention. Add the author's name and a note about why you love that word or phrase.

▶ After a brief time, ask a few volunteers to share. Add to the chart.

Summarize and Apply

Summarize the learning. Remind students to collect memorable words and phrases to inspire their own writing.

> During independent writing time today, add another memorable word or phrase to this section from a book we read together or one you are reading on your own. Or, if you get a writing idea from one of the words or phrases you have written in your notebook, write about it on the next clean page in Section 4. Bring your writer's notebook to share when we meet later.

Memorable Words/Quotes/ Phrases (include author's name)	Why I Love It
"bodega" "clap-clop on the sidewalk" —Laura Platas Scott	I think about shopping with my grandma. I can "hear" the shoes.
"quinceañera" "twinkly lights" "cha-cha-cha" —Laura Platas Scott	The words sound festive. I can write a story with fun-sounding words.

Confer

▶ During independent writing, move around the room to confer briefly with students about collecting memorable words or phrases. Use prompts such as the following as needed.

- *Share a memorable word or phrase you have collected. What made it stand out to you?*
- *Why do you love this word? Make a note about that.*
- *How might you use this phrase in your writing?*

Share

Following independent writing, gather students in the meeting area to share their notebook entries.

> In groups of three, share the memorable words and phrases you wrote in your writer's notebook. If you hear a word or phrase that you like from someone in your group, add it to your own writer's notebook.

**Writer's Notebook:
Getting Inspiration from
Writers and Artists**

You Will Need

- copies of two short poems glued onto pages 44 and 46 of your writer's notebook and into each student's writer's notebook (see Minilesson)
- writer's notebooks
- document camera (optional)
- chart paper and markers

Academic Language / Important Vocabulary

- writer's notebook
- poem
- inspire
- inspiration

Continuum Connection

- Continue to learn from other writers by borrowing ways with words, phrases, and sentences
- Learn ways of using language and constructing texts from other writers (reading books and hearing them read aloud) and apply understandings to one's own writing
- Use a writer's notebook or booklet as a tool for collecting ideas, experimenting, planning, sketching, or drafting
- Use sketching, webs, lists, and freewriting to think about, plan for, and try out writing
- Have topics and ideas for writing in a list or notebook

GOAL

Collect poems in a writer's notebook to notice writer's craft and inspire writing ideas.

RATIONALE

Poems provide ideas and examples of memorable language that can inspire ideas for writing. Show students how to collect and respond to poems in their writer's notebooks to spark writing ideas.

WRITER'S NOTEBOOK/WRITING FOLDER

Students will learn to find ideas for writing from poems they collect in their writer's notebooks.

ASSESS LEARNING

- Look for evidence that students collect poems to inspire writing ideas.
- Notice evidence that they can use vocabulary such as *writer's notebook*, *poem*, *inspire*, and *inspiration*.

MINILESSON

Students will need their writer's notebooks with two poems glued inside (pp. 44 and 46 in *Writer's Notebook, Intermediate*) for the minilesson. You can choose the same poems for all students, or have each student choose two favorite poems. To help students think about the minilesson principle, use a writer's notebook to model how to get ideas from poems. Here is an example.

- Ahead of time, have students glue or rewrite poems, each on a left-hand page, in Section 2.

  We are going to look at how you can get ideas for writing from a poem. Notice what I do, and then you can try it out in your own notebook.

- Display and read the first poem.

  The words "lazy little shadow" make me think about how part of me always wants to stay in my cozy bed when it's still dark. I wrote about that in my response to the poem.

- Display and read your response to the poem.
- Have students turn to the poem in Section 2 of their notebooks (p. 44 in *Writer's Notebook, Intermediate*).

  Now it is your turn. Write a response to your poem. It could be a list of ideas inspired by the poem or something about the poet's message. Or, you could write your own poem in response.

- After students have time to work, ask a few volunteers to share.

Have a Try

Invite students to notice ways they can use poems for inspiration.

▶ Display the second poem. Read it and your model response. Then have students turn to their second poems (p. 46 in *Writer's Notebook, Intermediate*).

> Look at your second poem. With your partner, talk about the word or line you might write about. Circle it.

▶ After a brief time, ask a few students to share what they circled and what it makes them think about.

Summarize and Apply

Summarize the learning and remind students to use their writer's notebooks to collect poems to get ideas for writing.

> There are other ways you can respond to poems. You could make a sketch, write a story inspired by the poem, or use a word or line from the poem to write your own poem.

> During independent writing time today, choose a way to respond to the second poem. Bring your writer's notebook to share when we meet later.

Confer

▶ During independent writing, move around the room to confer briefly with students about their responses to poems. Use prompts such as the following as needed.

- *What will you write or draw about this poem?*
- *What does the poet make you think about?*
- *Why do you love this word (line) in the poem?*

Share

Following independent writing, gather students in the meeting area. Ask as many students as time allows to share a poem and their response to it.

> Turn and talk to a partner about how you used a poem to inspire your writing.

---

from "My Shadow"

One morning, very early, before the
    sun was up,
I rose and found the shining dew on
    every buttercup;
But my lazy little shadow, like an
    arrant sleepy-head,
Had stayed at home behind me and
    was fast asleep in bed.

—Robert Lewis Stevenson

Many people have to get up early for work. I admire them. If I wake up before sunrise, I go back to sleep. Maybe I am an arrant sleepy-head. (Arrant means extreme. I looked it up!)

---

from "The Rainy Day"

Be still, sad heart! and cease repining;
Behind the clouds is the sun still shining;
Thy fate is the common fate of all,
Into each life some rain must fall,
Some days must be dark and dreary.

—H. W. Longfellow

"Behind the clouds is the sun still shining." This line gives me hope. No matter how dark and gray things seem, there is always some light somewhere.

Writing Minilesson Principle
Use books or parts of books to inspire writing ideas.

Writer's Notebook: Getting Inspiration from Writers and Artists

You Will Need

- two familiar books, such as the following from Text Set: Figuring Out Who You Are:
  - *Heroes* by Ken Mochizuki
  - *A Boy and a Jaguar* by Alan Rabinowitz
- writer's notebooks
- chart paper and markers

Academic Language / Important Vocabulary

- writer's notebook
- inspire
- lesson
- quick write
- opening line

Continuum Connection

- Continue to learn from other writers by borrowing ways with words, phrases, and sentences
- Use sketching, webs, lists, and freewriting to think about, plan for, and try out writing
- Use a writer's notebook or booklet as a tool for collecting ideas, experimenting, planning, sketching, or drafting

GOAL

Understand that writers use ideas and passages from books to inspire their writing.

RATIONALE

Writers are a source of inspiration for each other. Show students how to collect and respond in their writer's notebooks to a whole book or to a line or passage from a book to spark writing ideas. Once you teach them how, they can do it on their own.

WRITER'S NOTEBOOK/WRITING FOLDER

Students will learn to use their writer's notebooks to collect ideas for writing that they get from books.

ASSESS LEARNING

- Look for evidence that students collect ideas for writing inspired by books or parts of books.
- Notice evidence that they can use vocabulary such as *writer's notebook*, *inspire*, *lesson*, *quick write*, and *opening line*.

MINILESSON

Students will need their writer's notebooks for the minilesson. To help students think about the minilesson principle, use a writer's notebook to model how to collect ideas for writing from books. Here is an example.

- Revisit part of a familiar book that lends itself to writing a response, such as the last few pages in *Heroes*.

- Have students open their writer's notebooks to Section 2 (p. 48 in *Writer's Notebook, Intermediate*).

  What lesson did Donnie learn?

  Donnie learned to appreciate the heroes in his own family. What does that make you think about or wonder? You might think about a time that you learned a lesson, maybe a lesson about your own family, like Donnie. You might think about another lesson or about someone you consider a hero. Or, you might have a different thought. Let's do a quick write in response to the last part of *Heroes*. I will write in my notebook as you write in yours.

- Write alongside students in your own notebook or on chart paper. After several minutes, read what you wrote and ask a few volunteers to share their quick writes.

- Encourage students to turn to a clean page in Section 4 of their notebooks to jot down any ideas from classmates that inspire them.

Have a Try

Invite students to use an opening line from a book for writing inspiration.

> Another way to get an idea for writing is to write the opening line of a book in your writer's notebook and then write something about it. Let's try this with the opening line in *A Boy and a Jaguar*, which says, "I'm standing in the great cat house at the Bronx Zoo."

▶ Have students turn to Section 2 in their writer's notebooks (p. 50 in *Writer's Notebook, Intermediate*) and write the opening line, the book title, and the author's name. Then have them start writing about the line or use the line to begin a new story. Write alongside them. After a few minutes, ask a few students to share.

Summarize and Apply

Summarize the learning. Remind students that they can use books as inspiration for writing.

> How else might you use books to inspire writing ideas?

▶ Write the principle at the top of the chart paper and begin a list of ideas.

> When you write today, add on to what you started in your writer's notebook, or choose part of another book you enjoyed and try responding in one of the ways listed on the chart. Bring your notebook to share when we meet later.

> ### Use books or parts of books to inspire writing ideas.
>
> - Write about a time you learned a lesson like a character did in the book.
> - Make a list of things the book makes you wonder.
> - Write something the story makes you think about.
> - Write about a time you felt the same way as a character in the story.
> - Use an opening line and write a story from that.
> - Write the words the writer used to create a strong mental picture. Then make a sketch of the picture.

Confer

▶ During independent writing, move around the room to confer briefly with students about using books to get ideas for writing. Use prompts such as the following as needed.

- *What does this part of the book make you wonder? Make a list. Then see which idea inspires you to write.*
- *Have you ever felt like the main character in this book? That is something you could write about in your writer's notebook.*

Share

Following independent writing, gather students in the meeting area to share their writing.

> Who would like to share what you wrote in your writer's notebook today?

Writing Minilesson Principle
Use song lyrics to inspire writing ideas.

You Will Need

- recordings of two songs your students will enjoy
- copies of the lyrics for the two songs glued into your writer's notebook and each student's writer's notebook
- writer's notebooks
- chart paper and markers

Academic Language / Important Vocabulary

- writer's notebook
- song lyrics
- inspire

Continuum Connection

- Choose topics that are interesting to the writer
- Use a writer's notebook or booklet as a tool for collecting ideas, experimenting, planning, sketching, or drafting
- Use sketching, webs, lists, and freewriting to think about, plan for, and try out writing
- Have topics and ideas for writing in a list or notebook

GOAL

Understand that writers can use song lyrics to inspire writing ideas.

RATIONALE

Song lyrics can inspire thinking that in turn can be used as the basis for writing. Guide students to learn how to collect song lyrics and respond to them in their writer's notebooks to spark writing ideas.

WRITER'S NOTEBOOK/WRITING FOLDER

Students will learn to use their writer's notebooks to collect ideas for writing from song lyrics.

ASSESS LEARNING

- Look for evidence that students are using their writer's notebooks to collect and reflect on song lyrics to inspire writing ideas.
- Notice evidence that they can use vocabulary such as *writer's notebook*, *song lyrics*, and *inspire*.

MINILESSON

Students will need their writer's notebooks for the minilesson. To help students think about the minilesson principle, use a writer's notebook to model how to get ideas from songs. Glue one song in Section 2 (p. 54 in *Writer's Notebook, Intermediate*) and the other on the next clean page in Section 4. Here is an example.

- Have students turn to the lyrics of the first song.

  Turn to Section 2 in your writer's notebook. Follow along with these lyrics as you listen to the song.

- Play the recording of the first song as students follow along with the lyrics. This example uses "Happy" by Pharrell Williams, but you can choose any song that you think your students would enjoy. Share an idea of how the lyrics inspire your writing. This is just an example.

  I have always loved this song because it makes me think about what makes me happy. This song mentions clapping along, so it makes me think about how a positive approach to life can help you deal with challenges. That is something I might write about in my writer's notebook.

  The lyrics might mean the same thing or something different to you. Write briefly what these lyrics mean to you on the next page in your writer's notebook. I will do the same thing in my notebook.

- After a few minutes, ask several volunteers to share their writing. Point out that there are different ways of responding; there is no right answer.

Have a Try

Invite students to use their writer's notebooks to respond to song lyrics.

▶ Have students turn to the song lyrics for the second song in their writer's notebooks as you play the recording.

What story idea do these lyrics make you think about? This time, write an idea for a story or start a story in your notebook that the lyrics inspire while I do the same thing in my notebook.

▶ After students have had time to get started, ask a few volunteers to share what they are writing about.

Summarize and Apply

Summarize the learning and remind students to use song lyrics as inspiration for writing.

How can you use song lyrics to inspire writing ideas?

▶ Write the principle at the top of the chart paper and then begin a list of ideas.

When you write today, add on to what you started in your writer's notebook. Or choose lyrics from another song you love and write about them in one of the ways on the chart. Bring your writer's notebook to share when we meet later.

> ### Use song lyrics to inspire writing ideas.
>
> • Write a poem inspired by the lyrics.
>
> • Sketch something the song makes you think of.
>
> • Write what the lyrics mean to you.
>
> • Write what the lyrics make you think about.
>
> • Start your own story inspired by the lyrics.
>
> • Write song lyrics with the same message.

Confer

▶ During independent writing, move around the room to confer briefly with students about their responses to song lyrics. Use prompts such as the following as needed.

• *What does this song make you think about? Tell about a sketch you could make about that.*

• *Do these song lyrics inspire you to write a poem? Describe the poem idea.*

Share

Following independent writing, gather students in the meeting area to talk about their notebook entries.

What song inspired your writing today? Share what you wrote.

Writing Minilesson Principle
Use art to inspire writing ideas.

GOAL

Understand that writers can use works of art to inspire and generate writing ideas in a writer's notebook.

RATIONALE

Although art, whether professional or amateur, is a visual medium, it can prompt thoughts that can be used for writing. Teach students how to reflect on and respond to a piece of art in their writer's notebooks.

WRITER'S NOTEBOOK/WRITING FOLDER

Students will learn to use their writer's notebooks to collect ideas for writing that they get from art.

ASSESS LEARNING

▶ Look for evidence that students are using their reflections on art as a way to inspire ideas for writing.

▶ Notice evidence that they can use vocabulary such as *writer's notebook*, *art*, *sketch*, and *inspire*.

MINILESSON

Students will need their writer's notebooks for the minilesson. To help students think about the minilesson principle, use a writer's notebook to model how to use art to inspire ideas for writing. Below is an example based on the art shown in a biography about an artist.

▶ Show pages 10–11 from *Mosaic Master*. Prepare students to make a quick sketch that captures the main idea of the art.

> You can draw and write ideas you get from art in your writer's notebooks. Look at this piece of art that was created by the artist Antoni Gaudí. How would you describe it?

▶ Have students turn to Section 2 in their writer's notebooks (p. 56 in *Writer's Notebook, Intermediate*).

> Make a quick sketch that captures the main idea of the mosaic art gecko fountain.

▶ After a few moments, ask several volunteers to share their sketches.

> Now turn to the next page in your writer's notebook and write anything that the art makes you think about. I will be doing the same thing in my notebook.

▶ After students have had some time to get started, pause and ask a few volunteers to share ideas.

Have a Try

Invite students to use their writer's notebooks to respond to art.

▶ Show page 4 from *Mosaic Master*.

> Turn to the next clean page in Section 4 of your writer's notebook. Write the date and then make a quick sketch to remind yourself about this building that Antoni Gaudí designed. Then write about what the design makes you think about. Or, you might choose another idea, like writing about an animal the building makes you think about when you look at the wavy lines. I will be working in my writer's notebook, too.

▶ After students have had time to get started, ask a few volunteers to share what they are writing about.

Summarize and Apply

Summarize the learning and remind students to use art as inspiration for writing.

> What are some kinds of art you can use to inspire your writing ideas?

▶ Write the principle at the top of the chart paper. Then begin a list of ideas. Include the name of the student who suggested the idea.

> When you write today, add on to what you started in your writer's notebook. Or, write about a different piece of art. Bring your writer's notebook when we meet later.

Confer

▶ During independent writing, move around the room to confer briefly with students about how they might use art to inspire writing. Use prompts such as the following as needed.

- *Tell about the art sketch you made and what it makes you think about.*
- *What does this mosaic make you think of?*
- *Which painting will you use for inspiration?*

Share

Following independent writing, gather students in the meeting area to talk about their writing.

> Talk about the art you looked at and what it inspired you to write.

Use art to inspire writing ideas.

Sculpture	Camila
Watercolor	Bowie
Mary Cassatt painting	Nova
Sister's fingerpainting	Elian
Mosaic in the school hallway	Wells
Magazine photograph	Imran

Section 5: Writing Process

Assessment

After you have taught the minilessons in this umbrella, observe students as they write and talk about their writing. Use *The Fountas & Pinnell Literacy Continuum* to notice, teach for, and support students' learning as you observe their attempts at writing.

▶ What evidence do you have of students' new understandings related to using a writer's notebook?

- Are they collecting memorable words and phrases in their writer's notebooks?
- Can they use poems to inspire writing?
- Are they using books or parts of books for writing ideas?
- Can they use song lyrics for writing inspiration?
- Are they using art to generate writing ideas?
- Do they understand and use vocabulary such as *writer's notebook, memorable, collect, words, phrases, inspire, poem, inspiration, quick write, lesson, opening line, song lyrics, art,* and *sketch*?

▶ In what other ways, beyond the scope of this umbrella, are students using a writer's notebook?

- Do they get ideas for memoirs from their lists and webs?
- Do they try out craft moves in their writer's notebooks?

Use your observations to determine the next umbrella you will teach. You may also consult Suggested Sequence of Lessons (pp. 665–682) for guidance.

EXTENSIONS FOR WRITER'S NOTEBOOK: GETTING INSPIRATION FROM WRITERS AND ARTISTS

▶ From time to time while reading aloud, suggest that students listen for memorable words or phrases and write them in their writer's notebooks.

▶ Encourage students to repeat any of the writing activities they have done in the first two sections of the writer's notebook in Section 4.

▶ The tab for Section 2 in *Writer's Notebook, Intermediate,* has quotations from writers. Have students write a response to one of the quotations in their writer's notebooks.

▶ Many art museums show some of their collections online. Visit their websites to provide inspiration for students' writing.

Minilessons in This Umbrella

WML1 Make lists of topics you know, are interested in, and care about.

WML2 Use webs to explore and focus a topic.

WML3 Make a list of questions and wonderings about a topic.

WML4 Take notes about your topic in your own words.

WML5 Interview or watch an expert on your topic and take notes.

WML6 Choose and sketch a few objects to represent the big ideas of your topic.

Writer's Notebook

Before Teaching Umbrella 4 Minilessons

The purpose of the minilessons in this umbrella is to help students use the tools in their writer's notebooks to plan and prepare for nonfiction writing. Teach these lessons as students prepare to write informational texts, such as multimedia presentations and feature articles (GEN.U9 and GEN.U10), and already know the topic they want to write about. However, students who haven't already chosen a topic will find WML1 helpful.

Throughout this umbrella, students will be learning how to collect and try out ideas for writing in their writer's notebooks. The minilessons are based on Section 3: Becoming an Expert in *Writer's Notebook, Intermediate* (Fountas and Pinnell 2023). If students are using a plain notebook, prepare a similar section in their notebooks (see pp. 89–90). Students will be writing alongside you and some of the lessons involve multiple steps, so they are longer than usual. You may want to break them down and teach them over a few days. As students research and take notes on their topics, they will need access to resources to find information.

Before teaching this umbrella, you will also want to read and discuss engaging informational books about a variety of topics that will interest your class.

As you read and enjoy informational texts together, help students

- talk about what they learn from each text,

- share their questions and wonderings about the topic, and

- discuss their own ideas for writing.

Section 5: Writing Process

WML1

WPS.U4.WML1

Writing Minilesson Principle
Make lists of topics you know, are interested in, and care about.

Writer's Notebook: Becoming an Expert

You Will Need

- two sheets of chart paper prepared with two-column charts (or projected Section 3 tab and p. 59 in *Writer's Notebook, Intermediate*):

  - *Topics I Want to Learn More About* with a list of a few topics you are interested in

  - *Use Lists to Get Ideas for Topics You Want to Learn About* with the beginning of a list of interesting facts

- markers
- document camera (optional)
- writer's notebooks

Academic Language / Important Vocabulary

- writer's notebook
- topic
- fascinate

Continuum Connection

- Use a writer's notebook or booklet as a tool for collecting ideas, experimenting, planning, sketching, or drafting
- Use sketching, webs, lists, and freewriting to think about, plan for, and try out writing

GOAL

Make a list of topics of interest to inspire ideas for nonfiction writing.

RATIONALE

When students keep a list of topics they are interested in, it helps them become more aware of their own interests and have a source of ideas for informational writing. They will be more likely to write about topics they are interested in, will be more engaged in the writing process, and will write with more voice and authenticity.

WRITER'S NOTEBOOK/WRITING FOLDER

Students will list topics and facts in their writer's notebooks to build a collection of ideas for writing nonfiction.

ASSESS LEARNING

- Observe whether students add to a list of topics of interest from time to time.
- Notice whether they refer to their lists when choosing a topic for writing.
- Look for evidence that they can use vocabulary such as *writer's notebook, topic,* and *fascinate.*

MINILESSON

Students will need their writer's notebooks for the minilesson. This lesson uses Section 3: Becoming an Expert. To help students think about the minilesson principle, share and discuss your own topics of interest, and then invite students to write down and share theirs. Here is an example.

- Display the chart paper prepared with the title *Topics I Want to Learn More About* or project your writer's notebook page.

  Anytime you come across a topic you care about or want to learn more about, you can add it to a list in your writer's notebook.

- Tell students about the topics you wrote on your list.

  There are plenty of topics that I would like to learn more about and write about: birds because I sometimes like to go bird-watching, gardening because I just moved into a house with a backyard, and volcanoes because I read an interesting book about the eruption of Mount Vesuvius in Pompeii, Italy.

- Invite students to start making a list in their writer's notebooks of topics they are interested in and want to know more about.

  Who would like to share one of the topics you wrote on your list?

- Add students' responses to the chart.

  Why might it be helpful to you, as a writer, to make a list of topics?

Have a Try

Invite students to talk in pairs about facts they find fascinating.

▶ Display the chart paper (or project the page) prepared with the title *Use Lists to Get Ideas for Topics You Want to Learn About*.

> I came across these facts in a book, so I wrote them on a list because I want to know more about them and might decide to write about them. Turn and talk to a partner about these facts or any other interesting fact that you know. Write a fact that fascinates you in your writer's notebook.

▶ Refer students to page 59 in *Writer's Notebook, Intermediate*. After students turn and talk, invite a few students to share. Add a few more facts to the chart.

Summarize and Apply

Summarize the learning and remind students to make lists of topics and facts that interest them.

> Whenever you think of a new topic or come across a fact that interests you, add it to your lists. Look at these lists to get ideas for your writing when you are choosing a topic for a nonfiction piece.

> Today during independent writing time, write about one of the topics on your list. Write what interests you about it or what you know about it, or use it in a story or poem. Do your writing on the next clean page in Section 4 of your writer's notebook.

Topics I Want to Learn More About	
Birds	Earthquakes
Volcanoes	Airplanes
Gardening	Microbes
World War II	Insects
Hiccups	Mt. Everest
Stars	Hurricanes

Use Lists to Get Ideas for Topics You Want to Learn About

Facts That Fascinate	This fact makes me want to learn more about . . .
Most people fall asleep in seven minutes.	Why we need to sleep
Your feet produce about a pint of sweat every day.	Why people sweat
A tsunami wave can travel as fast as an airplane.	Tsunamis

Confer

▶ During independent writing, move around the room to confer briefly with students about topics and facts that interest them. Use prompts such as the following as needed.

- *What are some topics you know or care about?*
- *What do you like to read books about?*
- *What fascinating facts have you learned recently?*
- *What does that make you want to learn more about?*

Share

Following independent writing, gather students in the meeting area to share their lists. Ask all students to share one topic from their lists.

> If something you heard from a classmate interests you, add it to your list.

Writing Minilesson Principle
Use webs to explore and focus a topic.

Writer's Notebook: Becoming an Expert

You Will Need

▸ two sheets of chart paper prepared with blank webs, one labeled *Use Webs to Explore Your Topic* and one labeled *Use Webs to Focus Your Topic*

▸ markers

▸ an idea for a topic for a nonfiction writing

▸ writer's notebooks

Academic Language / Important Vocabulary

▸ web

▸ focus

▸ topic

Continuum Connection

▸ Use a writer's notebook or booklet as a tool for collecting ideas, experimenting, planning, sketching, or drafting

▸ Use sketching, webs, lists, and freewriting to think about, plan for, and try out writing

GOAL

Use webs as a tool to explore and narrow down ideas for topics for nonfiction writing.

RATIONALE

A web can be a useful tool for deciding on the focus of a topic for nonfiction writing. Students will begin by using a web to think about the "big ideas" of a topic and then use additional webs to explore each idea in further detail. This will help them decide whether to write about a large topic more generally or a subtopic more deeply.

WRITER'S NOTEBOOK/WRITING FOLDER

Students will make webs in their writer's notebooks to explore and focus a topic.

ASSESS LEARNING

▸ Observe whether students use webs to explore and focus ideas for nonfiction writing.

▸ Look for evidence that they can use vocabulary such as *web*, *focus*, and *topic*.

MINILESSON

Because this lesson will help students focus a topic for informational writing, they should have in mind the topic they have selected. To help students think about the principle, model using webs to decide the focus of a topic. Below is an example. If you are using *Writer's Notebook, Intermediate*, the webs are on pages 60 and 61.

▸ Display the first blank web. Write *Volcanoes* in the center. Model thinking aloud about what to write on the spokes of the web.

> I wrote a topic from my list in the center of the web. Now, I will explore my topic by writing some subtopics on the spokes. I know a bit about how volcanoes form and that volcanoes go through different stages. I read a book about the eruption of Mount Vesuvius in Pompeii, so I'll add that. I could also write about different kinds of volcanoes.

> If I wrote about all of this, that would be a lot! Instead, I will focus on one subtopic–the eruption of Mount Vesuvius.

▸ Display the second blank web, and write *Eruption of Mount Vesuvius* in the center. Model thinking aloud what to write on the spokes.

> I could write about what Pompeii was like before the eruption, what happened the day of the eruption, the effects of the eruption, and how we know when this eruption happened. How did I use webs to focus my topic?

> Making the webs helped me see what I could write about and decide whether there was enough or too much to write about.

Have a Try

Invite students to make a web to explore a topic in their writer's notebooks (p. 60 in *Writer's Notebook, Intermediate*).

> Choose a topic from your list. In your writer's notebook, write the topic in the center of a web. Write all the subtopics, or smaller topics, you already know at the ends of the spokes. Then turn and talk to your partner about your web.

Summarize and Apply

Help students summarize the learning and invite them to use webs to help focus a topic (pp. 61–62 in *Writer's Notebook, Intermediate*).

> Why is it helpful to use webs to explore a topic? How could this help you write nonfiction?

> Today during independent writing time, look at the web you just made. Choose one of the subtopics on your web and make a new web with that subtopic at the center. Write what you know about that subtopic. Then do the same thing with another subtopic. Finally, look at all your webs and decide what you would like to write about. Bring your notebook to share when we meet later.

▶ Save the charts for WML3.

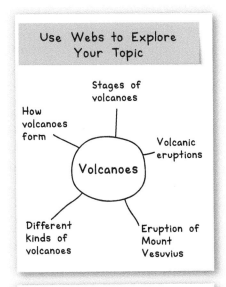

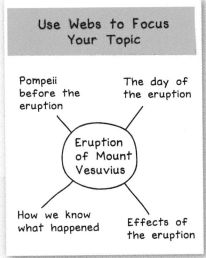

Confer

▶ During independent writing, move around the room to confer briefly with students about their webs. Use prompts such as the following as needed.

- *What topic is your web about?*
- *Which subtopic would you like to explore in greater detail?*
- *Is there enough information about that subtopic to create a piece of writing?*
- *Would you like to write a nonfiction piece about the whole topic or one of the subtopics you explored? Which subtopic? Why?*

Share

Following independent writing, gather students in the meeting area to share their webs with a partner.

> Share your web and talk to your partner about your plans for writing an informational piece.

Section 5: Writing Process

Writing Minilesson Principle
Make a list of questions and wonderings about a topic.

You Will Need

▶ the webs from WML2

▶ chart paper and markers

▶ writer's notebooks

Academic Language / Important Vocabulary

▶ writer's notebook

▶ question

▶ wondering

▶ topic

Continuum Connection

▶ Use a writer's notebook or booklet as a tool for collecting ideas, experimenting, planning, sketching, or drafting

▶ Use sketching, webs, lists, and freewriting to think about, plan for, and try out writing

GOAL

Make a list of questions and wonderings about a topic to help define the research focus.

RATIONALE

Listing questions and wonderings about a topic helps students identify their specific areas of interest and gaps in their knowledge, which in turn will help them to know what to look for when they do research on the topic.

WRITER'S NOTEBOOK/WRITING FOLDER

Students will explore their topics further by writing questions and wonderings in their writer's notebooks.

ASSESS LEARNING

▶ Notice whether students make lists of questions and wonderings about a topic.

▶ Look for evidence that they can use vocabulary such as *writer's notebook*, *question*, *wondering*, and *topic*.

MINILESSON

Students will need their writer's notebooks for this lesson. To help students think about the principle, model making a list of questions and wonderings about a topic. Here is an example.

▶ Display the webs from WML2.

> I made webs to focus my nonfiction writing about volcanoes. I thought about what I already know about this topic, and I decided to write about the eruption of Mount Vesuvius. There is a lot I already know about this topic, but there's also a lot that I don't know and that I need to find out before I start writing. I'm going to think about the questions I have and what I wonder about Mount Vesuvius. For example, I could ask myself, "What kind of volcano is Mount Vesuvius? When and how did it form? How many times has it erupted? How much did the people of Pompeii know about volcanoes?" I'm going to write my questions in my writer's notebook so I'll remember to do research to find the answers.
>
> Does anyone have any other questions about Mount Vesuvius or volcanoes in general? What do you wonder about this topic?

▶ Record each question and wondering discussed on chart paper.

Have a Try

Invite students to start making a list of questions and wonderings in their writer's notebooks (p. 64 in *Writer's Notebook, Intermediate*).

> Turn to Section 3 in your writer's notebook, and look at the webs you made. What do you already know about your topic? What do you want to find out? Write one or two questions or wonderings you have about your topic. Then turn and talk to a partner about what you wrote.

▶ After time for discussion, invite a few students to share their questions and wonderings.

Summarize and Apply

Write the principle at the top of the chart. Summarize the learning and invite students to add to their list of questions and wonderings.

> Why is it helpful to make a list of questions and wonderings about your topic before you write nonfiction?

> Making a list of questions and wonderings will help you know what to look for when you research your topic. What other questions or wonderings do you have? Add them to your list. Bring your notebook to share when we meet later.

> **Make a list of questions and wonderings about a topic.**
>
> • What kind of volcano is Mount Vesuvius?
>
> • When and how did it form?
>
> • How many times has it erupted?
>
> • How much did the people of Pompeii know about volcanoes?
>
> • Is Mount Vesuvius likely to erupt again anytime soon?
>
> • What happened to the people when the volcano erupted?
>
> • How hot was the lava?

Confer

▶ During independent writing, move around the room to confer briefly with students about their questions and wonderings. Use prompts such as the following as needed.

- *What do you already know about your topic?*
- *What do you want to learn about your topic?*
- *What do you wonder about your topic?*
- *Is there anything you think you know about your topic but that you need to check to make sure it's correct?*

Share

Following independent writing, gather students in the meeting area to share their lists.

> Who would like to share your list of questions and wonderings?

> Does anyone have any other questions or wonderings about _____'s topic?

Writing Minilesson Principle
Take notes about your topic in your own words.

Writer's Notebook: Becoming an Expert

You Will Need

- a topic for a model nonfiction text (e.g., volcanoes)
- a book or website about the topic
- chart paper and markers
- sticky notes
- writer's notebooks

Academic Language / Important Vocabulary

- writer's notebook
- expert
- topic
- notes

Continuum Connection

- Understand that to write an expository text, the writer needs to become very knowledgeable about a topic
- Use a writer's notebook or booklet as a tool for collecting ideas, experimenting, planning, sketching, or drafting
- Use sketching, webs, lists, and freewriting to think about, plan for, and try out writing

GOAL

Learn to take notes on a topic without copying the author's words.

RATIONALE

When you teach students to conduct research for their nonfiction writing, they begin to understand that nonfiction authors must first learn about a topic before they can write about it. They learn that anyone can become an expert on a topic with the right tools.

WRITER'S NOTEBOOK/WRITING FOLDER

Students will take notes about their topic in their writer's notebooks.

ASSESS LEARNING

- Notice whether students take notes in their writer's notebooks using their own words.
- Look for evidence that they can use vocabulary such as *writer's notebook*, *expert*, *topic*, and *notes*.

MINILESSON

To help students think about the minilesson principle, model gathering information about a topic and taking concise notes in your own words. Here is an example.

> Now that I have decided on the focus of my topic and I know what I need to learn about it, I will find out more information by reading and taking notes.

▶ Display a book or website about your topic. Read a short section aloud, and think aloud about the notes you will take.

> This website says that Mount Vesuvius is a kind of volcano called a stratovolcano. It says the eruption in the year 79 AD destroyed the cities of Pompeii and Herculaneum and changed the way the Sarno River flowed. It also changed Mount Vesuvius itself—it killed many of the plants that grew there and changed the way the top of the mountain looked. I'd like to remember all this information, so I'm going to write it in my writer's notebook. I don't want to write down everything the website says, just the most important ideas. I'm going to write these ideas in my own words on a sticky note. I can move the sticky notes around when it comes time to organize my notes.

▶ Model writing the notes on sticky notes and placing them on chart paper or in your writer's notebook (p. 66 in *Writer's Notebook, Intermediate*).

▶ Continue in a similar manner with at least one more section of text.

> What did you notice about how I took notes about my topic?

> Be sure to write the notes in your own words. If you copy words, place quotation marks around the words.

Have a Try

Invite students to talk to a partner about taking notes.

▶ Read aloud another section of text.

What information might I want to remember from this section? How could I take notes about that in my writer's notebook? Turn and talk to your partner about this.

▶ After time for discussion, invite a few pairs to share their thinking. Write the suggested notes on sticky notes and place them on the chart paper.

Summarize and Apply

Write the principle at the top of the chart. Summarize the learning. Students will need access to information about their topics so that they can take notes in their writer's notebooks (p. 66 in *Writer's Notebook, Intermediate*).

What did you learn today about how and why to take notes about a topic for nonfiction writing?

Today during independent writing time, look for information about your topic in books or on the internet. Then write short notes on sticky notes and put them in your writer's notebook. Remember to use your own words when you write the notes. Bring your notebook to share when we come back together.

Confer

▶ During independent writing, move around the room to confer briefly with students about taking notes for their nonfiction writing. Use prompts such as the following as needed.

• *Where could you find information about _____?*

• *What does that website say about _____?*

• *How could you record that information in your writer's notebook?*

• *How could you put that in your own words?*

Share

Following independent writing, gather students in the meeting area to share their research in groups of three or four.

Share the notes you took with your group.

Section 5: Writing Process

WML5

WPS.U4.WML5

Writing Minilesson Principle
Interview or watch an expert on your topic and take notes.

**Writer's Notebook:
Becoming an Expert**

You Will Need

- a topic for a nonfiction text (e.g., volcanoes)
- excerpt from a video or podcast of an expert talking about the topic
- chart paper and markers
- writer's notebooks

Academic Language / Important Vocabulary

- writer's notebook
- expert
- interview
- topic
- notes

Continuum Connection

- Use a writer's notebook or booklet as a tool for collecting ideas, experimenting, planning, sketching, or drafting
- Use sketching, webs, lists, and freewriting to think about, plan for, and try out writing

GOAL

Seek information from an expert about a topic.

RATIONALE

Information isn't found only in books or on websites. Consider having students learn about their topics from an expert, whether in person, via videoconference, from a video, or from a podcast. To get the most from the expert, guide students to develop a list of questions. Having a list of questions will prepare students to listen attentively for the information they need.

WRITER'S NOTEBOOK/WRITING FOLDER

Students will write questions they would ask an expert in their writer's notebooks.

ASSESS LEARNING

- Notice whether students can develop productive questions to get the information they need.
- Observe whether the notes they take are useful and in their own words.
- Look for evidence that they can use vocabulary such as *writer's notebook*, *expert*, *interview*, *topic*, and *notes*.

MINILESSON

To help students think about the minilesson principle, guide them to develop questions they would want to ask an expert about a topic. Then play an excerpt from a video or podcast about the topic and model taking notes. Here is an example.

> One way to become an expert on your topic is to interview someone who is already an expert. What does it mean to interview someone?

> When you interview an expert, you ask questions and the expert answers them. Sometimes, you might not be able to find an expert to interview. You could also watch a video of an expert talking about your topic. I searched online for an expert on the eruption of Mount Vesuvius, and I found a video by an archaeologist who studies Pompeii. Before we watch the video, let's think about questions we would want to ask the archaeologist about Pompeii. Two related questions I have are, "What artifacts have you found in Pompeii? What have you learned about Pompeii from them?"

- Write the questions on chart paper. Then invite students to pose their own questions on the topic, and add them to the chart.

> Now that we've thought about questions we would want to ask the expert, we are ready to watch the video. As you watch, pay close attention and notice if any of our questions are answered. Take notes about what you are learning.

- Play the video. Pause regularly to help students notice when a question has been answered and to model taking notes about the answers.

Have a Try

Invite students to talk to a partner about interviewing an expert.

> What questions about your topic would you want to ask an expert? Turn and talk to your partner about your ideas.

> ▶ After students turn and talk, invite a few students to share their thinking.

Summarize and Apply

Write the principle at the top of the chart. Summarize the learning and invite students to develop questions they would want to ask an expert.

> Why is it important to write down your questions and notes about the expert's answers?

> Today during independent writing time, turn to Section 3 in your writer's notebook (p. 68 in *Writer's Notebook, Intermediate*). Write some questions you would like to ask an expert about your topic. Bring your questions to share when we meet later.

Interview or watch an expert on your topic and take notes.

1. What artifacts have you found in Pompeii? What did you learn about Pompeii from these objects?

   - jewelry, artwork, buildings, skeletons
   - tells us what life was like in Pompeii

2. What are the strangest things archaeologists have found in Pompeii?

   - the bones of a giraffe
   - loaves of bread

3. How many people survived the eruption of Mount Vesuvius?

4. What did the people of Pompeii know about Mount Vesuvius?

   - didn't know it was a volcano (hadn't erupted for 600 years)

Confer

> ▶ During independent writing, move around the room to confer briefly with students about questions they would want to ask an expert. Use prompts such as the following as needed.

> - *What kind of expert could you interview about your topic?*
> - *What questions would you want to ask?*
> - *What are you wondering about?*
> - *What can you do to remember their answers?*

Share

Following independent writing, gather students in the meeting area to share their questions.

> What would you want to ask an expert about your topic?

> How could you find an expert on your topic?

Writing Minilesson Principle
Choose and sketch a few objects to represent the big ideas of your topic.

Writer's Notebook: Becoming an Expert

You Will Need

- a chosen topic for a model nonfiction text (e.g., volcanoes)
- chart paper and markers
- writer's notebooks

Academic Language / Important Vocabulary

- writer's notebook
- topic
- artifact
- object
- represent
- vocabulary

Continuum Connection

- Use some vocabulary specific to the topic
- Use a writer's notebook or booklet as a tool for collecting ideas, experimenting, planning, sketching, or drafting
- Use sketching, webs, lists, and freewriting to think about, plan for, and try out writing

GOAL

Choose and sketch a few important objects to focus thinking about a topic for nonfiction writing.

RATIONALE

Choosing and sketching a few important objects related to a topic can help students develop their thinking around the topic and decide what to include in their informational writing. It can also give them ideas for illustrations and topic-related vocabulary to include.

WRITER'S NOTEBOOK/WRITING FOLDER

Students will sketch objects and list vocabulary related to their topics in their writer's notebooks.

ASSESS LEARNING

- Notice whether students sketch important objects related to their topics.
- Look for evidence that they can use vocabulary such as *writer's notebook*, *topic*, *artifact*, *object*, *represent*, and *vocabulary*.

MINILESSON

Students will need their writer's notebooks for the lesson (p. 72 in *Writer's Notebook, Intermediate*). To help students think about the minilesson principle, model choosing and sketching a few objects related to your topic. Then invite students to begin sketching objects related to their own topics. Below is an example.

> Thinking about objects or artifacts that are important to your topic can help you think what to write. Ask yourself the question, "What objects would help someone learn about my topic?" My topic is the eruption of Mount Vesuvius, so I started to think about what objects you might see in a museum exhibit about the eruption. You might see a map of Italy that shows where Pompeii is. You might see a piece of volcanic rock from Mount Vesuvius. You might also see artifacts that have been found in Pompeii, such as jugs, vases, or coins. I'm going to sketch these important things so I remember to write about them.

> Turn to Section 3 in your writer's notebook. As I sketch, think about objects that would help someone learn about your topic. Begin to sketch them in your writer's notebook. Label your sketches.

▸ After students have had time to sketch, invite a few students to share their sketches.

> What did you sketch?

> Why is a _____ important to your topic?

Have a Try

Invite students to start making a list of topic-related vocabulary (p. 73 in *Writer's Notebook, Intermediate*).

> If someone is learning about the eruption of Mount Vesuvius, I think they should know important words such as *ash*, *lava*, *stratovolcano*, *artifact*, and *archaeologist*. What vocabulary should people know about your topic? Start making a list of these words in your writer's notebook.

Summarize and Apply

Write the principle at the top of the chart. Summarize the learning and invite students to add to their sketches and lists.

> During independent writing time today, continue to sketch important objects that represent your topic and to add important vocabulary words to your list. Also jot definitions in case you want to make a glossary. Later, when it comes time to write, your sketches and lists will help you remember what information you want to include in your writing. Bring your writer's notebook to share when we meet later.

Choose and sketch a few objects to represent the big ideas of your topic.

Important Words About My Topic

- ash
- lava
- stratovolcano
- artifact
- archaeologist

Pompeii

Confer

▷ During independent writing, move around the room to confer briefly with students about preparing for nonfiction writing. Use prompts such as the following as needed.

- *What objects or artifacts do you think of when you think of your topic?*
- *What artifacts might you see in a museum exhibit about your topic?*
- *Why is that object important to your topic?*
- *What are some important words readers should know about your topic?*

Share

Following independent writing, gather students in groups of three in the meeting area to share their sketches and lists.

> Tell your group about the objects and words you wrote in your writer's notebook. Remember to tell them why the objects are important to your topic.

Assessment

After you have taught the minilessons in this umbrella, observe students as they draw, write, and talk about their writing. Use *The Fountas & Pinnell Literacy Continuum* to notice, teach for, and support students' learning as you observe their preparation for informational writing.

> What evidence do you have of students' new understandings related to using the writer's notebook to prepare for and plan nonfiction writing?
>
> - Do students make lists of topics they are interested in?
> - Do they use webs to focus a topic for nonfiction writing?
> - Do they make lists of questions and wonderings about topics?
> - Can they take notes about a topic in their own words?
> - Can they develop questions they would want to ask an expert about a topic?
> - Have they tried sketching objects that represent the big ideas of their topic?
> - Do students understand and use vocabulary such as *writer's notebook*, *topic*, *web*, *focus*, *notes*, and *interview*?
>
> In what other ways, beyond the scope of this umbrella, are students ready to explore nonfiction writing?
>
> - How are students interested in sharing their writing?
> - Would they benefit from learning ways to expand their nonfiction writing?

Use your observations to determine the next umbrella you will teach. You may also consult Suggested Sequence of Lessons (pp. 665–682) for guidance.

EXTENSIONS FOR WRITER'S NOTEBOOK: BECOMING AN EXPERT

> Teach students how to organize information using different text structures (e.g., sequence, question and answer, problem and solution) as the main structure or as an underlying structure and choose the one(s) most appropriate for their topic.

> Enlist the aid of the school or local librarian to model how to find information effectively in books and/or online.

> Invite a local expert on a class science or social studies topic to give a presentation to your class. Have students develop questions in advance, and prepare them to take notes.

Minilessons in This Umbrella

Writer's Notebook

WML1	Search online efficiently and effectively to find information.
WML2	Evaluate whether you have found the information you need and record it.
WML3	Evaluate the credibility of the source of the information you find online.
WML4	Check your sources against each other.

Before Teaching Umbrella 5 Minilessons

With the constant explosion of new technologies, children and teenagers spend more and more time reading in digital environments. Although the growth of digital technologies offers myriad benefits, it also presents a number of challenges. A different set of skills is needed for reading in digital environments than for reading print publications. Students need to be taught how to locate, evaluate, and analyze content using digital resources such as websites, databases, e-books, and apps.

Some of the lessons in this umbrella overlap with SAS.U7: Reading in Digital Environments in *The Reading Minilessons Book, Grade 4* (Fountas and Pinnell 2020). If you are using both books, it is not necessary to teach both umbrellas.

We recommend teaching this umbrella when students are writing nonfiction so they can apply their new learning to something they are researching. Consider whether you want students to take notes about the information they locate in their writer's notebooks or on separate note-taking sheets to be kept in their writing folders.

Before teaching the minilessons in this umbrella, determine how and when your students will have access to digital devices during the school day, and put procedures in place for ensuring that they can use them safely. You might, for example, have students use a student-friendly search engine or give them lists of safe, trustworthy websites about different topics. Consider involving the technology coordinator at your school to assist with students' use of technology.

Researching in Digital Environments

You Will Need

- a computer or tablet with internet access (connected to a projector, if possible)
- chart paper and markers
- writer's notebooks

Academic Language / Important Vocabulary

- website
- online
- search engine
- keywords

Continuum Connection

- Use different search strategies to increase the effectiveness of your searches including keywords, search engine filters, and symbols
- Locate websites that fit one's needs and purpose

GOAL

Use different search techniques to increase the effectiveness of searches, including keywords, search engine filters, and symbols.

RATIONALE

Many students understand the basics of searching online for information but often find it challenging to find the information they actually need. When students are armed with a toolkit of effective searching techniques–for example, using filters and symbols, knowing how to phrase inquiries, and knowing how to perform multistep searches–they are more likely to find the information they need for their nonfiction writing.

WRITER'S NOTEBOOK/WRITING FOLDER

As students search online for information, they can take notes on their findings in their writer's notebooks.

ASSESS LEARNING

- Notice whether students are able to effectively search for and find the information they need online.
- Look for evidence that they can use vocabulary such as *website*, *online*, *search engine*, and *keywords*.

MINILESSON

To help students think about the minilesson principle, engage them in an interactive demonstration of how to search effectively for information online. Below is an example. This lesson assumes the use of Google as a search engine.

- Display Google or another search engine for students to see.

  When researching your nonfiction writing topic, you may want to search online. There is a large amount of information online, but sometimes it can be hard to find exactly what you need. What are some of the problems or challenges you've had when searching for information online?

- List students' responses on chart paper. Then discuss each problem, inviting students to offer possible solutions. Add solutions in a second column. Offer your own search tips, as needed.

  These are all excellent ideas. Let's research the topic of whales.

- Search using the keyword *whales*.

  The search engine found about half a billion results for the topic! What do you think I should search for to find the largest type of whale?

- Search for *biggest whale* and share your results.

Have a Try

Invite students to talk to a partner about another search inquiry.

> Turn and talk to your partner about what you would search for to find out if more people live in China or in India.

▶ If necessary, explain that some topics need to be broken down into multiple steps. Demonstrate searching for *population of China* (or *how many people live in China*) and then do the same for India.

Summarize and Apply

Write the principle at the top of the chart. Summarize the learning and remind students to use these tips and techniques when doing online searches.

> What did you learn today about how to search online for information?

> During independent writing time today, work on a piece of nonfiction writing. Try searching online for information about your topic. You can take notes about the information you find in your writer's notebook.

Search online efficiently and effectively to find information.	
Problem	**Solution**
I don't know what to write in the search box.	• Type only the <u>most important</u> <u>keywords</u>.
I can't find what I'm looking for.	• Is there another way to say what you're looking for? Use <u>synonyms</u>. • Make your search terms <u>more specific or less specific</u>.
I don't know how to spell the thing I'm looking for.	• The search engine can often guess what word you mean, but <u>get as close as you can to</u> <u>accuate spelling</u>.
I want to search for words in an exact order.	• Use <u>quotation marks</u> if you want to find websites that have your keywords in the same order. **"by the dawn's early light"**
The results are about something completely different from what I'm looking for.	• Use a <u>minus sign</u> (-) in front of words you want to exclude. If you are looking for websites about Mars the planet, not the candy company, type this: **-candy mars**
The websites are too hard to read—they're for adults.	• Type the word <u>kids</u> after your search terms to find websites that are for kids. **dinosaurs kids**

Confer

▶ During independent writing, move around the room to confer briefly with students about their writing and research. Use prompts such as the following as needed.

- *What are you writing about today?*
- *What could you search for online to find information about _____?*
- *How could you make your keywords more specific?*

Share

Following independent writing, gather students in the meeting area to talk about searching online for information.

> Talk about how you did your search for information. Did you find what you were looking for?

WML2
WPS.U5.WML2

Writing Minilesson Principle
Evaluate whether you have found the information you need and record it.

Researching in Digital Environments

You Will Need

- a computer or tablet with internet access (connected to a projector, if possible)
- chart paper and markers
- writer's notebooks

Academic Language / Important Vocabulary

- website
- online
- evaluate
- search engine
- source

Continuum Connection

- Locate websites that fit one's needs and purposes
- Identify the purposes of a website

GOAL

Evaluate whether you have found the appropriate information and take notes about it.

RATIONALE

When students are able to evaluate whether they have found the information they need after conducting an online search, they spend more time reading relevant, interesting information and working on their writing and less time searching for information or going off task.

WRITER'S NOTEBOOK/WRITING FOLDER

As students search online, they should use their writer's notebooks to record the information they find and the source of the information.

ASSESS LEARNING

- Notice whether students can quickly evaluate whether a search result contains the information they need and record the relevant information in their writer's notebooks.
- Look for evidence that they can use vocabulary such as *website*, *online*, *evaluate*, *search engine*, and *source*.

MINILESSON

To help students think about the minilesson principle, engage them in a demonstration and discussion about how to evaluate and take notes about search results. Here is an example.

- Display Google (or another search engine) for students to see.

    In my nonfiction book about colors in nature, I plan to have a section about why the sky is blue. What should I type into the search box?

- Think aloud as you choose a result to click on. Note that your search results may differ from this example.

    I see an article from NASA, an organization I trust. Below the title and web address, I see a few sentences that seem to be about what I'm looking for. What did you notice about how I chose which search result to click on?

- Record students' responses on chart paper.
- Click on the search result and think aloud to evaluate the source for relevancy. Point out any important words or phrases, subheadings, and text features.

    This website has what I need, so I'll read the whole article more closely. What did you notice about what I did after I chose a website to click on?

    What do you think you should do if you determine that a website doesn't have the information you need?

- Record responses on the chart.

Have a Try

Invite students to talk to a partner about recording information.

▶ Read aloud a small section of relevant information from the chosen website.

> This information is exactly what I need. What should I write down in my writer's notebook so I'll remember this information? Turn and talk to your partner about this.

▶ After students turn and talk, invite a few students to share their thinking. Model taking notes about the information you read and recording the source of the information.

> Why is it important to record the source of the information you found?

Summarize and Apply

Write the principle at the top of the chart. Summarize the learning and remind students to evaluate the relevancy of search results.

> What did you learn today about searching online for information?

> If you search online for information to help with your nonfiction writing today, remember first to evaluate whether you have found the information you need and then to record the information and source in your writer's notebook.

Evaluate whether you have found the information you need and record it.

1. Decide which website to click on.
   - Check out the web address/source.
   - Read the title and short description.
   - Click on the website that seems most likely to have the information you need.

2. Evaluate whether the website has the information you need.
   - Skim the website.
   - Does the website have the information you need? If so, read it closely.
   - If not, choose another search result.

3. Record the information.
   - Read closely.
   - Take notes about information that answers your question.
   - Write down the source (title, author, web address).

Confer

▶ During independent writing, move around the room to confer briefly with students about their writing and research. Use prompts such as the following as needed.

- *What do you want to find out? What could you search for to find that?*
- *Do you think this result has the information you need? What makes you think that?*
- *What could you write in your writer's notebook to help you remember that information?*

Share

Following independent writing, gather students in the meeting area to talk about how they searched for information.

> Who would like to tell about how you found information online?

Writing Minilesson Principle

Evaluate the credibility of the source of the information you find online.

Researching in Digital Environments

You Will Need

- a computer or tablet with internet access (connected to a projector, if possible)
- chart paper and markers
- writer's notebooks

Academic Language / Important Vocabulary

- website
- online
- credibility
- source
- content creator
- perspective

Continuum Connection

- Determine when a website was last updated
- Determine whether a website presents one perspective or multiple perspectives
- Be alert to an author's point of view and bias, and validate an author's authority on the topic

GOAL

Evaluate the credibility of sources of the information read online.

RATIONALE

When you teach students how to evaluate the credibility of online sources, they are more likely to access and use accurate information for their nonfiction writing. Additionally, the ability to critically evaluate information will serve them in all aspects of their lives, whether they are reading print or digital publications or are engaged in discourse.

WRITER'S NOTEBOOK/WRITING FOLDER

Encourage students to continue taking notes in their writer's notebooks as they conduct online research.

ASSESS LEARNING

- Observe for evidence that students can evaluate the credibility of online resources.
- Look for evidence that they can use vocabulary such as *website*, *online*, *credibility*, *source*, *content creator*, and *perspective*.

MINILESSON

To help students think about the minilesson principle, model evaluating the credibility of a website. Here is an example.

- Display a search engine, such as Google. Type the words *are zoos good for animals* or a question about another topic of your choice.

  I want to make sure I choose a credible, or trustworthy, source that will give me accurate information. Which of these results do you think will be credible? What makes you think that?

- If necessary, guide students to notice any results from well-known, credible sources. Click on one of them.

  How could you go about finding out if this site is credible?

- Guide students to understand how to check the content creator's credentials, bibliography, and the date the website was last updated (if available).

- Read aloud a few important passages from the website that show whether it presents one perspective or multiple perspectives.

  What does the creator of this website think about zoos? How can you tell?

  How someone feels about a topic is called perspective. Does this website give one perspective or multiple perspectives about zoos?

  Which makes a better website, one that offers one perspective or more than one perspective?

Have a Try

Invite students to talk to a partner about how to evaluate the credibility of a website.

> What did we think about when we evaluated the credibility of a website? What questions did we ask ourselves? Turn and talk to your partner about this.

▶ After time for discussion, invite several pairs to share their thinking. Summarize the learning on chart paper.

Summarize and Apply

Write the principle at the top of the chart. Summarize the learning and remind students to evaluate the credibility of online sources.

> Why is it important to evaluate the credibility of sources when you're doing online research for your nonfiction writing?

> During independent writing time today, work on a nonfiction piece. If you search online for information, remember to evaluate the credibility of the websites you find. When you find a credible website with the information you need, remember to take notes on what you read in your writer's notebook. If your notes have direct quotes, use quotation marks.

Evaluate the credibility of the source of the information you find online.

- Who created this website? Is the person or organization a trusted source (for example, a government agency, a university, or a major publication)? Web addresses that end in .gov or .edu are usually—but not always—trustworthy.

- Who is the author? Is that person an expert on the topic?

- Does the author list or link to credible sources of information (a bibliography)?

- When was the website last updated? Is the information current?

- Does the website present one perspective or multiple perspectives about the topic?

Confer

▶ During independent writing, move around the room to confer briefly with students about their writing and research. Use prompts such as the following as needed.

- *What are you working on today?*
- *Which websites seem to be credible sources? What makes you think that?*
- *Does this website give one perspective or multiple perspectives about the topic?*

Share

Following independent writing, gather students in the meeting area to share how they evaluated the credibility of online sources.

> Did anyone do online research today for your writing?

> How did you evaluate the credibility of the websites you found?

Researching in Digital Environments

You Will Need

- a computer or tablet with internet access (connected to a projector, if possible)
- two websites about the same topic, with at least one piece of information that is different between them
- chart paper and markers
- writer's notebooks and writing folders

Academic Language / Important Vocabulary

- online
- website
- source
- accurate

Continuum Connection

- Locate, evaluate, and analyze literary and informational content using approved digital resources such as websites, public and subscription-based databases, e-books, and apps

GOAL

Understand how to check online resources for accuracy.

RATIONALE

When you teach students how to check online resources against each other, they will understand that information published on the internet is not always accurate and must be verified with other sources. They will think critically about the information they read online and be more likely to include accurate information in their own nonfiction writing.

WRITER'S NOTEBOOK/WRITING FOLDER

Encourage students to continue taking notes in their writer's notebooks as they conduct online research and work on drafts of nonfiction writing from their writing folders.

ASSESS LEARNING

- Notice whether students use multiple credible sources to verify the accuracy of information they read online.
- Look for evidence that they can use vocabulary such as *online*, *website*, *source*, and *accurate*.

MINILESSON

To help students think about the minilesson principle, model checking two online sources against each other. Here is an example.

- Display two websites about the same topic side by side.

    I am doing a report on Brazil, a country in South America. I found these two websites with information about Brazil. Both say that Brazil is the fifth largest country in the world. That makes me think that this information is probably accurate.

    However, I also noticed some differences between these two websites. This website seems to give more information than this other website. Also, I see that this website says that the population of Brazil is around 215 million, but this one says it's 205 million. I want to make sure I include the correct population in my report. How can I know which number is correct?

- Discuss ways of verifying information, such as evaluating the credibility of each website (see WML3), checking each creator's sources, checking the date the information was updated, checking against a third website, and checking against print resources.

    Which website do you think is more likely to be accurate? Why?

    What should I search for to verify that this information is accurate?

- Demonstrate checking the information against a third credible source.

Have a Try

Invite students to talk to a partner about how to check sources against each other.

> How did we check the two websites against each other? What did we think about and ask ourselves? Turn and talk to your partner about this.

▶ After students turn and talk, invite several pairs to share their responses. Summarize the learning on chart paper.

Summarize and Apply

Summarize the learning and remind students to check their sources against each other.

> How can you be sure your information is accurate?

▶ Write the principle at the top of the chart.

> Continue working on your nonfiction writing today. If you search online for information for your writing, remember to read more than one website and check them against each other. If you find any different or conflicting information between them, determine the correct information by checking with at least one more website or print resource.

Check your sources against each other.

- Compare the information on two or more websites.

- What information is the same?

- What information is different? If there are differences, determine which is more accurate.

  o Evaluate the credibility of both websites. Is one from a more credible source than the other?

  o Check each author's sources, if listed.

  o Check the date the information was updated, if given.

  o Check another website or a print resource.

Confer

▶ During independent writing, move around the room to confer briefly with students about their writing and research. Use prompts such as the following as needed.

- *What information are you looking for today?*
- *Can you find another website about the same topic?*
- *Let's look at these two websites closely. What information is the same on both? What information is different?*
- *How can you find out which piece of information is correct?*

Share

Following independent writing, gather students in the meeting area to share how they checked sources against each other.

> Talk about how you went about your online research today.

Assessment

After you have taught the minilessons in this umbrella, observe students as they write and talk about their writing. Use *The Fountas & Pinnell Literacy Continuum* to notice, teach for, and support students' learning as you observe their reading and writing behaviors.

▶ What evidence do you have of students' new understandings related to researching in digital environments?

- Are students able to use search engines effectively? If their initial search fails to yield relevant results, are they able to revise their search strategy?
- Are they able to evaluate whether they have found the information they need?
- Do they evaluate the credibility of online resources?
- Do they check their sources against each other?
- Do they understand and use terms such as *online*, *source*, *website*, *keywords*, *search engine*, and *evaluate*?

▶ In what other ways, beyond the scope of this umbrella, are students exploring the writing process?

- Are they ready to create a multimedia presentation?
- Have they experimented with adding book and print features to their writing?

Use your observations to determine the next umbrella you will teach. You may also consult Suggested Sequence of Lessons (pp. 665–682) for guidance.

EXTENSIONS FOR RESEARCHING IN DIGITAL ENVIRONMENTS

▶ Teach students how to create a works cited page or a bibliography.

▶ Help students incorporate what they learned from their digital research into their own writing. Demonstrate how to restate information in one's own words.

▶ Encourage students to explore digital writing (see GEN.U17: Exploring Digital Writing).

Minilessons in This Umbrella

WML1   Think about your purpose and message.

WML2   Think about your audience.

WML3   Think about the kind of writing you want to do.

Before Teaching Umbrella 6 Minilessons

The goal of this umbrella is to make students aware of the relationship between purpose, audience, and genre or form. Purpose and audience are separate ideas, yet they are intertwined because they both influence the type of writing (genre or form) an author chooses to use. Prior to beginning this umbrella, students should have an idea of the topic they want to write about so they can think about and make a connection between their purpose, audience, and genre (form). In order to help them make topic decisions, have students reread their writer's notebooks for ideas. As well, it is suggested that you have formally taught several genres so that students will have a repertoire of genres from which to choose. When thinking about audience, encourage students to think beyond the school community (see WML2). These minilessons build on each other, so it is recommended that you teach them in order.

Students should have read a variety of genres and talked about the choices that the writers made. For mentor texts, use the books listed below from *Fountas & Pinnell Classroom™ Interactive Read-Aloud Collection* or books from the classroom library.

Interactive Read-Aloud Collection

Empathy

The Boy and the Whale by Mordicai Gerstein

Step Right Up: How Doc and Jim Key Taught the World About Kindness by Donna Janell Bowman

Illustration Study: Craft

Giant Squid by Candace Fleming

Eye to Eye: How Animals See the World by Steve Jenkins

Magnificent Birds by Narisa Togo

Friendship

Mangoes, Mischief, and Tales of Friendship: Stories from India by Chitra Soundar

Genre Study: Memoir

The Scraps Book: Notes from a Colorful Life by Lois Ehlert

As you read and enjoy these texts together, help students

- talk about what purpose the author may have had for writing, and

- talk about who the writer's intended audience might be.

Interactive Read-Aloud
Empathy

Illustration Study: Craft

Friendship

Genre Study: Memoir

Writer's Notebook

Section 5: Writing Process

Writing Minilesson Principle
Think about your purpose and message.

You Will Need

- two mentor texts that have the same topic but are different genres, such as the following:
  - *The Boy and the Whale* by Mordicai Gerstein, from Text Set: Empathy
  - *Giant Squid* by Candace Fleming, from Text Set: Illustration Study: Craft
- samples of different kinds of writing (e.g., persuasive, functional)
- markers
- writer's notebooks
- To download the following online resources for this lesson, visit **fp.pub/resource**:
  - Persuasive Essays (see GEN.U12.WML1)
  - Sample Letters (see GEN.U1.WML1)

Academic Language / Important Vocabulary

- reason
- topic
- purpose
- message

Continuum Connection

- Write for a specific purpose: e.g., to inform, entertain, persuade, reflect, instruct, retell, maintain relationships, plan
- Have clear goals and understand how the goals will affect the writing

---

GOAL

Understand that writers write for a reason.

RATIONALE

Writers write to communicate with an audience. What they want to communicate, their message or information, is their purpose for writing. When students understand that writers write for a reason, they begin to think about why and what they want to write.

WRITER'S NOTEBOOK/WRITING FOLDER

Students can write their ideas about their purpose for writing in their writer's notebooks.

ASSESS LEARNING

- ▶ Observe whether students are talking about different purposes for writing.
- ▶ Look for evidence that students can use vocabulary such as *reason, topic, purpose, and message*.

MINILESSON

Make sure students know what they will write about. To help students think about the minilesson principle, use mentor texts, including the two online resources, to engage them in a discussion about purposes for writing. Here is an example.

▶ Show the covers of *The Boy and the Whale* and *Giant Squid*.

> What is similar about the topic of each of these books?
>
> Why do you think the authors wrote their books?

▶ Engage students in a conversation about the authors' purposes, guiding them to recognize that Mordicai Gerstein's main purpose was to entertain (though he also gave some information) and Candace Fleming's main purpose was to give information (though she wrote her book with poetic language).

> Both authors wanted to give their readers a message about ocean animals, but one wanted to entertain readers with a story and the other wanted to inform readers using poetic language. The authors' purposes for writing helped them decide how to deliver their messages.

▶ On chart paper, start a list of purposes for writing.

▶ Continue to establish the purpose of other types of writing, such as directions for how to do or make something, a persuasive essay, and a letter. Record more purposes on the chart.

The Writing Minilessons Book, Grade 4

Have a Try

Invite students to turn and talk about purposes for writing.

> What purpose do you have for writing? Turn and talk to your partner about that.

▶ After time for discussion, ask several students to share their purposes for writing.

Summarize and Apply

Summarize the lesson. Encourage students to think about their purposes for writing. Write the principle at the top of the chart.

> A purpose is the reason for doing something. Before you write, think about your purpose for choosing to write about your topic. What message or information do you want to give? What way of writing is best for that? For example, do you want to tell a story, or give directions for how to do something? In your writer's notebook, write some ideas you have for your purpose for writing. Plan to share your ideas when we meet later.

Think about your purpose and message.	
Purposes for Writing	
• tell a story • entertain	• give information by telling a story
• give information	• explain
• convince someone	• change something
• perform a practical task • plan something	• teach how to do something
• express feelings • have someone feel something	• describe something using the senses

Confer

▶ During independent writing, move around the room to confer briefly with students about a purpose for writing. Use the following prompts as needed.

- *What ideas do you have for writing about this topic?*
- *What is your purpose for writing?*
- *Let's talk about your message and how you want to write about it.*

Share

Following independent writing, gather students in the meeting area to share their ideas.

> In groups of three, share your ideas about your purpose for writing.

Thinking About Purpose, Audience, and Genre/ Form

You Will Need

▸ several mentor texts with a clear audience, such as the following:

- *Mangoes, Mischief, and Tales of Friendship* by Chitra Soundar, from Text Set: Friendship

- *Eye to Eye* by Steve Jenkins, from Text Set: Illustration Study: Craft

▸ chart paper prepared with these headings: *Larger Community, Family, Classmates and Friends*

▸ markers

▸ writer's notebooks

Academic Language / Important Vocabulary

▸ audience

▸ purpose

▸ topic

Continuum Connection

▸ Write with specific readers or audience in mind

▸ Understand that writing is shaped by the writer's purpose and understanding of the audience

▸ Plan and organize information for the intended readers

▸ Understand audience as all readers rather than just the teacher

GOAL

Understand that writers think about their intended audience to further define their purpose.

RATIONALE

Once students have decided on a topic and purpose, they need to think whom they want to read their writing and how that affects what they write, such as understanding what the audience needs to know or adjusting the word choice (e.g., using simple words for young children).

WRITER'S NOTEBOOK/WRITING FOLDER

Students can write their ideas about their intended audience in their writer's notebooks.

ASSESS LEARNING

▸ Notice whether students understand that they need to adapt their writing to suit their audience.

▸ Look for evidence that students understand and use vocabulary such as *audience*, *purpose*, and *topic*.

MINILESSON

Students should already have a topic to write about. To help students think about the minilesson principle, use a mentor text and provide an interactive lesson about audience. Here is an example.

▸ Read aloud a few pages of *Mangoes, Mischief, and Tales of Friendship*.

Who do you think would like this book? Why?

You can tell that Chitra Soundar wrote the book for older children because she uses words that would be too difficult for younger children to read or understand, and she includes interesting drawings that older children might enjoy. Older children are her audience.

▸ Repeat with *Eye to Eye*.

An audience is the person or group of people you think would like to read something that you write or would enjoy hearing your writing read aloud.

▸ Show and read the prepared audience chart.

An audience can be small, perhaps one friend or classmate. An audience can also be big. An audience can be people you know, like friends or family, and it can also be people you don't know. Turn and talk about some people you would like to read your writing.

▸ After time for discussion, ask a few volunteers to share. Write each of the examples on the chart in the corresponding category.

Have a Try

Invite students to turn and talk about writing for an audience. Model talking about the way a writer might choose an audience using the topics chosen by several students in your class. This is just an example.

> Think about the different audiences you could write for. Brielle, your topic is enchiladas. You could write a recipe for enchiladas for the class. Ricardo, you could write a letter to a dolphin advocates' group asking how kids can help.

> Turn and talk about the audience you want to write for, what your audience might want to know, and what questions they might have.

▶ After time for discussion, ask students to share their ideas.

Summarize and Apply

Summarize the lesson. Encourage students to think about the audience they want to write for. Write the principle at the top of the chart.

> You have a topic and a purpose. Now think about your audience. During independent writing time, write down the audience you might like to write for in your writer's notebook near the purposes you wrote. Also write some things your audience might want to know and what questions they might have. Bring the ideas you have when we meet later.

▶ Add the three questions shown on the chart. Keep the chart posted.

Confer

▶ During independent writing, move around the room to confer briefly with students about writing for their audience. Use the following prompts as needed.

- *Who will be reading this?*
- *What does your audience know already? What do you think your audience would like to know more about? What words might your audience not know?*

Share

Following independent writing, gather students in the meeting area.

> Each of you will share your topic, purpose, and audience.

Think about your audience.

**Larger Community
(formal writing)**
local newspaper or website
school or school district leaders
author
expert

**Family
(less formal writing)**
sister
babysitter
uncle or aunt
parent

**Classmates and Friends
(casual writing)**

Who is the audience?

What would the audience want to know?

What questions does my audience have?

Writing Minilesson Principle

Think about the kind of writing you want to do.

Thinking About Purpose, Audience, and Genre/Form

You Will Need

▸ several mentor texts that have a clear purpose and audience, such as the following:

- *Step Right Up* by Donna Janell Bowman, from Text Set: Empathy

- *The Scraps Book* by Lois Ehlert, from Text Set: Genre Study: Memoir

- *Magnificent Birds* by Narisa Togo, from Text Set: Illustration Study: Craft

▸ chart paper prepared with a four-column chart with the headings *Author and Topic, Purpose, Audience*, and *Type of Writing*

▸ markers

▸ writer's notebooks and writing folders

Academic Language / Important Vocabulary

▸ topic   ▸ purpose

▸ choice   ▸ audience

Continuum Connection

▸ Tell whether a piece of writing is functional, narrative, informational, or poetic

▸ Understand how the purpose of the writing influences the selection of genre

▸ Select the genre for the writing based on the purpose

GOAL

Understand the relationship of the genre or form of writing to the purpose and the audience.

RATIONALE

When students learn to choose the type of writing they want to do by thinking about how it best suits their purpose and audience, they write effectively and with authenticity.

WRITER'S NOTEBOOK/WRITING FOLDER

Students should store their drafts in their writing folders. They may need their writer's notebooks to check for ideas to use in their writing.

ASSESS LEARNING

▸ Observe whether students recognize that their purpose and audience will help them decide what type of writing they want to do.

▸ Look for evidence that students can use vocabulary such as *topic, choice, purpose*, and *audience*.

MINILESSON

To help students think about the type of writing they want to do, use mentor texts and model the process. Here is an example.

▸ Show the covers of *Step Right Up*, *The Scraps Book*, and *Magnificent Birds*.

> Turn and talk to your partner about the purpose and audience for each of these books.

▸ Show the prepared chart. Ask volunteers to provide suggestions for the topic, purpose, audience, and type of writing for *Step Right Up*. Add their ideas to the chart. Repeat for the remaining two books.

▸ Choose one of the text examples and ask students to think about changing the purpose, audience, and type of writing for one of the topics. Model how to do this by contrasting the book with a student's plans for writing. Here is an example.

> Both Narisa Togo and Shelby are interested in writing about birds. Narisa Togo's purpose was to inform, so she wrote an informational book that might appeal to students or adults who want to learn more about birds. Shelby's purpose might be to describe the characteristics of birds, so she might write a poem for the class.

▸ Add the example to the chart.

> Authors decide how they will write about a topic. When you write, choose the way that makes sense for your purpose and audience. You can even write about the same topic more than once and choose a different type of writing each time.

Have a Try

Invite students to turn and talk about purpose, audience, and type of writing.

> Turn and talk about what type of writing would be best for your purpose and audience and why.

▶ After time for discussion, ask a few volunteers to share their ideas. Add to the chart.

▶ You may want to keep the chart posted and have other students fill it in with their ideas.

Summarize and Apply

Summarize the lesson. Remind students to think about what type of writing best fits their purpose and audience. Write the principle at the top of the chart.

> Remember that the type of writing you choose depends on your topic, purpose, and audience. You have made some notes about purpose and audience in your writer's notebook. Use your notes to choose the type of writing you want to do. You might also have notes about your topic in your writer's notebook. When you are ready, get a piece of draft paper and begin writing. Bring your writing to share when we meet later.

\multicolumn{4}{c}{Think about the kind of writing you want to do.}			
Author and Topic	Purpose	Audience	Type of Writing
Donna Janell Bowman: Doc and Jim Key	Inform by telling a story	Students	Biography
Lois Ehlert: Her life	Tell about her life	Young people	Memoir
Narisa Togo: Birds	Inform	Students or Adults	All-About Book
Shelby: Birds	Describe	Class	Poetry
Brielle: Enchiladas	Teach	Students	How-to book
Ricardo: Dolphins	Change something	Adult expert	Letter
My-Duyen: Holidays	Invite	Family	Invitation

Confer

▶ During independent writing, move around the room to confer briefly with students about their writing. Use the following prompts as needed.

- *Talk about why this type of writing is best for your purpose and audience.*
- *You have chosen a topic. Let's look at the chart and talk about how you might choose the type of writing.*

Share

Following independent writing, gather students in the meeting area to share their writing.

> In pairs, share your topic, purpose, audience, and type of writing. Then read what you have written so far.

Assessment

After you have taught the minilessons in this umbrella, observe students as they write and talk about writing. Use *The Fountas & Pinnell Literacy Continuum* to notice, teach for, and support students' learning as you observe their attempts at writing.

▶ What evidence do you have of students' new understandings related to purpose and audience?

- Do students' writing behaviors show that they are thinking about purpose and audience?

- Are they thinking about purpose and audience when they decide what kind of writing they want to do?

- Are they using vocabulary such as *reason*, *purpose*, *genre*, *audience*, and *choice*?

▶ In what ways, beyond the scope of this umbrella, are students showing an interest in making independent writing choices?

- Do they show an interest in choosing their own topics?

- Are they showing an interest in writing in a variety of genres?

Use your observations to determine the next umbrella you will teach. You may also consult Suggested Sequence of Lessons (pp. 665–682) for guidance.

EXTENSIONS FOR THINKING ABOUT PURPOSE, AUDIENCE, AND GENRE/FORM

▶ Share other types of writing with students that have different purposes and intended audiences and have them talk about the purpose and audience (e.g., recipes, news stories, greeting cards).

▶ Have students add to the audience chart as they think of new examples of each audience.

▶ If you are using *The Reading Minilessons Book, Grade 4* [Fountas and Pinnell 2020], consider teaching about author's purpose through the lens of a reader (see LA.U8: Thinking About the Author's Purpose and Message).

Minilessons in This Umbrella

WML1   Write your prediction.

WML2   Sketch and take notes about your observations.

WML3   Write a procedure.

WML4   Analyze and write about the results.

Writer's Notebook

Before Teaching Umbrella 7 Minilessons

This umbrella starts laying the foundation for students to think and write like scientists, eventually writing lab reports or scientific articles. WML3 provides an introduction to writing procedural texts. The understandings that start here will later be built upon in GEN.U2: Writing Procedural Texts. However, this umbrella can also be taught after GEN.U2 if that better suits your students or curriculum.

Before teaching the minilessons in this umbrella, you will need to choose, plan, and gather materials for a science experiment that you will do with the students during WML2. You can use any experiment that is relevant to your class's science curriculum; however, these minilessons use as an example an experiment in which the students explore the relationship between potential energy and kinetic energy. They will investigate how the distance a rubber band is stretched (potential energy) affects the distance the rubber band flies after being released (kinetic energy). You can find more information about this science experiment by searching online for keywords such as "rubber band energy science experiment."

You might also want to read and discuss nonfiction books related to the science topic you have chosen.

As you read and enjoy science texts together, help students

- make predictions and inferences,
- notice and discuss details in the illustrations, and
- pose questions and wonderings about the topic.

Section 5: Writing Process

Writing Minilesson Principle
Write your prediction.

You Will Need

- a plan and materials for a science experiment
- chart paper and markers
- writer's notebooks and writing folders

Academic Language / Important Vocabulary

- science
- experiment
- prediction
- centimeter (cm)

Continuum Connection

- Use vocabulary appropriate for the topic
- Generate and expand ideas through talk with peers and teacher

GOAL

Write a prediction for a science project.

RATIONALE

When you help students write a prediction for a science experiment, they learn that scientists use what they already know about a topic to make a prediction about what will happen. They also learn that scientists use writing for a purpose—to record their predictions in order to have a permanent, written record of their scientific process.

WRITER'S NOTEBOOK/WRITING FOLDER

Have students write their predictions in their writer's notebooks. If students have extra time, they can work on an ongoing writing project in their writing folders.

ASSESS LEARNING

- Notice whether students can make and write a prediction for a science experiment.
- Look for evidence that they can use vocabulary such as *science*, *experiment*, *prediction*, and *centimeter (cm)*.

MINILESSON

Introduce the science experiment that you will use for these lessons (see Before Teaching for more information) and help students make predictions. Here is an example.

- Introduce the topic of the experiment and help students review what they know about it.

    What different kinds of energy do you know about? What is the difference between potential and kinetic energy?

    We will stretch a rubber band to show potential, or stored, energy, and let it go to convert potential energy to kinetic energy, which is energy in motion.

- Show the materials for the science experiment and explain the procedure.

    To do this experiment, we will need a rubber band and a ruler. We will stretch a rubber band to three different lengths—10 cm, 20 cm, and 30 cm. Then we will release the rubber band and measure how far it flies. Will the amount we stretch the rubber band affect the amount of kinetic energy? What is your prediction about that? Your prediction is a statement of what you think will happen in the experiment.

- Choose several students to offer their predictions. Write the predictions on chart paper.

Have a Try

Invite students to talk to a partner about making predictions.

> How do you know what to predict? Turn and talk to your partner about the thinking behind your prediction.

▶ After students turn and talk, invite a few pairs to share their thinking. Make sure students understand that making predictions involves using known information to think about what will happen.

Summarize and Apply

Write the principle at the top of the chart. Summarize the learning and remind students to record their predictions.

> Why do you think it's important to write down your prediction for a science experiment?

> Write your prediction in your writer's notebook so you will remember it. After you see the results of the experiment, read your prediction to see if you correctly predicted what would happen. When you finish writing your prediction, continue working on a writing project that you've already started or start a new one.

Write your prediction.

• I think the rubber band will fly the farthest when it is stretched to 30 cm because it will have more potential energy.

• I predict that the rubber band will fly only a few feet when it is stretched to 10 cm because it won't have much potential energy.

• I predict that the more you stretch a rubber band, the farther it will fly. Stretching it more will give it more potential energy.

Confer

▶ During independent writing, move around the room to confer briefly with students about their predictions. Use prompts such as the following as needed.

- *Think about what you know already when you write your prediction.*
- *Is your prediction written clearly enough that another person could understand it?*

Share

Following independent writing, gather students in the meeting area to share their predictions.

> Who would like to read aloud your prediction for the science experiment?

WML2
WPS.U7.WML2

Writing Minilesson Principle
Sketch and take notes about your observations.

Observing and Writing Like a Scientist

You Will Need

- materials for a science experiment
- chart paper and markers
- writer's notebooks
- To download the following online resource for this lesson, visit **fp.pub/resources**:
  - chart art (optional)

Academic Language / Important Vocabulary

- sketch
- observe
- observation
- label
- scientist

Continuum Connection

- Make scientific observations, use notes and sketches to document them, and talk with others about connections and patterns

GOAL

Observe carefully and use drawing and writing to accurately record observations.

RATIONALE

When you help students record their scientific observations, they learn to look closely at a subject; make precise, detailed observations; and record their observations accurately. They begin to understand the importance of keeping a record of their scientific observations.

WRITER'S NOTEBOOK/WRITING FOLDER

Have students add their sketches and notes near their predictions in their writer's notebooks.

ASSESS LEARNING

- Notice whether students sketch and take notes about their observations.
- Look for evidence that they can use vocabulary such as *sketch*, *observe*, *observation*, *label*, and *scientist*.

MINILESSON

Students will need their writer's notebooks for this lesson. Demonstrate the planned science experiment and, at the appropriate point, model using drawing and writing to record scientific observations. Here is an example based on the rubber band experiment.

- Take students outdoors to do the rubber band experiment. Demonstrate stretching a rubber band beyond its size to 10, 20, and 30 cm and releasing it. Perform three or four trials of each distance. Invite a volunteer to measure how far the rubber band flies each time. Bring something outside on which to record the distances, and have students bring their writer's notebooks and pencils.

  We've recorded our scientific observations. Let's also make some sketches so we will remember what we did and observed. What could we draw?

  Labels will help readers understand our sketches and will help us remember what we did. What could we label?

- Add labels to the sketch. Also add today's date.

Have a Try

Invite students to talk to a partner about recording scientific observations.

> I wrote today's date above our observations. Why is it important to write the date when you record scientific observations? Turn and talk to your partner about this.

▶ After time for discussion, invite several pairs to share their thinking. Although less important for this experiment, best practice is to date a science report. For some experiments, different conditions over time could affect results.

Summarize and Apply

Summarize the learning. Remind students to sketch and take notes about their scientific observations.

> How can you remember the results of a science experiment?

▶ Write the principle at the top of the observations. Save the observations for WML4.

> Today during independent writing time, you will do the same experiment in a small group and sketch and record your observations in your writer's notebook. Remember to aim the rubber band away from people. Bring your notes to share when we come back together.

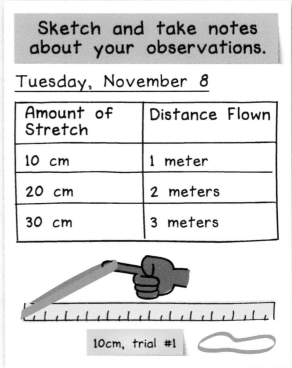

Sketch and take notes about your observations.

Tuesday, November 8

Amount of Stretch	Distance Flown
10 cm	1 meter
20 cm	2 meters
30 cm	3 meters

10cm, trial #1

Confer

▶ During independent writing, confer briefly with students about their scientific observations. Use prompts such as the following as needed.

- *What did you write about the experiment?*
- *Talk about what you drew to show what happened in the experiment.*
- *Are your notes and sketches clear enough for someone else to read?*

Share

Following independent writing, gather students in the meeting area to share their observations.

> What did you write and draw to record your scientific observations?

> Why is it important to record your scientific observations?

Writing Minilesson Principle
Write a procedure.

Observing and Writing Like a Scientist

You Will Need

- chart paper and markers
- writer's notebooks

Academic Language / Important Vocabulary

- science experiment
- procedure
- materials
- steps

Continuum Connection

- Understand that a procedural text often shows one item under another item and may include a number or letter for each item
- Write steps of a procedure with appropriate sequence and explicitness, using number words or transition words

GOAL

Write the procedure used for a science experiment so that others can replicate it.

RATIONALE

Writing the procedure used for a science experiment so that it can be replicated means that the writing has to be clear and precise. Students learn the importance of accuracy in writing about scientific subjects. This lesson could serve as an introduction or a follow-up to procedural writing (see GEN.U2).

WRITER'S NOTEBOOK/WRITING FOLDER

Have students write the procedure for a science experiment in their writer's notebooks.

ASSESS LEARNING

- Notice whether students can accurately recall and write the procedure they followed for a science experiment.
- Look for evidence that they can use vocabulary such as *science experiment*, *procedure*, *materials*, and *steps*.

MINILESSON

This minilesson should be taught shortly after students have observed or conducted a science experiment (see WML2). To help students think about the minilesson principle, use shared writing to begin writing the procedure for the experiment. Below is an example. Students will finish writing the procedure on their own during independent writing.

> If other people wanted to do the same experiment that we did, how would they know what to do?

> We could write the procedure we followed so other people could follow it. What is the first thing they would need to know in order to do this experiment?

> They would need to know what materials they need to do the experiment. What did we use for the experiment?

▶ Using students' input, write a materials list on chart paper.

> What do you notice about how I wrote the materials?

> I wrote a list of the materials. Each material is on its own line.

> What else would people need to know?

> They would need to know what to do. What would the first step be? What did we do after that?

▶ Use students' responses to write the first few steps of the procedure. Tell students that they will finish writing the procedure during independent writing.

Have a Try

Invite students to talk to a partner about how to write a procedure.

> What did you notice about how we wrote the procedure for the science experiment? Turn and talk to your partner about this.

▶ After time for discussion, invite several pairs to share their thinking. Use their responses to summarize the learning on a separate sheet of chart paper. Write the principle at the top.

Summarize and Apply

Summarize the learning. Invite students to write the procedure for the science experiment they conducted.

> Why is it important for scientists to write the procedure they followed for an experiment?

> If you write the procedure you followed, other people can do the same experiment exactly the same way you did it. If other people do the same experiment and get the same results, then you will know that your results are accurate. This can help you prove that your predictions were correct.

> Today during independent writing time, write the whole procedure for the science experiment in your writer's notebook. Bring your writing to share when we come back together.

Confer

▶ During independent writing, move around the room to confer briefly with students about writing a procedure. Use prompts such as the following as needed.

- *What would someone need to know to do the experiment?*
- *What materials did we use for the experiment?*
- *How should you write the materials?*
- *How can you make the order of the steps clear?*

Share

Following independent writing, gather students in the meeting area to share their writing.

> Who would like to read aloud the procedure you wrote?

> How did _____ make the procedure clear for other people to do the experiment?

Energy in Rubber Bands

Materials
- ruler
- rubber band
- chalk
- measuring tape

Procedure
1. Gather your supplies and go outside. Find a place with lots of space to do this experiment.
2. Draw a line in front of your toes with the chalk.
3. Hook the rubber band onto the front edge of the ruler, stretch it back to 10 cm, and then let go to launch the rubber band.
4.
5
6.

Write a procedure.

- Write a list of the materials needed.

- Write exactly what to do in the correct order.

- Number the steps.

- Start each step with a verb (action word).

Section 5: Writing Process

WML4

Writing Minilesson Principle
Analyze and write about the results.

Observing and Writing Like a Scientist

You Will Need

- the chart from WML2
- a book or website related to the topic of the science experiment
- chart paper and markers
- writer's notebooks

Academic Language / Important Vocabulary

- science experiment
- results
- analyze

Continuum Connection

- Make scientific observations, use notes and sketches to document them, and talk with others about connections and patterns

GOAL

Provide an explanation of and evidence for the results of a science experiment.

RATIONALE

When you guide students to analyze and write about the results of a science experiment, they begin to understand how scientists make connections between what they already know and what they observed in order to draw conclusions and advance scientific knowledge.

WRITER'S NOTEBOOK/WRITING FOLDER

Have students write their analyses of the science experiment in their writer's notebooks.

ASSESS LEARNING

- Notice whether students can draw on their background knowledge to provide a plausible explanation for the results of a science experiment.
- Look for evidence that they can use vocabulary such as *science experiment*, *results*, and *analyze*.

MINILESSON

To help students think about the minilesson principle, engage them in a discussion about the results of the science experiment conducted in WML2, and use shared writing to write an explanation for the results. Here is an example.

- Show the chart from WML2.

    What do you notice about the results of our science experiment? How did the length we stretched the rubber band affect how far the rubber band flew?

    When scientists do experiments, they make a prediction, do the experiment, and carefully record their observations. Afterward, they think very carefully about what happened and why it happened. They also think about whether their prediction was correct and try to understand why or why not.

    Let's think about why the rubber band flew farther the more it was stretched. We can use what we know about energy to analyze the results of our experiment.

- Read a portion of a grade-appropriate book or website that explains the difference between potential and kinetic energy.

    Why do you think stretching the rubber band farther made it fly farther? Does this website help you understand anything about what happened?

- Engage students in a discussion about their explanations. Encourage them to provide evidence for their thinking.

- Summarize the class's conclusions on chart paper.

Have a Try

Invite students to talk to a partner about how to analyze the results of a science experiment.

> How did we analyze and write about the results of our science experiment? What did we think about and do? Turn and talk to your partner about this.

▶ After students turn and talk, invite several pairs to share their thinking. Record their thinking on chart paper along with the principle.

Summarize and Apply

Summarize the learning and invite students to write their own explanations for what happened.

> During independent writing time today, write a paragraph in your writer's notebook analyzing the results of our science experiment. Use what you know about energy to explain your thinking. Even if you agree with everything we wrote on the chart, remember to write your own explanation in your own words. Bring your writing to share when we come back together.

Confer

▶ During independent writing, move around the room to confer briefly with students about their analyses. Use prompts such as the following as needed.

- *How does writing an analysis help you understand the results of an experiment?*
- *What could you write about why the results happened?*
- *What reasons or evidence can you give to support your thinking?*

Share

Following independent writing, gather students in the meeting area to share their analyses with a partner before sharing with the class.

> Turn to a partner to share your analysis.

Analysis of the Experiment

Potential energy was stored in the rubber band when it was at rest. When we stretched the rubber band, we increased its potential energy. When we released the rubber band and it started to move, the potential energy was converted into kinetic energy. The more potential energy the rubber band has, the more kinetic energy it will have, and the farther it will fly. Therefore, stretching a rubber band farther makes it fly farther.

Analyze and write about the results.

- Look at your observations.
- Think about what you know about the science.
- Read your prediction and notice if it was correct.
- Think about how the experiment supports what you know about the science. Write about that.
- Think about how you might use the information you learned from the experiment. Write about that.

Umbrella 7: Observing and Writing Like a Scientist

Assessment

After you have taught the minilessons in this umbrella, observe students as they write and talk about their writing. Use *The Fountas & Pinnell Literacy Continuum* to notice, teach for, and support students' learning as you observe their attempts at writing.

▶ What evidence do you have of students' new understandings related to observing and writing like a scientist?

- Can students write a prediction for a science experiment?

- Do they accurately write and sketch their scientific observations?

- Can they write the procedure for a science experiment they have conducted so that is it clear to the readers?

- Can they analyze and write about the results of a science experiment?

- Do students understand and use vocabulary such as *scientist*, *prediction*, *observation*, *procedure*, and *analyze*?

▶ In what other ways, beyond the scope of this umbrella, are students ready to write like scientists?

- Are they ready to write different kinds of texts about scientific topics (e.g., informational books, procedural texts, slide presentations)?

Use your observations to determine the next umbrella you will teach. You may also consult Suggested Sequence of Lessons (pp. 665–682) for guidance.

EXTENSIONS FOR OBSERVING AND WRITING LIKE A SCIENTIST

▶ Have students take photographs instead of sketching their observations.

▶ Encourage students to pose questions and wonderings based on their scientific observations. Then help them conduct research or do additional experiments to answer some of their questions and wonderings.

▶ Teach students how to create graphs to present scientific data.

▶ Incorporate writing into science class. Encourage students to write procedural texts about how to do a science experiment or informational books about a science topic.

Minilessons in This Umbrella

WML1 Use revising tools to add to your writing.

WML2 Add describing words or phrases to help readers picture the idea.

WML3 Add details to slow down the exciting or important part of the story.

WML4 Add sentences, words, and phrases to connect ideas in your writing.

WML5 Add information to support your ideas and help readers understand your topic.

Perseverance

Before Teaching Umbrella 8 Minilessons

These minilessons help students expand their thinking about ways to revise their writing: one way to revise writing is to add information that will explain and clarify. It is not necessary to teach the lessons consecutively. Instead, you might choose to teach them throughout the year because revision is a high-level concept and students will need multiple exposures to the concept.

These lessons use mentor texts and samples of your own writing to model how to look back at writing to find areas for improvement. Use the following texts from *Fountas & Pinnell Classroom™ Interactive Read-Aloud Collection,* or choose books from the classroom library that your students will enjoy.

Telling a Story with Photos

Face to Face with Whales by Flip and Linda Nicklin

Interactive Read-Aloud Collection

Genre Study: Memoir

Twelve Kinds of Ice by Ellen Bryan Obed

Perseverance

Strong to the Hoop by John Coy

Barbed Wire Baseball: How One Man Brought Hope to the Japanese Internment Camps of WWII by Marissa Moss

Telling a Story with Photos

Face to Face with Whales by Flip and Linda Nicklin

Innovative Thinking and Creative Problem Solving

Parrots Over Puerto Rico by Susan L. Roth and Cindy Trumbore

Innovative Thinking

As you read and enjoy these texts together, help students

* think about the author's process to write and revise a book,

* notice interesting details and word choices, and

* discuss what makes the book interesting or exciting.

Section 5: Writing Process

Writing Minilesson Principle
Use revising tools to add to your writing.

Adding Information to Your Writing

You Will Need

- a sample piece of writing (your own or class-made shared writing) that demonstrates a variety of tools for adding to writing (e.g., carets, sticky notes, strips of paper, numbered items on a separate page)
- chart paper and markers
- writing folders
- To download the following online resource for this lesson, visit **fp.pub/resources**:
  - chart art (optional)

Academic Language / Important Vocabulary

- revise
- add
- tool
- caret

Continuum Connection

- Add words, letters, phrases, or sentences using a variety of techniques: e.g., caret, sticky notes, spider's legs, numbered items on a separate page, word processing
- Use a number to identify a place to add information and an additional paper with numbers to write the information to insert

GOAL

Learn to use a variety of tools for adding information to a piece of writing.

RATIONALE

By teaching students a variety of ways to add to their writing, you make the act of revising more accessible. When students are armed with the tools they need to revise their writing, they will be able to communicate their ideas more effectively.

WRITER'S NOTEBOOK/WRITING FOLDER

Students will revise a longer piece of writing from their writing folders.

ASSESS LEARNING

- Notice whether students effectively use a variety of tools to add to their writing.
- Look for evidence that they can use vocabulary such as *revise*, *add*, *tool*, and *caret*.

MINILESSON

To help students think about the principle, use a piece of your own writing or a piece of shared writing to demonstrate ways they can add to their writing. Teach the tool(s) that you prefer your class to use. Here is an example.

- Display the writing sample.

  What does it mean to revise your writing?

  When you revise your writing, you reread it and make changes to improve it for your readers. Sometimes, you might need to add new words, phrases, sentences, or even paragraphs to explain something more clearly.

- Show a section of your writing that demonstrates one tool for adding to writing (e.g., a caret).

  What do you notice about how I added these words?

  A caret looks like an upside-down *V*. Place it right where you want the new word or phrase to go. Then write the word or phrase above the caret.

- Record a description and an example of using the tool on chart paper.
- Demonstrate the use of another tool (e.g., a spider leg).

  What do you notice about how I added to my writing on this page?

  This tool is called a spider leg! What could you use a spider leg for?

- Add the tool to the chart. Continue in a similar manner to teach other tools for adding to writing (e.g., sticky notes, numbered items at the bottom of a page or on a separate page).

Have a Try

Invite students to talk to a partner about how to add information to their writing.

> I would like to add a whole new section to my writing about _____. Turn and talk to your partner about how I could do that.

▶ After time for discussion, invite a few pairs to share their thinking. Discuss how best to add a lot of information and add to the chart.

Summarize and Apply

Summarize the learning and remind students to use different tools to add to their writing.

> What will you think about when you are deciding which tool to use to add to your writing?

▶ Write the principle at the top of the chart.

> During independent writing time today, reread a piece of writing from your writing folder. Think about whether there is anything you could add to your writing to improve it. If so, choose the best way to add that information. Bring your writing to share when we meet later.

Use revising tools to add to your writing.		
Tool	**What You Can Add**	**What It Looks Like**
Caret	A word or a few words	The edge was as as a thorn sharp.
Spider leg	A sentence	
Sticky note	A few sentences	
Numbers	More information when there's not enough space on the page	My parents immigrated to the United States from Ethiopia.¹ I was born two years later. ¹ Ethiopia is a country in East Africa.
New page	A lot more information	

Confer

▶ During independent writing, move around the room to confer briefly with students about adding to their writing. Use prompts such as the following as needed.

- *What could you add to your writing to help readers better understand _____?*
- *Is there anything you would like to add to this page/paragraph? How could you add that?*
- *I see you used a sticky note to add to your writing here. Why did you choose that tool?*

Share

Following independent writing, gather students in the meeting area to share their writing.

> Who would like to share how you added to your writing today?

> What did you add? How did you add it? Why did you choose that tool?

Writing Minilesson Principle
Add describing words or phrases to help readers picture the idea.

Adding Information to Your Writing

You Will Need

▸ a familiar book with strong examples of descriptive language, such as *Twelve Kinds of Ice* by Ellen Bryan Obed, from Text Set: Genre Study: Memoir

▸ chart paper prepared with a few basic sentences to which description could be added (see chart)

▸ markers

▸ writing folders

Academic Language / Important Vocabulary

▸ describing

▸ word

▸ phrase

▸ picture

Continuum Connection

▸ Add descriptive words (adjectives, adverbs) and phrases to help readers visualize and understand events, actions, processes, or topics

▸ Add words, phrases, or sentences to make the writing more interesting or exciting for readers

GOAL

Learn to revise writing by adding adjectives, adverbs, or descriptive phrases.

RATIONALE

When students notice the information they gain from the descriptive language that authors use in their writing, they understand the importance of it in their own writing. They will begin to use craft techniques they have observed in mentor texts in their own writing.

WRITER'S NOTEBOOK/WRITING FOLDER

Students will revise a longer piece of writing from their writing folders.

ASSESS LEARNING

▸ Observe whether students can identify and discuss descriptive language in other authors' writing.

▸ Notice whether students effectively use descriptive language in their own writing.

▸ Look for evidence that they can use vocabulary such as *describing*, *word*, *phrase*, and *picture*.

MINILESSON

Students will need their writing folders for this lesson. To help students think about the minilesson principle, use a familiar mentor text to engage them in an inquiry around noticing and using descriptive language. Here is an example.

▸ Show the cover of *Twelve Kinds of Ice* and read the title. Read pages 18–20, pausing frequently to draw students' attention to the author's use of descriptive language. Ask questions such as the following:

  • *How does the author help you make a picture in your mind of the Great Pond?*

  • *How does she describe the sounds the ice makes?*

  • *How does she help you understand how fast they are skating?*

  • *What do you think of when you hear this sentence: "Our minds burst with silver while the winter sun danced silver down our bending backs"?*

▸ Display the prepared chart paper.

  When you're revising your writing, you can add describing words or phrases to help your readers imagine what is happening. What words or phrases could you add to these sentences to help readers picture the idea? Turn and talk to your partner about your ideas.

▸ After time for discussion, invite several students to share their ideas. Add descriptive language to the sentences.

Have a Try

Invite students to talk to a partner about adding descriptive language.

▶ Make sure students have their writing folders.

> Read aloud a page of your writing from your writing folder to your partner. Then ask your partner to help you identify places where the reader gets a clear picture of what is happening and places where you might want to add more descriptive language.

Summarize and Apply

Summarize the learning and remind students to add descriptive language to their writing.

> Why do authors add describing words and phrases to their writing? How does this help readers?

▶ Write the principle at the top of the chart.

> During independent writing time today, revise the piece of writing that you discussed with your partner. Think about places where the reader might need or want more details, and try adding some describing words and phrases. Be careful not to add too many details—just enough to make your writing clear to your readers. Bring your writing to share when we come back together.

> Add describing words or phrases to help readers picture the idea.
>
>   like diamonds   dark
> The stars sparkled in the night sky.
>
>   as as ice
> My hands were cold.
>
> plump, juicy as   as candy
> The apple tasted sweet.
>
> eagerly   great big bear
> I gave my grandpa a hug as soon as
> I saw him.

Confer

▶ During independent writing, move around the room to confer briefly with students about adding to their writing. Use prompts such as the following as needed.

- *What words or phrases could you add to your writing to help readers picture _____?*
- *Could you help readers picture _____ by making a comparison with something else?*
- *What words could you use to describe how _____ looked [sounded, smelled, tasted, felt]?*
- *What tool could you use to add those words to your writing?*

Share

Following independent writing, gather students in the meeting area to share their writing.

> Who would like to share how you added describing words or phrases to your writing today?

> What do you notice about the words _____ used to describe _____?

Writing Minilesson Principle
Add details to slow down the exciting or important part of the story.

Adding Information to Your Writing

You Will Need

- two familiar fiction books, such as the following from Text Set: Perseverance:
  - *Strong to the Hoop* by John Coy
  - *Barbed Wire Baseball* by Marissa Moss
- chart paper and markers
- writing folders

Academic Language / Important Vocabulary

- detail
- exciting
- important
- character
- setting

Continuum Connection

- Identify the most exciting part of a story
- Add words, phrases, or sentences to make the writing more interesting or exciting for readers

GOAL

Understand that authors add details to slow down the key action in their stories.

RATIONALE

When you help students notice how authors use details to slow down the most exciting or important part of a story, they understand that they too can add extra details to their own stories to stretch out an exciting or important moment. Slowing down the most exciting part of the story engages the reader by creating interest or suspense.

WRITER'S NOTEBOOK/WRITING FOLDER

Students will revise a longer piece of writing from their writing folders.

ASSESS LEARNING

- Notice whether students add details to slow down the most exciting or important part of a story.
- Look for evidence that they can use vocabulary such as *detail*, *exciting*, *important*, *character*, and *setting*.

MINILESSON

Students will need their writing folders for this lesson. To help students think about the minilesson principle, use mentor texts to engage them in an inquiry around how authors slow down the most exciting or important part of a story. Here is an example.

- Show the cover of *Strong to the Hoop* and read the title.

  What is the most exciting part of this story?

- Read pages 20–28.

  When James plays basketball with the older boys, does he shoot a hoop right away?

  The basketball game goes on for several pages before James shoots a hoop. Why do you think the author makes you wait to see what happens?

  What did he do to make you wait?

  What kinds of details did he include about the game before James shoots a hoop?

- Help students understand that authors stretch out the action to make readers want to keep reading. Authors do this by including dialogue and/or details about what the characters are thinking, feeling, and doing.

- Continue in a similar manner with pages 29–36 of *Barbed Wire Baseball*.

- With students' input, make a list on chart paper of the types of details authors might include to slow down part of a story.

Have a Try

Invite students to identify the most exciting or important part of their own stories.

> Take your writing folder and choose a story you have written. Reread it and find the most exciting or important part. You may want to make a note of the most exciting part by drawing a star, smiley face, or another symbol next to it. Then turn and talk to your partner about what happens in that part of the story.

Summarize and Apply

Summarize the learning and invite students to add more details to slow down the most exciting or important part of their story.

> How can you make the most exciting part of your story last longer so readers will want to keep reading?

▶ Write the principle at the top of the chart.

> Today, think about details you could add to slow down and stretch out the exciting or important moment of your story. Add details using a tool you have learned about for adding information. Bring your writing to share when we meet later.

Add details to slow down the exciting or important part of the story.

Add details about . . .

- what the characters are thinking or feeling

- what the characters are doing

- what the characters are saying (dialogue)

- conflicts between the characters

- what the setting is like (describing words and phrases)

- what is going on around the main action

Confer

▶ During independent writing, move around the room to confer briefly with students about adding to their writing. Use prompts such as the following as needed.

- *What details could you add about the characters (setting)?*
- *What else might be going on while _____ happens?*
- *How can you add that to your writing?*

Share

Following independent writing, gather students together to share their writing with a partner. Then choose several to share with the whole class.

> Turn and talk to a different partner about how you revised your writing.

> What do you notice about how _____ slowed down the most exciting part of the story?

Writing Minilesson Principle

Add sentences, words, and phrases to connect ideas in your writing.

Adding Information to Your Writing

You Will Need

- a familiar nonfiction book, such as *Face to Face with Whales* by Flip and Linda Nicklin, from Text Set: Telling a Story with Photos
- chart paper and markers
- a brief sample of writing that contains examples of connecting words, phrases, and sentences
- highlighter
- writing folders

Academic Language / Important Vocabulary

- connecting word
- phrase
- sentence
- revise
- information

Continuum Connection

- Use common (simple) connectives and some sophisticated connectives (words that link ideas and clarify meaning) that are used in written texts but do not appear often in everyday oral language: e.g., *although, however, therefore, though, unless, whenever*

GOAL

Understand that writers use connecting words, phrases, and sentences to add information.

RATIONALE

When you help students notice how authors use connecting words, phrases, and sentences to connect ideas, they learn to do the same in their own writing. Connecting words, phrases, and sentences make writing flow smoothly and clearly show the relationships between different ideas.

WRITER'S NOTEBOOK/WRITING FOLDER

Students will revise a longer piece of writing from their writing folders.

ASSESS LEARNING

- Notice whether students can identify connecting words, phrases, and sentences in texts.
- Observe whether students effectively use a variety of connecting words, phrases, and sentences in their own writing.
- Look for evidence that they can use vocabulary such as *connecting word*, *phrase*, *sentence*, *revise*, and *information*.

MINILESSON

To help students think about the minilesson principle, use a mentor text to engage them in noticing and understanding how authors use connectives. Here is an example.

- Show the cover of *Face to Face with Whales* and read the title. Display page 17 and read the first paragraph aloud.

  At the beginning of this paragraph, the authors wrote about how male sperm whales leave their family groups and do not return for twenty years. At the end, they wrote how the whales rub up against each other with affection. How did they move from the first idea to the second one?

  The authors asked the question "How, we wondered, would the other whales interact with the male?" This sentence connects the two ideas and lets you know what information to expect next.

- Read pages 19–21.

  In the beginning of this section, the authors wrote about baleen whales. At the end, they wrote about toothed whales. How did they transition, or move, from baleen whales to toothed whales?

  How does the sentence "The other kind of whale has teeth instead of baleen" connect two ideas?

  The sentence lets readers know that the authors are finished writing about baleen whales and moving on to a different type of whale, which has teeth.

Have a Try

Invite students to talk to a partner about connecting words, phrases, and sentences.

▶ Display a piece of writing that has several examples of connecting words, phrases, and sentences.

> Here's what I wrote about jellyfish. How did I connect the ideas in my writing? Turn and talk to your partner about this.

▶ After students turn and talk, invite several students to share their responses. Highlight the connecting words, phrases, and sentences. Draw students' attention to how one word (e.g., *live*) is repeated in the next paragraph to show how one paragraph flows to another.

Summarize and Apply

Summarize the learning and remind students to use connecting words, phrases, and sentences when they add information to their writing.

> How do authors connect different ideas in their writing?

▶ Write the principle at the top of the chart.

> Today, reread a piece of nonfiction writing from your writing folder. Is there any information you would like to add? If so, remember to show how ideas are related. Bring your writing to share when we meet later.

Add sentences, words, and phrases to connect ideas in your writing.

Despite the name, jellyfish are neither fish nor made of jelly! But they do have a soft, jelly-like body, and, like fish, they live in the ocean.

Jellyfish live in all the world's oceans. Most prefer warm water. However, some species, like the lion's mane jellyfish, live in cold water.

There are more than 200 species. Some are barely larger than a sugar cube, while others are more than six feet across. A type of box jellyfish has tentacles up to ten feet long that can deliver a dangerous sting.

Jellyfish stings can be painful and sometimes deadly. Most stings, however, are not serious. In any case, if you get stung by a jellyfish, leave the water immediately and ask an adult for help.

Confer

▶ During independent writing, move around the room to confer briefly with students about adding to their writing. Use prompts such as the following as needed.

- *What information do you want to add to your writing? Where will you add it?*
- *How does _____ relate to _____ ? What word, phrase, or sentence could you write to show how they connect?*
- *Could you add a sentence here to show how these two ideas are connected?*

Share

Following independent writing, gather students in the meeting area to share their writing.

> Talk about how you added information to your writing.

WML 5

WPS.U8.WML5

Writing Minilesson Principle
Add information to support your ideas and help readers understand your topic.

Adding Information to Your Writing

You Will Need

- a familiar nonfiction book, such as *Parrots Over Puerto Rico* by Susan L. Roth and Cindy Trumbore, from Text Set: Innovative Thinking and Creative Problem Solving
- a short, simple piece of informational writing that is intentionally vague
- chart paper and markers
- writing folders

Academic Language / Important Vocabulary

- information
- support
- idea
- topic

Continuum Connection

- Add words, phrases, or sentences to provide more information to readers
- Add words, phrases, or sentences to clarify meaning for readers
- After reflection and rereading, add substantial pieces of text (paragraphs, pages) to provide further explanation, clarify points, add interest, or support points

GOAL

Add examples or evidence to support ideas and help readers understand the topic.

RATIONALE

When you model how to make informational writing clearer by adding details and examples to support the main ideas, students learn how to revise their own informational writing and communicate information more effectively.

WRITER'S NOTEBOOK/WRITING FOLDER

Students will revise a longer piece of writing from their writing folders.

ASSESS LEARNING

- Observe whether students reread their informational writing to identify parts that need supporting evidence or examples.
- Notice whether students show a willingness to add information to their writing.
- Look for evidence that they can use vocabulary such as *information*, *support*, *idea*, and *topic*.

MINILESSON

To help students think about the minilesson principle, use a mentor text to engage students in an inquiry around adding examples and evidence to informational writing. Here is an example.

- Show the cover of *Parrots Over Puerto Rico* and read the title. Then read page 12.

  What information tells about the idea that people from European countries tried to capture Puerto Rico? What did the authors write about the reason Europeans wanted Puerto Rico?

  The authors wrote, "The Boricuas protected their island." How did the authors support, or tell more about, this idea? How did the Boricuas protect their island?

  The authors gave specific details about how the Boricuas protected their island. Starting in 1539, they built a fort, and the fort grew to be 18 feet thick.

- Read page 24.

  It says on this page that the scientists built "special nesting boxes" for the parrots. What details did the authors provide to help you understand what was special about the boxes?

  The authors explained that the boxes were deep and dark, to seem like nesting holes in the wild. They also added that pearly-eyed thrashers like to see the bottoms of their nests, so they left the parrots' nesting boxes alone.

  The authors gave lots of specific details and examples to support the main ideas in the book.

Have a Try

Invite students to talk to a partner about adding information to an informational text.

▶ Display the prepared piece of informational writing and read it aloud.

> Is anything unclear, or is there anything you think readers would want to know more about? Turn and talk to your partner about this.

▶ After students turn and talk, invite several pairs to share their thinking. Using their suggestions, demonstrate adding additional information using the tools that students have been learning (see WML1).

Summarize and Apply

Summarize the learning and remind students to think about what information they could add to their informational writing.

> What should you think about when you are revising your nonfiction writing?

▶ Write the principle at the top of the chart.

> During independent writing time today, reread a piece of nonfiction writing from your writing folder. Think about whether you should add some additional information to support your ideas and help your readers better understand your topic. Bring your writing to share when we come back together.

> ### Add information to support your ideas and help readers understand your topic.
>
> #### Baleen Whales
>
> Baleen whales don't have teeth. Instead, they have baleen plates.[1] A baleen whale eats by taking in a big gulp of food and seawater, partially closing its mouth, squeezing the water out through its baleen plates, and swallowing its prey. Baleen whales usually eat small fish
>
> Krill are small, shrimp-like animals.
>
> and krill. There are many different species of baleen whales. For example, blue whales, gray whales, and humpback whales are baleen whales.
>
> ---
> [1] The baleen plates grow downward from the roof of the whale's mouth. They look like the teeth of a comb. Baleen is made of keratin, which is the same protein that makes up our hair and fingernails.

Confer

▶ During independent writing, move around the room to confer briefly with students about adding information to their writing. Use prompts such as the following as needed.

- *What could you add to help readers understand _____?*
- *What details could you add to explain this to people who don't know a lot about _____?*
- *What else might readers want to know about _____? How could you add that to your writing?*

Share

Following independent writing, gather students in the meeting area to share their writing.

> Talk about the information you added to your writing and why you added it.

Assessment

After you have taught the minilessons in this umbrella, observe students as they write and talk about their writing. Use *The Fountas & Pinnell Literacy Continuum* to notice, teach for, and support students' learning as you observe their writing skills.

▶ What evidence do you have of students' new understandings related to adding information to their writing?

- Do students understand that they can (and show a willingness to) revise their writing to make it better?

- Are they using tools (e.g., carets, spider legs, numbered items on a separate page) to add to their writing?

- Do they use describing and connecting words to make their writing clearer and more interesting?

- Do they understand what it means to slow down the most exciting or important part of a story?

- Are they using vocabulary such as *revise, detail, page, connecting word,* and *information*?

▶ In what other ways, beyond the scope of this umbrella, are students exploring the writing process?

- Are they ready to revise their writing in other ways?

- Are they showing an interest in writing informational texts?

Use your observations to determine the next umbrella you will teach. You may also consult Suggested Sequence of Lessons (pp. 665–682) for guidance.

EXTENSIONS FOR ADDING INFORMATION TO YOUR WRITING

▶ Pull together a small group of students who would benefit from guided instruction on adding to their writing.

▶ Teach students how to add to their writing when typing it on a computer.

▶ Suggest that students read their writing to a friend and then ask whether there is something that could be better explained by adding information.

Minilessons in This Umbrella

WML1 Take out information that does not add to the important ideas or message.

WML2 Skip time to focus your story.

WML3 Change words to make your writing more precise.

WML4 Organize your writing to make sure the order makes sense.

Before Teaching Umbrella 9 Minilessons

The minilessons in this umbrella do not need to be taught consecutively, so feel free to teach them when your students show a need for them. Because revision is a high-level concept, it is recommended that you teach each lesson more than once across the year, as students will benefit from multiple exposures to the concept of revision.

To model the minilesson principles, use the following familiar texts from *Fountas & Pinnell Classroom™ Interactive Read-Aloud Collection* and *Shared Reading Collection*, or choose suitable books from your classroom library.

Interactive Read-Aloud Collection
Genre Study: Historical Fiction

Dad, Jackie, and Me by Myron Uhlberg

The Buffalo Storm by Katherine Applegate

The Houdini Box by Brian Selznick

Taking Action, Making Change

Brothers in Hope: The Story of the Lost Boys of Sudan by Mary Williams

One Hen: How One Small Loan Made a Big Difference by Katie Smith Milway

Genre Study: Biography: Individuals Making a Difference

Farmer Will Allen and the Growing Table by Jacqueline Briggs Martin

Innovative Thinking and Creative Problem Solving

Ivan: The Remarkable True Story of the Shopping Mall Gorilla by Katherine Applegate

Shared Reading Collection

A Lifetime of Dance: A Biography of Katherine Dunham by Nnéka Nnolim

As you read and enjoy these texts together, help students notice that

- all the text on a page is relevant and connected to the main idea,
- authors often use specific and interesting word choices, and
- the writing is organized in an order that makes sense.

Taking Action,
Making Change

Genre Study:
Biography

Farmer Will Allen and the Growing Table by Jacqueline Briggs Martin

Innovative Thinking
and Creative Problem
Solving

Shared Reading

Writer's Notebook

Writer's Notebook

Section 5: Writing Process

WML1
WPS.U9.WML1

Writing Minilesson Principle
Take out information that does not add to the important ideas or message.

Revising to Focus and Organize Writing

You Will Need

- several familiar books with clear messages, such as the following from Text Set: Genre Study: Historical Fiction:
  - *Dad, Jackie, and Me* by Myron Uhlberg
  - *The Buffalo Storm* by Katherine Applegate
- chart paper prepared with a piece of writing that contains irrelevant or unimportant details
- markers
- writing folders

Academic Language / Important Vocabulary

- information
- idea
- purpose
- message

Continuum Connection

- Identify information that either distracts from or does not contribute to the central purpose and message
- Delete words or sentences that do not make sense or do not fit the topic or message
- Delete pages or paragraphs when information is not needed
- Reread and cross out words to ensure that meaning is clear

GOAL

Identify the important ideas and messages and take out information that does not fit.

RATIONALE

Some students may think that the more they write, the better their writing will be. However, including information that is not relevant weakens the writing. Once students learn this, they will begin to reread their own writing and remove extraneous information.

WRITER'S NOTEBOOK/WRITING FOLDER

Have students revise a piece of writing in their writing folders to take out unnecessary information.

ASSESS LEARNING

- Notice whether students can identify information that does not add to the important ideas.
- Look for evidence that they can use vocabulary such as *information*, *idea*, *purpose*, and *message*.

MINILESSON

To help students think about the minilesson principle, use mentor texts to help them notice that all the information on a page adds to the important ideas or message. Then model revising a brief text to take out unimportant information. Here is an example.

- Show the cover of *Dad, Jackie, and Me* and read the title.

  What is the purpose, or message, of this story?

  This story is about how Myron comes to understand the struggles that his father has with being deaf and that Jackie Robinson has as a Black athlete.

- Read pages 15–16 of the story.

  What are these pages about?

  Notice that everything here supports the purpose, or message, of the story.

- Repeat using *The Buffalo Storm*.
- Show the sample text that you prepared.

  I am working on a historical fiction story about a family member who came to the United States from Italy when she was a child. As I read, think about how I can make it better.

- Read the text aloud.

  What is the most important idea or message on this page?

  Is there anything that does not tell about my important idea?

- Using students' suggestions, cross out irrelevant parts of the story.

Have a Try

Invite students to talk to a partner about why they should revise their writing.

> Why is it a good idea to take out information that does not support the main ideas or message of your writing? Turn and talk to your partner about that.

▶ After time for discussion, invite several students to share their thinking.

Summarize and Apply

Summarize the learning and remind students to take out information that does not add to the important ideas or message.

> You may not want to take out words that you have written, but it's important to take out anything that does not add to the ideas or message of your writing.

▶ Write the principle at the top of the chart.

> During independent writing time today, reread a writing project from your writing folder. It could be one that you already started or one that you recently finished. Take out any information that does not add to the important ideas or message. Save any parts you take out. You could use them for pieces you write later. Bring your writing to share when we meet later.

Confer

▶ During independent writing, move around the room to confer briefly with students about revising their writing. Use prompts such as the following as needed.

- *What is the most important idea in this part of your writing?*
- *What do you want readers to understand from reading your writing?*
- *Does _____ add to this idea?*

Share

Following independent writing, gather students in the meeting area to discuss their writing.

> In groups of three, talk about any parts that you took out of your writing today.

> How did taking out some information improve your writing?

Take out information that does not add to the important ideas or message.

A Whole New World

The boat rocked day and night and made my stomach feel strange. I felt hungry and not hungry at the same time. I missed pasta. ~~I saw a lady walk by. She looked very nice in her blue dress. I had a blue dress packed in the bag.~~ I longed for food that I was used to, and I had no idea if there was pasta in New York.

We heard that it would be another three days until we got to New York. I missed my grandparents so much. I imagined my grandmother telling her funny stories each morning at breakfast. She would make breakfast for my brother and me. ~~My brother liked to whistle as he walked all over the ship. I wish I could whistle.~~

Revising to Focus and Organize Writing

You Will Need

- several familiar books with clear examples of skipping time, such as the following from Text Set: Genre Study: Historical Fiction:
  - *The Buffalo Storm* by Katherine Applegate
  - *Dad, Jackie, and Me* by Myron Uhlberg
  - *The Houdini Box* by Brian Selznick
- chart paper prepared with a piece of narrative writing that contains extra detail and does not skip time
- chart paper and markers
- writing folders

Academic Language / Important Vocabulary

- focus
- sequence
- skip
- transition

Continuum Connection

- Add transitional words and phrases to clarify meaning and make the writing smoother
- Reorder the information in a text to make the meaning clearer by cutting apart, cutting and pasting, laying out pages, using word processing
- Delete words, phrases, or sentences from a text (crossing out or using word processing) to make the meaning clearer

GOAL

Focus writing by using transitional words to skip time and remove unimportant details.

RATIONALE

When beginning narrative writing, students may write about everything that happens in a day, including many unimportant details. When you help them notice that authors often skip time and include only important details, they will begin to do the same in their own writing.

WRITER'S NOTEBOOK/WRITING FOLDER

Have students reread stories in their writing folders to find places they could revise to focus the writing.

ASSESS LEARNING

- Observe whether students focus their stories by using transitional words and removing unimportant details to skip time.
- Look for evidence that they can use vocabulary such as *focus*, *sequence*, *skip*, and *transition*.

MINILESSON

To help students think about the minilesson principle, use several familiar narrative books to discuss how authors skip time to focus their writing. Then revise a piece of writing together. Here is an example.

- Show the cover of *The Buffalo Storm* and read the title. Read pages 14–17.

  How can you tell that time has passed between when the storm came in the night and when the girl fell into the river?

  Why do you think the writer chose not to tell everything that happened between those two events?

  The author began a new section with the transition words "the next morning" to let us know that she was skipping time—probably several hours—and only telling us what we need to know. When you write your own stories, you don't have to describe everything that happens. You can skip minutes, hours, days, weeks, months, or even years to focus on the important events.

- On chart paper, begin a list of transition words that show that the writer has skipped time. Write the words *The next morning*.

  As I continue to read, raise your hand when the words indicate a skip in time.

- Continue reading the story. As students notice transition words that show that time has lapsed, pause to add each word to the list.

- As needed, repeat with several more stories that skip time, such as *Dad, Jackie, and Me* and *The Houdini Box*.

Have a Try

Invite students to revise a piece of writing together.

▶ Show the piece of writing that you prepared. Read it aloud.

> I wrote about my experience riding on a snowmobile when I was younger. What could I take out to focus my story on the important things? Turn and talk about that.

▶ After time for discussion, use shared writing to help students identify extraneous details, cross them out, and add transition words as needed. Add any new transition words to the chart.

Summarize and Apply

Summarize the learning. Remind students that they can skip time to focus their stories.

> Why do authors sometimes skip time in their stories?

▶ Write the principle at the top of the first chart.

> During independent writing time today, reread a story that you've already written. Look for places where you can skip time to focus your story on the most important events. Bring your writing to share when we meet later.

Confer

▶ During independent writing, move around the room to confer briefly with students about revising their stories. Use prompts such as the following as needed.

- *Read your story aloud, and then we can talk about places where you could skip time.*
- *Is _____ an important event? Does the reader need to know about this?*
- *What transition words could you add to show that you skipped time?*

Share

Following independent writing, gather students in the meeting area to share their writing.

> What transition words did you use today to show that you skipped time?

> How did leaving out part of a story make your writing even better? Share the part you left out.

Gliding Across the Snow

Over winter break, I rode on a snowmobile. At the rental place, there was a lot of waiting. ~~We waited about ten minutes in line and another ten minutes to fill out paperwork.~~ ~~Then we spent twenty minutes deciding which snowmobiles to rent.~~ After a long time, Dad chose our snowmobiles and told us to get ready. ~~I buttoned my jacket and put on my gloves. I pulled up my socks.~~ When I was all set, I jumped on with my older sister. What a feeling! We took the longest trail. ~~The sun began to set.~~ When it was late afternoon, we rode back to the rental place for some hot cocoa.

Writing Minilesson Principle
Change words to make your writing more precise.

Revising to Focus and Organize Writing

You Will Need

- several familiar books with precise word choices, such as the following:
  - *One Hen* by Katie Smith Milway and *Brothers in Hope* by Mary Williams, from Text Set: Taking Action, Making Change
  - *Farmer Will Allen and the Growing Table* by Jacqueline Briggs Martin, from Text Set: Genre Study: Biography: Individuals Making a Difference
- chart paper prepared with a writing piece that contains examples of generic language
- writer's notebooks and writing folders
- markers

Academic Language / Important Vocabulary

- precise
- reread

Continuum Connection

- Vary word choice to make the piece more interesting
- Identify vague parts and provide specificity

GOAL

Replace vague words to make writing more precise and interesting.

RATIONALE

When you help students notice the precise and powerful word choices used by mentor authors, they will be more likely to think carefully about the words they use in their own writing. They will reread their writing and identify and replace generic language.

WRITER'S NOTEBOOK/WRITING FOLDER

Have students reread their writing in their writer's notebooks or writing folders to find generic words that they could replace with words that are more precise or descriptive.

ASSESS LEARNING

- Look for evidence that students reread their writing, evaluate their word choices, and change words to make their writing more precise.
- Look for evidence that they can use vocabulary such as *precise* and *reread*.

MINILESSON

To help students think about the minilesson principle, use several mentor texts to engage them in an inquiry-based lesson on precise language. Then revise a piece of writing together. Here is an example.

- Show the cover of *One Hen* and read the title. Then read the second paragraph on page 11.

  How does Kojo hold his egg money?

  What does he find on the way home?

- Guide students to recognize that the author used the word *clutches* instead of *holds* because it helps readers understand just how tightly and carefully he holds his money. She wrote that he finds "loose grains and bits of fruit" instead of saying "food" because those words are more precise.

  When you use only the words that tell exactly what you want your readers to know, you are using precise language.

- Repeat with several other mentor texts that use precise language, such as *Brothers in Hope* and *Farmer Will Allen and the Growing Table*.

  Writers reread their writing to think about how they can say exactly what they want their readers to know. Using well-chosen words gives more information than using general, commonly used words.

Have a Try

Invite students to talk to a partner about how to revise a writing piece using words that are more precise.

▶ Display the prepared writing and read it aloud.

Which words would you change to make this writing more precise? Sometimes you might replace two or three words with just one word. Or you might replace one word with two or three. Turn and talk to your partner about how to revise this writing.

▶ After time for discussion, invite students to share their ideas. Make the changes using carets, sticky notes, or spider legs.

Summarize and Apply

Help students summarize the learning and remind them to reread their writing and think about using words that are more precise.

What is one way you can revise your writing?

▶ Write the principle at the top of the chart.

During independent writing time today, look at a writing project from your writing folder or at writing in your writer's notebook. If you find words that you can change for more precise words, make those changes. Bring your writing to share when we meet later.

Confer

▶ During independent writing, move around the room to confer briefly with students about revising their writing. Use prompts such as the following as needed.

• *Let's brainstorm some words that are more precise than _____.*

• *What is another word that means _____?*

• *Describe exactly what it looked like so that we can talk about a precise word you can use.*

Share

Following independent writing, gather students in the meeting area to share their writing.

In pairs, share the precise words you used today in your writing or that you wrote in your writer's notebook.

> **Change words to make your writing more precise.**
>
> Dear Ms. Fraser,
>
> We would like you to ~~think about and possibly~~ (consider) ~~decide on~~ getting extra snacks for the lunchroom. Most of us ~~eat~~ (only peck at) the school lunch, ~~but it is not our favorite.~~ We would like some extra choices. Some can be ~~good,~~ (tasty, like granola,) and some can be ~~good for you.~~ (healthy, like baby carrots.) We can help the ~~staff hand them out.~~ (distribute the snacks.)
>
> We would be ~~happier than we have ever felt before~~ (ecstatic) with this improvement.
>
> From,
> Room 34

Writing Minilesson Principle
Organize your writing to make sure the order makes sense.

You Will Need

- several familiar books with clear chronological sequences, such as the following:
  - *Ivan* by Katherine Applegate, from Text Set: Innovative Thinking and Creative Problem Solving
  - *A Lifetime of Dance* by Nnéka Nnolim, from *Shared Reading Collection*
- chart paper prepared with a simple text that has some sentences out of order
- markers
- writing folders

Academic Language / Important Vocabulary

- organize
- order

Continuum Connection

- Rearrange and revise writing to better express meaning or make the text more logical (reorder drawings, reorder pages, cut and paste)
- Reorder the information in a text to make the meaning clearer by cutting apart, cutting and pasting, laying out pages, using word processing

GOAL

Understand that writers revise their writing so that the order makes sense.

RATIONALE

When you teach students to reread their writing to make sure the order makes sense, they begin to think about the structure of their writing and they learn to communicate their ideas more effectively.

WRITER'S NOTEBOOK/WRITING FOLDER

Have students reread a piece of writing in their writing folders to make sure the order is correct.

ASSESS LEARNING

- Look for evidence that students reread their own writing to determine if the order makes sense.
- Notice whether students are open to revising their writing.
- Look for evidence that they can use vocabulary such as *organize* and *order*.

MINILESSON

To help students think about the minilesson principle, use several mentor texts to engage them in a discussion about how the order of events in a piece of writing should make sense. Then model how to revise a writing sample. Here is an example.

- Show the cover of *Ivan* and read the title. Show several pages of the book and help students summarize the major events of the story in order.

  Does the order of events that happen in the story make sense? Why or why not?

  The author organized the events in the same order that they happened and in a way that makes sense when you read the story.

- Show the cover of *A Lifetime of Dance* and briefly turn through the pages.

  In this biography, the author writes about Katherine Dunham's life.

  Does the order make sense?

  The author writes about her life from when she was a child to when she was an adult. This order makes sense.

Have a Try

Invite students to talk to a partner about how to change the order of a piece of writing.

- Display the prepared chart paper and read the writing sample.

  What do you notice about the order of my writing? Is there anything I should change? Turn and talk to your partner about that.

- After students turn and talk, invite a few pairs to share their thinking. Use their suggestions to demonstrate reorganizing the writing piece by circling words and using arrows.

Summarize and Apply

Write the principle at the top of the chart. Summarize the learning and remind students to reread their writing to make sure the order makes sense.

It is important to reread your writing to be sure the order makes sense. You might find it helpful to read your writing aloud.

During independent writing time today, reread a piece of writing from your writing folder. It can be fiction or nonfiction. Make sure the order of your writing makes sense. If it doesn't, mark your writing to show where the part that is out of order should go. Bring your writing to share when we meet later.

Confer

- During independent writing, move around the room to confer briefly with students about revising their writing. Use prompts such as the following as needed.

  - *Do your ideas connect?*
  - *Talk about what you have done to make sure your writing is well organized.*
  - *Are there any sentences that need to be moved? How can you show that?*

Share

Following independent writing, gather students in the meeting area to share their writing.

In groups of four, share an experience you had today with organizing your writing.

Why it is important to reread your writing to check that it makes sense?

Organize your writing to make sure the order makes sense.

Today I had so much fun with my students building a 3D solar system. When I was in middle school, I loved learning about the planets, and I realized I might want to be a teacher someday. Next week, I can't wait to move on to distant galaxies with the class. I remember flying on an airplane when I was six, and ever since then, I have loved everything above the ground.

Assessment

After you have taught the minilessons in this umbrella, observe students as they write and talk about their writing. Use *The Fountas & Pinnell Literacy Continuum* to notice, teach for, and support students' learning as you observe their attempts at writing.

▶ What evidence do you have of students' new understandings related to revising writing?

- Do students show a willingness to revise their writing?
- Are they able to identify information that does not add to the important ideas and remove it?
- Do they replace vague words with more precise word choices?
- How successful are students at skipping time in their narrative writing?
- Do they understand how to reorder writing?
- Do they understand and use vocabulary such as *idea, information, message, focus, sequence, skip, precise, organize,* and *order*?

▶ In what other ways, beyond the scope of this umbrella, are students exploring the writing process?

- Are they experimenting with writing different genres and subgenres?
- Are they including illustrations in their writing?

Use your observations to determine the next umbrella you will teach. You may also consult Suggested Sequence of Lessons (pp. 665–682) for guidance.

EXTENSIONS FOR REVISING TO FOCUS AND ORGANIZE WRITING

▶ Meet with a guided writing group of a few students who need further support for revising their writing.

▶ Help students understand the importance of deciding on the important idea or message before they begin writing so they can stay focused throughout.

▶ Model the process of how to revise on a computer.

Minilessons in This Umbrella

WML1 Make sure you communicate your ideas clearly.

WML2 Check your spelling using multiple resources.

WML3 Check your punctuation and capitalization.

WML4 Check your paragraphs to make sure they begin new ideas and group similar information together.

Before Teaching Umbrella 10 Minilessons

The goal of this umbrella is to help students understand how to proofread and edit their own writing. A basic checklist for editing and proofreading will be built as a chart across the minilessons. Decide whether students will use the online resource Editing and Proofreading Checklist throughout the minilessons or after all the minilessons have been presented. Students should keep the checklist in their writing folders.

Before teaching these lessons, make sure students have had many experiences writing and rereading their writing. It will also be helpful to have taught CNV.U1–CNV.U3. Throughout this umbrella, use writing samples written by students or by you. Make sure the samples are large enough for everyone to see—either project them or write them on chart paper. Use the books listed below from *Fountas & Pinnell Classroom*™ *Interactive Read-Aloud Collection* and *Shared Reading Collection*, or choose other enlarged texts (or projected books) to serve as models.

Interactive Read-Aloud Collection

Telling a Story with Photos

Face to Face with Whales by Flip and Linda Nicklin

Shared Reading Collection

Amazing Axolotls by Sherry Howard

Grannie's Coal Pot by Summer Edward

Migrate! Epic Animal Excursions by Michelle Garcia Andersen

As you read and enjoy these texts together, help students notice

- correct spelling,
- spaces between words,
- punctuation and capitalization, and
- print that makes sense.

Interactive Read-Aloud
Telling a Story with Photos

Face to Face with Whales by Flip and Linda Nicklin

Shared Reading

Section 5: Writing Process

Editing and Proofreading Writing

You Will Need

▸ a big book that has clear and simple writing, such as *Amazing Axolotls* by Sherry Howard, from *Shared Reading Collection*

▸ a writing sample with some parts that are not clear (e.g., Proofreading Sample 1) written on chart paper or projected

▸ chart paper and markers

▸ document camera (optional)

▸ writing folders

▸ To download the following online resources for this lesson, visit **fp.pub/resources**:

  ■ Editing and Proofreading Checklist (optional)

  ■ Proofreading Sample 1

Academic Language / Important Vocabulary

▸ make sense   ▸ cross out

▸ edit   ▸ caret

▸ proofread

Continuum Connection

▸ Delete words or sentences that do not make sense or do not fit the topic or message

▸ Add word, phrases, or sentences to clarify meaning for the reader

▸ Reread and change or add words to ensure that meaning is clear

▸ Reread writing to check for clarity and purpose

▸ Edit for grammar and sentence sense

GOAL

Edit writing to make sure ideas are communicated clearly.

RATIONALE

Writing is a form of communication from writers to their audience. For writing to be effective, it must make sense to the audience.

WRITER'S NOTEBOOK/WRITING FOLDER

Students will edit a piece of writing they are working on in their writing folders. If students will use the Editing and Proofreading Checklist in this lesson, make sure that a copy is fastened inside each student's writing folder.

ASSESS LEARNING

▸ Look for evidence that students understand that readers must be able to understand what they are reading.

▸ Observe for evidence that students proofread and edit their writing.

▸ Look for evidence that students can use vocabulary such as *make sense*, *edit*, *proofread*, *cross out*, and *caret*.

MINILESSON

To help students proofread and edit their work, model how writing can be corrected when it does not make sense. Here is an example that uses the online resource Proofreading Sample 1.

▸ Show the cover of *Amazing Axolotls* and then read page 14.

  Think about what the writer has written here. Does it make sense?

  The writer, Sherry Howard, proofread and edited her writing to make sure she communicated her ideas clearly. If something did not make sense, she edited, or made changes, to correct her work.

▸ Show the prepared writing sample.

  Let's look at this writing. Is it clear what the writer is writing about?

▸ Model the process by thinking aloud as you read the first sentence.

  Sometimes the spelling, punctuation, and capitalization are correct, but there might be words that aren't clear, or words might be left out or repeated.

▸ Edit the first sentence so that the meaning is clear. Show students how to use one line to cross out (not erase) extra words and a caret to add in missing words.

Have a Try

Invite students to turn and talk about checking writing to be sure it makes sense.

> Continue editing the writing. Are there other places readers might be confused? Turn and talk to your partner about that.

▶ After time for discussion, ask a few volunteers to share what they noticed. Show how to make the edits. Reread the writing and discuss whether it makes better sense after the edits.

Summarize and Apply

Summarize the lesson. Have students proofread and edit a longer piece of writing from their writing folders for sense.

> Today you learned that you should proofread and edit your work to make sure you communicate your ideas clearly to your readers.

▶ Begin a proofreading and editing checklist by writing the principle on chart paper. Keep the checklist posted and continue adding to it throughout this umbrella. You might also introduce the Editing and Proofreading Checklist from the online resources.

> During independent writing time today, read the writing you are working on quietly to yourself. If you hear or see any parts that might confuse your readers, cross out extra words or add in words so that the writing makes sense. Bring your writing when we meet later.

▶ Save the checklist for WML2.

Confer

▶ During independent writing, move around the room to confer briefly with students about proofreading and editing. You might wish to have them use the Editing and Proofreading Checklist. Use the following prompts as needed.

- *Reread this part. Are your ideas clear?*
- *Let's talk about words that could be added so that this makes sense.*
- *Are there any words that should be replaced so that your readers won't be confused?*

Share

Following independent writing, gather students in the meeting area to share their writing.

> Share an example of a part of your writing that you edited.

Editing and Proofreading Checklist

☐ Make sure you communicate your ideas clearly.

---

playing capture the flag
We were at camp. Sounds awesome, right. It wasn't. I was voted captain! of my team
to
I had decide the plan. My plan was
my team
to have one quarter of them
defend the flag and another
quarter get the other team's flag!

Writing Minilesson Principle
Check your spelling using multiple resources.

Editing and Proofreading Writing

You Will Need

- a big book, such as *Grannie's Coal Pot* by Summer Edward, from *Shared Reading Collection*

- a writing sample with spelling errors (e.g., Proofreading Sample 2) written on chart paper or projected

- chart from WML1 and markers

- document camera (optional)

- writing folders

- To download the following online resources for this lesson, visit **fp.pub/resources**:

  - Editing and Proofreading Checklist (optional)

  - Proofreading Sample 2

Academic Language / Important Vocabulary

- edit
- spelling
- proofread

Continuum Connection

- Use reference tools to check on spelling when editing final draft (dictionary, digital resources)

- Understand that a writer uses what is known to spell words

- Edit for spelling errors by circling words that do not look right and spelling them another way

- Edit for the conventional spelling of known words

- Understand the limitations of spell check and grammar check on the computer

---

GOAL

Reread writing to check or correct spelling so readers can understand the message.

RATIONALE

This lesson will help students understand the importance of making sure they have spelled words correctly and that it is the writer's responsibility to spell the words they know correctly. Encourage students to keep their momentum in writing and to use a more expansive vocabulary by using temporary approximated spellings of words with which they are unfamiliar with the understanding that the spelling will be checked at a later time.

WRITER'S NOTEBOOK/WRITING FOLDER

Students will proofread and edit a piece of writing they are working on in their writing folders. If students will use the Editing and Proofreading Checklist in this lesson, make sure that a copy is fastened inside each student's writing folder.

ASSESS LEARNING

- Observe whether students edit and proofread their work to check for correct spelling.

- Look for evidence that students can use vocabulary such as *edit*, *proofread*, and *spelling*.

MINILESSON

To help students learn how to edit and proofread their work, display mentor texts with proper spelling of words they know. Model how writing can be corrected when words they know are spelled incorrectly. Here is an example that uses the online resource Proofreading Sample 2.

- Show and read page 7 in *Grannie's Coal Pot*.

  What is a word you know on this page?

- Help students notice familiar words that are spelled correctly.

  You know the words *ocean* and *island*. Notice that they are spelled here the same way you would spell them. That's how you know what those words are. The words are spelled the same way each time they are written.

- Show the prepared writing sample.

  Are there any words that you think might not be spelled correctly?

- Guide the conversation to help students notice a few of the misspelled familiar words or content words they know (e.g., *there*, *Greek*, *myths*, *stories*). Model how to circle the words that don't look right and encourage students to try writing them correctly. Have them check spelling in places they know (e.g., online or print dictionary, digital resource, commonly misspelled words resource in their writing folders). Be sure they understand the limitations of using spell check on a computer and that it isn't a substitute for rereading their writing.

Have a Try

Invite students to turn and talk about how to correct misspelled words.

> Look at the writing. Turn and tell your partner about a word you know that should be fixed and how you would fix it.

▶ After time for a brief discussion, ask a few volunteers to share how they can fix any words that are misspelled. Show how to make the corrections.

Summarize and Apply

Summarize the lesson. Have students proofread and edit a longer piece of writing from their writing folders for spelling.

▶ Add to the editing and proofreading checklist you are using.

> Today you learned to proofread by checking to make sure the words you know are spelled correctly. When you do your own writing, it's important to write the words you know correctly so that your readers will understand what you wrote. During independent writing time today, check your spelling by rereading your writing. Bring your writing to share when we meet later.

▶ Save the checklist for WML3.

Confer

▶ During independent writing, move around the room to confer briefly with students about proofreading and editing their writing. You might wish to have them use the Editing and Proofreading Checklist. Use the following prompts as needed.

- *Read this sentence to make sure the words you know are spelled correctly.*
- *What do you notice about this sentence?*
- *How can you fix the spelling of this word?*
- *Show how you used the Editing and Proofreading Checklist.*

Share

Following independent writing, gather students in the meeting area to share their writing.

> Turn and talk with your partner about how you checked and fixed your spelling today.

Editing and Proofreading Checklist

☐ Make sure you communicate your ideas clearly.

☐ Check your spelling using multiple resources.

There   Greek
Their are many Greeke
legends and miths but I dont
have time to tell all of them
The Greeks mad up these
miths and storys because there
washt much to do to pass the
time and they just wanted to
find a way that the univers
began.

Section 5: Writing Process

Writing Minilesson Principle
Check your punctuation and capitalization.

Editing and Proofreading Writing

You Will Need

- a big book, such as *Migrate!* by Michelle Garcia Andersen, from *Shared Reading Collection*

- a writing sample with some missing punctuation marks and capitalization errors (e.g., Proofreading Sample 3) written on chart paper or projected

- chart from WML2 and markers

- document camera (optional)

- writing folders

- To download the following online resources for this lesson, visit **fp.pub/resources**:

  - Editing and Proofreading Checklist (optional)

  - Proofreading Sample 3

Academic Language / Important Vocabulary

- read aloud
- edit
- proofread
- dialogue
- punctuation
- capitalization

Continuum Connection

- Read one's writing aloud and think about where to place punctuation

- Use a capital letter in the first word of a sentence

- Use capital letters correctly in dialogue

- Reread writing to rethink and make changes

- Edit for capitalization and punctuation

GOAL

Reread your writing aloud and think where to place punctuation and capitalize letters.

RATIONALE

When students learn that reading aloud one's own writing can help them notice errors in punctuation and capitalization, they take ownership of their own writing and learn to think about conventions.

WRITER'S NOTEBOOK/WRITING FOLDER

Students will proofread and edit a piece of writing they are working on in their writing folders. If students will use the Editing and Proofreading Checklist in this lesson, make sure that a copy is fastened inside each student's writing folder.

ASSESS LEARNING

- Notice whether students read aloud their own writing to check for punctuation and capitalization.

- Look for evidence that students can use vocabulary such as *read aloud*, *edit*, *proofread*, *dialogue*, *punctuation*, and *capitalization*.

MINILESSON

To help students think about the minilesson principle, model and provide an interactive lesson about how to check for punctuation and capitalization and how to correct errors. Here is an example that uses the online resource Proofreading Sample 3.

- Show and read the text about hummingbirds on page 11 in *Migrate!*

  What do you notice about the punctuation and capitalization?

- Students should notice that the punctuation and capitalization are correct. You may want to point out the nonstandard use of capitalization on the map and in the caption and talk about why the author made those choices.

- Show the prepared writing sample.

  Notice how the writing looks as I read the first part of this writing sample.

- Read the first part of the sample and engage students in thinking about where the missing punctuation should go. Show how to insert it.

  What do you notice?

- Help students notice errors in punctuation and capitalization, especially in dialogue. Also help them check whether sentences are complete and how to correct run-on sentences. You may want to point out that sometimes, writers use incomplete sentences on purpose to show voice (e.g., "Awesome!").

Have a Try

Invite students to turn and talk about reading aloud a piece of writing to think about where to place punctuation marks and capital letters.

> With your partner, slowly read the rest of the writing quietly to yourselves. Talk about how to fix errors with punctuation and capitalization.

▶ After time for discussion, ask volunteers to share ideas. Show students how to use three lines under a lowercase letter to change it to an uppercase letter and a slash through an uppercase letter to change it to a lowercase letter.

Summarize and Apply

Summarize the learning. Have students read aloud a longer piece of writing from their writing folders as a way to check punctuation and capitalization.

▶ Add the principle to the editing and proofreading checklist you are using.

> During independent writing time today, choose a piece of writing you are working on in your writing folder. Read it aloud to yourself quietly and notice places where you need to fix punctuation and capitalization. Mark the errors the way I showed you. Bring your writing to share when we meet.

▶ Save the checklist for WML4.

Editing and Proofreading Checklist

☐ Make sure you communicate your ideas clearly.

☐ Check your spelling using multiple resources.

☐ Check your punctuation and capitalization.

"We have to go now, they don't let you play if you're late, jack Pleaded as he grabbed his helmet. "Dad, are you almost done" "I'm almost done." Then Jacks dad sprinted out to the car with Jack right behind him. Jack and his Father whipped open the door and sped off they did not look back"

Confer

▶ During independent writing, move around the room to confer briefly with students and invite them to read aloud their writing to help with proofreading and editing. Use the following prompts as needed.

- *Read this page aloud. Are there any places where you need to add punctuation?*
- *Where do the capital letters and punctuation marks go in this part with dialogue?*
- *Do you notice any place where a letter should be made uppercase (lowercase)?*

Share

Following independent writing, gather students in the meeting area to share their writing.

> How does reading your writing aloud help you check the punctuation marks and capital letters?

Writing Minilesson Principle
Check your paragraphs to make sure they begin new ideas and group similar information together.

Editing and Proofreading Writing

You Will Need

- a mentor text with clear paragraphs, such as *Face to Face with Whales* by Flip and Linda Nicklin from Text Set: Telling a Story with Photos
- a writing sample with some paragraph errors (e.g., Proofreading Sample 4) written on chart paper or projected
- chart from WML3 and markers
- document camera (optional)
- writing folders
- To download the following online resources for this lesson, visit **fp.pub/resources**:
  - Editing and Proofreading Checklist
  - Proofreading Sample 4

Academic Language / Important Vocabulary

- edit
- proofread
- paragraph
- main idea

Continuum Connection

- Understand and use paragraph structure (indented or block) to organize sentences that focus on one idea
- Organize and present information in paragraphs in a way that demonstrates clear understanding of their structure to group ideas
- Determine where new paragraphs should begin

GOAL

Reread your writing aloud and think about whether each paragraph focuses on one idea.

RATIONALE

When students learn that reading aloud one's own writing is helpful in checking paragraphs, they take ownership of their own writing and learn to think about conventions.

WRITER'S NOTEBOOK/WRITING FOLDER

Students will proofread and edit a piece of writing they are working on in their writing folders. If students will use the Editing and Proofreading Checklist in this lesson, make sure that a copy is fastened inside each student's writing folder.

ASSESS LEARNING

- Notice whether students are reading aloud their own writing to check whether each paragraph begins a new idea.
- Observe whether students are using paragraphs to group similar ideas together.
- Look for evidence that students can use vocabulary such as *edit*, *proofread*, *paragraph*, and *main idea*.

MINILESSON

To help students think about the minilesson principle, model the process of rereading writing to think about whether paragraphs begin new ideas and group similar information together. Here is an example that uses the online resource Proofreading Sample 4.

- Show pages 10–13 from *Face to Face with Whales*. Then read them aloud.

  What do you notice about how the authors used paragraphs?

- Guide students to recognize that each paragraph starts a new idea and that all of the information in a paragraph relates to the same idea.

  When you reread your writing, make sure you show where a new idea begins by starting a new paragraph. The information in each paragraph should be about the same idea. If that's not the case, mark your draft to show where new paragraphs begin.

- Show the prepared writing and read it aloud. Begin modeling the process of thinking aloud about paragraphs.

  The first idea in this writing is about Letty waking up confused. Where does the idea change?

- Show how to place the paragraph symbol to mark the beginning of a new paragraph.

Have a Try

Invite students to work with a partner to decide where new paragraphs should begin.

> With your partner, read the rest of the passage and discuss where the idea changes.

▶ After time for discussion, ask volunteers to share where a new paragraph should begin and why. Use the paragraph symbol to mark the new paragraph break.

Summarize and Apply

Summarize the learning. Have students proofread and edit paragraphs in a piece of writing from their writing folders.

▶ Add to the editing and proofreading checklist you are using.

> During independent writing time today, check the paragraphs in a piece of writing in your writing folder. Did you remember to start a new paragraph when the idea changed or for dialogue? Use the paragraph symbol to mark your draft. If you make a final version of that writing, you will know where to start a new paragraph. Bring your writing to share when we meet later.

Confer

▶ During independent writing, move around the room to confer briefly with students and invite them to read aloud their writing to help with proofreading and editing. Use the following prompts as needed.

- *Read this page aloud. Talk about the decisions about paragraphing that you made.*
- *Tell the main idea in each paragraph.*
- *Show how you have grouped similar information together in this paragraph.*

Share

Following independent writing, gather students in the meeting area to share their writing.

> How does having similar information grouped together in paragraphs help your readers understand what you wrote?

Editing and Proofreading Checklist

☐ Make sure you communicate your ideas clearly.

☐ Check your spelling using multiple resources.

☐ Check your punctuation and capitalization.

☐ Check your paragraphs to make sure they begin new ideas and group similar information together.

When Letty woke up, she was in a very bright room with a cast on her arm. She felt very confused and had no idea where she was or what had happened. ¶After what seemed like a very long time, a woman came in with a white coat. She spent a while adjusting some knobs on a machine behind Letty. She said she was Dr. Kerring and told Letty that she has broken arm from a crash. She pointed to the remote and told Letty she could use it to pass the time. ¶After Dr. Kerring left, Letty noticed something strange. The remote was glowing and changing colors. With a slight hesitation, Letty reached for it and pressed the flashing red button marked DANGER.

Assessment

After you have taught the minilessons in this umbrella, observe students in a variety of classroom activities. Use *The Fountas & Pinnell Literacy Continuum* to notice, teach for, and support students' learning as you observe their attempts at writing.

▶ What evidence do you have of students' new understandings related to editing and proofreading?

- Do students understand that they should reread their writing to make sure their readers will understand what they are reading?
- Are they using multiple resources to check their spelling?
- Do they check for correct punctuation and capitalization?
- Are they making sure their paragraphs stay focused on a main idea?
- Are you noticing evidence that they are using an editing and proofreading checklist?
- Are they using vocabulary such as *make sense, edit, proofread, cross out, caret, spelling, read aloud, punctuation, paragraph,* and *main idea*?

▶ In what ways, beyond the scope of this umbrella, are students showing an interest in the writing process?

- Are they revising and organizing their writing?
- Are they adding to and deleting from their writing?

Use your observations to determine the next umbrella you will teach. You may also consult Suggested Sequence of Lessons (pp. 665–682) for guidance.

EXTENSIONS FOR EDITING AND PROOFREADING WRITING

▶ Have students add the Editing and Proofreading Checklist (download from fp.pub/resources) to their writing folders. You may choose to teach WML5 in MGT.U3: Introducing the Writing Folder to further engage students in using the Editing and Proofreading Checklist.

▶ Form a small guided writing group of students who need support for a similar aspect of writing, such as checking for punctuation.

▶ If students type their work on a computer and use a program that marks potential grammar and spelling errors, remind them to think carefully before they choose the corrections suggested by the program because they are not always correct.

Minilessons in This Umbrella

WML1   Choose a title for your writing.

WML2   Add personal information to help your readers understand more about your writing.

WML3   Make endpapers for your book.

Before Teaching Umbrella 11 Minilessons

The minilessons in this umbrella introduce students to the ways they can get their writing ready to share with an audience by adding book and print features. Teach the minilessons when you observe that students are ready and have writing to which to apply their new learning, such as picture book biographies, rather than consecutively.

Before teaching these minilessons, give students plenty of opportunities to write and draw freely and without constraints. Read and discuss engaging books from a variety of genres. For these minilessons, use the following books from *Fountas & Pinnell Classroom™ Interactive Read-Aloud Collection*, or choose books with a variety of book and print features from the classroom library.

Interactive Read-Aloud Collection

Genre Study: Memoir

The Upside Down Boy by Juan Felipe Herrera

Figuring Out Who You Are

The Junkyard Wonders by Patricia Polacco

La Mariposa by Francisco Jiménez

Exploring Identity

The Royal Bee by Frances Park and Ginger Park

Rickshaw Girl by Mitali Perkins

Crown: An Ode to the Fresh Cut by Derrick Barnes

Genre Study: Biography: Individuals Making a Difference

Six Dots: A Story of Young Louis Braille by Jen Bryant

The Secret Kingdom: Nek Chand, a Changing India, and a Hidden World of Art by Barb Rosenstock

Genre Study: Historical Fiction

Dad, Jackie, and Me by Myron Uhlberg

As you read and enjoy these texts together, help students

- evaluate the effectiveness of the title,
- notice and talk about how authors share personal information, and
- share what they notice about endpapers.

Interactive Read-Aloud
Memoir

Figuring Out Who You Are

Exploring Identity

Biography

Historical Fiction

Writer's Notebook

Writing Minilesson Principle
Choose a title for your writing.

Adding Book and Print Features

You Will Need

- several familiar books with interesting and appropriate titles, such as the following:
  - *The Upside Down Boy* by Juan Felipe Herrera, from Text Set: Genre Study: Memoir
  - *The Junkyard Wonders* by Patricia Polacco and *La Mariposa* by Francisco Jiménez, from Text Set: Figuring Out Who You Are
- chart paper and markers
- writer's notebooks and writing folders
- To download the following online resource for this lesson, visit **fp.pub/resources**:
  - chart art (optional)

Academic Language / Important Vocabulary

- cover
- title

Continuum Connection

- Select an appropriate title for a poem, story, or informational book
- Generate multiple titles for the piece and select the one that best fits the content of an informational piece or the plot or characterization in a narrative
- Use engaging titles and language

GOAL

Learn how writers think about titling their writing.

RATIONALE

The title is often what entices a reader to pick up a book, so a writer must choose a title that gives a hint about the book's content as well as catches the reader's attention. As students study familiar books, talk about how and why authors title their books to prompt their thinking about titles for their own books and other writing.

WRITER'S NOTEBOOK/WRITING FOLDER

Students can try out titles for a current piece of writing in their writer's notebooks. Or, they can write a new title for a piece of writing from their writing folders.

ASSESS LEARNING

- Observe for evidence that students understand the purpose of and thought behind titles and add appropriate titles to their own writing.
- Look for evidence that students can use vocabulary such as *cover* and *title*.

MINILESSON

To help students think about the minilesson principle, use several familiar books with strong titles and provide an interactive lesson. Here is an example.

- Display the cover of *The Upside Down Boy*.

  The writer, Juan Felipe Herrera, chose the title *The Upside Down Boy*, which he wrote in both English and Spanish. Let's think about why the writer decided to call this story *The Upside Down Boy*. What is the story about?

- Guide students to recollect that the author wrote the story to share how he felt when he started school before he learned English. Because it was so confusing to learn a new language and new customs and because he felt different from the other students, he felt like he was upside down.

- Show and read pages 14–15.

  What do these words and this illustration tell you about how the author chose the title?

  Often, you will come up with your title after you finish writing. Juan Felipe Herrera might have done that because his title uses words from the book. Other times, you might think of a title before you finish and it helps you focus your writing.

The Writing Minilessons Book, Grade 4

Have a Try

Have students turn and talk about titles.

▶ Display several familiar books with interesting and appropriate titles, such as *The Junkyard Wonders* and *La Mariposa*.

> Turn and talk about whether you think these are good titles and what makes a good title.

▶ After time for discussion, invite students to share their ideas. Begin a list on chart paper of their thoughts about what makes a good title.

Summarize and Apply

Summarize the learning. Remind students to write a title for a writing piece they are working on. Write the principle at the top of the chart.

> During independent writing time, write a title for a piece you are working on. You can try out several titles in your writer's notebook and choose the one you like best. Maybe the title you choose will send your writing in a new direction. Or, you can revisit an older piece of writing from your writing folder and try out a new title. Bring your writing to share when we meet later.

Choose a title for your writing.

A good book title—

- Catches readers' attention
- Tells what the topic is
- Is symbolic
- Has multiple meanings
- Hints at the plot
- Is unique
- Is memorable
- Builds curiosity

Confer

▶ During independent writing, move around the room to confer briefly with students about choosing a title for their writing. Use the following prompts as needed.

- *What are you writing about?*
- *What are your ideas for a title? Which title do you think is the best? Why?*
- *What title might make your readers want to read more?*

Share

Following independent writing, gather students in the meeting area to share their titles.

> In groups of four, share a title you wrote today and why you chose that title.

Writing Minilesson Principle
Add personal information to help your readers understand more about your writing.

Adding Book and Print Features

You Will Need

- several familiar books with examples of author pages, author's notes, dedications, and acknowledgments, such as the following:
  - *The Royal Bee* by Frances Park and Ginger Park, *Rickshaw Girl* by Mitali Perkins, and *Crown* by Derrick Barnes, from Text Set: Exploring Identity
  - *The Upside Down Boy* by Juan Felipe Herrera, from Text Set: Genre Study: Memoir
- chart paper and markers
- writer's notebooks and writing folders

Academic Language / Important Vocabulary

- author page
- author's note
- dedication
- acknowledgments

Continuum Connection

- In anticipation of an audience, add book and print features during the publishing process: e.g., illustrations and other graphics, cover spread, title, dedication, table of contents, about the author piece, headings, subheadings

GOAL

Notice how authors share information about themselves.

RATIONALE

Guiding students to notice how and where authors share information about themselves and supporting them in doing the same helps them view themselves as writers.

WRITER'S NOTEBOOK/WRITING FOLDER

Students can use their writer's notebooks to try out different ways to share personal information. They can write author pages, author's notes, dedications, and acknowledgments for the book they are working on in their writing folders.

ASSESS LEARNING

- Look for evidence that students understand why some authors include personal information with their writing.
- Notice whether students sometimes include personal information with their writing.
- Look for evidence that students can use vocabulary such as *author page*, *author's note*, *dedication*, and *acknowledgments*.

MINILESSON

To help students think about the minilesson principle, engage then in an inquiry-based lesson on author pages, author's notes, dedications, and acknowledgments in several familiar texts. Here is an example.

- Read aloud the dedication and authors' note at the beginning of *The Royal Bee*.

  What does this part of the book tell you about?

  What do you learn about the authors, Frances Park and Ginger Park?

  What do you learn about what inspired them to write this book?

  These authors wrote a dedication and an authors' note.

- Record information that students learned from each part on chart paper.

- Show the cover of *Rickshaw Girl*. Read aloud the dedication at the beginning and the author's note and acknowledgments at the end.

  What information did the author, Mitali Perkins, include that helps you understand more about her writing?

  She wrote a dedication and acknowledgments.

- Record the type of information students learned on the chart.

- Repeat with the dedication at the beginning and note from the author at the end of *Crown* and the dedication and author page at the end of *The Upside Down Boy*.

Have a Try

Invite students to talk to a partner about what they would write on their own author page or in an author's note, a dedication, and/or acknowledgments.

> Think about what personal information you might include in a piece of writing you are working on or one that you have already written. What would you choose to share about yourself or about your writing? Turn and talk about that.

▶ After time for discussion, invite several students to share their thinking. Add new ideas to the chart.

Summarize and Apply

Summarize the learning. Remind students that they can write personal information that helps readers understand more about their writing.

> Why do writers decide to include personal information with their writing?

▶ Write the principle at the top of the chart.

> During independent writing time today, think some more about what you would like your readers to know about you. Write some type of personal information, such as an author page, author's note, dedication, or acknowledgments. Bring your writing to share when we come back together.

Add personal information to help your readers understand more about your writing.

Part of the Book	Kind of Information
Dedication	• Someone who taught you something • People you respect, love, or care about • Someone who helped you with something
Author's Note	• Inspiration for the book • Why the book is meaningful • Extra information about the book
Acknowledgments	• People who helped with ideas for writing • Someone who proofread or edited the writing • People who inspired the writer
Author Page	• Where the author lives • How the author got the idea for the book • Where the author went to school • A photo or illustration of the author • Other books the author has written

Confer

▶ During independent writing, move around the room to confer briefly with students about including personal information in the writing they are working on. Use prompts such as the following as needed.

- *What would you like your readers to know about you?*
- *What could you write to share why you wrote about this topic?*
- *Who helped you with or inspired your writing?*

Share

Following independent writing, gather students in the meeting area to share the personal information they are including in a book they are working on.

> In groups of three, share the personal information you included in your writing and why you decided to share that information.

WML3

WPS.U11.WML3

Writing Minilesson Principle
Make endpapers for your book.

Adding Book and Print Features

You Will Need

- familiar books with interesting endpapers, such as the following:
  - *Six Dots* by Jen Bryant from Text Set: Genre Study: Biography: Individuals Making a Difference
  - *Dad, Jackie, and Me* by Myron Uhlberg, from Text Set: Genre Study: Historical Fiction
- a mentor text without endpapers that lends itself to adding endpapers, such as the following:
  - *The Secret Kingdom* by Barb Rosenstock, from Text Set: Genre Study: Biography: Individuals Making a Difference
- chart paper and markers
- writer's notebooks and writing folders

Academic Language / Important Vocabulary

- endpapers

Continuum Connection

- In anticipation of an audience, add book and print features during the publishing process: e.g., illustrations and other graphics, cover spread, title, dedication, table of contents, about the author piece, headings, subheadings
- Create drawings that are related to the written text and increase readers' understanding and enjoyment

GOAL

Make endpapers that are related to the meaning of the text and increase readers' understanding and enjoyment.

RATIONALE

When students study endpapers and think about how they relate to the book's meaning, they gain an appreciation for the thought and care that went into creating every aspect of the book. They understand that they, too, can put the same thought and care into creating their own books by adding endpapers.

WRITER'S NOTEBOOK/WRITING FOLDER

Students can use writer's notebooks to try out different ideas for endpapers. They can make endpapers for the book they are working on in their writing folders.

ASSESS LEARNING

- Look for evidence that students understand that endpapers can add to the meaning of a text and increase the reader's enjoyment.
- Notice whether students add endpapers to their own books.
- Observe for evidence that students can use vocabulary such as *endpapers*.

MINILESSON

To help students think about the minilesson principle, have them study the endpapers in familiar texts. Here is an example.

- Show the cover of *Six Dots*. Open to the endpapers, helping students to notice they are at the beginning and end of the book.

  What do you notice about the beginning and final pages in this book?

  These pages are not part of the main text. Talk about why they are there and why they are important.

  The illustration shows the Braille alphabet. These pages tell or remind you that you are learning about Louis Braille. These are called endpapers. They come at one or both ends of a book.

  What might authors and illustrators show on the endpapers in their books?

- Begin a list on chart paper of why authors decide to illustrate the endpapers.

- Show the endpapers in *Dad, Jackie, and Me*.

  What do you notice about these endpapers?

- Add to the chart.

Have a Try

Invite students to talk to a partner about their own books.

▷ Briefly revisit *The Secret Kingdom*.

This book has no endpapers, but if it did, what might they show? Turn and talk about that.

▷ After students turn and talk, invite several to share their ideas. Encourage them to select an idea related to the story, such as a drawing of Nek Chand or a design using recycled materials. Using students' ideas and shared drawing, sketch one or more options.

Summarize and Apply

Summarize the learning. Remind students that they can make endpapers.

During independent writing time, use your writer's notebook to sketch some possible endpapers for a book you have written or are writing.

▷ Add the principle to the chart.

When you are ready, choose an idea, make the endpapers on paper, and then glue them into your book. Or, you can make them right in your book. Bring your book to share when we come back together.

> **Make endpapers for your book.**
>
> • Connect to the story
> • Show what the book is about
> • Decoration or design
> • Remind readers of what they learned
> • Give more information
> • Make the book more fun to read
> • Hook readers' attention

Confer

▷ During independent writing, move around the room to confer briefly with students about making endpapers. Use prompts such as the following as needed.

- *What might you draw that would help readers understand more about the topic?*
- *Look at the chart. What idea will you use for endpapers?*
- *Why did you decide to put _____ on your book's endpapers?*

Share

Following independent writing, gather students in the meeting area to share their endpapers.

What ideas for endpapers did you make or sketch? Tell about what you drew.

Assessment

After you have taught the minilessons in this umbrella, observe students as they draw, write, and talk about their writing. Use *The Fountas & Pinnell Literacy Continuum* to notice, teach for, and support students' learning as you observe their bookmaking skills.

▶ What evidence do you have of students' new understandings related to adding book and print features for an audience?

- Do students' titles relate to the contents of their books?
- Have they experimented with adding author pages, author's notes, dedications, and acknowledgments?
- Have they experimented with making endpapers for a book?
- Do they understand and use vocabulary such as *cover*, *title*, *author page*, *author's note*, *dedication*, *acknowledgments*, and *endpapers*?

▶ In what other ways, beyond the scope of this umbrella, are students exploring the writing process?

- Are they sharing their writing with others?
- Are they incorporating what they know about illustration to enhance the meaning of their writing?
- Are they publishing their writing in different ways?

Use your observations to determine the next umbrella you will teach. You may also consult Suggested Sequence of Lessons (pp. 665–682) for guidance.

EXTENSIONS FOR ADDING BOOK AND PRINT FEATURES

▶ If you are using *The Reading Minilessons Book, Grade 4* (Fountas and Pinnell 2020), you may want to teach LA.U12: Noticing Book and Print Features.

▶ Help students study front and back covers to learn the kind of information that is usually included. Then have them make front and back covers for their own books.

▶ Teach students how to make other book parts, such as a copyright page and a glossary.

▶ Students might revisit finished pieces in their writing folders to add a dedication, author page, or endpapers.

Minilessons in This Umbrella

WML1   Choose and prepare a piece of writing you want to publish.

WML2   Use a self-assessment rubric to think about your strengths and goals.

WML3   Develop a rubric for a type of writing.

WML4   Choose a piece of writing that shows your growth as a writer.

Writer's Notebook

Before Teaching Umbrella 12 Minilessons

We recommend teaching at least some of the minilessons in WPS.U11: Adding Book and Print Features before teaching WML1. It would also be helpful for you to prepare some sample writing projects to use for demonstrating this umbrella's principles. Teach the first minilesson when students have completed several writing pieces and are ready to choose one for a more formal publishing treatment. Teach the last three minilessons when students have a body of work that they can use to assess and reflect on how they are progressing as writers.

The purpose of the minilessons in this umbrella is to prepare students to choose pieces they are proud of to publish, share, and reflect upon. How you define "publishing" for fourth graders is up to you and your students. In some cases, students might enjoy publishing their work by typing and printing it, while in other cases they may rewrite their final draft in their best handwriting. Some teachers may prefer to help their students prepare a perfectly edited final product, while others may choose to have their students handle their own editing and proofreading.

Of course, not every piece of writing will be published. Whenever students are learning to write in a particular genre (e.g., memoirs), they should write more than one piece in that genre and then choose which among those they want to bring all the way through the writing process.

Students will need their writing folders to access longer pieces of writing for publishing and self-assessing. They will also need access to their finished writing, kept in hanging file folders (see pp. 53–54), from which they will choose a piece that shows how they have grown as writers.

Writing Minilesson Principle
Choose and prepare a piece of writing you want to publish.

Publishing and Self-Assessing Your Writing

You Will Need

- examples of writing (yours or students') that have been published in different ways (as a picture book, with cover, framed and mounted, etc.)
- chart paper and markers
- writing folders

Academic Language / Important Vocabulary

- publish
- audience
- type
- cover
- title page
- author page

Continuum Connection

- Understand publishing as the sharing of a piece of writing with a purpose and an audience in mind
- Select a poem, story, or informational book to publish in a variety of appropriate ways: e.g., typed/printed, framed and mounted or otherwise displayed
- Add cover spread with title and author information
- In anticipation of an audience, add book and print features during the publishing process: e.g., illustrations and other graphics, cover, spread, title, dedication, table of contents, about the author piece, headings, subheadings

GOAL

Select and prepare a piece to publish for an audience.

RATIONALE

Before students can "publish" their work, they must first choose which piece to publish and how to prepare it for publication. When you teach students different ways to publish their writing, they begin to understand that writing is a process that involves several steps beyond writing the words and drawing the illustrations. They begin to conceptualize the idea of writing not just for themselves but also for an audience.

WRITER'S NOTEBOOK/WRITING FOLDER

Students will select a draft from their writing folders to prepare it for publication.

ASSESS LEARNING

- Listen to students' reasons for choosing pieces to publish.
- Notice whether students experiment with different ways of publishing.
- Look for evidence that they can use vocabulary such as *publish, audience, type, cover, title page*, and *author page*.

MINILESSON

To help students think about the principle, discuss what it means to publish a piece of writing. Here is an example.

- Show students a piece of published writing by you or a student.

  What do you think it means to publish a piece of writing?

  Publishing a piece of writing means to get it ready so other people can read it. Authors carefully choose which pieces of writing to publish.

  I worked very hard on this piece of writing and I'm proud of it. I think it shows my best work, and it's about an important topic that I care a lot about. What do you notice about why I chose to publish this piece of writing?

- Record students' responses on chart paper.

  After deciding to publish my nonfiction picture book, I proofread and edited my writing to make sure there weren't any spelling or punctuation mistakes. Then I typed my writing on a computer to make it look nice and be easy to read. I added a title page and an author page. Finally, I put a cover on my book.

  What do you notice about how I prepared my writing to be published?

- Record on the chart what you did to prepare your writing.
- Display and discuss a few other pieces of writing that have been published in different ways (e.g., a framed and mounted poem, a spiral-bound book, a magazine article).

Have a Try

Invite students to talk to a partner about a piece of writing they would like to publish.

> Think about the pieces of writing you have worked on lately. Which one would you like to publish, and how would you like to publish it? What will you do to get it ready to be published? Turn and talk to your partner about this.

▶ After students turn and talk, invite several students to share their thinking. Add any new ideas to the chart.

Summarize and Apply

Write the principle at the top of the chart. Summarize the learning and invite students to choose a piece of writing to publish.

> Today you learned how to choose and prepare a piece of writing to be published. During independent writing time today, look through your writing folder and choose a piece of writing you would like to publish. Then decide how you want to publish it and start getting it ready to be published.

Choose and prepare a piece of writing you want to publish.

Choosing a Piece of Writing for Publishing	Preparing a Piece of Writing for Publishing
• You worked very hard on it.	• Decide how you want to publish it.
• You are proud of your work.	• Edit and proofread your writing.
• It shows your best work.	• Type it or write it in your best handwriting.
• You care a lot about the topic.	• Add book and print features (cover, title page, author page).
• You want other people to learn about the topic.	• Mount, frame, or bind it.
• You are excited about this piece of writing.	
• You want to share your writing with more people.	

Confer

▶ During independent writing, move around the room to confer briefly with students about publishing their writing. Use prompts such as the following as needed.

- *Which piece of writing will you publish? What are your reasons?*
- *How would you like to publish it?*
- *What do you need to do to get it ready to be published?*

Share

Following independent writing, gather students in the meeting area to talk about publishing their writing.

> Who would like to share the piece of writing you decided to publish and how you got it ready, or started to get it ready, to be published?

Writing Minilesson Principle
Use a self-assessment rubric to think about your strengths and goals.

Publishing and Self-Assessing Your Writing

You Will Need

- a sample memoir you have prepared
- a copy of the Rubric for Memoirs (Student) for you and each student
- markers
- writing folders
- To download the following online resource for this lesson, visit **fp.pub/resources**:
  - Rubric for Memoirs (Student)

Academic Language / Important Vocabulary

- assess
- self-assessment
- rubric

Continuum Connection

- Self-evaluate writing and talk about what is good about it and what techniques were used
- Notice what makes writing effective and name the craft or technique

---

GOAL

Use a self-assessment tool to reflect on areas of strength and determine goals for writing.

RATIONALE

When you teach students how to use a self-assessment rubric, they are able to independently evaluate their own work, reflect on areas of strength, and identify areas for future development.

WRITER'S NOTEBOOK/WRITING FOLDER

When students are ready to evaluate a finished piece of writing from their writing folders, provide the appropriate rubric.

ASSESS LEARNING

- Notice whether students think carefully about their work and can identify areas of strength and areas for future development.
- Look for evidence that they can use vocabulary such as *assess*, *self-assessment*, and *rubric*.

MINILESSON

To help students think about the minilesson principle, model using a self-assessment rubric to evaluate your writing. For the lesson, project a copy of the rubric or provide a copy to each student. (Students will need their own rubrics for Summarize and Apply.) Here is an example.

- Show the Rubric for Memoirs (Student).

  This is a rubric for writing memoirs. What do you think a rubric is?

  A rubric is a tool that you can use to self-assess your writing. When you self-assess your writing, you reread it and think carefully about what you did well and what you need to work on. What do you notice about this rubric?

- Show the sample memoir you prepared. Then model how to use the rubric.

  I reread my memoir, and now I'm going to use the rubric to self-assess my writing. The first section is titled Genre Understandings. This section is about how well you understand the type of writing and show the qualities of it in your own writing. The first row in this section is about whether I wrote about a special moment or memory. There are three choices. I think I stayed focused on a special moment or memory and showed why the memory is important to me. I will circle the fourth column in the first row.

  The row next to the word *Voice* is about whether I can hear my voice in my writing. I think I can sometimes hear my voice in my writing, but I could practice with this more, so I will circle the third column.

- Continue as needed to make sure students understand how to use the rubric.

Have a Try

Invite students to talk to a partner about how to use a self-assessment rubric.

> What did you notice about how I self-assessed my writing using the rubric? What did I do and think about? Turn and talk to your partner about what you noticed.

▶ After time for discussion, invite several pairs to share their thinking. Summarize the learning on chart paper.

Summarize and Apply

Summarize the learning and invite students to use the rubric to self-assess their own writing.

> Why is it important to self-assess your writing? How can this help you grow as a writer?

> During independent writing time today, use this self-assessment rubric to evaluate the last memoir you wrote. I will be available to help you.

How to Use a Rubric

- Reread your writing.

- Read across the first row of the rubric.

- Think about which description best fits your writing, and circle it.

- Repeat for each row of the rubric.

- Think about what you could do better next time.

Confer

▶ During independent writing, move around the room to confer briefly with students about self-assessing their writing. Use prompts such as the following as needed.

- *What is this row of the rubric asking you to notice?*

- *Do you think you shared meaningful thoughts and feelings about the memory? Can you share an example of where you did that?*

- *What interesting words or phrases did you use in your writing?*

- *Did you write many interesting details about the important parts of your story? Did you include any details that are not important? Where?*

Share

Following independent writing, gather students in the meeting area to talk about self-assessing their writing.

> How does using a rubric help you think about your writing?

Writing Minilesson Principle
Develop a rubric for a type of writing.

Publishing and Self-Assessing Your Writing

You Will Need

- the chart from GEN.U11.WML1 (or a prepared list of the qualities of a particular genre of writing)
- chart paper prepared with qualities of a genre of writing in the first of four columns (see chart)
- markers
- writer's notebooks
- To download the following online resources for this lesson, visit **fp.pub/resources**:
  - Rubric for Memoirs (Student)
  - Blank Rubric

Academic Language / Important Vocabulary

- rubric
- self-assess
- develop

Continuum Connection

- Self-evaluate writing and talk about what is good about it and what techniques were used
- Self-evaluate pieces of writing in light of what is known about a genre
- Notice what makes writing effective and name the craft or technique

GOAL

Collaborate to develop a self-assessment rubric based on the defining qualities of a genre.

RATIONALE

When students help develop a rubric for writing in a particular genre, they will be more personally invested in the success criteria and more motivated to achieve them. Before this lesson, students should already be very familiar with using a self-assessment rubric (WML2). They should also have already done an inquiry into the qualities of the chosen genre and written several pieces in that genre. This lesson focuses on opinion writing as an example (see GEN.U11), but it can be applied to any genre.

WRITER'S NOTEBOOK/WRITING FOLDER

Have students work in small groups to develop one of the criteria for the rubric. They can take notes in their writer's notebooks.

ASSESS LEARNING

- Notice whether students understand how to develop a rubric for writing.
- Look for evidence that they can use vocabulary such as *rubric*, *self-assess*, and *develop*.

MINILESSON

To help students think about the minilesson principle, use shared writing to create a rubric for opinion writing (or another genre with which students are very familiar). Here is an example.

- Show the Rubric for Memoirs (Student).

  What is the purpose of a rubric?

  Today we're going to develop our own rubric for opinion writing. To start, we can use the qualities of this genre that we noticed when we studied opinion writing.

- Display the chart from GEN.U11.WML1 and the prepared chart paper. Model writing criteria in the first row of the rubric, using students' input.

  The fourth column is labeled "I can teach someone about this." This is the column you would circle if you think you did a very good job at stating your opinion at the beginning of your piece. What could we write for the description for this column?

  The second column is labeled "I need help with this." If you feel that you could do a better job stating your opinion with some assistance, this is the column that you would circle. What could we write for the description?

  What should we write under "I need more practice with this"?

Have a Try

Invite students to talk to a partner about how to develop a rubric.

> What did you notice about how we developed the first row of our rubric for opinion writing? Turn and talk to your partner about this.

▶ After students turn and talk, invite several pairs to share their thinking. Confirm that they understand the process, and clear up any misunderstandings.

Summarize and Apply

Summarize the learning and invite students to work with a small group to develop one row of the rubric.

> During independent writing time today, you will work with a group of your classmates to develop another row of our rubric. With your group, decide what should go in each of the three labeled columns for one of the qualities of opinion writing. Write the three descriptions in your writer's notebook. When we come back together, you will share your ideas, and we will finish filling in the rubric together.

▶ Divide students into small groups, and assign each group one of the remaining rows on the rubric.

Rubric for Opinion Writing

	I need help with this.	I need more practice with this.	I can teach someone about this.
The writer states the opinion clearly, usually at the beginning.	I did not state my opinion at the beginning of the piece.	I tried to state my opinion at the beginning of the piece, but it is not clear.	I clearly stated my opinion in the beginning of the piece.
The writer supports the opinion with reasons and evidence.	I did not provide reasons and evidence for my opinion.	I provided one or two reasons for my opinion.	I provided several reasons and pieces of evidence for my opinion.
The writer uses personal experience to support the opinion.	I did not write about a personal experience.	I wrote about a personal experience, but it doesn't clearly support my opinion.	I used personal experiences that clearly support my opinion.
The writer uses connecting words to show how ideas are related.	I did not use connecting words to connect different ideas.	I tried using a few connecting words to connect different ideas.	I often used connecting words that show how ideas are related.
The writer summarizes the opinion at the end.	I did not summarize my opinion at the end of the piece.	I tried to summarize my opinion at the end, but it is not clear.	I clearly summarized my opinion at the end of the piece.

Confer

▶ During independent writing, move around the room to confer briefly with groups about developing a rubric. Use prompts such as the following as needed.

- *What would it look like if a writer has succeeded at _____?*
- *What could you write in the first column for this quality?*
- *If a writer needs more practice with _____, what might that look like?*

Share

Following independent writing, gather students in the meeting area to share their ideas. Invite each group to share the criteria they chose for their assigned row of the rubric. Discuss the criteria as a class. Add it to the rubric.

> Choose a member of your group to share how you filled in your row of the rubric.

Writing Minilesson Principle

Choose a piece of writing that shows your growth as a writer.

Publishing and Self-Assessing Your Writing

You Will Need

- a sample piece of your writing and a prepared reflection on the writing
- chart paper and markers
- writer's notebooks and writing folders

Academic Language / Important Vocabulary

- growth
- reflect

Continuum Connection

- Notice what makes writing effective and name the craft or technique
- Select examples of best writing in all genres attempted

GOAL

Select a piece of writing and reflect on how the piece shows growth.

RATIONALE

In addition to reflecting on their work regularly throughout the writing process, it is also helpful for students to select a piece of writing specifically for looking at their growth as a writer a few times a year (e.g., quarterly). This allows them to see and reflect on the "big picture" of their writing progress.

WRITER'S NOTEBOOK/WRITING FOLDER

Students will select a piece of writing from their writing folders, writer's notebooks, or their hanging files, reflect on how it shows their growth as a writer, and note what they have learned.

ASSESS LEARNING

- Notice whether students select a piece of writing that shows their growth as a writer and explain why they selected it.
- Look for evidence that they can use vocabulary such as *growth* and *reflect*.

MINILESSON

A few times a year, have students write a longer reflection about a piece of writing that shows their growth as writers and illustrators. More frequently, you will have students write short reflections on the writing folder resource What I Have Learned to Do as a Writer and Illustrator (see MGT.U3.WML2). This example lesson shows how you might do the former.

- Read aloud and show the sample piece of writing you prepared. Then explain why you chose to reflect on this piece of writing.

   I chose this persuasive essay to reflect on because it's a new type of writing for me, and it shows that I can organize my writing better than I used to. I worked hard on it, and I'm very proud of it. Listen as I read my reflection.

- Show and read the prepared reflection.

   Why did I choose this piece of writing to write a reflection on?

   What else might you think about when you choose a piece of writing to reflect on?

- Record responses on chart paper.

   What do you notice about my reflection? What did I include in it?

- Record responses on the chart.

Have a Try

Invite students to talk to a partner about a piece of writing that shows their growth as a writer.

> Think about the writing projects that you have worked on lately. Which piece of writing shows your growth as a writer? How does it show growth? Turn and talk to your partner about this.

▶ After time for discussion, invite a few volunteers to share their thinking.

Summarize and Apply

Write the principle at the top of the chart. Summarize the learning and invite students to reflect on their writing progress.

> During independent writing time today, you will spend some more time reflecting on your growth as a writer. Look through the writing you have done lately and choose a piece of writing that shows how you have improved as a writer. Then write at least one or two paragraphs explaining how it shows growth. Bring your reflection to share when we meet later.

Choose a piece of writing that shows your growth as a writer.

Reasons to Choose a Piece of Writing

- You tried a new type of writing.
- You worked very hard on it.
- You're proud of it.
- You tried something new in your writing.
- It shows how you have improved as a writer.

What to Include in a Reflection

- Explain why you chose the piece.
- Describe what you think you did well.
- Give specific examples.
- Tell how it shows your growth as a writer.

Confer

▶ During independent writing, move around the room to confer briefly with students about their growth as a writer. Use prompts such as the following as needed.

- *Which piece of writing shows how you have grown as a writer?*
- *Why did you choose this piece of writing?*
- *Did you try something new in this piece of writing?*
- *What makes you proud of this piece of writing?*

Share

Following independent writing, gather students in the meeting area to share their reflections.

> Who would like to share the reflection you wrote today?

Assessment

After you have taught the minilessons in this umbrella, observe students as they write and talk about their writing. Use *The Fountas & Pinnell Literacy Continuum* to notice, teach for, and support students' writing development.

▶ What evidence do you have of students' new understandings related to publishing and self-assessing writing?

- How are students explaining their choices of what to publish?
- How do they prepare and publish their writing?
- Do they develop and use self-assessment rubrics to reflect on their work?
- Are they able to notice and reflect on their growth as a writer?
- Do students understand and use vocabulary such as *publish*, *self-assessment*, *rubric*, and *growth*?

▶ In what other ways, beyond the scope of this umbrella, are students exploring the writing process?

- Are they revising, editing, and proofreading their writing?
- Are they adding book and print features to their books?

Use your observations to determine the next umbrella you will teach. You may also consult Suggested Sequence of Lessons (pp. 665–682) for guidance.

EXTENSIONS FOR PUBLISHING AND SELF-ASSESSING YOUR WRITING

▶ Dedicate a section of the classroom library or area of the school (e.g., hallway or lobby) to displaying and celebrating students' published writing projects.

▶ Teach students how to publish a collection of several of their stories or poems and/or help them work together to create a class anthology.

▶ When students write a longer reflection on a separate piece of paper, attach it to the piece of writing and place in their hanging file folders. You may find it helpful to have two or three writing pieces with reflections available for when you hold conferences with parents and caregivers. For more frequent, shorter reflections, use the writing folder online resource What I Have Learned to Do as a Writer and Illustrator (see MGT.U3.WML2).

▶ Consider using the assessment forms Guide to Observing and Noting Writing Behaviors, available for both individual students and the class. Download the forms from fp.pub/resources.

Appendix:
Suggested Sequence of Lessons

The Suggested Sequence of Lessons is also available on the Fountas & Pinnell Online Resources site (**fp.pub/resources**).

Suggested Sequence of Lessons

This sequence shows when you might teach the writing minilessons across the year. It also aligns the lessons with the texts from *Fountas & Pinnell Classroom™ Shared Reading Collection* and *Interactive Read-Aloud Collection*, as well as the reading minilesson umbrellas from *The Reading Minilessons Book, Grade 4*. You do not need these other resources to teach the writing minilessons in this book, but if you have any of them, this comprehensive sequence helps you see how the pieces can fit together and think about how you might organize reading and writing across the year.

You will notice that there are more writing minilessons than days in the year. Because learners are on a continuum of understanding and development in writing, the lessons in this book are designed to give you choices about what to teach based on the writers in front of you. **We have listed all the umbrellas in the order we would recommend teaching them, but you will need to make your own choices about which umbrellas and lessons to teach and which to omit.**

Suggested Sequence of Lessons

Months	Texts from *Fountas & Pinnell Classroom™ Shared Reading Collection*	Text Sets from *Fountas & Pinnell Classroom™ Interactive Read-Aloud Collection*	Reading Minilessons (RML) Umbrellas	Writing Minilessons (WML) Umbrellas	Teaching Suggestions for Extending Learning
Months 1 & 2	Stinky, Slimy, Sludgy Poems	Friendship Figuring Out Who You Are	MGT.U1: Being a Respectful Member of the Classroom Community	**MGT.U1: Being a Respectful Member of the Classroom Community**	If you have taught the first umbrellas in the Management and Literary Analysis sections of *The Reading Minilessons Book, Grade 4*, you may not need to teach similar lessons in WML MGT.U1 because the RML and WML books establish the same basic routines. The lessons in WML MGT.U1 provide a context for applying the umbrella's behaviors and routines by inviting students to interview classmates and create slides to introduce them to the class. They are also invited to make public service announcements about their class values.

Key
CFT: Craft • CNV: Convention • GEN: Genres and Forms • LA: Literary Analysis • MGT: Management • SAS: Strategies and Skills • WAR: Writing About Reading • WPS: Writing Process

Months	Texts from *Fountas & Pinnell Classroom™ Shared Reading Collection*	Text Sets from *Fountas & Pinnell Classroom™ Interactive Read-Aloud Collection*	Reading Minilessons (RML) Umbrellas	Writing Minilessons (WML) Umbrellas	Teaching Suggestions for Extending Learning
Months 1 & 2 (cont.)	My Typhoon	Empathy	MGT.U2: Getting Started with Independent Reading WAR.U1: Introducing a Reader's Notebook MGT.U3: Living a Reading Life	**WPS.U1: Introducing and Using a Writer's Notebook, WML1–WML4**	We recommend introducing a writer's notebook as soon as you can in the school year so that students can write in it daily. Teach most of this umbrella at one time or interweave these lessons with MGT.U1 or MGT.U2. Consider teaching more than one minilesson a day for the first couple of weeks of school. For example, teach a lesson from MGT.U1 or MGT.U2 and WPS.U1 on the same day. Leave the last lesson in WPS.U1 until you have introduced most sections of the writer's notebook thoroughly.
				MGT.U2: Establishing Independent Writing	Students can work in their writer's notebooks as they apply the lessons in MGT.U2.
	A Cuban American Familia		WAR.U2: Using a Reader's Notebook	**WPS.U2: Writer's Notebook: Getting Ideas from Your Life**	The lessons in WPS.U2 are designed to teach students ways to get ideas for their writing and to develop the habit of writing every day in their notebooks for at least ten minutes. You can teach these lessons to begin writers' workshop or use them outside of writers' workshop as a quick writing prompt. Teach these lessons all at once, or teach them over time to inspire new writing ideas. This umbrella corresponds to Section 1 in the *Fountas & Pinnell Writer's Notebook, Intermediate*.
	The Breadfruit Bonanza		WAR.U3: Writing Letters to Share Thinking About Books, RML1–RML2	**GEN.U1: Writing Letters, WML1–WML2**	Teach the first two lessons in this umbrella at the beginning of the year. If you are using *The Reading Minilessons Book, Grade 4*, these lessons will support students in writing their reading letters (WAR.U3). Teach the other two lessons in the umbrella later in the year when students have more experience with letter writing and more topics to use in formal letters and emails. Note that some of the lessons refer to mentor texts that fall later in the suggested sequence for the *Interactive Read-Aloud Collection* and *Shared Reading Collection*. It is fine if you have not read these books in their entirety.

Months	Texts from *Fountas & Pinnell Classroom™ Shared Reading Collection*	Text Sets from *Fountas & Pinnell Classroom™ Interactive Read-Aloud Collection*	Reading Minilessons [RML] Umbrellas	Writing Minilessons [WML] Umbrellas	Teaching Suggestions for Extending Learning
Months 1 & 2 [cont.]		Genre Study: Memoir	LA.U13: Studying Memoir	**CNV.U1: Writing Words**	Teach only the lessons students need. The lessons are designed to support, not replace, your phonics and word study instruction and to help students transfer those concepts to writing. Students will need explicit instruction in phonics and word study in addition to these Conventions minilessons.
			LA.U5: Understanding Fiction and Nonfiction Genres	**GEN.U5: Writing Memoirs**	Students revisit ideas they have collected in WPS.U2 to find ideas for memoirs. Encourage them to write several memoirs, trying both small-moment writing and a collection of vignettes. If you are using *The Reading Minilessons Book, Grade 4*, consider teaching LA.U13 slightly before GEN.U5.
			WAR.U3: Writing Letters to Share Thinking About Books, RML3	**CFT.U4: Using Dialogue in Writing**	Students can apply the minilessons in this umbrella to the memoirs they are writing. Encourage them to try out dialogue in their writer's notebooks. Teach lessons about punctuating and paragraphing dialogue from CNV.U2 and CNV.U3 now or later in the year during more in-depth studies of punctuation and paragraphing.
	Pangaea: The World's Biggest Puzzle	Author/ Illustrator Study: Allen Say	LA.U3: Studying Authors and Their Processes, RML1	**WPS.U8: Adding Information to Your Writing, WML1–WML2**	Teach any of the lessons in this umbrella as needed. We recommend teaching the first two lessons early in the year so students learn tools for revising and begin to understand what it means to revise. Students can apply these lessons to one of the memoirs they have written or to writing in their writer's notebooks.
	Space Junk			**WPS.U11: Adding Book and Print Features, WML1**	We recommend teaching WML1 early in the year so students learn how to select meaningful titles for their writing. Students can apply this lesson to a memoir they plan to publish. The rest of the lessons in WPS.U11 are best taught while students are engaged in bookmaking.

Months	Texts from *Fountas & Pinnell Classroom™ Shared Reading Collection*	Text Sets from *Fountas & Pinnell Classroom™ Interactive Read-Aloud Collection*	Reading Minilessons (RML) Umbrellas	Writing Minilessons (WML) Umbrellas	Teaching Suggestions for Extending Learning
Months 1 & 2 (cont.)	Amazing Axolotls		LA.U1: Getting Started with Book Clubs	**WPS.U12: Publishing and Self-Assessing Your Writing**	Invite students to publish one of the memoirs they have been working on. Consider having them apply a rubric to the piece before publishing it. To show their growth as a writer (WML4), students can choose a published piece of writing or a writing piece that is still in process.
			WAR.U3: Writing Letters to Share Thinking About Books, RML4–RML5	**MGT.U3: Introducing the Writing Folder, WML1–WML4**	Have students record the memoirs they have written on their writing projects list. After self-assessing their writing (WPS.U12), help them establish writing goals using the goals sheet (available in the online resources). We recommend teaching the last lesson in this umbrella after you have taught more lessons on revising and editing from the Writing Process section.
Months 3 & 4	The Power and Influence of Color	Illustration Study: Craft	SAS.U1: Solving Multisyllable Words	**GEN.U13: Making Poetry Anthologies, WML1–WML2**	Teach the first two lessons in this umbrella early in the year to get poetry anthologies established. Anthologies give students a place in addition to their writer's notebooks to collect, respond to, and write poetry. Teach the rest of this umbrella across a few weeks to give students time to collect poetry in between lessons. Consider hosting a poetry workshop biweekly or monthly to teach poetry-focused minilessons and to integrate poetry throughout the year.
		Illustrator Study: Floyd Cooper		**CFT.U1: Learning from Writers and Illustrators**	The lessons in this umbrella are designed to help students read like writers and illustrators–to notice the craft moves that writers and illustrators make. This umbrella will support the work of the next couple of umbrellas as well as provide a foundation for LA.U10 and LA.U11 (taught later in the year) in *The Reading Minilessons Book, Grade 4*.

Months	Texts from *Fountas & Pinnell Classroom™ Shared Reading Collection*	Text Sets from *Fountas & Pinnell Classroom™ Interactive Read-Aloud Collection*	Reading Minilessons (RML) Umbrellas	Writing Minilessons (WML) Umbrellas	Teaching Suggestions for Extending Learning
Months 3 & 4 (cont.)	Mosaic Master: Antoni Gaudí	Biography: Artists	LA.U11: Studying Illustrators and Analyzing an Illustrator's Craft	**WPS.U3: Writer's Notebook: Getting Inspiration from Writers and Artists**	The minilessons in this umbrella build on the idea that writers can use mentor texts to inspire ideas and build their writer's notebooks. Teach the minilessons consecutively or over the next few weeks, as students need inspiration. This umbrella corresponds to Section 2 in *Writer's Notebook, Intermediate*.
			LA.U2: Learning Conversational Moves in Book Club	**CFT.U14: Adding Meaning Through Illustrations**	Invite students to make picture books. They might choose a story idea from their writer's notebooks or turn something they have written (e.g., a memoir) into picture book form. Encourage them to use their writer's notebooks to try techniques learned in CFT.U14. You may also choose to teach or revisit this umbrella when students are learning to make picture book biographies. Some of these lessons overlap with LA.U11 in *The Reading Minilessons Book, Grade 4*. Select only the lessons your students need.
		Telling a Story with Photos	SAS.U4: Maintaining Fluency	**CFT.U5: Crafting Powerful Leads and Endings**	Whether students are writing fiction or nonfiction, they will benefit from studying how authors craft strong leads and endings. Invite them to apply these lessons to a current writing project or to writing in their writer's notebooks.
	Get the Scoop! Plans and Poems for Making Compost		LA.U25: Understanding Plot	**CFT.U7: Exploring Plot Structures, WML1**	CFT.U7.WML1 forms the basis for narrative plot structure. This umbrella is best taught over time to allow students time to experiment with each plot structure. We have placed it here in the sequence to build on understandings developed in LA.U25 in *The Reading Minilessons Book, Grade 4*. However, lessons from this umbrella can be taught at any time your students are engaged in narrative writing (e.g., memoir, realistic fiction, biography).

Months	Texts from *Fountas & Pinnell Classroom™ Shared Reading Collection*	Text Sets from *Fountas & Pinnell Classroom™ Interactive Read-Aloud Collection*	Reading Minilessons (RML) Umbrellas	Writing Minilessons (WML) Umbrellas	Teaching Suggestions for Extending Learning
Months 3 & 4 (cont.)	A Whirling Swirl of Poems		LA.U26: Understanding Characters' Feelings, Motivations, and Intentions	**CNV.U2: Learning About Punctuation and Capitalization**	The minilessons in this umbrella can be taught all at once as a part of a comprehensive study of capitalization and punctuation or over time as needed. Besides learning the conventions of writing, the minilessons in this umbrella help students see how a writer's capitalization and punctuation decisions influence meaning.
	Grannie's Coal Pot		WAR.U5: Introducing Different Genres and Forms for Responding to Reading, RML1–RML3	**WPS.U6: Thinking About Purpose, Audience, and Genre/Form**	The minilessons in this umbrella help students make meaningful choices about which genre and form best suit their purpose and audience. To keep their writing fresh, give students the opportunity to choose the genre and form of their writing between genre studies. Revisit this umbrella throughout the year as necessary.
	Swarm! When Animals Move as One		SAS.U5: Summarizing, RML1	**CFT.U10: Choosing a Point of View**	This umbrella builds on students' experience in writing from the first-person point of view in memoirs. Invite them to change something they have written from first person to third person to see how it changes the story or invites a different perspective. If you are using *The Reading Minilessons Book, Grade 4*, you might also reference the ideas taught in LA.U26 because changing point of view can affect readers' insight into characters' feelings, motivations, and intentions.

Months	Texts from *Fountas & Pinnell Classroom™ Shared Reading Collection*	Text Sets from *Fountas & Pinnell Classroom™ Interactive Read-Aloud Collection*	Reading Minilessons (RML) Umbrellas	Writing Minilessons (WML) Umbrellas	Teaching Suggestions for Extending Learning
Months 3 & 4 (cont.)	Migrate! Epic Animal Excursions	Author/ Illustrator Study: Douglas Florian	WAR.U5: Introducing Different Genres and Forms for Responding to Reading, RML4–RML5	CNV.U3: Learning to Paragraph	Teach the minilessons in this umbrella when students are writing longer pieces that require more paragraphing. The lessons can be taught consecutively or across the year as needed.
				WPS.U10: Editing and Proofreading Writing	Teach and revisit this umbrella any time students need help with proofreading and editing for conventions. It is best taught after you have introduced all the Conventions umbrellas.
			SAS.U2: Using Context and Word Parts to Understand Vocabulary	MGT.U3: Introducing the Writing Folder, WML5	Teach this lesson after WPS.U10 with a focus on the parts of the lesson related to the proofreading checklist (available in the online resources), and then repeat the lesson when you introduce the revising checklist later in the year. Or, wait until you have introduced more revision lessons and teach how to use both checklists at the same time.
			Revisit LA.U3: Studying Authors and Their Processes, RML1	GEN.U15: Writing Different Kinds of Poems, WML1–WML2	Teach the lessons in GEN.U15 over time at any time of the year. Consider using these lessons in a poetry workshop every other week or once a month. If you are using the *Interactive Read–Aloud Collection*, you might find it helpful to teach WML1 and WML2 after studying Douglas Florian. His rhyming poems provide a contrast to free verse poetry, and his concrete poems can be used as mentor texts in WML2.
				WPS.U4: Writer's Notebook: Becoming an Expert	The minilessons in this umbrella help students research and develop topics of interest for nonfiction writing. This umbrella addresses Section 3 in *Writer's Notebook, Intermediate*.
				GEN.U9: Making Informational Multimedia Presentations	GEN.U9 teaches students how to develop a multimedia presentation to share what they have learned about a topic. It is very helpful to teach WPS.U4 before GEN.U9 so students have topics to select for the presentations.

Months	Texts from *Fountas & Pinnell Classroom*™ *Shared Reading Collection*	Text Sets from *Fountas & Pinnell Classroom*™ *Interactive Read-Aloud Collection*	Reading Minilessons (RML) Umbrellas	Writing Minilessons (WML) Umbrellas	Teaching Suggestions for Extending Learning
Months 5 & 6	More Than Sleeping: A Hibernation Journey Through Poems	Genre Study: Poetry	SAS.U3: Understanding Connectives	**WPS.U1: Introducing and Using a Writer's Notebook, WML5**	Around this time of the year, you may find it helpful to teach students how to continue to build their writer's notebooks by revisiting the prompts and sections they have used. In addition to teaching this lesson, you may want to revisit lessons in WPS.U2 and WPS.U3 to inspire new writing.
				GEN.U13: Making Poetry Anthologies, WML3	In this minilesson, students learn to write poems that connect to other poems for a new section in their poetry anthologies.
	If Rivers Could Speak		LA.U6: Studying Poetry	**GEN.U14: Writing Poetry, WML1–WML3**	If you have taught LA.U6 in *The Reading Minilessons Book, Grade 4*, you may not need to teach similar lessons in GEN.U14. You might choose to teach these lessons in biweekly or monthly poetry workshops. Fourth graders benefit from exposure to poetry all year long instead of in a one-time poetry unit. However, it is also beneficial to dive deep into poetry with a genre study as suggested in LA.U6 and GEN.U14.
	First Class: How Elizabeth Lange Built a School		LA.U20: Understanding Realistic Fiction	**GEN.U7: Writing Realistic Fiction Stories**	Building on what students have learned about narrative writing from writing memoirs, GEN.U7 helps them explore the characteristics of realistic fiction, create realistic characters, and develop a feasible plot. This umbrella complements the lessons in LA.U20 in *The Reading Minilessons Book, Grade 4*. Skip lessons that feel repetitive or that students don't need in either the reading or writing umbrellas.
				CFT.U7: Exploring Plot Structures, WML2–WML3	The lessons in CFT.U7 can be taught any time students are engaged in narrative writing. Invite them to apply these lessons to their realistic fiction stories.

Months	Texts from *Fountas & Pinnell Classroom™ Shared Reading Collection*	Text Sets from *Fountas & Pinnell Classroom™ Interactive Read-Aloud Collection*	Reading Minilessons (RML) Umbrellas	Writing Minilessons (WML) Umbrellas	Teaching Suggestions for Extending Learning
Months 5 & 6 (cont.)	A Spark of Genius: A Biography of Richard Turere	Genre Study: Historical Fiction	LA.U24: Thinking About the Setting in Fiction Books	CFT.U2: Describing Characters	Teach the lessons in CFT.U2 that you think will benefit students as they experiment with writing realistic fiction. Invite them to try out the lessons in their writer's notebooks and apply them to their realistic fiction stories. Another option is to wait to teach this umbrella when you address LA.U27: Understanding a Character's Traits and Development in *The Reading Minilessons Book, Grade 4*.
				CFT.U7: Exploring Plot Structures, WML4–WML5	The last two lessons in CFT.U7 explore sophisticated plot structures. Consider using these lessons in guided writing with small groups of students if the whole class is not ready for them. Students can experiment with these ideas in their writer's notebooks and apply them to the realistic fiction stories they are writing.
		Exploring Identity	WAR.U5: Introducing Different Genres and Forms for Responding to Reading, RML6	CFT.U3: Crafting a Setting	CFT.U3 builds on understandings developed in LA.U24 in *The Reading Minilessons Book, Grade 4*. Encourage students to use their writer's notebooks to try out ideas from these lessons. They can apply the understandings they develop to any type of narrative writing, so you can revisit this umbrella throughout the year. At this time of the year, students might apply these concepts to realistic fiction stories or, later, to picture book biographies.
			LA.23: Studying Historical Fiction		
		Perseverance	LA.U10: Reading Like a Writer: Analyzing the Writer's Craft	GEN.U14: Writing Poetry, WML4–WML5	Help students see that they can use figurative language in both poetry and prose. Teach both lessons in coordination with LA.U10 (especially the lessons that address metaphor and personification) in *The Reading Minilessons Book, Grade 4*, or teach them individually as part of your biweekly or monthly poetry workshop.
			LA.U27: Understanding a Character's Traits and Development	GEN.U13: Making Poetry Anthologies, WML4	Invite students to continue to apply their learning from GEN.U14 as they write poems for their poetry anthologies. Teach this lesson after GEN.U14 or as part of a biweekly or monthly poetry workshop.

Months	Texts from *Fountas & Pinnell Classroom™ Shared Reading Collection*	Text Sets from *Fountas & Pinnell Classroom™ Interactive Read-Aloud Collection*	Reading Minilessons (RML) Umbrellas	Writing Minilessons (WML) Umbrellas	Teaching Suggestions for Extending Learning
Months 5 & 6 (cont.)	A Lifetime of Dance: A Biography of Katherine Dunham	Genre Study: Biography: Individuals Making a Difference	WAR.U5: Introducing Different Genres and Forms for Responding to Reading, RML7–RML8	**CFT.U8: Making Powerful Word Choices**	Students can apply these lessons to both fiction and nonfiction writing. This umbrella complements concepts taught in LA.U10 in *The Reading Minilessons Book, Grade 4*. Consider also revisiting CFT.U1: Learning from Writers and Illustrators.
			LA.U14: Studying Biography	**GEN.U6: Writing Picture Book Biographies**	LA.14 in *The Reading Minilessons Book, Grade 4* is designed to immerse students in a study of biographies using a variety of picture books. Using these as mentor texts, GEN.U6 invites students to learn about writing biographies alongside bookmaking. Students can use Section 3 of *Writer's Notebook, Intermediate* to guide them in researching their subjects. Revisit any lessons in WPS.U4: Writer's Notebook: Becoming an Expert that you think will be helpful.
			SAS.U5: Summarizing, RML2	**CFT.U16: Exploring Design Features and Text Layout**	This umbrella invites students to consider the choices they have for designing illustrations and composing the pages of a book, including the layout of the illustrations and print. Consider revisiting CFT.U14: Adding Meaning Through Illustrations with the whole group or with guided writing groups to help students think about how the pictures and words can work together to convey meaning. Invite students to apply all of these lessons to their picture book biographies.
				CFT.U11: Writing with Voice in Fiction and Nonfiction	Invite students to apply these lessons in their writer's notebooks or to any writing they are working on (e.g., picture book biographies).
				WPS.U8: Adding Information to Your Writing, WML3	This lesson in WPS.U8 can be taught at any time to help students revise their writing. Invite them to apply WML3 to their biographies or to any writing in process.

The Writing Minilessons Book, Grade 4

Months	Texts from *Fountas & Pinnell Classroom™ Shared Reading Collection*	Text Sets from *Fountas & Pinnell Classroom™ Interactive Read-Aloud Collection*	Reading Minilessons (RML) Umbrellas	Writing Minilessons (WML) Umbrellas	Teaching Suggestions for Extending Learning
Months 5 & 6 (cont.)			LA.U7: Exploring Different Kinds of Poetry	**WPS.U9: Revising to Focus and Organize Writing, WML1–WML2**	Through the lessons in this umbrella, students learn a variety of ways to revise their writing. Teach the lessons over the course of the year as they apply to your students' writing. Invite them to apply WML1 and WML2 to any of their writing (e.g., picture book biographies, writer's notebooks).
				WPS.U11: Adding Book and Print Features, WML2–WML3	The last two minilessons in this umbrella are best applied to bookmaking. Invite students to apply what they learn from these lessons when they publish their picture book biographies.
				GEN.U15: Writing Different Kinds of Poems, WML3	Building on understandings developed in LA.U7, GEN.U15.WML3 introduces students to writing lyrical poems. Consider whether to teach the rest of the lessons in GEN.U15 in coordination with LA.U7 or whether to introduce the rest of the lessons over time in poetry workshop.
				GEN.U14: Writing Poetry, WML6	Crafting a title for a poem helps students further understand how a title impacts meaning for a reader. Teach this lesson whenever it is helpful for students.
Months 7 & 8	Change-makers: Voices of the Future

Incredible, Edible Insects

The Water Finder | Taking Action, Making Change

Innovative Thinking and Creative Problem Solving | SAS.U6: Monitoring Comprehension of Difficult Texts

LA.U4: Reading Graphic Texts | **GEN.U11: Exploring Opinion Writing** | This umbrella provides a foundation for persuasive writing. Later in the year, students will build on this umbrella by writing persuasive essays. You may want to revisit some of the lessons in WPS.U2: Writer's Notebook: Getting Ideas from Life and WPS.U4: Writer's Notebook: Becoming an Expert to help students think about topics they have strong opinions about. |
| | | | | **CFT.U9: Writing Clear and Interesting Sentences** | Teach the minilessons in this umbrella any time you think it would benefit your students. Students can apply these lessons to fiction or nonfiction writing. This umbrella revisits and builds on concepts developed earlier in the year in SAS.U3: Understanding Connectives in *The Reading Minilessons Book, Grade 4*. |

Months	Texts from *Fountas & Pinnell Classroom™ Shared Reading Collection*	Text Sets from *Fountas & Pinnell Classroom™ Interactive Read-Aloud Collection*	Reading Minilessons (RML) Umbrellas	Writing Minilessons (WML) Umbrellas	Teaching Suggestions for Extending Learning
Months 7 & 8 (cont.)	Buried Beneath			**WPS.U8: Adding Information to Your Writing, WML4**	This minilesson can be taught at any time of the year. It may be particularly helpful for students working on connecting ideas in their opinion pieces. Also consider revisiting SAS.U3: Understanding Connectives in *The Reading Minilessons Book, Grade 4*.
	Island Life to City Life		LA.U8: Thinking About the Author's Purpose and Message	**GEN.U1: Writing Letters, WML3–WML4**	Building on the understandings developed in GEN.U11 and CFT.U9, students learn how to write clear, formal letters about their opinions and things they care about.
	Eyewitness			**GEN.U15: Writing Different Kinds of Poems, WML4**	Consider introducing poems for two voices during poetry workshop while students are exploring opinion writing. Invite them to consider making the two voices in the poem represent opposing opinions.
				GEN.U3: Writing to a Prompt: Getting Ready for Test Writing	This umbrella prepares students for state tests or writing assessments that require responding to a prompt. Teach it when it makes sense for your testing schedule.
	Big River's Daughter: The Legend of Keelboat Annie	Series: Vanishing Cultures	LA.U12: Noticing Book and Print Features	**GEN.U4: Writing to a Prompt: Extended Responses**	This umbrella builds on GEN.U3 by teaching students how to write a more extended response to a writing prompt. Teach only as necessary to prepare students for testing.
				GEN.U16: Making Photo Essays	This umbrella invites students to try a unique form of composition. You might choose to revisit WPS.U11: Adding Book and Print Features and LA.U12 from *The Reading Minilessons Book, Grade 4* and invite students to apply the lessons to their photo essays.
			SAS.U7: Reading in Digital Environments	**GEN.U15: Writing Different Kinds of Poems, WML5**	During a poetry workshop, invite students to explore the natural world with haiku. They might focus on a topic related to work you are doing in science or to a topic they explored in their photo essays.

Months	Texts from *Fountas & Pinnell Classroom™ Shared Reading Collection*	Text Sets from *Fountas & Pinnell Classroom™ Interactive Read-Aloud Collection*	Reading Minilessons (RML) Umbrellas	Writing Minilessons (WML) Umbrellas	Teaching Suggestions for Extending Learning
Months 7 & 8 (cont.)		Coping with Loss	LA.U17: Reading Informational Text Like a Scientist	WPS.U7: Observing and Writing Like a Scientist	Use WPS.U7 to integrate writing into your science curriculum at any time. WPS.U7 also provides a foundation for when students write procedural texts later in the year.
				WPS.U5: Researching in Digital Environments	In preparation for writing feature articles, students will benefit from learning about how to research in online environments. Revisit lessons from WPS.U4: Writer's Notebook: Becoming an Expert as needed to help students identify a topic to research. If you are teaching reading minilessons, consider whether you can omit lessons that are similar to those in SAS.U7: Reading in Digital Environments.
			LA.U16: Noticing How Nonfiction Authors Choose to Organize Information	GEN.U10: Writing Feature Articles	Encourage students to use a topic they have researched to write at least one feature article. Students learn that voice is an important characteristic of feature articles. Revisit CFT.U11: Writing with Voice in Fiction and Nonfiction as necessary.
			WAR.U4: Using Graphic Organizers to Share Thinking About Books, RML1	CFT.U13: Making Nonfiction Writing Interesting	Invite students to apply these lessons to the feature articles they are writing or to any nonfiction writing, including any in their writer's notebooks. Students can also use their writer's notebooks to try out the lessons before applying them directly to their writing.

Months	Texts from *Fountas & Pinnell Classroom™ Shared Reading Collection*	Text Sets from *Fountas & Pinnell Classroom™ Interactive Read-Aloud Collection*	Reading Minilessons (RML) Umbrellas	Writing Minilessons (WML) Umbrellas	Teaching Suggestions for Extending Learning
Months 7 & 8 (cont.)			LA.U19: Using Text Features to Gain Information LA.U18: Learning Information from Illustrations/Graphics	**CFT.U6: Exploring Text Structures in Nonfiction Writing**	CFT.U6 revisits ideas developed in the reading minilesson umbrella LA.U16: Noticing How Nonfiction Authors Choose to Organize Information. This umbrella comes after students have had several experiences reading and writing nonfiction so they can make sophisticated choices about the way they organize information in their writing. Encourage them to choose a nonfiction topic from their writer's notebooks and to try out different text structures. They can also revisit any of the feature articles they have written to try a different text structure.
		The Idea of Home	WAR.U4: Using Graphic Organizers to Share Thinking About Books, RML2	**CFT.U12: Using Text Features in Nonfiction Writing**	Students can experiment with text features in their writer's notebooks before adding them to a current writing project (e.g., a feature article). This umbrella complements some of the understandings students have developed about text features as readers in LA.U19.
Months 9 & 10		What It Means to Be a Family	SAS.U5: Summarizing, RML3	**CFT.U15: Illustrating and Using Graphics in Nonfiction Writing**	This umbrella builds on concepts developed in LA.U18 in *The Reading Minilessons Book, Grade 4*, in which readers learn how to get information from illustrations and graphics. In CFT.U15, students learn how to integrate illustrations and graphics into their own nonfiction writing. Encourage them to add graphics to their feature articles or to other nonfiction writing. Another possibility is for them to revisit informational multimedia presentations (GEN.U9) and create interesting illustrations and graphics for their slides.

Months	Texts from *Fountas & Pinnell Classroom™ Shared Reading Collection*	Text Sets from *Fountas & Pinnell Classroom™ Interactive Read-Aloud Collection*	Reading Minilessons (RML) Umbrellas	Writing Minilessons (WML) Umbrellas	Teaching Suggestions for Extending Learning
Months 9 & 10 (cont.)		Author Study: Patricia McKissack	LA.U3: Studying Authors and Their Processes, RML1–RML4	**GEN.U15: Writing Different Kinds of Poems, WML6**	Invite students to write an informational poem on a topic they have researched.
				GEN.U17: Exploring Digital Writing	This umbrella allows writers to put together everything they have learned about researching online and writing nonfiction texts. Revisit the lessons in WPS.U4: Writer's Notebook: Becoming an Expert as necessary.
			LA.U15: Exploring Persuasive Texts	**GEN.U12: Writing Persuasive Essays**	GEN.U12 builds on what students have learned about opinion writing in GEN.U11 and what they have learned about reading persuasive texts from LA.U15 in *The Reading Minilessons Book, Grade 4*.
			WAR.U5: Introducing Different Genres and Forms for Responding to Reading, RML9	**WPS.U8: Adding Information to Your Writing, WML5**	WPS.U8.WML5 can be taught whenever students need support in revising their writing for more detailed examples. You may find this very helpful to teach while students are revising their persuasive essays to make them more convincing.
				WPS.U9: Revising to Focus and Organize Writing, WML3	Though this lesson can be taught anytime and repeated as it applies to students' writing, it will be particularly meaningful to apply it to persuasive writing because word choice is such an important part of being convincing.
			LA.U9: Thinking About Themes WAR.U4: Using Graphic Organizers to Share Thinking About Books, RML3	**GEN.U2: Writing Procedural Texts**	The end of the year is a nice time for students to identify something they want to teach to an audience and to choose a creative way to teach it. For example, they might decide to make a video, plan a presentation, make a how-to book, or create a board game with instructions. Schedule times throughout the rest of the year for students to present their procedural texts to the class.

Suggested Sequence of Lessons (cont.)

Months	Texts from *Fountas & Pinnell Classroom™ Shared Reading Collection*	Text Sets from *Fountas & Pinnell Classroom™ Interactive Read-Aloud Collection*	Reading Minilessons (RML) Umbrellas	Writing Minilessons (WML) Umbrellas	Teaching Suggestions for Extending Learning
Months 9 & 10 (cont.)	Zarah and the Zemi The Golden Swan: A Story from the Jataka Tales Little Deer and the Little People The Dragon Alliance	Genre Study: Fantasy	LA.U21: Studying Fantasy	**WPS.U9: Revising to Focus and Organize Writing, WML4**	This lesson can be taught anytime; however, it will be helpful for students to apply it to their procedural writing because the order of instructions is often essential.
		Genre Study: Fairy Tales Cinderella Stories	LA.U22: Studying Fairy Tales	**GEN.U8: Writing Fairy Tales**	If you are teaching reading minilessons, teach LA.U22 before GEN.U8 to build a strong understanding of the qualities of the fairy tale genre. Invite students to brainstorm ideas for fairy tales in their writer's notebooks. Consider having them write their own Cinderella tales inspired by the stories in the *Interactive Read-Aloud Collection*.
			WAR.U4: Using Graphic Organizers to Share Thinking About Books, RML4–RML5	Revisit any of the following umbrellas: **CFT.U2: Describing Characters** **CFT.U3: Crafting a Setting** **CFT.U4: Using Dialogue in Writing** **CFT.U7: Exploring Plot Structures**	As students write fairy tales, it might be helpful to revisit any of these craft lessons. Students can try out the lessons in their writer's notebooks before applying them to their fairy tales.
				Revisit **WPS.U12: Publishing and Self-Assessing Your Writing**	End the year with another opportunity for students to evaluate their writing and reflect on their growth across the year.

Glossary

alliteration The repetition of identical or similar initial consonant sounds in consecutive or nearby words or syllables.

assessment A means for gathering information or data that reveals what learners control, partially control, or do not yet control consistently.

assonance The repetition of identical or similar vowel sounds in stressed syllables in words that usually end with different consonant sounds. Compare with *consonance* and *rhyme*.

audience The readers of a text. Often a writer crafts a text with a particular audience in mind.

behaviors Actions that are observable as students read or write.

biography A biographical text in which the story (or part of the story) of a real person's life is written and narrated by another person. Biography is usually told in chronological sequence but may be in another order.

bold / boldface Type that is heavier and darker than usual, often used for emphasis.

book and print features The physical attributes of a text (for example, font, layout, and length). Also, elements of a book (for example, acknowledgments, author page, dedication, and endpapers). See also *text features*.

character An individual, usually a person or animal, in a text.

character sketch A brief written piece that describes a character's personality and physical traits. It may also include a drawing of the character.

chronological sequence An underlying structural pattern used especially in nonfiction texts to describe a series of events in the order they happened in time.

circular plot A plot structure in which a sense of completeness or closure results from the way the end of a piece returns to the subject matter, the wording, or other similarity found at the beginning of the story.

compare and contrast An underlying structural pattern used especially in nonfiction texts to compare two ideas, events, or phenomena by showing how they are alike and how they are different.

concrete poetry Poems with words (and sometimes punctuation) arranged to present a concrete picture of the idea the poem is conveying. See also *shape poem*.

connective A word or phrase that clarifies relationships and ideas in language. Simple connectives appear often in both oral and written language (e.g., *and*, *but*, *because*). Sophisticated connectives are used in written texts but do not appear often in everyday oral language (e.g., *although*, *however*, *yet*).

consonance The repetition of the final consonant sounds in words with different vowels. Compare with *assonance* and *rhyme*.

conventions In writing, formal usage that has become customary in written language. Grammar, usage, capitalization, punctuation, spelling, handwriting, and text layout are categories of writing conventions.

craft In writing, how an individual piece of writing is shaped. Elements of craft are organization, idea development, language use, word choice, and voice. Compare with *style* and *voice*.

cursive A form of handwriting in which letters are connected.

dialogue Spoken words, usually set off with quotation marks in text. See also *speaker tag*.

directions (how-to) Part of a procedural nonfiction text that shows the steps involved in performing a task. A set of directions may include diagrams or drawings with labels. See also *procedural text*.

draft An early version of a writer's composition.

drafting and revising The process of getting ideas down on paper and shaping them to convey the writer's message.

editing and proofreading The process of polishing the final draft of a written composition to prepare it for publication.

elements of fiction Important elements of fiction include narrator, characters, plot, setting, theme, and style.

elements of poetry Important elements of poetry include figurative language, imagery, personification, rhythm, rhyme, repetition, alliteration, assonance, consonance, onomatopoeia, and aspects of layout.

English learners People whose native language is not English and who are acquiring English as an additional language.

fairy tale A folktale involving magic, magical creatures, and a conflict between good and evil.

feature article An expository text that presents information organized around a central theme or idea or one particular aspect of a topic. A feature article may use one or more structural patterns to weave a cohesive sequence of ideas. Feature articles usually are published in newspapers and magazines.

fiction Invented, imaginative prose or poetry that tells a story. Fiction texts can be organized into the categories realism and fantasy. Along with nonfiction, fiction is one of two basic genres of literature.

figurative language An element of a writer's style, figurative language changes or goes beyond literal meaning. Two common types of figurative language are metaphor (a direct comparison) and simile (a comparison that uses *like* or *as*).

flashback A literary device in which the action moves suddenly into the past to relate events that have relevance for understanding the present.

font In printed text, a collection of type (letters) in a particular style.

form A kind of text that is characterized by particular elements. Mystery, for example, is a form of writing within the realistic fiction genre. Another term for *form* is *subgenre*.

formal letter In writing, a functional nonfiction text usually addressed to a stranger, in which the form (for example, a business letter or email) follows specific conventions.

free verse A form of poetry with irregular meter. Free verse may include rhyme, alliteration, and other poetic sound devices.

friendly letter In writing, a functional nonfiction text usually addressed to friends or family that may take the form of notes, letters, invitations, or email.

functional text A nonfiction text intended to accomplish a practical task, for example, labels, lists, letters, and directions with steps (how-to).

genre A category of written text that is characterized by a particular style, form, or content.

grammar Complex rules by which people can generate an unlimited number of phrases, sentences, and longer texts in that language. *Conventional grammar* refers to the accepted grammatical conventions in a society.

graphic feature In fiction texts, graphic features are usually illustrations. In nonfiction texts, graphic features include photographs, paintings and drawings, charts, diagrams, tables and graphs, maps, and timelines.

guided writing Instructional support for a small, temporary group of writers who have similar needs.

haiku An ancient Japanese form of non-rhyming poetry that creates a mental picture and makes a concise emotional statement.

high-frequency words Words that occur often in spoken and written language (for example, *because*).

high point The most significant or exciting part of a story.

how-to See *directions (how-to)* and *procedural text.*

illustration Graphic representation of important content (for example, art, photos, maps, graphs, charts) in a fiction or nonfiction text.

independent writing A text written by students independently with teacher support as needed. Also, a time during writers' workshop for students to write on their own.

informational text A nonfiction text in which a purpose is to inform or give facts about a topic. Informational texts include the following genres: biography, autobiography, memoir, and narrative nonfiction, as well as expository texts, procedural texts, and persuasive texts.

interactive read-aloud An instructional context in which students are actively listening and responding to an oral reading of a text.

italic (italics) A styling of type that is characterized by slanted letters.

label A written word or phrase that names the content of an illustration.

layout The way the print and illustrations are arranged on a page.

learning zone The level at which it is most productive to aim one's teaching for each student (the zone of proximal development).

lowercase letter A small letterform that is usually different from its corresponding capital or uppercase form.

main idea The central underlying idea, concept, or message that the author conveys in a nonfiction text. See also *message.*

memoir A biographical text in which a writer takes a reflective stance in looking back on a particular time or person. Usually written in the first person, memoirs are often briefer and more intense accounts of a memory or set of memories than the accounts found in biographies and autobiographies.

mentor texts Books or other texts that serve as examples of excellent writing. Mentor texts are read and reread to provide models for literature discussion and student writing.

message An important idea that an author conveys in a fiction or nonfiction text. See also *main idea*.

metaphor A type of figurative language that describes one thing by comparing it to something else without using the words *like* or *as*. Compare with *simile*.

modeled writing An instructional technique in which a teacher demonstrates the process of composing a particular genre, making the process explicit for students.

mood Language and events that convey an emotional atmosphere in a text, affecting how the reader feels. An element of a writer's style, mood is established by details, imagery, figurative language, setting, and illustration (color).

multimedia A type of communication involving more than one medium, for example, a combination of print, video, and audio.

narrative nonfiction A nonfiction text that tells a story using a narrative structure and literary language to make a topic interesting and appealing to readers.

narrative text structure A method of organizing a text. A simple narrative structure follows a traditional sequence that includes a beginning, a problem, a series of events, a resolution of the problem, and an ending. Alternative narrative structures may include devices such as flashback or flash-forward to change the sequence of events or allow for multiple narrators.

nonfiction Prose or poetry that provides factual information. According to their structures, nonfiction texts can be organized into the categories of narrative and nonnarrative. Along with fiction, nonfiction is one of the two basic genres of literature.

nonnarrative text structure A method of organizing a text. Nonnarrative structures are used especially in three genres of nonfiction—expository texts, procedural texts, and persuasive texts. In nonnarrative nonfiction texts, underlying structural patterns include description, cause and effect, chronological sequence, temporal sequence, categorization, compare and contrast, problem and solution, and question and answer. See also *organization*, *text structure*, and *narrative text structure*.

onomatopoeia The representation of sound with words.

onset In a syllable, the part (consonant, consonant cluster, or consonant digraph) that comes before the vowel (e.g., the *cr* in *cream*). See also *rime*.

opinion writing A type of writing whose purpose is to express a belief. Compare with *persuasive writing*.

organization The arrangement of ideas in a text according to a logical structure, either narrative or nonnarrative. Another term for *organization* is *text structure*.

organizational tools and sources of information A design feature of nonfiction texts. Organizational tools and sources of information help a reader process and understand nonfiction texts. Examples include tables of contents, headings, indexes, glossaries, appendices, author bios, and references.

personification A figure of speech in which an animal is spoken of or portrayed as if it were a person, or in which a lifeless thing or idea is spoken of or portrayed as a living thing. Personification is one type of figurative language.

perspective The angle from which the story is told, usually the first person (the narrator is a character in the story) or the third person (the unnamed narrator is not a character in the story). Another term for perspective is *point of view*.

persuasive writing A nonfiction text intended to convince the reader of the validity of a set of ideas—usually a particular point of view. Compare with *opinion writing*.

phonogram A phonetic element represented by graphic characters or symbols (e.g., *-ack, -ight*).

photo essay A form of nonfiction text in which meaning is carried by a series of photographs with no text or very spare text.

picture book An illustrated fiction or nonfiction text in which pictures work with the text to tell a story or provide information.

planning and rehearsing The process of collecting, working with, and selecting ideas for a written composition.

plot The events, action, conflict, and resolution of a story presented in a certain order in a fiction text. A simple plot progresses chronologically from start to end, whereas more complex plots may shift back and forth in time.

poetry Compact, metrical writing characterized by imagination and artistry and imbued with intense meaning. Along with prose, poetry is one of two broad categories into which all literature can be divided.

point of view See *perspective*.

principle A generalization that is predictable. It is the key idea that students will learn and be invited to apply.

print feature In nonfiction texts, features that include the color, size, style, and font of type, as well as various aspects of layout.

procedural text A nonfiction text that explains how to do something. Procedural texts are almost always organized in temporal sequence and take the form of directions (or how-to texts) or descriptions of a process. See also *directions (how-to)*.

prompt A question, direction, or statement designed to encourage the student to say more about a topic.

publishing The process of making the final draft of a written composition public.

punctuation Marks used in written text to clarify meaning and separate structural units. The comma and the period are common punctuation marks.

purpose A writer's overall intention in creating a text, or a reader's overall intention in reading a text. To tell a story is one example of a writer's purpose, and to be entertained is one example of a reader's purpose.

question and answer A structural pattern used especially in nonfiction texts to organize information in a series of questions with responses. Question-and-answer texts may be based on a verbal or written interview or on frequently arising or logical questions about a topic.

quick write Informal writing in which students write their immediate thoughts and feelings, usually in response to a prompt or something they have read.

repetition Repeated words or phrases that help create rhythm and emphasis in poetry or prose.

resolution/solution The point in the plot of a fiction story when the main conflict is solved.

rhyme The repetition of vowel and consonant sounds in the stressed and unstressed syllables of words in verse, especially at the ends of lines.

rhythm The regular or ordered repetition of stressed and unstressed syllables in poetry, other writing, or speech.

rime In a syllable, the ending part containing the letters that represent the vowel sound and the consonant letters that follow (e.g., the *eam* in *dream*). See also *onset*.

sequence See *chronological sequence* and *temporal sequence*.

setting The place and time in which a fiction text or biographical text takes place.

shape poem Poetry with words (and sometimes punctuation) arranged in interesting ways that may be tied to the poem's meaning. See also *concrete poetry*.

shared reading An instructional context in which the teacher involves a group of students in the reading of a particular big book to introduce aspects of literacy (such as print conventions), develop reading strategies (such as decoding or predicting), and teach vocabulary.

shared writing An instructional context in which the teacher involves a group of students in the composing of a coherent text together. The teacher writes while scaffolding students' language and ideas.

sidebar Information that is additional to the main text, placed alongside the text and sometimes set off from the main text in a box.

simile A type of figurative language that makes a comparison of two different things using the words *like* or *as*. Compare with *metaphor*.

slide presentation A series of slides or pages often prepared on a computer and presented on a screen. Slides contain minimal print and (if on a computer) possible audio or video that can be played to enhance the presentation.

small moment Part of a memory that a writer focuses on. For example, rather than writing about a whole event, the writer writes in detail about one thing that happened during the event.

speaker tag The words at the beginning, at the end, or in the middle of dialogue that identify the speaker (e.g., *said Grace*).

speech bubble A shape, often rounded, containing the words a character says in a cartoon or other text. Another term for *speech bubble* is *speech balloon*.

split dialogue Written dialogue in which a "*said* phrase" divides the speaker's words (e.g., "Come on," said Mom. "Let's go home.").

story A series of events in narrative form, either fiction or nonfiction.

story arc A representation of the rise and fall of the sequence of events in a story.

style The way a writer chooses and arranges words to create a meaningful text. Aspects of style include sentence length, word choice, and the use of figurative language and symbolism. Compare with *craft* and *voice*.

subtopic A subject or idea that is part of a larger, more general topic.

syllable A minimal unit of sequential speech sounds composed of a vowel sound or a consonant-vowel combination. A syllable always contains a vowel or vowel-like speech sound (e.g., *pen/ny*). See also *onset* and *rime*.

temporal sequence An underlying structural pattern used especially in nonfiction texts to describe the sequence in which something always or usually occurs, such as the steps in a process or a life cycle. See also *procedural text*.

test writing A type of functional writing in which students are prompted to write a short constructed response (sometimes called *short answer*) or an extended constructed response (or *essay*).

text features Parts of a text designed to help the reader access or better understand it (for example, tables of contents, headings, sidebars, captions). See also *book and print features*.

text structure The overall architecture or organization of a piece of writing. Another term for *text structure* is *organization*.

thought bubble A shape, often rounded, containing the words (or sometimes an image that suggests one or more words) a character thinks in a cartoon or other text. Another term for *thought bubble* is *thought balloon*.

tools In writing, resources that support the writing process (writer's notebook, writing folder, pens, pencils). Also, a physical means of revising or editing a piece of writing, such as a caret, a spider leg, or a numbered list.

topic The subject of a piece of writing.

uppercase letter A large letterform that is usually different from its corresponding lowercase form. Another term for *uppercase letter* is *capital letter*.

viewing self as writer Having attitudes and using practices that support a student in becoming a lifelong writer.

vignette A short description or account; a scene.

voice In writing, the unique way a writer "sounds" as a result of word choice, point of view, and arrangement of words and sentences. Compare with *craft* and *style*.

word choice In writing, the craft of choosing words to convey precise meaning.

writer's notebook A notebook of bound pages in which students gather ideas for writing and experiment with writing. A writer's notebook is a record of students' writing across the year. It may have several different sections to serve a variety of purposes.

writers' workshop A classroom structure that begins with a whole-group minilesson; continues with independent writing, individual conferences, and small-group instruction; and ends with a whole-group share.

writing Students engaging in the writing process and producing pieces of their own writing in many genres.

writing about reading Students responding to reading a text by writing and sometimes drawing.

writing folder A two-pocket folder with brads in the middle. Writing that is in progress is stored in the pockets. Resources, such as checklists and spelling lists, are fastened in the middle. When a piece of writing is finished, it is removed from the folder and placed in a hanging file.

writing process Key phases of creating a piece of writing: planning and rehearsing, drafting and revising, editing and proofreading, and publishing.

Credits

All Penguin Random House covers reproduced courtesy of Penguin Random House.

Cover of *A Boy and a Jaguar*. Text and illustrations © 2014 Alan Rabinowitz and Catia Chien. Reprinted with permission of HarperCollins Publishers.

Cover of *A Little Book of Sloth* by Lucy Cooke. © 2013 Lucy Cooke. Reprinted with the permission Margaret K. McElderry Books, an imprint of Simon & Schuster Children's Publishing Division. All rights reserved.

Cover of *A Place to Start a Family: Poems About Creatures That Build*. Text and illustrations © 2018 David L. Harrison and Giles Laroche. Used with permission by Charlesbridge Publishing, Inc., 9 Galen Street, Watertown, MA 02472. (617) 926-0329. www.charlesbridge.com. All rights reserved.

Cover of *A Symphony of Whales*. Text and illustrations © 1999 Steve Schuch and Peter Sylvada. Reprinted with permission of HarperCollins Publishers.

Cover of *Action Jackson* by Jan Greenberg and Sandra Jordan, illustrated by Robert Andrew Parker. Text and illustrations © 2002 Jan Greenberg, Sandra Jordan, and Robert Andrew Parker. Reprinted by permission of Roaring Brook Press, a division of Holtzbrinck Publishing Holdings Limited Partnership. All Rights Reserved.

Cover of *Barbed Wire Baseball* by Marissa Moss, illustrated by Yuko Shimizu. Text and illustrations © 2013 Marissa Moss and Yuko Shimizu. Used by permission of Abrams, an imprint of Harry N. Abrams, Inc. New York. All rights reserved.

Cover of *Be Water, My Friend: The Early Years of Bruce Lee*. Text and illustrations © 2006 Ken Mochizuki and Dom Lee. Permission arranged with LEE & LOW BOOKS Inc., New York, NY 10016. All rights reserved. Learn more at leeandlow.com.

Cover of *Beauty and the Beast*. Text and illustrations © 1989 Jan Brett Studios, Inc. Reprinted with permission of Clarion Books, an imprint of HarperCollins Publishers.

Cover of *Brave Red, Smart Frog*. Text and illustrations © 2018 Emily Jenkins and Rohan Daniel Eason. Reproduced by permission of the publisher, Candlewick Press, Somerville, MA.

Cover of *Brothers in Hope: The Story of the Lost Boys of Sudan*. Text and illustrations © 2005 Mary Williams and R. Gregory Christie. Permission arranged with LEE & LOW BOOKS Inc., New York, NY 10016. All rights reserved. Learn more at leeandlow.com.

Cover of *Cendrillon* by Robert D. San Souci, illustrated by Brian Pinkney. Text and illustrations © 1998 Robert D. San Souci and Brian Pinkney. Reprinted with the permission of Simon & Schuster Books for Young Readers, an imprint of Simon & Schuster Children's Publishing Division. All rights reserved.

Cover of *Crow Call* by Lois Lowry, illustrated by Bagram Ibatoulline. Text and illustrations © 2009 Lois Lowry and Bagram Ibatoulline. Reprinted by permission of Scholastic Inc.

Works Cited

Fletcher, Ralph. 2003. *A Writer's Notebook: Unlocking the Writer Within You*. New York: HarperCollins.

———. 2017. *Joy Write: Cultivating High-Impact, Low-Stakes Writing*. Portsmouth, NH: Heinemann.

Fountas, Irene C., and Gay Su Pinnell. 2012. *Genre Study: Teaching with Fiction and Nonfiction Books*. Portsmouth, NH: Heinemann.

———. 2017, 2022. *The Fountas & Pinnell Literacy Continuum: A Tool for Assessment, Planning, and Teaching*. Portsmouth, NH: Heinemann.

———. 2017. *Guided Reading: Responsive Teaching Across the Grades*, 2nd ed. Portsmouth, NH: Heinemann.

———. 2018. *The Literacy Quick Guide: A Reference Tool for Responsive Literacy Teaching*. Portsmouth, NH: Heinemann.

———. 2020. *Fountas & Pinnell Classroom™ Interactive Read-Aloud Collection*. Portsmouth, NH: Heinemann.

———. 2020. *Fountas & Pinnell Classroom™ System Guide, Grade 4*. Portsmouth, NH: Heinemann.

———. 2020. *Fountas & Pinnell Word Study System, for Grade 4*. Portsmouth, NH: Heinemann.

———. 2020. *The Reading Minilessons Book, Grade 4*. Portsmouth, NH: Heinemann.

———. 2023. *Fountas & Pinnell Classroom™ Shared Reading Collection*. Portsmouth, NH: Heinemann.

Glover, Matt. 2009. *Engaging Young Writers, Preschool–Grade 1*. Portsmouth, NH: Heinemann.

Heard, Georgia. 1999. *Awakening the Heart: Exploring Poetry in Elementary and Middle School*. Portsmouth, NH: Heinemann.

———. 2016. *Heart Maps: Helping Students Create and Craft Authentic Writing*. Portsmouth, NH: Heinemann.

Heard, Georgia, and Jennifer McDonough. 2009. *A Place for Wonder: Reading and Writing Nonfiction in the Primary Grades*. Portsmouth, NH: Stenhouse.

VanDerwater, Amy. 2018. *Poems Are Teachers: How Studying Poetry Stengthens Writing in All Genres*. Portsmouth, NH: Heinemann.

Vygotsky, Lev. 1979. *Mind in Society: The Development of Higher Psychological Processes*. Cambridge, MA: Harvard University Press.